Oz Clarke's
POCKET **WINE** BOOK

2003

The **world** of **wine** from **A-Z**

WEBSTERS

timewarner
books

A TIME WARNER/WEBSTERS BOOK

This edition first published in 2002 by
Time Warner Books UK
Brettenham House
Lancaster Place
LONDON WC2E 7EN
www.TimeWarnerBooks.co.uk

Created and designed by
Websters International Publishers Limited
Axe and Bottle Court
70 Newcomen Street
London SE1 1YT
www.websters.co.uk
www.ozclarke.com

11th edition. First published in 1992. Revised editions published annually.

A CIP catalogue for this book is available from the
British Library.

ISBN 0-316-85962-1

Printed and bound in Belgium

CORPORATE SALES
**Companies, institutions and other organizations wishing to make
bulk purchases of this or any other Oz Clarke title published by
Time Warner Books UK should contact Andrew Hally on
+44 (0)20-7911 8933.**

Thanks are due to the following people for their invaluable help with
the 2003 edition and the generous spirit in which they have shared
their knowledge: Stephen Brook, Bob Campbell MW, Elizabeth Eyre, Tom
Hyland, James Lawther MW, Angela Lloyd, Dan McCarthy, Dave
McIntyre, Sally Marden, David Moore, Jasper Morris, Stuart Pigott,
Victor de la Serna, Patricio Tapia, Phillip Williamson.

CONTENTS

HOW TO USE THE A–Z

The **A–Z** section starts on page 44 and includes over 1600 entries on wines, producers, grapes and wine regions from all over the world. It is followed on page 289 by a **Glossary** of some of the more common winemaking terms that are often seen on labels.

Detailed **Vintage Charts** with information on which of the world's top wines are ready for drinking in 2003 can be found on the inside front and back covers; the front chart features vintages back to 1992; the back chart covers a selection of older vintages for premium wines.

Glass Symbols   These indicate the wines produced.

● Red wine   ◒ Rosé wine   ○ White wine

The order of the glasses reflects the importance of the wines in terms of volume produced. For example:

◔ White followed by rosé wine

◓ Red followed by white wine

◕ Red followed by rosé, then white wine

Grape Symbols   These identify entries on grape varieties.

⠿ Red grape   ⠿ White grape

Star Symbols   These indicate wines and producers that are highly rated by the author.

★   A particularly good wine or producer in its category
★★   An excellent wine or producer in its category – one
       especially worth seeking out
★★★   An exceptional, world-class wine or producer

Best Years   Recommended vintages are listed for many producer and appellation entries. Those listed in bold, e.g. **2001**, **99**, indicate wines that are ready for drinking now, although they may not necessarily be at their best; those appearing in brackets, e.g. (2001), (00), are preliminary assessments of wines that are not yet ready for drinking.

Cross References   To help you find your way round the A–Z, wine names, producers and regions that have their own entries elsewhere in the A–Z are indicated by SMALL CAPITALS. Grape varieties are not cross-referred in this way, but more than 70 varieties, from Albariño to Zinfandel, are included.

Special Features   The A–Z section includes special 2-page features on the world's most important wine styles, regions and grape varieties. These features include recommended vintages and producers, as well as lists of related entries elsewhere in the A–Z.

Index   The Index, starting on page 297, will help you find over 4000 recommended producers, including all of those that don't have their own entry in the A–Z. Some of the world's most famous brand names are also included.

INTRODUCTION

Some years it's all planes and boats and trains. I seem to do nothing but tear from one part of the world to the next, with my friends sniggering – 'Hey, off to work on your tan again?' I wish. I can see their point when I'm heading off to South Africa, Chile, Argentina or wherever in the middle of a bitter European winter. But they should come with me. The pace of change is so hectic in so many parts of the world – above all in the southern hemisphere – that if I'm going to see even half of what's new, I am *never* going to get to the beach. And this year there was so much to see, so many places to visit, that I didn't even get a single full night's sleep on my travels. The beach? Forget it.

But I'm not complaining. However exhausting the trips, they're exhilarating too. And several of the trips I made have resulted in considerable changes to the book this year. But let's start closer to home, with Austria. It's easy to forget just how good Austrian wine is because so much of it gets drunk on the spot. But there's an ambitious mood sweeping the country – not only in the classic areas for fine dry whites like Wachau on the Danube, but in other areas like Burgenland, already famous for sweet wines and now producing some remarkable reds. So Austria gets increased coverage.

And so does South Africa. A new generation of wine people is making its presence felt in the Cape, which up till now has been one of the most unselfcritical of the New World regions. Not any more. Problems are being addressed and worn-out traditions discarded, at the same time as new zones, new grape varieties and new wine styles are being skilfully and excitingly interwoven with the best of the old.

The best of the old is not particularly relevant in South America. Although Chile has historically produced some fine wine, the other countries haven't, and even in Chile's case, the new star wines are so much more exciting than even the best of the old stuff that there's really no need to look back. But look forward, and the prospects are dazzling. Chile is developing new areas at the same time as radically re-vamping and re-thinking her marvellous old-established vineyards. The result is wines of a personality and style that no other country can imitate. Argentina's wine industry dramatically reinvented itself during the 1990s and Uruguay is just beginning to carve out her own niche. The whole mood of determination and imagination in the three countries is so infectious that we've expanded coverage of all of them.

We've squeezed in a fistful of new entries for some of California's important producers and wine regions, too. On a trip there I was very pleased to see lots of old vines (such as Zinfandel in Dry Creek Valley) as well as serious amounts of new plantings.

So, this year we've got more countries, more estates, more wine regions; and new grape varieties like Carmenère and Nero d'Avola are given their own entries. Basically, for everything that seems good in the world of wine, we've tried to increase coverage.

But not everything is good. The last 12 months have seen a rash of mergers and takeovers, creating global giants whose likely benefits will be experienced solely by the shareholders, and precious little by consumers facing less choice, dumbed down, homogenized flavours, and a boom and bust cycle of price war followed by price hike.

Which makes it ever more important to support the good guys by drinking their wine. I'll start with **South America**. **Chile** may be producing more wine each vintage, but she's producing better wine each vintage. Stunning Cabernets from **Maipo**, impressive Merlots, Carmenères and Syrahs from **Colchagua** and irresistible **Casablanca** whites – I'll drink 'em all. And I'll drink marvellous deep Malbecs, Cabernets, Syrahs and Bonardas from a resurgent **Argentina**. The country's having a tough time at the moment. Give the winemakers a boost. Drink their wine. And throw in a bottle or two of gutsy red from **Uruguay** while you're about it.

In **California**, I'll give the big volume brands a miss because I can't tell one from another any more. But by trading up, I can get some stunning stuff – at a price. The Pinot Noirs have never been better; there's a slew of Syrahs coming on stream, many of them really tasty; and the Cabernet Sauvignons have taken a leap forward since the great 1997 vintage. In **Washington** and **Oregon**, you'll more likely see me with a glass of Semillon or Pinot Gris. Just that bit further north, in **Canada's Okanagan Valley**, it'll be Pinot Blanc or Chardonnay.

South Africa has made a massive improvement in her wine in the last few years, and she's now producing some of the best Chardonnays and Sauvignons in the southern hemisphere. **New Zealand** won't like to hear that, but will probably relish the challenge. Will **Australia** relish the challenge? I hope so, but for the first time in years I'll be drinking less Australian wine, and what I do drink will be from individual producers and independent companies still committed to the old Australian ideal of super flavours at a fair-dinkum price.

In Europe, I'll be turning more of my attention to **Italy**, where the individualism which marks so much of her national character is now being seen more and more in her wines. **Sicily** and **Puglia** lead the way, but right through **Campania**, **Umbria** and **Tuscany** up to **Piedmont** and the **Veneto**, exciting wines are being made.

In **Spain**, I'll spend more time in **Castilla y León**, where some interesting grape varieties are being given up-to the-minute treatment. And in **Andalucía**, where **sherry** is one of the world's classic yet underappreciated wines. In **Portugal** I'll stay south to get my share of the exciting reds coming out of the **Alentejo** and **Ribatejo**.

As I head north, I shall drink the occasional bottle of **Bordeaux**, but the price/pleasure ratio is so out of control it'll just be the occasional bottle. And it'll be at the upper end of quality because Bordeaux really does struggle at the bottom end. **Burgundy**, too, doesn't excel at the lower level, but is making consistently good wine higher up. I shall revel in a series of good vintages and revitalized winemakers in the **Rhône** and in the red wine appellations of **Languedoc-Roussillon**.

All of that warm-blooded red will leave me panting for something cool and fragrant and refreshing. It could be **Champagne**, but it's much more likely to be the peppery, green-streaked Grüner Veltliner of **Austria** and the perfectly balanced Kabinett and Spätlese Rieslings of **Germany's Mosel Valley**. And that should be that for another year – but the world of wine doesn't stand still and neither shall I. I'll be off again, seeking out the best, most interesting wines from countries old and new – and trying to work on my tan.

PICK OF THE YEAR

Every year – on my travels, at tastings and at home – I taste countless hundreds of wines, always on the lookout for thrilling flavours. These are some of the wines I've enjoyed most this year. Some are widely available; others are very rare, and can only be obtained from the winery, but if you get the chance to try them, grab it! You can find out more about them in the A–Z on pages 44 to 288: the cross-references in SMALL CAPITALS will guide you to the relevant entries.

WORLD CLASS WINES THAT DON'T COST THE EARTH
- Tim ADAMS Shiraz, CLARE VALLEY, Australia
- CONO SUR 20 Barrels Reserva Merlot, Chile
- Forrest Estate Sauvignon Blanc, MARLBOROUGH, New Zealand
- NYETIMBER Classic Cuvée, England
- SANTA RITA Triple C, MAIPO, Chile
- STEENBERG Merlot, CONSTANTIA, South Africa
- VALDESPINO Inocente Fino, Spain

BEST LOOKALIKES TO THE CLASSICS
Bordeaux-style red wines
- Larose, STONYRIDGE, WAIHEKE ISLAND, New Zealand
- Sorella, ANDREW WILL, WASHINGTON STATE, USA
- VERGELEGEN, STELLENBOSCH, South Africa

Burgundy-style white wines
- Allandale Chardonnay, HUNTER VALLEY, Australia
- CA' DEL BOSCO Chardonnay, Italy
- GROSSET, Piccadilly Chardonnay, Australia
- VELICH, Tiglat Chardonnay, Austria

Champagne-style wines
- IRON HORSE Blanc de Blancs, CALIFORNIA, USA
- PIPERS BROOK Pirie, TASMANIA, Australia
- ROEDERER ESTATE L'Ermitage, CALIFORNIA, USA

REGIONS TO WATCH
- ALENTEJO, Portugal
- CASTILLA Y LEON, Spain
- COLCHAGUA Valley, Chile
- CORBIERES, France
- COSTIERES DE NIMES, France
- GREAT SOUTHERN, Australia
- Luján de Cuyo, MENDOZA, Argentina
- OKANAGAN VALLEY, Canada

- SICILY, Italy
- Waipara, CANTERBURY, New Zealand

PRODUCERS TO WATCH
- CHAPEL DOWN, England
- CRAGGY RANGE, HAWKES BAY, New Zealand
- Diemersfontein, PAARL, South Africa
- Hewitson, BAROSSA, Australia
- LA AGRICOLA, MENDOZA, Argentina
- PLANETA, SICILY, Italy
- Rijckaert, BURGUNDY WHITE WINES, France
- Telmo RODRIGUEZ, Spain
- Horst SAUER, Franken, Germany
- Tatachilla, MCLAREN VALE, Australia
- Terrabianca, CHIANTI CLASSICO, Italy

TOP VALUE WINES
- Argentinian Bonarda
- CAVA fizz from Spain
- FAIRVIEW Pinotage, South Africa
- Heartland Shiraz, LIMESTONE COAST, Australia
- Incyon NERO D'AVOLA, SICILY, Italy
- La Palmeria Merlot, LA ROSA, RAPEL, Chile
- Peter LEHMANN Grenache, Australia
- Los Robles Carmenère, CURICO, Chile
- MONTANA Sauvignon Blanc, New Zealand
- Trincadeira, ALENTEJO, Portugal

AUSTRALIA
- Tim ADAMS Aberfeldy Shiraz
- CAPE MENTELLE Cabernet Sauvignon
- Freycinet Pinot Noir, TASMANIA
- GROSSET Watervale Riesling
- HENSCHKE HILL OF GRACE Shiraz
- LEEUWIN ESTATE Art Series Chardonnay

- MORRIS Old Premium Liqueur Tokay
- PETALUMA Tiers Chardonnay
- PLANTAGENET Shiraz
- TYRRELL'S Vat 1 Semillon
- WYNNS John Riddoch Cabernet Sauvignon

BORDEAUX

- Ch. ANGELUS (red)
- Ch. CHEVAL-BLANC (red)
- Ch. DUCRU-BEAUCAILLOU (red)
- Ch. GRAND-PUY-LACOSTE (red)
- Ch. LAFAURIE-PEYRAGUEY (sweet)
- Les Forts de LATOUR (red)
- Ch. LEOVILLE-BARTON (red)
- Ch LYNCH-BAGES (red)
- Ch. PICHON-LONGUEVILLE-LALANDE (red)
- Ch. SMITH-HAUT-LAFITTE (white)

BURGUNDY

- CARILLON, Bienvenues-BATARD-MONTRACHET (white)
- R Chevillon, NUITS-ST-GEORGES les Perrières (red)
- COCHE-DURY, CORTON-CHARLEMAGNE (white)
- Dugat-Py, Charmes-CHAMBERTIN (red)
- J-N GAGNARD, BATARD-MONTRACHET (white)
- Anne Gros, CLOS DE VOUGEOT (red)
- LAFON, VOLNAY Santenots (red)
- D Mortet, GEVREY-CHAMBERTIN Lavaux-St-Jacques (red)
- M Rollin, CORTON-CHARLEMAGNE (white)
- E Rouget, ECHEZEAUX (red)

CALIFORNIA

- AU BON CLIMAT Chardonnay Le Bouge d'àcôté
- CAIN Five
- LAUREL GLEN Cabernet Sauvignon
- NEWTON Le Puzzle
- Pahlmeyer Red, NAPA VALLEY
- QUPE Bien Nacido Reserve Syrah
- RIDGE Santa Cruz Mountains Chardonnay
- Sausalito Canyon Zinfandel, SAN LUIS OBISPO COUNTY
- SHAFER Hillside Select Cabernet Sauvignon
- Viader, NAPA VALLEY

ITALIAN REDS

- ALLEGRINI AMARONE
- Fattoria di Basciano CHIANTI RUFINA Riserva
- Caggiano, TAURASI
- GAJA LANGHE Sperss
- ISOLE E OLENA Cepparello
- PLANETA Santa Cecilia
- POLIZIANO Le Stanze
- Le Pupille Saffredi (see SUPER-TUSCANS)
- SELVAPIANA CHIANTI RUFINA Riserva Bucerchiale

RHÔNE AND SOUTHERN FRANCE

- Ch. de BEAUCASTEL Roussanne Vieilles Vignes (white)
- Dom. du Chêne, ST-JOSEPH
- CLOS DES PAPES, CHATEAUNEUF-DU-PAPE
- CUILLERON, CONDRIEU les Chaillets
- GRAILLOT, CROZES-HERMITAGE la Guiraude
- JAMET, COTE-ROTIE
- Dom. de la Janasse, CHATEAUNEUF-DU-PAPE Vieilles Vignes
- Ch. de St-Cosme, CONDRIEU
- VERSET, CORNAS

CABERNET SAUVIGNON

- Clos Quebrada de Macul, Domus Aurea, MAIPO Valley, Chile
- GAJA Darmagi, PIEDMONT, Italy
- Ch. GRAND-PUY-LACOSTE, PAUILLAC, France
- Les Forts de LATOUR, PAUILLAC, France
- Long Meadow Ranch, NAPA VALLEY, CALIFORNIA, USA
- RIDGE Monte Bello, CALIFORNIA, USA
- STAG'S LEAP WINE CELLARS SLV, CALIFORNIA, USA
- Terrazas de los Andes, Gran Cabernet Sauvignon, MENDOZA, Argentina
- WYNNS John Riddoch, COONAWARRA, Australia

CHARDONNAY

- AU BON CLIMAT Les Nuits Blanches, CALIFORNIA, USA
- CA DEL BOSCO, FRANCIACORTA, Italy
- CARILLON, Bienvenues-BATARD-MONTRACHET, France
- COCHE-DURY, CORTON-CHARLEMAGNE, France

- CONCHA Y TORO Amelia, Chile
- J-N GAGNARD, BATARD-MONTRACHET, France
- GROSSET Piccadilly, ADELAIDE HILLS, Australia
- KISTLER Kistler Vineyard, CALIFORNIA, USA
- KUMEU RIVER, AUCKLAND, New Zealand
- NEWTON Unfiltered, CALIFORNIA, USA
- M Rollin, CORTON-CHARLEMAGNE, France

MERLOT

- ANDREW WILL, WASHINGTON, USA
- Ch. ANGELUS, ST-EMILION, France
- Ch. AUSONE, ST-EMILION, France
- CONO SUR Reserva, Chile
- Ch. GAZIN, POMEROL, France
- LEONETTI CELLAR, WASHINGTON, USA
- ORNELLAIA Masseto, TUSCANY, Italy
- Ch. PETRUS, POMEROL, France

PINOT NOIR

- ATA RANGI, MARTINBOROUGH, New Zealand
- R Chevillon, NUITS-ST-GEORGES les St-Georges, France
- Dugat-Py, Charmes-CHAMBERTIN, France
- FELTON ROAD, CENTRAL OTAGO, New Zealand
- Freycinet, TASMANIA, Australia
- Anne Gros, CLOS DE VOUGEOT, France
- LAFON, VOLNAY Santenots, France
- Rex Hill Reserve, OREGON, USA
- E Rouget, ECHEZEAUX, France

RIESLING

- H DONNHOFF Niederhäuser Hermannshöhle, NAHE, Germany
- GROSSET Watervale, CLARE VALLEY, Australia
- GUNDERLOCH Nackenheimer Rothenberg, RHEINHESSEN, Germany
- Fritz HAAG Brauneberger Juffer Sonnenuhr, MOSEL, Germany
- Dr LOOSEN Erdener Prälat, MOSEL, Germany
- Mount Horrocks, CLARE VALLEY, Australia
- Horst SAUER Escherndorfer Lump, FRANKEN, Germany
- TRIMBACH, Clos St-Hune, ALSACE France

SAUVIGNON BLANC

- Clifford Bay, MARLBOROUGH, New Zealand
- CONCHA Y TORO Terrunyo, Chile
- Lucien CROCHET, SANCERRE, France
- Didier DAGUENEAU, POUILLY-FUME, France
- Forrest Estate, MARLBOROUGH, New Zealand
- PALLISER ESTATE, Martinborough, New Zealand
- Ch. SMITH-HAUT-LAFITTE, PESSAC-LEOGNAN, France
- STEENBERG, CONSTANTIA, South Africa
- VERGELEGEN, STELLENBOSCH, South Africa

SYRAH/SHIRAZ

- Tim ADAMS Aberfeldy, CLARE VALLEY, Australia
- BOEKENHOUTSKLOOF, FRANSCHHOEK, South Africa
- BROKENWOOD Graveyard, HUNTER VALLEY, Australia
- CHAVE, HERMITAGE, France
- HENSCHKE HILL OF GRACE, Eden Valley, Australia
- JAMET, COTE-ROTIE, France
- MONTES Folly, COLCHAGUA, Chile
- Ojai, SANTA BARBARA COUNTY, CALIFORNIA, USA
- PENFOLDS GRANGE, Australia
- QUPE Bien Nacido Reserve, CALIFORNIA, USA
- VERSET, CORNAS, France

SPARKLING WINE

- BILLECART-SALMON Cuvée N-F Billecart CHAMPAGNE, France
- CLOUDY BAY Pelorus, MARLBOROUGH, New Zealand
- DEUTZ Blanc de Blancs CHAMPAGNE, France
- Alfred GRATIEN Vintage CHAMPAGNE, France
- Charles HEIDSIECK Mis en Caves CHAMPAGNE, France
- Charles MELTON Sparkling Shiraz, BAROSSA, Australia
- NYETIMBER, England
- PIPERS BROOK Pirie, TASMANIA, Australia
- POL ROGER Vintage CHAMPAGNE, France
- ROEDERER ESTATE L'Ermitage, CALIFORNIA, USA

MODERN WINE STYLES

Not so long ago, if I were to outline the basic wine styles, the list would have been strongly biased towards the classics – Bordeaux, Burgundy, Sancerre, Mosel Riesling, Champagne. But the classics have, over time, become expensive and unreliable – thus opening the door to other, less established regions, and giving them the chance to offer us wines that may or may not owe anything to the originals. *These* are the flavours to which ambitious winemakers the world over now aspire.

WHITE WINES

Ripe, up-front, spicy Chardonnay Fruit is the key here: round, ripe, apricot, peach, melon, pineapple and tropical fruits, spiced up with the vanilla and butterscotch richness of some new oak – often American oak – to make a delicious, approachable, easy-to-drink fruit cocktail of taste. Australia created this style and still effortlessly leads the field.

Green, tangy Sauvignon New Zealand was the originator of this style – all zingy, grassy, nettles and asparagus and then green apples and peach – and South Africa now has its own tangy, super-fresh examples. Chile has the potential to produce something similar and there are hopeful signs in southern France. Bordeaux and the Loire are the original sources of dry Sauvignon wines, and at last we are seeing an expanding band of committed modern producers matching clean fruit with zippy green tang.

Bone-dry, neutral whites This doesn't sound very appetizing, but as long as it is well made it will be thirst-quenching and easy to drink. Many Italian whites fit this bill. Southern French wines, where no grape variety is specified, will be like this; so will many wines from Bordeaux, the South-West, Muscadet and Anjou. Modern young Spanish whites and Portuguese Vinho Verdes are good examples, as are Swiss Fendant (Chasselas) and southern German Trocken (dry) wines. I don't like seeing too much neutrality in New World wines, but cheap South African and California whites are 'superneutral'.

White Burgundy By this I mean the nutty, oatmealy-ripe but dry, subtly oaked styles of villages like Meursault at their best. Few people do it well, even in Burgundy itself, and it's a difficult style to emulate. California makes the most effort. Washington, Oregon and New York State each have occasional successes, as do top Australian and New Zealand Chardonnays.

Perfumy, off-dry whites Gewurztraminer, Muscat and Pinot Gris from Alsace will give you this style and in southern Germany Gewürztraminer, Scheurebe, Kerner, Grauburgunder (Pinot Gris) and occasionally Riesling may also do it. Riesling in Australia is often aromatic and mildly fruity. In New Zealand Riesling and Gewürztraminer can be excellent. Irsai Oliver from Hungary and Torrontés from Argentina are both heady and perfumed.

Mouthfuls of luscious gold Good sweet wines are difficult to make. Sauternes is the most famous, but the Loire, and sometimes Alsace, can also come up with rich, intensely sweet wines that can live for decades. Germany's top sweeties are stunning; Austria's are similiar in style to Germany's, but weightier. Hungarian Tokaji has a wonderful sweet-sour smoky flavour. Australia, California and New Zealand also have some exciting examples.

RED WINES

Spicy, warm-hearted reds Australia is out in front at the moment through the ebullient resurgence of her Shiraz reds – ripe, almost sweet, sinfully easy to enjoy. France's Rhône Valley is also on the up and the traditional appellations in the far south of France are looking good. In Italy Piedmont is producing delicious beefy Barbera and juicy exotic Dolcetto. Spain's Ribera del Duero and Toro, and Portugal's south also deliver the goods, as does Malbec in Argentina. California Zinfandel made in its most powerful style is spicy and rich.

Juicy, fruity reds This used to be the Beaujolais spot, but there hasn't been much exciting Beaujolais recently. Grenache and Syrah vins de pays are better bets, as are grassy, sharp Loire reds. Modern Spanish reds from Valdepeñas and La Mancha do the trick, as do some Garnachas from Aragón, while in Italy young Chianti and Teroldego hit home. Argentina has some good fresh examples from Sangiovese, Tempranillo and other Italian and Spanish grape varieties.

Blackcurranty Cabernet Chile has climbed back to the top of the Cabernet tree, knocking Australia off its perch, though there are still some good examples from Australia. New Zealand also strikes the blackcurrant bell in a much greener, sharper way. California only sometimes hits the sweet spot, and often with Merlot rather than Cabernet. Eastern Europe, in particular Hungary, is doing well, as is southern France. And what about Bordeaux? Only a few of the top wines reach the target; for the price, Tuscan Cabernet is often more exciting.

Tough, tannic long-haul boys Bordeaux does lead this field, and the best wines are really good after 10 years or so – but don't expect wines from minor properties to age in the same way. It's the same in Tuscany and Piedmont – only the top wines last well – especially Chianti Classico, Barolo and Barbaresco. In Portugal there's plenty of tannin and some increasingly good long-lasting Douro reds.

Soft, strawberryish charmers Good Burgundy definitely tops this group. Rioja in Spain can sometimes get there, as can Navarra and Valdepeñas. Pinot Noir in California, Oregon and New Zealand is frequently delicious, and Chile and Australia increasingly get it right too. Germany hits the spot with Spätburgunder (Pinot Noir) now and then. Italy's Lago di Caldaro often smooches in; and over in Bordeaux, of all places, both St-Émilion and Pomerol can do the business.

SPARKLING AND FORTIFIED WINES

Fizz This can be white or pink or red, dry or sweet, and I sometimes think it doesn't matter what it tastes like as long as it's cold enough and there's enough of it. Champagne can be best, but frequently isn't – and there are lots of new-wave winemakers making good-value lookalikes. Australia is tops for tasty bargains, followed by California and New Zealand. Spain pumps out oceans of good basic stuff.

Fortified wines For once in my life I find myself saying that the old ways are definitely the best. There's nothing to beat the top ports and sherries in the deep, rich, sticky stakes – though for the glimmerings of a new angle look to Australia, California and South Africa. The Portuguese island of Madeira produces fortifieds with rich, brown smoky flavours and a startling acid bite – and don't forget the luscious Muscats made all round the Mediterranean.

11

MATCHING FOOD AND WINE

Give me a rule, I'll break it – well, bend it anyway. So when I see the proliferation of publications laying down rules as to what wine to drink with what food, I get very uneasy and have to quell a burning desire to slosh back a Grand Cru Burgundy with my chilli con carne.

The pleasures of eating and drinking operate on so many levels that hard and fast rules make no sense. What about mood? If I'm in the mood for Champagne, Champagne it shall be, whatever I'm eating. What about place? If I'm sitting gazing out across the shimmering Mediterranean, hand me anything, just as long as it's local – it'll be perfect.

Even so, there are some things that simply don't go well with wine: artichokes, asparagus, spinach, kippers and mackerel, chilli, salsas and vinegars, chocolate, all flatten the flavours of wines. The general rule here is avoid tannic red wines and go for juicy young reds, or whites with plenty of fruit and fresh acidity. And for chocolate, liqueur Muscats and Asti Spumante are just about the only things that work. Don't be afraid to experiment. Who would guess that salty Roquefort cheese and rich, sweet Sauternes would go together? But they do, and it's a match made in heaven. So, with these factors in mind, the following pairings are not rules – just my recommendations.

FISH

Grilled or baked white fish
White Burgundy or other fine Chardonnay, Pessac-Léognan or Graves, Viognier, Australian and New Zealand Riesling.

Grilled or baked oily or 'meaty' fish (e.g. salmon, trout, tuna, swordfish) Alsace Riesling, fruity New World Chardonnay or Semillon, Chinon or Bourgueil, New World Pinot Noir.

Fried/battered fish Simple, fresh whites, e.g. Soave, Mâcon-Villages, Pinot Gris, white Bordeaux, or a Spätlese from the Rheingau or Pfalz.

Shellfish Chablis or unoaked Chardonnay, Pinot Blanc; *clams and oysters* Aligoté, Vinho Verde, Seyval Blanc; *crab* Riesling Spätlese, Viognier; *lobster, scallops* white Burgundy or other fine Chardonnay, Champagne, Viognier; *mussels* Muscadet, Italian Pinot Grigio.

Smoked fish Ice-cold basic fizz, manzanilla or fino sherry, Alsace Gewurztraminer or Pinot Gris, lightly oaked Chardonnay, New World Riesling.

MEAT

Beef/steak *Plain roasted or grilled* tannic reds, top Bordeaux, New World Cabernet Sauvignon, Ribera del Duero, Super-Tuscans, South African Pinotage.

Lamb *Plain roasted or grilled* top red Burgundy, top red Bordeaux, especially Pauillac or St-Éstephe, Rioja Reserva, fine New World Pinot Noir or Merlot.

Pork *Plain roasted or grilled* full, spicy dry whites, e.g. Alsace Pinot Gris, lightly oaked Chardonnay; smooth reds, e.g. Rioja, Alentejo; *ham and bacon* young, fruity reds, e.g. Beaujolais, Teroldego, unoaked Tempranillo, Mendoza Malbec, Lambrusco; *sausages, salami, pâté* rustic/young reds from Beaujolais, Provence, Puglia, and from Merlot, Zinfandel, Pinotage grapes.

Veal *Plain roasted or grilled* full-bodied whites, e.g. Alsace, German, Austrian Pinot Gris, Grüner Veltliner, Vouvray, Châteauneuf-du-Pape; soft reds, e.g. Dolcetto, Baden Pinot Noir, or mature Rioja, Burgundy or Margaux; *with cream-based sauce* full, ripe whites, e.g.

Alsace Pinot Blanc or Pinot Gris, Vouvray, oaked New World Chardonnay; *with rich red-wine sauce* (e.g. *osso buco*) young Italian reds, Zinfandel.

Venison *Plain roasted or grilled* Barolo, St-Estèphe, Pomerol, Côte de Nuits, Hermitage, big Zinfandel, Alsace or German Pinot Gris; *with red-wine sauce* Piedmont and Portuguese reds, Pomerol, St-Émilion, New World Syrah/Shiraz or Pinotage, Priorat.

Chicken and turkey *Plain roasted or grilled* fine red or white Burgundy, red Rioja Reserva, New World Chardonnay or Semillon.

Duck *Plain roasted* Pomerol, St-Émilion, Côte de Nuits or Rhône reds, New World Syrah/Shiraz (including sparkling) or Merlot; also full, soft whites such as Austrian Riesling; *with orange* German Riesling Auslese, or Barsac.

Game birds *Plain roasted or grilled* top reds from Burgundy, Rhône, Tuscany, Piedmont, Ribera del Duero, New World Cabernet; also full whites such as New World Semillon.

Casseroles and stews Match the dominant ingredient, e.g. red wine for *boeuf bourguignon* or *coq au vin*, dry whites for a fricassee. The weight of the wine should match the richness of the sauce. For strong tomato flavours see Pasta.

ETHNIC CUISINES

Chinese Riesling or Gewürztraminer, unoaked New World Chardonnay; mild German and Austrian reds.

Indian/Tex-Mex Spicy whites, e.g. Gewürztraminer, Mosel Kabinett or Spätlese, New World Sauvignon Blanc, Viognier; non-tannic reds, such as Rioja, Valpolicella, Merlot, Grenache, Syrah/Shiraz.

South-East Asian Alsace Pinot Gris, New World Sauvignon Blanc, California Zinfandel.

Thai Riesling, Gewürztraminer, New World Sauvignon Blanc. Rich, oaky Australian or California Chardonnay can cope with coconut.

EGGS

Champagne and traditional-method fizz; light, fresh reds such as Beaujolais or Chinon; full, dry unoaked whites; New World rosé.

PASTA

With tomato sauce Barbera, Soave, Verdicchio, New World Sauvignon Blanc; *with meat-based sauce* north or central Italian reds, French or New World Syrah/Shiraz, Zinfandel; *with cream- or cheese-based sauce* soft, full, dry unoaked whites from northern Italy, light Austrian reds; *with seafood/fish sauce* dry, tangy whites, e.g. Verdicchio, Vermentino, Grüner Veltliner, Muscadet; *with pesto* New World Sauvignon Blanc, Dolcetto, Minervois.

SALADS

Sharp-edged whites, e.g. New World Sauvignon Blanc, Chenin Blanc, dry Riesling, Vinho Verde.

CHEESES

Hard Full reds from Italy, France or Spain, New World Merlot or Zinfandel, dry oloroso sherry, tawny port.

Soft LBV port, rich, fruity Rhône reds, Shiraz, Zinfandel, Alsace Pinot Gris, Gewürztraminer.

Blue Botrytized sweet whites such as Sauternes, vintage port, old oloroso sherry, Malmsey Madeira.

Goats' Sancerre, Pouilly-Fumé, New World Sauvignon Blanc, Chinon, Saumur-Champigny.

DESSERTS

Chocolate Australian Liqueur Muscat, Asti Spumante.

Fruit-based Sauternes, Eiswein, Moscatel de Valencia.

MATCHING WINE AND FOOD _____

With very special bottles, when you have found an irresistible bargain or when you are casting around for culinary inspiration, it can be a good idea to let the wine dictate the choice of food.

Although I said earlier that rules in this area are made to be bent if not broken, there are certain points to remember when matching wine and food. Before you make specific choices, think about some basic characteristics and see how thinking in terms of grape varieties and wine styles can point you in the right direction.

In many cases, the local food and wine combinations that have evolved over the years simply cannot be bettered (think of ripe Burgundy with *coq au vin* or *boeuf bourguignon*; Chianti Riserva with *bistecca alla Fiorentina*; Muscadet and Breton oysters). Yet the world of food and wine is moving so fast that it would be madness to be restricted by the old tenets. Californian cuisine, fusion food, and the infiltration of innumerable ethnic influences coupled with the re-invigoration of traditional wines, continuous experiment with new methods and blends and the opening up of completely new wine areas mean that the search for perfect food and wine partners is, and will remain, very much an on-going process.

Here are some of the characteristics you need to consider, plus a summary of the main grape varieties and their best food matches.

Body/weight As well as considering the taste of the wine you need to match the weight or body of the wine to the intensity of the food's flavour. A heavy alcoholic wine will not suit a delicate dish; and *vice versa*.

Acidity The acidity of a dish should balance the acidity of a wine. High-acid flavours, such as tomato, lemon or vinegar, need matching acidity in their accompanying wines. Use acidity in wine to cut through the richness of a dish but for this to work, make sure the wine is full in flavour.

Sweetness Sweet food makes dry wine taste unpleasantly lean and acidic. With desserts and puddings find a wine that is at least as sweet as the food (sweeter than the food is fine). However, many savoury foods, such as carrots, onions and parsnips, taste slightly sweet and dishes in which they feature prominently will go best with ripe, fruity wines that have a touch of sweetness.

Salt Salty foods and sweet wines match, but salty foods and tannin are definitely best avoided.

Age/Maturity The bouquet of a wine is only acquired over time and should be savoured and appreciated: with age many red wines acquire complex flavours and perfumes and a similar degree of complexity in the flavour of the food is often a good idea.

Tannin Rare red meat can have the effect of softening tannic wine. Avoid eggs and fish.

Oak Oak flavours in wine vary from the satisfyingly subtle to positively strident. This latter end of the scale can conflict with food, although it may be suitable for smoked fish (white wines only) or full-flavoured meat or game.

Wine in the food If you want to use wine in cooking it is best to use the same style of wine as the one you are going to drink with the meal (it can be an inferior version though).

RED GRAPES

Barbera Wines made to be drunk young have high acidity that can hold their own with sausages, salami, ham, and tomato sauces. Complex older wines from the top growers need to be matched with rich Piemontese food: beef casseroles and game dishes.

Cabernet Franc Best drunk with plain rather than sauced meat dishes, or, slightly chilled, with grilled or baked salmon or trout. Try it with Indian food.

Cabernet Sauvignon All over the world the Cabernet Sauvignon makes full-flavoured reliable red wine: the ideal food wine. Classic combinations include Cru Classé Pauillac with roast lamb; Super-Tuscan *vini da tavola* with *bistecca alla Fiorentina;* softer, riper New World Cabernet Sauvignons with roast turkey or goose. Cabernet Sauvignon seems to have a particular affinity for lamb but it partners all plain roast or grilled meats and game well and would be an excellent choice for many sauced meat dishes such as *boeuf bourguignon*, steak and kidney pie or rabbit stew and any substantial dishes made with mushrooms.

Dolcetto Dolcetto produces fruity purple wines that go beautifully with hearty local north Italian meat dishes such as calves' liver and onions or casseroled game with polenta.

Gamay The grape of red Beaujolais, Gamay, makes wine you can drink whenever, wherever, however and with whatever you want. It goes particularly well with charcuterie products such as pâtés and sausages because its acidity provides a satisfying foil to their richness. It would be a good choice for many vegetarian dishes. If in doubt you are unlikely to go far wrong with Gamay.

Grenache Generally blended with other grapes, Grenache nonetheless dominates, with its high alcoholic strength and rich, spicy flavours. These are wines readily matched with food: casseroles, charcuterie and grills for concentrated older wines; almost anything – from light vegetarian dishes to *soupe de poissons* – for lighter reds and rosés.

Merlot The Bordeaux grape that has come into its own all over the world, Merlot makes soft, rounded, fruity wines that are some of the easiest red wines to enjoy without food, yet are also a good choice with many kinds of food. Spicier game dishes, herby terrines and pâtés, pheasant, pigeon, duck or goose all blend well with Merlot; substantial casseroles made with wine are excellent with top Pomerol châteaux; and the soft fruitiness of the wines is perfect for pork, liver, turkey, and savoury foods with a hint of sweetness such as honey-roast or Bayonne ham.

Nebbiolo Fruity, fragrant, early-drinking styles of Nebbiolo wine are best with local salami, pâtés, *bresaola* and lighter meat dishes. The best Barolos and Barbarescos need substantial food: *bollito misto*, rich hare or beef casseroles and *brasato al Barolo* (a large piece of beef marinated then braised slowly in Barolo) are just the job in Piedmont, or anywhere else for that matter.

Pinot Noir The great grape of Burgundy has taken its food-friendly complexity all over the wine world. However, nothing can beat the marriage of great wine with sublime local food that is Burgundy's heritage, and it is Burgundian dishes that spring to mind as perfect partners for the Pinot Noir: *coq au vin, boeuf bourguignon*, rabbit with mustard, braised ham, chicken with tarragon, steaks from prized Charolais cattle with a rich red-wine sauce ... the list is endless.

Pinot Noir's subtle flavours make it a natural choice for complex meat dishes but it is also excellent with plain grills and roasts and, in its lighter manifestations from, say, the Loire or Oregon, a good match for salmon or salmon trout.

In spite of the prevalence of superb cheese in Burgundy, the best Pinot Noir red wines are wasted on cheese.

Sangiovese Tuscany is where Sangiovese best expresses the qualities that can lead it, in the right circumstances, to be numbered among the great grapes of the world. And Tuscany is very much food with wine territory. Sangiovese wines such as Chianti, Rosso di Montalcino, Vino Nobile di Montepulciano, and the biggest of them all, Brunello, positively demand to be drunk with food. Drink them with *bistecca alla Fiorentina*, roast meats and game, calves' liver, casseroles, hearty pasta sauces, *porcini* mushrooms and Pecorino cheese.

Syrah/Shiraz Whether from France (in the Northern Rhône), Australia, California or South Africa, this grape always makes powerful, rich, full-bodied wines that are superb with full-flavoured food. The classic barbecue wine, Shiraz/Syrah also goes with roasts, game, hearty casseroles

and charcuterie. It can also be good with tangy cheeses such as Manchego or Cheshire.

Tempranillo Spain's best native red grape makes aromatic wines for drinking young, and matures well to a rich (usually) oaky flavour. Tempranillo is good with game, local cured hams and sausages, casseroles and meat grilled with herbs; it is particularly good with lamb. It can partner some Indian dishes and goes well with strong soft cheeses such as ripe Brie.

Zinfandel California's much-planted, most versatile grape is used for a bewildering variety of wine styles from bland, slightly sweet pinks to rich, elegant, fruity reds. And the good red Zinfandels themselves may vary greatly in style. If they aren't too oaky they are good with barbecued meats, venison and roast chicken. The hefty old-style wines are a great match with the spicy, mouthfilling San Francisco cuisine, or with game casseroles. The pale blush style of Zin goes well with tomato sauce.

WHITE GRAPES

Albariño Light, crisp, aromatic with apricots and grapefruit, this goes well with crab and prawn dishes as well as Chinese-style chicken dishes.

Aligoté This Burgundian grape can, at its best, make very versatile food wine. It goes well with many fish and seafood dishes, smoked fish, salads and snails in garlic and butter.

Chardonnay More than almost any other grape Chardonnay responds to different climatic conditions and to the winemaker's art. This, plus the relative ease with which it can be grown, accounts for the marked gradation of flavours and styles: from steely, cool-climate austerity to almost tropical lusciousness. The relatively sharp end of the spectrum is one of the best choices for simple fish dishes; most Chardonnays are superb with roast chicken or other white meat; the really full, rich, New World blockbusters need rich fish and seafood dishes. Oaky Chardonnays are a good choice for smoked fish.

Chenin Blanc One of the most versatile of grapes, Chenin Blanc makes wines ranging from averagely quaffable dry whites to the great sweet whites of the Loire. The lighter wines can be good as apéritifs or with light fish dishes or salads. The sweet wines are good with most puddings and superb with those made with slightly tart fruit.

Gewürztraminer Spicy and perfumed, Gewürztraminer has the weight and flavour to go with such hard-to-match dishes as *choucroute* and smoked fish. It is also a good choice for Chinese or indeed any oriental food.

Marsanne These rich, fat wines are a bit short of acid so match them with simply prepared chicken, pork, fish or vegetables.

Muscadet The dry, light Muscadet grape (best wines are *sur lie*) is perfect with seafood.

Muscat Fragrant, grapy wines ranging from delicate to downright syrupy. The drier ones are more difficult to pair with food; the sweeties come into their own with most desserts. Sweet Moscato d'Asti, delicious by itself, goes well with rich Christmas pudding or mince pies.

Pinot Blanc Clean, bright and appley, Pinot Blanc is very food-friendly. Classic white wine dishes, modern vegetarian dishes, pasta and pizza all match up well.

Pinot Gris Rich, fat wines that need rich, fat food. Go (in Alsace) for *choucroute*, *confit de canard*, rich pork dishes. The Italian Pinot Gris (Grigio) wines are lighter and more suited to pizza or pasta.

Riesling Good dry Rieslings are delicious by themselves, but also excellent with spicy cuisine. Sweet Rieslings are best enjoyed for their own lusciousness but are suitable partners to fruit-based desserts. In between, those with a slight acid bite can counteract the richness of, say, goose or duck, and the fuller examples can be good with oriental food and otherwise hard-to-match salads.

Sauvignon Blanc This grape makes wines with enough bite and sharpness to accompany quite rich fish dishes as well as being an obvious choice for seafood. The characteristic acid intensity makes a brilliant match with dishes made with tomato, but the best match of all is Sancerre and local Loire goats' cheese.

Sémillon/Semillon Dry Bordeaux Blancs are excellent with fish and shellfish; fuller, riper New World Semillons are equal to spicy food and rich sauces, often going even better with meat than with fish; sweet Sémillons can partner many puddings, especially rich, creamy ones. Sémillon also goes well with many cheeses, and Sauternes with Roquefort is a classic combination.

Viognier A subtle and characterful grape, Viognier is at its best as an apéritif. It can also go well with spicy Indian dishes.

17

MAKING THE MOST OF WINE

Most wine is pretty hardy stuff and can put up with a fair amount of rough handling. Young red wines can knock about in the back of a car for a day or two and be lugged from garage to kitchen to dinner table without coming to too much harm. Serving young white wines when well chilled can cover up all kinds of ill-treatment – a couple of hours in the fridge should do the trick. Even so, there are some conditions that are better than others for storing your wines, especially if they are on the mature side. And there are certain ways of serving wines which will emphasize any flavours or perfumes they have.

STORING

Most wines are sold ready for drinking, and it will be hard to ruin them if you store them for a few months before you pull the cork. Don't stand them next to the central heating or the cooker, though, or on a sunny windowsill.

Light and extremes of temperature are also the things to worry about if you are storing wine long-term. Some wines, Chardonnay for instance, are particularly sensitive to exposure to light over several months, and the damage will be worse if the bottle is made of pale-coloured glass. The warmer the wine, the quicker it will age, and really high temperatures can spoil wine quite quickly. Beware in the winter of garages and outhouses, too: a very cold snap – say –4°C (25°F) or below – will freeze your wine, push out the corks and crack the bottles. An underground cellar is ideal, with a fairly constant temperature of 10°–12°C (50°–53°F). And bottles really do need to lie on their sides, so that the cork stays damp and swollen, and keeps out the air.

TEMPERATURE

The person who thought up the rule that red wine should be served at room temperature certainly didn't live in a modern, centrally heated flat. It's no great sin to serve a big beefy red at the temperature of your central heating, but I prefer most reds just a touch cooler. Over-heated wine tastes flabby, and may lose some of its more volatile aromas. In general, the lighter the red, the cooler it can be. Really light, refreshing reds, such as Beaujolais, are nice lightly chilled. Ideally, I'd serve Burgundy and other Pinot Noir wines at larder temperature (about 15°C/59°F), Bordeaux and Rioja a bit warmer (18°C/64°F), Rhône wines and New World Cabernet at a comfortable room temperature, but no more than 20°C/68°F.

Chilling white wines makes them taste fresher, emphasizing their acidity. White wines with low acidity especially benefit from chilling, and it's vital for sparkling wines if you want to avoid exploding corks and a tableful of froth. Drastic chilling also subdues flavours, however – a useful ruse if you're serving basic wine, but a shame if the wine is very good. A good guide for whites is to give the cheapest and lightest a spell in the fridge, but serve bigger and better wines – Australian Chardonnays or top white Burgundies – perhaps half-way between fridge and central-heating temperature. If you're undecided, err on the cooler side, for whites or reds. To chill wine quickly, and to keep it cool, an ice bucket is more efficient if filled with a mixture of ice and water, rather than ice alone.

18

OPENING THE BOTTLE

There's no corkscrew to beat the Screwpull, and the Spinhandle Screwpull is especially easy to use. Don't worry if bits of cork crumble into the wine – just fish them out of your glass. Tight corks that refuse to budge might be loosened if you run hot water over the bottle neck to expand the glass. If the cork is loose and falls in, push it right in and don't worry about it.

Opening sparkling wines is a serious business – point the cork away from people! Once you've started, never take your hand off the cork until it's safely out. Remove the foil, loosen the wire, hold the wire and cork firmly and twist the bottle. If the wine froths, hold the bottle at an angle of 45 degrees, and have a glass at hand.

AIRING AND DECANTING

Scientists have proved that opening young to middle-aged red wines an hour before serving makes no difference whatsoever. The surface area of wine in contact with air in the bottle neck is too tiny to be significant. Decanting is a different matter, because sloshing the wine from bottle to jug or decanter mixes it up quite thoroughly with the air. The only wines that really need to be decanted are those that have a sediment which would cloud the wine if they were poured directly – mature red Bordeaux, Burgundy and vintage port are the commonest examples. Ideally, if you are able to plan that far in advance, you need to stand the bottle upright for a day or two to let the sediment settle in the bottom. Draw the cork extremely gently. As you tip the bottle, shine a bright light through from underneath as you pour in a single steady movement. Stop pouring when you see the sediment approaching the bottle neck.

Contrary to many wine buffs' practice, I would decant a mature wine only just before serving; elderly wines often fade rapidly once they meet with air, and an hour in the decanter could kill off what little fruit they had left. By contrast, a good-quality young white wine can benefit from decanting.

GLASSES

If you want to taste wine at its best, to enjoy all its flavours and aromas, to admire its colours and texture, choose glasses designed for the purpose and show the wine a bit of respect. The ideal wine glass is a fairly large tulip shape, made of fine, clear glass, with a slender stem. When you pour the wine, fill the glass no more than halfway to allow space for aromas. For sparkling wines choose a tall, slender glass, as it helps the bubbles to last longer.

KEEPING LEFTOVERS

Leftover white wine keeps better than red, since the tannin and colouring matter in red wine is easily attacked by the air. Any wine, red or white, keeps better in the fridge than in a warm kitchen. And most wines, if well made in the first place, will be perfectly acceptable, if not pristine, after 2 or 3 days re-corked in the fridge. But for better results it's best to use one of the gadgets sold for this purpose. The ones that work by blanketing the wine with heavier-than-air inert gas are much better than those that create a vacuum in the air space in the bottle.

FRANCE

I've visited most of the wine-producing countries of the world by now, but the one I come back to again and again, with my enthusiasm undimmed by time, is France. The sheer range of its wine flavours, the number of wine styles produced, and indeed the quality differences, from very best to very nearly worst, continue to enthral me, and as each year's vintage nears, I find myself itching to leap into the car and head for the vineyards of Champagne, of Burgundy, of Bordeaux and the Loire. France is currently going through a fascinating period – with an eye on the New World, she's redefining her ideas of what makes a wine great, and what makes her wines different from all the others.

CLIMATE AND SOIL
France lies between the 40th and 50th parallels north, and the climate runs from the distinctly chilly and almost too cool to ripen grapes in the far north near the English Channel, right through to the swelteringly hot and almost too torrid to avoid grapes overripening in the far south on the Mediterranean shores. In the north the most refined and delicate sparkling wine is made in Champagne. In the south, rich, luscious dessert Muscats and fortified wines dominate. In between is just about every sort of wine you could wish for.

The factors that influence a wine's flavour are the grape variety, the soil and climate, and the winemaker's techniques. Most of the great wine grapes, like the red Cabernet Sauvignon, Merlot, Pinot Noir and Syrah, and the white Chardonnay, Sauvignon Blanc, Sémillon and Viognier, find conditions in France where they can ripen slowly but reliably – and slow, even ripening always gives better flavours to a wine. Since grapes have been grown for over 2000 years in France, the most suitable varieties for the different soils and meso-climates have naturally evolved. And since winemaking was brought to France by the Romans, generation upon generation of winemakers have refined their techniques to produce the best possible results from their different grape types. The great wines of areas like Bordeaux and Burgundy are the results of centuries of experience and of trial and error, which winemakers from other countries of the world now use as role models in their attempts to create good wine.

WINE REGIONS
White grapes generally ripen more easily than red grapes and they dominate the northern regions. Even so, the chilly Champagne region barely manages to ripen its red or white grapes on its chalky soil. But the resultant acid wine is the ideal base for sparkling wine, and the acidity of the young still wine can, with good winemaking and a few years' maturing, transform into a golden honeyed sparkling wine of incomparable finesse.

Alsace, on the German border, is warmer and drier than Champagne (the vineyards sit in a rain shadow created by the Vosges mountains that rise above the Rhine Valley) but still produces mainly dry white wines, from grapes such as Riesling, Pinot Gris and Gewurz-traminer that are not widely encountered elsewhere in France. With its clear blue skies, Alsace can provide ripeness, and therefore the higher alcoholic strength of the warm south, but also the perfume and fragrance of the cool north.

South-east of Paris, Chablis marks the northernmost tip of the Burgundy region, and the Chardonnay grape here produces very dry wines, usually with a streak of green acidity, but nowadays with a fuller softer texture to subdue any harshness.

It's a good 2 hours' drive further south to the heart of Burgundy – the Côte d'Or which runs between Dijon and Chagny. World-famous villages such as Gevrey-Chambertin and Vosne-Romanée (where the red Pinot Noir dominates) and Meursault and Puligny-Montrachet (where Chardonnay reigns) here produce the great Burgundies that have given the region renown over the centuries. Lesser Burgundies – but they're still good – are produced further south in the Côte Chalonnaise, while between Mâcon and Lyon are the white Mâconnais wine villages (Pouilly-Fuissé and St-Véran are particularly good) and the villages of Beaujolais, famous for bright, easy-going red wine from the Gamay grape. The 10 Beaujolais Crus or 'growths' are the most important vineyard sites and should produce wine with more character and structure.

South of Lyon in the Rhône Valley red wines begin to dominate. The Syrah grape makes great wine at Hermitage and Côte-Rôtie in the north, while in the south the Grenache and a host of supporting grapes (most southern Rhône reds will include at least Syrah, Cinsaut or Mourvèdre in their blends) make full, satisfying reds, of which Châteauneuf-du-Pape is the most famous. The white Viognier makes lovely wine at Condrieu and Château-Grillet in the north.

Main vineyard areas

0   50   100 km
0   50 miles

The whole of the south of France is now changing and improving at a bewildering rate, prompted by a new generation or a change in ownership, often bringing in foreign investment to the region. Provence and the scorched Midi vineyards are learning how to produce exciting wines from unpromising land and many of France's tastiest and most affordable wines now come under a Vin de Pays label from the south. In the Languedoc the red wines from traditional vineyards of Grenache, Syrah, Mourvèdre and Carignan can be exceptional, and in the Roussillon the sweet Muscats and Grenache-based fortifieds are equally fine.

The South-West of France is dominated by the wines of Bordeaux, but has many other gems benefiting from the cooling influence of the Atlantic. Dry whites from Gascony and Bergerac can be exciting. Jurançon down in the Basque country produces some remarkable dry and sweet wines, while Madiran, Cahors and Bergerac produce good to excellent reds.

But Bordeaux is the king here. The Cabernet Sauvignon and Merlot are the chief grapes, the Cabernet dominating the production of deep reds from the Médoc peninsula and its famous villages of Margaux, St-Julien, Pauillac and St-Estèphe. Round the city of Bordeaux are Pessac-Léognan and Graves, where Cabernet and Merlot blend to produce fragrant refined reds. On the right bank of the Gironde estuary, the Merlot is most important in the plump rich reds of St-Émilion and Pomerol. Sweet whites from Sémillon and Sauvignon Blanc are made in Sauternes, with increasingly good dry whites produced in the Entre-Deux-Mers, and especially in Graves and Pessac-Léognan.

The Loire Valley is the most northerly of France's Atlantic wine regions but, since the river rises in the heart of France not far from the Rhône, styles vary widely. Sancerre and Pouilly in the east produce tangy Sauvignon whites, the centre of the river produces fizzy wine at Vouvray and Saumur, sweet wine at Vouvray and the Layon Valley (Chenin Blanc is used for everything here from sparkling wines to botrytized ones), red wines at Chinon and Bourgueil, and dry whites virtually everywhere, while down at the mouth of the river, as it slips past Nantes into the Atlantic swell, the vineyards of Muscadet produce one of the world's most famous and often least memorable dry white wines.

CLASSIFICATIONS

France has an intricate but eminently logical system for controlling the quality and authenticity of its wines. The system is divided into 4 broad classifications (in ascending order): Vin de Table, Vin de Pays, VDQS (Vin Délimité de Qualité Supérieure) and AC (Appellation Contrôlée). Within the laws there are numerous variations, with certain vineyards or producers singled out for special mention. The 1855 Classification in Bordeaux or the Grands Crus of Alsace or Burgundy are good examples. The intention is a system which rewards quality. Vin de Pays and VDQS wines can be promoted to AC, for example, after a few years' good behaviour. The AC system is now under increasing attack from critics, both inside and outside France, who feel that it is outmoded and ineffectual and that too many poor wines are passed as of Appellation Contrôlée standard.

2001 VINTAGE REPORT

The 2000 vintage in Bordeaux was a difficult act to follow but 2001 looks generally to be a good year. Winemakers are calling it 'classical' and making comparisons with 1996 and 1998 rather than the riper 1990 or 2000. The best reds have good colour and firm tannins. After last year's disappointment, Sauternes and other sweet wine appellations have made some exceptional wines. Hot, dry, sunny weather in August through to October again made up for a dismal early season. Rain fell on 2 or 3 days during the harvest and the possibility of rot was a worry. Quality is therefore likely to vary according to the work undertaken in the vineyards (green harvesting, leaf plucking) during the summer months.

The cool wet weather in early September took the edge off what could have been another fine vintage for Burgundy. However, the weather cheered up towards the end of the month and most producers are happy with what they have in their cellars – just lamenting the absence of one extra week of fine sunny weather in mid-September which might have made the difference. Expect decent reds and whites but not a glamour vintage.

2001 looks set to be another fine year for both reds and whites throughout the Rhône Valley, creating a remarkable run of good vintages. Whites from the north are looking particularly impressive, and the reds have good balance and should prove to be fine cellaring prospects. Reds from the south should be every bit as good as those from the 2000 vintage. Conditions also look favourable throughout Provence.

Dry, sunny weather and the drying *vent du Nord* produced wines with huge ripeness and concentration in the Languedoc-Roussillon. Growers say they haven't seen such phenomenal conditions since 1982. The Carignan, Cinsaut, Grenache and Mourvèdre are all excellent, with only the Syrah suffering from the lack of rain in certain zones. The natural alcohol potential was high, making these big, powerful wines that will need some bottle age.

Conditions were variable throughout the Loire, with the better weather to be found at the western end, resulting in some very good Muscadet – although volume will be down due to late spring frosts. Anjou and Touraine look promising, with less rain and rot than 2000, and a number of good sweet wines should be produced. Sancerre and Pouilly-Fumé were challenging: the best producers focused on reducing yields to ensure quality.

In Alsace a fine summer was followed by a wet September, provoking both noble and ignoble rot. However, a fine sunny October saved the day, and overall quality promises to be very good, with well-balanced wines.

Champagne experienced the wettest harvest in over a century. The crop was enormous but quality is likely to be modest, except where growers have rigorously eliminated rotten and swollen grapes. It's certainly unlikely to be a year for vintage wines.

See also ALSACE, BORDEAUX RED WINES, BORDEAUX WHITE WINES, BURGUNDY RED WINES, BURGUNDY WHITE WINES, CHAMPAGNE, CORSICA, JURA, LANGUEDOC-ROUSSILLON, LOIRE VALLEY, MIDI, PROVENCE, RHONE VALLEY, ROUSSILLON, SAVOIE, SOUTH-WEST FRANCE; and individual wines and producers.

ITALY

The cultivation of the vine was introduced to Italy over 3000 years ago, by the Greeks (to Sicily and the south) and by the Etruscans (to the north-east and central zones). Despite their great tradition, Italian wines as we know them today are relatively young. New attitudes have resulted, in the last 30 years or so, in a great change in Italian wine. The whole industry has been modernized, and areas like Tuscany are now among the most dynamic of any in the world. With her unique characteristics, challenging wine styles and mass of grape varieties, Italy is now ready again to take on the role of leadership she has avoided for so long.

GRAPE VARIETIES AND WINE REGIONS

Vines are grown all over Italy, from the Austrian border in the north-east to the island of Pantelleria in the far south, nearer to North Africa than to Sicily. The north-west, especially Piedmont, is the home of many of the best Italian red grapes, like Nebbiolo (the grape of Barolo and Barbaresco), Dolcetto and Barbera, while the north-east (Friuli-Venezia Giulia, Alto Adige and the Veneto) is more noted for the success of native white varieties like Garganega, Tocai and Ribolla, reds like Corvina, and imports like Pinot Grigio, Chardonnay

and Sauvignon. The central Po Valley is Lambrusco country. Moving south, Tuscany is best known for its red Chianti, Brunello di Montalcino and Vino Nobile di Montepulciano wines from the native Sangiovese grape as well as its famed Super-Tuscans. South of Rome, where the Mediterranean climate holds sway, modern winemakers are revelling in the chance to make exciting wines from both traditional and international varieties. The islands too have their own varieties: Nero d'Avola in Sicily, red Cannonau and Carignano and white Vermentino in Sardinia.

CLASSIFICATIONS

Vino da Tavola, or 'table wine', is used for a wine that is produced either outside the existing laws, or in an area where no delimited zone exists. Both cheap, basic wines and inspired innovative creations like Tignanello, Sassicaia and other so-called Super-Tuscans used to fall into this anonymous category. Now the fancy wines have become either DOC (particularly in Piedmont with its Langhe DOC) or IGT (a lot of Super-Tuscans are now IGT). Remaining Vino da Tavola are labelled simply as *bianco*, *rosso* or *rosato* without vintages or geographical indications.

IGT (Indicazione Geografica Tipica) began taking effect with the 1995 vintage to identify wines from certain regions or areas as an equivalent of the French Vin de Pays. A great swathe of both ordinary and premium wines traded their Vino da Tavola status for a regional IGT.

DOC (Denominazione di Origine Controllata) is the main classification for wines from designated zones made following traditions that were historically valid but often outdated. Recently the laws have become more flexible, encouraging producers to lower yields and modernize techniques, while bringing quality wines under new appellations that allow for recognition of communes, estates and single vineyards.

DOCG (Denominazione di Origine Controllata e Garantita) was conceived as a 'super-league' for DOCs with a guarantee of authenticity that promised high class but didn't always provide it. Still, despite some dubious promotions to this élite category, wines must be made under stricter standards that have favoured improvements. The best guarantee of quality, however, remains the producer's name.

2001 VINTAGE REPORT

A potentially outstanding vintage in Piedmont was spoilt slightly by hail and intermittent rain from early September onwards, but for many producers this makes the seventh very good vintage on the trot (starting with 1995). Late spring frosts and a very dry, hot summer have reduced quantities here and in much of northern and central Italy, especially Tuscany. Generally a better vintage for early-ripening varieties, although Sangiovese from well-tended vineyards will be excellent. Quality will be more mixed in the north-east. While very promising in the hot, sunny south, some vines there were stressed due to excessive heat, and some fruit was overripe.

See also ABRUZZO, ALTO ADIGE, CALABRIA, CAMPANIA, EMILIA-ROMAGNA, FRIULI-VENEZIA GIULIA, LAZIO, LIGURIA, LOMBARDY, MARCHE, PIEDMONT, PUGLIA, ROMAGNA, SARDINIA, SICILY, TRENTINO, TUSCANY, UMBRIA, VALLE D'AOSTA, VENETO; and individual wines and producers.

GERMANY

Dull, semi-sweet wines with names like Liebfraumilch, Niersteiner Gutes Domtal and Piesporter Michelsberg used to dominate the export market, but they are rapidly vanishing off all but the most basic radar screens. Though producers at present find exports difficult, single-estate wines, with a greatly improved quality, are now the focus of sales abroad. Throughout Germany, both red and white wines are year by year, region by region, grower by grower, becoming fuller, better balanced and drier.

GRAPE VARIETIES

Riesling makes the best wines, in styles ranging from dry to intensely sweet. Other white wines come from Grauburgunder/Ruländer (Pinot Gris), Weissburgunder (Pinot Blanc), Gewürztraminer, Silvaner and Scheurebe, although the widely planted Müller-Thurgau produces much of the simpler wine. In the past decade plantings of red grape varieties have doubled. Good reds can be made in the south of the country from Spätburgunder (Pinot Noir) or blends based on Lemberger.

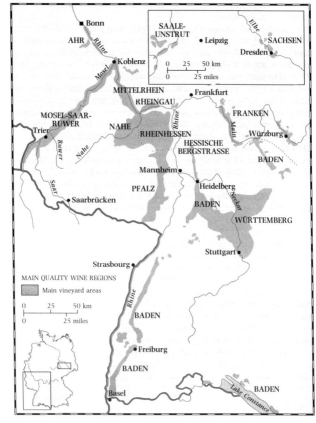

26

WINE REGIONS

Many of the most delectable Rieslings come from villages such as Bernkastel, Brauneberg, Ürzig and Wehlen on the Mosel, and Eltville, Johannisberg and Rüdesheim in the Rheingau. The Nahe also makes superb Rieslings in Schlossböckelheim and Niederhausen, and Traisen has the best vineyards in the entire region. Rheinhessen is unfortunately better known for its sugary Niersteiner Gutes Domtal than it is for the excellent racy Rieslings produced on steep slopes in the villages of Nackenheim, Nierstein and Oppenheim. Franken is the one place the Silvaner grape excels, often made in a powerful, dry, earthy style. The Pfalz is climatically similar to Alsace and has a similar potential for well-rounded, dry whites, plus rapidly improving reds. Baden produces wine styles which appeal to an international market increasingly reared on fuller, drier wines. In Württemberg most of the red wines are thin and dull, but there are a few producers who understand the need for weight and flavour in red winemaking. The other smaller wine regions make little wine and little is exported.

CLASSIFICATIONS

Germany's classification system is based on the ripeness of the grapes and therefore their potential alcohol level.

Tafelwein (table wine) is the most basic term, used for any blended wine, accounting for only a tiny percentage of production.

Landwein (country wine) is a slightly more up-market version, linked to 17 regional areas. These must be Trocken (dry) or Halbtrocken (medium-dry).

QbA (Qualitätswein bestimmter Anbaugebiete) is 'quality' wine from one of 13 designated regions, but the grapes don't have to be very ripe, and sugar can be added to the juice to increase alcoholic content.

QmP (Qualitätswein mit Prädikat) or 'quality wine with distinction' is the top level. There are 6 levels of QmP (in ascending order of ripeness): Kabinett, Spätlese, Auslese, Beerenauslese, Eiswein, Trockenbeerenauslese. The addition of sugar is strictly forbidden.

In 2000, 2 new designations for dry wine were introduced: **Classic** for 'good' varietal wines and **Selection** for 'top quality' varietal wines.

The Rheingau has introduced an official classification – Erstes Gewächs (First Growth) – for its best sites. Other regions are evolving unofficial classifications – currently called Grosses Gewächs or Erste Lage – in the hope that these, too, will become law.

2001 VINTAGE REPORT

The northerly regions of Germany, most particularly the Mosel, Nahe, Mittelrhein, Rheingau and Franken, hit the jackpot when the wet September turned into a genuinely golden October and fine November. The late-picked Riesling wines look to be the best since 1990, maybe even since 1959. Further south, the Rieslings are less homogenously good, but the Burgunders (Pinots) gave good results.

See also AHR, BADEN, FRANKEN, HESSISCHE BERGSTRASSE, MITTELRHEIN, MOSEL-SAAR-RUWER, NAHE, PFALZ, RHEINGAU, RHEINHESSEN, SAALE-UNSTRUT, SACHSEN, WURTTEMBERG; and individual wine villages and producers.

AUSTRIA

I can't think of a European nation where the wine culture has changed so dramatically over a generation as it has in Austria. Austria still makes great sweet wines, but a new order based on world-class dry whites and increasingly fine reds has emerged. Austria suddenly seems positively New World in its ambition and innovation.

WINE REGIONS AND GRAPE VARIETIES

The Danube runs through Niederösterreich, scene of much of Austria's viticulture. The Wachau produces great Riesling and excellent pepper-dry Grüner Veltliner. Next along the Danube are Kremstal and Kamptal, also fine dry white regions with a few good reds. Burgenland, south of Vienna, produces the best reds and also, around the Neusiedler See, superb dessert wines. Further south, in Steiermark, Chardonnay and Sauvignon are increasingly oak-aged.

CLASSIFICATIONS

Wine categories are similar to those in Germany, beginning with **Tafelwein** (table wine) and **Landwein** (country wine, like the French Vin de Pays). **Qualitätswein** must come from a region specified on the label: this may be from one of the 16 main producing regions or a village or vineyard within the region. Like German wines, quality wines may additionally have a special category: Kabinett, Auslese, Beerenauslese, Ausbruch, Trockenbeerenauslese.

2001 VINTAGE REPORT

The golden October and November of 2001 yielded dry Riesling, Grüner Veltliner and Sauvignon Blanc wines which marry concentration with elegance. The dessert wine harvest in Burgenland generally promises high quality. Though the reds were more affected by September's rain, the top growers report small crops of solid quality.

See also BURGENLAND, CARNUNTUM, DONAULAND, KAMPTAL, KREMSTAL, STEIERMARK, THERMENREGION, WACHAU, WIEN; and individual wine villages and producers.

SPAIN

The late 1990s provided a dramatic turnaround in the quality of Spain's long-neglected wines. A drastic modernization of winemaking technology has now allowed regions like Priorat, Ribera del Duero, La Mancha, Rueda and Toro to muscle into the limelight, alongside Rioja and Jerez, with potent fruit-driven wines with the impact and style to convert the modern consumer.

WINE REGIONS

Galicia in the green, hilly north-west grows Spain's most aromatic whites. The heartland of the great Spanish reds, Rioja, Navarra and Ribera del Duero, is situated between the central plateau and the northern coast. Travelling west along the Duero, Rueda produces fresh whites and Toro good ripe reds. Cataluña is principally white wine country (much of it sparkling Cava), though there are some great reds in Priorat and increasingly in Terra Alta and new DO Montsant. Aragón's reds and whites are looking good too. The central plateau of La Mancha makes mainly cheap reds and whites, though non-DO producers are improving spectacularly. Valencia in the south-east can rival La Mancha for fresh, unmemorable but inexpensive reds and whites. Andalucía's specialities are the fortified wines, sherry, Montilla and Málaga.

CLASSIFICATIONS

Vino de Mesa, the equivalent of France's Vin de Table, is the lowest level, but is also used for a growing number of non-DO 'Super-Spanish'.
Vino de la Tierra is Spain's equivalent of France's Vin de Pays.
DO (Denominación de Origen) is the equivalent of France's AC, regulating grape varieties and region of origin.
DOC (Denominación de Origen Calificada) is a super-category. For a long time Rioja was the only region to have been promoted to DOC, but it has recently been joined by Priorat.

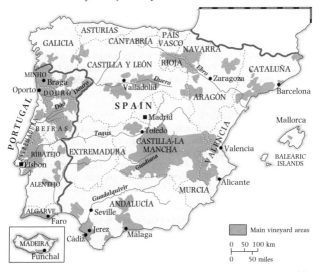

29

2001 VINTAGE REPORT
In central and southern Spain, drought conditions were so intense that grape growth was often affected, resulting in a reduced crop and uneven quality. In Rioja and Ribera del Duero, ripening conditions were far better, giving rise to an outstanding if smallish crop – quality levels have been compared with those of 1994 and even 1964.

PORTUGAL

Investment and a new dynamic approach seem to be paying off in this varied and attractive country, with climates that vary from the mild, damp Minho region in the north-west to the subtropical island of Madeira. Innovative use of native grape varieties means that Portugal is now a rich source of inexpensive yet characterful wines.

WINE REGIONS
The lush Vinho Verde country in the north-west gives very different wine from the parched valleys of the neighbouring Douro, with its drier, more continental climate. The Douro, home of port, is also the source of some of Portugal's best unfortified red wines. In Beiras, which includes Bairrada and Dão, soils are more important in determining the character of the wines. Estremadura and Ribatejo supply generous quantities of wine from regions either influenced by the maritime climate, or softened by the river Tagus. South of Lisbon, the Terras do Sado and Alentejo produce some exciting table wines. And Madeira is unique, a volcanic island 400km (250 miles) out in the Atlantic Ocean.

CLASSIFICATIONS
Vinho Regional is equivalent to French Vin de Pays, with laws and permitted varieties much freer than for IPR and DOC.
IPR (Indicação de Proveniência Regulamentada) is the intermediate step for wine regions hoping to move up to DOC status. Many were promoted in 1999, leaving just 9 IPRs. Their wines are referred to as Vinhos de Qualidade Produzidos em Região Determinada (VQPRD).
DOC (Denominação de Origem Controlada) Equivalent to France's AC. There are now 38 DOC regions and sub-regions.

2001 VINTAGE REPORT
Portugal's very wet winter resulted in landslides and flood damage in the Douro, and will be remembered for the tragic bridge collapse over the river on 4 March. Yet the rain did stop, and a successful flowering and a hot summer made for good quantity. Despite rain in some regions at harvest, quality seems generally good to very good, if not at the level of the small but outstanding 2000 vintage.

See also (SPAIN) ANDALUCIA, ARAGON, BALEARIC ISLANDS, CANARY ISLANDS, CASTILLA-LA MANCHA, CASTILLA Y LEON, CATALUNA, GALICIA; (PORTUGAL) ALENTEJO, ALGARVE, BEIRAS, ESTREMADURA, PORT, RIBATEJO, TERRAS DO SADO, TRAS-OS-MONTES; and individual wines and producers.

USA

The United States has more varied growing conditions for grapes than any other country in the world, which isn't so surprising when you consider that the 50 states of the Union cover an area that is larger than Western Europe; and although Alaska doesn't grow grapes in the icy far north, Washington State does in the north-west, as does Texas in the south and New York State in the north-east, and even Hawaii, lost in the pounding surf of the Pacific Ocean, manages to grow grapes and make wine. Altogether there are over 40 states that make wine of some sort or another; it ranges from some pretty dire offerings which would have been far better distilled into brandy or used for marinating the sirloin, to some of the greatest and most original wine flavours to be found in the world today.

GRAPE VARIETIES AND WINE REGIONS

California is far and away the most important state for wine production. In its determination to match the best red Bordeaux and white Burgundy, California proved that it was possible to take the classic European role models and successfully re-interpret them in an area thousands of miles away from their home. However, there is

more to California than this. The Central Valley produces the majority of the simple beverage wines that still dominate the American market. Napa and Sonoma counties north of San Francisco Bay do produce great Cabernet and Chardonnay, but grapes like Zinfandel and Merlot are making their mark and Carneros and Russian River Valley are highly successful for Pinot Noir, Chardonnay and sparkling wines. In the north, Mendocino and Lake Counties produce good grapes, while south of San Francisco, in the cool, foggy valleys between Santa Cruz and Santa Barbara, exciting cool-climate flavours are appearing, especially from Chardonnay, Pinot Noir and Syrah.

There are those that say that much of California is too hot for the best table wines – and many of the critics are based in Oregon and Washington, both keen to wrest the quality crown from California. Oregon, with a cooler but capricious climate, perseveres with Pinot Noir, Chardonnay, Pinot Gris, Pinot Blanc and Riesling with patchy success. Washington, so chilly and misty on the coast, becomes virtual desert east of the Cascade Mountains and it is here, in irrigated vineyards, that superb reds and whites can be made with thrillingly focused fruit.

New Yorkers are showing that Long Island has all the makings of a classic region: this warm, temperate claw of land to the east of New York City is well suited to Merlot, Cabernet Franc and Chardonnay. Finger Lakes and the Hudson Valley are increasingly turning from hybrid to vinifera grapes and have made a name with Riesling, Chardonnay and sparklers, and improved vineyard management has led to advances with reds, especially Pinot Noir and Cabernet Franc.

Of the other states, Texas has the most widespread plantings of classic vinifera wine varieties, but producers of excellence also exist in Virginia, Maryland and Pennsylvania on the east coast, and Idaho, Arizona and New Mexico in the west.

CLASSIFICATIONS

A rudimentary appellation system was established during the 1970s. AVA (American Viticultural Area) merely defines a spread of land and decrees that at least 85% of the wine's volume must be derived from grapes grown within that AVA. There are currently over 135 AVAs, more than 80 of which are in California.

2001 VINTAGE REPORT

2001 started on a terrible note for California, with the worst spring frosts in 30 years. Carneros was the worst hit, with a few growers losing as much as 40% of their crop. Warmer areas such as upper Napa Valley and Alexander Valley suffered only minimal damage. The damage to fruit set followed by summer heatwaves meant a smallish crop. While the harvest began early, cool autumn weather meant the grapes received extra hangtime, aiding the overall sugar/acid balance and consequent flavour. Overall the best wines should be the big reds such as Cabernet and Zinfandel, as small berries mean excellent skin/juice ratio. Chardonnays and Pinot Noirs would seem to be not as finely balanced as those from 1999 or 2000.

In Washington State, late-summer heatwaves delayed ripening and led to uneven ripening within clusters. A long, warm harvest resulted in high-alcohol, low-acid wines. In Oregon, a prolific flowering caused the largest cluster size in the state's history and heavy thinning was needed to avoid overcropping. The harvest was sunny and clear. Longer ripening time led to higher alcohol levels. The result is good to very good wines but not as concentrated as 2000 or 1999.

The growing season in 2001 was ideal all along the East Coast. Virginia winemakers were ecstatic over a vintage that could eclipse even the 1998, while New York enjoyed a long, cool season and an extended, dry harvest.

See also CALIFORNIA, NEW YORK STATE, OREGON, TEXAS, WASHINGTON STATE; and individual wine areas and wineries.

AUSTRALIA

Australian wine today enjoys a reputation still well out of proportion to the quantity of wine produced (total output is about one-tenth of Italy's), though volumes are mushrooming. The heavy, alcoholic wines of the past are long gone; sheer volume of fruit aroma and flavour is the hallmark of today's fine white, red and sparkling styles. Water plays a crucial role in the Australian wine industry. There's more than enough sunshine and not nearly enough rain to grow the grapes, so growers rely heavily on irrigation. Dynamic and innovative winemakers ensure a steady supply of new wines, wineries and even regions, but consolidation and internationalization of larger operators is a cause for concern.

GRAPE VARIETIES

Semillon and Shiraz have long been key varietals and are overtaking Chardonnay and Cabernet Sauvignon as the most fashionable. The use of small oak barrels for aging is important in modern reds as well as Chardonnays. Pinot Noir is enjoying some local success, though Riesling is the real darling of the moment.

WINE REGIONS

Western Australia is a vast state, virtually desert except for its south-western coastal strip. The sun-baked region near Perth was best suited to throaty reds and fortified wines but winery and vineyard expertise is so sophisticated that good dry whites are now being made. The most exciting wines, both red and white, come from Margaret River and Great Southern down towards the coast.

33

South Australia dominates the wine scene – it grows the most grapes, makes the wine and is home to most of the nation's biggest wine companies. There is more to it, however, than attractive, undemanding, gluggable wine. Clare Valley is an excellent producer of 'cool-climate' wines, but local climates enable Shiraz and Cabernet to be just as good as Clare Riesling. The Barossa is home to some of the planet's oldest vines, particularly Shiraz and Grenache. Eden Valley, in the hills to the east of Barossa, excels at crisp, steely Rieslings. Padthaway and Coonawarra also make some thrilling wines.

Victoria was Australia's major producer for most of the 19th century until her vineyards were devasted by the phylloxera louse. It's only recently that Victoria has regained her position as provider of some of the most startling wine styles in the country: stunning liqueur Muscats; the thrilling dark reds of Central Victoria; and the urbane Yarra Valley and Mornington Peninsula reds and whites.

New South Wales was home to the revolution that propelled Australia to the front of the world wine stage (in the Hunter Valley, an area that remains a dominant force). However, the state is a major bulk producer along the Murrumbidgee River, and a clutch of new regions in the Central Ranges are grabbing headlines.

Tasmania, with its cooler climate, is attracting attention for top-quality Pinot Noirs and Champagne-method sparkling wines. Riesling and Gewurztraminer would almost certainly be excellent, if the producers would give them a chance.

CLASSIFICATIONS
Formal appellation control, restricting certain grapes to certain regions, is virtually unknown; regulations are more of a guarantee of authenticity than a guide to quality. In a country so keen on inter-regional blending for its commercial brands, a system resembling France's AC could be problematic. However, the Label Integrity Program (LIP) guarantees all claims made on labels and the Geographical Indications (GI) committee is busy clarifying zones, regions and sub-regions – albeit with plenty of lively, at times acrimonious, debate about where some regional borders should go.

2002 VINTAGE REPORT
'Towards the end of 2001, all was doom and gloom as experts predicted a massive oversupply of grapes. However, any talk of wine lakes was quickly quashed by Mother Nature, who awarded the bulk of Australia's best-known wine regions an uncharacteristically cool summer. The South Aussie stalwarts of Adelaide Hills, the Barossa, Clare and McLaren Vale and Victoria's Yarra Valley and Mornington Peninsula were expecting yields to drop by anything up to 70 per cent; a classic case of top quality, but very limited quantity. Conversely, the relatively low temperatures have been a blessing to the normally parched Riverina and Riverland areas, giving them some excellent fruit in 2002. Other regions looking forward to a better than average haul included Rutherglen, Mudgee, Cowra and Queensland.

See also NEW SOUTH WALES, QUEENSLAND, SOUTH AUSTRALIA, TASMANIA, VICTORIA, WESTERN AUSTRALIA and individual wineries.

NEW ZEALAND

New Zealand's wines are characterized by intense fruit flavours, zesty acidity and pungent aromas – the product of cool growing conditions and high-tech winemaking. Styles are diverse due to regional differences, vintage variation and winemaking philosophy.

GRAPE VARIETIES AND WINE REGIONS

Nearly 1600km (1000 miles) separate New Zealand's northernmost wine region from the country's (and the world's) most southerly wine region, Central Otago. In terms of wine styles it is useful to divide the country into two parts. Hawkes Bay and further north, including Gisborne, Auckland and Northland, produce the best Cabernet Sauvignon, Merlot, Cabernet Franc and Syrah. From Martinborough and further south, including Marlborough, Nelson, Canterbury and Central Otago, come the best Sauvignon Blanc, Riesling, Pinot Noir and fizz. Chardonnay and Pinot Gris perform well everywhere, with riper, fleshier styles in the north and finer, zestier styles to the south.

CLASSIFICATIONS

A new system guarantees geographic origin. The broadest designation is New Zealand, followed by North or South Island. Next come the 10 or so regions. Labels may also name specific localities and individual vineyards.

2002 VINTAGE REPORT

The largest vintage on record. Good weather during flowering, but most regions experienced cool, wet pre-vintage conditions, followed by better weather. Average quality in the North Island; slightly better in the later-ripening South Island regions.

NORTH ISLAND
Matakana
AUCKLAND
Kumeu/Huapai
Henderson
Auckland
Waiheke Island
BAY OF PLENTY
WAIKATO
GISBORNE
HAWKES BAY
Nelson
NELSON
Blenheim
MARLBOROUGH
WELLINGTON
Martinborough
Wellington
CANTERBURY
Waipara
Christchurch
SOUTH ISLAND
OTAGO
Dunedin

Main vineyard areas

0   100   200 km
0   100 miles

See also AUCKLAND, CANTERBURY, CENTRAL OTAGO, GISBORNE, HAWKES BAY, KUMEU/HUAPAI, MARLBOROUGH, MARTINBOROUGH, NELSON, WAIHEKE ISLAND; and individual wineries.

SOUTH AMERICA

The only two countries to have proved their ability to make fine wine are Chile and Argentina, though clearly Uruguay is going to try to join them. Elsewhere it's largely a story of heat, humidity and the indifference of a local population much keener on spirits than wine.

ARGENTINA
Argentina is the fifth largest producer in the world but, until recently, one of the least known. This was partly because she used to drink all that she produced but also because her political and economic turmoil discouraged foreigners from attempting to do business with her. The economic turmoil took a welcome respite during the 1990s and the Argentine wine industry took the opportunity to modernize. Mendoza is the hub of wine activity and old plantings of grapes like Malbec, Sangiovese, Tempranillo and Bonarda as well as new ones of Syrah and Cabernet are producing a rich selection of reds. There are good whites too – from Chardonnay, Sauvignon and Torrontés – especially from the Uco Valley, but the best white conditions are far south in Río Negro or far north in Cafayate.

CHILE
Over the years Chile has boasted of having the world's most perfect conditions for grape growing. Reliable sunshine, no rain, irrigation

from the Andes – and no disease in the vineyards. Which is all very well, but most of the world's great wines have been made from grapes grown in far more taxing conditions, and until recently you could accuse Chile of simply having things too easy to excel. Oceans of soft, pleasant reds and whites flooded out, but nothing to make the heart miss a beat. There is now a new generation of wine people in charge here, keen to meet the challenge of upping quality, and results get more exciting every year. Though vineyards extend for over 1100 km (685 miles) north to south, the majority of grapes are grown from just north of Santiago at Aconcagua, down to Maule, with the most important quality areas being cool-climate Casablanca, Maipo and Rapel. Cabernet Sauvignon is the most famous and most widely planted grape, but Merlot, Carmenère (often mislabelled as Merlot), Syrah, Pinot Noir and others perform well here. Whites are more patchy, but Casablanca gives superb results with Chardonnay and Sauvignon, as do some of the southern vineyards.

URUGUAY
The least-known high-quality South American wine country, Uruguay suffers from relatively high rainfall in a relatively cool climate, and the majority of the vines are on clay soil near Montevideo. This may explain why the thick-skinned, rot-resistant black Tannat grape from South-West France is the leading variety. However, there is a clutch of modern wineries working hard at adapting vineyard practices to the conditions. Expect to see greatly improved, snappy Sauvignon Blanc and full, balanced Chardonnay as well as Merlot, Cabernet Franc, Cabernet Sauvignon – and even Shiraz and Nebbiolo – in the near future. Best producers include Carrau, Castillo Viejo, Filgueira, Irurtia, Juanico, de Lucca, Pisano, Stagnari.

OTHER COUNTRIES
Look at Brazil, how vast it is. Yet in all this expanse, running from 33° South to 5° North, there's nowhere ideal to site a vineyard. The best attempts are made down towards the Uruguayan border. Peru has seemingly good vineyard sites in the Ica Valley south of Lima, but nothing exciting winewise. Bolivia has few vineyards, but they're good, and incredibly high. Venezuela's chief claim to fame is that some of her subtropical vines give three crops a year!

2002 VINTAGE REPORT
In Chile the season started dry and warm during flowering. It was a hot vintage, with grapes ripening about a week earlier than in 2001. Most of the white grapes were already picked when heavy rains started to fall in the south of Central Valley, especially in Curicó and Maule, affecting red varieties such as Syrah, Malbec and Merlot. Rain was not a problem in Maipo, Casablanca and Aconcagua valleys, where the vintage is likely to be as good as it was in 2001. In Argentina, Mendoza producers are proclaiming their best red-wine vintage in 10 years.

See also (ARGENTINA) MENDOZA, UCO VALLEY; (CHILE) CASABLANCA, CENTRAL, COLCHAGUA, CURICO, MAIPO, MAULE, RAPEL; and individual wineries.

SOUTH AFRICA _____

There is a mood of confidence and optimism in South Africa. The changes being wrought in the vineyards are dramatic and the wines themselves are transformed. Bursting with vibrant fruit, sensitively tempered by oak and actually starting to speak of a sense of place – the French idea of *terroir* is firmly at the heart of the new South African agenda. A flood of new private producers is also leading the drive for quality. Between 1997 and 2000, about 80 new wineries started up. They are still in a minority, however; co-operatives continue to process about 85% of the country's grape crop.

GRAPE VARIETIES AND WINE REGIONS
The Cape's winelands run roughly 400km (250 miles) north and east of Cape Town. The major grape varieties are planted over the entire Cape; Chenin Blanc, though declining, still dominates. Cabernet Sauvignon, Chardonnay, Merlot, Pinotage and Sauvignon Blanc now register more strongly on the dial. Shiraz would probably top the lot in terms of producers' enthusiasm but there is a shortage of vine material. The swing towards classic, international varieties now includes small quantites of Viognier, Mourvèdre, Malbec, Nebbiolo and Sangiovese. The current vogue for Rhône varieties means that the spotlight is on Grenache, although little is currently grown here, and old bush vine plantings of Cinsaut. There is little typicity of origin, although some areas are historically associated with specific varieties or styles. Stellenbosch currently produces some of the best red wines; Constantia, with its sea-facing slopes, is acknowledged as ideal for Sauvignon Blanc; cooler areas also include Walker Bay in the Overberg district, where the focus is Pinot Noir. New areas such as Durbanville, Darling Hills, Elgin and Elim (at the tip of Africa) are beginning to show promise. The inland, warmer areas are noted for fortifieds, both Muscadel (Muscat) and port styles.

CLASSIFICATION
The Wine of Origin (WO) system – introduced in 1973, with major modifications in 1993 – divides wine-producing areas into regions, districts and wards. Wines can be traced back to their source, but quality is not guaranteed. Varietal wines for export must be made from at least 85% of the named grape. To qualify as an 'estate' wine, the producer's vines must be grown on a single piece of land and the wine vinified, matured and bottled on the property.

2002 VINTAGE REPORT
Welcome winter rains broke the 3-year drought but then continued late into spring, causing downy mildew in major wine-producing areas. Those who took the correct action at the correct time minimized the problem, but some growers suffered heavy losses. Rain in January also caused rot, both noble and sour, in the ripening grapes. The traditional heatwave struck with a vengeance towards the end of February, which will have affected whites more than reds. Given the varied conditions, choosing a good producer will be key.

See also CONSTANTIA, FRANSCHHOEK, OVERBERG, PAARL, ROBERTSON, STELLENBOSCH; and individual wineries.

OTHER WINE COUNTRIES

ALGERIA The western coastal province of Oran produces three-quarters of Algeria's wine, including soft but muscular wines of the Coteaux de Tlemcen, and dark, beefy reds of the Coteaux de Mascara. Around 80% of the vines are over 40 years old, and with recent substantial replantings there should be great potential here.

BULGARIA After success in the 1980s and disarray in the 90s, the roller coaster seems to have stopped. New World influence implies a brighter future, but there is still more disappointment than not. International varieties (Cabernet Sauvignon, Merlot, Chardonnay) dominate but local grapes – plummy Mavrud, meaty Gamza, deep Melnik, mild-mannered, fruity white Dimiat and Misket – can be good. Best wineries include BOYAR ESTATES, KHAN KRUM and SUHINDOL.

CANADA The strict VQA (Vintners Quality Alliance) maintains high standards in British Columbia and Ontario, and there has been enormous progress in the 2 most important regions – OKANAGAN VALLEY in British Columbia and the NIAGARA PENINSULA in Ontario – where the move from hybrid to vinifera varieties is rapid. Sweet icewine is still Canada's main trump card. Pinot Gris, Chardonnay, Riesling and Gewürztraminer lead the way in non-sweet whites; Merlot, Cabernet Franc, Cabernet Sauvignon, even Syrah, show potential in reds.

CHINA Though China officially promotes wine, its potential remains unfulfilled as the Chinese are reluctant to drink it. Plantings, mainly international grapes with some traditional Chinese, German and Russian varieties, are expanding rapidly, yet only 10% of the harvest is crushed for wine. In the next 15 years output could double – or treble – who knows? Major Western and Chinese investment (Beijing Friendship/Pernod Ricard, Dynasty/Rémy-Martin, Great Wall/TORRES, HUADONG/Allied Domecq) leads the way.

CROATIA Inland Croatia has an undercurrent of rising potential: bulk whites dominate but small private producers are emerging. What the country needs now is more investment, more technology in the vineyard and winery and a fair price for the grapes. The best vineyards are on the Dalmatian coast, where international varieties are being planted alongside gutsy Peljesac and Faros reds; deep, tannic Plavac Mali has long produced the top red wines. GRGICH of California has a winery on the Peljesac peninsula.

CYPRUS The island has not had a high reputation for wine since the Crusades, when COMMANDARIA was reputedly a rich, succulent nectar worth risking your neck for. However, Cyprus is modernizing and, supported by the government, regional press houses and wineries are being built in or near the vineyards. A 3-year restructuring plan and investment by companies like Etko, Keo, Loel and Sodap is at last producing tasty modern reds and whites. For the first time we are seeing varietal wines, and the first efforts with grapes like Cabernet Sauvignon and Sémillon are impressive. Look for the Island Vines label.

THE CZECH REPUBLIC The vineyards of Bohemia in the north-west and Moravia in the south-east are mainly planted with white varieties

– Grüner Veltliner, Müller-Thurgau, Riesling, Pinot Blanc – with pockets of red such as St-Laurent and Lemberger. Lack of direction is a problem, but Western investment and consultancy is helping.

ENGLAND The wine industry has come of age, with around 1000ha (2470 acres) of vineyards and 115 wineries. Producers are more focused: what will and will not work in this unpredictable cool climate is becoming clearer, and some outstanding white and sparkling wines are being produced. The most widely grown grape variety is Müller-Thurgau, the most successful is the hybrid Seyval Blanc, plus German crosses that can hold off disease, such as Bacchus, Huxelrebe, Schönburger. New inter-specific cross-vine varieties must still only be labelled as table wine. The best white wines are delicate and aromatic, with enough ripeness and depth to balance the crisp acidity. Some excellent late-harvest botrytized dessert wines are made, and red varieties are also becoming more popular. 50% of sales are gate sales. The most popular winemaking counties are Kent (Biddenden, CHAPEL DOWN, Davenport), Sussex (BREAKY BOTTOM, Hidden Spring, Nutbourne, NYETIMBER, RIDGEVIEW), Berkshire (VALLEY VINEYARDS), Gloucestershire (THREE CHOIRS), Hampshire (Northbrook Springs, Wickham, Woolings), Oxfordshire (Chiltern Valley), Somerset (Staplecombe) and Surrey (DENBIES).

GEORGIA Georgia faces many challenges – lack of regulation, resistance to change, counterfeiting – but its diverse climates (from subtropical to moderate continental) and soils produce every style imaginable. International and indigenous varieties abound; the peppery, powerful red Saperavi shows promise. Most wine is still pretty rustic, but investment is beginning to have an effect. GWS (Georgian Wines & Spirits Company, 50% owned by Pernod Ricard) benefits from the flair of Australian winemaker David Nelson.

GREECE There is life beyond the decline of RETSINA. A new generation of winemakers and grape growers, many of them trained in France, Australia or California, have a clear vision of the flavours they want to achieve and their wines are modern but marvellously original too. Polarization between cheap bulk and expensive boutique wines continues, but large companies such as Boutari, Kourtakis and Tsantalis are upping the quality stakes and flavours improve every vintage, although many labels are still difficult to understand. International plantings have led to surprising blends with indigenous varieties such as Agiorgitiko, Xynomavro, Assyrtiko, Moschofilero and Roditis. Quality areas: Naousa and Nemea for reds, SAMOS for sweet Muscats, Patras for dessert Mavrodaphne. Wineries to watch include: ANTONOPOULOS, DOMAINE CONSTANTIN LAZARIDI, Gentilini, Hatzimichali, GEROVASSILIOU, Papaïoannou and Strofilia.

HUNGARY Hungary has an image problem, although superb quality whites abound and red plantings are increasing. Stringent regulations and investment/advice from Australian and western European companies and consultants, particularly in TOKAJI, have put Hungary, with its 22 designated appellations, back on the international wine map. There is renewed interest in native varieties such as Furmint, Irsai

Oliver, Kékfrankos and Kadarka, and top Hungarian winemakers – Tibor Gál, Akos Kamocsay, Vilmos Thummerer and others – are now a solid force. There is a refreshing balance between those who are determined to push individual regional and vineyard potential and those who offer good general quality at an affordable price.

INDIA This large country has a tiny wine industry, partly due to its climate. Less than 10% of the 50,000ha (123,500 acres) of vines is used for wine; both international varieties and ancient Indian ones, such as Arkesham and Arkavati, are planted. Château Indage, with vineyards in the Maharashtra hills east of Mumbai (Bombay), controls 75% of the market and produces still and sparkling wines, in particular OMAR KHAYYAM. Bordeaux superstar Michel Rolland advises Grover Vineyards in Bangalore.

ISRAEL Much of Israel's wine is sweet red, but good dry wines and sparklers are produced at GOLAN HEIGHTS and Carmel, the oldest and largest winery. Smaller producers are making Bordeaux-style reds, and there is a move towards Merlot. Some of Israel's most promising wines now come from Castel in the Judean Hills, Galil Mountain in Galilee and Tishbi in Shomron.

JAPAN Wine can be made from locally grown or imported grapes, juice or wine – and the labels don't help you tell which is which. Wine is produced in almost every province, though many are too humid. SUNTORY is in the best region, Yamanashi. Other main players are Mercian, Sapporo and Mann, whose Chateau Lumière produces a fine Bordeaux-style red blend.

LEBANON CHATEAU MUSAR, Kefraya and Ksara survived the 25-year war. Peace has brought a new generation of producers and improved quality from the older companies – the new releases of wines from Ksara are vastly different to those produced just a few years ago.

LUXEMBOURG This small, cool country produces pleasant still and sparkling whites from Rivaner, Riesling, Pinot Gris and Elbling, grown along 42km (26 miles) of the Moselle.

MEXICO In the far north-west of Mexico, in Baja California, some good reds are made by L A CETTO as well as by smaller companies such as Monte Xanic. In the rest of the country, only high-altitude areas such as the Parras Valley and Zacatecas have the potential for quality wines. Promising grape varieties include Nebbiolo, Petite Sirah, Tempranillo, Zinfandel and Barbera, with Viognier and Chardonnay also planted.

MOLDOVA Standards of winemaking and equipment still leave much to be desired, but the quality of fruit is good, and international players including PENFOLDS, and winemakers Jacques Lurton, Hugh Ryman and Alain Thiénot, have worked with local winemakers to produce encouraging whites. However, chaotic social conditions have led to many attempts being abandoned. You may still find an occasional mature Rochu or Negru red from Purkar.

MONTENEGRO This red-wine-dominated part of the former Yugoslavia shows some potential in the beefy Vranac grape with its bitter cherry flavours.

MOROCCO Known for big, sweet-fruited reds that once found a ready blending market in France. Since the 1990s massive investment by Castel Frères is instigating a rebirth: the first fruits are excellent Syrah and Cabernet reds.

ROMANIA This ancient wineland, of enormous potential, 10th in world production, is slowly getting the message that its strength lies in its *terroir*: Dealul Mare, MURFATLAR and COTNARI all have ancient reputations. International backed ventures are a sign of the mini-revolution, but challenges remain. Huge investment from Halewood, as in the undemanding Prahova Valley range, is helping, but there is a long way to go.

SLOVAKIA The eastern part of the old Czechoslovakia, with its cool-climate vineyards, is dominated by white varieties: Pinot Blanc, Riesling, Grüner Veltliner, Irsai Oliver. Western investment, particularly at the state winery at Nitra and smaller wineries such as Gbelce and Hurbanovo near the Hungarian border at Komárno, is rapidly improving the quality.

SLOVENIA Many of the old Yugoslav Federation's best vineyards are here. On the Italian border, Brda and Vipava have go-ahead co-operatives, and Kraski Teran is a red wine of repute. The Movia range, from the Kristancic family, looks promising. A well-policed quality wine scheme allows only the best wines to be bottled and exported.

SWITZERLAND Fendant (Chasselas) is the main grape for snappy, neutral whites from the VALAIS. Like the fruity DOLE reds, they are best drunk very young. German-speaking cantons produce light reds and rosés from Pinot Noir (Blauburgunder), and whites from Müller-Thurgau (Rivaner). Italian-speaking TICINO concentrates on Merlots, juicy at best but often lean and grassy. Serious wines use Cabernet, Chardonnay and traditional varieties like Amigne and Petite Arvine. See also NEUCHATEL and VAUD.

TUNISIA Ancient wine traditions have had an injection of new life from international investment, and results so far are encouraging.

TURKEY The world's fifth-largest grape producer, but 97% ends up as raisins. State-owned companies dominate wine production, making basic reds and whites. Producers such as Diren, Kavaklidere and Doluca are using modern technology to produce very drinkable wines.

UKRAINE The Crimea's vineyards, producing hearty reds, are the most important. The Odessa region is successful with its sparkling wines. Future European investment is said to be in the pipeline.

ZIMBABWE Despite the present political and economic upheaval, the small wine industry is doing quite well. Summer rain can be more of a problem. There are just two companies: Mukuyu and Stapleford.

A–Z

OF WINES,
PRODUCERS, GRAPES
& WINE REGIONS

In the following pages there are over
1600 entries covering the world's top wines, as well as
leading producers, main wine regions and grape
varieties, followed on page 289 by a glossary of wine
terms and classifications.

*On page 4 you will find a full explanation of
How to Use the A–Z. On page 297 there is an index
of all wine producers in the book, to help you find the
world's best wines.*

ABRUZZO *Italy* East of Rome, this region stretches from the Adriatic coast to the mountainous Apennine interior. White Trebbiano d'Abruzzo DOC is usually dry and neutral; the MONTEPULCIANO D'ABRUZZO DOC is sometimes rosé called Cerasuolo, but generally a strapping, peppery red of real character. Overproduction is a problem, but there are a number of good producers.

ACACIA *Carneros AVA, California, USA* Leading producer of Chardonnay and Pinot Noir from the CARNEROS region for almost 2 decades. The regular Carneros Chardonnay is restrained but attractive. Pinot Noirs include the stunning DeSoto★★★ as well as a Beckstoffer Vineyard★★ and a Carneros★ – the wines have moved to a riper, meatier style of late. Also a voluptuous Carneros Viognier★ and Brut fizz. Best years: (Pinot Noir) 2000 99 **98 97 96 95**.

TIM ADAMS *Clare Valley, South Australia* Important maker of fine, old-fashioned wine from his own and bought-in local grapes. Classic dry Riesling★★, oaky Semillon★★, and rich, opulent Shiraz★★ and Cabernet★★. The botrytis Semillon★ can be super, The Fergus★★ is a glorious Grenache-based blend, and minty, peppery Aberfeldy Shiraz★★★ is a remarkable, at times unnerving, mouthful of brilliance from 100-year-old vines growing near WENDOUREE. Best years: (Aberfeldy Shiraz) (1999) 98 97 96 95 **94 93 92**.

ADELAIDE HILLS *South Australia* Small and exciting region 30 minutes' drive from Adelaide. High altitude affords a cool, moist climate ideal for fine table wines and superb sparkling wine. Consistently good Sauvignon Blanc and Chardonnay, plus promising Pinot Noir. Best producers: Ashton Hills★, CHAIN OF PONDS, HENSCHKE★★, LENSWOOD VINEYARDS★★, Nepenthe★, PETALUMA★★, SHAW & SMITH★★, Geoff WEAVER★★.

ADELSHEIM VINEYARD *Willamette Valley AVA, Oregon, USA* This vineyard first hit the headlines with wine labels depicting various local beauties, including the owner's daughter. Adelsheim has established a reputation for excellent, generally unfiltered, Pinot Noir – especially cherry-scented Elizabeth's Reserve★★ and Seven Springs Vineyard★★ – and rich Chardonnay Reserve★★. Also a bright, fresh Pinot Gris★. Best years: (Elizabeth's Reserve) 2001 00 99 98 **96 94**.

AGE *Rioja DOC, Rioja, Spain* A huge investment to build Rioja's largest vinification plant may yet improve the whole range. The Siglo Saco red Crianza is its best-known wine, perhaps because it comes wrapped in a hessian sack – but, luckily, this doesn't seem to cause sack taint. Best years: (reds) 2000 99 **98 96 95 94**.

AGLIANICO DEL VULTURE DOC *Basilicata, Italy* Red wine from the Aglianico grape grown on the steep slopes of Mt Vulture. Despite being one of Italy's most southerly DOCs the harvest is later than in BAROLO, 750km (470 miles) to the north-west, because the Aglianico grape ripens very late. The best wines are structured, complex and long-lived. Best producers: Basilium★, Consorzio Viticoltori Associati del Vulture (Carpe Diem★), D'Angelo★★, Cantine del Notaio★★, Paternoster★★, Le Querce★. Best years: 2000 99 98 97 **95 94 93 90 88**.

AHR *Germany* The Ahr Valley is a small, mainly red wine region south of Bonn. Chief grape varieties are the Spätburgunder (Pinot Noir) and (Blauer) Portugieser. Most Ahr reds used to be made sweet for the day-trippers from Bonn and Cologne, but this style is on the way out. Meyer-Näkel has achieved a certain international reputation by making serious dry reds.

AIRÉN Spain's – and indeed the world's – most planted white grape can make fresh modern white wines, or thick, yellow, old-fashioned brews. Airén is grown all over the centre and south of Spain, especially in LA MANCHA, VALDEPENAS and ANDALUCIA (where it's called Lairén). Any new plantings are now forbidden in the CASTILLA-LA MANCHA region.

ALBAN *Edna Valley AVA, California, USA* A Rhône specialist in the Arroyo Grande district of Edna Valley, John Alban first produced Viognier in 1991. Today he offers 2 bottlings, an Estate★★ and a Central Coast★. Roussanne★★ from estate vineyards is laden with honey notes. Syrah is also represented by 2 bottlings: Reva★★ and the more expensive Lorraine★★. An intense Grenache★★ rounds out the line-up. Best years: (Syrah) (2000) 99 98 97 96 **95**.

ALBANA DI ROMAGNA DOCG *Romagna, Italy* In the hills south of Bologna and Ravenna, Italy's first white DOCG was a 'political' appointment that caused outrage among wine enthusiasts because of the totally forgettable flavours of most Albana wine. Though also made in dry and sparkling styles, the sweet *passito* version is the best. Best producers: (passito) Celli, Conti, Ferrucci, Giovanna Madonia (Chimera★), Paradiso, Riva, Tre Monti, Uccellina★, Zerbina (Scacco Matto★★).

ALBARIÑO Possibly Spain's most characterful white grape. It grows in GALICIA in Spain's rainy north-west and, as Alvarinho, in Portugal's VINHO VERDE region. When well made, Albariño wines have fascinating flavours of apricot, peach, grapefruit and Muscat grapes, refreshingly high acidity, highish alcohol – and unrefreshingly high prices.

ALCAMO DOC *Sicily, Italy* DOC for white wines based on the indigenous Catarratto grape of western Sicily, grown between MARSALA and Palermo. The few good examples are dry, nutty and rounded. Drink young. Best producers: Firriato, Rapitalà★, Spadafora.

ALEATICO Rarely seen, ancient, native Italian grape that produces sweet, high-alcohol after-dinner wines in central and southern Italy. Best producers: AVIGNONESI, Candido (delicious Aleatico di Puglia★).

ALENQUER DOC *Estremadura, Portugal* Maritime-influenced hills north of Lisbon, producing wines from, mostly, local grape varieties, but also Cabernet and Chardonnay. Many wines are simply labelled ESTREMADURA. Best producers: Quinta da Abrigada★, D F J VINHOS★, Quinta de Pancas★, Casa SANTOS LIMA★. Best years: (reds) (2001) 00 **99 97 96 95**.

ALENTEJO *Portugal* A large chunk of southern Portugal east of Lisbon and, along with the DOURO, one of Portugal's fastest improving red wine regions. Has had its own DOC since 1999, and there are also 8 DOCs for sub-regions: Borba, Évora, Granja-Amareleja, Moura, Portalegre, Redondo, Reguengos and Vidigueira. Potential is far from realized but already some of Portugal's finest reds come from here. Best producers: (reds) Caves ALIANCA (Quinta da Terrugem★★), Fundação Eugénio de Almeida (Cartuxa★, Pera Manca★★), Borba co-op, Quinta do CARMO★, Herdade dos Coelheiros★,

45

CORTES DE CIMA★★, D F J VINHOS★★, Vinha d'Ervideira★, ESPORAO★★, José Maria da FONSECA★, J P VINHOS★, Mouchão★, Quinta do Mouro★, João Portugal RAMOS★★, Reguengos de Monsaraz co-op. Best years: (reds) (2001) 00 **99 97 95 94 91 90 89**.

ALEXANDER VALLEY AVA *Sonoma County, California, USA* Important AVA, centred on the Russian River, which is fairly warm with only patchy summer fog. Cabernet Sauvignon is highly successful here, with lovely, juicy fruit not marred by an excess of tannin. Chardonnay may also be good but is often overproduced and lacking in ripe, round flavours. Zinfandel and Merlot can be outstanding from hillside vineyards. Best producers: Alexander Valley Vineyards★, Chateau Souverain, CLOS DU BOIS★, GEYSER PEAK★, JORDAN★, Murphy-Goode★★, SEGHESIO★★, SILVER OAK★★, SIMI★. See also Russian River Valley AVA, Sonoma County. Best years: (reds) (2000) 99 97 **95 94 93 92 91 90 88**.

ALGARVE *Portugal* Holiday region with feeble-flavoured, mostly red wines in 4 DOCs: Lagoa, Lagos, Portimão and Tavira. The broad Vinho Regional Algarve classification suffices for D F J VINHOS' ripe-fruited Cataplana★. Look out for the new red from (Sir) Cliff Richard, made by David Baverstock.

ALIANÇA, CAVES *Beira Litoral, Portugal* Based in BAIRRADA, Aliança makes crisp, fresh whites and soft, approachable red Bairradas. Also made, either from its own vineyards or bought-in grapes or wines, are reds from the DAO and DOURO. The top reds, though, are those from an estate in ALENTEJO, Quinta da Terrugem★★. Aliança also markets varietal Merlot★★, Touriga Nacional★★ and Tinta Roriz★★ (and a Reserva★★ blend of the three) from Quinta da Cortezia in ESTREMADURA.

ALIGOTÉ French grape, found mainly in Burgundy, whose basic characteristic is a lemony tartness. It can make extremely nice wine, especially from old vines, but is generally rather dull and lean. In ripe years it can resemble Chardonnay, especially if a little new oak is used. The best comes from Bouzeron in the COTE CHALONNAISE. Bouzeron is the only village in Burgundy with its own appellation for Aligoté. Occasionally also found in Moldova and Bulgaria. Drink young. Best producers: (Burgundy) Denis Bachelet, COCHE-DURY★, A Ente★, JAYER-GILLES★, Denis Mortet★, RION★, TOLLOT-BEAUT, Villaine★.

ALLEGRINI *Valpolicella, Veneto, Italy* High-profile producer in VALPOLICELLA Classico, making single-vineyard La Grola★★ and Palazzo della Torre★★. These are now sold under the regional IGT – partly to further distance them from the continuing low regard in which much of Valpolicella is held. These, and the barrique-aged La Poja★★★, are made solely with the Corvina grape and show the great potential that exists in Valpolicella. Outstanding AMARONE★★★ and RECIOTO (Giovanni Allegrini★★). Best years: (Amarone) 1997 **96 95 94 93 90 88 86 85**.

THIERRY ALLEMAND *Cornas, Rhône Valley, France* Thierry Allemand has a smallholding of some 3ha (7.5 acres) of vines taken over from Noël VERSET. He is determined to keep yields low and to avoid making harsh, tannic wines. With careful vinification he produces 2 supple and intense unfiltered expressions of CORNAS at its dense and powerful best: Chaillot★★ is marginally the lighter; Reynard★★ is from a parcel of very old Syrah. Best years: (Reynard) (2000) 99 98 97 96 95 94 **91 90**.

ALLENDE *Rioja DOC, Rioja, Spain* The ebullient Miguel Angel de Gregorio has made his modest, young winery and vineyards in Briones into one of the most admired new names in RIOJA. Scented, uncompromisingly concentrated reds include Aurus★★★, Calvario★★ and the affordable Allende★. There is also a delicate white★. Best years: (reds) (2000) 99 **98 97 96**.

ALL SAINTS *Rutherglen, Victoria, Australia* Old winery revived with great flair by Peter Brown of the BROWN BROTHERS family since 1998. Superb fortifieds Rare Tokay★★★, Muscat★★, Tawny★★, Madeira★★ and Amontillado★ have rediscovered past glory. Grand★★ fortifieds are very good but younger. Table wines are big, American oak bruisers.

ALMAVIVA★★ *Valle del Maipo, Chile* Joint venture between CONCHA Y TORO and Baron Philippe de Rothschild, and currently Chile's most expensive red. Purposeful investment in the winery and a careful choice of vineyard sites are paying dividends as the wines improve with every vintage. Unreleased 2001 could be the best yet. Can be drunk at 5 years but should age for 10. Best years: (2001) (00) (99) **98 97 96**.

ALOXE-CORTON AC *Côte de Beaune, Burgundy, France* An important village at the northern end of the COTE DE BEAUNE producing mostly red wines from Pinot Noir. Its reputation is based on the 2 Grands Crus, CORTON (mainly red) and CORTON-CHARLEMAGNE (white only). Other vineyards in Aloxe-Corton used to be a source of tasty, good-value Burgundy, but nowadays the reds rarely exhibit their former characteristic blend of ripe fruit and appetizing savoury dryness. Almost all the white wine is sold as Grand Cru; straight Aloxe-Corton Blanc is very rare. Best producers: CHANDON DE BRIAILLES★★, M Chapuis★, Marius Delarche★, Dubreuil-Fontaine★, Follin-Arvelet★, Antonin Guyon★, JADOT★, Rapet★, Comte Senard★, TOLLOT-BEAUT★★, Michel Voarick★. Best years: (reds) 1999 98 **97** 96 **95 93 90**.

ALSACE AC *Alsace, France* Tucked away on France's eastern border with Germany, Alsace produces some of the most individual white wines of all, rich in aroma and full of ripe, distinctive flavours. Alsace is almost as far north as Champagne, but its climate is considerably warmer. Since 1975 the best vineyard sites can call themselves Grands Crus; there are currently 50 of these. Riesling, Muscat, Gewurztraminer and Pinot Gris are generally considered the finest varieties in Alsace and are permitted for Grand Cru wines, as is Sylvaner from 2001. Pinot Blanc can produce good wines, too, but Pinot Noir, the area's only red grape, is usually confined to less well-appointed vineyards and produces pale wines that are closer to a rosé than a red BURGUNDY. Alsace was one of the first regions to label its wines by grape variety. Apart from Edelzwicker (a blend), and CREMANT D'ALSACE, all Alsace wines are made from a single grape variety. Best producers: L Albrecht, J Becker, Léon Beyer, P BLANCK, Bott-Geyl, A Boxler, E Burn, DEISS, Dirler, HUGEL, Josmeyer, Kientzler, Kreydenweiss, KUENTZ-BAS, S Landmann, Lorentz, A MANN, Meyer-Fonné, MURÉ, Ostertag, Pfaffenheim co-op, Rolly Gassmann, M Schaetzel, Schlumberger, SCHOFFIT, Bruno Sorg, M Tempé, TRIMBACH, TURCKHEIM co-op, WEINBACH, ZIND-HUMBRECHT. Best years: (2001) 00 99 98 **97** 96 **95 94 90 89 88 85 83**. See also Alsace Vendange Tardive.

ALSACE VENDANGE TARDIVE *Alsace, France* Vendange Tardive means 'late-harvest'. The grapes (Riesling, Muscat, Pinot Gris or Gewurztraminer) are picked late and almost overripe, giving higher

47

sugar levels and potentially more intense flavours. The resulting wines are usually rich and mouthfilling and often need 5 years or more to show their personality. A further sub-category of Alsace wines is Sélection de Grains Nobles – late-harvest wines made exclusively from super-ripe grapes of the same varieties. Invariably sweet and usually affected by noble rot, they are among Alsace's finest, but are very expensive to produce (and to buy). Best producers: Léon Beyer★★, P BLANCK★★★, Bott-Geyl★★★, E Burn★★★, DEISS★★★, Rolly Gassmann★★, HUGEL★★★, Kientzler★★★, Kreydenweiss★★★, MURÉ★★, Ostertag★★★, SCHOFFIT★★, Tempé★★★, WEINBACH★★, ZIND-HUMBRECHT★★★. Best years: (2001) 00 98 97 96 95 94 **93 92 90 89 88 85 76**.

ALTARE *Barolo DOCG, Piedmont, Italy* Elio Altare crafts some of the most stunning of Alba's wines: excellent Dolcetto d'Alba★★ and BARBERA D'ALBA★ and even finer BAROLO Vigneto Arborina★★★ and new Barolo Brunate★★★. Though a professed modernist, his wines are intense, full and structured while young, but with clearly discernible fruit flavours, thanks largely to tiny yields. He also makes 3 barrique-aged wines under the LANGHE DOC: Arborina★★★ (Nebbiolo), Larigi★★★ (Barbera) and La Villa★★ (Nebbiolo-Barbera). Also one of 7 producers that make a version of L'Insieme★★ (a Nebbiolo-Cabernet-Barbera blend). Best years: (Barolo) (2000) (99) 98 96 95 **94 93 90 89 88 86 85**.

ALTO ADIGE *Trentino-Alto Adige, Italy* A largely German-speaking province, originally called Südtirol. The region-wide DOC covers 25 types of wine. Reds are almost invariably varietal and range from light and perfumed when made from the Schiava grape, to fruity and more structured from the Cabernets or Merlot, to dark and velvety if Lagrein is used. Whites include Chardonnay, Pinot Bianco, Pinot Grigio, Riesling and Sauvignon, and are usually fresh and fragrant. There is also some good sparkling wine. Much of the wine comes from well-run co-ops. Sub-zones include the previously independent DOCs at SANTA MADDALENA and Terlano. Best producers: Abbazia di Novacella★, Caldaro co-op★, Casòn Hirschprunn★, Colterenzio co-op★★, Peter Dipoli★, Giorgio Grai★★, Franz Haas★, Hofstätter★★, LAGEDER★★, Laimburg★, J Niedermayr★, Ignaz Niedriest★, Peter Pliger-Kuenhof★★, Prima & Nuova/Erste & Neue★, Hans Rottensteiner★, San Michele Appiano co-op★★, Tiefenbrunner★, Elena Walch★, Baron Widmann★. See also Trentino.

ALVARINHO See Albariño.

AMA, CASTELLO DI *Chianti Classico DOCG, Tuscany, Italy* Model estate of CHIANTI CLASSICO, with outstanding single-vineyard bottlings★★ (Bellavista and La Casuccia). L'Apparita★★★ is one of Italy's best Merlots; less impressive Il Chiuso is made from Pinot Nero. Also good Chardonnay Al Poggio★. Best years: (Chianti Classico) (2000) 99 **98 97 96 95 94 93 91 90 88 85**.

AMARONE DELLA VALPOLICELLA *Valpolicella DOC, Veneto, Italy* A brilliantly individual, bitter-sweet style of VALPOLICELLA made from grapes shrivelled on mats for months after harvest. The wine, which can reach up to 16% of alcohol, differs from the sweet RECIOTO DELLA VALPOLICELLA in that it is fermented to dryness. Classico is generally the best, though an exception can be made for DAL FORNO.

Best producers: Stefano Accordini★★, ALLEGRINI★★★, Bertani★★, Brigaldara★★, Brunelli★, Tommaso Bussola★★, Michele Castellani-I Castei★★, DAL FORNO★★★, Guerrieri-Rizzardi★★, MASI★, QUINTARELLI★★★, Le Ragose★, Le Salette★★, Serègo Alighieri★, Speri★★, Tedeschi★★, Tommasi★, Villa Monteleone★★, Zenato★★. Best years: (2000) 97 **95 93 90 88**.

AMIGNE Swiss grape variety that is virtually limited to the region of Vétroz in the VALAIS. The wine has an earthy, nutty intensity and benefits from a few years' aging. Best producers: Germanier Bon Père, Granges Frères (Escalier de la Dame), Caves Imesch.

AMITY VINEYARDS *Willamette Valley AVA, Oregon, USA*   Myron Redford was one of the pioneers in OREGON, opening his winery in 1976. The Gewürztraminer★★ is outstanding and Riesling★ is almost as good. The showpiece is the Pinot Noir, notably the Winemakers Reserve★. Pinot Blanc★ has replaced Chardonnay. Fruity, floral Gamay Noir remains fine value. Best years: (Pinot Noir) 2000 99 **98 97 96**.

ANDALUCÍA *Spain*   Fortified wines, or wines naturally so strong in alcohol that they don't need fortifying, are the speciality of this southern stretch of Spain. Apart from sherry (JEREZ Y MANZANILLA DO), there are the lesser, sherry-like wines of Condado de Huelva DO and MONTILLA-MORILES DO, and the rich, sometimes treacly-sweet wines of MALAGA DO. These regions now also make some modern but bland dry whites; the best are from Condado de Huelva. Red wine is now appearing from producers in the Málaga, Granada and Almeria provinces.

ANDERSON VALLEY AVA *California, USA*   Small appellation (less than 245ha/600 acres) in western MENDOCINO COUNTY that produces brilliant wines. Most vineyards are within 15 miles of the Pacific Ocean, making this one of the coldest AVAs in California. Delicate Pinot Noirs and Chardonnays, and one of the few places in the state for first-rate Gewürztraminer. Superb sparkling wines with healthy acidity and creamy yeast are highlights as well. Best producers: Greenwood Ridge★, HANDLEY★★, Lazy Creek★, Navarro★★, PACIFIC ECHO★, ROEDERER ESTATE★★.

ANDREW WILL WINERY *Washington State, USA*   Winemaker Chris Camarda makes delicious Merlots and powerful Cabernet Sauvignons from a range of older WASHINGTON vineyards. At the top are the complex Champoux Vineyard★★★, the opulent Ciel du Cheval★★★ and the tannic yet ageworthy Klipsun★★★. Wines from the WALLA WALLA vineyards of Pepper Bridge★★ and Seven Hills★ are fruity and drink well early. Sorella★★★, a BORDEAUX blend, is outstanding with age. White wines vary and seem more a pastime than a portfolio. Best years: (reds) 2000 99 97 96 **95 94 93**.

CH. ANGÉLUS★★★ *St-Émilion Grand Cru AC, 1er Grand Cru Classé, Bordeaux, France*   One of the best-known ST-ÉMILION Grands Crus with an energetic owner and talented winemaker. Increasingly gorgeous wines throughout the 80s, recognized by promotion to Premier Grand Cru Classé in 1996. Best years: 2000 99 98 97 96 95 **94 93 92 90 89 88**.

MARQUIS D'ANGERVILLE *Volnay AC, Côte de Beaune, Burgundy, France*   With over half a century's experience and meticulous attention to detail, Marquis Jacques d'Angerville produces an exemplary range of elegant Premiers Crus from VOLNAY, the classiest of the CÔTE DE BEAUNE's red wine appellations. Clos des Ducs and Taillepieds are ★★★. All should be kept for at least 5 years. Best years: (top reds) 1999 98 **97** 96 95 93 **91 90 89**.

CH. D'ANGLUDET★ *Margaux AC, Cru Bourgeois, Haut-Médoc, Bordeaux, France* This English-owned château makes a gentle, unobtrusive but extremely attractive red that is generally of Classed Growth standard and is never overpriced. It ages well for up to a decade. Best years: 2000 98 96 **95 94 90 89 88 86 85 83 82**.

ANJOU BLANC AC *Loire Valley, France* Ill-defined AC; ranges from bone dry to sweet, from excellent to dreadful; the best are dry. Up to 20% Chardonnay or Sauvignon can be added, but many of the leading producers use 100% Chenin. Best producers: M Angeli★★, Bidet, Cady, Fesles★, Haute-Perche, Montgilet/V Lebreton, Ogereau★, Pierre-Bise★, J Pithon★★, RICHOU★, Soucherie/P-Y Tijou★, Yves Soulez★, la Varière★. Best years: (top wines) (2001) 00 **99 98 97 96 95**.

ANJOU ROUGE AC *Loire Valley, France* Anjou is best known for ROSÉ D'ANJOU but reds (from Cabernets Sauvignon and Franc or Pineau d'Aunis) are increasingly successful. Usually fruity, easy-drinking wine, with less tannin than ANJOU-VILLAGES. Wines made from Gamay are sold as Anjou Gamay. Best producers: M Angeli★, Fesles, J Pithon★, RICHOU★, Yves Soulez, Touche Noire. Best years: (top wines) (2001) 00 99 **98 97 96 95**.

ANJOU-VILLAGES AC *Loire Valley, France* Since 1985, 46 villages have been entitled to the AC Anjou-Villages, only for red wine from Cabernet Franc and Cabernet Sauvignon. Some extremely attractive dry, fruity reds are emerging in the region, with better aging potential than ANJOU ROUGE. Anjou-Villages Brissac is a superior sub-appellation. Best producers: Bablut★, P Baudouin★, Closel★, P Delesvaux★, Haute-Perche★, Laffourcade, Montgilet/V Lebreton★, Ogereau★, Pierre-Bise★, Putille★, RICHOU (Vieilles Vignes★★), Rochelles/J-Y Lebreton★★, Pierre Soulez★, Tigné★, la Varière★. Best years: (2001) 00 **99 98 97 96 95 90 89**.

ANSELMI *Soave DOC, Veneto, Italy* Roberto Anselmi, with PIEROPAN, has shown that much-maligned SOAVE can have personality when carefully made. Using ultra-modern methods he has honed the fruit flavours of his San Vincenzo★ and Capitel Foscarino★★ and introduced small-barrel-aging for single-vineyard Capitel Croce★★ and luscious, Sauternes-like I Capitelli★★ (sometimes ★★★). All sold under the regional IGT. Best years: (I Capitelli) 1999 **98 97 96 95 93 92 90 88**.

ANTINORI *Tuscany, Italy* World-famous Florentine family firm that has been involved in wine since 1385, but it is Piero Antinori, the current head, who has made the Antinori name synonymous with quality and innovation. The quality of its CHIANTI CLASSICO wines like Badia a Passignano★ (Riserva★★), Pèppoli★, Tenute Marchese Riserva★★ and Villa Antinori is consistently good, but it was its development of the SUPER-TUSCAN concept of superior wines outside the DOC that launched a quality revolution during the 1970s. Introducing small-barrel-aging to Tuscany, TIGNANELLO★★ (Sangiovese-Cabernet) and SOLAIA★★★ (Cabernet-based) can be great wines. Other interests include VINO NOBILE, La Braccesca★★ and BOLGHERI's Guado al Tasso★★ (Cabernet-Merlot). Ownership further afield includes PRUNOTTO in Piedmont, Pian delle Vigne in BRUNELLO DI MONTALCINO, the Tormaresca wines from PUGLIA, and ATLAS PEAK in California. Best years: (reds) 2000 99 **98 97 96 95 94 93 90**. See also Castello della Sala.

ANTONOPOULOS *Patras AO, Peloponnese, Greece*   Boutique winery producing barrel-fermented Chardonnay★★, Cabernet Nea Dris (New Oak)★, a blend of Cabernets Sauvignon and Franc, and Private Collection★, a promising Agiorgitiko-Cabernet blend.

ARAGÓN *Spain*   Most of Aragón, stretching from the Pyrenees south to Spain's central plateau, used to be responsible for much of the country's cheap red wine. There have been improvements, especially in the cooler, hilly, northern SOMONTANO DO. Further south, winemaking is improving in Campo de Borja DO, Calatayud DO and, particularly, CARINENA DO; these 3 areas have the potential to be a major budget-price force in a world mad for beefy reds.

ARAUJO *Napa Valley AVA, California, USA*   Boutique winery whose great coup was to buy the Eisele vineyard, traditionally a source of superb Cabernet under the Joseph Phelps label. Araujo Cabernet Sauvignon★★★ is now one of California's most sought-after reds, combining great fruit intensity with powerful but digestible tannins. There is also an attractively zesty Sauvignon Blanc★ and a tiny amount of impressive estate Syrah★★ produced as well.

ARBOIS AC *Jura, France*   The largest of the specific ACs in the Jura region. The whites are made from Chardonnay or the local Savagnin, which can give the wines a sherry-like flavour that is most concentrated in *vin jaune*. There is also a rare, sweet *vin de paille*. Good sparkling CREMANT DE JURA is made mainly from Chardonnay. Best reds and sparklers are from the commune of Pupillin. Best producers: Ch. d'Arlay★, Aviet★, Bourdy★, Désiré★, Dugois★, J Foret★, F Lornet★, H Maire★, P Overnoy★, la Pinte★, J Puffeney★, Pupillin co-op★, Rijckaert★, Rolet★, A & M Tissot★, J Tissot★, Tournelle★. Best years: (2001) 00 99 **98 97 96 95**.

ARCHERY SUMMIT *Willamette Valley AVA, Oregon, USA*   Owned by the Andrus family of PINE RIDGE, with more than 40ha (100 acres) in 3 estate vineyards, the focus here is on deeply coloured, heavily oaked Pinot Noir. Single-vineyard Pinot Noirs from Archery Summit Estate★, Red Hills★ and Arcus Estate★ top the list. A white wine labelled Vireton★ is a blend of Pinot Gris, Pinot Blanc and Chardonnay. Best years: (Pinot Noir) 2000 99 98 **96 94**.

ARGIANO *Brunello di Montalcino DOCG, Tuscany, Italy*   The mini-renaissance continues: renewed investment and the hand of Giacomo Tachis can be seen in radically refashioned BRUNELLO★★ (Riserva★★★) that is both rich and accessible, and scintillating Solengo★★★ (a blend of Cabernet, Merlot, Sangiovese and Syrah). Good ROSSO DI MONTALCINO★, too. Best years: (Brunello) 1997 95 **94 93 91 90**.

ARGIOLAS *Sardinia, Italy*   Sardinian star making DOC wines Cannonau (Costera★), Monica (Perdera) and Vermentino (Costamolino★) di Sardegna, but the best wines are the IGT Isola dei Nuraghi blends – Turriga★★ and Korem★ are powerful, spicy reds, Angialis★★ a golden, sweet white. All the wines are good value.

ARNEIS   Italian grape grown in the ROERO hills in PIEDMONT. Arneis is DOC in Roero, producing dry white wines which, at best, have an attractive nutty, herbal perfume. They can be expensive. Best producers: Araldica/Alasia★, Brovia★, Cascina Chicco★, Correggia★, Deltetto★, GIACOSA★, Malvirà★, Angelo Negro★, PRUNOTTO★, Vietti★, Gianni Voerzio★.

51

CH. L'ARROSÉE★★ *St-Émilion Grand Cru AC, Grand Cru Classé, Bordeaux, France* This small property, just south-west of the small historic town of ST-ÉMILION, makes really exciting wine: rich, chewy and wonderfully luscious, with a comparatively high proportion (40%) of Cabernet Sauvignon. Drink after 5 years, but may be cellared for 10 or more. Best years: 2000 98 **97** 96 **95 94 90 89 88 86 85**.

ARROWOOD *Sonoma Valley AVA, California, USA* Dick Arrowood was the winemaker at CHATEAU ST JEAN during its glory years of Chardonnay. In 1988 he started his own winery, which was purchased in 2000 by MONDAVI. The wines have mostly been tip-top – beautifully balanced Cabernet★★ (Reserve★★), superb Merlot★★, a deeply fruity Syrah★★, lovely, velvety Chardonnay★★ and a crisp, fragrant Viognier★★. Whites should be drunk young, reds with a little age. Best years: (Cabernet Sauvignon) (2000) 99 98 97 **96 95 94 91 90**.

ISMAEL ARROYO *Ribera del Duero DO, Castilla y León, Spain* This family bodega is one of the best RIBERA DEL DUERO producers, making long-lived, tannic wines, headed by Val Sotillo Reserva★★, Gran Reserva★★ and Crianza★. Best years: (Val Sotillo Reserva) **1996 95 94 91**.

ARTADI *Rioja DOC, País Vasco, Spain* Under demanding new boss Juan Carlos López de Lacalle, this former co-op is now producing RIOJA's deepest, most ambitious reds. These include Grandes Añadas★★★, Viña El Pisón★★★, Pagos Viejos★★ and Viñas de Gain. Best years: (2000) 99 **98 96 95 94 91**.

ASCHERI *Piedmont, Italy* Winemakers in PIEDMONT for at least 5 centuries, the Ascheri style is forward and appealingly drinkable, whether it be BAROLO (Vigna dei Pola★, Sorano★★), Dolcetto d'Alba (Vigna Nirane★) or NEBBIOLO D'ALBA. New are Syrah and Viognier sold as Montelupa Rosso and Bianco. The Cristina Ascheri MOSCATO D'ASTI is delightful.

ASTI DOCG *Piedmont, Italy* Asti Spumante, the world's best-selling sweet sparkling wine, was long derided as light and cheap, though promotion to DOCG signalled an upturn in quality. Made in the province of Asti south-east of Turin, under the new appellation (which includes the rarer MOSCATO D'ASTI) the wine is now called simply Asti. Its light sweetness and refreshing sparkle make it ideal with fruit, rich cakes and a wide range of sweet dishes. Drink young. Best producers: Araldica, Bera★, Cinzano★, Contero, Giuseppe Contratto★★, Cascina Fonda★, FONTANAFREDDA, Gancia★, Martini & Rossi★, Cascina Pian d'Or★.

ATA RANGI *Martinborough, North Island, New Zealand* Small, high-quality winery run by 2 families. Stylish, concentrated wines include big, rich Craighall Chardonnay★★, seductively perfumed cherry/plum Pinot Noir★★★ and an impressive Cabernet-Merlot-Syrah blend called Célèbre★★. Young Vines Pinot Noir is not of the same standard, but new Syrah★★ is promising. Best years: (Pinot Noir) (2001) 00 99 98 97 96.

ATLAS PEAK *Atlas Peak AVA, Napa, California, USA* These hillside vineyards, managed by ANTINORI of Italy, are demonstrating a new sense of direction after several years adrift. The 100% Sangiovese has been improving throughout the 1990s, as has Consenso★, a tasty Cabernet-Sangiovese blend. Both can age for 5–10 years. Chardonnay and Cabernet are recent additions. Best years: (reds) (1999) 98 97 **96 95**.

AU BON CLIMAT *Santa Maria Valley AVA, California, USA* Pace-setting winery in this cool region, run by the talented Jim Clendenen, who spends much time in BURGUNDY and PIEDMONT. The result is lush Chardonnay★★, intense Pinot Noir★★ (Isabelle bottling can be ★★★) and BORDEAUX styles under the Vita Nova label. Watch out for Italian varietals under the Il Podere dell' Olivos label and Cold Heaven Viogniers. QUPE operates from the same winery. Best years: (Pinot Noir) (2000) 99 98 **97 96 95 94 91 90**; (Chardonnay) (2001) 00 **99 98 97 95 92**.

AUCKLAND *North Island, New Zealand* Vineyards in the region of Auckland are concentrated in the districts of Henderson, KUMEU/HUAPAI, Matakana and WAIHEKE ISLAND. Clevedon, south of Auckland, is a fledgling area that shows promise. Best producers: COLLARDS★, Heron's Flight. Best years: (Cabernet Sauvignon) 2000 99 **98 96 94 93 91**.

CH. AUSONE★★★ *St-Émilion Grand Cru AC, 1er Grand Cru Classé, Bordeaux, France* This beautiful property, situated on what are perhaps the best slopes in ST-ÉMILION, made a much-vaunted return to form in the 1980s, and has maintained high standards. Owner Alain Vauthier's richly textured wines gain added complexity from the high proportion (50%) of Cabernet Franc. Production is a tiny 2000 cases a year. Best years: 2000 99 98 97 96 95 94 **90 89 88 86 85 83 82**.

AUXEY-DURESSES AC *Côte de Beaune, Burgundy, France* Auxey-Duresses is a backwater village up in the hills behind MEURSAULT. The reds should be light and fresh but can often lack ripeness. At its best, and at 3–5 years, the white is dry, soft, nutty and hinting at the creaminess of a good Meursault, but at much lower prices. Of the Premiers Crus, Les Duresses is the most consistent. Best producers: (reds) Comte Armand★★, J-P Diconne★, Jessiaume Père et Fils, Maison LEROY, Duc de Magenta★, M Prunier★, P Prunier★; (whites) R Ampeau★, d'Auvenay (Dom. LEROY)★★, J-P Diconne★, DROUHIN★★, J-P Fichet★, Olivier LEFLAIVE★, Maison LEROY★, Duc de Magenta★, M Prunier★. Best years: (reds) 1999 98 **96 95 93 90**; (whites) 2000 99 **97 96 95**.

AVIGNONESI *Vino Nobile di Montepulciano DOCG, Tuscany, Italy* The Falvo brothers led Montepulciano's revival as one of TUSCANY's best zones. Although VINO NOBILE★★ is often the best of the dry wines, for a time the international wines, Il Marzocco★ (Chardonnay) and Desiderio★★ (previously Merlot, now Merlot-Cabernet), received more attention. The VIN SANTO★★★ is the most sought-after in Tuscany; there's also a rare red version from Sangiovese, Occhio di Pernice★★★. Best years: (Vino Nobile) 1999 98 97 **96 95 94 93 91 90 88**.

AYL *Saar, Germany* A top Saar village. The best-known vineyard in Ayl is Kupp, which produces classy, slaty off-dry and sweet Rieslings on its steep slopes. Best producers: Bischöflicher Konvikt, Peter Lauer★, Dr Heinz Wagner★. Best years: (2001) **99 97 95 94 93 90**.

BABICH *Henderson, North Island, New Zealand* Family-run winery with some prime vineyard land in MARLBOROUGH and HAWKES BAY. Irongate Chardonnay★ is an intense, steely wine that needs plenty of cellaring, while intense, full-flavoured varietal reds under the Winemakers Reserve label show even greater potential for development. Flagship label Patriarch features Chardonnay★★ and Cabernet Sauvignon★★, both from Hawkes Bay. Marlborough wines include a stylish Sauvignon Blanc★, a tangy Riesling and a light, fruity Pinot Gris. Best years: (premium Hawkes Bay reds) 2000 99 **98 96 94**.

BAD DÜRKHEIM *Pfalz, Germany* This spa town has some good vineyards and is the headquarters of the dependable Vier Jahreszeiten Kloster Limburg co-op. Best producers: DARTING★, Fitz-Ritter, Pflüger★, Karl Schaefer★. Best years: (Riesling Spätlese) (2001) 99 98 **97 96 93 92**.

BAD KREUZNACH *Nahe, Germany* Spa town with 22 individual vineyard sites, the best wines coming from the steepest sites such as Brückes, Kahlenberg and Krötenpfuhl. Not to be confused with the NAHE district Bereich Kreuznach. Best producers: Paul Anheuser, Anton Finkenauer, Carl Finkenauer, Reichsgraf von Plettenberg. Best years: (Riesling Spätlese) 1999 98 **97 93 90**.

BADEN *Germany* Very large wine region stretching from FRANKEN to the Bodensee (Lake Constance). Its dry whites and reds show off the fuller, softer flavours Germany can produce in the warmer climate of its southerly regions. Many of the best non-Riesling German wines of the future will come from here, as well as many of the best barrel-fermented and barrel-aged wines. Good co-operative cellars at Achkarren, Bickensohl, Bötzingen, Durbach, Königsschaffhausen and Sasbach.

BAGA Important red grape in BAIRRADA, which is one of the few regions in Portugal to rely mainly on one variety. Also planted in much smaller quantities in DAO and the RIBATEJO. It can give deep, blackberryish wine, but aggressive tannin is a continual problem.

BAILEYS *North-East Victoria, Australia* Old, traditional winery at Glenrowan, where Australia's most famous bush bandit, Ned Kelly, made his last stand. Now part of Beringer Blass and, after a shaky start, showing real improvement (1920s Block Shiraz★). Also some of Australia's most luscious fortified Muscat and Tokay (Winemakers Selection★★) – still heavenly and irresistible stickies, but I can't help thinking they were better a few years ago.

BAIRRADA DOC *Beira Litoral, Portugal* Bairrada, along with the DOURO and ALENTEJO, is the source of many of Portugal's best red table wines. These can brim over with intense raspberry and blackberry fruit, though the tannin levels are severe and may take quite a few years to soften. The whites are coming on fast with modern vinification methods. Best producers: (reds) Caves ALIANCA, Quinta das Bágeiras★, Quinta do Carvalhinho★, Gonçalves Faria★★, Caves Messias (Garrafeira★), Luis PATO★★, Caves Primavera (Garrafeira★), Quinta da Rigodeira★, Casa de Saima★, Caves SAO JOAO★★, SOGRAPE, Sidónio de Sousa★★; (whites) Quinta da Rigodeira★, Casa de Saima★, SOGRAPE (Reserva★★, Quinta de Pedralvites★). Best years: (reds) (2001) 00 97 **96 95 94 92 91 90**.

BALATONBOGLÁR WINERY *Transdanubia, Hungary* The dominant winery in the Lake Balaton region, benefiting from heavy investment and the expertise of viticulturist Richard Smart and wine consultant Kym Milne, has improved quality, particularly in the inexpensive, inoffensive range sold under the Chapel Hill label in the UK. Owned by Henkell & Söhnlein, a large German sparkling wine producer.

BALEARIC ISLANDS *Spain* Medium-bodied reds and soft rosés were the mainstays of Mallorca's 2 DO areas, Binissalem and Plà i Llevant, until the Anima Negra winery began turning out its stunning, deep reds from the native Callet grape. Best producers: Anima Negra★, Franja Roja (J L Ferrer), Herederos de Ribas, Son Bordils★.

BANDOL AC *Provence, France* A lovely fishing port with vineyards high above the Mediterranean, producing some of the best reds and rosés in Provence. The Mourvèdre grape gives Bandol its character – gentle raisin and honey softness with a herby fragrance. The reds happily age for 10 years, sometimes more, but can be very good at 3–4. The rosés, delicious and spicy but often too pricy, should be drunk young. There is a small amount of neutral, overpriced white. Best producers: (reds) Bastide Blanche★★, la Bégude★, Bunan★, Frégate★, le Galantin★, J P Gaussen★★, Gros' Noré★★, l'Hermitage★, Lafran-Veyrolles★, Mas Redorne★, la Noblesse★, PIBARNON★★, Pradeaux★★, Ray-Jane★★, Roche Redonne★, Romassan★, Ste-Anne★, des Salettes★, de Souviou★★, la Suffrène★★, TEMPIER★★, Terrebrune★★, la Tour de Bon★, Vannières★. Best years: (2001) 00 99 98 **97 96 95 93 90 89 88**.

BANFI *Brunello di Montalcino DOCG, Tuscany, Italy* High-tech American-owned firm which is now a force in Italy. Noted winemaker Ezio Rivella (here from 1977 to 1999) did much to establish Banfi's reputation. BRUNELLO★, Chardonnay (Fontanelle★★), Cabernet (Tavernelle★★) and Merlot (Mandrielle★) are very successful, but even better are Brunello Riserva Poggio all'Oro★★ and SUPER-TUSCANS Summus★★ (a blend of Sangiovese, Cabernet and Syrah) and Excelsus★★ (Cabernet-Merlot). Also has cellars (Vigne Regali) in PIEDMONT for GAVI and fizz. Best years: (top reds) 1999 97 **96 95 94 93 90**.

BANNOCKBURN *Geelong, Victoria, Australia* The experience gleaned from vintage stints at Burgundy's Dom. DUJAC is reflected in Gary Farr's powerful, gamy Pinot Noir★ and MEURSAULT-like Chardonnay★★, which are among Australia's best or most notorious wines – depending on your view. I prefer the complex and classy Shiraz★★, influenced by Rhône's Alain GRAILLOT. (Note that there was no estate-grown wine in 1998 due to a freak hailstorm.) Best years: (Shiraz) 1998 97 **96 95 94 92 91 90 89 88 86**.

BANYULS AC *Roussillon, France* One of the best *vin doux naturels*, made mainly from Grenache, with a strong plum and raisin flavour. Rimage – vintaged early bottlings – and tawny styles are the best. Generally served as an apéritif in France and deserves a wider audience. Try sampling it mid-afternoon with some macaroons or plain cake. Best producers: Casa Blanca, Cellier des Templiers★, Clos des Paulilles★, l'Étoile★, Mas Blanc★★, la RECTORIE★★, la Tour Vieille★, Vial Magnères★.

BARBADILLO *Jerez y Manzanilla DO, Andalucía, Spain* The largest sherry company in the coastal town of Sanlúcar de Barrameda makes a wide range of good to excellent wines, in particular salty, dry manzanilla styles (Solear★★) and intense, nutty, but dry amontillados and olorosos, led by Amontillado Principe★★ and Oloroso Cuco★★. Neutral dry white Castillo de San Diego is a best seller in Spain.

BARBARESCO DOCG *Piedmont, Italy* This prestigious red wine, grown near Alba in the LANGHE hills south-east of Turin, is often twinned with its neighbour BAROLO to demonstrate the nobility of the Nebbiolo grape. Barbaresco can be a shade softer and less powerful. The wine usually takes less time to mature and is often considered the most approachable of the two, as exemplified by the international style of GAJA. But, as in Barolo, traditionalists also excel, led by Bruno GIACOSA. Even though the area is relatively compact (509ha/1257 acres), wine styles can differ significantly between vineyards and producers. Best vineyards: Asili, Bricco di Neive, Costa Russi, Crichet Pajè, Gallina, Marcorino, Martinenga, Messoirano, Moccagatta,

Montestefano, Ovello, Pora, Rabajà, Rio Sordo, San Lorenzo, Santo Stefano, Serraboella, Sorì Paitin, Sorì Tildìn. Best producers: Barbaresco co-op★★, Piero Busso★, CERETTO★★, Cigliuti★★, Stefano Farina★★, Fontanabianca★★, GAJA★★★, GIACOSA★★★, Marchesi di Gresy★★, Moccagatta★★, Fiorenzo Nada★★, Castello di Neive★★, Paitin★★, Oddero★, Pelissero★★, Pio Cesare★★, PRUNOTTO★, Albino Rocca★★, Bruno Rocca★★, Sottimano★★, La Spinetta★★, Vietti★★. Best years: (2001) 00 99 98 97 96 **95 93 90 89 88 86 85 82**.

BARBERA A native of north-west Italy, Barbera vies with Sangiovese as the most widely planted red grape in the country. When grown for high yields its natural acidity shows through, producing vibrant quaffers. Low yields from the top PIEDMONT estates create intensely rich and complex wines. Oaked versions can be stunning.

BARBERA D'ALBA DOC *Piedmont, Italy* Some of the most outstanding Barbera comes from this appellation. The most modern examples are supple and generous and can be drunk almost at once. More intense, dark-fruited versions require a minimum 3 years' age, but might improve for as much as 8. Best producers: G Alessandria★★, ALTARE★, Azelia★★, Boglietti★★, Brovia★, Cascina Chicco★, CERETTO★, Cigliuti★, CLERICO★, Elvio Cogno★★, Aldo CONTERNO★★, Giacomo CONTERNO★, Conterno-Fantino★, Corino★★, Correggia★★, Elio Grasso★, Giuseppe MASCARELLO★, Moccagatta★, M Molino★★, Monfalletto-Cordero di Montezemolo★★, Oberto★★, Parusso★★, Pelissero★, F Principiano★★, PRUNOTTO★★, Albino Rocca★★, Bruno Rocca★, SANDRONE★★, P Scavino★★, La Spinetta★★, Vajra★★, Mauro Veglio★★, Vietti★★, Gianni Voerzio★★, Roberto VOERZIO★★★. Best years: 2000 99 **98 97 96 95**.

BARBERA D'ASTI DOC *Piedmont, Italy* While Dolcetto d'Asti is usually light and simple, wines made from Barbera show a greater range of quality. Unoaked and barrique-aged examples can compete with the best BARBERA D'ALBA and rival some of the better Nebbiolo-based reds. Best examples can be kept for 5–6 years, occasionally longer. Best producers: Araldica/Alasia★, La Barbatella★★, Pietro Barbero★★, Bava★, Bertelli★★, Braida★★, Cascina Castlèt★, Coppo★★, Hastae (Quorum★), Il Mongetto★★, Martinetti★★, PRUNOTTO★★, Cantine Sant'Agata★, Scarpa★★, La Spinetta★★, Vietti★★. Best years: (2001) 00 99 98 **97 96 95**.

BARDOLINO DOC *Veneto, Italy* Substantial zone centred on Lake Garda, giving, at best, light, scented red and rosé (chiaretto) wines to be drunk young, from the same grape mix as neighbouring VALPOLICELLA. Best producers: Cavalchina★, Corte Gardoni★, Guerrieri-Rizzardi★, MASI, Le Vigne di San Pietro★, Fratelli Zeni.

BAROLO DOCG *Piedmont, Italy* Renowned red wine, named after a village south-west of Alba, from the Nebbiolo grape grown in 1284ha (3272 acres) of vineyards in the steep LANGHE hills. Its status as 'king of wines and wine of kings' for a time proved to be more of a burden than a benefit among Italians, who considered its austere power too much for modern palates, with tough, chewy tannins which took years of cask-aging to soften. But for over a decade, many winemakers have applied new methods to make Barolo that is fresher, cleaner, better balanced and ready sooner, with greater colour, richer fruit and softer tannins yet without sacrificing Barolo's noble character. Distinct styles of wine are made in the zone's villages. Barolo and La Morra make the most perfumed wines; Monforte and Serralunga the most structured; Castiglione Falletto strikes a balance between the two. Barolo is nowadays frequently labelled by vineyards, though the producer's reputation often carries more weight. Best vineyards: Bricco delle Viole, Brunate, Bussia Soprana, Cannubi Boschis, Cerequio, Conca dell'Annunziata, Fiasco, Francia, Giachini, Ginestra, Monfalletto, Monprivato, Rocche dell'Annunziata, Rocche di Castiglione, Santo Stefano di Perno, La Serra, Vigna Rionda, Villero. Best producers: C Alario★★, G Alessandria★★, ALTARE★★, Azelia★★, Boglietti★★, Bongiovanni★★, Brovia★★, CERETTO★★, CHIARLO★, CLERICO★★, Aldo CONTERNO★★★, Giacomo CONTERNO★★, Conterno-Fantino★★, Corino★★, Luigi Einaudi★★, GAJA★★★, GIACOSA★★, Elio Grasso★★, M Marengo★★, Bartolo MASCARELLO★★★, Giuseppe MASCARELLO★★★, Monfalletto-Cordero di Montezemolo★★, Oberto★★, Oddero★★, Parusso★★, Pio Cesare★★, Pira★★, E Pira & Figli★★, F Principiano★, PRUNOTTO★★, Renato RATTI★, Revello★★, Rocche dei Manzoni★★, SANDRONE★★★, P Scavino★★, M Sebaste★★, Vajra★★, Mauro Veglio★★, Vietti★★, Vigna Rionda★★, Gianni Voerzio★★, Roberto VOERZIO★★. Best years: (2001) (00) 99 97 96 95 **93 90 89 88 86 85**.

BAROSSA VALLEY See pages 58–9.

BAROSSA VALLEY ESTATE *Barossa, South Australia* Half owned by local grape growers, half by industry giant BRL HARDY. Flagship reds are huge, gutsy BAROSSA beauties E&E Black Pepper Shiraz★★, Ebenezer Shiraz★★ and E&E Sparkling Shiraz★★, all of them bursting with ripe plum fruit, spice and plenty of vanilla oak. There's also Ebenezer Cabernet Sauvignon★ and Chardonnay★★ and intense, full-flavoured sparkling Pinot Noir★ in the same range. Moculta, a second label, offers a good value range of wines.

JIM BARRY *Clare Valley, South Australia* Formerly more of a white wine outfit, with the famous Florita vineyard as the source of perfumed, classy Rieslings★. However, it is for rich and complex reds such as Cabernet Sauvignon, McCrae Wood Shiraz★, and the heady, palate-busting Armagh Shiraz★★ that it is now known. Best years: (Armagh Shiraz) (1999) 98 96 **95 93 92 91 90**.

BARSAC AC *Bordeaux, France* Barsac, largest of the 5 communes in the SAUTERNES AC, also has its own AC, which is used by most, but by no means all, of the top properties. In general, the wines are a little less luscious than other Sauternes, but from good estates they can be marvellous. Best producers: CLIMENS★★★, COUTET★★, DOISY-DAENE★★, Doisy-Dubroca★, DOISY-VÉDRINES★★, Myrat★, NAIRAC★★, Piada, Suau★. Best years: (2001) 99 98 97 **96 95 90 89 88 86 83**.

BASEDOW *Barossa Valley, South Australia* Basedow has changed hands a few times in recent years but now seems settled. The lush, wood-aged Semillon★★ is partnered by a soft, rich Shiraz★ and Cabernet★, a heavyweight Chardonnay and a new super-premium Johannes Shiraz★★. Best years: (Johannes Shiraz) 1998 **96**.

BASSERMANN-JORDAN *Deidesheim, Pfalz, Germany* Since the arrival of winemaker Ulrich Mell with the 1996 vintage, this famous estate has resumed making the rich yet elegant Rieslings of ★ and ★★ quality which long made its name synonymous with great Deidesheim and FORST wines. Best years: (2001) 00 **99 98 97** 96 90 89 88 86 81 79 76 71.

CH. BASTOR-LAMONTAGNE★ *Sauternes AC, Cru Bourgeois, Bordeaux, France* Luscious, honeyed sweet wine at a price which allows us to enjoy high-class SAUTERNES without taking out a second mortgage. Best years: (2001) 99 98 97 **96 95 94 90** 89 88 86 85 83.

BAROSSA

South Australia

The Barossa Valley, an hour or so's drive north of Adelaide in South Australia, is the heart of the Australian wine industry. Penfolds, Orlando, Beringer Blass, Seppelt, Yalumba and other giants have their headquarters here, alongside around 50 or so smaller wineries, producing or processing up to 60% of the nation's wine. However, this percentage is based mostly on grapes trucked in from other regions, because the Barossa's vineyards themselves grow less than 10% of Australia's grapes. Yet Barossa-grown grapes, once rejected as uneconomical for their low yields, are now increasingly prized for those same low yields.

Why? Well, it's highly likely that the world's oldest vines are in the Barossa. The valley was settled in the 1840s by Prussian immigrants who brought with them vines from Europe, most importantly, as it turned out, cuttings from the Syrah (or Shiraz) variety of France's Rhône Valley. And because Barossa has never been affected by the phylloxera louse, which destroyed much of the world's vineyards in the late 19th century, today you can still see gnarled, twisted old vines sporting just a few tiny bunches of priceless fruit that were planted by refugees from Europe all of a century-and-a-half ago, and are still tended by their descendants. A new wave of winemakers has taken up the cause of the Barossa vines with much zeal and no small amount of national pride, and they now produce from them some of the deepest, most fascinating wines, not just in Australia, but in the world.

GRAPE VARIETIES

Shiraz is prized above all other Barossa grapes, able to conjure headswirling, palate-dousing flavours. Barossa is the main source of Shiraz grapes for Penfolds Grange, the wine that began the revolution in Australian red wine in the 1950s. Cabernet Sauvignon is also excellent and similarly potent, as are the Rhône varieties of heady Grenache and deliciously earthy Mourvèdre; some of the most exciting examples are from the original vines planted in the 19th century. All these varieties are largely grown on the hot, dry, valley floor, but just to the east lie the Barossa Ranges, and in these higher, cooler vineyards, especially in those of the neighbouring Eden Valley, some of Australia's best and most fashionable Rieslings are grown, prized for their steely attack and lime fragrance. There is also some excellent Semillon and Chardonnay. But even here you can't get away from Shiraz, and some thrilling examples come from the hills, not least Henschke's Hill of Grace.

CLASSIFICATIONS

The Barossa was among the first zones to be ratified within the Australian system of Geographical Indications and comprises the regions of Barossa Valley and Eden Valley. The Barossa lies within South Australia's collective 'super zone' of Adelaide.

See also GRANGE, SOUTH AUSTRALIA; and individual producers.

(Barossa Valley Shiraz) (2001) 99 98 97 **96 95 94 91 90 88 87**; (Eden Valley Riesling) **2001 00 99 98 97 96 95 94 92 91 90 88 87**

BEST PRODUCERS

Shiraz-based reds
BAROSSA VALLEY ESTATE, BASEDOW, Bethany, Grant BURGE, Charles Cimicky (Signature), Elderton (Command), Glaetzer, Greenock Creek (Block Shiraz, Seven Acres), HENSCHKE, Hewitson, Jenke, Trevor Jones, Peter LEHMANN, Charles MELTON, Miranda (Show Reserve Old Vine Shiraz), MOUNTADAM, ORLANDO, PENFOLDS (RWT, GRANGE), ROCKFORD, ST HALLETT, Saltram (No. 1 Shiraz), Three Rivers, Torbreck, Turkey Flat, VERITAS, The Willows, YALUMBA (Octavius).

Riesling
Bethany, Grant BURGE, Leo Buring (Leonay), Heggies (Botrytis Riesling), HENSCHKE, Hewitson, Peter LEHMANN, MOUNTADAM, ORLANDO, Ross Estate, YALUMBA (Contour).

Cabernet Sauvignon-based reds
Grant BURGE, Greenock Creek, HENSCHKE, Peter LEHMANN, ST HALLETT, VERITAS.

Other reds (containing Grenache, Mourvèdre, Shiraz)
Burge Family (Olive Hill), Grant BURGE, Charles Cimicky (Grenache), Elderton (CSM), Jenke (Mourvèdre), Peter LEHMANN, Charles MELTON, PENFOLDS (Old Vine), Torbreck (Juveniles, The Steading), Turkey Flat (Butcher's Block, Grenache Noir), VERITAS.

Semillon
BASEDOW, Grant BURGE, Craneford, HENSCHKE, Jenke, Peter LEHMANN, ROCKFORD, Turkey Flat, The Willows.

CH. BATAILLEY★ *Pauillac AC, 5ème Cru Classé, Haut-Médoc, Bordeaux, France* A byword for value for money and reliability among the Pauillac Classed Growth estates. Marked by a full, obvious blackcurrant fruit, not too much tannin and a luscious overlay of creamy vanilla. Lovely to drink at only 5 years old, the wine continues to age well for up to 15 years. Best years: 2000 96 **95 94 90 89 88 86 85 83 82**.

BÂTARD-MONTRACHET AC *Grand Cru, Côte de Beaune, Burgundy, France* This Grand Cru produces some of the world's greatest whites – they are full, rich and balanced, with a powerful mineral intensity of fruit and fresh acidity. There are 2 associated Grands Crus: Bienvenues-Bâtard-Montrachet and the minuscule Criots-Bâtard-Montrachet. All can age for a decade. Best producers: Blain-Gagnard★★★, CARILLON★★★, DROUHIN★★★, J-N GAGNARD★★★, GAGNARD-DELAGRANGE★★★, JADOT★★★, V & F Jouard★★, LATOUR★★, Dom. LEFLAIVE★★★, Olivier LEFLAIVE★★, Marc Morey★★★, Pierre Morey★★★, Michel Niellon★★★, RAMONET★★★, SAUZET★★★, VERGET★★★. Best years: (2001) 00 99 98 97 96 95 **92 90 89**.

DOM. DES BAUMARD *Coteaux du Layon, Loire Valley, France* Excellent domaine established nearly 400 years ago. The heart of the domaine is its sweet wines: sensational QUARTS DE CHAUME★★★ which requires aging, as well as rich, honeyed, impeccably balanced COTEAUX DU LAYON Clos de Ste Cathérine★★. Also, a fine steely, mineral-scented SAVENNIERES Clos du Papillon★★. CRÉMANT DE LOIRE and ANJOU reds are okay but a touch unexciting. Best years: (Quarts de Chaume) 1999 97 96 95 **93 90 89 88 85 83 81 78 76 71 70 69 66 64 62 59 47**.

DOM. DE LA BAUME *Vin de Pays d'Oc, Languedoc, France* The French outpost of BRL HARDY, chiefly making varietal wines. The whites★ regularly outperform the reds, but none excel. Chardonnay, Sauvignon Blanc, Merlot, Cabernet Sauvignon and Shiraz are sold under the La Baume label, and include contract fruit; there are also 2 premium estate wines, a Merlot and a Chardonnay-Viognier blend, under the Domaine de la Baume label.

LES BAUX-DE-PROVENCE AC *Provence, France* This AC has proved that organic farming can produce spectacular results mainly due to the warm dry climate. Good fruit and intelligent winemaking produce some of the more easily enjoyable reds in Provence. Best producers: Mas de la Dame★, Mas de Gourgonnier★, Mas Ste-Berthe★, Romanin★, Terres Blanches★. Best years: (2001) 00 99 98 **97 96 95 94 93**.

BÉARN AC *South-West France* While the rest of South-West France has been busy producing some unusual and original flavours in recent years, Béarn hasn't managed to cash in. The wines (90% red and rosé) just aren't special enough, despite some decent grape varieties. The 2000 vintage saw an upswing in quality. Best producers: Bellocq co-op, Cauhapé, Guilhermas, Lapeyre, Nigri.

CH. DE BEAUCASTEL *Châteauneuf-du-Pape AC, Rhône Valley, France* François Perrin makes some of the richest, most tannic reds★★★ in CHATEAUNEUF-DU-PAPE, with an unusually high percentage of Mourvèdre and Syrah, which can take at least a decade to show at their best. The white Vieilles Vignes★★★, made almost entirely from Roussanne, is exquisite, too. Perrin also produces COTES DU RHONE Coudelet de Beaucastel red★ and white★ and a range of southern reds under the Domaine Perrin label. Best years: (reds) (2000) 99 98 97 96 95 **94 93 90 89 88 86 85 83 82 81**; (whites) (2000) 99 98 97 96 95 **94 93 92 90 89 88**.

BEAUJOLAIS AC *Beaujolais, Burgundy, France*   Famous red wine from a large area of rolling hills and valleys in southern Burgundy. In the north, toward Mâcon, most of the reds qualify either as BEAUJOLAIS-VILLAGES or as a single Cru (10 villages which produce better but more expensive wine: BROUILLY, CHENAS, CHIROUBLES, COTE DE BROUILLY, FLEURIE, JULIENAS, MORGON, MOULIN-A-VENT, REGNIE, ST-AMOUR). In the south, toward Lyon, most of the wine is simple AC Beaujolais, a light red to be drunk very young, which should be lovely and fresh but is now too often dilute. Much Beaujolais appears as BEAUJOLAIS NOUVEAU. Beaujolais Supérieur means wine with a minimum strength of 1% more alcohol than basic Beaujolais. A little white is made from Chardonnay. The Éventail de Vignerons Producteurs is a high-profile marketing group. Best producers: (reds) DUBOEUF, DROUHIN, Éventail de Vignerons Producteurs, H Fessy★, JADOT, de la Madone★, Terres Dorées/J-P Brun, Vissoux/P-M Chermette★. Best years: (2001) **00 99**.

BEAUJOLAIS NOUVEAU *Beaujolais AC, Burgundy, France*   Often known as Beaujolais Primeur, this is the first release of bouncy, fruity Beaujolais on the third Thursday of November after the harvest. Once a simple celebration of the new vintage, then a much-hyped beano, now increasingly *passé*. Quality is generally reasonable. The wine usually improves by Christmas and the New Year, and the best ones are perfect for summer picnics.

BEAUJOLAIS-VILLAGES AC *Beaujolais, Burgundy, France*   Beaujolais-Villages can come from any one of 38 villages in the north of the region. Carefully made, it can represent all the simple excitement of the Gamay grape at its best. Best villages: Beaujeu, Lancié, Lantignié, Leynes, Quincié, St-Étienne-des-Ouillières, St-Jean-d'Ardières. Best producers: Daumas★, G Descombes★, DUBOEUF, Éventail de Vignerons Producteurs, Janin★, Lacondemine★, Miolane★, Dom. Perrier★, J-C Pivot★, M Tête★, Ch. Thivin★. Best years: (2001) **00 99 98**.

BEAULIEU VINEYARD *Napa Valley AVA, California, USA*   The late André Tchelistcheff had a major role in creating this icon for Napa Cabernet Sauvignon as winemaker from the late 1930s to the late 60s. After he left, Beaulieu missed a few beats and lived on its reputation for too long, even though Tchelistcheff continued to consult. However, recent bottlings of the Private Reserve Cabernet Sauvignon★★ signal a return to form. A meritage red called Tapestry★★ is also top-notch. Recent bottlings of Chardonnay★ and Pinot Noir★ from CARNEROS and Syrah★ have been a pleasant surprise. Best years: (Private Reserve) (2000) 99 98 97 96 95 94 92 91 **90 87 86 85 84**.

BEAUMES-DE-VENISE *Rhône Valley, France*   Area famous for its sweet wine, MUSCAT DE BEAUMES-DE-VENISE. The local red wine is also very good, one of the meatier COTES DU RHONE-VILLAGES, with a ripe, plummy fruit in warm years. Best producers: (reds) Bernardins, les Goubert★, Beaumes-de-Venise co-op.

BEAUNE AC *Côte de Beaune, Burgundy, France*   Beaune gives its name to the southern section of the COTE D'OR, the COTE DE BEAUNE. Most of the wines are red, with delicious, soft red-fruits ripeness. There are no Grands Crus but some excellent Premiers Crus (Boucherottes, Bressandes, Clos des Mouches, Fèves, Grèves, Marconnets, Teurons, Vignes Franches). There's an increasing production of white – DROUHIN makes an outstandingly good, creamy, nutty Clos des Mouches★★★. Best producers: (growers) GERMAIN★★, LAFARGE★★, Albert Morot★★, TOLLOT-BEAUT★★; (merchants) BOUCHARD PERE ET FILS★★ (since 1996),

Champy★★, Chanson★, DROUHIN★★, Camille Giroud★★, JADOT★★, JAFFELIN, LABOURE-ROI, THOMAS-MOILLARD★. Best years: (reds) (2001) 99 98 **97** 96 **95 93 90**; (whites) (2001) 00 99 **97** 96 **95**.

CH. BEAU-SÉJOUR BÉCOT★★ *St-Émilion Grand Cru AC, 1er Grand Cru Classé, Bordeaux, France* Demoted from Premier Grand Cru Classé in 1986 and promoted again in 1996, this estate is now back on top form. Brothers Gérard and Dominique Bécot produce firm, ripe, richly textured wines that need at least 8–10 years to develop. Best years: 2000 98 97 96 95 **94 90 89 88 86 85**.

BEAUX FRÈRES *Willamette Valley AVA, Oregon, USA* A venture that has generated much interest due to the participation of wine critic Robert Parker; co-owner and winemaker Mike Etzel is his brother-in-law (hence the name). The aim has been to make ripe, unfiltered Pinot Noir★★ that expresses the essence of the grape and vineyard. Its immediate success has attracted a cult following. Second label Belles Soeurs★ is also good. Best years: 2001 00 99 98 **97 96 94 93**.

GRAHAM BECK WINES *Robertson WO, South Africa* This two-cellar operation is one of the Cape's most exciting. In ROBERTSON, Pieter Ferreira concentrates on Cap Classique sparkling, including an elegant, rich NV Brut from Chardonnay and Pinot Noir, and a toastily fragrant, creamy barrel-fermented Blanc de Blancs★. Shiraz★ carries the flag for reds, while the flavourful, balanced Chardonnay★ does the same for still white wine; also a promising Viognier. Charles Hopkins runs the FRANSCHHOEK cellar: his Graham Beck Coastal range – much from old-vine STELLENBOSCH fruit – is making waves with Shiraz, The Old Road Pinotage★ and Cabernet Sauvignon★

J B BECKER *Walluf, Rheingau, Germany* Hajo Becker makes some of the raciest and longest-living dry Rieslings – usually ★, some Spätlese trocken ★★ – in the RHEINGAU. He also makes impressive dry Spätburgunder (Pinot Noir) reds matured without any new oak. Best years: (Riesling Spätlese trocken) (2001) 99 98 **97 96 94 92 90**.

BEDELL CELLARS *Long Island, New York State, USA* Winemaker Kip Bedell earned a reputation in the 1980s for high-quality, BORDEAUX-styled Merlot★ (Reserve★★), Cabernet Sauvignon★ and a red blend called Cupola★★. In the 90s, other wineries began imitating Bedell's vineyard management techniques, contributing to a quality increase throughout the region. Bedell sold the winery in 2000, but remains as winemaker. Best years: (reds) (2001) (00) **98 97 95 94**.

BEIRAS *Portugal* This large, central Portuguese province includes the leading DOCs of DAO and BAIRRADA, as well as new DOCs Távora/Varosa and Beira Interior. A number of important wines are made at the Vinho Regional level, using Portuguese red and white grape varieties along with international grapes such as Cabernet Sauvignon and Chardonnay. Best producers: Caves ALIANCA (Galeria), D F J VINHOS, Quinta do Encontro★, Figueira de Castelo Rodrigo co-op, Quinta de Foz de Arouce★, Luis PATO★★, Caves SAO JOAO (Quinta do Poco do Lobo).

CH. BELAIR★ *St-Émilion Grand Cru AC, 1er Grand Cru Classé, Bordeaux, France* Belair is located on ST-ÉMILION's limestone plateau next to AUSONE. Under the direction of winemaker Pascal Delbeck the estate has been run biodynamically since 1994, and the effects are beginning to be felt with the soft, stylish wines on good form. Best years: 2000 98 **95 94 90 89 88 86 85 83 82**.

BELLAVISTA *Franciacorta DOCG, Lombardy, Italy* Winemaker Mattia Vezzola specializes in FRANCIACORTA sparkling wines with a very good Cuvée Brut★★ and 4 distinctive Gran Cuvées★★ (including an excellent rosé). Riserva Vittorio Moretti Extra Brut★★ is made in exceptional years. Also produces lovely still wines, including white blend Convento dell'Annunciata★★★, Chardonnay Uccellanda★★ and red Casotte★ (Pinot Nero) and Solesine★★ (Cabernet-Merlot).

BELLET AC *Provence, France* A tiny AC in the hills behind Nice; the wine, mostly white, is usually overpriced. Ch. de Crémat★ and Ch. de Bellet★ are the most important producers but my favourite is Delmasso★. Best years: (2001) **00 99 98 97 96 95**.

BENDIGO *Central Victoria, Australia* Warm, dry, former gold-mining region, which produced some decent wines in the 19th century. Triumphantly resurrected by Balgownie in 1969, and other small-scale, high-quality wineries followed (including Chateau Leamon, Water Wheel, Heathcote, Jasper Hill, Passing Clouds, Wild Duck Creek, YELLOWGLEN). The best wines are rich, ripe, distinctively minty Shiraz and Cabernet. Best years: (Shiraz) (2001) 00 99 98 **97 95 94 93 91 90**.

BERBERANA *Rioja DOC, Rioja, Spain* A dynamic new boss has transformed one of RIOJA's largest companies. Berberana has bought Lagunilla and formed a partnership with MARQUES DE GRINON, and is making a pleasant, lightly oaked Crianza and respectable Reservas and Gran Reservas. The name of the whole group is Arco Bodegas Unidas but Berberana remains the brand name for most of its Rioja wines. Best years: (Reserva) **1996 95 94 91**.

BERCHER *Burkheim, Baden, Germany* The Bercher brothers run one of the top estates of the KAISERSTUHL. The high points are the powerful oak-aged Spätburgunder (Pinot Noir) reds★★ and Grauburgunder★★ (Pinot Gris) dry whites, which marry richness with perfect balance. Drink young or cellar for 3–5 years or more. Best years: (whites) (2001) **99 98 97 96 94 93**; (reds) (2001) (99) **97 96 93**.

BERGERAC AC *South-West France* Bergerac is the main town of the Dordogne and the overall AC for this underrated area on the eastern edge of Bordeaux. The grape varieties are mostly the same as those used in the BORDEAUX ACS. The red is generally like a light, fresh claret, a bit grassy but with a good, raw blackcurrant fruit and hint of earth. Recent vintages have shown more ripe fruit character. Côtes de Bergerac AC wines must have a higher minimum alcohol level. In general drink young although a few estate reds can age for at least 3–5 years. The whites are generally lean and dry for quick drinking. Best producers: l'Ancienne Cure★, Bélingard, la Colline★, Court-les-Mûts, Eyssards, Gouyat, la Jaubertie, Moulin Caresse, Panisseau, TOUR DES GENDRES★, Tour des Verdots★, Tourmentine. Best years: (reds) 2000 **98 96 95 90**.

BERINGER *Napa Valley AVA, California, USA* Beringer produces a full range of wine, but, in particular, offers a spectacular range of top-class Cabernet Sauvignons. The Private Reserve Cabernet can be ★★★ and is one of NAPA VALLEY's finest yet most approachable; the Chabot Vineyards★★, when released under its own label, can be equally impressive. The Knight's Valley Cabernet Sauvignon★ is made in a lighter style and is good value. Beringer makes red★★ and white★

Alluvium (meritage wines) from Knight's Valley. The Private Reserve Chardonnay★★ is a powerful wine that ages well. HOWELL MOUNTAIN Merlot★★ from Bancroft Ranch is also very good. Best years: (Cabernet Sauvignon) (2000) 99 98 97 96 **95 94 93 91 90 87 86 85 84 81**.

BERNKASTEL *Mosel, Germany* Both a town in the Middle Mosel and a large Bereich. Top wines, however, will come only from vineyard sites within the town – the most famous of these is the overpriced DOCTOR vineyard. Many wines from the Graben and Lay sites are as good or better and cost a fraction of the price. Best producers: Hansen-Lauer★, Dr LOOSEN★★, J J PRUM★★, Dr H Thanisch★, WEGELER★★. Best years: (2001) 00 99 98 **97** 95 **93 90 88**.

BEST'S *Grampians, Victoria, Australia* Small winery run by Viv Thomson, who makes attractive wines from estate vineyards first planted in 1868. Tasty, clear-fruited Great Western Bin No. 0 Shiraz★ and Great Western Cabernet★ are good, and the Riesling★ shows flashes of brilliance. Tropical-fruity, finely balanced Chardonnay★ is variable, delicious at best; Thomson Family Reserve★★ is a super-Shiraz label. Best years: (Thomson Family Reserve) 1998 97 96 95 94 **92**.

BETHEL HEIGHTS *Willamette Valley AVA, Oregon, USA* OREGON winery with a reputation for stylish Pinot Noirs★★ which are delicious young but can also age surprisingly well; the Southeast Block Reserve★★★ is the star. Subtle Chardonnay Reserve★ is gathering acclaim too, and Pinot Gris★★ filled with citrus and mineral scents is crisp and immensely drinkable. Best years: (Pinot Noir) 2000 99 98 **96 94**.

CH. BEYCHEVELLE★ *St-Julien AC, 4ème Cru Classé, Haut-Médoc, Bordeaux, France* At its best, this château can make wine of Second Growth quality. The wine has a charming softness even when young, but takes at least a decade to mature into the cedarwood and blackcurrant flavour for which ST-JULIEN is famous. In the best years it is worth its high price and, after a period of inconsistency, quality has become more regular since the late 1990s. Second wine: Réserve de l'Amiral. Best years: 2000 99 98 96 **95 90 89 86 85 83 82**.

BEYERSKLOOF *Stellenbosch WO, South Africa* Red wine maestro Beyers Truter concentrates on only 2 wines at this property he owns in partnership with the Krige brothers of KANONKOP. The striking, supple Cabernet Sauvignon-based Beyerskloof★★ is made in boutique quantities. The Pinotage★ is bountiful in quantity and ripe juiciness, showing delightfully pure Pinotage character. Quaffable when young, recent vintages show more aging ability. Best years: (Beyerskloof) **1999 98 97 96 95 94 93**.

BIANCO DI CUSTOZA DOC *Veneto, Italy* Dry white wine similar to neighbouring SOAVE. Drink young. Best producers: Cavalchina★, Gorgo★, Montresor★, Le Vigne di San Pietro★.

BIENVENUES-BÂTARD-MONTRACHET AC See Bâtard-Montrachet.

BIERZO DO *Castilla y León, Spain* Sandwiched between the rainy mountains of GALICIA and the arid plains of CASTILLA Y LEON, Bierzo makes mostly commonplace reds. However, the recent arrival of Alvaro PALACIOS, of PRIORAT fame, with his inspired Corullón★★ red sheds an entirely new and exciting light on the potential of the Mencía grape. Best producers: Pérez Caramés, Descendientes de José Palacios★★, Pittacum★, Prada a Tope.

JOSEF BIFFAR *Deidesheim, Pfalz, Germany* Gerhard Biffar runs this reliable estate, making dry and sweet Rieslings from top sites in Deidesheim, Ruppertsberg and WACHENHEIM. Consistent ★ quality from recent vintages. Drink young or cellar for 5 years or more. Best years: (Riesling Spätlese) (2001) **99** 98 **97 96 94 93 92 90**.

BILLECART-SALMON *Champagne AC, Champagne, France* Top-notch CHAMPAGNE house and one of the few still under family control. The wines are extremely elegant, fresh and delicate, becoming simply irresistible with age. The non-vintage Brut★★, non-vintage Brut Rosé★★, Blanc de Blancs★★★, vintage Cuvée N-F Billecart★★★ and Cuvée Elisabeth Salmon Rosé★★ are all excellent. Best years: (1996) 95 **91 90 89 88 86 85 82**.

BINGEN *Rheinhessen, Germany* This is a small town and also a Bereich, the vineyards of which fall in both the NAHE and RHEINHESSEN. The best vineyard in the town is the Scharlachberg, which produces some exciting wines, stinging with racy acidity and the whiff of coal smoke. Best producer: Villa Sachsen. Best years: (Riesling Spätlese) (2001) 00 **99** 98 **97 96 90**.

BIONDI-SANTI *Brunello di Montalcino DOCG, Tuscany, Italy* Estate that in less than a century created both a legend and an international standing for BRUNELLO DI MONTALCINO. The modern dynamism of the zone owes more to other producers, however, since quality has slipped over the last 2 decades. Yet the very expensive Riserva★★, with formidable levels of extract, tannin and acidity, deserves a minimum 10 years' further aging after release before serious judgement is passed on it. Franco Biondi-Santi's son, Jacopo, has created his own range of wines, including Sassoallora★★, a barrique-aged Sangiovese, and Cabernet-based blend Schidione★★. Best years: (Riserva) 1990 88 85 83 82 **75 71 64 55 45 25**.

BLAGNY AC *Côte de Beaune, Burgundy, France* The red wine from this tiny hamlet above MEURSAULT and PULIGNY-MONTRACHET can be fair value, if you like a rustic Burgundy. Actually much more Chardonnay than Pinot Noir is grown here, but this is sold as Puligny-Montrachet, Meursault Premier Cru or Meursault-Blagny. Best producers: R Ampeau★★, Lamy-Pillot★★, Matrot★★. Best years: (2001) 99 **97** 96 **95 93 90**.

DOM. PAUL BLANCK *Alsace AC, Alsace, France* Philippe Blanck and his winemaker cousin Frédéric had a run of good vintages in the 1990s and the Blanck wines are improving all the time. From a huge range, Vieilles Vignes Riesling★★★ and Gewurztraminer★★★ from the Furstentum Grand Cru stand out. Riesling Schlossberg★★★ and Pinot Gris Altenberg★★ also offer depth and finesse. Best years: (Grand Cru Riesling) (2001) 00 99 98 **97** 96 **95 94 93 92 90 89 88**.

BLANQUETTE DE LIMOUX AC *Languedoc-Roussillon, France* Many southern white wines are singularly flat and dull, but this fizz is sharp and refreshing. The secret lies in the Mauzac grape, which makes up over 80% of the wine and gives it its striking 'green apple skin' flavour – the balance is made up of Chardonnay and Chenin Blanc. The Champagne method is used to create the sparkle. The more rustic *méthode rurale*, finishing off the original fermentation inside the bottle, is used under a separate appellation – Blanquette Méthode Ancestrale. Best producers: Collin, Fourn★, Guinot, Martinolles, SIEUR D'ARQUES CO-Op★, les Terres Blanches. See also Crémant de Limoux AC and pages 258–9.

WOLF BLASS *Barossa Valley, South Australia*   Wolf Blass stands as one of the most important men in the modern Australian wine world for mastering reds and whites of high quality and consistency which were nonetheless *easy* to enjoy. Now part of Beringer Blass, Wolf Blass reds can still have a delicious mint and blackcurrant, easy-going charm, but are showing signs of stretching. The Rieslings are soft and sweetish, and other whites also possess juicy fruit and sweet oak. Gold Label Riesling★★ from CLARE and Eden Valleys is impressively intense and consistently good. Black Label★, the top label for reds released at 4 years old, is expensive but good. New single-vineyard varietals look promising. Best years: (Black Label) 1998 **96 95 94 92 91 90 88 86 82**.

BLAUBURGUNDER   See Pinot Noir.

BLAUER LEMBERGER   See Blaufränkisch.

BLAUFRÄNKISCH   Good, ripe Blaufränkisch has a taste similar to raspberries and white pepper or even beetroot. It does well in Austria, where it is the principal red wine grape of BURGENLAND. The Hungarian vineyards (where it is called Kékfrankos) are mostly just across the border on the other side of the Neusiedlersee. Called Lemberger in Germany, where almost all of it is grown in WURTTEMBERG. Also successful in WASHINGTON STATE.

BOEKENHOUTSKLOOF *Franschhoek WO, South Africa*   Perched high in the FRANSCHHOEK mountains, this small winery, named after the surrounding Cape beech trees, captivates as much for its spectacular scenery as Marc Kent's individual wines. His punchy Syrah★★ resonates with black pepper, chocolate plum and herb savouriness. Cabernet Sauvignon★★ is deep and powerful and built for the long term. The barrel-fermented Semillon★★, from 100-year-old bush vines, is scented and sophisticated and could become a classic. Second label Porcupine Ridge range offers cheaper but excellent, more fruit-focused drinking. Best years (Cabernet Sauvignon): **1999 98 97**.

BOISSET *Burgundy, France*   Jean Claude Boisset bought his first vineyards in 1964 and began a négociant company whose extraordinary success has enabled him to swallow up many other long-established names such as Jaffelin, Ponelle, Ropiteau and Heritier Guyot in the CÔTE D'OR, Moreau in CHABLIS; Cellier des Samsons and Mommessin in BEAUJOLAIS and others elsewhere in France. None of these companies has delivered much in the way of quality wine to date. With these acquisitions came various vineyards which have been grouped together as Domaine de la Vougeraie, producing excellent wines (notably Clos Blanc de VOUGEOT★★★ and CORTON-CHARLEMAGNE★★ whites and CLOS DE VOUGEOT★★, GEVREY-CHAMBERTIN les Evocelles★, le MUSIGNY★★ and VOUGEOT les Cras★★ reds) under the capable stewardship of Pascal Marchand.

BOLGHERI DOC *Tuscany, Italy*   In 1994, this zone near the coast south of Livorno extended its DOC beyond simple white and rosé to cover red wines based on Cabernet, Merlot and Sangiovese in various combinations, while creating a special category for SASSICAIA. The DOC Rosso Superiore now covers wines from the prestigious estates of Grattamacco★★, Le Macchiole★★, ORNELLAIA★★★, Michele Satta★★ and ANTINORI's Guado al Tasso★★. Best years: (since 1994): (reds) (2001) 00 99 98 97 **96 95 94**.

BOLLINGER *Champagne AC, Champagne, France* One of the great CHAMPAGNE houses, with good non-vintage (Special Cuvée★★) and vintage wines (Grande Année★★★), made in a full, rich, rather old-fashioned style that you love or hate. (Bollinger is one of the few houses to ferment its base wine in barrels.) It also produces a range of rarer vintage Champagnes, including a Vintage RD★★★ and Vieilles Vignes Françaises Blanc de Noirs★★ from ancient, ungrafted Pinot Noir vines. Best years: (Grande Année) (1995) **92 90 89 88 85 82 79**.

BONNES-MARES AC *Grand Cru, Côte de Nuits, Burgundy, France* A large Grand Cru straddling the communes of CHAMBOLLE-MUSIGNY and MOREY-ST-DENIS. Less famous than many Grands Crus, but commendably consistent over the last few decades. Bonnes-Mares generally has a deep, ripe, smoky plum fruit, which starts rich and chewy and matures over 10–20 years. Best producers: d'Auvenay (Dom. LEROY)★★★, BOUCHARD PERE ET FILS★★, Champy★★, DROUHIN★★, DUJAC★★★, Robert Groffier★★★, JADOT★★★, D Laurent★★★, J-F Mugnier★★, ROUMIER★★★, VOGUE★★★, Vougeraie★★. Best years: (2001) 00 99 98 97 96 95 93 **90 89 88 85 78**.

CH. BONNET *Entre-Deux-Mers AC, Bordeaux, France* Pioneering estate for quality and consistency in the ENTRE-DEUX-MERS region. Large volumes of good, fruity, affordable Entre-Deux-Mers★, and BORDEAUX AC rosé and red, particularly the barrel-aged Merlot-Cabernet Réserve★. Drink this at 3–4 years and the others young. A new special cuvée Dominus was launched with the 2000 vintage. Owner André Lurton is also the proprietor of La LOUVIERE and other properties in PESSAC-LEOGNAN.

BONNEZEAUX AC *Loire Valley, France* One of France's great sweet wines, Bonnezeaux is a zone within the larger COTEAUX DU LAYON AC. Like SAUTERNES, the wine is influenced by noble rot, but the flavours are different, as only Chenin Blanc is used. Extensive recent plantings have made quality less reliable. It can age very well in good vintages. Best producers: M Angeli★★★, Fesles★★★, Godineau★★, des Grandes Vignes★★, Laffourcade, Petits Quarts★★, Petit Val★★, René Renou★★, Terrebrune★★, la Varière★★. Best years: (2001) 00 99 **97** 96 **95 94 93 90** 89 88 85 83 79 78 76 71 64 59 47.

BONNY DOON *Santa Cruz Mountains AVA, California, USA* Iconoclastic operation under Randall Grahm, who revels in the unexpected. He has a particular love for RHONE, Italian and Spanish varietals and for fanciful brand names: Le Cigare Volant★★ is a blend of Grenache and Syrah and is Grahm's homage to CHATEAUNEUF-DU-PAPE. Old Telegram★★ is 100% Mourvèdre. Particularly delightful are his Ca' del Solo Italianate wines, especially a bone-dry Malvasia Bianca★ and a white blend, Il Pescatore★, his answer to VERDICCHIO. He also makes a lovely Syrah from Santa Maria★★, Cardinal Zin★ Zinfandel, a pure Riesling from WASHINGTON and eaux de vie. Grahm has now spread his net even wider and has 3 new wines from European vineyards: a MADIRAN★, a Vin de Pays d'Oc Syrah and a Grenache from NAVARRA. Best years: (Old Telegram) (2000) 99 98 97 **96 95 94 92 91 90**.

CH. LE BON PASTEUR★★ *Pomerol AC, Bordeaux, France* Small château which has established an excellent reputation under the ownership of Michel Rolland, one of Bordeaux's leading winemakers. Wines from le Bon Pasteur have been expensive in recent years, but they are always deliciously soft and full of lush fruit. Best years: 2000 99 98 96 **95 94 93 90 89 88 85 83 82**.

BORDEAUX RED WINES

Bordeaux, France

This large area of South-West France, centred on the historic city of Bordeaux, produces a larger volume of fine red wine than any other French region. Wonderful Bordeaux-style wines are produced in California, Australia, South Africa and South America, but the home team's top performers still just about keep the upstarts at bay. Around 600 million bottles of red wine a year are produced here. The best wines, known as the Classed Growths, account for a tiny percentage of this figure, but some of their lustre rubs off on the lesser names, making this one of the most popular wine styles.

GRAPE VARIETIES

Bordeaux's reds are commonly divided into 'right' and 'left' bank wines. On the left bank of the Gironde estuary, the red wines are dominated by the Cabernet Sauvignon grape, with varying proportions of Cabernet Franc, Merlot and Petit Verdot. At best they are austere but perfumed with blackcurrant and cedarwood. The most important left bank areas are the Haut-Médoc (especially the communes of Margaux, St-Julien, Pauillac and St-Estèphe) and, south of the city of Bordeaux, the ACs of Pessac-Léognan and Graves. On the right bank, Merlot is the predominant grape, which generally makes the resulting wines more supple and fleshy than those of the left bank. The key areas for Merlot-based wines are St-Émilion and Pomerol.

CLASSIFICATIONS

Red Bordeaux is made all over the region. At its most basic, the wine is simply labelled Bordeaux or Bordeaux Supérieur. Above this are the more specific ACs covering sub-areas (such as the Haut-Médoc) and individual communes (such as Pomerol, St-Émilion or Margaux). Single-estate Crus Bourgeois are the next rung up on the quality ladder, followed by the Crus Classés (Classed Growths) of the Médoc, Graves and St-Émilion. The famous classification of 1855 ranked the top red wines of the Médoc (plus one from Graves) into 5 tiers, from First to Fifth Growths (Crus); there has been only one change, in 1973, promoting Mouton-Rothschild to First Growth status. Since the 1950s the Graves/Pessac-Léognan region has had its own classification, for red and white wines. St-Émilion's classification (for red wines only) has been revised several times, the last modification being in 1996; the possibility of re-grading can help to maintain quality. Curiously, Pomerol, home of Château Pétrus, arguably the most famous red wine in the world, has no official pecking order. Many top Bordeaux châteaux also make 'second wines', which are cheaper versions of their Grands Vins.

See also BORDEAUX, BORDEAUX-COTES DE FRANCS, BORDEAUX SUPERIEUR, CANON-FRONSAC, COTES DE BOURG, COTES DE CASTILLON, FRONSAC, GRAVES, HAUT-MEDOC, LALANDE-DE-POMEROL, LISTRAC-MEDOC, LUSSAC-ST-EMILION, MARGAUX, MEDOC, MONTAGNE-ST-EMILION, MOULIS, PAUILLAC, PESSAC-LEOGNAN, POMEROL, PREMIERES COTES DE BLAYE, PREMIERES COTES DE BORDEAUX, PUISSEGUIN-ST-EMILION, ST-EMILION, ST-ESTEPHE, ST-GEORGES-ST-EMILION, ST-JULIEN; and individual châteaux.

BEST YEARS

(2001) 00 98 96 95 **90 89 88 86 85 83 82 78 70 66 62 61**

BEST PRODUCERS

Graves, Pessac-Léognan
Dom. de CHEVALIER, HAUT-BAILLY, HAUT-BRION, la LOUVIERE, la MISSION-HAUT-BRION, PAPE-CLEMENT, SMITH-HAUT-LAFITTE, la Tour-Haut-Brion.

Margaux BRANE-CANTENAC, FERRIERE, MALESCOT ST-EXUPERY, Ch. MARGAUX, PALMER, RAUZAN-SEGLA.

Pauillac GRAND-PUY-LACOSTE, LAFITE-ROTHSCHILD, LATOUR, LYNCH-BAGES, MOUTON-ROTHSCHILD, PICHON-LONGUEVILLE, PICHON-LONGUEVILLE-LALANDE, PONTET-CANET.

Pomerol le BON PASTEUR, Certan-de-May, Clinet, la CONSEILLANTE, l'EGLISE-CLINET, l'EVANGILE, la FLEUR-PETRUS, GAZIN, LAFLEUR, LATOUR-A-POMEROL, PETIT-VILLAGE, PETRUS, le PIN, TROTANOY, VIEUX-CHATEAU-CERTAN.

St-Émilion ANGELUS, l'ARROSEE, AUSONE, BEAU-SEJOUR BECOT, Beauséjour, CANON, CANON-LA-GAFFELIERE, CHEVAL BLANC, la Dominique, FIGEAC, Grand Mayne, MAGDALAINE, La Mondotte, Moulin St-Georges, PAVIE, PAVIE-MACQUIN, TERTRE-ROTEBOEUF, TROPLONG-MONDOT, VALANDRAUD.

St-Estèphe CALON-SEGUR, COS D'ESTOURNEL, HAUT-MARBUZET, MONTROSE.

St-Julien BRANAIRE, DUCRU-BEAUCAILLOU, GRUAUD-LAROSE, LAGRANGE, LANGOA-BARTON, LEOVILLE-BARTON, LEOVILLE-LAS-CASES, LEOVILLE-POYFERRE, ST-PIERRE, TALBOT.

BORDEAUX WHITE WINES

Bordeaux, France

This is France's largest fine wine region but, except for the sweet wines of Sauternes and Barsac, Bordeaux's international reputation is based solely on its reds. From 52% of the vineyard area in 1970, white wines now represent only 13.5% of the present 116,900ha (288,860 acres) of vines. Given the size of the region, the diversity of Bordeaux's white wines should come as no surprise. There are dry, medium and sweet styles, ranging from dreary to some of the most sublime white wines of all. Bordeaux's temperate southern climate – moderated by the influence of the Atlantic and of 2 rivers, the Dordogne and the Garonne, is ideal for white wine production, particularly south of the city along the banks of the Garonne.

GRAPE VARIETIES

Sauvignon Blanc and Sémillon, the most important white grapes, are both varieties of considerable character and are usually blended together. They are backed up by smaller quantities of other grapes, the most notable of which is Muscadelle (unrelated to Muscat), which lends perfume to sweet wines and spiciness to dry.

DRY WINES

With the introduction of new technology and new ideas, many of them influenced by the New World, Bordeaux has become one of France's most exciting white wine areas. The wines have improved beyond recognition over the last decade. At their best, dry Bordeaux whites have fresh fruit flavours of apples, peaches and apricots, balanced by a light grassiness.

SWEET WINES

Bordeaux's most famous whites are its sweet wines made from grapes affected by noble rot, particularly those from Sauternes and Barsac. The noble rot concentrates the flavours, producing rich, honeyed wines replete with pineapple and peach flavours, and which develop a nut-oiliness and greater honeyed richness with age. On the other side of the Garonne river, Cadillac, Loupiac and Ste-Croix-du-Mont also make sweet wines; these rarely attain the richness or complexity of a top Sauternes, but they are considerably less expensive.

CLASSIFICATIONS

The two largest dry white wine ACs in Bordeaux are Bordeaux Blanc and Entre-Deux-Mers. There are plenty of good dry wines in the Graves and Pessac-Léognan regions; the Pessac-Léognan AC, created in 1987, contains all the dry white Classed Growths. The great sweet wines of Sauternes and Barsac were classified as First or Second Growths in 1855.

> See also BARSAC, BORDEAUX, BORDEAUX-COTES DE FRANCS, BORDEAUX SUPERIEUR, CADILLAC, CERONS, COTES DE BLAYE, COTES DE BOURG, ENTRE-DEUX-MERS, GRAVES, GRAVES SUPERIEURES, LOUPIAC, PESSAC-LEOGNAN, PREMIERES COTES DE BLAYE, PREMIERES COTES DE BORDEAUX, STE-CROIX-DU-MONT, SAUTERNES; and individual châteaux.

GRAND VIN SEC DE BORDEAUX

CHATEAU BONNET

ENTRE-DEUX-MERS
Appellation Entre-Deux-Mers Contrôlée

2000

S.C.E.A. LES VIGNOBLES
ANDRÉ LURTON
VITICULTEUR A GRÉZILLAC · GIRONDE · FRANCE
MIS EN BOUTEILLE AU CHATEAU

PRODUIT DE FRANCE

12% vol   75 cl

Nº 14025 B

71

BORDEAUX AC *Bordeaux, France*   One of the most important ACs in France. It can be applied to reds and rosés as well as to the dry, medium and sweet white wines of the entire Gironde region. Most of the best wines are allowed more specific district or commune ACs (such as MARGAUX or SAUTERNES) but a vast amount of Bordeaux's wine – delicious, atrocious and everything in between – is sold as Bordeaux AC. At its best, straight red Bordeaux is marked by bone-dry grassy fruit and an attractive earthy edge, but far more frequently the wines are tannic and raw – and often overpriced. Good examples usually benefit from a year or so of aging. Bordeaux Blanc, once a byword for flabby, fruitless and oversulphured brews, is joining the modern world with an increasing number of refreshing, pleasant, clean wines. These may be labelled as Bordeaux Sauvignon. Drink as young as possible. Bordeaux Clairet is a pale red wine, virtually rosé but with a little more substance. Best producers: (reds) BONNET★, Dourthe (Numéro 1), Ducla, Sirius, Thieuley★, Tour de Mirambeau, le Trébuchet; (whites) l'Abbaye de Ste-Ferme★, CARSIN★, DOISY-DAENE★, Dourthe (Numéro 1), d:vin★, LYNCH-BAGES★, MARGAUX (Pavillon Blanc★★), Premius, REYNON★, Roquefort★, Sours, Thieuley★, Tour de Mirambeau★. See also pages 68–71.

BORDEAUX-CÔTES DE FRANCS AC *Bordeaux, France*   There's been quite a bit of investment in this tiny area east of ST-ÉMILION, and the top wines are looking good value. The Thienpont family (Ch. Puygueraud) continues to be the driving force here. Best producers: les Charmes-Godard★, Laclaverie★, Francs★, Marsau, Moulin la Pitié, Pelan★, la Prade, Puygueraud★★. Best years: 2000 98 **97 96 95 94 90 89 88 86**.

BORDEAUX SUPÉRIEUR AC *Bordeaux, France*   This AC covers the same area as the BORDEAUX AC but the wines must have an extra 0.5% of alcohol, a lower yield and a longer period of maturation. Many of the best petits châteaux are labelled Bordeaux Supérieur. Best producers (reds): l'Abbaye de Ste-Ferme, les Arromans, Barreyre★, de Bouillerot★, de Courteillac★, Laville, Parenchère★, Penin★, Reignac★, de Seguin.

BOSCARELLI *Vino Nobile di Montepulciano DOCG, Tuscany, Italy*   Arguably Montepulciano's best producer, Paola de Ferrari and her sons Luca and Niccolò, with guidance from star enologist Maurizio Castelli, craft rich and stylish reds. VINO NOBILE★★, Riserva del Nocio★★ and the barrique-aged Sangiovese Boscarelli★★ are all brilliant. Best years: (2000) 99 **98 97 96 95 94 93 91 90 88 85**.

BOSCHENDAL *Paarl WO, South Africa*   Owners Anglo American plc are looking for a buyer for this historic farm, currently going through a dull patch. Chief reds are Shiraz, Merlot and a Cabernet Sauvignon-based BORDEAUX blend called Grand Reserve. Flavoursome Chardonnay and Sauvignon Blanc lead the whites. Le Grand Pavillon NV and rich vintage Boschendal Brut remain sound Cap Classique bubblies.

BOUCHARD FINLAYSON *Walker Bay, Overberg WO, South Africa*   Winemaker Peter Finlayson continues to produce dry but classy Pinot Noirs 'domaine' Galpin Peak★ and barrel selection Tête de Cuvée★. Chardonnays (Kaimansgaat★ and home-grown Missionvale★) are full, nutty and passably Burgundian. Sauvignon Blanc★ is flinty and fresh. Best years: (Pinot Noir) (2001) **00 99 98 97 96 95**.

BOUCHARD PÈRE ET FILS *Beaune, Burgundy, France*   Important merchant and vineyard owner, with vines in some of Burgundy's most spectacular sites, including CORTON, CORTON-CHARLEMAGNE, Chevalier-Montrachet and le MONTRACHET. The firm is owned by Champagne whiz-kid Joseph Henriot, who is starting to realize the full potential here.

Wines from the company's own vineyards are sold under the Domaines du Château de Beaune label. Don't touch anything pre-1996. Best years: (top reds) (2001) 00 99 98 **97** 96.

BOUCHES-DU-RHÔNE, VIN DE PAYS DES *Provence, France* Wines from 3 areas: the coast, a zone around Aix-en-Provence and the Camargue. Mainly full-bodied, spicy reds, but rosé can be good. Best producers: Château Bas, de Boujeu, l'Île St-Pierre, Mas de Rey, TREVALLON★★, Valdition. Best years: (reds) (2001) 00 **99 98 97** 96.

BOURGOGNE AC *Burgundy, France* Bourgogne is the French name anglicized as 'Burgundy'. This generic AC mops up all the Burgundian wine with no AC of its own, resulting in massive differences in style and quality. The best wines will usually come from a single grower's vineyards just outside the main village ACs of the CÔTE D'OR. In today's world of high prices such wines may be the only way we can afford the joys of fine Burgundy. If the wine is from a grower, the flavours should follow a regional style. However, if the address on the label is that of a négociant, the wine could be from anywhere in Burgundy. Pinot Noir is the main red grape, but Gamay from a declassified BEAUJOLAIS cru is allowed. Red Bourgogne is usually light, fruity in an upfront strawberry and cherry way, and should be drunk young (within 2–3 years). The rosé (from Pinot Noir) can be pleasant but little is produced. Bourgogne Blanc is a bone-dry Chardonnay wine and most should be drunk within 2 years. Bourgogne Passe-tout-Grains is made from Gamay with a minimum 33% of Pinot Noir, while Bourgogne Grand Ordinaire is the most basic appellation of all – rarely more than a quaffing wine, drunk in local bars. Best producers: (reds/growers) COCHE-DURY★, Dugat-Py★★, J-P Fichet★, GERMAIN, LAFARGE★, MEO-CAMUZET★★, Pierre Morey★, Patrice Rion★★, ROUMIER★; (reds/merchants) DROUHIN★, GIRARDIN, JADOT★, LABOURE-ROI, Maison LEROY★★; (reds/co-ops) BUXY★, les Caves des Hautes-Côtes★; (whites/growers) M Bouzereau★, Boyer-Martenot★, COCHE-DURY★★, Henri Gouges★★, P Javillier★★, Ch. de Meursault, Guy Roulot★, SAUZET★, TOLLOT-BEAUT★; (whites/merchants) DROUHIN★, FAIVELEY, JADOT★, Olivier LEFLAIVE, RODET★; (whites/co-ops) BUXY, les Caves des Hautes-Côtes. Best years: (reds) (2001) 00 99 **98 97** 96; (whites) (2001) 00 **99**. See also pages 76–9.

BOURGOGNE ALIGOTÉ AC See Aligoté.

BOURGOGNE-CÔTE CHALONNAISE AC *Côte Chalonnaise, Burgundy, France* These vineyards have gained in importance, mainly because of spiralling prices on the CÔTE D'OR to the north. This AC covers vineyards to the west of Chalon-sur-Saône around the villages of Bouzeron, RULLY, MERCUREY, GIVRY and MONTAGNY. Best producers: X Besson, BUXY co-op★, Villaine★. Best years: (2001) 00 **99**.

BOURGOGNE-HAUTES-CÔTES DE BEAUNE AC *Burgundy, France* The hills behind the great CÔTE DE BEAUNE have been a source of affordable Burgundy since the 1970s. The red wines are lean but drinkable, as is the slightly sharp Chardonnay. Best producers: D & F Clair★, les Caves des Hautes-Côtes★, J-Y Devevey★, L Jacob★, J-L Joillot★, Ch. de Mercey (RODET)★, Naudin-Ferrand★, M Serveau★. Best years: (reds) (2001) 00 99 **96**; (whites) (2001) 00 99 **97**.

BOURGOGNE-HAUTES-CÔTES DE NUITS AC *Burgundy, France* Attractive, lightweight wines from the hills behind the CÔTE DE NUITS. The reds are best, with an attractive cherry and plum flavour. The whites tend to be rather dry and flinty. Best producers: (reds) FAIVELEY★, A-F Gros★, M Gros★, A Guyon★, les Caves des Hautes-Côtes★,

B Hudelot★, JAYER-GILLES★★, THOMAS-MOILLARD★; (whites) les Caves des Hautes-Côtes★, Y Chaley★, Champy★, J-Y Devevey★, B Hudelot★, JAYER-GILLES★★, Thévenot-le-Brun★, THOMAS-MOILLARD★, A Verdet★. Best years: (reds) (2001) 00 99 **98 97 96**; (whites) (2001) 00 **99 97**.

BOURGOGNE-IRANCY AC See Irancy AC.

BOURGUEIL AC *Loire Valley, France* Fine red wine from between Tours and Angers. Made with Cabernet Franc, topped up with a little Cabernet Sauvignon; in hot years results can be superb. Given 5–10 years of age, the wines can develop a wonderful raspberry fragrance. Best producers: (reds) l'Abbaye★, Yannick Amirault★, Audebert (estate wines★), T Boucard★, P Breton★, la Butte★, Caslot★, Caslot-Galbrun★, Max Cognard★, J-F Demont★, DRUET★★, Forges★, La Lande/Delaunay★, Lamé-Delisle-Boucard★, Nau Frères★, Raguenières★. Best years: (2001) 00 99 **97 96 95 90 89 88 86 85**. See also St-Nicolas-de-Bourgueil.

BOUVET-LADUBAY *Saumur AC, Loire Valley, France* Fizz producer owned by the Champagne house TAITTINGER. The basic range (Bouvet Brut, Bouvet Rosé) is good. Cuvée Saphir, the top-selling wine, is over-sweet, but Trésor (Blanc★ and Rosé★), fermented in oak casks, is very good. Weird and wonderful Rubis★ sparkling red is worth trying. Also sells non-sparkling wine from VOUVRAY and SAUMUR.

BOUVIER Austrian and Slovenian grape short on acidity and so mainly used for sweet to ultra-sweet wines, where it achieves richness but rarely manages to offer any other complexity. Best producers: Weinkellerei Burgenland, KRACHER★, OPITZ★.

BOUZY *Coteaux Champenois AC, Champagne, France* A leading CHAMPAGNE village growing good Pinot Noir, which is used mainly for *white* Champagne. However, in outstanding years a little still red wine is made. It is light and high in acidity. Best producers: Bara★, E Barnaut★, A Clouet★. Best years: (2000) 99 98 96 **95 90 89**.

BOWEN ESTATE *Coonawarra, South Australia* Doug Bowen can make some of COONAWARRA's best peppery Shiraz★★ and blackcurranty Cabernet★; however, recent releases have seemed less consistent. Chardonnay★ is a good Coonawarra example. Best years: (Shiraz) (1999) 98 **97 96 94 93 92 91 89 88 87**.

BOYAR ESTATES *Bulgaria* The leading distributor of Bulgarian wines, selling more than 65 million bottles worldwide each year. It also has extensive vineyard holdings of 1000ha (2470 acres), and wineries at Iambol, Shumen, Sliven (new, state-of-the-art Blueridge) and – following its merger with Vinprom – at Rousse. So far Boyar has stressed its internationalist intentions, with a range of quite attractive reds led by Cabernet Sauvignon and Merlot.

BRACHETTO Piedmontese grape revived in dry versions and in sweet, frothy types with a Muscat-like perfume, as exemplified by Brachetto d'Acqui DOCG. Best producers: (dry) Correggia★, Scarpa★; (Brachetto d'Acqui) BANFI★, Braida★, G Marenco★.

CH. BRANAIRE★★ *St-Julien AC, 4ème Cru Classé, Haut-Médoc, Bordeaux, France* After a long period of mediocrity Branaire chose the difficult 93 and 94 vintages to signal its renewed ambition. Subsequent vintages have confirmed a welcome return to full, soft, chocolaty form. Best years: 2000 99 98 96 95 **94**.

BRAND'S *Coonawarra, South Australia* COONAWARRA firm, owned by MCWILLIAM'S, with 100ha (250 acres) of new vineyards as well as some ancient vines now over 100 years old. An unsubtle, peachy Chardonnay is good, and ripe Cabernet★ and Cabernet-Merlot★ are increasingly attractive; Patron's Reserve Cabernet★★ is excellent. New life has been breathed into Shiraz★, and Stentiford's Reserve★★ shows how good Coonawarra Shiraz can be. Best years: (reds) 1998 **97 96 94 92 90**.

CH. BRANE-CANTENAC★★ *Margaux AC, 2ème Cru Classé, Haut-Médoc, Bordeaux, France* Early signs from the late 90s suggest Brane-Cantenac is back on form after a prolonged downturn. Henri Lurton has taken over the family property and is making some superb wines, particularly the 2000. The property now merits its 2nd Growth status, and I am delighted that I can once more enjoy what used to be one of my favourite Bordeaux. Best years: 2000 99 98 97 96 95 **90 89 88 86**.

BRAUNEBERG *Mosel, Germany* Small village with 2 famous vineyard sites, Juffer and Juffer Sonnenuhr, whose wines have a honeyed richness and creamy gentleness rare in the Mosel. Best producers: Bastgen★★, Fritz HAAG★★★, Willi Haag★, Paulinshof★, M F RICHTER★★. Best years: (Riesling Spätlese) (2001) 00 99 98 **97** 95 **93 90**.

BREAKY BOTTOM *Sussex, England* Small vineyard in the South Downs near Lewes, badly flooded in 2000. Peter Hall is a quirky, passionate grower, making dry, nutty Seyval Blanc★ that becomes creamy and BURGUNDY-like after 3–4 years. His crisp Müller-Thurgau★ is full of hedgerow pungency and sparkling Seyval Blanc is delicious.

BREGANZE DOC *Veneto, Italy* Small DOC in the hills north of Vicenza for a Merlot-based red, a dry white based on Tocai Friulano, and a range of varietals, including Cabernet and Vespaiolo. Best producers: Bartolomeo da Breganze co-op, MACULAN★★, Vigneto Due Santi.

GEORG BREUER *Rüdesheim, Rheingau, Germany* Medium-sized estate run by Bernhard Breuer, producing quality dry Riesling from vines on the RÜDESHEIMER Berg Schlossberg★★ and RAUENTHALer Nonnenberg★★. Also a barrique-aged Pinot Gris and Pinot Noir. Best years: (Berg Schlossberg) (2001) 00 99 98 **97** 96 **95 94 93 90**.

BRIGHT BROTHERS *Ribatejo, Portugal* The Fiúza-Bright winemaking operation is located in the town of Almeirim in the RIBATEJO and Fiúza-labelled wines are made from local vineyards planted to both Portuguese and French varieties. Australian Peter Bright also sources grapes (exclusively Portuguese varieties) from, chiefly, Palmela (Reserva★) and DOURO (TFN★) for the Bright Brothers label. Bright also makes a range of wines for PENAFLOR in Argentina.

JEAN-MARC BROCARD *Chablis AC, Burgundy, France* Dynamic winemaker who has built up this 80ha (200-acre) domaine almost from scratch. Except for Premiers Crus (including Montée de la Tonnerre★★, Montmains★★) and slow-evolving Grands Crus (les Clos★★ stands out), all the fruit is machine-picked and vinified in steel tanks. Vieilles Vignes★ is usually the best of the regular CHABLIS. Brocard also produces a range of BOURGOGNE Blancs★ from different soil types.

BROKENWOOD *Hunter Valley, New South Wales, Australia* High-profile winery with delicious aged HUNTER Semillon★★ and Chardonnay★. Best wine is classic Hunter Graveyard Vineyard Shiraz★★★; the Rayner Vineyard MCLAREN VALE Shiraz★★ is also a stunning wine. Cricket Pitch★ reds and whites are cheerful, fruity ready-drinkers. Best years: (Graveyard Vineyard Shiraz) 1999 98 96 95 94 **93 91 90 89 88 86 85 83**.

BURGUNDY RED WINES

Burgundy, France

 Rich in history and gastronomic tradition, the region of Burgundy (Bourgogne in French) covers a vast tract of eastern France, running from Auxerre, south-east of Paris, to the city of Lyon. As with its white wines, Burgundy's red wines are extremely diverse. The explanation for this lies partly in the fickle nature of Pinot Noir, the area's principal red grape, and partly in the historical imbalance of supply and demand between growers – who grow the grapes and make and bottle much of the best wine – and merchants, whose efforts have established the reputation of the wines internationally.

GRAPE VARIETIES

Pinot Noir is prone to mutation – there are several dozen variations in Burgundy alone – and the range of flavours you get from the grape vividly demonstrates this. A red Épineuil from near Auxerre in the north of the region will be light, chalky, strawberry-flavoured; a Pinot from the Mâconnais toward Lyon will be rustic and earthy; and in between in the Côte d'Or – the heartland of red Burgundy – the flavours sweep through strawberry, raspberry, damson and cherry to a wild, magnificent maturity of Oriental spices, chocolate, mushrooms and truffles.

WINE REGIONS

The top red Burgundies come from the Côte d'Or. The greatest of all – the world-famous Grand Cru vineyards such as Clos de Vougeot, Chambertin, Musigny and Richebourg – are in the Côte de Nuits, the northern part of the Côte d'Or, from Nuits-St-Georges up toward Dijon. Other fine reds – especially Volnay, Pommard and Corton – come from the Côte de Beaune. The Côte Chalonnaise produces solid reds from Givry and Mercurey, while lighter examples are to be found further south in the Mâconnais and to the north around Auxerre. The Beaujolais should really be considered as a separate region, growing Gamay on acidic soils rather than Pinot Noir on limestone.

CLASSIFICATIONS

A large part of Burgundy has 5 increasingly specific levels of classification: regional ACs (e.g. Bourgogne), specified ACs covering groups of villages (e.g. Côte de Nuits-Villages), village wines taking the village name (Pommard, Vosne-Romanée), Premiers Crus (good village vineyard sites) and Grands Crus (the best individual vineyard sites).

See also ALOXE-CORTON, AUXEY-DURESSES, BEAUJOLAIS, BEAUNE, BLAGNY, BONNES-MARES, BOURGOGNE, BOURGOGNE-COTE CHALONNAISE, BOURGOGNE-HAUTES-COTES DE BEAUNE, CHAMBERTIN, CHAMBOLLE-MUSIGNY, CHASSAGNE-MONTRACHET, CHOREY-LES-BEAUNE, CLOS DE LA ROCHE, CLOS ST-DENIS, CLOS DE VOUGEOT, CORTON, COTE DE BEAUNE, COTE DE NUITS, COTE D'OR, CREMANT DE BOURGOGNE, ECHEZEAUX, FIXIN, GEVREY-CHAMBERTIN, GIVRY, LADOIX, MACON, MARSANNAY, MERCUREY, MEURSAULT, MONTHELIE, MOREY-ST-DENIS, MOULIN-A-VENT, MUSIGNY, NUITS-ST-GEORGES, PERNAND-VERGELESSES, POMMARD, PULIGNY-MONTRACHET, RICHEBOURG, La ROMANEE-CONTI, ROMANEE-ST-VIVANT, RULLY, ST-AUBIN, ST-ROMAIN, SAVIGNY-LES-BEAUNE, La TACHE, VOLNAY, VOSNE-ROMANEE, VOUGEOT; and individual producers.

DOMAINE PIERRE DAMOY
1999
Chambertin Clos de Bèze
Grand Cru
Appellation Chambertin Clos de Bèze Contrôlée

Mise en bouteille...Pierre Damoy propriétaire à Gevrey-Chambertin - Côte d'Or - France

PRODUCT OF FRANCE   750 ml

BEST PRODUCERS

Côte de Nuits B Ambroise, Dom. de l'Arlot, Robert Arnoux, Denis Bachelet, G Barthod, Burguet, Charlopin, R Chevillon, CLAIR, J-J Confuron, C Dugat, B Dugat-Py, DUJAC, Engel, Sylvie Esmonin (formerly Michel Esmonin & Fille), Geantet-Pansiot, Gouges, GRIVOT, Anne Gros, Hudelot-Noëllat, JAYER-GILLES, Dom. LEROY, H Lignier, MEO-CAMUZET, Denis Mortet, Mugneret-Gibourg, Mugnier, Perrot-Minot, Ponsot, RION, Dom. de la ROMANEE-CONTI, Roty, Rouget, ROUMIER, ROUSSEAU, Sérafin, Dom. THOMAS-MOILLARD, de VOGUE, Vougeraie.

Côte de Beaune Ampeau, d'ANGERVILLE, Comte Armand, J-M Boillot, CHANDON DE BRIAILLES, COCHE-DURY, Courcel, GERMAIN, Michel LAFARGE, LAFON, Montille, Albert Morot, Pousse d'Or, TOLLOT-BEAUT.

Côte Chalonnaise Brintet, H & P Jacqueson, Joblot, M Juillot, Lorenzon, Raquillet, Thénard, Villaine.

Merchants BOUCHARD PERE ET FILS (since 1996), Champy, DROUHIN, DUBOEUF, FAIVELEY, Féry-Meunier, V GIRARDIN, Camille Giroud, JADOT, LABOURE-ROI, D Laurent, Olivier LEFLAIVE, Maison LEROY, Nicolas Potel, RODET.

Co-ops BUXY, les Caves des Hautes-Côtes.

77

BURGUNDY WHITE WINES

Burgundy, France

 White Burgundy has for generations been thought of as the world's leading dry white wine. The top wines have a remarkable succulent richness of honey and hazelnut, melted butter and sprinkled spice, yet are totally dry. Such wines are all from the Chardonnay grape and the finest are generally produced in the Côte de Beaune, the southern part of the Côte d'Or, in the communes of Aloxe-Corton, Meursault, Puligny-Montrachet and Chassagne-Montrachet, where limestone soils and the aspect of the vineyard provide perfect conditions for even ripening of grapes.

WINE STYLES

However, Burgundy encompasses many more wine styles than this, even if no single one quite attains the peaks of quality of those 4 villages on the Côte de Beaune.

Chablis in the north traditionally produces very good steely wines, aggressive and lean when young, but nutty and rounded – though still very dry – after a few years. Modern Chablis is generally a softer, milder wine, easy to drink young, and sometimes enriched with aging in new oak barrels.

There is no doubt that Meursault and the other Côte de Beaune villages can produce stupendous wine, but it is in such demand that unscrupulous producers are often tempted to maximize yields and cut corners on quality. Consequently white Burgundy from these famous villages must be approached with caution. Lesser-known villages such as Pernand-Vergelesses and St-Aubin often provide good wine at lower prices. There are also good wines from some villages in the Côte de Nuits, such as Morey-St-Denis, Nuits-St-Georges and Vougeot, though amounts are tiny compared with the Côte de Beaune.

South of the Côte d'Or the Côte Chalonnaise is becoming more interesting for quality white wine as a result of more widespread use of better equipment for temperature control and now that oak barrels are being used more often for aging. Rully and Montagny are the most important villages, though Givry and Mercurey can produce nice white, too.

The minor Aligoté grape makes some reasonable acidic wine, especially in Bouzeron. Further south, the Mâconnais is a large region, two-thirds planted with Chardonnay. The wine used to be dull and flat and not all that cheap, but there is some fair sparkling Crémant de Bourgogne, and some very good vineyard sites, in particular in St-Véran and in Pouilly-Fuissé. Increasingly stunning wines can now be found.

See also ALOXE-CORTON, AUXEY-DURESSES, BATARD-MONTRACHET, BEAUJOLAIS, BEAUNE, BOURGOGNE, BOURGOGNE-COTE CHALONNAISE, CHABLIS, CHASSAGNE-MONTRACHET, CORTON, CORTON-CHARLEMAGNE, COTE DE BEAUNE, COTE DE NUITS, COTE D'OR, CREMANT DE BOURGOGNE, FIXIN, GIVRY, LADOIX, MACON, MARSANNAY, MERCUREY, MEURSAULT, MONTAGNY, MONTHELIE, MONTRACHET, MOREY-ST-DENIS, MUSIGNY, NUITS-ST-GEORGES, PERNAND-VERGELESSES, POUILLY-FUISSE, POUILLY-LOCHE, PULIGNY-MONTRACHET, RULLY, ST-AUBIN, ST-ROMAIN, ST-VERAN, SAVIGNY-LES-BEAUNE, VOUGEOT; and individual producers.

1998 1998

PRODUCE OF FRANCE

Chablis Grand Cru

LES CLOS
APPELLATION CHABLIS GRAND CRU CONTRÔLÉE

MIS EN BOUTEILLE PAR
J-M. BROCARD à PREHY - 89800 CHABLIS FRANCE

BEST PRODUCERS

Chablis J-C Bessin, Billaud-Simon, A & F Boudin/de Chantemerle, J-M BROCARD, D Dampt, R & V DAUVISSAT, D & E Defaix, DROIN, DURUP, W Fèvre, J-P Grossot, Laroche, Louis MICHEL, G Picq, RAVENEAU, Simonnet-Febvre, Vocoret.

Côte d'Or (Côte de Beaune) G Amiot, R Ampeau, d'Auvenay (LEROY), Blain-Gagnard, Jean Boillot, J-M Boillot, Bonneau du Martray, M Bouzereau, Y Boyer-Martenot, CARILLON, CHANDON DE BRIAILLES, COCHE-DURY, Marc Colin, Colin-Deléger, Arnaud Ente, J-P Fichet, Fontaine-Gagnard, J-N GAGNARD, GAGNARD-DELAGRANGE, P Javillier, F Jobard, R Jobard, LAFON, R Lamy-Pillot, Dom. LEFLAIVE, Dom. Matrot, F Mikulski, Bernard Morey, Marc Morey, Pierre Morey, M Niellon, P Pernot, J & J-M Pillot, RAMONET, M Rollin, G Roulot, SAUZET, VERGET.

Côte Chalonnaise S Aladame, H & P Jacqueson.

Mâconnais D & M Barraud, Bonhomme, Corsin, Deux Roches, J A Ferret, Ch. FUISSE, la Greffière, Guffens-Heynen (VERGET), J-J Litaud, O Merlin, Robert-Denogent, Saumaize-Michelin, Soufrandière, Thévenet, Valette.

Merchants BOUCHARD PERE ET FILS, Champy, DROUHIN, FAIVELEY, V GIRARDIN, JADOT, LABOURE-ROI, Louis LATOUR, Olivier LEFLAIVE, Maison LEROY, Rijckaert, RODET, VERGET.

Co-ops BUXY, la CHABLISIENNE.

79

BROUILLY AC *Beaujolais, Burgundy, France* Largest of the 10 BEAUJOLAIS Crus; at its best, the wine is soft, fruity and gluggable. Best producers: la Chaize★, DUBOEUF (Combillaty, Ch. de Nervers★), Hospices de Beaujeu★, A Michaud★, Ch. des Tours★. Best years: (2001) **00 99**.

BROWN BROTHERS *North-East Victoria, Australia* Highly successful family winery that has outgrown its small producer tag. There is a huge range of varietal table wines, vintage fizz is consistently good and stickies are superb, especially the Very Old Muscat★★, Port★ and Tokay★★ range. Focusing on cool King Valley and mountain-top Whitlands for its premium grapes.

BRÜNDLMAYER *Kamptal, Niederösterreich, Austria* Willi Bründlmayer makes wine in a variety of Austrian and international styles, but his dry Riesling (Alte Reben★★) from the great Heiligenstein vineyard and Grüner Veltliner (Ried Lamm★★★) are the best; some recent vintages have been very high in alcohol. Good Sekt. Best years: (Zöbinger Heiligenstein Riesling) (2001) 99 98 **97 95 94 93 92 91**.

BRUNELLO DI MONTALCINO DOCG *Tuscany, Italy* Powerful red wine produced from Sangiovese (known locally as Brunello). Traditionally needed over 10 years to soften, but modern practices result in more fruit-rich wines, yet still tannic enough to age spectacularly. Best producers: Altesino★ (Montosoli★★), ARGIANO★★, BANFI★★, Barbi★, Baricci★, BIONDI-SANTI★★, La Campana★★, Caparzo★★, Casanova di Neri★★, CASTELGIOCONDO★★, Centolani (Friggiali★, Pietranera★★), Cerbaiona★★, Ciacci Piccolomini d'Aragona★★, Donatella Cinelli Colombini-Casato★★, Col d'Orcia★★, COSTANTI★★, Fuligni★★, La Gerla★, Gorelli-Due Portine★★, Maurizio Lambardi★★, Lisini★★, Mastrojanni★★, Siro Pacenti★★★, Pian delle Vigne★★/ANTINORI, Agostina Pieri★★, Pieve Santa Restituta★★★, La Poderina★★, Poggio Antico★★, Poggio di Sotto★★, Il Poggiolo★★, Il Poggione★★, Salvioni-La Cerbaiola★★, Livio Sassetti-Pertimali★★, Scopetone★, Soldera★, Talenti★★, Valdicava★, Val di Suga★. Best years: (2000) (99) (98) 97 **95 93 91 90 88 85**.

BUCELAS DOC *Estremadura, Portugal* A tiny but historic DOC. The wines are whites based on the Arinto grape (noted for its high acidity). For attractive, modern examples try Quinta da Murta or Quinta da Romeira (Morgado de Santa Catherina★).

VON BUHL *Deidesheim, Pfalz, Germany* Large estate, leased to the Japanese Sanyo group. The wines are rarely subtle, but have full fruit and a confident Riesling character.

BUITENVERWACHTING *Constantia WO, South Africa* Time slows down at this beautiful property, part of the Cape's original CONSTANTIA wine farm. The traditional, Old World-style wines also take time to unfold: a ripe, fruit-laden Chardonnay★★, penetrating, zesty Sauvignon Blanc★ and light, racily dry Riesling. Aristocratic red blend Christine★ is regularly one of the Cape's most accurate BORDEAUX lookalikes. Best years: (Christine) **1998 96 95 94 93 92 91**.

BULL'S BLOOD *Hungary* Kékfrankos (Blaufränkisch) grapes sometimes replace robust Kadarka in the blend, thinning the blood; some producers blend with Cabernet Sauvignon, Kékoporto or Merlot. New stringent regulations should improve quality in the 2 permitted regions, Eger and Szekszárd. Winemakers Tibor Gàl (of Egervin) and Vilmos Thummerer are working hard on this front.

GRANT BURGE *Barossa Valley, South Australia* A leading producer in the BAROSSA, making chocolaty Filsell Shiraz★ and Cameron Vale Cabernet★, opulent Summers Chardonnay★, fresh Thorn Riesling★ and oaky Zer

Semillon. Top label is rich but somewhat oak-dominated Meshach
Shiraz★★. Shadrach Cabernet★★ and continually improving RHONE-
style blend, Holy Trinity★, are recent additions. Best years: (Meshach)
1998 **96 95 94 91 90**.

BURGENLAND *Austria*   4 regions: Neusiedlersee, including Seewinkel for
sweet Prädikat wines; Neusiedlersee-Hügelland, famous for sweet wines,
now also big reds and fruity dry whites; Mittelburgenland, for robust
Blaufränkisch reds; and Südburgenland, for good reds and dry whites. Best
producers: FEILER-ARTINGER★★★, Gernot Heinrich★, Hans Igler★, Juris★,
Kollwentz★★, KRACHER★★★, Krutzler★★, M & A Nittnaus★★, OPITZ★, Peter
Schandl★, Ernst Triebaumer★★, Umathum★★, VELICH★★, Robert Wenzel★.

BURGUNDY See Bourgogne AC and pages 76–9.
BÜRKLIN-WOLF *Wachenheim, Pfalz, Germany*   With nearly 100ha (250
acres) of vineyards, this is one of Germany's largest privately owned
estates. Under director Christian von Guradze, a champion of vineyard
classification, it has shot back up to the first rank of the region's
producers since the 1994 vintage. The powerful, spicy dry Rieslings
are now ★ to ★★, with the magnificent dessert wines ★★★. Best years:
(Grosses Gewächs Rieslings) (2001) 98 **97** 96 **95** 94 93.
BURMESTER *Port DOC, Douro, Portugal*   Shipper established since 1730
and recently on the up. Vintage PORT★★ is much improved, as is the
Vintage released under the Quinta Nova de Nossa Senhora do Carmo★
label. This highly regarded quinta was purchased by Burmester in
1991. As well as refined 10- and 20-year-old tawnies, there are some
outstanding old colheitas★★ which extend back over 100 years. Also
good recent Late Bottled Vintage★ and oak-aged DOURO red, Casa
Burmester★. Best years: (Vintage) (2000) 97 **95** 94.
BURRWEILER *Pfalz, Germany*   Burrweiler is the PFALZ's only wine village
with a slate soil like the MOSEL, most notably in the excellent Schäwer
site. Elegant dry Rieslings and some fine dessert wines. Best producer:
Herbert Messmer★. Best years: (2001) 99 98 **97** 94 93.
BUXY, CAVE DES VIGNERONS DE *Côte Chalonnaise, Burgundy, France*
Based in the Côte Chalonnaise, this ranks among Burgundy's top co-
operatives, producing affordable, well-made Chardonnay and Pinot
Noir. The light, oak-aged BOURGOGNE Pinot Noir★ and the red and
white Clos de Chenôves★, as well as the nutty, white MONTAGNY★, are
all good, reasonably priced, and best with 2–3 years' age.
BUZET AC *South-West France*   Good Bordeaux-style red wines from the
same mix of grapes and at a lower price. There is very little rosé and
the whites are rarely exciting. Best producers: les Vignerons de Buzet
(especially Baron d'Ardeuil, Ch. de Gueyze and Cuvée 44), Tissot.
BYRON *Santa Maria Valley AVA, California, USA*   After new owner MONDAVI
built a new winery and acquired more vineyards, founder Ken 'Byron'
Brown has been making better-than-ever Pinot Noir and Chardonnay.
His Nielson Vineyard (formerly Estate) Pinot★★ is full of spicy cherry
fruit, and the Nielson Vineyard Chardonnay★★ with mineral notes and
fine balance can age for several years. Regular Chardonnay is often good
value, as is a vibrant Pinot Gris★★. Io★, a robust Rhône blend, is off to
a promising start. Best years: (Nielson Pinot Noir) (2000) 99 98 **97 96** 95.
CA' DEL BOSCO *Franciacorta DOCG, Lombardy, Italy*   Model estate,
headed by Maurizio Zanella, making some of Italy's finest and most
expensive wines: outstanding sparklers in FRANCIACORTA Brut★★,

Dosage Zero★, Satén★★ and the prestige Cuvée Annamaria Clementi★★; good Terre di Franciacorta Rosso★, remarkably good Chardonnay★★★, Pinero★★ (Pinot Nero) and a BORDEAUX blend, Maurizio Zanella★★★. Also promising varietal Carmenère, Carmenero★★.

CABARDÈS AC *Languedoc, France* Next door to MINERVOIS but, as well as the usual Mediterranean grape varieties, Cabernet Sauvignon and Merlot are allowed. At best, full-bodied, chewy and rustically attractive. AC status granted in 1999. Best producers: Cabrol★, Jouclary, Penautier, Salitis, Ventenac.

CABERNET D'ANJOU AC *Loire Valley, France* Can be made from both Cabernets and generally demi-sec. Now made to drink young, but there are still a few remarkable old vintages from the 1940s and 50s around. Best producers: Bablut, Ogereau, Passavant, Putille, Tigné.

CABERNET FRANC Often unfairly dismissed as an inferior Cabernet Sauvignon, Cabernet Franc comes into its own in cool zones or areas where the soil is damp and heavy. It can have a leafy freshness linked to raw but tasty blackcurrant-raspberry fruit. In France it thrives in the LOIRE VALLEY and BORDEAUX, especially ST-EMILION and POMEROL where it accounts for 19% of the planting. Successful in northern Italy, especially ALTO ADIGE and FRIULI, although some plantings here have turned out to be Carmenère. Experiments with Cabernet Franc on CALIFORNIA's North Coast and in WASHINGTON STATE show promise. There are also some good South African, Chilean and Australian examples.

CABERNET SAUVIGNON See pages 84–5.

CADILLAC AC *Bordeaux, France* Sweet wine from the southern half of the PREMIERES COTES DE BORDEAUX. Styles vary from fresh, semi-sweet to richly botrytized. The wines have greatly improved in recent vintages. Drink young. Best producers: CARSIN, Cayla★, Ch. du Juge/Dupleich, Manos★, Mémoires★, REYNON, Ste-Catherine.

CAHORS AC *South-West France* Important South-West red wine region. This dark, often tannic wine is made from at least 70% Auxerrois (Bordeaux's Malbec) and has an unforgettable, rich plummy flavour when ripe and well made. Ages well. Best producers: la Caminade, Cayrou★, CEDRE★, Clos la Coutale★, Clos de Gamot★, Clos Triguedina★, Côtes d'Olt co-op, Gaudou, Gautoul★, Haute-Serre★, les Ifs★, LAGREZETTE★, Lamartine★, les Rigalets★. Best years: 2000 98 **96 95 94 90 89 88 86 85**.

CAIN CELLARS *Napa Valley AVA, California, USA* This Spring Mountain estate appears to be solidly on track. Cain Five★★ is a particularly pleasing, slow-maturing red BORDEAUX blend. Cain Concept★ is a red Bordeaux blend made from hillside vineyards. Also attractive are lower-priced drink-me-now red Cain Cuvée★ and strongly flavoured white Sauvignon Musqué★. Best years: (Cain Five) (2000) 99 97 95 94 **93 92 91 90 87**.

CALABRIA *Italy* One of Italy's poorest regions. CIRO, Donnici, Savuto and Scavigna reds from the native Gaglioppo grape, and whites from Greco, are much improved thanks to greater winemaking expertise. The leading producer is the Librandi family, who have recently added what is one of southern Italy's most exciting new reds – Magno Megonio★★ from the obscure Magliocco variety – to an already fine range.

CALERA *San Benito, California, USA* A pace-setter for California Pinot Noir with 4 different estate wines: Reed Vineyard★★, Selleck Vineyard★★, Jensen Vineyard★★ and Mills★★. They are complex, fascinating wines with power and originality and capable of aging. Mt Harlan Chardonnay★★ is excitingly original too. Small amounts of Viognier★★ are succulent with sensuous fruit. Best years: (Pinot Noir) 2000 99 98 **97 96 95 94 91 90 88 87 86**; (Chardonnay) (2001) 00 99 **98 97 96 95**.

CALIFORNIA *USA* California's importance is not simply in being the leading wine producer in the USA and the fourth largest in the world. Most of the great revolutions in technology and style that have transformed the expectations and achievements of winemakers in every country of the world – including France – were born in the ambitions of a band of Californian winemakers during the 1960s and 70s. They challenged the old order with its regulated, self-serving elitism, democratizing the world of fine wine, to the benefit of every wine drinker. This revolutionary fervour is less evident now. And there are times when Californians seem too intent on establishing their own particular New World old order. A few figures: there are more than 200,000ha (500,000 acres) of wine grapes, producing over 500 million gallons of wine annually, about 90% of all wine made in the USA. A large proportion comes from the hot, inland CENTRAL VALLEY. See also Central Coast, Mendocino County, Monterey County, Napa Valley, San Luis Obispo County, Santa Barbara County, Sonoma County.

CALITERRA *Curicó, Chile* A joint venture between MONDAVI and Chadwick (as is SENA), which has never really lived up to its potential. Few of the wines have expressed any great Chilean character, though Reserva Cabernet Sauvignon and new Arboleda Carmenère aren't bad. Must try harder, I'd say.

CH. CALON-SÉGUR★★ *St-Estèphe AC, 3ème Cru Classé, Haut-Médoc, Bordeaux, France* Long considered one of ST-ESTEPHE's leading châteaux but in the mid-1980s the wines were not as good as they should have been. Recent vintages have been more impressive, with better fruit and a suppler texture. Second wine: Marquis de Ségur. Best years: 2000 99 98 96 95 **90 89 86 82**.

CAMBRIA WINERY *Santa Maria Valley AVA, California, USA* The biggest winery in SANTA BARBARA COUNTY. Most of the production is Chardonnay (Katherine's Vineyard★★ and Reserve★★), with the remainder devoted to Pinot Noir, Syrah★, Viognier and Sangiovese. Look for fine Julia's Vineyard Pinot Noir★. Best years: (Chardonnay) (1999) **98 97 96 95**.

CAMPANIA *Italy* Until recently Italy's south was a desert for the wine lover, but now 3 regions lead the revolution there. While many have been clamouring for the new wines of PUGLIA and SICILY, in Campania moves toward quality have been underpinned by the likes of enologist Riccardo Cotarella. Other producers besides the venerable MASTROBERARDINO have finally begun to realize the potential of its soil, climate and grapes, especially the red Aglianico. DOCs of note are FALERNO DEL MASSICO, Fiano di Avellino, Greco di Tufo, Ischia, TAURASI and VESUVIO. The leading wines are Montevetrano★★★ (Cabernet, Merlot and Aglianico) and Galardi's Terra di Lavoro★★★ (Aglianico and Piedirossa) but also look for top Aglianico reds from De Concilis★, Luigi Maffini★ and Orazio Rillo★ and others that fall outside the main DOCs.

CABERNET SAUVIGNON _____

 Wine made from Cabernet Sauvignon in places like Australia, California, Chile, Bulgaria, even in parts of southern France, has become so popular now that many people may not realize where it all started – and how Cabernet has managed to become the great, all-purpose, omnipresent red wine grape of the world.

WINE STYLES

Bordeaux Cabernet It all began in Bordeaux. With the exception of a clutch of Merlot-based beauties in St-Émilion and Pomerol, all the greatest red Bordeaux wines are based on Cabernet Sauvignon, with varying amounts of Merlot, Cabernet Franc, and possibly Petit Verdot also blended in. The blending is necessary because by itself Cabernet makes such a strong, powerful, aggressive and assertive wine. Dark and tannic when young, the great Bordeaux wines need 10–20 years for the aggression to fade, the fruit becoming sweet and perfumed as fresh blackcurrants, with a fragrance of cedarwood, of cigar boxes mingling magically among the fruit. It is this character which has made red Bordeaux famous for at least 2 centuries.

Cabernet worldwide When winemakers in other parts of the world sought role models to try to improve their wines, most of them automatically thought of Bordeaux and chose Cabernet Sauvignon. It was lucky that they did, because not only is this variety easy to grow in almost all conditions – cool or warm, dry or damp – but that unstoppable personality always powers through. The cheaper wines are generally made to accentuate the blackcurrant fruit and the slightly earthy tannins. They are drinkable young, but able to age surprisingly well. The more ambitious wines are aged in oak barrels, often new ones, to enhance the tannin yet also to add spice and richness capable of developing over a decade or more. Sometimes the Cabernet is blended – usually with Merlot, sometimes with Cabernet Franc, and occasionally with other grapes: Shiraz in Australia, Sangiovese in Italy.

European Cabernets Many vineyards in southern France now produce good, affordable Cabernet Sauvignon. Some of the best wines from Spain have been Cabernet blends, and Portugal has also had success. Italy's red wine quality revolution was sparked off by the success of Cabernet in Tuscany, and all the leading regions now grow it. Austria is starting to use it as a blender and even southern Germany is having a go. Eastern Europe grows lots of Cabernet, but of widely varying quality, while the Eastern Mediterranean (Cyprus, Lebanon, Israel) and North Africa are beginning to produce tasty examples.

New World Cabernets California's reputation was created by its strong, weighty Cabernets. Recently some producers have eased up, making examples that bring out the fruit flavours and can be drunk young, while others have intensified their styles. Both Australia and New Zealand place more emphasis on upfront fruit in their Cabernets. Chile has made the juicy, blackcurranty style very much her own, and Argentina is showing it wants to join in too. New clones, producing riper fruit and tannins, show South Africa will be capable of mixing with the best.

THELEMA

1997
Cabernet Sauvignon

WINE OF ORIGIN STELLENBOSCH

Produced and bottled by
THELEMA MOUNTAIN VINEYARDS,
HELSHOOGTE, STELLENBOSCH.

PRODUCE OF SOUTH AFRICA

750 ml   13.5% Alc.Vol.

BEST PRODUCERS

France

Bordeaux Dom. de CHEVALIER, COS D'ESTOURNEL, GRAND-PUY-LACOSTE, GRUAUD-LAROSE, LAFITE-ROTHSCHILD, LATOUR, LEOVILLE-LAS-CASES, LYNCH-BAGES, Ch. MARGAUX, MOUTON-ROTHSCHILD, PICHON-LONGUEVILLE, RAUZAN-SEGLA; *Midi* RICHEAUME, TREVALLON.

Other European Cabernets

Italy BANFI, CA' DEL BOSCO, Col d'Orcia (Olmaia), GAJA, LAGEDER, MACULAN, ORNELLAIA, RAMPOLLA, SASSICAIA, SOLAIA, TASCA D'ALMERITA.

Spain Blecua, MARQUES DE GRINON, TORRES.

New World Cabernets

Australia BRAND'S, CAPE MENTELLE, CULLEN, Giaconda, HOWARD PARK, MOSS WOOD, MOUNT MARY, PENFOLDS (Bin 707), PETALUMA, WYNNS, YARRA YERING.

New Zealand Esk Valley, GOLDWATER, MATUA VALLEY, STONYRIDGE, TE MATA, VILLA MARIA.

USA (California) ARAUJO, BERINGER, Bryant Family, CAYMUS, DALLA VALLE, DIAMOND CREEK, DOMINUS, DUNN, Grace Family, HARLAN, LAUREL GLEN, Long Meadow Ranch, Peter MICHAEL, MINER, MONDAVI, NEWTON, PHELPS, RIDGE, SCREAMING EAGLE, SHAFER, SILVER OAK, SPOTTSWOODE, STAG'S LEAP, Viader; (Washington) ANDREW WILL, LEONETTI, QUILCEDA CREEK, WOODWARD CANYON.

Chile ALMAVIVA, CARMEN (Nativa), Clos Quebrada de Macul (Domus Aurea), CONCHA Y TORO (Don Melchor, Terrunyo), CONO SUR (20 Barrels), VIÑA CASABLANCA (Santa Isabel).

Argentina CATENA, Terrazas de los Andes (Gran Cabernet Sauvignon).

South Africa BEYERSKLOOF, BOEKENHOUTSKLOOF, BUITEN-VERWACHTING, Neil ELLIS, KANONKOP, MEERLUST, RUSTEN-BERG, SAXENBURG, THELEMA, VEENWOUDEN, VERGELEGEN.

85

CAMPILLO *Rioja DOC, País Vasco, Spain* An up-market subsidiary of Bodegas FAUSTINO, producing some exciting new red RIOJAS★. The wines are often Tempranillo-Cabernet Sauvignon blends, with masses of ripe, velvety fruit. Best years: (Reserva) 1996 **95 94**.

CAMPO VIEJO *Rioja DOC, Rioja, Spain* The largest producer of RIOJA. Reservas★ and Gran Reservas★ are reliably good, as are the elegant, all-Tempranillo Reserva Viña Alcorta★ and the barrel-fermented white Viña Alcorta★. Albor Tempranillo is a good modern young Rioja, packed with fresh, pastilley fruit. Best years: (Reserva) **1996 95 94**.

CANARY ISLANDS *Spain* Tacoronte-Acentejo, Lanzarote, La Palma, Hierro, Abona, Valle de Güimar, Valle de la Orotava and Ycoden-Daute-Isora: a total of 8 DOs for the Canaries – there's local politics for you! The sweet Malvasia from Lanzarote or La Palma is worth a try, otherwise stick with the young reds, made mostly from Listán Negro. Best producers: El Grifo, Bodegas Monje, Viña Norte.

CANBERRA DISTRICT *New South Wales, Australia* Cool, high altitude (800m/2600ft) may sound good, but excessive cold and frost can be problematic. Lark Hill and Helm make exciting Riesling, Lark Hill and Brindabella Hills some smart Cabernet blends and Clonakilla increasingly sublime Shiraz (with a dollop of Viognier). BRL HARDY is pouring money in here. Best producers: Brindabella Hills★, Clonakilla (Shiraz★★), Doonkuna★, Helm, Lark Hill★.

DOM. CANET-VALETTE *St-Chinian AC, Languedoc, France* Marc Valette is uncompromising in his quest to make great wine: organic cultivation, low yields, gravity-fed grapes and traditional *pigeage* (foot-stomping) are just some of his methods. The wines offer a fabulously rich expression of ST-CHINIAN's Mediterranean grape varieties and clay-limestone soils. Cuvées include Mille et Une Nuits (1001 Nights)★ and the powerful, complex Syrah-Grenache Le Vin Maghani★★. Best years: (Le Vin Maghani) 2000 99 98 **97 95**.

CANNONAU Sardinian grape variety essentially the same as Spain's Garnacha and France's Grenache Noir. In SARDINIA it produces deep, tannic reds but lighter, modern, dry red wines are gaining in popularity, although traditional sweet and fortified styles can still be found. Best producers: (modern reds) ARGIOLAS, SELLA & MOSCA, Dolianova, Dorgali, Jerzu, Ogliastra, Oliena, Santa Maria La Palma and Trexenta co-ops.

CANOE RIDGE VINEYARD *Columbia Valley AVA, Washington, USA* Successful WASHINGTON outpost of California's CHALONE group, with reliable and tasty Chardonnay★, fruit-filled Merlot★★ and solid Cabernet Sauvignon★★. Recent vintages have focused on red wine production and the results are significant, yielding sturdy, ageworthy bottlings. Best years: (reds) 2000 99 98 97 **96 95**.

CH. CANON★ *St-Émilion Grand Cru AC, 1er Grand Cru Classé, Bordeaux, France* Canon can make some of the richest, most concentrated ST-ÉMILIONS, but it went into steep decline before being purchased in 1996 by Chanel. Signs are that things are returning to form. The 3.5-ha (8.65-acre) vineyard of Grand Cru Classé Ch. Curé-Bon has recently been added to the estate. In good vintages the wine is tannic and rich at first but is worth aging 10–15 years. Second wine: Clos J Kanon. Best years: 2000 98 96 95 **90 89 88 86 85 83 82**.

CANON-FRONSAC AC *Bordeaux, France* This AC is the heart of the
FRONSAC region. The wines are quite sturdy when young but can age
for 10 years or more. Best producers: Barrabaque★, Canon★, Canon-
de-Brem★, Canon-Moueix★, Cassagne-Haut-Canon★, la Fleur-Cailleau,
Grand-Renouil★, Moulin-Pey-Labrie★, Pavillon, Vrai-Canon-Bouché.
Best years: 2000 98 97 96 **95 94 90 89 88**.

CH. CANON-LA-GAFFELIÈRE★★ *St-Émilion Grand Cru AC, Grand Cru
Classé, Bordeaux, France* Owner Stephan von Neipperg has placed
this property, located at the foot of the town of ST-ÉMILION, at the top
of the list of Grands Crus Classés. The wines are firm, rich and
concentrated. Under the same ownership are Clos l'Oratoire★, Ch.
l'Aiguilhe★ in the COTES DE CASTILLON, and the remarkable *micro-cuvée*
La Mondotte★★. Best years: 2000 99 98 **97** 96 **95 94 93 90 89 88 85**.

CH. CANTEMERLE★ *Haut-Médoc AC, 5ème Cru Classé, Bordeaux, France*
With la LAGUNE, the most southerly of the Crus Classés. The wines are
delicate in style and excellent in ripe vintages. Second wine:
Villeneuve de Cantemerle. Best years: 2000 99 96 **95 90 89 83 82**.

CANTERBURY *South Island, New Zealand* The long, cool ripening
season of the arid central coast of South Island favours white varieties,
particularly Chardonnay, Pinot Gris, Sauvignon Blanc and Riesling, as well
as Pinot Noir. The northerly Waipara district produces Canterbury's most
exciting wines, especially from Riesling and Pinot Noir. Best producers:
GIESEN★, Mountford★, PEGASUS BAY★★, Daniel Schuster★, Waipara West★.
Best years: (Pinot Noir) (2001) 00 99 **98 97 96 95**; (Riesling) (2001) 00 **99 98 96**.

CAPEL VALE *Geographe, Western Australia* Radiologist Peter Pratten's
winery makes fine Riesling★, Chardonnay★ and Semillon-Sauvignon
Blanc★, often blending Capel fruit with Mount Barker. Connoisseur
range whites and reds are increasingly classy, especially Whispering
Hill Riesling★★ and Howecroft Cabernet-Merlot★ and Frederick
Chardonnay★. Best years: (Whispering Hill Riesling) 1999 **98 97**.

CAPE MENTELLE *Margaret River, Western Australia* Leading MARGARET
RIVER winery, owned by French luxury giant LVMH. Cape Mentelle's
founder, David Hohnen, and winemaker John Durham produce full-
throttle Cabernet★★ and Shiraz★★, impressive Chardonnay★★, tangy
Semillon-Sauvignon Blanc★★ and wonderfully chewy Zinfandel★★
which effectively expresses Hohnen's CALIFORNIA training. All wines
benefit from cellaring – whites up to 5 years, reds 8–10. Best years:
(Cabernet Sauvignon) 1998 96 95 **94 93 91 90 88 86 83 82**.

CH. CARBONNIEUX *Pessac-Léognan AC, Cru Classé de Graves, Bordeaux,
France* Carbonnieux is the largest of the GRAVES Classed Growth
properties, now part of the PESSAC-LEOGNAN AC. The white★ is a pleasant,
mildly oaked wine. The red is generally balanced and enjoyable but
rarely memorable. Second wine: la Tour-Léognan. Best years: (whites)
2000 99 **98 96 95 94 90 89 88**; (reds) 2000 98 96 **95 90 89 88 86**.

CAREMA DOC *Piedmont, Italy* Lighter than most other Nebbiolos, these
wines can have great elegance and perfume. Production is confined to
the local co-op (Carema Carema★) and Luigi Ferrando (White Label★,
Black Label★★). Best years: (2000) 99 98 **97** 96 **95 93 90 88 85**.

CARIGNAN The dominant red grape in the south of France is responsible
for much boring, cheap, harsh wine. But when made by carbonic
maceration, the wine can have delicious spicy fruit. Old vines are capable

of thick, rich, impressive reds, with which it is now having the odd success in CALIFORNIA and Chile. There is also some interest in South Africa. Although initially a Spanish grape (as Cariñena or Mazuelo), it is not that widespread there, but is useful for adding colour and acidity in RIOJA and CATALUNA, and has gained unexpected respect in PRIORAT.

CARIGNANO DEL SULCIS DOC *Sardinia, Italy*
Carignano is now starting to produce wines of quite startling quality. Rocca Rubia★, a barrique-aged Riserva from the co-op at Santadi, with rich, fleshy and chocolaty fruit, is one of SARDINIA's best reds. In a similar vein, but a step up, is Baie Rosse★★; even better is the more structured and concentrated Terre Brune★★. Best producer: Santadi co-op. Best years: (reds) (2001) 00 99 **98 97 96 95**.

LOUIS CARILLON & FILS *Puligny-Montrachet AC, Côte de Beaune, Burgundy, France* Excellent family-owned estate in PULIGNY-MONTRACHET. The emphasis here is on traditional, finely balanced whites of great concentration, rather than new oak. Look out for the Premiers Crus les Referts★★, Champs Canet★★ and les Perrières★★★, and the tiny but exquisite production of Bienvenues-BATARD-MONTRACHET★★★. Reds from CHASSAGNE-MONTRACHET★, ST-AUBIN★ and MERCUREY★ are good, too. Best years: (whites) (2001) 00 99 97 96 **95 92 90**.

CARIÑENA DO *Aragón, Spain* The largest DO of ARAGON, baking under the mercilessly hot sun in inland eastern Spain, Cariñena has traditionally been a land of cheap, deep red, alcoholic wines from the Garnacha grape. However, a switch to Tempranillo grapes has begun, and some growers now pick earlier. International grape varieties like Cabernet Sauvignon are being planted widely. Best producers: Bodegas San Valero (Monte Ducay, Don Mendo), Señorío de Urbezo.

CARMEN *Maipo, Chile* Sister winery to SANTA RITA. Innovative young winemaker Alvaro Espinoza has left after an 8-year stint; now led by Pilar Gonzalez, ex-SANTA CAROLINA. Both Chardonnay★ and Sauvignon Blanc★ are good, but it is the reds that really shine. Excellent, blackcurranty, organic Nativa Cabernet Sauvignon★★, throaty, deep Carmenère-Cabernet Sauvignon★★ and Winemaker's Reserve★★ blend of 5 varieties lead the way. Single-vineyard Cabernet Sauvignon Gold Reserve★★ is also excellent.

CARMENÈRE A minor constituent of BORDEAUX blends in the 19th century, historically known as Grande Vidure. Planted in Chile, it was generally labelled as Merlot until 1998. When ripe and made with care, it has rich blackberry, plum and spice flavours, with an unexpected but delicious bunch of savoury characters – grilled meat, soy sauce, celery, coffee – thrown in. A true original.

CARMENET VINEYARD *Sonoma Valley AVA, California, USA* Carmenet sets out to make BORDEAUX-style reds and whites and succeeds brilliantly with its Moon Mountain Estate Reserve★★ and Reserve Sauvignon Blanc★★. The Dynamite line of wines (Cabernet★) are softer and more approachable. Best years: (reds) (2000) 99 98 97 96 95 94 **92 91 90 88 87 86**.

CARMIGNANO DOCG *Tuscany, Italy* Red wine from the west of Florence, renowned since the 16th century and revived in the 1960s by Capezzana. The blend (85% Sangiovese, 15% Cabernet) is one of Tuscany's more refined wines and can be very long-lived. Although Carmignano is DOCG for its red wine, notable as Riserva, DOC applies to a lighter red Barco Reale, a rosé called Vin Ruspo and fine VIN SANTO. Best producers: Ambra★ (Vigne Alte★★), Artimino★, Capezzana★★, Le Farnete/E Pierazzuoli★ (Riserva★★), Il Poggiolo★, Villa di Trefiano★. Best years: 2000 99 98 **97 96 95 94 93 90 88 85**.

CARMO, QUINTA DO *Alentejo, Portugal* Well-established estate, part-owned by Domaines Rothschild since 1992. Estate red★ used to be complex and ageworthy, but quality from vintages in the 90s has been very ordinary, especially given its inflated price. And that's not really acceptable when you can supposedly call upon top Bordeaux expertise and finance. Second label: Dom Martinho. Best years: (2000) (99) **95 94**

CARNEROS AVA *California, USA* Hugging the northern edge of San Francisco Bay, Carneros includes parts of both NAPA and SONOMA Counties. Windswept and chilly with morning fog off the Bay, it is a top cool-climate area, suitable for Chardonnay and Pinot Noir as both table wine and a base for sparkling wine. Merlot and even Syrah are also coming on well, but vineyard expansion is beginning to worry me. Best producers: ACACIA★★, Buena Vista, Carneros Creek★, DOMAINE CARNEROS★★, MUMM NAPA (Winery Lake)★, David Ramey★★, RASMUSSEN★★, SAINTSBURY★★. Best years: (Pinot Noir) (2001) 00 99 **98 97 96 95 94**.

CARNUNTUM *Niederösterreich, Austria* Wine region south of Danube and east of Vienna, with a strong red wine tradition. Best producers: Walter Glatzer, Markowitsch, Pitnauer★.

CH. CARSIN *Premières Côtes de Bordeaux AC, Bordeaux, France* With an Australian winemaker – Mandy Jones – and a winery designed and built by an Australian engineering company, what could you expect other than aromatic and fruity New World-style wines? Carsin delivers the goods with well-oaked, drink-young white Cuvée Prestige★ and red Cuvée Noire★. Also peach and citrus vin de table Etiquette Gris★ and a sweet CADILLAC. Best years: (Cuvée Noire) 2000 99 **98 97 96 95 94**.

CASABLANCA, VALLE DE *Aconcagua, Chile* Coastal valley with a cool-climate personality that is Chile's strongest proof of regional style. Whites dominate, with best results from Chardonnay, Sauvignon Blanc and Gewürztraminer. Even so, the rare reds, Pinot Noir especially, are very good. Best producers: (whites) CONCHA Y TORO★, CASA LAPOSTOLLE★, ERRAZURIZ★, Morandé, Veramonte★★, VILLARD ESTATE, VIÑA CASABLANCA★★. Best years: (whites) **2001 00 99 98**.

CASA LAPOSTOLLE *Rapel, Chile* Joint venture between Marnier-Lapostolle and Chile's Rabat family, with Michel Rolland at the winemaking helm. Cuvée Alexandre Merlot★★ and Chardonnay★ both have the intensity for several years' aging. Clos Apalta★★★ is a world-class Merlot- and Carmenère-based blend.

DOM. LA CASENOVE *Côtes du Roussillon AC, Roussillon, France* Former photojournalist Étienne Montès, with the help of consultant enologist Jean-Luc COLOMBO, has developed an impressive range of wines, including a perfumed white Vin de Pays Catalan made from Macabeu and Torbat, MUSCAT DE RIVESALTES★, RIVESALTES★ and 2 red COTES DU ROUSSILLON: Tradition★ and the predominantly Syrah Commandant François Jaubert★★. Drink this with at least 5 years' bottle age. Best years: (Cdt François Jaubert) 2000 99 98 **97 96 95**.

CASSIS AC *Provence, France*   A picturesque fishing port near Marseille. Because of its situation, its white wine is the most overpriced on the French Riviera. Based on Ugni Blanc and Clairette, the wine can be good if fresh. The red wine is dull but the rosé can be pleasant (especially from a single estate). Best producers: Bagnol★, Clos Ste-Magdelaine★, Ferme Blanche★, Fontblanche, Mas de Boudard, Mas Fontcreuse. Best years: (2001) **00 99 98 97 96**.

CASTEL DEL MONTE DOC *Puglia, Italy*   An arid, hilly zone, and an ideal habitat for the Uva di Troia grape, producing long-lived red wine of astonishing character. There is also varietal Aglianico, some good rosé, and the whites produced from international varieties are improving. Best producers: RIVERA★, Santa Lucia, Tormaresca/ANTINORI, Torrevento★. Best years: (2001) 00 99 98 **97 96 95 94 93**.

CASTELGIOCONDO *Brunello di Montalcino DOCG, Tuscany, Italy* FRESCOBALDI's estate is the source of merely adequate BRUNELLO, superior Brunello Riserva★ and Merlot Lamaione★★. The vineyards are also providing grapes for the much-trumpeted joint venture with MONDAVI, Luce, a Sangiovese-Merlot blend; so far, I'm unconvinced, but the addition of a second wine, Lucente, may help.

CASTELLARE *Chianti Classico DOCG, Tuscany, Italy*   Publisher Paolo Panerai's fine estate in the west of the Classico zone produces excellent Chianti Classico★ and deeper, richer Riserva★★. Canonico di Castellare★ (Chardonnay), Coniale di Castellare★★ (Cabernet Sauvignon), and Spartito di Castellare★ (Sauvignon Blanc) are all ripe and fruity. Top wine I Sodi di San Niccolò★★ is an unusual Sangiovese-Malvasia blend, intense but finely perfumed.

CASTELLO DI BORGHESE/HARGRAVE VINEYARD *Long Island, New York State, USA*   It took Hargrave's thrilling reds and whites produced from an old potato plantation to establish LONG ISLAND as a serious wine region in the 1980s and spark a grape-growing explosion on the island's North Fork. The vineyard changed hands in 1999, and the new Italian owners, Castello di Borghese, have begun planting the region's first Sangiovese.

CASTILLA-LA MANCHA *Spain*   The biggest wine region in Spain; hot, dry country with poor clay-chalk soil. The DOs of the central plateau, La MANCHA and VALDEPEÑAS, make white wines from the Airén grape, and some good reds from the Cencibel (Tempranillo). Méntrida DO, the new Manchuela DO and Almansa DO make mostly rustic reds. The most ambitious wines made here fall outside the DOs: those from MARQUES DE GRINON's Dominio de Valdepusa★★ estate and the Dehesa del Carrizal★ estate, both in the Toledo mountains, Uribes Madero's Calzadilla★ in Cuenca province and Manuel Manzaneque's Sierra de Alcaraz★★ vineyards in Albacete province are of the highest standard.

CASTILLA Y LEÓN *Spain*   This is Spain's harsh, high plateau, with long cold winters and hot summers (but always cool nights). A few rivers, notably the Duero, temper this climate and afford fine conditions for viticulture. After many decades of winemaking ignorance, with a few exceptions like VEGA SICILIA, the situation has changed radically for the better in 2 of the region's DOs, RIBERA DEL DUERO and RUEDA, and is rapidly improving in the other 3, BIERZO, Cigales and TORO. Dynamic winemakers such as Telmo RODRIGUEZ and Mariano García of MAURO have won huge critical acclaim for the region.

CATALUÑA *Spain* Standards vary among the region's DOs. PENEDES, between Barcelona and Tarragona, has the greatest number of technically equipped wineries in Spain, but doesn't make a commensurate number of superior wines. In the south, mountainous, isolated PRIORAT DOC has become a new icon for its heady, raging reds, and the neighbouring DOs of Montsant and Terra Alta are following in its footsteps. Inland COSTERS DEL SEGRE and CONCA DE BARBERA make potentially excellent reds and whites. Up the coast, Alella makes attractive whites and Ampurdán-Costa Brava (Empordá-Costa Brava), by the French border, is showing signs of life. Cataluña also makes most of Spain's CAVA sparkling wines. The Catalunya DO allows inexpensive blends from anywhere in the region.

NICOLÁS CATENA *Mendoza, Argentina* Argentina's most progressive export-orientated wine producer. Top-end stuff has always been good to excellent, but the basic range was sluggish; it is now greatly improved, and led by the Argento brand of Chardonnay and Malbec★ – both fresh, modern and perfumed. Catena-owned Esmeralda produces good international-style Chardonnay, oak-aged Cabernet Sauvignon and powerful Agrelo vineyard Malbec, with second-label Alamos providing a rather leaner interpretation. Soft, juicy Malbec and Merlot under the Rutini label, and gob-stopping Bonarda El Mirador★. However, the star wines come from Catena's spectacular Zapata winery in Agrelo. Using a variety of grape sources – from some of Argentina's older Malbec at Lunlunta, right up to new, high-altitude Tupungato fruit – the Alta range of Chardonnay★★, Cabernet★★ and Malbec★★, topped by new Catena Zapata★★, is top-flight. Expect ★★★ some time soon.

DOM. CAUHAPÉ *Jurançon AC, South-West France* Henri Ramonteu has been a major influence in JURANÇON, proving that the area can make complex dry whites as well as more traditional sweet wines. Dry, unoaked Jurançon Sec is labelled Chant des Vignes★; the oaked version is Sève d'Automne★. Top wines are sweet Noblesse du Temps★★ and barrel-fermented Quintessence★★★.

CAVA DO *Spain* Cava, the Catalan and hence Spanish name for CHAMPAGNE-method fizz, is made in 159 towns and villages in northern Spain, but more than 95% are in CATALUÑA. Grapes used are the local trio of Parellada, Macabeo and Xarel-lo. The best-value, fruitiest Cavas are generally the youngest, with no more than the minimum 9 months' aging. Some good Catalan Cavas are made with Chardonnay and maybe Pinot Noir. A number of top-quality wines are now produced but are seldom seen abroad, since their prices are too close to those of Champagne to attract international customers. Best producers: Can Feixes, Can Ràfols dels Caus, Castellblanch, Castell de Vilarnau, CODORNIU★, FREIXENET, JUVE Y CAMPS★, Marques de Monistrol, Parxet, RAIMAT, Raventós i Blanc, Rovellats, Agustí Torelló, Jané Ventura.

CAYMUS VINEYARDS *Napa Valley AVA, California, USA* Caymus Cabernet Sauvignon is a ripe, intense and generally tannic style that is good in its regular bottling★ and can be outstanding as a Special Selection★★★. Conundrum★ is an exotic, full-flavoured blended white. Mer Soleil★★, a new label for MONTEREY Chardonnay, was an instant success. Best years: (Special Selection) (2000) (99) 98 97 **95 94 92 91 90 87 86 85 84**.

DOM. CAZES *Rivesaltes, Roussillon, France* The Cazes brothers make outstanding MUSCAT DE RIVESALTES★★, RIVESALTES Vieux★★ and the superb Aimé Cazes★★, but also produce a wide range of red and white

91

table wines, mainly as COTES DU ROUSSILLON and Vin de Pays des Côtes Catalanes. Look out for the soft, fruity red Le Canon du Maréchal★, the Cabernet-based Le Credo★ and the small production of barrel-fermented Chardonnay.

CH. DU CÈDRE *Cahors AC, South-West France* Pascal Verhaegue is the leader of a new generation of CAHORS winemakers, producing dark, richly textured wines with a generous coating of chocolaty oak. There are 3 cuvées: Tradition★, Le Prestige★ and the 100% Auxerrois (Malbec) Le Cèdre★★, which is aged in new oak barrels for 20 months. All 3 benefit from at least 4–5 years' bottle age. Best years: (Le Cèdre) 2000 99 98 **97 96**.

CELLIER LE BRUN *Marlborough, New Zealand* Champagne-method specialist, with vintage Blanc de Blancs★★, and tasty blended vintage and non-vintage bubblies. Founder Daniel Le Brun has now sold up and established a new MARLBOROUGH winery. Le Brun Family Cellars. Best years: (Blanc de Blancs) **1996 95 93 92 91 90**.

CENCIBEL See Tempranillo.

CENTRAL COAST AVA *California, USA* Huge AVA covering virtually every vineyard between San Francisco and Los Angeles, with a number of sub-AVAs, such as SANTA CRUZ MOUNTAINS, Santa Ynez Valley, SANTA MARIA VALLEY and Monterey, which include some excellent cooler areas for Pinot Noir and Chardonnay. See also Monterey County, San Luis Obispo County, Santa Barbara County.

CENTRAL OTAGO *South Island, New Zealand* The only wine region in New Zealand with a continental rather than maritime climate. Technically the ripening season is long and cool, suiting Pinot Noir, Gewürztraminer and Chardonnay, but there are usually periods of considerable heat during the summer to intensify flavour. Long autumns have also produced some excellent Rieslings. There are already well over 30 wineries and an explosion of plantings, some in good areas like Bannockburn and Gibbston Valley, others in areas that could prove decidedly marginal. A region to watch. Best producers: Chard Farm★, FELTON ROAD★★, Gibbston Valley★, Mount Difficulty★, Mount Edwards★, Quartz Reef★, Rippon Vineyards★. Best years: (Pinot Noir) (2001) **99 98**.

VALLE CENTRAL *Chile* The heart of Chile's wine industry, encompassing the valleys of MAIPO, RAPEL, CURICO and MAULE. Most major producers are located here, and the key factor determining mesoclimate differences is the distance relative to the coastal and Andean Cordilleras.

CENTRAL VALLEY *California, USA* This vast area grows over 50% of California's wine grapes, used mostly for cheaper styles of wine, along with brandies and grape concentrate. Viewed overall, the quality has improved over the past few years, but it is a hot area, where irrigated vineyards tend to produce excess tonnages of grapes. It has often been said that it is virtually impossible to produce exciting wine in the Central Valley, but in fact the climatic conditions in the northern half are not that unlike those in many parts of Spain and southern France. During the 1990s, growers in the Lodi AVA expanded vineyards to 23,000ha (57,000 acres), making Lodi the volume leader for Chardonnay, Merlot, Zinfandel and Cabernet. Lodi Zinfandel shows some potential. Other sub-regions with claims to quality are the Sacramento Valley and the Delta area. Best producers: MONDAVI Woodbridge, SUTTER HOME.

CENTRAL VICTORIA *Victoria, Australia*
Comprising the regions of BENDIGO, Goulburn Valley and the Central Victorian Mountain Country around the Strathbogie Ranges, the mostly warm conditions of Central Victoria produce powerful and individual wines. The few wineries on the banks of the serene

thread of the Goulburn River produce fine RHONE varieties, particularly white Marsanne, while reds from the marginal mountain country are well structured, tight and tannic. Best producers: DELATITE★★, MITCHELTON★★, Paul Osicka★★, Plunkett's, TAHBILK★.

CERETTO *Piedmont, Italy*   This merchant house, run by brothers Bruno and Marcello Ceretto, has gained a reputation as one of the chief modern producers in BAROLO. With the help of enologist Donato Lanati, Barolo (from Bricco Rocche★★, Brunate★★ and Prapò★★), BARBARESCO (Bricco Asili★★), BARBERA D'ALBA Piana★ and white Arneis Blangè are living up to their reputation. Ceretto also produce an oak-aged LANGHE red, Monsordo★★, from Cabernet, Merlot, Pinot Nero and Nebbiolo. An unoaked white counterpart, l'Arbarei, is based on Riesling. A good Chardonnay, La Bernardina★, was last produced in 1999.

CÉRONS AC *Bordeaux, France*   An AC for sweet wine in the GRAVES region of Bordeaux. The soft, mildly honeyed wine is not quite as sweet as SAUTERNES and not so well known, nor so highly priced. Most producers now make dry wine under the Graves label. Best producers: Ch. de Cérons★, Chantegrive, Grand Enclos du Château de Cérons★, Seuil. Best years: (2001) 99 98 **97 96 95 90 89**.

L A CETTO *Baja California, Mexico*   Mexico's most successful winery relies on mists and cooling Pacific breezes to temper the heat of the Valle de Guadalupe. Italian Camilo Magoni makes ripe, fleshy Petite Sirah, oak-aged Cabernet Sauvignon, Zinfandel and Nebbiolo. Chardonnay lacks acidity but, paradoxically, Cetto makes a decent stab at fizz.

CHABLAIS *Vaud, Switzerland*   A sub-region of the VAUD, south-east of Lake Geneva. Most of the vineyards lie on the alluvial plains but 2 villages, Yvorne and Aigle, benefit from much steeper slopes and produce tangy whites and good reds. Most of the thirst-quenchingly dry whites are made from Chasselas, or Dorin as it is called locally. The reds are made from Pinot Noir, as is a rosé speciality, Oeil de Perdrix, an enjoyable summer wine. Drink whites and rosés young. Best producers: Henri Badoux, Delarze, Grognuz, J & P Testuz.

CHABLIS AC *Burgundy, France*   Chablis, as close to CHAMPAGNE as to the COTE D'OR, is Burgundy's northernmost outpost. When not destroyed by frost or hail, the Chardonnay grape makes a crisp, dry white wine with a steely mineral fruit which can be delicious. Several producers are experimenting with barrel-aging for their better wines, resulting in some full, toasty, positively rich dry whites. Others are intentionally producing a soft, creamy, early drinking style, which is nice but not really Chablis. The outlying areas come under the Petit Chablis AC and should be drunk young. The better straight Chablis AC should be drunk at 3–5 years, while a good vintage of a leading Chablis Premier Cru may take 5 years to show its full potential. About a quarter of Chablis is designated as Premier Cru, the best vineyards on the rolling limestone slopes being Fourchaumes, Mont de Milieu, Montmains, Montée de Tonnerre and Vaillons. Best producers: Barat★, J-C Bessin

93

(Fourchaume★★), Billaud-Simon (Mont de Milieu★★), Pascal Bouchard★, A & F Boudin★★, BROCARD★, la CHABLISIENNE★ (Mont de Milieu★★), Collet★, Dampt★, R & V DAUVISSAT★★, D & E Defaix★, DROIN★, DROUHIN★, DURUP★, W Fèvre★, J-P Grossot (Côte de Troesme★★), Laroche★★, Malandes (Côte de Léchêt★), MICHEL (Montmains★★), Picq (Vaucoupin★★), L Pinson★, RAVENEAU (Montée de Tonnerre★★), Vocoret★★. Best years: (Chablis Premier Cru) (2001) 00 99 **98 96 95 90**.

CHABLIS GRAND CRU AC *Burgundy, France* The 7 Grands Crus (Bougros, les Preuses, Vaudésir, Grenouilles, Valmur, les Clos and les Blanchots) facing south-west across the town of Chablis are the heart of the AC. Oak barrel-aging takes the edge off taut flavours, adding a rich warmth to these fine wines. DROIN and Fèvre are the most enthusiastic users of new oak, but use it less than they used to. Never drink young: 5–10 years is needed before you can see why you spent your money. Best producers: J-C Bessin★★, Billaud-Simon★★, la CHABLISIENNE★★, J Dauvissat★★, R & V DAUVISSAT★★★, D & E Defaix★★, DROIN★★, Laroche★★★, Long-Depaquit★★, MICHEL★★★, Pinson★★, RAVENEAU★★★, Servin★, Simonnet-Febvre★★, Vocoret★★. Best years: (2001) 00 99 98 97 96 **95 92 90**.

LA CHABLISIENNE *Chablis, Burgundy, France* Substantial co-op producing nearly a third of all CHABLIS. The wines are reliable and can aspire to greatness. The best are the oaky Grands Crus – especially les Preuses★★ and Grenouilles (sold as Ch. Grenouille★★) – but the basic unoaked Chablis★, the Cuvée Vieilles Vignes★★ and the numerous Premiers Crus★ are good, as is the red BOURGOGNE Épineuil. Best years: (whites) (2001) 00 **99 98 97 96 95**; (reds) (2001) 00 **99 98**.

CHAIN OF PONDS *Adelaide Hills, South Australia* The Amadio family's 120ha (300-acre) vineyard supplies grapes to other wine companies, including PENFOLDS, but the cream of the crop is reserved for their own finely crafted range, including Chardonnay★★, Riesling★, Sauvignon Blanc-Semillon★, Semillon★, Amadeus Cabernet Sauvignon★★, Ledge Shiraz★, Pinot Noir★ and Novello Rosso rosé. From vines on Kangaroo Island, south-west of Adelaide, Florance Cabernet-Merlot★ is probably the best wine the island has yet produced.

CHALONE *Monterey County, California, USA* Producers of full-blown but slow-developing Chardonnay★★ and concentrated Pinot Noir★★ from vineyards on the arid eastern slope of the Coastal Range in mid-MONTEREY COUNTY. Also makes very good Pinot Blanc★★ and Chenin Blanc★, as well as Reserve bottlings of Pinot Noir★★ and Chardonnay★★. These are strongly individualistic wines. Best years: (Chardonnay) (2001) 00 99 98 97 **96 95 94 93 92 91 90 89 85**; (Pinot Noir) 2000 99 98 **96 95 94 92 91 90 88 86 83**.

CHAMBERS *Rutherglen, Victoria, Australia* Legendary family winery making sheer nectar in the form of Muscat and Tokay. The secret is Bill Chambers' ability to draw on ancient stocks put down in wood by earlier generations. His 'Special'★★ and 'Rare'★★★ blends are national treasures. The Cabernet and Shiraz are good, the whites pedestrian.

CHAMBERTIN AC *Grand Cru, Côte de Nuits, Burgundy, France* The village of GEVREY-CHAMBERTIN, the largest COTE DE NUITS commune, has no fewer than 8 Grands Crus (Chambertin, Chambertin-Clos-de-Bèze, Chapelle-Chambertin, Charmes-Chambertin, Griotte-Chambertin, Latricières-Chambertin, Mazis-Chambertin and Ruchottes-Chambertin), which can produce some of Burgundy's greatest and most intense red wine. Its rough-hewn fruit, seeming to war with fragrant perfumes for its first few years, creates remarkable flavours a the wine ages. Chambertin and Chambertin-Clos-de-Bèze are the greatest sites, but overproduction is a recurrent problem with some producers. Best producers: Denis Bachelet★★, BOUCHARD PERE ET FILS★★, Charlopin★, CLAIR★★★, P Damoy★, DROUHIN★★, Dugat-Py★★★, FAIVELEY★★, R Groffier★★, JADOT★★, D Laurent★★★, Dom. LEROY★★★, Denis Mortet★★★, H Perrot-Minot★★, Ponsot★★, Rossignol-Trapet★, J Roty★, ROUMIER★★, ROUSSEAU★★★, Jean Trapet★. Best years: (2001) 00 99 98 97 96 95 93 **91** 90 **89 88 85**.

CHAMBERTIN-CLOS-DE-BÈZE AC See Chambertin AC.

CHAMBOLLE-MUSIGNY AC *Côte de Nuits, Burgundy, France* AC with the potential to produce the most fragrant, perfumed red Burgundy, when not over-cropped. Encouragingly, more young producers are now bottling their own wines. Best producers: G Barthod★★, DROUHIN★★, DUJAC★★, R Groffier★★, Hudelot-Noëllat★★, JADOT★★, Dom. LEROY★★, Marchand-Grillot★★, D Mortet★★, J-F Mugnier★, RION★★, ROUMIER★★ VOGUE★★. Best years: (2001) 00 99 98 **97** 96 **95 93 90**.

CHAMPAGNE See pages 96–7.

CHAMPAGNE ROSÉ *Champagne, France* Good pink CHAMPAGNE has a delicious fragrance of cherries and raspberries. The top wines can age well, but most should be drunk on release. Best producers: (vintage) BILLECART-SALMON★★, BOLLINGER★★, Charbaut★, Gosset★★★, Charles HEIDSIECK★★, JACQUESSON★★, LAURENT-PERRIER★★, MOET & CHANDON★★, POL ROGER★★, Louis ROEDERER★★, VEUVE CLICQUOT★★; (non-vintage) Paul Bara★, E Barnaut★★, Beaumont des Crayères★, BILLECART-SALMON★★, Egly-Ouriet★, Jacquart★, KRUG★★, LANSON★, LAURENT-PERRIER★★, MOET & CHANDON★, PERRIER-JOUET★, RUINART★, TAITTINGER★, Vilmart★. Best years: (1999) (98) (96) 95 **91 90 89 88 85 82**. See also pages 96–7.

CHANDON DE BRIAILLES *Savigny-lès-Beaune AC, Côte de Beaune, Burgundy, France* The de Nicolays, mother and daughter, combine modern sophistication with traditional values to produce rich but refined reds from SAVIGNY-LES-BEAUNE★, PERNAND-VERGELESSES★★, ALOXE-CORTON★★ and CORTON★★★, and an equally good range of whites from Pernand-Vergelesses★★, Corton★★★ and CORTON-CHARLEMAGNE★★★. Best years: (reds) (2001) 99 98 96 **95 93 90**.

CHAPEL DOWN *Kent, England* A merger with Carr Taylor (including Lamberhurst) has created New Wave Wines, with Owen Elias as chief winemaker. Grapes are from their own vineyards in Kent, and bought in from 25 vineyards across southern England. The range includes good, inexpensive sparkling wines (Brut non-vintage and Vintage★) and still wines under the Curious Grape label: fruity white blends, varietal Bacchus and a wood-aged red Epoch I.

CHAPEL HILL *McLaren Vale, South Australia* Pam Dunsford makes powerful, classy wines at her hilltop winery. She blends mature MCLAREN VALE fruit and COONAWARRA in her Cabernet Sauvignon★★, while Shiraz★★ is all McLaren Vale. Good unwooded Chardonnay★ (Reserve★★), and fascinating, bone-dry, honey-scented Verdelho★★. Owned by the Swiss Thomas Schmidheiny group, which also owns CUVAISON in California. Best years: (Shiraz) 1998 97 **96 95 94 93 91**.

CHAPELLE-CHAMBERTIN AC See Chambertin AC.

LA CHAPELLE LENCLOS *Madiran AC, South-West France* Patrick Ducournau has tamed the savage Tannat grape with controlled oxygenation during barrel aging. The Chapelle Lenclos★★ and Dom. Mouréou★ reds are ripe and concentrated, though they still need at least 5 years to mature. Best years: 2000 99 98 **96 95 94 93 90**.

CHAMPAGNE AC
Champagne, France

The Champagne region produces the most celebrated sparkling wines in the world. East of Paris, it is the most northerly AC in France – a place where grapes struggle to ripen fully. Champagne is divided into 5 distinct areas – the best are the Montagne de Reims, where the Pinot Noir grape performs brilliantly, and the Chardonnay-dominated Côte des Blancs south of Épernay. In addition to Chardonnay and Pinot Noir, the only other grape permitted for the production of Champagne is Pinot Meunier.

The wines undergo a second fermentation in the bottle which produces carbon dioxide, contained under pressure. It is through this method that Champagne acquires its crisp, long-lasting bubbles and a distinctive yeasty, toasty dimension to its flavour. If you buy a bottle of Coteaux Champenois, a still wine from the area, you can see why they decided to make bubbly instead; it usually tastes mean and tart, but is transformed by the Champagne method into some of the most delightfully exhilarating wines of all.

That's the theory anyway, and for 150 years or so the Champenois have suavely persuaded us that their product is second to none. It can be, too, except when it is released too young or sweetened to make up for a lack of richness. A combination of high prices and competition from other sparkling wines has produced a glut of Champagne. But as Champagne expertise begins to turn out exciting sparklers in California, Australia and New Zealand, the Champagne producers must re-focus on quality or lose much of their market for good.

The Champagne trade is dominated by large companies or houses, called négociants-manipulants, recognized by the letters NM on the label. The récoltants-manipulants (recognized by the letters RM) are growers who make their own wine.

STYLES OF CHAMPAGNE

Non-vintage Most Champagne is a blend of 2 or more vintages. Quality varies enormously, depending on who has made the wine and how long it has been aged. Most Champagne is sold as Brut, which is a dry, but not bone-dry style. Strangely, Extra Dry denotes a style less dry than Brut.

Vintage Denotes Champagne made with grapes from a single vintage. As a rule, it is made only in the best years, but far too many mediocre years were declared in the 1990s.

Blanc de Blancs A lighter, and at best highly elegant, style of Champagne made solely from the Chardonnay grape.

Blanc de Noirs A white Champagne, but made entirely from black grapes, either Pinot Noir, Pinot Meunier, or a combination of the two. Generally rather solid.

Rosé Pink Champagne, made either from black grapes or (more usually) by mixing a little still red wine into white Champagne.

De luxe cuvée In theory the finest Champagne and certainly always the most expensive, residing in the fanciest bottles.

See also CHAMPAGNE ROSE; and individual producers.

BEST PRODUCERS

Houses BILLECART-SALMON, BOLLINGER, Cattier, Charbaut, Delamotte, Delbeck, DEUTZ, Drappier, Duval-Leroy, Gosset, Alfred GRATIEN, Charles HEIDSIECK, Henriot, Jacquesson, KRUG, LANSON, LAURENT-PERRIER, Bruno PAILLARD, Joseph PERRIER, PERRIER-JOUET, Philipponnat, POL ROGER, POMMERY, Louis ROEDERER, RUINART, Salon, TAITTINGER, VEUVE CLICQUOT.

Growers Bara, Barnaut, Beaufort, Beerens, Callot, Charpentier, Chartogne-Taillet, Diebolt Vallois, Daniel Dumont, Egly-Ouriet, René Geoffroy, Gimonnet, André Jacquart, Lamiable, Larmandier, Larmandier-Bernier, Launois, Margaine, Mathieu, G Michel, Moncuit, Alain Robert, Secondé, Selosse, de Sousa, Tarlant, Vilmart.

Co-ops Beaumont les Crayères, Chouilly (Nicolas Feuillatte), Jacquart, Mailly.

De luxe cuvées Belle Époque (PERRIER-JOUET), N-F Billecart (BILLECART-SALMON), Blanc de Millénaires (Charles HEIDSIECK), Clos des Goisses (Philipponnat), Clos de Mesnil (KRUG), Comtes de Champagne (TAITTINGER), Cristal (Louis ROEDERER), Cuvée Josephine (Joseph PERRIER), Cuvée Sir Winston Churchill (POL ROGER), Cuvée William Deutz (DEUTZ), Dom Pérignon (MOET & CHANDON), Dom Ruinart (RUINART), Grand Siècle (LAURENT-PERRIER), Grande Dame (VEUVE CLICQUOT), Noble Cuvée (LANSON), Vintage RD (BOLLINGER).

M CHAPOUTIER *Rhône Valley, France* These days, Chapoutier is very much in the vanguard of progress, both in viticulture and in winemaking, and is producing a full range of serious and exciting wines. The HERMITAGE la Sizeranne★★, l'Ermite★★ and le Pavillon★★★, white Hermitage Cuvée de l'Orée★★ and le Méal★★★, CROZES-HERMITAGE les Varonniers★★, ST-JOSEPH les Granits★★ and CHATEAUNEUF-DU-PAPE Barbe Rac★★ are all good, but some of them show a surfeit of new oak. Jointly owns Dom. des Béates (Cuvée Terra d'Or★★) in PROVENCE. Best years: (la Sizeranne) (2000) 99 98 96 95 **94 92 91 90 89 88**.

CHARDONNAY See pages 100–101.

CHARMES-CHAMBERTIN AC See Chambertin AC.

CHASSAGNE-MONTRACHET AC *Côte de Beaune, Burgundy, France* Some of Burgundy's greatest white wine vineyards (part of le MONTRACHET and BATARD-MONTRACHET, all of Criots-Bâtard-Montrachet) are within the village boundary. The white Chassagne Premiers Crus are not as well known, but can offer nutty, toasty wines, especially if aged for 4–8 years. Ordinary white Chassagne-Montrachet is usually enjoyable; the red is a little earthy, peppery and plummy and can be an acquired taste. Look out for reds from the following Premiers Crus: Clos de la Boudriotte, Clos St-Jean and Clos de la Chapelle. Best producers: (whites) F d'Allaines★, G Amiot★★, Blain-Gagnard★★, M Colin★★, Colin-Deléger★★, Fontaine-Gagnard★★, J-N GAGNARD★★, GAGNARD-DELAGRANGE★★, V GIRARDIN★★, F & V Jouard★★, H Lamy★, Duc de Magenta★★, B Morey★★, M Morey★★, M Niellon★★★, RAMONET★★; (reds) G Amiot★★, CARILLON★, R Clerget★, V GIRARDIN★★, B Morey★★, RAMONET★★. Best years: (whites) (2001) 00 99 **98 97** 96 **95 92**; (reds) 1999 98 **97** 06 **95 93 90**.

CHASSELAS Chasselas is considered a table grape worldwide. Only in BADEN (where it is called Gutedel) and Switzerland (called Dorin, Perlan or Fendant) is it thought to make decent light, dry wines with a slight prickle for everyday drinking. A few Swiss examples, such as those from Louis Bovard, rise above this.

CH. CHASSE-SPLEEN★ *Moulis AC, Cru Bourgeois, Haut-Médoc, Bordeaux, France* Chasse-Spleen is not a Classed Growth – but during the 1980s it built a tremendous reputation for ripe, concentrated and powerful wines under the late proprietor, Bernadette Villars. The château is now run by Villars' daughter Céline, and recent vintages have again found the form of the old days. Second wine: l'Ermitage de Chasse-Spleen. Best years: 2000 99 96 **95 94 90 89 88 86 83 82**.

CHÂTEAU-CHALON AC *Jura, France* The most prized – and pricy – *vin jaune*, it is difficult to find, even in the Jura. But if you do find a bottle, beware – the awesome flavour will shock your tastebuds like no other French wine. Not released until 6 years after the vintage, it can be kept for much longer. Best producers: Baud★★, Berthet-Bondet★★, Bourdy★★, Chalandard★★, Credoz★, Durand-Perron★★, J Maclé★★, H Maire★★. Best years: (1994) 93 92 **91 90 89 88 87 85**.

CHÂTEAU-GRILLET AC★★ *Rhône Valley, France* This rare and *very* expensive RHONE white, made from Viognier, has a magic reek of orchard fruit and harvest bloom when young and it can age well. However, it does not warrant a price premium above the top CONDRIEUS, many of which consistently make superior wine. Best years: (2001) 00 **99 98 97 96 95**.

CHATEAU MONTELENA *Napa Valley AVA, California, USA* Napa winery producing well-balanced Chardonnay★★ and a Cabernet★★ that is impressive, if slow to develop. There is also a fascinating, soft Zinfandel-Sangiovese blend, St Vincent★★. Best years: (Chardonnay) (2001) 00 99 **98 97 96 95 94**; (Cabernet) (2000) 99 98 97 96 **95 94 93 92 91 90 87 86 85 84.**

CHATEAU MUSAR *Ghazir, Lebanon* Founded by Gaston Hochar in the 1930s and now run by his Bordeaux-trained son Serge, Musar is famous for having made wine every year bar two (1976 and 84) throughout Lebanon's civil war. From an unlikely blend of Cabernet Sauvignon, Cinsaut and Syrah comes a wine of real, if wildly exotic, character, with sweet, spicy fruit and good aging potential: Hochar says that red Musar★ 'should be drunk at 15 years'. Some recent vintages have not quite lived up to expectations. There is also a rosé, and a white from local grape varieties Obaideh and Merwah – Chardonnay and Sémillon lookalikes respectively. Trial plantings of Merlot may result in a Cinsaut-Merlot blend. Best years: (red) (1998) (97) **96 95 94 93 91 90 89 88**; (white) **1996**.

CHATEAU ST JEAN *Sonoma Valley AVA, California, USA* Once known almost entirely for its range of Chardonnays (Belle Terre★★ and Robert Young★★), St Jean has emerged as a producer of delicious reds including a meritage-style red called Cinq Cepages★★ and a Reserve Merlot★★. Best years: (Chardonnay) (2001) 00 99 **98 97 96 95 94 91 90**; (Cabernet) (2000) 99 97 96 **95 94**.

CHATEAU STE MICHELLE *Washington State, USA* A pioneering winery with an enormous range of wines, including several attractive vineyard-designated Chardonnays★, Cabernet Sauvignons★ and Merlots★, especially Cold Creek Vineyard★★ wines. Good Riesling, both dry and sweet, and increasingly interesting red Meritage★ and white Sauvignon. Partnership with Italy's ANTINORI and Germany's Ernst LOOSEN have produced dark, powerful red Col Solare★, a lovely dry Riesling Eroica★ and a thrilling sweet version, TBA★★★, made in tiny quantities. Best years: (premium reds) 2000 99 98 97 **96 95 94**.

CHÂTEAUNEUF-DU-PAPE AC *Rhône Valley, France* A large vineyard area between Orange and Avignon that used to be one of the most abused of all wine names. Now, much Châteauneuf comes from single estates and deservedly ranks as one of France's top reds. Always get an estate wine, distinguished by the papal coat of arms embossed on the neck of the bottle. Only 5% of Châteauneuf is white. Made mainly from Grenache Blanc, Bourboulenc and Clairette, these wines can be surprisingly good. The top reds, particularly the increasing number of old-vine cuvées, will age for 8 years or more, while the whites are best young. Best producers: (reds) P Autard★★, L Barrot★★, BEAUCASTEL★★★, Beaurenard★★, H Bonneau★★ (Réserve des Célestins★★★), Bois de Boursan★★, Bosquet des Papes★★, Dom. du Caillou★★, les Cailloux★★, Chante Perdrix★★, CHAPOUTIER★★, la Charbonnière★★, G Charvin★★, Clos du Mont Olivet★★, CLOS DES PAPES★★★, Font du Loup★★, FONT DE MICHELLE★★, Fortia★★, la Gardine★★, Grand Tinel★★, la Janasse★★, Marcoux★★, Monpertuis★★, Mont-Redon★★, la Nerthe★★, Pégaü★★, RAYAS★★★, la Roquette★★, Roger Sabon★★, Tardieu-Laurent★★, P Usseglio★★, la Vieille-Julienne★★, Vieux Donjon★★, VIEUX TELEGRAPHE★★★, Villeneuve★★; (whites) BEAUCASTEL★★★, CLOS DES PAPES★★, FONT DE MICHELLE★★, Grand Veneur★★, Marcoux★★, RAYAS★★, St-Cosme★, VIEUX TELEGRAPHE★★. Best years: (reds) (2001) 00 99 98 **97 96 95 94 90 89 88**.

CHARDONNAY

I never thought I'd see myself write this. Yes, we are getting bored with Chardonnay. Not all Chardonnay: there's probably more top Chardonnay being produced right now than ever before. And for millions of wine drinkers the Chardonnay revolution (easy to pronounce, easy to swallow) has only just begun. But in the heart of the wine world – the middle market, where people care about flavour but also care about price – we're getting fed up. Far too much sugary, over-oaked, unrefreshing junk has been dumped into our laps recently, from countries and producers who should know better. Add to this the increasingly desperate dirt-cheap offerings at the rump end of the market, and you'll see why I think the great golden goose of Chardonnay has the carving knife of cynicism and greed firmly held against its neck. It's now the fourth most-planted variety in the world. The next few years will show whether it wishes to be the supremely versatile all-rounder or the sloppy jack of all trades and master of none.

WINE STYLES
France Although a relatively neutral variety if left alone (this is what makes it so suitable as a base wine for top-quality Champagne-method sparkling wine), the grape can ripen in a surprising range of conditions, developing a subtle gradation of flavours going from the sharp apple-core greenness of Chardonnay grown in Champagne or the Loire, through the exciting, bone-dry yet succulent flavours of white Burgundy, to a round, perfumed flavour in Languedoc-Roussillon.

Other regions Italy produces Chardonnay that can be bone dry and lean or fat, spicy and lush. Spain does much the same. California and Australia virtually created their reputations on great, viscous, almost syrupy, tropical fruits and spice-flavoured Chardonnays; the best producers are now moving away from this style. Some of the best New World Chardonnays, dry but ripe and subtly oaked, are coming from South Africa. New Zealand is producing rich, deep, but beautifully balanced Chardonnays, while Chile and Argentina have found it easy to grow and are rapidly learning how to make fine wine from it too. Add Germany, Austria, Canada, New York State, Greece, Slovenia, Moldova, Romania, even China, and you'll see it can perform almost anywhere.

Using oak The reason for all these different flavours lies in Chardonnay's wonderful susceptibility to the winemaker's aspirations and skills. The most important manipulation is the use of the oak barrel for fermenting and aging the wine. Chardonnay is the grape of the great white Burgundies and these are fermented and matured in oak (not necessarily new oak); the effect is to give a marvellous round, nutty richness to a wine that is yet savoury and dry. This is enriched still further by aging the wine on its lees.

The New World winemakers sought to emulate the great Burgundies, planting Chardonnay and employing thousands of oak barrels (mostly new), and their success – and the enthusiasm with which wine drinkers embraced the wine – has caused winemakers everywhere else to see Chardonnay as the perfect variety – easy to grow, easy to turn into wine and easy to sell to an adoring public

BEST PRODUCERS

France *Chablis* J-C Bessin, A & F Boudin, DAUVISSAT, DROIN, Laroche, MICHEL, RAVENEAU; *Côte d'Or* G Amiot, R Ampeau, J-M Boillot, Bonneau du Martray, BOUCHARD, M Bouzereau, CARILLON, COCHE-DURY, Marc Colin, DROUHIN, Arnaud Ente, J-N GAGNARD, GAGNARD-DELAGRANGE, V GIRARDIN, JADOT, F Jobard, R Jobard, LAFON, R Lamy-Pillot, Louis LATOUR, Dom. LEFLAIVE, Bernard Morey, M Niellon, RAMONET, M Rollin, G Roulot, SAUZET, VERGET; *Mâconnais* D & M Barraud, Guffens-Heynen (VERGET), O Merlin, Thévenet, Valette.

Other European Chardonnays

Austria E & M TEMENT, VELICH.

Germany JOHNER, REBHOLZ.

Italy BELLAVISTA, CA' DEL BOSCO, GAJA, LAGEDER, Vie di Romans, Castello della SALA.

Spain ENATE, Manzaneque, TORRES, Señorío de Otazu.

New World Chardonnays

Australia Allandale, CULLEN, Giaconda, GROSSET, HOWARD PARK, LEEUWIN, LENSWOOD, MOUNTADAM, PENFOLDS, PETALUMA, PIERRO, ROSEMOUNT, TYRRELL'S.

New Zealand CLOUDY BAY, DRY RIVER, FELTON ROAD, ISABEL, KUMEU RIVER, MORTON ESTATE, NEUDORF, PEGASUS BAY, SERESIN, TE MATA, VAVASOUR, WITHER HILLS.

USA ARROWOOD, AU BON CLIMAT, BERINGER, CALERA, CHALONE, CHATEAU ST JEAN, FERRARI-CARANO, FLOWERS, KISTLER, MARCASSIN, MATANZAS CREEK, MERRYVALE, Peter MICHAEL, NEWTON, Pahlmeyer, David Ramey, RIDGE, ROCHIOLI, SAINTSBURY, SANFORD, SHAFER, STEELE, TALBOTT.

South Africa BUITENVERWACHTING, GLEN CARLOU, HAMILTON RUSSELL, MEERLUST, MULDERBOSCH, THELEMA, VERGELEGEN.

South America CATENA, CONCHA Y TORO (Amelia), VIÑA CASABLANCA.

101

JEAN-LOUIS CHAVE *Rhône Valley, France* Jean-Louis Chave, son of founder Gérard, has deservedly achieved superstar status in recent years. His red HERMITAGE★★★ is one of the world's great wines, surpassed only by the Cuvée Cathelin★★★, produced only in exceptional years. His wonderful white Hermitage★★★ sometimes even outlasts the reds, as it quietly moves toward its honeyed, nutty zenith. Also produces a small amount of excellent red ST-JOSEPH★★ and an occasional stunning traditional sweet Vin de Paille★★. Expensive, but worth the money. Best years: (reds) (2000) 99 98 97 96 95 94 **92** 91 90 89 **88 86 85 83 82 81 79 78**; (whites) (2000) 99 98 97 96 95 94 **93 92 91 90 89 88 83**.

CHÉNAS AC *Beaujolais, Burgundy, France* The smallest of the BEAUJOLAIS Crus, Chénas wines, usually quite tough when young, benefit from 2 or more years' aging, when they take on chocolaty tones. Best producers: G Braillon★, L Champagnon★, DUBOEUF (Manoir des Journets)★, G Granger★, H Lapierre★, Daniel Robin★, B Santé★. Best years: (2001) **00 99 98 97 96 95**.

CHENIN BLANC One of the most underrated white wine grapes in the world. In the LOIRE VALLEY, where it is also called Pineau de la Loire, it is responsible for the great sweet wines of QUARTS DE CHAUME and BONNEZEAUX, as well as being the variety for VOUVRAY, sweet or dry, and much other Anjou white. It is also the main grape for the Loire sparkling wines. In South Africa, although showing an annual decline, Chenin (also known as Steen) accounts for 21% of the vineyard area and is used for everything from easy-drinking, dryish whites through botrytized desserts to modern barrel-fermented versions, and also for brandy. CALIFORNIA, with a few exceptions like Chappellet, only employs it as a useful blender. New Zealand and Australia have produced good varietal examples.

CH. CHEVAL BLANC★★★ *St-Émilion Grand Cru AC, 1er Grand Cru Classé, Bordeaux, France* Along with AUSONE, the leading ST-ÉMILION estate. Right on the border with POMEROL, it seems to share some of its sturdy richness, but with an extra spice and fruit that is impressively, recognizably unique. An unusually high percentage (60%) of Cabernet Franc can be used in the blend. Best years: 2000 99 98 97 96 95 94 **90 89 88 86 85 83 82**.

CHEVALIER-MONTRACHET AC See Montrachet AC.

DOM. DE CHEVALIER *Pessac-Léognan AC, Cru Classé de Graves Bordeaux, France* This estate, mainly devoted to red, can produce some of Bordeaux's finest wines. The red★★ always starts out dry and tannic but over 10–20 years gains heavenly cedar, tobacco and black currant flavour. The brilliant white★★★ is both fermented and aged in oak barrels; in the best vintages it will still be improving at 15–20 years. Best years: (reds) 2000 99 98 96 95 **90 89 88**; (whites) (2000) 99 98 97 96 95 **94 90 89 88**.

CHEVERNY AC *Loire Valley, France* A little-known area south of Blois. The local speciality is the white Romorantin grape, which makes bone-dry wine under the AC Cour-Cheverny, but the best whites are from Chardonnay. Also pleasant Sauvignon, Pinot Noir and Gamay and a bracing Champagne-method fizz. Drink young. Best producers: Cazin, Cheverny co-op, Courtioux, Gendrier★, Gueritte, Salvard, Sauger, P Tessier/la Desoucherie, Tue-Boeuf★.

CHIANTI DOCG *Tuscany, Italy* The most famous of all Italian wines, but there are many styles, depending on what grapes are used, where they are grown, and by which producer. It can be a light, fresh, easy-drinking red wine, but with a characteristic hint of bitterness, or it can be an intense, structured yet sleek wine in the same league as the best BORDEAUX. The vineyards are scattered over central Tuscany. There are 8 sub-zones: Classico (with its own DOCG), Colli Aretini, Colli Fiorentini, Colli Senesi, Colline Pisane, Montalbano, Montespertoli and Rufina. Sangiovese is the main grape; traditionally it was blended with the red Canaiolo and white Malvasia and Trebbiano. Modern wine-makers often ignored the others, especially the whites, and made Chianti from Sangiovese alone or blended with 10–15% of Cabernet, Merlot or Syrah. The DOCG for CHIANTI CLASSICO sanctions this, and other zones are expected to follow suit. See also Chianti Colli Fiorentini, Chianti Colli Senesi, Chianti Rufina, Super-Tuscans.

CHIANTI CLASSICO DOCG *Tuscany, Italy* The original (if slightly enlarged) CHIANTI zone in the hills between Florence and Siena. Classico has led the trend in making richer, more structured and better-balanced wines. Nonetheless, many producers use their best grapes for high-profile SUPER-TUSCANS. Since the 96 vintage, Classico can be made from 100% Sangiovese; the Riserva may now be aged in barrel for 2 instead of 3 years but must only use red grapes. The finest Riserva wines can improve for a decade or more. Many of the estates also offer regular bottlings of red wine, round and fruity, for drinking about 2–5 years after the harvest. Best producers: (Riservas) Castello di AMA★★, ANTINORI★, Badia a Coltibuono★★, Brancaia★, Cacchiano★, Capaccia★★, Casaloste★★, CASTELLARE★★, Castell'in Villa★, Cecchi (Villa Cerna★), Cennatoio★, Collelungo★★, Colombaio di Cencio★★, Dievole★, Casa Emma★★, FELSINA★★, Le Filigare★, FONTERUTOLI★★★, FONTODI★★, ISOLE E OLENA★★, La Massa★★, Melini★, Monsanto★★, Monte Bernardi★, Il Palazzino★★, Paneretta★★, Panzanello★★, Poggerino★★, Poggiopiano★, Poggio al Sole (Casasilia★★★), Querceto★, QUERCIABELLA★★, Castello di RAMPOLLA★★, RICASOLI (Castello di Brolio★★), RIECINE★★, Rocca di Castagnoli★★, Rocca di Montegrossi★★, RUFFINO★★, San Felice★★, San Giusto a Rentennano★★, San Polo in Rosso★, Terrabianca★, Valtellina★★, Vecchie Terre di Montefili★★, Verrazzano★, Vicchiomaggio★★, Vignamaggio★, Villa Cafaggio★★, VOLPAIA★★. Best years: (2001) 00 **99 98 97 96 95 93 90 88**.

CHIANTI COLLI FIORENTINI *Chianti DOCG, Tuscany, Italy* Colli Fiorentini covers the hills around Florence. The wines traditionally are made to drink young, though some estates make Riservas of real interest. Best producers: Baggiolino★, Le Calvane, Il Corno, Corzano e Paterno★, Lanciola★, Pasolini dall'Onda★, Poppiano★, La Querce, Sammontana, San Vito in Fior di Selva.

CHIANTI COLLI SENESI *Chianti DOCG, Tuscany, Italy* This CHIANTI sub-zone consists of a vast area of Siena province (including the towns of Montalcino, Montepulciano and San Gimignano). Wines range from everyday quaffers to fairly elegant Riservas. Best producers: Campriano, Carpineta Fontalpino★, Casabianca, Casale-Falchini★, Farnetella★, Ficomontanino★, Pacina★, Paradiso★, Pietraserena.

CHIANTI RUFINA *Chianti DOCG, Tuscany, Italy* Smallest of the CHIANTI sub-zones, situated in an enclave of the Apennine mountains to the east of Florence, where wines were noted for exceptional strength, structure and longevity long before they joined the ranks of Chianti.

Today the wines, particularly the long-lived Riserva from SELVAPIANA and Montesodi from the ancient FRESCOBALDI estate of Castello di Nipozzano, match the best of CHIANTI CLASSICO. Pomino is a small (100ha/247-acre) high-altitude zone almost entirely surrounded by Chianti Rufina; dominated by Frescobaldi, it makes greater use of French varieties such as Merlot, Cabernet and Chardonnay. Best producers: (Riservas) Basciano★★, Tenuta di Bossi★, Colognole, FRESCOBALDI★★, Grignano★, Lavacchio★, SELVAPIANA★★, Castello del Trebbio★. Best years: (2001) 00 99 **98 97 96 95 94 93 90 88 86 85**.

MICHELE CHIARLO *Piedmont, Italy* From his winery base south of Asti, Michele Chiarlo produces stylish wines from several PIEDMONT zones. Single-vineyard BAROLOS★★ and BARBARESCOS★ top the list, but BARBERA D'ASTI★ and GAVI★ are reliable, too. Piedmont's new Monferrato DOC embraces Countacc!★, a Nebbiolo-Barbera-Cabernet Sauvignon blend.

CHIMNEY ROCK *Stags Leap District AVA, California, USA* After a shaky start, winemaker Doug Fletcher stepped in to put Chimney Rock on the right track, with powerful yet elegantly shaped Cabernet Sauvignon★★, Reserve Cabernet Sauvignon★★ and a meritage blend called Elevage★★. A tangy Sauvignon Blanc★ is also made. Best years: (Elevage) (2000) (99) 98 97 96 **95 94 92 91 90**.

CHINON AC *Loire Valley, France* Best red wine of the LOIRE VALLEY, made mainly from Cabernet Franc. Full of raspberry fruit and fresh summer earth when young, can improve for 20 years; always worth buying a single-estate wine. Best producers: Philippe Alliet★★, B Baudry★★, J & C Baudry★, P Breton★, Coulaine★, COULY-DUTHEIL★, Delaunay★, DRUET★★, La Grille★, Charles Joguet★, Lenoir★, Moulin à Tan★, Noblaie★, la Perrière★, J-M Raffault★, Olga Raffault★, Rousse★, Sourdais★. Best years: (2001) 00 99 97 96 95 90 89 85 83 82 78 76.

CHIROUBLES AC *Beaujolais, Burgundy, France* Lightest, most delicately fragrant of the BEAUJOLAIS Crus; expensive for only a notionally superior BEAUJOLAIS-VILLAGES. Best producers: Cheysson★, de la Grosse Pierre★, G Passot★, J Passot★. Best years: (2001) 00 99.

CHIVITE *Navarra DO, Navarra, Spain* The longtime leader in wine exports from NAVARRA, owned and run by the Chivite family. The wine is reliable to good but the reds, in particular, could be a bit more lively. The top range is called Colección 125 and includes a red Reserva★, white Blanco★★ made from Chardonnay, and a characterful sweet Vendimia Tardía★★ from Moscatel (Muscat Blanc à Petits Grains).

CHOREY-LÈS-BEAUNE AC *Côte de Beaune, Burgundy, France* One of those tiny, forgotten villages that make good, if not great, Burgundy at prices most of us can still afford, with some committed producers too. Can age for 5–8 years. Best producers: Arnoux Père et Fils★, DROUHIN★, GERMAIN★★, Maillard Père et Fils★, TOLLOT-BEAUT★★. Best years: (2001) 99 **98 97 96 95**.

CHURCHILL *Port DOC, Douro, Portugal* Established in 1981, it was the first new PORT shipper for 50 years. The wines are very good, notably Vintage★★, LBV★, Crusted★★, single-quinta Agua Alta★★ and well-aged quirky dry white ports. Quinta da Gricha (purchased in 1999) is a new source of Vintage port. Also new is a red DOURO table wine. Best years: (Vintage) (2000) 97 94 **91 85**; (Agua Alta) 1998 96 **95 92 87**.

CHURCH ROAD *Hawkes Bay, New Zealand* Church Road (formerly known as The McDonald Winery) is a premium-wine project owned by MONTANA, New Zealand's largest producer. There's a dry but balanced Cabernet Sauvignon-Merlot★ blend and a plummy Reserve Merlot★

Super-premium blend Tom★, first released in 1999, has BORDEAUX-style austerity but good depth. Stylish Reserve Chardonnay★ is rich and smooth with flavours of peach, grapefruit and hazelnut. Best years: (Cabernet Sauvignon-Merlot) 2000 98 **96 95 94**.

CINSAUT Also spelt Cinsault. Found mainly in France's southern RHONE, PROVENCE and the MIDI, giving a light wine with fresh, but rather fleeting, neutral fruit. Popular as a blender in South Africa and Lebanon's CHATEAU MUSAR.

CIRÒ DOC *Calabria, Italy* The fact that this was the wine offered to champions in the ancient Olympics seemed a more potent reason to buy it than for quality. Yet Cirò Rosso, a full-bodied red from the Gaglioppo grape, has improved remarkably of late. New wines, such as Librandi's Gravello★★ (an oak-aged blend with Cabernet), are genuinely exciting. The DOC also covers a dry white from Greco and a rare dry rosé. Best producers: Caparra & Siciliani★, Librandi★ (Riserva★★), San Francesco★. Best years: (reds) (2000) 99 **97 96 95 93**.

BRUNO CLAIR *Marsannay, Côte de Nuits, Burgundy, France* Based in MARSANNAY, Bruno Clair produces a large range of excellent wines from a broad span of vineyards there, as well as in GEVREY-CHAMBERTIN, GIVRY, SAVIGNY and VOSNE-ROMANEE. Most of his wine is red, but there is a small amount of white (CORTON-CHARLEMAGNE★★) and a delicious Marsannay rosé★. Top wines are CHAMBERTIN Clos de Bèze★★★, Gevrey-Chambertin Clos St-Jacques★★★ and vineyard-designated Marsannay reds★★. Best years: (top reds) (2001) 00 99 98 96 **95 93 90**.

CLAIRETTE DE DIE AC *Rhône Valley, France* One of the undeservedly forgotten sparkling wines of France, made from a minimum of 75% Muscat, off-dry with a creamy bubble and an orchard-fresh fragrance. The *méthode Dioise* is used, which preserves the Muscat scent. Drink young. Best producers: Achard-Vincent★, Clairette de Die co-op★, Jacques Faure, Georges Raspail★. See also Crémant de Die.

A CLAPE *Cornas, Rhône Valley, France* The leading estate in CORNAS. Clape's wines★★ are consistently among the best in the RHONE – dense, tannic and full of rich, roasted fruit. Clape also makes fine COTES DU RHONE, both red★ and white★, and decent ST-PERAY★. Best years: (Cornas) (2000) 99 98 97 96 **95 94 92 91 90 89 88 86 85**.

LA CLAPE *Coteaux du Languedoc AC, Languedoc, France* The mountain of La Clape rears unexpectedly from the flat coastal fields south-east of Narbonne. The vineyards here are a Cru within the COTEAUX DU LANGUEDOC AC and produce some of the best Hérault wines. There are excellent whites from Bourboulenc and Clairette, plus some good reds and rosés, mainly from Carignan. The whites and reds can age. Best producers: l'Hospitalet★, Mire l'Étang, Négly, Pech-Céleyran★, Pech Redon★, Vires. Best years: (reds) 2000 99 98 **96 95 93 91 90**.

CLARENDON HILLS *McLaren Vale, South Australia* Controversial MCLAREN VALE winery with a name for high-priced, highly extracted, unfined, unfiltered and unobtainable reds. At the top is single-vineyard Astralis (a controversial ★★★), a hugely concentrated Shiraz from old vines aged in 100% French new oak. Other Shiraz★★ labels offer slightly better value, while Merlot★★ and Cabernet Sauvignon★★ aim to rub shoulders with great red BORDEAUX – although I'm not sure which ones. Several cuvées of Old Vines Grenache★★ are marked by saturated black cherry fruit and high alcohol. Best years: (Astralis) 1998 96 95 **94**.

CLARE VALLEY *South Australia* Historic upland valley north of Adelaide with a deceptively moderate climate, able to grow fine, aromatic Riesling, marvellously textured Semillon, rich, robust Shiraz and Cabernet blends and peppery but voluptuous Grenache. Best producers: (whites) Tim ADAMS★★, Jim BARRY★, Wolf BLASS (Gold Label★★), Leo Buring (Leonay★★), Crabtree, Galah, GROSSET★★★, KNAPPSTEIN★★, LEASINGHAM★, MITCHELL★, Mount Horrocks★★, PETALUMA★★, Pikes; (reds) Tim ADAMS★★, Jim BARRY★★, LEASINGHAM★, MITCHELL★, Pikes★, WENDOUREE★★★. Best years: (Shiraz) (2000) 99 98 **97 96 94 91 90 88 86**; (Riesling) 2001 **00 99 98 97 96 95 94 92 91 90**.

CH. CLARKE *Listrac-Médoc AC, Bordeaux, France* This property had millions spent on it by the late Baron Edmond de Rothschild during the late 1970s, and the wines have reaped the benefit. And from the 98 vintage, leading Bordeaux winemaker Michel Rolland has been consultant enologist. The wines have an attractive blackcurrant fruit, though they never quite escape the typical LISTRAC earthiness. But with a name like Clarke, how could they possibly fail to be seductive? There is also a small production of dry white wine, le Merle Blanc. Best years: 2000 99 98 **96 95 90 89 88**.

DOMENICO CLERICO *Barolo DOCG, Piedmont, Italy* Domenico Clerico has been one of the top BAROLO producers for more than a decade. He produces consistently superlative Barolos (Ciabot Mentin Ginestra★★★, Pajana★★★, Percristina★★★) and one of the best Barberas★ (Trevigne★★), all wonderfully balanced. His range also includes LANGHE Arte★★, a barrique-aged blend of Nebbiolo and Barbera. Best years: (Barolos) (2000) (99) 98 97 96 **95 94 93 92 91 90 89 88**.

CH. CLIMENS★★★ *Barsac AC, 1er Cru Classé, Bordeaux, France* The leading estate in BARSAC, with a deserved reputation for fabulous, sensuous wines, rich and succulent yet streaked with lively lemon acidity. Easy to drink at 5 years, but a good vintage will be richer and more satisfying after 10–15 years. Second wine: les Cyprès (also delicious). Best years: (2001) 99 98 97 **96 95 90 89 88 86 83 76 75**.

CLOS BAGATELLE *St-Chinian AC, Languedoc-Roussillon, France* For long a reference for quality wines in ST-CHINIAN. Now run by siblings Luc and Christine Simon, who produce 5 red cuvées and a MUSCAT DE ST-JEAN-DE-MINERVOIS. Top wine La Gloire de Mon Père★ is made from Syrah, Mourvèdre and Grenache, and aged in 100% new oak barrels; Sélection in only 25%. Unoaked Marie et Mathieu★ is fruit-driven; Cuvée Camille has spicy, herbal aromas; Tradition is a traditional St-Chinian, a Carignan-Cinsaut-Grenache blend.

CLOS DU BOIS *Alexander Valley AVA, California, USA* Winery showcasing gentle, fruit-dominated flavours of SONOMA Chardonnay, Merlot and Cabernet. Top vineyard selections can be exciting, especially the Calcaire★★ and Flintwood★ Chardonnays, as well as the rich, strong Briarcrest Cabernet Sauvignon★★ and Marlstone★★, a red BORDEAUX-style blend. Best years: (reds) (2000) 99 **97 96 95 94 91 90 88 87 86**.

CLOS CENTEILLES *Minervois AC, Languedoc-Roussillon, France* Daniel Domergue and his wife Patricia Boyer are producing excellent MINERVOIS La Livinière and innovative vins de pays. The impressive Clos de Centeilles★★ is their top wine; Capitelle de Centeilles★ and

Carignanissime★ are 100% Cinsaut and Carignan respectively. Best years: 2000 99 98 **97 96 95 94 93**.

CLOS DE LA COULÉE-DE-SERRANT *Savennières AC, Loire Valley, France*
Fine estate of only 7ha (17 acres) which merits its own AC within the boundaries of SAVENNIÈRES. The Joly family runs the property on fervently biodynamic lines and the estate wine★★ is a concentrated, long-lived, very pricy Chenin Blanc with a honeyed, floral bouquet. Also produces better-value Savennières Roche aux Moines★★ and Becherelle★. Best years: 2000 99 **97** 96 **95 93 90 89 88 85 83 82**.

CLOS MOGADOR *Priorat DO, Cataluña, Spain* René Barbier Ferrer was one of the pioneers who relaunched the reputation of PRIORAT in the 80s. The wine★★ is a ripe, intense, brooding monster built to age. He also acts as consultant at nearby Clos Erasmus★★★, where the wine receives extended oak aging. Best years: 1999 98 97 96 **95 94 93 92 91 90**.

DOM. DU CLOS NAUDIN *Vouvray, Loire Valley, France* Philippe Foreau runs this first-rate VOUVRAY domaine. Depending on the vintage, Foreau produces a range of styles: dry★★, medium-dry★★ and sweet★★ (Réserve★★★), as well as Vouvray Mousseux★★ and Pétillant★★. The wines are supremely ageworthy, though in their relative youth are rather softer in style than the more structured Vouvrays of HUET. Best years: (Moelleux Réserve) 1997 96 **95 90 89 88 85 83 78 76 75 70**.

CLOS DES PAPES *Châteauneuf-du-Pape AC, Rhône Valley, France* Paul Avril is one of the outstanding CHATEAUNEUF-DU-PAPE producers. The red★★★ has an unusually high proportion of Mourvèdre (20%), which can give greater structure and complexity and confers potential longevity. Nevertheless, there is enough Grenache to ensure the wine's approachability in its youth and provide an initial blast of fruit. The white★★ takes on the nutty character of aged Burgundy after 5 or 6 years. Best years: (red) (2000) 99 98 97 96 **95 94 93 92 90 89 88 83 81 79**.

CLOS DE LA ROCHE AC *Grand Cru, Côte de Nuits, Burgundy, France* The best and biggest of the 5 MOREY-ST-DENIS Grands Crus. It has a lovely, bright, red-fruits flavour when young, and should become richly chocolaty or gamy with age. Best producers: DROUHIN★★★, DUJAC★★★, Léchenaut★★★, Dom. LEROY★★★, H Lignier★★★, Henri Perrot-Minot★★, Ponsot★★★, ROUSSEAU★★. Best years: (2001) 00 99 98 97 96 95 93 **90 89 88**.

CLOS ST-DENIS AC *Grand Cru, Côte de Nuits, Burgundy, France* This small (6.5ha/16-acre) Grand Cru, which gave its name to the village of MOREY-ST-DENIS, produces wines which are sometimes light, but should be wonderfully silky, with the texture that only great Burgundy, so far, can give. Best after 10 years or more. Best producers: Bertagna★★, Charlopin★★, DUJAC★★★, JADOT★★, Georges Lignier★★, Ponsot★★★. Best years: (2001) 00 99 98 97 96 95 **93 90**.

CLOS UROULAT *Jurançon AC, South-West France* Charles Hours makes stunningly good Jurançon, but in tiny quantities. Dry Cuvée Marie★★ balances ripe fruit with a deliciously refreshing finish. The richly textured sweet Jurançon★★ pulls together lemon, lime, honey and apricot: enjoyable young, but magnificent when aged. Best years: (sweet) 2000 99 **98 96 95 93 90 89**.

CLOS DU VAL *Napa Valley AVA, California, USA* A sometimes overlooked producer of elegant Cabernet Sauvignon★, Chardonnay★ (Reserve★), Merlot★ and Zinfandel★ (Palisade Vineyard★ from STAGS LEAP DISTRICT). The Reserve Cabernet★ can age well. Ariadne★★, a Semillon-Sauvignon Blanc blend, is a lovely aromatic white. Best years: (Reserve Cabernet) (2000) 99 97 96 **95 94 91 90 87 86 85 84**.

CLOS DE VOUGEOT AC *Grand Cru, Côte de Nuits, Burgundy, France*
Enclosed by Cistercian monks in the 14th century, and today a considerable tourist attraction, this large (50ha/125-acre) vineyard is now divided among 82 owners. As a result of this division, Clos de Vougeot has become one of the most unreliable Grand Cru Burgundies; the better wine tends to come from the upper and middle parts. When it is good it is wonderfully fleshy, turning dark and exotic after 10 years or more. Best producers: B Ambroise★★★, Amiot-Servelle★★, Chopin-Groffier★★★, J-J Confuron★★★, R Engel★★★, FAIVELEY★★, GRIVOT★★★, Anne Gros★★★, Haegelen-Jayer★, JADOT★★★, Dom. LEROY★★★, MEO-CAMUZET★★★, D Mortet★★★, Mugneret-Gibourg★★★, Raphet★★, Vougeraie★★. Best years: (2001) 00 99 98 97 96 95 93 **91 90 88**.

CLOUDY BAY *Marlborough, South Island, New Zealand* New Zealand's most successful winery, Cloudy Bay achieved cult status with the first release of its zesty, herbaceous Sauvignon Blanc★★ in 1985. New and very different Sauvignon Blanc Te Koko★★ is a rich, creamy, oak-matured, bottle-aged wine. Cloudy Bay also makes Chardonnay★★, a late-harvest Riesling★★, Pinot Noir★ and vintage Pelorus★★, a high-quality old-style Champagne-method fizz. First releases of non-vintage Pelorus★★ are excellent. Best years: (Sauvignon Blanc) **2001 00 99 97 96**.

J-F COCHE-DURY *Meursault, Côte de Beaune, Burgundy, France* Jean-François Coche-Dury is a modest superstar, quietly turning out some of the finest wines on the COTE DE BEAUNE. His best wines are his CORTON-CHARLEMAGNE★★★ and MEURSAULT Perrières★★★, but everything he makes is excellent, even his BOURGOGNE Blanc★★. His red wines, from VOLNAY★★ and MONTHELIE★, tend to be significantly cheaper than the whites and should be drunk younger, too. Best years: (whites) (2001) 00 99 97 96 95 **92 90 89**.

COCKBURN *Port DOC, Douro, Portugal* Best known for its Special Reserve ruby, Cockburns has much more than that to offer. Cockburns Vintage★★ is stylishly cedary and Quinta dos Canais★★ is a fine single quinta, while the aged tawnies★★ are famously refined and nutty. Best years: (Vintage) (2000) 97 94 **91 83 70 67 63 60 55**; (dos Canais) 1995 **92**.

CODORNÍU *Cava DO, Cataluña, Spain* The biggest Champagne-method sparkling wine company in the world. Anna de Codorníu★ and Jaume Codorníu★ are especially good, but all the sparklers are better than the CAVA average. Drink young for freshness. Codorníu also owns the RAIMAT estate in COSTERS DEL SEGRE, Masía Bach in the PENEDES and Bodegas Bilbaínas in RIOJA, and has purchased 25% of Scala Dei in PRIORAT. It also owns the quality-conscious California winery Artesa and a new winery in Argentina, Septima.

COLCHAGUA, VALLE DE *Rapel, Chile* RAPEL sub-region and home to many exciting estates, such as the acclaimed Apalta vineyard, where CASA LAPOSTOLLE, MONTES and others have plantings. Merlot, Syrah and Carmenère do very well here. San Fernando and Chimbarongo are the best-known sub-zones. Best producers: CASA LAPOSTOLLE★★, Casa Silva★★, CONO SUR★★, MONTES★, MONT GRAS★, Viu Manent★.

COLDSTREAM HILLS *Yarra Valley, Victoria, Australia* Founded by Australian wine guru James Halliday, Coldstream Hills has been owned by Southcorp since 1996. Standards remain high: Halliday keeps a close eye on winemaking. Pinot Noir★ is consistently good (Reserve★★): sappy and smoky with cherry fruit and clever use of all-

French oak. Chardonnay★ (Reserve★★) has subtlety and delicacy but real depth as well. Reserve Cabernet★ is good, though not always ripe. Best years: (Reserve Pinot Noir) **1998 97 96 94 92 88**.

COLLARDS *Henderson, Auckland, New Zealand*
White wine is the greatest strength of this small family winery, including Rothesay Chardonnay★ and Sauvignon Blanc★, HAWKES BAY Chardonnay★, and MARLBOROUGH Chardonnay★, Sauvignon★ and Riesling★. The dry Chenin Blanc★ is one of New Zealand's better examples. Red wines are less interesting, with the exception of light, fruity Marlborough Queen Charlotte Pinot Noir. Best years: (Chardonnay) (2001) 00 **99 98 96 94**.

COLLI BOLOGNESI DOC *Emilia-Romagna, Italy*
Wines from this zone in the Apennine foothills near Bologna were traditionally slightly sweet and frothy in style. Today some winemaking concessions have begun to be made to international taste, resulting in fine Cabernets★★ from Bonzara and Terre Rosse. Other good red wines are produced from Merlot, and increasing amounts of dry white wine are made from Sauvignon, Pignoletto and Pinot Bianco. Best producers: Bonzara (Cabernet★, Merlot★), Santarosa★, Terre Rosse★★, Vallona★. Best years: (reds) 2000 99 98 **97 96 95 94 93**.

COLLI EUGANEI DOC *Veneto, Italy* The sheer hills south of Padova produce an array of DOC wines, still and sparkling, that are mainly taken lightly. One serious exception is the Vignalta estate, for Merlot-Cabernet blend Gemola★★. Best producers: Ca' Lustra★, Vignalta★★, Villa Sceriman. Best years: (reds) 2000 99 98 **97 95 94 93 90**.

COLLI ORIENTALI DEL FRIULI DOC *Friuli-Venezia Giulia, Italy* This DOC covers 20 different types of wine. Best known are the sweet whites from Verduzzo in the Ramandolo sub-zone and the delicate Picolit, but it is the reds, from the indigenous Refosco and Schioppettino, as well as imports like Cabernet and dry whites, from Tocai, Ribolla, Pinot Bianco and Malvasia Istriana, that show how exciting the wines can be. Prices are high. Best producers: Ca' Ronesca★, Dario Coos★, Dorigo★, Dri★, Le Due Terre★★, Livio FELLUGA★★, Walter Filiputti★, Adriano Gigante★, Livon★, Meroi★, Miani★, Davide Moschioni★★, Rocca Bernarda★, Rodaro★, Ronchi di Cialla★, Ronchi di Manzano★★, Ronco del Gnemiz★★, Scubla★, Specogna★, Le Vigne di Zamò★★, Zof★. Best years: (whites) (2001) **00 99 98 97**.

COLLI PIACENTINI DOC *Emilia-Romagna, Italy* Home to some of Emilia-Romagna's best wines, this DOC covers 11 different types, the best of which are Cabernet Sauvignon and the red Gutturnio (a blend of Barbera and Bonarda) as well as the medium-sweet white and bubbly Malvasia. Best producers: Luretta★, Lusenti, Castello di Luzzano/Fugazza★, Il Poggiarello★, La Stoppa★ (Cabernet★★), Torre Fornello★, La Tosa (Cabernet Sauvignon★). Best years: (reds) (2001) 00 **99 98 97 96 95 94**.

COLLINES RHODANIENNES, VIN DE PAYS DES *Rhône Valley, France*
Region between Vienne and Valence. The best wines are varietal Gamay and Syrah, although there are some good juicy Merlots, too. Best producers: COLOMBO★, P Gaillard★, Pochon★, ST-DESIRAT co-op, TAIN-L'HERMITAGE co-op, Vernay★, les Vins de Vienne (Sotanum)★★. Best years: (reds) (2001) 00 **99 98 97**.

COLLIO DOC *Friuli-Venezia Giulia, Italy* These hills are the home of some of Italy's best and most expensive dry white wines. The zone produces 19 types of wine, including 17 varietals, which range from the local Tocai and Malvasia Istriana to international types. The best white and red wines are ageworthy. Best producers: Borgo Conventi★, Borgo del Tiglio★★, La Castellada★, Damijan★, Livio FELLUGA★★, Marco Felluga★, Fiegl★, GRAVNER★★★, JERMANN★★, Edi Keber★, Renato Keber★★, Livon★, Matijaz Tercic★, Primosic★, Princic★, Puiatti★, Russiz Superiore★, SCHIOPETTO★★, Venica & Venica★★, Villanova★, Villa Russiz★★. Best years: (whites) (2001) 00 **99 98 97 96 95**.

COLLIOURE AC *Roussillon, France* This tiny fishing port tucked away in the Pyrenean foothills only a few miles from the Spanish border is also an AC, and makes a throat-warming red wine that is capable of aging for a decade but is marvellously rip-roaring when young. Best producers: (reds) Baillaury★, Casa Blanca, Cellier des Templiers★, Clos des Paulilles★, Mas Blanc★★, la RECTORIE★★, la Tour Vieille★, Vial Magnères★. Best years: 2000 99 **98 96 95 94 93 91 90**.

COLOMBARD In France, Colombard traditionally has been distilled to make Armagnac and Cognac, but has now emerged as a table wine grape in its own right, notably as a Vin de Pays des COTES DE GASCOGNE. At its best, it has a lovely, crisp acidity and fresh, aromatic fruit. The largest plantings of the grape are in CALIFORNIA, where it generally produces rather less distinguished wines. South Africa can produce attractive basic wines and Australia also has some fair examples.

JEAN-LUC COLOMBO *Cornas AC, Rhône Valley, France* Colombo is a modernist who has caused controversy with his criticism of traditional methods. His powerful, rich CORNAS has far less tannic grip than some. Top cuvées are les Ruchets★★ and the lush late-harvest la Louvée★★, made in tiny quantities. Among négociant wines now produced, CHATEAUNEUF-DU-PAPE les Bartavelles★, red HERMITAGE★★ and the white Hermitage le Rouet★★ stand out, although some lesser labels don't always seem fully ripe. Also produces fragrant ST-PERAY la Belle de Mai★★, good COTES DU RHONE★ and vins de pays from the RHONE and ROUSSILLON. Best years: (Cornas) (2000) 99 98 **97 95 94 91 90 88**.

COLUMBIA CREST *Washington State, USA* Columbia Crest started life as a second label for CHATEAU STE MICHELLE but has evolved into a full-scale producer of good-value, good-quality wines. Grand Estates Merlot★ and Grand Estates Chardonnay★ are strong suits. For fruit intensity, drink both with 2–3 years' age. There is also a promising, intense Syrah★. Best years: (Grand Estates reds) (2000) (99) 98.

COLUMBIA VALLEY AVA *Washington State, USA* The largest of WASHINGTON's viticultural regions, covering a third of the landmass in the state and encompassing both the YAKIMA VALLEY and WALLA WALLA regions. It produces 98% of the state's wine grapes: Merlot is the most widely planted variety, with Cabernet Sauvignon and Chardonnay following close behind. Best producers: ANDREW WILL★★, CHATEAU STE MICHELLE★★, COLUMBIA CREST★, Matthews Cellars★★, QUILCEDA CREEK★★. Best years: (reds) 2000 99 98 97 **96**.

COLUMBIA WINERY *Columbia Valley AVA, Washington State, USA* Under the guidance of David Lake MW, Columbia produces an assortment of decent wines along with several standouts from Red Willow Vineyard. The best include deeply fruited, built-to-last Cabernet Sauvignon★ and a fruity, smoky-styled Syrah★★. Merlot★ has improved in recent vintages. Best years: (Red Willow reds) (1999) 98 97 **95**.

COMMANDARIA *Cyprus* Dark brown, treacly wine made from red Mavro and white Xynisteri grapes, sun-dried for 2 weeks before vinification and solera aging. Pretty decent stuff but only potentially one of the world's great rich wines. A lighter, drier style is also produced.

CONCA DE BARBERÁ DO *Cataluña, Spain* Quality wine area, but most of its production is sold to CAVA producers. Cool climate here is ideal and TORRES grows excellent Chardonnay, Cabernet Sauvignon, Pinot Noir, Merlot and Tempranillo. Best producers: Sanstravé (Gasset Chardonnay★), TORRES (Milmanda★★, Grans Muralles★★).

CONCHA Y TORO *Maipo, Chile* Chile's biggest winery has 3200ha (7900 acres) of vineyards and the talented Ignacio Recabarren (ex-VIÑA CASABLANCA) behind some of its excellent wines. Top whites include Amelia★★ and Terrunyo★★ Chardonnays and Terrunyo Sauvignon Blanc★. Don Melchor Cabernet Sauvignon★★ leads the reds, along with spicy Terrunyo Cabernet Sauvignon★★ – and keep an eye on Terrunyo Carmenère★★. Revitalized Marqués de Casa Concha★ range is also exciting. See also Almaviva.

CONDRIEU AC *Rhône Valley, France* Because of the demand for this wonderfully fragrant wine made entirely from Viognier, Condrieu is decidedly expensive. But quality, from the single domaines at least, is becoming more consistent. Condrieu is a sensation everyone should try at least once, but make sure you choose a good producer. Best drunk young. Best producers: Gilles Barge★★, P & C Bonnefond★★, du Chêne★★, L Chèze★★, COLOMBO★★, CUILLERON★★★, DELAS★★, P Dumazet★★, C Facchin★★, Y Gangloff★★, GUIGAL★★★, Monteillet★★, Niéro★, A Paret★★, A Perret★★★, C Pichon★★, ROSTAING★★, St-Cosme★★, G Vernay★★, F Villard★★. Best years: **2001 00 99 98**.

CONO SUR *Rapel, Chile* Dynamic sister winery to CONCHA Y TORO, whose Chimbarongo Pinot Noir★ put both grape and region on the Chilean map. The new, partly CASABLANCA-sourced 20 Barrels Pinot★★ is rich and perfumed and the 20 Barrels Limited Edition★★ is positively unctuous. Reserva Merlot★★ and Cabernet Sauvignon★★, under both 20 Barrels and Visión labels, are excellent. Isla Negra offers drier, leaner, more 'European' flavours.

CH. LA CONSEILLANTE★★ *Pomerol AC, Bordeaux, France* Elegant, exotic, velvety wine that blossoms beautifully after 5–6 years but can age much longer. Best years: 2000 99 98 96 **95 94 90 89 88 86 85**.

CONSTANTIA WO *South Africa* The historical heart of South African wine: Groot Constantia, KLEIN CONSTANTIA and BUITENVERWACHTING form part of Simon van der Stel's original 1685 land grant. STEENBERG was also one of the earliest wine farms. Despite the crowding of upmarket houses, vying for space with vineyards, there are several new names springing up along these famous slopes. Sauvignon Blanc has thrust this cool-climate area into the limelight, but Chardonnays are good and Steenberg succeeds with reds. Klein Constantia makes a fortified wine based on the 18th-century Constantia. Best producers: BUITENVERWACHTING★, Constantia-Uitsig★, KLEIN CONSTANTIA★, STEENBERG★★. Best years: (whites) **2001 00 99 98 97**.

ALDO CONTERNO *Barolo DOCG, Piedmont, Italy* Arguably BAROLO's finest producer. He makes good Dolcetto d'Alba★, excellent BARBERA D'ALBA Conca Tre Pile★★, a barrique-aged LANGHE Nebbiolo Il Favot★★, blended red Quartetto★★ and 2 Langhe Chardonnays, unoaked

111

Printaniè and Bussia d'Or★, fermented and aged in new wood. Pride of the range, though, are his Barolos from the hill of Bussia. In top vintages he produces Barolos Vigna Colonello★★★, Vigna Cicala★★★ and excellent Granbussia★★★, as well as a blended regular Barolo called Bussia Soprana★★. All these Barolos, though accessible when young, need several years to show their true majesty, but retain a remarkable freshness. Best years: (Barolo) (2000) 99 98 97 96 **95 93 90 89 88 86 85 82**.

GIACOMO CONTERNO *Barolo DOCG, Piedmont, Italy* Aldo's elder brother Giovanni has always taken a more traditional approach to winemaking. His flagship wine is BAROLO Monfortino★★★ (only released after some 6 or 7 years in large oak barrels) but Barolo Cascina Francia★★★ is also superb. Powerful, earthy Dolcetto d'Alba★ and BARBERA D'ALBA★ are also made. Best years: (Monfortino) (1995) 90 89 88 **87 86 85 82 79 78 74 71**.

CONTINO *Rioja DOC, Rioja, Spain* An estate on some of the finest RIOJA land, half-owned by CVNE. The wines, including a Reserva★, a single-vineyard Viña del Olivo★★ and an innovative Graciano★ varietal, are made by CVNE. Skipped the 92 and 93 vintages to solve cellar problems. Best years: (Reserva) **1996 95 94 86 85**.

COONAWARRA *South Australia* On a flat limestone belt thinly veneered with terra rossa soil, Coonawarra can produce sublime Cabernet with blackcurrant leafy flavours and spicy Shiraz that age for years. Chardonnay and Riesling can be good. An export-led boom has seen hundreds of new vineyards planted, many of which are outside the legendary terra rossa strip. In view of some disappointing light reds, and a hotly contested boundary dispute, I wonder if Coonawarra's great reputation is not at risk. Best producers: Balnaves, BRAND'S★, BOWEN★, HOLLICK★, KATNOOK★, LECONFIELD★, LINDEMANS★★, Majella★★, ORLANDO★, PARKER★, PENFOLDS★★, PENLEY★★, PETALUMA★★★, ROSEMOUNT★, WYNNS★★, Zema★★. Best years: (Cabernet Sauvignon) (2000) 99 98 97 **96 94 92 91 90 88 86**.

COOPERS CREEK *Auckland, New Zealand* A specialist in wines from HAWKES BAY and MARLBOROUGH grapes, and successful producer of Chardonnay★, especially Swamp Reserve Chardonnay★, and tangy Marlborough Sauvignon Blanc★. Dry Riesling★ and Late Harvest Riesling★★ styles are also good. A smart range of Reserve reds from Hawkes Bay includes complex Merlot★ and elegant Cabernet Sauvignon★. Best years: (Chardonnay) 2000 **99 98**.

CORBANS *Auckland, Gisborne and Marlborough,*  *New Zealand* New Zealand's second-largest wine company was bought by the largest, MONTANA, in 2000. Brands include Cooks, Stoneleigh, Longridge, Huntaway and Robard & Butler. Stoneleigh Sauvignon Blanc★ shows good MARLBOROUGH style but Stoneleigh Riesling★★ is a more exciting example. Private Bin Chardonnay★, Noble Riesling★★ and Merlot★ are good, small-production wines. There's a consistently good Champagne-method sparkler called Amadeus★. Flagship wines from all major wine regions are now produced under the Cottage Block label.

CORBIÈRES AC *Languedoc, France* This huge AC now produces some of the best reds in the LANGUEDOC, with juicy fruit and more than a hint of wild hillside herbs. Excellent young, wines from the best estates can age for years. White Corbières is adequate – drink as young as possible. Best producers: (reds) Baillat★, Bel Eveque★, Caraguilhes★, Ch. Cascadais★, Étang des Colombes★, Fontsainte★, Grand Crès★, Grand Moulin★, Haut-Gléon, Hélène★, l'Ille★, LASTOURS★, Mansenoble★, MONT TAUCH co-op★, les Palais★, St-Auriol★, Vaugelas★, VOULTE-GASPARETS★. Best years: (reds) 2000 **99 98 96 95 93**.

CORNAS AC *Rhône Valley, France* Northern Rhône's up-and-coming star, whose wines are especially attractive since those of neighbouring HERMITAGE and COTE-ROTIE have spiralled upward in price recently. When young, the wine is a thick, impenetrable red, almost black in the ripest years. Most need 10 years' aging. Best producers: ALLEMAND★★, R Balthazar★★, CLAPE★★, COLOMBO★★, Courbis★★, DELAS★★, E & J Durand★★, Fauterie★, JABOULET★, J Lemenicier★, LIONNET/Rochepertuis★★, TAIN L'HERMITAGE co-op★, Tardieu-Laurent★, Tunnel★★, VERSET★★, A Voge★. Best years: (2001) 00 99 98 97 **96 95 94 91 90 89 88 85 83**.

CORSE AC, VIN DE *Corsica, France* Overall AC for Corsica with 5 superior sub-regions: Calvi, Cap Corse, Figari, Porto Vecchio and Sartène. Ajaccio and Patrimonio are entitled to their own ACs. The most distinctive wines, mainly red, come from local grapes (Nielluccio and Sciacarello for reds, Vermentino for whites). There are some rich sweet Muscats – especially from Muscat de Cap Corse. Best producers: Arena★, Catarelli★, Clos d'Alzeto★, Clos Capitoro, Clos Culombu★, Clos Landry★, Clos Nicrosi★, Gentile★, Leccia★, Maestracci★, Orenga de Gaffory★, Comte Peraldi★, Renucci★.

CORSICA *France* This Mediterranean island has made some pretty dull and undistinguished wines in the past. The last decade has seen a welcome trend toward quality, with co-ops and local growers investing in better equipment and planting noble grape varieties – such as Syrah, Merlot, Cabernet Sauvignon and Mourvèdre for reds, and Chardonnay and Sauvignon Blanc for whites – to complement the local Nielluccio, Sciacarello and Vermentino. Whites and rosés are pleasant for drinking young; reds are more exciting and can age for 3–4 years. See also Corse AC.

CORTES DE CIMA *Alentejo, Portugal* Dane Hans Kristian Jørgensen and his American wife Carrie make excellent modern-style Portuguese reds in the heart of the ALENTEJO. Local grape varieties – Aragonez (Tempranillo), Trincadeira and Periquita – are used for spicy, fruity Chaminé★, oaked red Cortes de Cima★ and a splendid dark, smoky Reserva★★. A little Cabernet, Touriga and Syrah are also grown, the latter for Incógnito★★, a promising gutsy, black-fruited blockbuster. Best years: (2001) 00 **99 98 97**.

CORTESE White grape variety planted primarily in south-eastern PIEDMONT in Italy; it can produce good, fairly acidic, dry whites. Sometimes labelled simply as Cortese del Piemonte, it is also used for GAVI.

CORTON AC *Grand Cru, Côte de Beaune, Burgundy, France* This is the only red Grand Cru in the COTE DE BEAUNE and ideally the wines should have the burliness and savoury power of the top COTE DE NUITS wines, combined with the more seductively perfumed fruit of Côte de Beaune. Red Corton should take 10 years to mature, but too many modern examples never make it. Very little white Corton is made. Best producers: B Ambroise★★, Bonneau du Martray★★, CHANDON DE

BRIAILLES★★★, Dubreuil-Fontaine★★, FAIVELEY★★, Guyon★★, JADOT★★★, Dom. LEROY★★★, MEO-CAMUZET★★★, Rapet★★, Senard★★, TOLLOT-BEAUT★★★. Best years: (reds) (2001) 00 99 98 **97** 96 95 **93 91 90 89 88**.

CORTON-CHARLEMAGNE AC *Grand Cru, Côte de Beaune, Burgundy, France* Corton-Charlemagne, at the top of the famous Corton hill, is the largest of Burgundy's white Grands Crus. It can produce some of the most impressive white Burgundies – rich, buttery and nutty with a fine mineral quality. The best show their real worth only at 10 years or more. Best producers: B Ambroise★★, Bonneau du Martray★★★, BOUCHARD PERE ET FILS★★, Champy★★, CHANDON DE BRIAILLES★★★, COCHE-DURY★★★, DROUHIN★★, FAIVELEY★★, V Girardin★★★, JADOT★★, LATOUR★★, Rapet★★, Rollin★★★, ROUMIER★★, TOLLOT-BEAUT★★★, VERGET★★. Best years: (2001) 00 99 98 97 96 95 **92 90 89**.

CH. COS D'ESTOURNEL★★★ *St-Estèphe AC, 2ème Cru Classé, Haut-Médoc, Bordeaux, France* Top name in ST-ESTEPHE, and one of the leading châteaux in all Bordeaux. Despite a high proportion of Merlot (just under 40%), the wine is classically made for aging and usually needs 10 years to show really well. Recent vintages have been dark, brooding and packed with long-term potential. Second wine: les Pagodes de Cos. Best years: 2000 99 98 97 96 95 **94 93 90 89 88 86 85 83 82**.

COSTANTI *Brunello di Montalcino DOCG, Tuscany, Italy* One of the original, highly respected Montalcino estates, run by Andrea Costanti, making first-rate BRUNELLO★★ and Rosso★★, as well as a tasty partially barrique-aged Sangiovese called Vermiglio★. The archetypal Brunello of this zone is austere, elegant and long-lived, epitomized by the Costanti Riserva★★. New Calbello wines from the hill of Montosoli include excellent Rosso★★ and promising Merlot-Cabernet blend Ardingo★★. Best years: (Brunello) 1997 95 94 93 **91** 90 **88 86 85 82**.

COSTERS DEL SEGRE DO *Cataluña, Spain* DO created for the RAIMAT estate near Lleida in western CATALUNA. A great array of grape varieties is grown, with the accent on French varieties. Quality is generally good and prices moderate. Best producers: Celler de Cantonella★★, Castell del Remei★★, RAIMAT★. Best years: (reds) (2000) 99 **98 96** 95 94.

COSTIÈRES DE NÎMES AC *Languedoc, France* Improving AC between Nîmes and Arles. The reds are generally bright and perfumed, rosés are good young gluggers. Only a little white is produced, usually tasty versions of Marsanne and Roussanne. Best producers: l'Amarine★, Grande Cassagne★, Mas des Bressades★, Mas Carlot, Mourgues du Grès★, Nages★, la Tuilerie★. Best years: 2001 00 **99 98 96** 95 94 93.

CÔTE DE BEAUNE *Côte d'Or, Burgundy, France* Southern part of the COTE D'OR; beginning at the hill of Corton, north of the town of BEAUNE, the Côte de Beaune progresses south as far as les Maranges, with white wines gradually taking over from red.

CÔTE DE BEAUNE AC *Côte de Beaune, Burgundy, France* Small AC for reds and white Burgundy, high on the hill above the city of Beaune, named to ensure confusion with the title for the whole region. Best producers: Allexant, Vougeraie★.

CÔTE DE BEAUNE-VILLAGES AC *Côte de Beaune, Burgundy, France* Red wine AC covering 16 villages, such as AUXEY-DURESSES, LADOIX, MARANGES. Most producers use their own village name, but if the wine is a blend from several villages it is sold as Côte de Beaune-Villages. It can also cover the red wine production of mainly white wine villages such as MEURSAULT. Best producers: DROUHIN★, J-P Fichet★, JADOT★. Best years: 1999 **98 97 96** 95.

CÔTE DE BROUILLY AC *Beaujolais, Burgundy, France*   A steep hill in the middle of the BROUILLY AC, producing extra-ripe grapes. The wine is good young but can age well for several years. Best producers: Conroy★, H Fessy★, Lacondemine★, J-C Pivot★, O Ravier★, Ch. Thivin (Geoffray)★★, Viornery★. Best years: (2001) 00 **99 98**.

CÔTE CHALONNAISE   See Bourgogne-Côte Chalonnaise.

CÔTE DE NUITS *Côte d'Or, Burgundy, France*   This is the northern part of the great CÔTE D'OR and is *not* an AC. Almost entirely red wine country, the vineyards start in the southern suburbs of Dijon and continue south in a narrow swath to below the town of NUITS-ST-GEORGES. The villages are some of the greatest wine names in the world – GEVREY-CHAMBERTIN, VOUGEOT and VOSNE-ROMANÉE etc.

CÔTE DE NUITS-VILLAGES AC *Côte de Nuits, Burgundy, France*   This AC is specific to the villages of Corgoloin, Comblanchien and Prémeaux in the south of the CÔTE DE NUITS and Brochon and FIXIN in the north. Although not much seen, the wines (mostly red) are often good, not very deep in colour but with a nice cherry fruit. Best producers: (reds) D Bachelet★, Chopin-Groffier★, J-J Confuron, JADOT, JAYER-GILLES★, RION★, P Rossignol★. Best years: (reds) (2000) 99 98 **97 96 95**.

CÔTE D'OR *Burgundy, France*   Europe's most northern great red wine area and also the home of some of the world's best dry white wines. The name, meaning 'golden slope', refers to a 48-km (30-mile) stretch between Dijon and Chagny which divides into the CÔTE DE NUITS in the north and the CÔTE DE BEAUNE in the south.

CÔTE ROANNAISE AC *Loire Valley, France*   In the upper Loire; the nearest large town is Lyon, the capital of BEAUJOLAIS, and so it is logical that the chief grape variety here is Gamay. Most of the wine produced is red and should generally be drunk young. Best producers: A Baillon, J-C Chaucesse, Demon★, Lapandéry, M Lutz, J Plasse, R Sérol, P & J-M Vial.

CÔTE-RÔTIE AC *Rhône Valley, France*   The Côte-Rôtie, or 'roasted slope', produces one of France's greatest red wines. The Syrah grape bakes to super-ripeness on these steep slopes, and the small amount of white Viognier sometimes included in the blend gives an unexpected exotic fragrance. Lovely young, it is better aged for 10 years. Best producers: G Barge★★, P & C Bonnefond★★, Bonserine★, B Burgaud★★, Clusel-Roch★★, CUILLERON★★, DELAS★★, Duclaux★★, Gallet★★, V Gasse★★, J-M Gerin★, GUIGAL★★, JAMET★★★, Jasmin★★, M Ogier★, ROSTAING★★, Tardieu-Laurent★★, Vidal-Fleury★★, F Villard★, Vins de Vienne★★. Best years: (2001) 00 99 98 97 **96 95 94 91 90 89 87 85**.

COTEAUX D'AIX-EN-PROVENCE AC *Provence, France*   This AC was the first in the south to acknowledge that Cabernet Sauvignon can enormously enhance the traditional local grape varieties such as Grenache, Cinsaut, Mourvèdre, Syrah and Carignan. The red wines produced here can age. Some quite good fresh rosé is made, while the white wines, mostly still traditionally made, are pleasant but hardly riveting. Best producers: Ch. Bas★, les Bastides★, des Béates★★, Calissanne★, Fonscolombe★, des Gavelles★, Revelette★, Vignelaure★. Best years: (reds) (2001) 00 **99 98 97 96 95 94 93 90**.

COTEAUX DE L'ARDÈCHE, VIN DE PAYS DES *Rhône Valley, France*   Wines from the southern part of the Ardèche. Look out for the increasingly good varietal red wines made from Cabernet Sauvignon, Syrah, Merlot or Gamay and dry, fresh white wines from Chardonnay, Viognier or Sauvignon Blanc. Best producers: Colombier, Louis LATOUR, Pradel, ST-DESIRAT co-op, les Vignerons Ardèchois.

COTEAUX DE L'AUBANCE AC *Loire Valley, France*   Smallish AC parallel to the COTEAUX DU LAYON AC. It is enjoying a renaissance for its sweet or semi-sweet white wines made from Chenin Blanc. Sweet styles can improve for 10–25 years. Best producers: Bablut★★, Charbotières★, Haute Perche★, Montgilet/V Lebreton★★, RICHOU★★, Rochelles/J-Y Lebreton, la Varière★. Best years: (2001) 00 99 **97 96 95 93 90**.

COTEAUX CHAMPENOIS AC *Champagne, France*   The AC for still wines from Champagne. Fairly acid with a few exceptions, notably from BOUZY and Ay. The best age for 5 years or more. Best producers: Bara★, BOLLINGER★, Egly-Ouriet★, LAURENT-PERRIER, Joseph PERRIER, Ch. de Saran★ (MOET & CHANDON). Best years: (1999) 98 96 **95 90 89**.

COTEAUX DU LANGUEDOC AC *Languedoc, France*   A large and increasingly successful AC situated between Montpellier and Narbonne in the LANGUEDOC, producing around 60 million bottles of beefy red and tasty rosé wines. Eleven of the best villages (crus) can now add their own names to the AC name, including Cabrières, la CLAPE, Montpeyroux, PIC ST-LOUP, St-Drézery and St-Georges-d'Orques. Best producers: Abbaye de Valmagne, l'Aiguelière★★, Aupilhac★, Calage★, Cazeneuve★, Clavel★, la Coste★, l'HORTUS★, Jougla★, Lascaux★, MAS BRUGUIERE★, Mas des Chimères★, MAS JULLIEN★, Lavabre★, Mas de Mortiès★, PEYRE ROSE★★, PRIEURÉ DE ST-JEAN DE BÉBIAN★★, Puech-Haut★, St-Martin de la Garrigue★, Terre Megère★. Best years: 2001 00 **99 98 96 95 93 91 90**.

COTEAUX DU LAYON AC *Loire Valley, France*   Sweet wine from the Layon Valley south of Angers. The wine is made from Chenin Blanc grapes that, ideally, are attacked by noble rot. In great years like 1990 and 89, and from a talented grower, this can be one of the world's exceptional sweet wines. Seven villages are entitled to use the Coteaux du Layon-Villages AC (one of the best is Chaume) and put their own name on the label, and these wines are definitely underpriced for the quality. Two sub-areas, BONNEZEAUX and QUARTS DE CHAUME, have their own ACs. Best producers: P Aquilas★★, P Baudouin★★★, BAUMARD★★, Bergerie★★, Bidet★, Breuil★, Cady★★, P Delesvaux★★★, Forges★★, Guimonière (Fesles)★★, Ogereau★★, Passavant★★, Pierre-Bise★★, J Pithon★★★, J Renou★★, Roulerie (Fesles)★★, Sablonettes★★, Sauveroy★, Soucherie/P-Y Tijou★★, Yves Soulez★★, Touche Noire★. Best years: (2001) 00 99 **97 96 95 90 89 88 85 83 76**.

COTEAUX DU LYONNAIS AC *Burgundy, France*   Good, light, BEAUJOLAIS-style reds and a few whites and rosés from scattered vineyards between Villefranche and Lyon. Drink young.

COTEAUX DU TRICASTIN AC *Rhône Valley, France*   From the southern Drôme these are bright, fresh reds and rosés with attractive juicy fruit. Only a little of the nutty white is made but is worth looking out for. Drink it young. Best producers: Grangeneuve★, Lônes, St-Luc, la Tour d'Elyssas, Vieux Micocoulier. Best years: (2001) 00 **99 98 95**.

COTEAUX VAROIS AC *Provence, France*   An area to watch with new plantings of classic grapes. Best producers: Alysses★, Bremond, Calisse★, Deffends★, Garbelle, Routas★, Ch. St-Estève, St-Jean-le-Vieux, St-Jean-de-Villecroze★, Triennes★. Best years: (2001) 00 99 **98 97 96 95 94 93 90**.

CÔTES DE BERGERAC AC   See Bergerac AC.

CÔTES DE BLAYE AC *Bordeaux, France*   AC for white wines from the right bank of the Gironde estuary produced from Colombard and Sauvignon. Almost all the best whites are now dry. Drink young. Best producer: Cave de Marcillac.

CÔTES DE BOURG AC *Bordeaux, France*
Mainly a red wine area to the south of the COTES DE BLAYE, where the best producers and the local co-op at Tauriac make great efforts. The reds are earthy but blackcurranty and can age for 6–10 years. Very little white is made, most of which is dry and dull. Best producers: Barbe, Brulesécaille★, Bujan, FALFAS★, Fougas★, Guerry, Haut-Guiraud, Haut-Macô★, Macay, Nodoz★, ROC DE CAMBES★★, Rousset, Tauriac co-op, Tayac★. Best years: 2000 99 98 **96 95 94** 90 89 88.

CÔTES DE CASTILLON AC *Bordeaux, France* Red wine area just to the east of ST-EMILION. As the price of decent red Bordeaux climbs ever upward, Côtes de Castillon wines have remained a good, reasonably priced alternative – a little earthy but full and round. Depending on the vintage the wine is enjoyable between 3 and 10 years after the vintage. Best producers: Domaine de l'A★, Aiguilhe★, Belcier★, Cap-de-Faugères, la Clarière Laithwaite, Clos de l'Eglise★, Côte-Montpezat, Lapeyronie★, Poupille★, Robin★, Veyry★, Vieux-Ch.-Champs-de-Mars. Best years: 2000 99 98 **96 95 94** 90 89.

CÔTES DE DURAS AC *South-West France* AC between ENTRE-DEUX-MERS and BERGERAC, with 2 very active co-ops which offer good, fresh, grassy reds and whites from traditional BORDEAUX grapes. Drink young. Best producers: Amblard, Clos du Cadaret, Cours, Duras co-op, Grand Mayne, Lafon, Landerrouat co-op, Laulan. Best years: (reds) 2000 **98 96 95**.

CÔTES DE FRANCS See Bordeaux-Côtes de Francs.

CÔTES DU FRONTONNAIS AC *South-West France* From north of Toulouse, some of the most distinctive reds – often superb and positively silky in texture – of South-West France. Négrette is the chief grape, but certain producers coarsen it with Cabernet, which rather defeats the object. Best producers: Baudare, Bellevue-la-Forêt★, Cahuzac★, la Colombière, Ferran, Flotis, Laurou, Montauriol, la Palme, Plaisance, le Roc★, St-Louis. Best years: 2000 99 **98 97 96 95**.

CÔTES DE GASCOGNE, VIN DE PAYS DES *South-West France* Mainly white wines from the Gers *département*. This is Armagnac country, but the tangy-fresh, fruity table wines are tremendously good – especially when you consider that they were condemned as unfit for anything but distillation a decade ago. Best producers: Aurin, Brumont, GRASSA★, Producteurs PLAIMONT★, de Joy, St-Lannes.

CÔTES DU JURA AC *Jura, France* The regional AC for Jura covers a wide variety of wines, including local specialities *vin jaune* and *vin de paille*. The Savagnin makes strong-tasting whites and Chardonnay is used for some good dry whites and Champagne-method fizz. Reds and rosés can be good when made from Pinot Noir, but with the local Poulsard and Trousseau the wines can be a bit odd. Drink young. Best producers: Ch. d'Arlay★★, Berthet-Bondet★★, Bourdy★★, Chalandard★, Clavelin★, Durand-Perron★★, Ch. de l'Étoile★, Joly★, A Labet★★, J Maclé★★, Reverchon★, Rijckaert★★, Rolet★★, A & M Tissot★.

CÔTES DU LUBÉRON AC *Rhône Valley, France* Wine production is dominated by the co-ops east of Avignon. The light, easy wines are refreshing and for drinking young. Best producers: Ch. la Canorgue, la Citadelle★, Fontenille★, Ch. de l'Isolette★, la Tour-d'Aigues co-op, Val Joanis, la Verrerie★. Best years: (2001) **00 99 98 95**.

CÔTES DU MARMANDAIS AC *South-West France* Marmandais producers aim to make BORDEAUX lookalikes, and the red wines achieve a fair amount of success. Syrah is also permitted. Best producers: Beaulieu, Cave de Beaupuy, Cocumont co-op, Elian Da Ros (Chante Coucou, Clos Baquey★).

CÔTES DE MONTRAVEL AC See Montravel AC.

CÔTES DE PROVENCE AC *Provence, France* Large AC mainly for fruity reds and rosés to drink young, showing signs of improvement in recent years. Whites are mostly forgettable. Best producers: Barbanau★, la Bernarde★, Commanderie de Bargemore★, Commanderie de Peyrassol★, la Courtade★★, Coussin Ste-Victoire★, Dragon★, Esclans★, Féraud★, des Garcinières★, Gavoty★, Maravenne★, Ott★, Rabiega★, Réal Martin★, RICHEAUME★, Rimauresq★, les Maîtres Vignerons de St-Tropez, Sorin★, Élie Sumeire★, Vannières★. Best years: (reds) (2001) 00 **99 98 97 96 95 94 93 91 90**.

CÔTES DU RHÔNE AC *Rhône Valley, France* The general appellation for the whole RHONE VALLEY. Over 90% is red and rosé mainly from Grenache with some Cinsaut, Syrah, Carignan and Mourvèdre to add lots of warm, spicy southern personality. Modern winemaking has revolutionized the style, and today's wines are generally juicy, spicy and easy to drink, ideally within 2 years. Most wine is made by co-ops and there are now many examples with depth and structure. Best producers: (reds) d'Andézon★, les Aphillanthes★, A Brunel★, CLAPE★, COLOMBO★, Coudoulet de BEAUCASTEL★, Cros de la Mûre★, Fonsalette★★, FONT DE MICHELLE★, Gramenon★★, Grand Moulas★, Grand Prebois★, GUIGAL, JABOULET, la Janasse★, LIONNET★, J-M Lombard★, Mas de Libian★, Mont Redon, la Mordoreé★, REMEJEANNE★, M Richaud★, Ste-Anne★, Santa Duc★, Tardieu-Laurent★, Tours★; (whites) CLAPE★, P Gaillard★, REMEJEANNE★, Ste-Anne★. Best years: (reds) (2001) **00 99 98 95**.

CÔTES DU RHÔNE-VILLAGES AC *Rhône Valley, France* AC for wines with a higher minimum alcohol content than straightforward COTES DU RHONE, covering 16 villages in the southern Rhône that have traditionally made superior wine (especially Cairanne, Séguret, Valréas, Sablet, Visan, Chusclan, Laudun). Almost all the best are spicy reds that can age well. Best producers: Achiary★, Alary★, l'Ameillaud★, Amouriers★, Beaurenard★, Bressy-Masson★, Brusset★, de Cabasse★, Cave de Cairanne★, D Charavin★, Charbonnière★, Chaume-Arnaud★, Combe★, Cros de la Mûre★, Estézargues co-op★, les Goubert★, Gourt de Mautens★★, Gramenon★, Grand Moulas★, les Hautes Cances★, JABOULET★, la Janasse★, l'ORATOIRE ST-MARTIN★, Pélaquié★, Piaugier★, Rabasse-Charavin★, REMEJEANNE★, M Richaud★, ST-GAYAN★, Ste-Anne★, la Soumade★, Tours★, Trapadis★, Verquière★. Best years: (reds) (2001) 00 **99 98 95 90**.

CÔTES DU ROUSSILLON AC *Roussillon, France* Large AC covering much of ROUSSILLON. Mainly red wine; most of the white is unmemorable. Production is dominated by the co-ops, some enlightened, but estates are making their presence felt. Best producers: (reds) Vignerons Catalans, CASENOVE★, CAZES★, Chênes★, J-L COLOMBO★, Ferrer-Ribière★, Forca Réal GAUBY★★, Jau, Joliette, Laporte★, Mas Crémat★, Piquemal★, Rivesaltes co-op, Salvat, Sarda-Malet★. Best years: (reds) 2000 **99 98 96 95**.

CÔTES DU ROUSSILLON-VILLAGES AC *Roussillon, France* AC for red wines from the best sites in the northern part of COTES DU ROUSSILLON. Villages Caramany, Latour-de-France, Lesquerde and Tautavel may add their own name, but wines from Caramany and Latour have been poo lately. Best producers: Agly co-op, Vignerons Catalans, CAZES★, Chênes★, Clos des Fées★, Fontanel★★, Forca Réal, Gardiès★, GAUBY★★, Jau, Joliette, Mas Crémat★, Schistes★. Best years: (reds) 2000 99 98 **96 95**.

CÔTES DE ST-MONT VDQS *South-West France* A good VDQS for firm but fruity reds and some fair rosés and dry whites. Best producer: Producteurs PLAIMONT.

CÔTES DE THONGUE, VIN DE PAYS DES *Languedoc, France* Mainly red wines, from north-east of Béziers. Most are dull quaffers made from Carignan, but recent plantings of classic grapes by dynamic estates can produce excellent results. Best producers: l'Arjolle★, Bellevue, les Chemins de Bassac★, Condamine l'Evêque, Croix Belle.

CÔTES DU VENTOUX AC *Rhône Valley, France* Increasingly successful AC, with vineyards on the slopes of Mt Ventoux in the RHONE VALLEY near Carpentras. When the wine is well made from a single estate or blended by a serious merchant, the reds can have a lovely juicy fruit, or in the case of JABOULET and Pesquié, some real stuffing. There is only a little white. Best producers: Anges★, Brusset, Cascavel, Champ-Long, JABOULET, Pesquié★, Valcombe, Union des Caves du Ventoux, la Verrière, la Vieille Ferme. Best years: (reds) 2000 **99 98**.

CÔTES DU VIVARAIS AC *Rhône Valley, France* In the northern Gard and Ardèche, typical southern Rhône grapes (Grenache, Syrah, Cinsaut, Carignan) produce mainly light, fresh reds and rosés for drinking young. Best producers: Chais du Vivarais, Vigier, Vignerons Ardèchois.

COTNARI *Romania* The warm mesoclimate of this hilly region, close to the border with Moldova, encourages noble rot. Once – but not now – on a footing with TOKAJI, Cotnari's principal local varieties are Grasa, Tamîîoasă, Francusa and Fetească Albă.

CÔTTO, QUINTA DO *Douro DOC and Port DOC, Douro, Portugal* Table wine expert in Lower DOURO. Basic red and white Quinta do Côtto are reasonable, and its Grande Escolha★★ is one of Portugal's best reds, oaky and powerful when young, rich and cedary when mature. Best years: (Grande Escolha) 1997 **95 94 90 87 85**.

COULY-DUTHEIL *Chinon, Loire Valley, France* Large merchant house responsible for 10% of the CHINON AC. Uses its own vineyards for the best wines, particularly Clos de l'Écho★ and Clos de l'Olive★. Top négociant blend is la Baronnie Madeleine★, which combines delicious raspberry fruit with a considerable capacity to age. Also sells a range of other Touraine wines. Best years: (reds) 2000 99 **97 96 95 90 89 86 85**.

PIERRE COURSODON *St-Joseph AC, Rhône Valley, France* Family-owned domaine, much improved in recent years, producing rich ST-JOSEPH from very old vines. The red wines★ need up to 5 years to show all the magnificent cassis and truffle and violet richness of the best Rhône reds, especially the top wine, la Sensonne★★. Whites are good too. Best years: (reds) (2000) 99 98 97 **96 95 94 90 89 88 86 85 83**.

CH. COUTET★★ *Barsac AC, 1er Cru Classé, Bordeaux, France* BARSAC'S largest Classed Growth property has languished behind its neighbour CLIMENS for a generation, but has shown great improvement in recent years. Extraordinarily intense Cuvée Madame★★★ is made in exceptional years. Best years: (2001) 99 98 97 **96 95 90 89 88**.

COWRA *New South Wales, Australia* Rapidly emerging district with a reliable warm climate and good water supplies for irrigation. It produces soft, peachy Chardonnay and spicy, cool-tasting Shiraz. Best producers: Cowra Estate, Hamilton's Bluff, Richmond Grove, ROTHBURY★, Charles Sturt University★, Windowrie Estate.

CRAGGY RANGE *Hawkes Bay, North Island, New Zealand* Exciting new venture funded by a wealthy American family and managed by brilliant viticulturist Steve Smith. Extensive vineyards in HAWKES BAY and MARTINBOROUGH are being established. So far contract grapes have been used to make some impressive wines: ripe, pungent Sauvignon Blanc★★, tangy Rapaura Road Riesling★ and vibrant Strugglers Flat Pinot Noir★ all come from MARLBOROUGH grapes. Elegant Apley Road Vineyard Chardonnay★★ is from grapes grown in Hawkes Bay.

CRASTO, QUINTA DO *Douro DOC and Port DOC, Douro, Portugal* Well-situated property belonging to the Roquette family. Very good traditional LBV★★ and Vintage★★ port and thoroughly enjoyable red DOURO★, especially Reserva★★ and varietal Touriga Nacional★★. New flagship reds, Vinha da Ponte★★ and Doña Maria Teresa★★, though first made in the modest 1998 vintage, show further promise. Best years: (port) (2000) (99) 97 **95 94**; (Reserva red) (2000) (99) **97 96 95 94**.

CRÉMANT D'ALSACE AC *Alsace, France* Good Champagne-method sparkling wine from Alsace, usually made from Pinot Blanc. Reasonable quality, if not great value for money. Best producers: BLANCK★, Dopff au Moulin★, Dopff & Irion, J Gross★, KUENTZ-BAS, MURÉ★, Ostertag★, Pfaffenheim co-op, P Sparr★, A Stoffel★, TURCKHEIM co-op★.

CRÉMANT DE BOURGOGNE AC *Burgundy, France* Most Burgundian Crémant is white and is made either from Chardonnay alone or blended with Pinot Noir. The result, especially in ripe years, can be full, soft, almost honey-flavoured – if you give the wine the 2–3 years' aging needed for mellowness to develop. The best rosé comes from Chablis and Auxerre in northern Burgundy. Best producers: A Delorme, Lucius-Grégoire, Parigot-Richard, Simonnet-Febvre; and the co-ops at Bailly★ (the best for rosé), Lugny★, St-Gengoux-de-Scissé and Viré.

CRÉMANT DE DIE AC *Rhône Valley, France* AC for traditional-method fizz made entirely from the Clairette Blanche grape. Less aromatic than CLAIRETTE DE DIE. Best producers: Clairette de Die co-op, Jacques Faure.

CRÉMANT DE JURA AC *Jura, France* AC for fizz from Jura. Largely Chardonnay-based, with Poulsard for the pinks. Best producers: Ch. de l'Étoile★, de la Pinte, Pupillin co-op★.

CRÉMANT DE LIMOUX AC *Languedoc-Roussillon, France* Sparkling wine made from a blend of Chardonnay, Chenin Blanc and Mauzac; the wines generally have more complexity than straight BLANQUETTE DE LIMOUX. Drink young. Best producers: l'Aigle★, Antech, Fourn★, Guinot, Laurens★, Martinolles★, SIEUR D'ARQUES★, Valent.

CRÉMANT DE LOIRE AC *Loire Valley, France* The AC for Champagne-method sparkling wine in Anjou and Touraine, with more fruit and yeast character than those of VOUVRAY and SAUMUR. The wine is good to drink as soon as it is released and can be excellent value. Best producers: BAUMARD★, Berger Frères★, Brizé★, la Gabillière, Girault, GRATIEN & MEYER★, Lambert★, Langlois-Château★, Michaud★, Oisly-et-Thésée co-op★, Passavant★.

CRIOTS-BÂTARD-MONTRACHET AC See Bâtard-Montrachet AC.

CRISTOM *Willamette Valley AVA, Oregon, USA* Named after the owners' children, Chris and Tom, this medium-sized winery, nestled in the Eola Hills, makes fine Pinot Noir. Two of the outstanding reserve Pinot Noirs are from Marjorie Vineyard★★ and Jessie Vineyard★★★. Good white wines include Chardonnay from Celilo Vineyard★ (in WASHINGTON), Pinot Gris and Viognier. Best years: (Pinot Noir) 2000 99 98 **97 96 94**.

LUCIEN CROCHET *Sancerre AC, Loire Valley, France* Textbook SANCERRE, both red and white. Best are the domaine-bottled wines, including ripe, perfumed red la Croix du Roy★ and zesty, gooseberryish white le Chêne★. Premium Cuvée Prestige white and red (both ★★), made from late-harvested old vines, have the depth and structure to age. Best years: (Cuvée Prestige) 2001 **00 99 97 96 95**.

CROFT *Port DOC, Douro, Portugal* Vintage ports★★ can be deceptively light in their youth, but they develop into subtle, elegant wines. Single-quinta Quinta da Roêda★★ is fine in the most recent vintages. Part of the Taylor Fonseca group since 2001. Best years: (Vintage) 1994 **91 77 70 66 63 60 45 35 27**; (Roêda) 1997 **95**.

CROZES-HERMITAGE AC *Rhône Valley, France* The largest of the northern Rhône ACs. Ideally, the reds should have a full colour and a strong, meaty but rich flavour. You can drink them young but in ripe years from a hillside site the wine improves greatly for 2–5 years. The best whites are fresh, clean and racy. In general drink white Crozes young before the floral perfume disappears. Best producers: (reds) A Belle★★, CHAPOUTIER★, B Chave★ (Tête de Cuvée★★), Colombier★, Combier★ (Clos des Grives★★), DELAS★, O Dumaine★, Entrefaux★, Fayolle★, GRAILLOT★★, JABOULET★, Pavillon-Mercurol★, Pochon★ (Ch. Curson★★), Remizières★★, G Robin★★, M Sorrel★, Tardieu-Laurent★★, Vins de Vienne★; (whites) B Chave★, Colombier★, Combier★★, DELAS★, O Dumaine★, Ferraton★, GRAILLOT★★, JABOULET★, Pochon★ (Ch. Curson★★), Pradelle★, Remizières★★, M Sorrel★. Best years: (reds) (2001) 00 **99 98 97 96 95 94 91 90 89 88**; (whites) (2001) **00 99 98 97 96**.

DR CRUSIUS *Traisen, Nahe, Germany* Dr Peter Crusius produces Rieslings from the Traiser Bastei★ and SCHLOSSBÖCKELHEIMER Felsenberg★ vineyards which manage to be rich, clean and flinty all at the same time.

YVES CUILLERON *Condrieu AC, Rhône Valley, France* With wines like Cuilleron's you can understand CONDRIEU's fame and perhaps even forgive it its high price. Les Chaillets Vieilles Vignes★★★ is everything wine made from Viognier should be: opulent and rich, with perfumed honey and apricot aromas. La Petite Côte★★ is also exceptional, and the late-harvest les Ayguets★★★ is an extraordinary sweet whirl of dried apricots, honey and barley sugar. Condrieu's young star also turns a hand to ST-JOSEPH reds★★ and whites★★ and tiny quantities of ripe, dark, spicy COTE-ROTIE★★. A joint venture, les Vins de Vienne, with partners Pierre Gaillard and François Villard, produces a range of wines including Vin de Pays des COLLINES RHODANIENNES Sotanum★★ from ancient vineyard terraces in Seyssuel, just north of Vienne. Best years: (Condrieu) **2000 99 98 97 96 95**.

CULLEN *Margaret River, Western Australia* One of the original and best MARGARET RIVER vineyards, run by the wonderful Cullen women: winemaker Vanya and her mother Diana. The Chardonnay★★ is one of the region's richest and most complex; the Semillon-Sauvignon blend★★, also stellar, has a long-lasting, nutty aftertaste. Their Cabernet Sauvignon-Merlot★★★ is gloriously soft, deep and scented; this wine is now justifiably regarded as one of Australia's greats, especially since the Reserve bottling was discontinued. Best years: (Cabernet Sauvignon-Merlot) 1999 98 97 **96 95 94 92 91 90 86 84 82**.

CURICÓ, VALLE DE *Valle Central, Chile* Most of the big producers here have planted Cabernet Sauvignon, Merlot, Chardonnay and Sauvignon Blanc. The long growing season provides good fruit concentration. Best producers: Canepa★, Echeverría★, Los Robles★, MONTES★, SAN PEDRO★, Miguel TORRES★, VALDIVIESO★.

CUVAISON *Napa Valley AVA, California, USA* Cuvaison built a reputation for brooding red wines in the 1970s. Now, in a more modern style, it produces tasty, focused Merlot★, sound Cabernet Sauvignon★ and good Chardonnay. The silky Reserve Chardonnay★ is worth seeking out, as is the delicate Pinot Noir★. Most should be drunk young. Best years: (Merlot) 1999 98 **97 96 95 94 92 91 90**.

CVNE *Rioja DOC, Rioja, Spain* Compañía Vinícola del Norte de España is the full name of this firm, but it's usually known as 'coonay'. Viña Real★ is one of RIOJA's only remaining well-oaked whites; the Viña Real Reserva★ and Gran Reserva★ reds can be rich and meaty, and easily surpass the rather commercial Crianzas; the top Imperial Gran Reserva★★ is long-lived and impressive. Marqués de Haro★ is a new premium red. Best years: (reds) **1996 95 94 92 91 90 89 88 87 86 85 81**.

DIDIER DAGUENEAU *Pouilly-Fumé AC, Loire Valley, France* Didier Dagueneau is known as the wild man of POUILLY-FUMÉ. In fact he is a much-needed innovator and quality fanatic in a complacent region. His wines generally benefit from 4 or 5 years' aging and, although at times unpredictable, are generally intense and complex. Top-quality barrel-fermented Sauvignon Blanc called Silex★★, En Chailloux★★, Buisson Renard★★ and Pur Sang★★. Best years: (2001) 00 99 98 **97 96**.

ROMANO DAL FORNO *Valpolicella DOC, Veneto, Italy* On his small estate at Illasi, outside the VALPOLICELLA Classico area, Romano Dal Forno makes one of the most impressive wines of the appellation. His Valpolicella Superiore★★ from the Monte Lodoletta vineyard is a model of power and grace, though his RECIOTO DELLA VALPOLICELLA★★★ and AMARONE★★★, from the same source, are even more voluptuous. Best years: (Amarone) (1997) 96 95 94 93 **91 90 89 88 86 85**.

DALLA VALLE *Napa Valley AVA, California, USA* Stunning hillside winery, producing some of NAPA's most esteemed Cabernets. Foremost among them is Maya★★★, a magnificent blend of Cabernet Sauvignon and Cabernet Franc. The straight Cabernet Sauvignon★★★ is almost as rich. New Pietre Rosse★★ is richly cherryish 100% Sangiovese. Cabernet-based reds drink well at 10 years, but will keep for 20 or more. Best years: (Maya) (2000) (99) 98 97 96 95 94 **93 92 91 90**.

DÃO DOC *Beira Alta, Portugal* Dão has steep slopes ideal for vineyards, and a great climate for growing local grape varieties; yet only in the last decade have white wines been freshened up, and reds begun to realize their long-promised potential – but many still have a long way to go. Best years: (reds) Caves ALIANCA, Boas Quintas (Fonte do Ouro★), Quinta de Cabriz★ (Virgilio Loureiro★★), Quinta das Maias★ Quinta da Pellada (Tinta Roriz, Touriga Nacional★), Quinta dos ROQUES★★, Quinta de Sães★, Caves SAO JOAO★★, SOGRAPE★; (whites) Quinta de Cabriz, Quinta das Maias★, Quinta dos ROQUES★, Quinta de Sães★, SOGRAPE★. Best years: (reds) (2001) 00 99 **97 96 95 94 92**.

D'ARENBERG *McLaren Vale, South Australia* Chester Osborn makes blockbuster Dead Arm Shiraz★★, Footbolt Old Vine Shiraz★, Custodian Grenache★ and numerous blends from very low-yielding old vines. These are big, brash, character-filled wines, but seem to have lost a little heft recently. Best years: (Dead Arm Shiraz) 1999 98 97 **96 95 94**.

KURT DARTING *Bad Dürkheim, Pfalz, Germany*   Helmut Darting makes
full, four-square wines in BAD DURKHEIM (Spielberg), Ungstein
(Ungsteiner Herrenberg Riesling Spätlese★★) and WACHENHEIM
(Mandelgarten), including rich, peachy Kabinett★ from Dürkheim.
Best years: (Riesling Spätlese) (2001) 99 98 97 96 **93 92**.

RENÉ & VINCENT DAUVISSAT *Chablis AC, Burgundy, France*   One of the
top domaines in CHABLIS. This is Chablis at its most complex –
refreshing, seductive and beautifully structured, with the fruit
balancing the subtle influence of mostly older oak. Look out in
particular for la Forest★★, the more aromatic Vaillons★★★ and the
powerful les Clos★★★. Best years: (2001) 00 99 98 97 96 95 **92 90 89**.

MARCO DE BARTOLI *Sicily, Italy*   Marco De Bartoli is most noted for a
dry but unfortified MARSALA-style wine called Vecchio Samperi; his
version of what he believes Marsala was before the first English
merchant, John Woodhouse, fortified it for export. Particularly fine are
the 20★★- and 30-year-old★★ Riserva wines – dry, intense and
redolent of candied citrus peel, dates and old, old raisins. Also
excellent is the MOSCATO PASSITO DI PANTELLERIA Bukkuram★★.

DE BORTOLI *Riverina, New South Wales, Australia*   Large, family-owned
winery producing a truly sublime botrytized Noble One Semillon★★★
that is head and shoulders above the rest of a vast range of
inexpensive RIVERINA quaffers. In the YARRA VALLEY De Bortoli is also
crafting some fine Chardonnay★, Shiraz★, Cabernet★ and Pinot
Noir★★. Good-value second labels are Windy Peak and Gulf Station.
Best years: (Noble One) 1999 98 97 96 95 **94 91 90 87 84 82**.

DEHLINGER *Russian River Valley AVA, California, USA*   Outstanding Pinot
Noir★★★ from vineyards in the cool RUSSIAN RIVER region a few miles
from the Pacific, best at 5–10 years old. Also solid Chardonnay★★ and
bold, peppery Syrah★★. Recent vintages of Cabernet★★ and Bordeaux
Blend★★ (Cabernet-Merlot) reflect a surge in quality. Best years: (Pinot
Noir) (2001) 00 99 98 97 **96 95 94 93 92 91 90**.

MARCEL DEISS *Alsace AC, Alsace, France*   For many years Jean-Michel
Deiss has been fanatical about distinctions of *terroir*, so it was not
surprising when in 1998 the estate became biodynamic. The finest
wines are the Rieslings★★★ from the Grands Crus Altenberg and
Schoenenbourg, which in top years also yield stunning Sélection de
Grains Nobles★★★. Although Deiss claims to be less interested in
Pinot Gris★★, his wines from this variety, as well as his
Gewurztraminers★★★, Pinot Noirs★★ and blended Grand Vin
d'Altenberg de Bergheim★, are vibrant and delicious. Best years:
(Grand Cru Riesling) (2001) (00) 98 97 96 **95 94 93 92 90 89 88**.

DELAS FRÈRES *Rhône Valley, France*   An underrated and rapidly
improving merchant based near Tournon, now part of DEUTZ, selling
wines from the entire RHONE VALLEY. Wines from its own northern
Rhône vineyards have improved greatly in recent vintages. Look out
for the aromatic CONDRIEU★★, as well as its single-vineyard, dense,
powerful red HERMITAGE★★ (les Bessards★★★), which needs as much as
a decade to reach its peak, and the perfumed single-vineyard COTE-
ROTIE la Landonne★★★. The CROZES-HERMITAGE Tour d'Albon★★ is an
increasingly good bet, as is the COTES DU RHONE St-Esprit. Best years:
(premium reds) (2000) 99 98 97 **96 95 94 91 90 89 88 86 85 83 78**.

DELATITE *Mansfield, Central Victoria, Australia*   The Ritchies' high-
altitude vineyard, in sight of VICTORIA's snowfields, grows delicate,
aromatic Riesling★★ and Gewürztraminer★★; there is also subtle

123

Chardonnay★ and extravagantly fruity reds. The Pinot Noir★ is perfumed, and Devil's River★★ is a very smart, minty BORDEAUX blend. Best years: (Riesling) 2000 99 **97 96 94 93 87 86 82**.

DELEGAT'S *Henderson, Auckland, North Island, New Zealand* Family winery specializing in Chardonnay, Cabernet-Merlot and Sauvignon Blanc from the HAWKES BAY and MARLBOROUGH (under Oyster Bay★ label) regions. Prices are generally fair and quality is good but not thrilling. Best are Reserve Chardonnay★ and Reserve Merlot★.

DENBIES *Surrey, England* England's largest vineyard, with 107ha (265 acres), is planted on chalky soils outside Dorking. Winemaker John Worontschak has encouraged new plantings and created more blends. Sparkling wines are good; the whites enormously improved after a long period when they really didn't measure up; encouraging releases of dry rosé, decent reds and excellent botrytized sweet white★.

DEUTZ *Champagne AC, Champagne, France* Probably better known for its New Zealand fizz than for its Champagne. Unfairly so, perhaps, because this small company, now owned by ROEDERER, produces excellent, medium-priced Champagne. The non-vintage★ is always reliable, but the top wines are the classic Blanc de Blancs★★ and the weightier Cuvée William Deutz★★. Best years: (1996) **95 93 90 89 88**.

DÉZALEY *Lavaux, Vaud, Switzerland* The top wine commune in the VAUD, making surprisingly powerful, mineral wines from the Chasselas grape. Best producers: Louis Bovard★, Conne, Dubois Fils★, Les Frères Dubois★, J D Fonjallaz (l'Arbalète)★, Pinget★, J & P Testuz.

D F J VINHOS *Portugal* In the early 1990s, UK wine shippers D & F began working with one of Portugal's finest winemakers, José Neiva, in 1999 this relationship evolved into D F J Vinhos, with a range that is now available both locally and internationally. The Bela Fonte brand includes varietal reds Baga, Jaen★ and Touriga Franca★ and a white Bical, all from BEIRAS. Other labels include Manta Preta★ from ESTREMADURA, Rocha do Monte from TERRAS DO SADO, Senda do Vale★ from RIBATEJO, and an ALGARVE red, Cataplana★. At the top end are the Grand'Arte reds, including an intensely fruity, peppery Trincadeira★★.

DIAMOND CREEK VINEYARDS *Napa Valley AVA, California, USA* Small estate specializing in Cabernet: Volcanic Hill★★★, Red Rock Terrace★★ and Gravelly Meadow★★. Traditionally huge, tannic wines that, when tasted young, I swear won't ever come round. Yet there's usually a sweet inner core of fruit that envelops the tannin over 10–15 years, and recent releases show wonderful perfume and balance in their youth. Best years: (2000) 99 98 97 96 95 94 92 91 90 **87 86 85 84 80**.

DIEL, SCHLOSSGUT *Burg Layen, Nahe, Germany* Armin Diel made his name with dry wines, and some of Germany's finest new oak-aged whites during the 1980s. However, since 1990 it has been classic-style Rieslings which have been attracting headlines. Spätlese and Auslese from Dorsheim's top sites are regularly ★★, Eiswein ★★★. Best years: (Riesling Spätlese) (2001) 00 99 98 **97** 96 **95 93 90** 89 88.

DISTELL *Stellenbosch, South Africa* This company, formed by the merger between Distillers Corporation and South Africa's largest merchant-producer, Stellenbosch Farmers' Winery, controls almost 30% of Cape table wine production and is still finding its feet, but some of the labels

– such as Neethlingshof★, STELLENZICHT★ and Durbanville Hills★ – are already performing well. Fleur du Cap is also upgrading itself, and other promising labels are Zonnebloem Fine Art, Stellenryck★ and Pongrácz★ Cap Classique fizz. Two wineries in PAARL (Nederburg and Plaisir de Merle★) are run separately. After a recent slump, Nederburg is busy reinventing itself; its best-known botrytized dessert, Edelkeur★, is sold only through an annual auction. Plaisir de Merle, after a great start, lost its way, but signs are that it is on the way back.

CH. DOISY-DAËNE★★ *Sauternes AC, 2ème Cru Classé, Bordeaux, France*
A consistently good property in BARSAC (although it uses the SAUTERNES AC for its wines) and unusual in that the sweet wine is made exclusively from Sémillon. It ages well for 10 years or more. The extra-rich Extravagant★★★ is produced in exceptional years. Doisy-Daëne Sec★ is a good, perfumed, dry white. Drink young. **Best years:** (sweet) (2001) 99 98 97 **96 95 90 89 88 86 83**; (dry) 1999 **98 96 95 94 90**.

CH. DOISY-VÉDRINES★★ *Sauternes AC, 2ème Cru Classé, Bordeaux, France* Next door to DOISY-DAENE, Doisy-Védrines is a richly botrytized wine, fatter and more syrupy than most BARSAC wines. Like its neighbour, it also sells its wines under the SAUTERNES AC. **Best years:** (sweet) (2001) 99 98 97 **96 95 90 89 88 86 85 83**.

DOLCETTO One of Italy's most charming native grapes, producing purple wines bursting at the seams with fruit. Virtually exclusive to PIEDMONT, it is DOC in 7 zones, with styles ranging from intense and rich in Alba, Ovada and Dogliani, to lighter, more perfumed versions in Acqui and ASTI. Usually best drunk within 1–2 years, top wines can age up to 4 years. **Best producers:** (Alba) Alario★★, ALTARE★★, Boglietti★, Bongiovanni★★, Bricco Maiolica★, Brovia★★, Elvio Cogno★★, Aldo CONTERNO★, Giacomo CONTERNO★, Conterno-Fantino★★, B Marcarini★, Bartolo MASCARELLO★, Giuseppe MASCARELLO★★, Paitin★, Pelissero★★, PRUNOTTO★, Albino Rocca★★, SANDRONE★★, Vajra★★, Vietti★, Gianni Voerzio★, Roberto VOERZIO★★; (Dogliani) M & E Abbona★, Chionetti★★, Luigi Einaudi★★, Pecchenino★★, San Fereolo★★, San Romano★.

DÔLE *Valais, Switzerland* Red wine from the Swiss VALAIS that must be made from at least 51% Pinot Noir, the rest being Gamay. Dôle is generally a light wine – the deeper, richer (100% Pinot Noir) styles have the right to call themselves Pinot Noir. Most should be drunk young, and can be lightly chilled in summer. **Best producers:** M Clavien, J Germanier, Caves Imesch, Mathier, Caves Orsat.

DOMAINE CARNEROS *Carneros AVA, California, USA* From its founding in 1987, this TAITTINGER-owned sparkling wine house has shown great promise. Both the vintage Brut★ and the Blanc de Blancs★★ now match if not surpass Taittinger's fizz from Champagne. De luxe Le Rêve★★ blanc de blancs is made in the best years, and there's a tasty still Pinot Noir★.

DOMAINE CHANDON *Napa Valley AVA, California, USA* The first French-owned (MOET & CHANDON) sparkling wine producer in California has shown remarkable consistency and good quality with reasonably priced non-vintage bubblies. The Reserve★ bottlings, rich and creamy, are especially good. Blanc de Blancs★, made entirely from CARNEROS Chardonnay, is a welcome addition. Étoile★★ is an aged de luxe wine, and is also made as a flavourful Rosé★★ as well. Shadow Creek is the budget line.

DOMAINE CONSTANTIN LAZARIDI *Drama, Greece* This state-of-the-art, Bordeaux-inspired winery was conceived with an eye on the historic evidence of this area's potential. Winemaker Vasilis Tsaktsarlis makes good use of indigenous and international varieties in wines ranging from the fresh gooseberry Amethystos white★ (Sauvignon, Semillon and Assyrtiko) to a fascinatingly intense experimental Viognier★ with a stunning, oily, peach kernel finish, tasty Château Julia Chardonnay and the fine Amethystos Cava★, an oak-aged Cabernet Sauvignon from very low yields. A winery to watch.

DOMAINE DROUHIN OREGON *Willamette Valley AVA, Oregon, USA* Burgundy wine merchant Robert DROUHIN bought 40ha (100 acres) in OREGON in 1987, with plans to make fine Pinot Noir, and this has certainly been achieved. The regular Pinot Noir★ is silky smooth, and the de luxe Pinot Noir Laurène★★ is supple, voluptuous, and one of Oregon's finest. Chardonnay★ has established itself well since its first release in 1996. Best years: (Pinot Noir) 2000 99 98 97 **96 94 93**.

DOMAINE VISTALBA *Argentina* All the reds from this French-owned company have dark, concentrated fruit, increasing in complexity through the Fabre Montmayou range. The almost black, chocolate-and-damsons Grand Vin★★ is a splendidly topsy-turvy BORDEAUX blend: Malbec plus Merlot and Cabernet Sauvignon. Cuvée Diane★★ is denser and richer still. The reds from a second MENDOZA winery, Altos de Temporada, are also potentially excellent. Dual-variety reds from Río Negro, under the Infinitus label, are erratic.

DOMECQ *Jerez y Manzanilla DO, Andalucía and Rioja DOC, País Vasco, Spain* The largest of the sherry companies, best known for its reliable fino, La Ina★. At the top of the range, dry Amontillado 51-1A★★★, Sibarita Palo Cortado★★★ and Venerable Pedro Ximénez★★ are spectacular. Domecq also makes light, elegant RIOJA, Marqués de Arienzo★.

DOMINUS★★ *Napa Valley AVA, California, USA* Red wine only from this property owned by Christian MOUEIX, director of Bordeaux superstar PETRUS. Wines are based on Cabernet with leavenings of Merlot and Cabernet Franc. Early vintages were mercilessly tannic, but recent ones show great improvement. Best years: (2000) 99 97 96 95 94 91 **90**.

DONAULAND *Niederösterreich, Austria* Amorphous wine region on both banks of the Danube stretching from just north of Vienna west to St Polten. Best are the dry Grüner Veltliners from the Wagram area. Best producers: Karl Fritsch, Wimmer-Czerny.

DÖNNHOFF *Oberhausen, Nahe, Germany* Helmut Dönnhoff is the quiet winemaking genius of the NAHE, conjuring from a string of top sites some of the most mineral dry and naturally sweet Rieslings in the world. The very best are the subtle, long-lived wines from the Niederhäuser Hermannshöhle★★★ vineyard. Eiswein★★★ is equally exciting. Best years: (Hermannshöhle Riesling Spätlese) (2001) 00 **99** 98 **97** 96 95 **94 93 90** 89 83 76 **71**.

DOURO DOC *Douro, Portugal* As well as a flood of port and basic table wine, some of Portugal's top, soft-textured red wines come from here. Also good whites, made from the more aromatic white port grape varieties. White wines are best young, but red wines may improve for 10 years or even more. Best producers: (reds) Caves ALIANÇA (Foral Grande Escolha★), Maria Doroteia Serôdio Borges (Fojo★★), BRIGHT BROTHERS (TFN★), Quinta do COTTO (Grande Escolha★★), Quinta do CRASTO★★, FERREIRA★ (Barca Velha★★, Quinta da Leda★★), Quinta da Gaivosa★★, NIEPOORT (Passadouro★★, Redoma★★), Quinta do NOVAL★,

Quinta do Portal (Grande Reserva★), Quinta da Portela da Vilariça (Touriga Nacional★), Quinta de la ROSA★, SOGRAPE, Quinta do Vale Dona Maria★★, Quinta do Vale da Raposa (single varietals★), Vallado★. Best years: (reds) (2001) 00 99 **97 96 95 94 92 91 90**.

DOW *Port DOC, Douro, Portugal*   The grapes for Dow's Vintage PORT★★★ come mostly from the Quinta do Bomfim, which is also the name of the excellent single quinta★★★. Dow ports are relatively dry compared with those of GRAHAM and WARRE (the 2 other major brands belonging to the Symington family), and there are some excellent aged tawnies★★. Impressive young port has also been produced under the Quinta Senhora da Ribeira label from the 40ha (100-acre) vineyard opposite VESUVIO since 1998. Best years: (Vintage) 1997 94 **91 85 83 80 77 70 66 63 60 55 45**; (Bomfim) (1999) 98 95 92 **90 87 86 84**.

JEAN-PAUL DROIN *Chablis AC, Burgundy, France*   Jean-Paul Droin sells some of his production to NUITS-ST-GEORGES merchant LABOURE-ROI, but bottles 14 different wines under his own label. Apart from CHABLIS★ and Petit Chablis, all of Droin's wines are fermented and/or aged in oak barrels. The best wines are the big, buttery Chablis Premiers Crus (Montmains★★, Vosgros★★) and Grands Crus (Vaudésir★★, Grenouilles★★). Best years: (top crus) (2001) 00 99 98 97 **96 95 90**.

DROMANA ESTATE *Mornington Peninsula, Victoria, Australia*   In 20 years, Garry Crittenden has built Dromana into the MORNINGTON PENINSULA's major producer, with two dozen wines and a growing raft of brands. Winemaking, thankfully, remains on track with fragrant, restrained Pinot Noir★ and Reserve Chardonnay★★ and leafy, fruity Cabernet-Merlot★. Italian varietals under the Garry Crittenden 'i' label, mostly from King Valley grapes, are of special interest, particularly Sangiovese★, Barbera★ and Arneis. Best years: (Reserve Chardonnay) 1999 **98 97 96 94 91**.

JOSEPH DROUHIN *Beaune, Burgundy, France*   One of the best Burgundian merchants, now Japanese-owned, with substantial vineyard holdings in CHABLIS and the COTE D'OR, and DOMAINE DROUHIN OREGON, USA. Drouhin makes a consistently good, if expensive, range of wines from all over Burgundy. Look for BONNES-MARES★★, ROMANEE-ST-VIVANT★★★, BEAUNE Clos des Mouches (red★★ and white★★★), le Musigny★★★ and le MONTRACHET★★★ from the Dom. du Marquis de Laguiche. Drouhin offers better value in Chablis★ and less glamorous Burgundian ACs, such as RULLY★ and ST-AUBIN★. The BEAUJOLAIS is always good, but overall Drouhin's whites are (just) better than the reds. Quality reds and whites should be aged for at least 5 years, often better nearer 10.

PIERRE-JACQUES DRUET *Bourgueil, Loire Valley, France*   A passionate producer of BOURGUEIL and small quantities of CHINON. Druet makes 5 Bourgueils – les Cent Boisselées★, Cuvée Beauvais★★, Cuvée Grand Mont★★, Cuvée Reservée★★ and Vaumoreau★★ – each a complex expression of the Cabernet Franc grape. Best aged for at least 3–5 years. Best years: (top cuvées) (2000) 99 **97 96 95 90 89 88 85**.

DRY CREEK VALLEY AVA *Sonoma, California, USA*   Best known for Sauvignon Blanc, Zinfandel and Cabernet Sauvignon, this valley runs west of ALEXANDER VALLEY AVA, and similarly becomes hotter moving northwards. Best producers: DRY CREEK VINEYARD★, Duxoup★, FERRARI-CARANO★★, GALLO (Zinfandel★, Cabernet Sauvignon★), Michel-Schlumberger★, Nalle★★, Pezzi King★, Preston★, QUIVIRA★★, Rafanelli (Zinfandel★★). Best years: (reds) (2000) 99 98 97 **96 95 94 92 91**.

127

DRY CREEK VINEYARD *Dry Creek Valley AVA, California, USA* An early advocate of Fumé Blanc, Dave Stare remains faithful to the brisk racy style of Fumé★ and also makes a serious Reserve Fumé Blanc★ which improves with aging. A drink-young Chardonnay (Reserve★) is attractive, but the stars here are red Meritage★, Merlot★ and Old Vine Zinfandel★★. Best years: (Old Vine Zin) (2000) 99 **97 96 95 94 93 92 91**.

DRY RIVER *Martinborough, North Island, New Zealand* Low yields, careful selection and an uncompromising attitude to quality at this tiny winery, owned by the meticulous Dr Neil McCallum, have helped create some of the country's top Gewürztraminer★★★ and Pinot Gris★★, together with an intense and seductively smooth Pinot Noir★★★, a sleek Chardonnay★★ and powerful, long-lived Craighall Riesling★★★. Excellent Syrah★★ is made in tiny quantities. Best years: (Craighall Riesling) (2001) 00 **99 98 96 94**; (Pinot Noir) (2001) 00 **99 96 94**.

GEORGES DUBOEUF *Beaujolais, Burgundy, France* Known, with some justification, as the King of Beaujolais, Duboeuf is responsible for more than 10% of the wine produced in the region. Given the size of his operation, the quality of the wines is good. Duboeuf also makes and blends wine from the Mâconnais and the RHONE VALLEY. His BEAUJOLAIS NOUVEAU is usually reliable, but his top wines are those he bottles for small growers, particularly Jean Descombes★★ in MORGON, Dom. des Quatre Vents★, la Madone★ in FLEURIE and Dom. de la Tour du Bief★ in MOULIN-A-VENT. His ST-VERAN★ can be very good.

DUCKHORN *Napa Valley AVA, California, USA* This Californian winery has earned a reputation for a very chunky, tannic Merlot★ (Estate Merlot★★), now, thankfully, softer and riper, but the Cabernet Sauvignon★ and Sauvignon Blanc★ still provide easier drinking. Under the Goldeneye label there is also a ripe, oaky Pinot Noir. Paraduxx is a Zinfandel-Cabernet blend; Decoy is the budget line. Best years: (Three Palms Merlot) (1999) 98 97 96 95 94 **91 90 86**.

CH. DUCRU-BEAUCAILLOU★★★ *St-Julien AC, 2ème Cru Classé, Haut-Médoc, Bordeaux, France* Traditionally the epitome of ST-JULIEN, mixing charm and austerity, fruit and firm tannins. Vintages in the mid-1980s and early 90s were flawed, but recent vintages show vast improvement. Welcome back to the premier league. Second wine: la Croix de Beaucaillou. Best years: 2000 99 98 96 95 **94 85 83 82**.

DUJAC *Morey-St-Denis AC, Côte de Nuits, Burgundy, France* Owner Jacques Seysses is one of Burgundy's most influential winemakers. His estate is based in MOREY-ST-DENIS, and there are also some choice vineyards in CHAMBOLLE-MUSIGNY, ECHEZEAUX and GEVREY-CHAMBERTIN. The wines are all perfumed and elegant, including a small quantity of Morey-St-Denis★ white wine, but the outstanding Dujac bottlings are the Grands Crus – Échézeaux★★★, CLOS DE LA ROCHE★★★, BONNES-MARES★★★ and CLOS ST-DENIS★★★ – all of which will age for a decade or more. Best years: (Grands Crus) (2001) 00 99 98 96 95 **93 91 90 89 85**.

DUNN VINEYARDS *Howell Mountain AVA, California, USA* Massive, concentrated, hauntingly perfumed, long-lived Cabernet Sauvignon★★★ is the trademark of Randy Dunn's HOWELL MOUNTAIN wines. His NAPA VALLEY Cabernets★★ are less powerful but still scented. Best years: (2000) 99 97 96 95 94 93 92 91 90 **88 87 86 85 84 82**.

DURIF See Petite Sirah.

JEAN DURUP *Chablis, Burgundy, France*   The largest vineyard owner in
CHABLIS, Jean Durup is a great believer in unoaked Chablis, which
tends to be clean without any great complexity. Best are the Premiers
Crus Fourchaume★ and Montée de Tonnerre★★. Wines appear under
a variety of labels, including l'Eglantière, Ch. de Maligny and Valéry.

ÉCHÉZEAUX AC *Grand Cru, Côte de Nuits, Burgundy, France*   The village
of Flagey-Échézeaux, down in the plain away from the vineyards, is
best known for its 2 Grands Crus, Échézeaux and the smaller and more
prestigious Grands-Échézeaux, which are sandwiched between the
world-famous CLOS DE VOUGEOT and VOSNE-ROMANEE. Few of the 80
growers here have really made a name for themselves, but there are
some fine wines with a smoky, plum richness and a soft texture that
age well over 10–15 years to a gamy, chocolaty depth. Best producers:
R Arnoux★★, BOUCHARD Père et Fils★★, Cacheux-Sirugue★★★,
DROUHIN★★, DUJAC★★★, R Engel★★★, GRIVOT★★★, JAYER-GILLES★★★,
Mongeard-Mugneret★★, Mugneret-Gibourg★★★, Dom. de la ROMANEE-
CONTI★★★, E Rouget★★★. Best years: (2001) 00 99 98 97 96 95 **93 90 89**.

DOM. DE L'ECU *Muscadet Sèvre-et-Maine, Loire Valley, France*   One of the
finest producers in MUSCADET, Guy Bossard's biodynamically run estate
also produces GROS PLANT DU PAYS NANTAIS white, a red vin de pays blend
of Cabernets Franc and Sauvignon and a refreshing sparkler, Ludwig
Hahn. It is his Muscadet, though, that stands out, especially top
cuvées Boisée (oak aged) and Hermine d'Or★. Best years: (top
Muscadets) (2001) **00 99 98 97 96**.

EDEN VALLEY See Barossa, pages 58–9.

CH. L'ÉGLISE-CLINET★★★ *Pomerol AC, Bordeaux, France*   A tiny 5.5ha
(13-acre) domaine in the heart of the POMEROL plateau, l'Église-Clinet has
a very old vineyard – one of the reasons for the depth and elegance of the
wines. The other is the winemaking ability of owner Denis Durantou.
The wine is expensive and in limited supply, but worth seeking out. It
can be enjoyed young, though the best examples should be cellared for
10 years or more. Best years: 2000 99 98 97 96 **95 94 93 90 89 86 85**.

EIKENDAL *Stellenbosch WO, South Africa*   Winemaker Josef Krammer's
wines are unflamboyant, though individual and complex. The deep,
well-drained slopes of Helderberg produce an elegant, balanced
Chardonnay★ with an aging ability unusual in South Africa, and a
light-textured but tasty Merlot★. Best years: (Chardonnay) **2001 00 99
98 97 96**.

ELK COVE *Willamette Valley AVA, Oregon, USA*   Dating back to 1973,
rather early by OREGON standards, Elk Cove produces Pinot Noir★,
Cabernet Sauvignon, Pinot Gris★, Chardonnay, Gewürztraminer,
Viognier and Riesling★ from its own 27ha (65 acres) of vineyards. The
Reserve Pinot Noirs – Roosevelt, Windhill and La Boheme – have taken
a jump up in quality and compete with the elite from the state. Best
years: (Pinot Noir) 2000 99 98 **97 94**.

NEIL ELLIS *Stellenbosch WO, South Africa*   A leading winemaker/
négociant, and mentor for many of the Cape's younger winemakers,
renowned for powerful, invigorating Groenekloof Sauvignon Blanc★★
and striking Stellenbosch reds (blackcurranty Cabernet Sauvignon★★
and supple Cabernet-Merlot★), Ellis has now turned his attention to
Shiraz★. Ageworthy single-vineyard Shiraz★, Pinotage★ and
Cabernet★★ (from Jonkershoek fruit), and a subtly delicious
Chardonnay★ from cool Elgin confirm his versatility.

ELTVILLE *Rheingau, Germany*   This large wine town makes some of the RHEINGAU's most racy Riesling wines. Best producers: J B BECKER★, J Fischer, Langwerth von Simmern★. Best years: (2001) 00 **99 98 97 96 90**.

EMILIA-ROMAGNA *Italy*   Central-eastern region in Italy, divided into the provinces of Emilia (in the west) and ROMAGNA (in the east). It is chiefly infamous for LAMBRUSCO in Emilia. See also Colli Bolognesi, Colli Piacentini.

ENATE *Somontano DO, Aragón, Spain*   Enate and VINAS DEL VERO seem to be slugging it out for supremacy in the SOMONTANO DO. Barrel-fermented Chardonnay★ is rich, buttery and toasty, Gewürztraminer★ is exotic and convincing. Imported grape varieties also feature in the red Crianza, Reserva★ (100% Cabernet Sauvignon), Reserva Especial★★ (Cabernet-Merlot) and a new blockbuster, Enate Merlot-Merlot★★! Best years: (reds) 1999 **98 96 95 94**.

ENTRE-DEUX-MERS AC *Bordeaux, France*   This AC increasingly represents some of the freshest, snappiest dry white wine in France. In general, drink the latest vintage, though better wines will last a year or two. Sweet wines are sold as PREMIERES COTES DE BORDEAUX, St-Macaire, LOUPIAC and STE-CROIX-DU-MONT. Best producers: Bel Air, BONNET★, Castelneau, de Fontenille★, Launay, Moulin-de-Launay, Nardique-la-Gravière★, Ste-Marie★, Tour-de-Mirambeau, Toutigeac★, Turcaud★.

ERBACH *Rheingau, Germany*   Erbach's famous Marcobrunn vineyard is one of the top spots for Riesling on the Rhine. The village wines are elegant, off-dry; those from Marcobrunn more powerful and imposing. Best producers: Jakob Jung★, Knyphausen★, SCHLOSS REINHARTS-HAUSEN★, Schloss Schönborn★. Best years: (Riesling Spätlese) (2001) 00 **99** 98 **97** 96 **94 93 92**.

ERBALUCE DI CALUSO DOC *Piedmont, Italy*   Usually a dry or sparkling white from the Erbaluce grape, but Caluso Passito, where the grapes are semi-dried before fermenting, can be a great sweet wine. Best producers: (Caluso Passito) Cieck★, Ferrando★, Orsolani★.

ERDEN *Mosel, Germany*   Village in the Middle MOSEL, whose most famous vineyards are Prälat and Treppchen. The wines are rich and succulent with a strong mineral character. Best producers: J J Christoffel★★, Dr LOOSEN★★★, Meulenhof★, Mönchhof★★. Best years: (Riesling Spätlese) (2001) 00 **99 98 97** 96 **95 94 93 90**.

ERMITAGE   Swiss name for the Marsanne grape of the northern RHONE VALLEY. Mostly found in the central VALAIS, where it produces a range of wines from slightly sweet to lovely honeyed dessert wines. Best producers: Chappaz★, Dom. du Mont d'Or★, Orsat (Marsanne Blanche★).

ERRÁZURIZ *Aconcagua, Chile*   American winemaker Ed Flaherty has brought a welcome consistency to this producer's wines. Using red grapes from relatively low-yielding Aconcagua slopes north of Santiago, as well as traditional supplies from south of Santiago, there is a uniquely crunchy Merlot★★, reliably rich Cabernet Sauvignon★ from the Don Maximiano vineyards (also source of SEÑA) and smoky Syrah★. 'Wild Ferment' Chardonnay★ and Pinot Noir★ from CASABLANCA look good. Best years: (reds) **1999 98 97 96**.

ESPORÃO *Reguengos DOC, Alentejo, Portugal*   Huge estate in the heart of the ALENTEJO, with Australian David Baverstock producing a broad range of wines. The principal labels are Esporão (red★★ and white★

Reservas), Vinha da Defesa★, Monte Velho and Alandra, and there are some delightful varietals: Trincadeira★, Aragonês★★, Cabernet Sauvignon★ and Touriga Nacional★. Best years: (reds) (2001) 00 99 98 **97 96 95 94 92**.

EST! EST!! EST!!! DI MONTEFIASCONE DOC *Lazio, Italy* Modest white accorded its undeserved reputation because of an apocryphal story of a bishop's servant who thought he'd made a major discovery in this wine. The most credible exception is Falesco's Poggio dei Gelsi★. Far better is the same producer's barrique-aged Merlot Montiano★★. Best producers: Bigi (Graffiti), Falesco★, Mazziotti (Canuleio★).

CH. DES ESTANILLES *Faugères AC, Languedoc, France* The Louisons know that quality begins in the vineyard. Their best site is the Clos de Fou, with its very steep schistous slope planted with Syrah; the grape 'dominates' the top red cuvée★★ (i.e. 100% – but the AC regulations do not allow them to say so). Also a wood-fermented and aged rosé, plus fine COTEAUX DU LANGUEDOC white★.

ESTREMADURA *Portugal* Portugal's most productive region, occupying the western coastal strip and with an increasing number of clean, characterful wines. The leading area is ALENQUER, promoted to DOC status along with Arruda, Óbidos and Torres Vedras, and there are also the IPRs of Alcobaça and Encostas d'Aire. However, much of the wine, including some of the region's best, is simply labelled as Vinho Regional Estremadura. Spicy, perfumed reds are often based on Castelão, but Cabernet Sauvignon, Touriga Nacional and Tinta Roriz contribute to top examples, which can benefit from 4 or 5 years' age. Top producers also make fresh, aromatic whites. Best producers: Quinta da Abrigada★, Quinta da Cortezia★★ (Caves ALIANÇA), D F J VINHOS (Grand'Arte Touriga Nacional★, Manta Preta★), Quinta de Pancas★, Casa SANTOS LIMA★. See also Bucelas. Best years: (reds) (2001) 00 **99 97 96 95**.

L'ÉTOILE AC *Jura, France* A tiny area within the COTES DU JURA which has its own AC for whites, mainly Chardonnay and Savagnin, and for *vin jaune*. There is good Champagne-method fizz too. Best producers: Ch. l'Étoile★, Geneletti★, Joly★, Montbourgeau★★, Quintigny★.

CH. L'ÉVANGILE★★ *Pomerol AC, Bordeaux, France* A neighbour to PETRUS and CHEVAL BLANC, this estate is now wholly owned and managed by the Rothschilds of LAFITE-ROTHSCHILD. The wine is quintessential POMEROL – rich, fat and exotic. Recent vintages have been very good, but expect further improvement as the Rothschild effect kicks in. Best years: 2000 99 98 96 95 **94 93 90 89 88 85 83 82**.

EVANS & TATE *Margaret River, Western Australia* This important Western Australian winery relocated to MARGARET RIVER in 1997. The range includes nutty, creamy Two-Vineyards Chardonnay★, crisp Sauvignon-Semillon★, blackcurrant Cabernet-Merlot★ and concentrated yet irresistible Cabernet Sauvignon★★ and Shiraz★★. Best years: (Cabernet Sauvignon) 1998 97 **96 94 93 92 91**.

EYRIE VINEYARDS *Willamette Valley AVA, Oregon, USA* One of the leading Pinot Noir producers in OREGON, especially the Reserve★, but in poor years the wines can be withdrawn and thin. Chardonnay★ shows nice varietal fruit, while the popular Pinot Gris★ flies off the shelves. Best years: (Pinot Noir Reserve) (1999) 98 **97 96**.

FAIRVIEW *Paarl WO, South Africa* Owner Charles Back ensures that wine remains fun as well as a serious business. The latest consumer hit is Goats do Roam, a spoof on COTES DU RHONE: a red★, with Pinotage added to the blend of Rhône grape varieties, has now been joined by a spicy, partly barrel-fermented rosé and a lovely white★ featuring Viognier, Grenache Blanc and Clairette. Zinfandel-Cinsaut★ is another delightful idiosyncrasy. There is hardly a red grape Back isn't prepared to try, though the Rhône varieties are his passion, and he makes fine Shiraz★★, Carignan★, Malbec★, Merlot★★, Cabernet Sauvignon★ and Pinotage★ (Primo★★), among others. Good whites include Chenin Blanc★, Semillon★ (Oom Pagel★★) and Viognier★. Charles Back also owns the progressive SPICE ROUTE WINE COMPANY and acts as guiding light to the Fair Valley workers' empowerment project. Best years: (Shiraz) 2001 **00** 99 98 97 96 95 93.

JOSEPH FAIVELEY *Nuits-St-Georges, Côtes de Nuits, Burgundy, France*
This Burgundian merchant makes impressive but rather severely tannic, long-lived red wines (CORTON★★, CHAMBERTIN-Clos-de-Bèze★★★, Mazis-Chambertin★★), principally from its own substantial vineyard holdings. In lesser wines, the fruit may not hold out against the tannin, and even aging may not help. The much cheaper MERCUREY reds can also be attractive if on the lean side. The Côte Chalonnaise whites from RULLY★ and Mercurey★, and the oak-aged BOURGOGNE Blanc represent reasonably good value. Best years: (top reds) (2001) 00 99 98 97 96 **95 03 90 09**, (whites) (2001) 00 99 **97 96 95**.

FALERNO DEL MASSICO DOC *Campania, Italy* Falernian, from north of Naples, was one of the ancient Romans' superstar wines. The revived DOC, with a white Falanghina and reds from either Aglianico and Piedirosso or from Primitivo, looks promising. Best producers: Michele Moio★, Villa Matilde★ (Vigna Camarato★★). Best years: (reds) (2001) 00 99 **98 97 96 95**.

CH. FALFAS★ *Côtes de Bourg AC, Bordeaux, France* Biodynamic estate making concentrated, structured wine that needs 4–5 years to soften. Le Chevalier is an old-vines cuvée. Best years: 2000 99 98 **96 95 94 90**.

CH. DE FARGUES★★ *Sauternes AC, Cru Bourgeois, Bordeaux, France* Property run by the Lur-Saluces family, who until 1999 also owned Ch. d'YQUEM. The quality of this fine, rich wine is more a tribute to their commitment than to the inherent quality of the vineyard. Best years: 1997 96 95 **90 89 88 86 83**.

FAUGÈRES AC *Languedoc, France* Faugères, with its vineyards in the schistous hills north of Béziers in the Hérault, was the first of the LANGUEDOC communes to make a reputation of its own. Its ripe, soft, rather plummy flavour marks it out from other Languedoc reds. Best producers: Alquier★, Léon Barral★, Chenaie★, ESTANILLES★, Faugères co-op, Fraisse, Grézan, Haut-Fabrègues, la Liquière, Moulin de Ciffre★, Ollier-Taillefer (Cuvée Castel Fossibus★), St-Antonin. Best years: 2001 00 99 **98 96 95 94 93**.

FAUSTINO *Rioja DOC, País Vasco and Rioja, and Cava DO, Spain* Family-owned and technically very well equipped, this RIOJA company makes good Reserva V★ and Gran Reserva I★ red Riojas in distinctive dark, frosted bottles, as well as a more modern, oak-aged red, Faustino de Autor, and pleasant whites and rosés. In 1999 it introduced a fruit-driven Faustino de Crianza. Best years: (reds) 1998 **96 95 94 92 91 90 89 87 85 82 81**.

FEILER-ARTINGER *Rust, Neusiedlersee, Burgenland, Austria* Father and son team Hans and Kurt Feiler make Ausbruch-style dessert wines★★★ of great elegance. Their dry whites are ★. Solitaire★★ is an elegant red blend of Merlot with Blaufränkisch and Zweigelt.

Best years: (sweet whites) (2001) (00) 99 98 97 **96 95 94 93 91**; (Solitaire) (2000) 99 **97 95 94**.

LIVIO FELLUGA *Colli Orientali del Friuli DOC, Friuli-Venezia Giulia, Italy*   A younger generation has continued the great work of Livio Felluga, delivering both quality and quantity from this large Friuli estate. Pinot Grigio★, Picolit Riserva★★, Tocai★, Merlot-Cabernet blend Vertigo★★ and raspberryish straight Merlot Riserva Sossò★★ are all class acts. Sharjs★ combines Chardonnay with Ribolla and oak, but there's more to stimulate the palate in Terre Alte★★, an aromatic blend of Tocai, Pinot Bianco and Sauvignon. Best years (whites): (2001) **00 99 98 97 96**.

FELSINA, FATTORIA DI *Chianti Classico DOCG, Tuscany, Italy*   Full, chunky CHIANTI CLASSICO★★ wines which improve with several years' bottle age. Quality is generally outstanding; most notable are the single-vineyard Riserva Rancia★★★ and Sangiovese Fontalloro★★★. Also good Chardonnay I Sistri★★ and Cabernet Maestro Raro★★. Best years: (Fontalloro) (1999) 98 97 **95 94 93 90 88 86 85**.

FELTON ROAD *Central Otago, New Zealand*   Runaway success with vineyards in the old goldfields of Bannockburn. Intensely fruity, seductive Pinot Noir★★ is surpassed by very limited quantities of concentrated, complex Block 3 Pinot Noir★★★ and the equally limited edition Block 5★★★. Three classy Rieslings (all ★★) cover the range from dry to sweet. Mineral, citrus unoaked Chardonnay★★ is one of New Zealand's best; barrel-fermented Chardonnay★★ also impresses. Best years: (Pinot Noir) (2001) 00 **99 98 97**.

FENDANT *Valais, Switzerland*   Chasselas wine from the steep slopes of the Swiss VALAIS. Good Fendant should be ever so slightly *spritzig* with a spicy character. However, the average Fendant is thin and virtually characterless. It is best drunk *very* young, but a good example can age for years. Best producers: Chappaz, J Germanier, Gilliard, Caves Imesch, Maye & Fils, Caves Orsat.

FERRARI *Trento DOC, Trentino, Italy* Founded in 1902, the firm is a leader for sparkling wine. Consistent, classy wines include Ferrari Brut★, Maximum Brut★, Perlé★, Rosé★ and vintage Giulio Ferrari Riserva del Fondatore★★, aged 8 years on its lees and an Italian classic.

FERRARI-CARANO *Dry Creek Valley AVA, California, USA*   Delightful Chardonnay, with balanced, elegant fruit made in a regular and a Reserve style. The Reserve★★ is deeply flavoured with more than a touch of oak, while the regular bottling★★ has delicious apple-spice fruit. Red wines are equally impressive, including Siena★★ (a Cabernet Sauvignon-Sangiovese blend) and Tresor★★, a meritage red. Syrah★, Merlot★, Zinfandel★ and Fumé Blanc★ are also good. Reds can improve for 5–10 years. Best years: (reds) (2000) 99 98 97 96 **95 94 91**.

FERREIRA *Port DOC, Douro DOC, Douro, Portugal*   Old port house owned by SOGRAPE, who have taken a major role in modernizing Portugal's wine production. Ferreira is best known for excellent tawny ports: creamy, nutty Quinta do Porto 10-year-old★ and Duque de Braganza 20-year-old★★. The Vintage Port★★ is increasingly good. Ferreira's table wine operation, known as Casa Ferreirinha, produces Portugal's most sought-after red, Barca Velha★★; made from DOURO grape varieties (mainly Tinta Roriz), it is produced only in the finest years – just 12 vintages since 1953. Marginally less good years are now sold as Casa Ferreirinha Reserva★ (previously Reserva Especial). Quinta da Leda reds★★ are also good. Best years: (Vintage) 1997 95 94 91 **85 78 77 70 66 63**; (Barca Velha) **1991 85 83 82 81 78**.

CH. FERRIÈRE★★ *Margaux AC, 3ème Cru Classé, Haut-Médoc, Bordeaux,*
France The smallest classified growth in MARGAUX, Ferrière was leased
to its larger neighbour Ch. LASCOMBES until 1992, when it was
purchased by the Merlaut family, owners of Ch. CHASSE-SPLEEN. It is
now managed by Claire Villars, and the ripe, rich and perfumed wines
are among the best in Margaux AC. Best years: 2000 99 98 96 **95 94**.

FETZER VINEYARDS *Mendocino County, California, USA* Important
winery balancing quality and quantity. Basic wines are good, with a
tasty Syrah★; Barrel Select bottles are usually ★. Also a leader in
organic viticulture with the Bonterra range: Chardonnay★, Viognier★,
Merlot★, Roussanne★, Zinfandel★, Cabernet Sauvignon and Sangiovese.
Best years: (Barrel Select reds) 1999 98 **97 96 95 94**.

FIANO Exciting, distinctive, low-yielding southern Italian white grape
variety. Best producers: (Molise) Di Majo Norante; (Fiano di Avellino
DOC in Campania) Colli di Lapio★, Feudi di San Gregorio★★,
MASTROBERARDINO★, Terredora di Paolo★, Vadiaperti★; (others) L Maffini
(Kràtos★★), PLANETA (Cometa★★).

CH. DE FIEUZAL *Pessac-Léognan AC, Cru Classé de Graves, Bordeaux,*
France Recently purchased by Irish businessman Lochlainn Quinn,
this is one of the most up-to-date properties in the region. The red★ is
drinkable almost immediately, but has the structure to age. Less than
10% of the wine is white★★ but this gorgeous, perfumed (and
ageworthy) wine is the star performer here. Second wine (red and
white): l'Abeille de Fieuzal. Best years: (reds) 2000 98 96 **95 94 90 89 88
87 86 85 83 82**; (whites) 2000 99 98 96 **95 94 93**.

CH. FIGEAC★★ *St-Émilion Grand Cru AC, 1er Grand Cru Classé, Bordeaux,*
France Leading property whose wine traditionally has a delightful
fragrance and gentleness of texture. There is an unusually high
percentage of Cabernets Franc and Sauvignon (70%) in the wine,
making it more structured than other ST-ÉMILIONS. After an
unconvincing run of vintages from the mid-1980s, recent vintages
have been far more like the lovely Figeac of old. Second wine: la
Grangeneuve de Figeac. Best years: 2000 99 98 95 **90 89 88 86 85 83 82**.

FILLIATREAU *Saumur-Champigny, Loire Valley, France* One of the
leading growers in SAUMUR-CHAMPIGNY, producing 3 richly flavoured,
ageworthy Cabernet Francs – Jeunes Vignes★, Saumur-Champigny★
and Vieilles Vignes★ – as well as SAUMUR Rouge, called Château
Fouquet★. Best years: (Vieilles Vignes) (2001) 00 99 **97 96 95 90 89 85**.

FINGER LAKES AVA *New York State, USA* Cool region in central NEW
YORK STATE. Riesling, Chardonnay and sparkling wines are the trump
cards here, but Pinot Noir and Cabernet Franc are increasingly
successful. Best producers: FOX RUN★, Dr Konstantin Frank, Glenora,
LAMOREAUX LANDING★, Silver Thread, Wagner, Hermann J Wiemer.

FITOU AC *Languedoc-Roussillon, France* One of the success stories of the
1980s. Quality subsequently slumped, but with the innovative MONT
TAUCH co-op taking the lead, Fitou is once again an excellent place to
seek out dark, herb-scented reds. Best producers: Bertrand-Berge★, les
Fenals, Lerys★, Milles Vignes, MONT TAUCH co-op★, Nouvelles★
Rochelière, Rolland, Roudène★. Best years: 2000 99 **98 96 95 94 93**.

FIXIN AC *Côte de Nuits, Burgundy, France* Despite being next door to
GEVREY-CHAMBERTIN, Fixin rarely produces anything really magical. The
wines are often sold as CÔTE DE NUITS-VILLAGES. Recent vintages, though

have shown improvements, with best wines able to age for 5 years. Best producers: Champy★★, Pierre Gelin★, Alain Guyard★, Dominique Laurent★★, Naddef★. Best years: (reds) (2001) 00 99 98 **97** 96 **95**.

FLEURIE AC *Beaujolais, Burgundy,*
France The third-largest, but best-known BEAUJOLAIS Cru. Good Fleurie reveals the happy, carefree flavours of the Gamay grape at its best, plus heady perfumes and a delightful juicy sweetness. But demand has meant that many wines are overpriced and ordinary. Best producers: J-M

Aujoux★, Berrod★, M Chignard★, Clos de la Roilette★, Daumas★, Depardon★, Déprés★, DUBOEUF (named vineyards★), H Fessy★, Fleurie co-op★, Metrat★, A & M Morel★, Verpoix★, Vissoux/P-M Chermette★★. Best years: (2001) 00 **99 98 97 96 95**.

CH. LA FLEUR-PÉTRUS★★ *Pomerol AC, Bordeaux, France* Like the better-known PETRUS and TROTANOY, this is owned by the dynamic MOUEIX family. Unlike its stablemates, it is situated entirely on gravel soil and tends to produce tighter wines with less immediate fruit but considerable elegance and cellar potential. Among POMEROL's top dozen properties. Best years: 2000 99 98 97 96 **95 94 93 90 89 88 85 82**.

FLORA SPRINGS *Napa Valley AVA, California, USA* This winery started life as a white wine specialist, but after replanting is now best known for Cabernet Reserve★★, a red BORDEAUX blend called Trilogy★★ and Merlot★★. Chardonnay Reserve★★ tops the whites. The winery also works with Italian varietals; a weighty Pinot Grigio★ and a lightly spiced Sangiovese★ are consistent successes. Best years: (Trilogy) (2000) 99 97 96 95 94 **93 92 91**.

FLOWERS *Sonoma Coast AVA, California, USA* Small producer whose estate vineyard, Camp Meeting Ridge, a few miles from the Pacific Ocean, yields wines of great intensity. The Camp Meeting Ridge Pinot Noir★★★ and Chardonnay★★★ are usually made with native yeasts and offer wonderful exotic aromas and flavours. Wines from purchased fruit with a SONOMA COAST designation are ★★ in quality. Best years: (Chardonnay) (2001) 00 99 **98 97 96**; (Pinot Noir) 2000 99 **98** 97 96.

FONSECA *Port DOC, Douro, Portugal* Owned by the same group as TAYLOR FLADGATE & YEATMAN, Fonseca makes ports in a rich, densely plummy style. Fonseca Vintage★★★ is magnificent, and the aged tawnies★★ uniformly superb. Fonseca Guimaraens★★ is the name of the 'off-vintage' wine, but off vintages here are equal to all but the best offerings of other houses. Bin No. 27★ is one of the best examples of a premium ruby port. Best years: (Vintage) (2000) 97 94 92 **85 83 77 75 70 66 63 55**.

JOSÉ MARIA DA FONSECA *Terras do Sado, Portugal* One of Portugal's most go-ahead wineries. Its most exciting red wines come from Setúbal, south of Lisbon. As well as the famous though rustic red Periquita (better in the 1995 Clássico★ version), acceptable red and dry white Quinta de Camarate and good Primum white★ and red★ are produced. The top wines, however, are premium Garrafeiras RA★★, CO★ and FSF★★ and the famous sweet fortified Moscatel de SETUBAL, ★★ in its 20-year-old and vintage-dated 'superior' versions. Better still, if you can find it, is a superb blend of 3 outstanding 20th-century vintages (1900, 1934 and 1965) called Trilogia★★★.

135

FONTANAFREDDA *Barolo DOCG, Piedmont, Italy*   One of the largest PIEDMONT estates, based in the old BAROLO hunting lodge of the King of Italy. As well as Barolo Serralunga d'Alba★, it also produces a range of Piedmont varietals, several single-vineyard Barolos★ (La Delizia★★), 4 million bottles of ASTI and a good dry sparkler, Contessa Rosa. Best years: (Barolo) (1998) (97) 96 **90 89 88 85**.

DOM. FONT DE MICHELLE *Châteauneuf-du-Pape AC, Rhône Valley, France*   This much-improved estate is currently among the better performers in CHATEAUNEUF-DU-PAPE. The reds★★, in particular Cuvée Étienne Gonnet★★, and whites★ are stylish but still heady, with richness and southern herb fragrance – and not too expensive. Best years: (Étienne Gonnet red) (2000) 99 98 **97 95 90 89**.

FONTERUTOLI, CASTELLO DI *Chianti Classico DOCG, Tuscany, Italy*   This eminent estate has belonged to the Mazzei family since the 15th century. Now, in a dramatic gesture, it has focused production on CHIANTI CLASSICO Riserva★★★. The new wine replaces the fine SUPER-TUSCAN Concerto★★ (Sangiovese with 20% Cabernet) and previously outstanding Riserva Ser Lapo★★. The excellent Sangiovese-Merlot Siepi★★★ is being retained. Belguardo MORELLINO DI SCANSANO★ is a new venture in the southern Maremma.

FONTODI *Chianti Classico DOCG, Tuscany, Italy*   The Manetti family has built this superbly sited estate into one of the most admired in the CHIANTI CLASSICO area, with excellent *normale*★★, richer Riserva★★ and fine Riserva Vigna del Sorbo★★. SUPER-TUSCAN Flaccianello della Pieve★★★, produced from a single vineyard of old vines, has served as a shining example to other producers of how excellent Sangiovese can be without the addition of other varieties. Two varietals are made under the new Case Via label; of these, the Syrah★★ is most promising. Best years: (Flaccianello) (1999) 98 97 96 95 **94 93 91 90 88 86 85**.

FORADORI *Teroldego Rotaliano DOC, Trentino, Italy*   Producer of dark, spicy, berry-fruited wines, including a regular TEROLDEGO ROTALIANO★ and barrique-aged Granato★★. Foradori's interest in Syrah is producing excellent results, both in the varietal Ailanpa★★ and the smoky, black-cherry lushness of Cabernet-Syrah blend Karanar★. Best years: (Granato) (2000) 99 **97 96 95 93 91**.

FORST *Pfalz, Germany*   Village with 6 individual vineyard sites, including the Ungeheuer or 'Monster'; wines from the Monster can indeed be quite savage, with a marvellous mineral intensity and richness in the best years. Equally good are the Kirchenstück, Jesuitengarten, Freundstück and Pechstein. Best producers: BASSERMANN-JORDAN★★, von BUHL★, BURKLIN-WOLF★★, MOSBACHER★★, WEGELER★, Werlé★, WOLF★★. Best years: (Riesling Auslese) (2001) 99 98 **97 96 95 94 93 90**.

FOX CREEK *McLaren Vale, South Australia*   Impressive, opulent, superripe MCLAREN VALE reds. Reserve Shiraz★★ and Reserve Cabernet Sauvignon★★ have wowed the critics; JSM Shiraz-Cabernets★★ is rich and succulent; Merlot★★ is a little lighter but still concentrated and powerful. Vixen sparkling Shiraz★ is also lip-smacking stuff. Whites are comparatively ordinary, albeit fair value for money.

FOX RUN VINEYARDS *Finger Lakes AVA, New York State, USA*   A reliable producer of quality wines, including a complex ALSACE-style Gewürztraminer★★, an elegant Reserve Chardonnay★ and a delightfully quaffable semi-dry Riesling. There are also spicy, attractive reds from Pinot Noir and Cabernet Franc and, since 1996, a complex, fruit-forward red Meritage. Best years: 2000 **99 98 97**.

FRANCIACORTA DOCG *Lombardy, Italy* A Champagne-method sparkler made from Pinot and Chardonnay grapes that has held DOCG status since the mid-90s. Still whites from Pinot Bianco and Chardonnay and reds from Cabernet, Barbera, Nebbiolo and Merlot are all DOC with the appellation Terre di Franciacorta. Best producers: BELLAVISTA★★, CA' DEL BOSCO★★, Fratelli Berlucchi★, Guido Berlucchi★, Castellino★, Cavalleri★, La Ferghettina★, Enrico Gatti★, Monte Rossa★, Ricci Curbastro★, San Cristoforo★, Uberti★, Villa★.

FRANCISCAN *Napa Valley AVA, California, USA* Consistently good wines at fair prices, from the heart of the NAPA VALLEY. The Cuvée Sauvage Chardonnay★★ is a blockbusting, courageous mouthful, and the Cabernet Sauvignon-based meritage Magnificat★ is developing a very attractive style. Estancia is a separate label, with remarkably good-value Chardonnay★ from CENTRAL COAST and Cabernet Sauvignon★ from ALEXANDER VALLEY, as well as its own Meritage★. Franciscan also owns Mount Veeder Winery, where lean but intense Cabernet Sauvignon★★ of great mineral depth and complexity is made.

FRANKEN *Germany* Wine region incorporated into the kingdom of Bavaria at the beginning of the 19th century and specializing in dry wines. Easily recognizable by their squat, green Bocksbeutel bottles (now more familiar because of the Portuguese wine Mateus Rosé). Silvaner is the traditional grape variety, although Müller-Thurgau now predominates. The most famous vineyards are on the hillsides around WURZBURG and IPHOFEN.

FRANSCHHOEK WO *South Africa* A picturesque valley encircled by breathtaking mountain peaks, Franschhoek is a ward within the PAARL district. Huguenot refugees settled here in the 17th century and many of the wineries still bear French names. Semillon is a local speciality (a few vines are close to 100 years old) and the valley is best known for its white wines. However, a diverse range of reds is now showing promise, including BOEKENHOUTSKLOOF Syrah★★ and Cabernet Sauvignon★★, Cabrière Pinot Noir★, La Motte Shiraz★ and Stony Brook Cabernet Sauvignon Reserve. Best producers: BOEKENHOUTSKLOOF★★, Cabrière Estate★, Jean Daneel Wines, La Motte★, La Petite Ferme, L'Ormarins, Rupert & Rothschild Vignerons. Best years: (reds) **1999 98 97**.

FRASCATI DOC *Lazio, Italy* One of Italy's most famous whites, frequently referred to as Rome's quaffing wine. The wine is a blend of Trebbiano and Malvasia; the better examples have a higher proportion of Malvasia. Good Frascati is worth seeking out, most notably Vigna Adriana★★, from the revelationary Castel de Paolis. A number of producers are also reviving the sweet late-harvest style called Cannellino. Other light, dry Frascati-like wines come from neighbouring DOCs in the hills of the Castelli Romani and Colli Albani, including Marino, Montecompatri, Velletri and Zagarolo. Best producers: Casale Marchese★, Castel de Paolis★★, Colli di Catone★, Piero Costantini/Villa Simone★, Fontana Candida★, Zandotti★.

FREISA Italian PIEDMONT grape making sweet, foaming, 'happy juice' reds, now sadly rather out of fashion. Some producers are now making a dry style which is very tasty after 3 or 4 years. Best producers: Poderi Colla, Piero Gatti, Giuseppe MASCARELLO, Cantina del Pino, Scarpa★, Vajra★★, Rino Varaldo, Gianni Voerzio.

FREIXENET *Cava DO, Cataluña, Spain* The second-biggest Spanish sparkling wine company (after CODORNIU) makes the famous Cordon Negro Brut CAVA in a vast network of cellars in Sant Sadurní d'Anoia. Freixenet also owns the Castellblanch, Segura Viudas, Conde de Caralt and Canals & Nubiola Cava brands as well as PENEDES winery René Barbier. Its international expansion has gathered pace in recent years with interests in CHAMPAGNE, CALIFORNIA, Australia and BORDEAUX.

FRESCOBALDI *Tuscany, Italy* Florentine company selling large quantities of inexpensive blended CHIANTIS, but from its own vineyards (some 800 ha/1980 acres in total) it produces good to very good wines at Nipozzano (especially CHIANTI RUFINA Castello di Nipozzano Riserva★★ and Montesodi★★★), Tenuta di Pomino★, and CASTELGIOCONDO★ in BRUNELLO DI MONTALCINO. Castelgiocondo is also the early source for the much-ballyhooed new wine, Luce – a joint venture with MONDAVI. Best years: (premium reds) (2000) 99 98 97 96 **95 94 93 91 90 88 85**.

FRIEDRICH-WILHELM-GYMNASIUM *Trier, Ruwer, Germany* New director Helmut Kranich has brought this estate back on song after a serious lapse in performance in the early 1990s. The naturally sweet Rieslings all have an appealing delicacy and lightness, and most Spätlese and Auslese rate ★. Best years: (Riesling Spätlese) (2001) **99 98 97 95 90**.

FRIULI GRAVE DOC *Friuli-Venezia Giulia, Italy* DOC in western Friuli covering 19 wine types. Good affordable Merlot, Refosco, Chardonnay, Pinot Grigio, Traminer and Tocai. Best producers: Borgo Magredo★, Le Fredis★, Di Lenardo★, Orgnani★, Pighin★, Pittaro★, Plozner★, Pradio★, Russolo★, Vigneti Le Monde★, Villa Chiopris★, Vistorta★. Best years: (whites) (2001) **00 98**.

FRIULI ISONZO DOC *Friuli-Venezia Giulia, Italy* Classy southern neighbour of COLLIO with wines of outstanding value. The DOC covers 20 styles, including Merlot, Chardonnay, Pinot Grigio and Sauvignon. The best from neighbouring Carso are also good. Best producers: (Isonzo) Borgo San Daniele★, Colmello di Grotta★, Sergio & Mauro Drius★★, Masùt da Rive★ (Silvano Gallo), Lis Neris-Pecorari★★, Pierpaolo Pecorari★★, Giovanni Puiatti★, Ronco del Gelso★★, Tenuta Villanova★, Vie di Romans★★; (Carso) Castelvecchio, Edi Kante★★. Best years: (whites) (2001) **00 99 98 97**.

FRIULI-VENEZIA GIULIA *Italy* North-east Italian region bordering Austria and Slovenia. The hilly DOC zones of COLLIO and COLLI ORIENTALI produce some of Italy's finest whites from Chardonnay, Pinot Bianco, Pinot Grigio, Sauvignon and Tocai, and excellent reds mainly from Cabernet Merlot and Refosco. The DOCs of Friuli Aquileia, FRIULI ISONZO, Friuli Latisana and FRIULI GRAVE, in the rolling hills and plains, produce good-value wines

FRONSAC AC *Bordeaux, France* Small area west of POMEROL making good-value Merlot-based wines. The top producers have taken note of the feeding frenzy in neighbouring Pomerol and sharpened up their act accordingly, with finely structured, mineral wines, occasionally perfumed, and better with at least 5 years' age. Best producers: Dalem★, la Dauphine★, Fontenil★, la Grave★, Haut-Carles★, Mayne Vieil, Moulin-Haut-Laroque★, Puy Guilhem, la Rivière★, la Rousselle★, Tour du Moulin, les Trois Croix, la Vieille Cure★, Villars★. Best years: 2001 98 97 96 **95 94 90 89 88 86 85**.

CH. FUISSÉ *Pouilly-Fuissé, Mâconnais, Burgundy, France* Jean-Jacque Vincent has a reputation for rich, ripe, concentrated Chardonnays. To wines are the POUILLY-FUISSÉS: unoaked Cuvée Première, oak-fermente

Ch. Fuissé and Ch. Fuissé Vieilles Vignes. However, the last few vintages have been disappointing. He also makes ST-VERAN, and has a négociant business specializing in the wines of the Mâconnais.

FUMÉ BLANC See Sauvignon Blanc.

RUDOLF FÜRST *Bürgstadt, Franken, Germany* Paul Fürst's dry Rieslings★★ are unusually elegant for a region renowned for its earthy white wines, and his ageworthy Spätburgunder (Pinot Noir) reds★★ are some of the best in Germany. Sensual, intellectual wines with excellent aging potential. Best years: (Riesling Spätlese) 1999 98 **97 94 93 92 90 89 88**; (reds) (2001) 00 99 98 **97 94 90**.

JEAN-NOËL GAGNARD *Chassagne-Montrachet AC, Côte de Beaune, Burgundy, France* Caroline Lestimé has recently taken up the reins from her father, Jean-Noël Gagnard. They consistently make some of the best wines of CHASSAGNE-MONTRACHET. Top wine is rich, toasty BATARD-MONTRACHET★★★, but other whites are first rate, too, particularly Premiers Crus Caillerets★★★ and Morgeot★★. Gagnard's reds★ are not quite as good, but are still among the most enjoyable in Chassagne. All whites are capable of extended cellaring. Best years: (whites) (2001) 00 99 98 **97** 96 **95**.

GAGNARD-DELAGRANGE *Chassagne-Montrachet AC, Côte de Beaune, Burgundy, France* Jacques Gagnard-Delagrange heads a distinguished family of interrelated winemakers – Jacques' brother is Jean-Noël GAGNARD. Jacques makes excellent BATARD-MONTRACHET★★★ and CHASSAGNE-MONTRACHET Premiers Crus la Boudriotte★★ and Morgeot★★. His 2 daughters and their husbands are responsible for Domaines Blain-Gagnard (look out for Criots-Bâtard-Montrachet★★) and Fontaine-Gagnard (also Criots-Bâtard-Montrachet★★★ and several Chassagne-Montrachet Premiers Crus★★). Best years: (whites) (2001) 00 99 98 **97** 96 **95**.

GAILLAC AC *South-West France* The whites, mainly from Mauzac with its sharp but attractive green apple bite, are rather stern but, from a decent grower or the revitalized co-ops, can be extremely refreshing. Sweet whites are getting better as well. Some more serious reds are now being made, which require some aging. The star of Gaillac at the moment is the outstanding fizz, ideally not quite dry and packed with fruit. Drink as young as possible. Best producers: Albert, Bosc-Long, Causses-Marines★, Ch. Clément Termes, Escausses, de Gineste★, Labarthe★, Labastide-de-Lévis co-op, Mas Pignou, Plageoles★, Rotier, Técou co-op★, des Terrisses★.

GAJA *Barbaresco DOCG, Piedmont, Italy* Angelo Gaja brought about the transformation of PIEDMONT from an old-fashioned region that Italians swore made the finest red wine in the world yet the rest of the world disdained, to an area buzzing with excitement. He introduced international standards and charged staggeringly high prices, thus

giving other Piedmont growers the chance at last to get a decent return for their labours. Into this fiercely conservative area, full of fascinating grape varieties but proudest of the native Nebbiolo, he also introduced French grapes like Cabernet Sauvignon (Darmagi★★), Sauvignon Blanc (Alteni di Brassica★) and Chardonnay (Gaia & Rey★★). His latest coup has been to renounce the Barbaresco and Barolo DOCGs for his best wines! Gaja's traditional strength has been in single-vineyard wines from the BARBARESCO region: his Sorì San Lorenzo★★★, Sorì Tildìn★★★ and Costa Russi★★★, now sold under the LANGHE DOC, are often cited as Barbaresco's best. One single premium bottling of Barbaresco★★★ is now made. Sperss★★★ and Conteisa★★★ – from BAROLO, but sold as Langhe DOC wines – are also outstanding. Barbera Sito Rey★ and Nebbiolo-based Langhe Sito Moresco★ are less exciting. Gaja has also invested in BRUNELLO DI MONTALCINO (Pieve Santa Restituta) and BOLGHERI (Cà Marcanda). Best years: (Barbaresco) (2000) 99 98 97 96 **95 94 93 90 89 88 85 82 79 78 71 61**.

GALICIA *Spain* Up in Spain's hilly, verdant north-west, Galicia is renowned for its Albariño whites. There are 5 DOs: RIAS BAIXAS can make excellent, fragrant Albariño, with modern equipment and serious winemaking; Ribeiro DO has also invested heavily in new equipment, and better local white grapes are now being used, as is the case in the mountainous Valdeorras DO. Some young reds from the Mencía grape are also made there and in the new Ribeira Sacra DO. Monterrei DO, also new, is technically backward but shows some potential with its native white grape variety, Doña Blanca. Most wines are best consumed young.

E & J GALLO *Central Valley, California, USA* With the release of its upscale Sonoma Estate Chardonnay and Cabernet Sauvignon in the mid-1990s, Gallo, the world's biggest winery – known for cheap wines – is at last convincing doubters it can make fine wine. Both limited production wines came from Gallo's 800ha (2000 acres) of premium vineyards in key SONOMA COUNTY AVAs. Their success led to the establishment of Gallo of Sonoma, a new label for varietals such as Zinfandel and Cabernet Sauvignon from DRY CREEK VALLEY, Cabernet from ALEXANDER VALLEY and Chardonnay from several vineyards. New vineyards in RUSSIAN RIVER VALLEY have been planted to Pinot Noir. Yet despite this giant step up in quality, Gallo continues to produce oceans of low-priced wine that is at best ordinary. New labels such as Turning Leaf, Gossamer Bay and Garnet Point were launched in the 1990s, plus small-volume brands Anapamu (CENTRAL COAST Chardonnay), Rancho Zabaco (SONOMA COUNTY wines), Marcelina (NAPA wines) and Indigo Hills (MENDOCINO wines).

GALLUCCIO ESTATE VINEYARDS/GRISTINA WINERY *Long Island, New York State, USA* A long-standing producer acquired in 2000 by Vincent Galluccio, who immediately embarked on expanding facilities and plantings. Stars are the elegant Chardonnay★ and cherry-vanilla Merlot.

GAMAY The only grape allowed for red BEAUJOLAIS. In general Gamay wine is rather rough-edged and quite high in raspy acidity, but in Beaujolais so long as the yield is not too high, it can achieve a wonderful, juicy fruit gluggability, almost unmatched in the world of wine. Elsewhere in France, it is successful in the Ardèche and the Loire and less so in the Mâconnais. In Switzerland it is blended with Pinot Noir to create DOLE. In CALIFORNIA, the grape sold under the name of Gamay has now been identified as Valdiguié and the name Gamay is being phased out. There are occasional plantings in Canada and New Zealand, both countries where it could be interesting.

GARD, VIN DE PAYS DU *Languedoc, France*   Mainly reds and rosés from the western side of the RHONE delta. Most red is light, spicy and attractive. Rosés can be fresh when young, and with modern winemaking, whites can be good. Best producers: des Aveylans★, Baruel★, Cantarelles★, Coste Plane, Grande Cassagne★, Guiot★, Mas des Bressades★.

GARGANEGA   Italian white grape from the VENETO in north-east Italy; main component of SOAVE. Grown on hillsides, it can have class, but its reputation is tainted by excessive yields from the Veronese plain.

GARNACHA BLANCA   See Grenache Blanc.

GARNACHA TINTA   See Grenache Noir.

GATTINARA DOCG *Piedmont, Italy*   One of the most capricious of Italy's top red wine areas. The Nebbiolo wines should be softer and lighter than BAROLO, with a delicious, black plums, tar and roses flavour if you're lucky. Drink within 10 years. Vintages follow those for Barolo. Best producers: Antoniolo★, S Gattinara, Nervi★, Travaglini★.

DOM. GAUBY *Côtes du Roussillon-Villages AC, Roussillon, France*   Gérard Gauby used to make burly wines in which the fruit was hidden by very hard tannins. Recent vintages have been softer while still retaining concentration, and Gauby is now a hot property in ROUSSILLON. Highlights include powerful COTES DU ROUSSILLON-VILLAGES Vieilles Vignes★★ and Syrah-dominated la Muntada★★ as well as a vin de pays Viognier★★. Best years: (reds) 2000 99 98 **97 96 95 94 93**.

GAVI DOCG *Piedmont, Italy*   Fashionable and often overpriced, this Cortese-based, steely, lemony white can age up to 5 years, providing it starts life with sufficient fruit. La Scolca's Spumante Brut Soldati★ is an admirable sparkling wine. Best producers: Battistina★, Bergaglio★, Broglia★, La Chiara★, CHIARLO★, FONTANAFREDDA, La Giustiniana★★, Pio Cesare, San Pietro★, La Scolca★, Tassarolo★, Villa Sparina★.

CH. GAZIN★★ *Pomerol AC, Bordeaux, France*   One of the largest châteaux in POMEROL, next to the legendary PETRUS. The wine, traditionally a succulent, sweet-textured Pomerol, seemed to lose its way in the 1980s but is now showing real richness and a very individualistic character under the management of owner Nicolas de Bailliencourt. Best years: 2000 98 97 96 **95 94 90** 89 88.

GEELONG *Victoria, Australia*   Cool-climate, maritime-influenced region revived in the 1960s after destruction by phylloxera in the 19th century. Can be brilliant; potentially a match for the YARRA VALLEY. Impressive Pinot Noir, Chardonnay, Riesling, Sauvignon Blanc and Shiraz. Best producers: BANNOCKBURN★★, Idyll, Scotchmans Hill★★.

GEISENHEIM *Rheingau, Germany*   Village famous for its wine school, founded in 1872. It was here that the Müller-Thurgau grape, now one of Germany's most widely planted grapes, was bred in 1882. Geisenheim's most famous vineyard is the Rothenberg, which produces strong, earthy wines. Best producers: Johannishof, WEGELER, von Zwierlein. Best years: (Riesling Spätlese) (2001) 99 98 **97 96 93** 90.

GERMAIN PÈRE & FILS *Chorey-lès-Beaune, Côte de Beaune, Burgundy, France*   The sleepy village of CHOREY-LES-BEAUNE is the source of some of the COTE D'OR's best-value reds and, along with TOLLOT-BEAUT, François Germain is the AC's best-known producer. Makes elegant red Ch. de Chorey★, a series of richer BEAUNE Premiers Crus (Teurons★★ and Vignes Franches★★ are delicious) and reasonably priced PERNAND-VERGELESSES Blanc. The reds are best drunk after 2–6 years in bottle.

GEROVASSILIOU *Macedonia, Greece* Bordeaux-trained Evangelos Gerovassiliou is one of Greece's most respected enologists, with 33ha (81 acres) of vineyards in Epanomi in northern Greece. High-quality fruit results in superb RHONE-like reds, including a varietal Syrah★★ and Syrah-dominated Domaine Gerovassiliou red. Fresh, modern whites include a fine Viognier★ that lacks a little perfume but has fantastic fruit, and the Domaine Gerovassiliou★ white, an excellent Assyrtiko-Malagousia blend.

GEVREY-CHAMBERTIN AC *Côte de Nuits, Burgundy, France* There have been periods when the wines of Gevrey-Chambertin too often proved disappointing, but a new generation of growers has restored the reputation of Gevrey as a source of well-coloured, firmly structured, powerful, perfumed wines that become rich and gamy with age. Village wines should be kept for at least 5 years, Premiers Crus and the 8 Grands Crus for 10 years or more, especially CHAMBERTIN and Clos-de-Bèze. Look for the Premier Cru Clos St-Jacques, a wine worthy of promotion to Grand Cru. **Best producers:** Denis Bachelet★★, L Boillot★, A Burguet★★, CLAIR★★★, P Damoy★★, DROUHIN★★, C Dugat★★★, B Dugat-Py★★, DUJAC★★, S Esmonin★★, FAIVELEY★★, Fourrier★★, JADOT★★, Philippe Leclerc★★, Denis Mortet★★★, Rossignol★, J Roty★★, ROUSSEAU★★★, Sérafin★★, J & J-L Trapet★. **Best years:** (2001) 00 99 98 **97** 96 **95** 93 **90**.

GEWÜRZTRAMINER *Gewürz* means spice, and the wine certainly can be spicy and exotically perfumed, as well as being typically low in acidity. It is thought to have originated in the village of Tramin, in Italy's ALTO ADIGE, and the name Traminer is used by many producers. In parts of Germany and Austria it is known as Clevner and in Switzerland it is called Heida or Paien. It makes an appearance in many wine-producing countries; quality is mixed and styles vary enormously, from the fresh, light, florally perfumed wines produced in Italy to the rich, luscious, late-harvest ALSACE VENDANGE TARDIVE. Best in France's ALSACE and also impressive in the Styria region of Austria.

GEYSER PEAK *Alexander Valley AVA, California, USA* Australian winemaker Daryl Groom's wines tend to be accessible, fruity and fun. Typical are the fruity Sonoma County Cabernet★ and Merlot★ – ripe, juicy and delicious upon release. The Reserve Alexandre★★, a BORDEAUX-style blend, is made for aging, and the Shiraz Reserve★★ has a cult following. Block Collection features limited production, single-vineyard wines. **Best years:** (Alexandre) (2000) (99) 98 97 **95 94 92 91**.

GHEMME DOCG *Piedmont, Italy* Nebbiolo-based wine from the opposite bank of the Sésia to GATTINARA. The top examples are Cantalupo's Collis Carellae and Signore di Bayard. **Best producers:** Antichi Vigneti d Cantalupo★, G Bianchi★. **Best years:** (2000) (99) 98 97 96 **95** 93 90 89 88

BRUNO GIACOSA *Barbaresco DOCG, Piedmont, Italy* One of the grea winemakers of the LANGHE hills, and an unashamed traditionalist leaving his BARBARESCOS and BAROLOS in cask for up to 6 years. Superl Barbarescos Asili★★★, Santo Stefano★★★ and Rabaja★★★, and Barolo including Collina Rionda★★★ and Falletto★★. Also excellent Dolcette d'Alba★, Roero Arneis★, Moscato d'Asti★★ and sparkling Extra Brut★★

GIESEN *Canterbury, South Island, New Zealand* CANTERBURY's largest winery makes outstanding botrytized Riesling★★, as well as fine dry Riesling★, complex, oaky Chardonnay★, and an attractive Sauvignon Blanc★. Best years: (Reserve Chardonnay) (2001) 00 **99 98 97**.

GIGONDAS AC *Rhône Valley, France* Gigondas wines, mostly red and made mainly from Grenache, have fistfuls of chunky personality. Most drink well with 5 years' age; some need a little more. Best producers: la Boussière★★, Brusset★★, Cassan★★, Cayron★★, Clos des Cazaux★, Cros de la Mûre★★, DELAS★, des Espiers★★, Font-Sane★★, les Goubert★, Gour de Chaule★, Grapillon d'Or★★, GUIGAL★, JABOULET★, Longue-Toque★, Montvac★★, Moulin de la Gardette★★, les Pallières★, Piaugier★, Raspail-Ay★★, Redortier★★, St-Cosme★, ST-GAYAN★, Santa-Duc★★, Tardieu-Laurent★★, la Tourade★★, Trignon★★. Best years: (2001) 00 99 98 **97 95 93 90**.

CH. GILETTE★★ *Sauternes AC, Bordeaux, France* These astonishing wines are stored in concrete vats as opposed to the more normal wooden barrels. This virtually precludes any oxygen contact, and it is oxygen that ages a wine. Consequently, when released at up to 30 years old, they are bursting with life and lusciousness. Best years: **1981 79 78 76 75 70 67 61 59 55 53 49**.

GIPPSLAND *Victoria, Australia* Diverse wineries along the southern Victoria coast, all tiny but with massive potential. Results can be erratic, occasionally brilliant. Nicholson River's BURGUNDY-style Chardonnay can hit ★★, but only occasionally. McAlister★, a red BORDEAUX blend, has also produced some tasty flavours. Bass Phillip Reserve★★ and Premium★★ Pinots are among the best in Australia, with a cult following – in years like 1997 they approached the silky charm of the CÔTE DE NUITS.

VINCENT GIRARDIN *Santenay AC, Côte de Beaune, Burgundy, France* The best grower in SANTENAY and now a thriving négociant as well. Bright, glossy reds from Santenay★★, MARANGES★ and CHASSAGNE-MONTRACHET★★ are surpassed by excellent VOLNAY★★ and POMMARD Grands Epenots★★★. Chassagne-Montrachet whites (Morgeot★★ and Caillerets★★★) are well balanced with good fruit depth. CORTON-CHARLEMAGNE★★★ is exceptional. Best years: (reds) (2001) 99 98 **97 96 95**.

GISBORNE *North Island, New Zealand* Gisborne, with its hot, humid climate and fertile soils, delivers both quality and quantity. Local growers have christened their region 'The Chardonnay Capital of New Zealand' and Gewürztraminer and Chenin Blanc are also a success. Good reds, however, are hard to find. Best producers: CORBANS, MILLTON★★, MONTANA, Revington. Best years: (Chardonnay) **1999 98**.

GIVRY AC *Côte Chalonnaise, Burgundy, France* An important CÔTE CHALONNAISE village. The reds have an intensity of fruit and ability to age that are unusual in the region. In recent years the whites have improved considerably, and there are now some attractive, fairly full, nutty examples. Best producers: Bourgeon★, Chofflet-Valdenaire★, Joblot★★, F Lumpp★★, Parize★, Ragot★, Sarrazin★, Thénard★. Best years: (reds) 2000 99 98 **97 96 95**; (whites) 2000 99.

GLEN CARLOU *Paarl WO, South Africa* Extensive new vineyards, mainly Chardonnay, but also some Zinfandel, Tempranillo and Mourvèdre, reveal the bullish mood in this successful partnership between the Finlaysons and Donald Hess, owner of CALIFORNIA winery The HESS

143

COLLECTION. They also indicate winemaker David Finlayson's versatility: his elegant standard Chardonnay★ and richer toasty Reserve★★ version, the spicy, silky Pinot Noir★, and Grand Classique★★, a red BORDEAUX blend with excellent aging potential, have recently been joined by a rich, spicy Shiraz★★. Best years: (Chardonnay) **2000 99 98 97 96**.

CH. GLORIA★ *St-Julien AC, Cru Bourgeois, Haut-Médoc, Bordeaux, France*
An interesting property, created out of tiny plots of Classed Growth land scattered all round ST-JULIEN. Generally very soft and sweet-centred, the wine nonetheless ages well. Second wine: Peymartin. Best years: 2000 98 96 **95 94 90 89 88 86 85 83 82**.

GOLAN HEIGHTS WINERY *Golan Heights, Israel*   Israel's leading quality wine producer. Cool summers, high-altitude vineyards and modern winemaking with kosher standards have resulted in good Sauvignon Blanc and Cabernet Sauvignon★, excellent, oaky Chardonnay★ and good bottle-fermented fizz★. Yarden is the top label; Golan and Gamla are mid-range. Expansion to new vineyards in Galilee may offset the threat to the flagship winery as the Middle East peace process evolves.

GOLDMUSKATELLER   Moscato Giallo, a strain of Muscat Blanc à Petits Grains, is known as Goldmuskateller in the ALTO ADIGE. Here and elsewhere in Italy's north-east it makes scented wines in dry, off-dry and sweet (*passito*) styles. Best producers: Bolognani★, LAGEDER★, Obermoser.

GOLDWATER ESTATE *Waiheke Island, Auckland, New Zealand*   The founding vineyard established by Kim and Jeanette Goldwater on WAIHEKE ISLAND, New Zealand's premium red wine district. Intense, long-lived Cabernet-Merlot★★ and Esslin Merlot★★, made in an elegant, cedary style with considerable depth and structure. Newly released Zell Chardonnay★ from Waiheke shows promise. Also attractive MARLBOROUGH Dog Point Sauvignon Blanc★ and Roseland Chardonnay★ from grapes grown under contract. Best years: (Waiheke reds) (2000) **99 98 96**.

GONZÁLEZ BYASS *Jerez y Manzanilla DO, Andalucía, Spain*   Tio Pepe★, the high-quality fino brand of this huge top sherry firm, is the world's biggest-selling sherry. The top range of old sherries is superb: intense, dry Amontillado del Duque★★★, and 2 rich, complex olorosos, sweet Matusalem★★ and medium Apostoles★★. One step down is the Alfonso Dry Oloroso★. The firm pioneered the rediscovery of single-vintage (non-solera) dry olorosos★★.

GRAACH *Mosel, Germany*   Important Middle MOSEL wine village with 4 vineyard sites, the most famous being Domprobst (also the best) and Himmelreich. A third, the Josephshöfer, is wholly owned by the von KESSELSTATT estate in Trier. The wines have an attractive fullness to balance their steely acidity, and great aging potential. Best producers: von KESSELSTATT★★, Dr LOOSEN★★, Markus Molitor★, J J PRUM★★, Max Ferd RICHTER★, Willi SCHAEFER★★★, SELBACH-OSTER★★, Weins-Prüm★. Best years: (2001) 00 99 98 **97** 96 **95 94 93 90**.

GRACIANO   Rare, low-yielding but excellent Spanish grape, traditional in RIOJA, NAVARRA and, as Parraleta, in SOMONTANO. It makes dense, highly structured, fragrant reds, and its high acidity adds life when blended with low-acid Tempranillo. Two wineries, CONTINO and Viña Ijalba, now offer varietal examples. Also grown by BROWN BROTHERS in Australia.

GRAHAM *Port DOC, Douro, Portugal*   Part of the Symington empire, making rich, florally scented Vintage Port★★★, sweeter than DOW's and WARRE's, but with the backbone to age. In non-vintage years makes a fine wine called Malvedos★★. Six Grapes is one of the better premium rubies, and 10-year-old★ and 20-year-old★ tawnies are consistently good. Best years: (Vintage) (2000) 97 94 91 **85 83 80 77 75 70 66 63 60**; (Malvedos) (1999) 98 95 92 **90 87 86 84**.

ALAIN GRAILLOT *Crozes-Hermitage AC, Rhône Valley, France*   This excellent estate, established in 1985, stands out as a producer of powerfully concentrated, rich, fruity reds. The top wine is called la Guiraude★★, but the regular CROZES-HERMITAGE★★ is wonderful too, as are the ST-JOSEPH★★ and HERMITAGE★★ and a lovely fragrant white Crozes-Hermitage★★. Keep reds for 5 years, though the best will become even finer with longer aging. Best years: (la Guiraude) (2000) 99 **96 95 94 92 91 90 89 88**.

GRAMPIANS AND PYRENEES *Victoria, Australia*   This area centres on Great Western, a distinguished old viticultural area in central-western VICTORIA, historically known for its sparkling wine but now producing some of Australia's most characterful Shiraz – as cool-climate table wine, sparkling red and even port-style. Best producers: BEST'S★, Dalwhinnie★★, Garden Gully★, MOUNT LANGI GHIRAN★★, Redbank★, SEPPELT★★, TALTARNI★. Best years: (Shiraz) 2000 99 98 97 **96 95 94 91 90**.

CH. GRAND-PUY-DUCASSE★ *Pauillac AC, 5ème Cru Classé, Haut-Médoc, Bordeaux, France*   After great improvement in the 1980s, form dipped in the early 90s but recovered again in 95. Approachable after 5 years, but the wines can improve for considerably longer. Second wine: Artigues-Arnaud. Best years: 2000 96 **95 90 89 88 86 85**.

CH. GRAND-PUY-LACOSTE★★ *Pauillac AC, 5ème Cru Classé, Haut-Médoc, Bordeaux, France*   Classic PAUILLAC, with lots of blackcurrant and cigar-box perfume. As the wine develops, the flavours mingle with the sweetness of new oak into one of Pauillac's most memorable taste sensations. Second wine: Lacoste-Borie. Best years: 2000 99 98 **97** 96 95 **94 93 90 89 88 86 85 83 82**.

GRANDS-ÉCHÉZEAUX AC   See Échézeaux AC.

GRANGE★★★ *Barossa Valley, South Australia*   In 1950, Max Schubert, chief winemaker at PENFOLDS, visited Europe and came back determined to make a wine that could match the great BORDEAUX reds. Undeterred by a lack of Cabernet Sauvignon grapes and French oak barrels, he set to work with BAROSSA Shiraz and barrels made from the more pungent American oak. Initially ignored and misunderstood, Schubert eventually achieved global recognition for his wine, a stupendously complex, thrillingly rich red that only begins to reveal its magnificence after 10 years in bottle. Produced using the best grapes, primarily from the Barossa and MCLAREN VALE, it is acknowledged as Australia's greatest red. Best years: 1996 95 94 93 92 91 **90 88 86 84 83 80 76 71 67 66 63 62 55 53 52**.

GRANGEHURST *Stellenbosch WO, South Africa*   Boutique winery with a focused 3-wine range. The modern Pinotage★ and a Cabernet-Merlot★★ with powerful claret appeal have been joined by Nikela★, a blend of all 3 varieties – owner/winemaker Jeremy Walker's answer to the Cape blend. Best years: (Cabernet-Merlot) **1998 97 95 94 93 92**.

DOM. DE LA GRANGE DES PÈRES *Vin de Pays de l'Hérault, Languedoc, France*   It hasn't taken long for owner Laurent Vaillé to establish his tiny domaine as a LANGUEDOC legend – the first vintage was only in

1992. With only 500 cases produced each year, demand is high for the meticulously crafted unfiltered red★★. 1995 was the first vintage of a white★★ which is produced in even smaller quantities. Best years: (red) (2000) 99 98 **97 96 95 94 93 92**.

GRANS-FASSIAN *Leiwen, Mittel Mosel, Germany* LEIWEN owes its reputation largely to Gerhard Grans' success during the late 1980s. His naturally sweet Rieslings have gained in sophistication over the years: Spätlese★★ and Auslese★★ from TRITTENHEIMER Apotheke are particularly impressive. Eiswein is a speciality and ★★★ in good vintages. Best years: (Riesling Spätlese, Auslese) (2001) 99 98 **97 96 95 94 93 90**.

YVES GRASSA *Vin de Pays des Côtes de Gascogne, South-West France* Innovative COTES DE GASCOGNE producer, who transformed Gascony's thin raw whites into some of the snappiest, fruitiest, almost-dry wines in France. Grassa also makes oak-aged★ and late-harvest★ styles.

ALFRED GRATIEN *Champagne AC, Champagne, France* This small company makes some of my favourite CHAMPAGNE. Its wines are made in wooden casks, which is very rare nowadays. The non-vintage★★ blend is usually 4 years old when sold, rather than the normal 3 years. The vintage★★★ is deliciously ripe and toasty when released but can age for another 10 years. The prestige cuvée, Cuvée Paradis★★, is non-vintage. Best years: (1996) **95** 91 **90 89 88 87 85 83**.

GRATIEN & MEYER *Loire Valley, France* Owner of Champagne house Alfred GRATIEN, Gratien & Meyer is in turn owned by German sparkling wine company Henkell & Söhnlein. In the Loire the company's reputation rests on its Champagne-method SAUMUR MOUSSEUX, particularly its attractively rich, biscuity Cuvée Flamme★ and the Cuvée Flamme Rosé. Also a producer of still SAUMUR white and red SAUMUR-CHAMPIGNY, it produces a little CREMANT DE LOIRE★ – and the sparkling red Cuvée Cardinal is unusual and fun.

GRAVES AC *Bordeaux, France* The Graves region covers the area south of Bordeaux to Langon, but the generally superior villages in the northern half broke away in 1987 to form the PESSAC-LEOGNAN AC. Nowadays a new wave of winemaking is sweeping through the southern Graves, and there are plenty of clean, bone-dry white wines, with lots of snappy freshness, as well as more complex soft, nutty barrel-aged whites, and some juicy, quick-drinking reds. Sweet white wines take the Graves Supérieures AC; the best make a decent substitute for the more expensive SAUTERNES. Best producers: Archambeau, Ardennes★, le Bonnat, Brondelle★, Chantegrive★, Clos Floridène★, Dom. la Grave★, l'Hospital, Landiras, Magence, Magneau★, Rahoul★, Respide-Médeville★, St-Robert, Seuil★, Vieux-Ch.-Gaubert★, Villa Bel Air★; (sweet) Clos St-Georges, Léhoul. Best years: (reds) 2000 **98 96 95 94 90 89 88 86 85 83 82**; (dry whites) 2000 **98 96 95 94 90 89 88**; (sweet whites) 2001 **99 98 97 96 95 90 89 88 86**.

GRAVNER *Friuli-Venezia Giulia, Italy* Josko Gravner, FRIULI's most zealous winemaker, sets styles with wood-aged wines of uncommon stature though some remain outside the COLLIO DOC. Along with prized and high-priced Chardonnay★★, Sauvignon★★ and Ribolla Gialla★, he combines 6 white varieties in Breg★★. Reds are Rosso Gravner★ (predominantly Merlot) and Rujno★★ (Merlot-Cabernet Sauvignon)

GREAT SOUTHERN *Western Australia* A vast, cool-climate region encompassing Mount Barker, Frankland River, Denmark, Albany and the Porongurup Ranges. Riesling, Pinot Noir and Chardonnay all de well here, and there is some stunningly peppery Shiraz from warmer sites, as well as Cabernet Sauvignon in patches. Best producers: Alkoomi★, Frankland Estate★★, Goundrey★, HOUGHTON★, HOWARD PARK★★★, Jingalla★, Old Kent River★, PLANTAGENET★★, Wignalls★.

GRECHETTO Italian grape centred on UMBRIA, making tasty, anise-tinged dry whites. Also used in VIN SANTO in TUSCANY. Best producers: Antonelli, Barberani-Vallesanta, Caprai, Falesco★, Palazzone, Castello della SALA.

GRECO See Grechetto.

GREEN POINT VINEYARDS *Yarra Valley, Victoria, Australia* MOET & CHANDON's Aussie offshoot makes Pinot Noir-Chardonnay Champagne-method fizz, including regular Chandon Australia and premium sparklers under the Green Point label (Vintage Brut★★, Vintage Brut Rosé★★). Now also producing a sparkling red Pinot Noir-Shiraz★, as well as still wines from Chardonnay and Pinot Noir in a fairly oaky style. The Domaine Chandon label is used in the Australian market and is the name of the winery.

GRENACHE BLANC A common white grape in the south of France, but without many admirers. Except me, that is, because I love the pear-scented wine flecked with anise that a good producer can achieve. Generally best within a year of the vintage, although the odd old-vine example can age. Grown as Garnacha Blanca in Spain.

GRENACHE NOIR Among the world's most widely planted red grapes – the bulk of it in Spain, where it is called Garnacha Tinta. It is a hot-climate grape and in France it reaches its peak in the southern RHONE, especially in CHATEAUNEUF-DU-PAPE, where it combines great alcoholic strength with rich raspberry fruit and a perfume hot from the herb-strewn hills. It is generally given more tannin, acid and structure by blending with Syrah, Mourvèdre, Cinsaut or other southern French grapes. It can make wonderful rosé in TAVEL, LIRAC and COTES DE PROVENCE, as well as in NAVARRA in Spain. It takes centre stage in ARAGON's Calatayud, Campo de Borja and CARINENA, and forms the backbone of the impressive reds of PRIORAT; in RIOJA it adds weight to the Tempranillo. It is also the basis for the *vins doux naturels* of BANYULS and MAURY. Also grown in CALIFORNIA and SOUTH AUSTRALIA, where it has only recently been accorded much respect as imaginative winemakers realized there was a great resource (that no one was taking any notice of) of century-old vines capable of making wild and massively enjoyable reds. See also Cannonau.

GRGICH HILLS CELLAR *Rutherford AVA, California, USA* Mike Grgich was winemaker at CHATEAU MONTELENA when its Chardonnay shocked Paris judges by finishing ahead of French versions in the famous 1976 tasting. At his own winery he makes ripe, tannic Cabernet★ and a huge, old-style Zinfandel★, but his reputation has been made by big, ripe, oaky Chardonnay★★ that is one of NAPA's best-selling high-priced wines. Best years: (Chardonnay) 2000 99 **98 97 96 95 94 92 91 90**.

GRIOTTE-CHAMBERTIN AC See Chambertin AC.

JEAN GRIVOT *Vosne-Romanée, Côte de Nuits, Burgundy, France* Étienne Grivot took time to settle down but has now reconciled his father's traditional styles and former consultant Guy Accad's experimentation into a high-quality interpretation of his own. He has made brilliant wines since 1995, especially RICHEBOURG★★★ and NUITS-ST-GEORGES les Boudots★★. Expensive. Best years: (2001) 00 99 98 97 96 **95**.

GROS PLANT DU PAYS NANTAIS VDQS *Loire Valley, France* From the marshy salt-flats around Nantes, Gros Plant can be searing stuff, but this acidic wine is well suited to the seafood guzzled in the region. Look for a *sur lie* bottling and drink the youngest available. Best producers: Chiron, l'ECU, J Guindon, J Hallereau, Herbauges, la Preuille, Sauvion.

GROSSET *Clare Valley, South Australia* Jeffrey Grosset is a perfectionist, crafting tiny quantities of hand-made wines in his Auburn winery. A Riesling specialist, he bottles Watervale★★★ separately from Polish Hill★★★; both are supremely good and age well. Cabernet blend Gaia★★ is smooth and seamless. Also outstanding Piccadilly (ADELAIDE HILLS) Chardonnay★★★ and very fine Pinot Noir★★ and Semillon-Sauvignon★★. Best years: (Riesling) 2001 **00 99** 98 97 96 94 93 92 90.

GROVE MILL *Marlborough, New Zealand* Mid-sized producer with a strong quality focus. Full-bodied Sauvignon Blanc★ is a feature of their range, together with a ripe, rich, remarkably smooth Chardonnay★ and tangy, pungent Riesling★★. Best years: (Riesling) (2001) 00 **99 98 97** 96.

CH. GRUAUD-LAROSE★★ *St-Julien AC, 2ème Cru Classé, Haut-Médoc, Bordeaux, France* One of the largest ST-JULIEN estates, now owned by the same family as CHASSE-SPLEEN and HAUT-BAGES-LIBERAL. Until the 1970s these wines were classic, cedary St-Juliens. Since the early 80s, the wines have been darker, richer and coated with new oak, yet have also shown an unnerving animal quality. They're certainly impressive, but it is hard to say whether the animal or the cedar will prevail after 20 years or so of aging in bottle. Second wine: Sarget de Gruaud-Larose. Best years: 2000 99 98 97 96 95 **94 93 90 89 88 86 85**.

GRÜNER VELTLINER Austrian grape, also grown in Slovakia and Hungary. The grape is at its best, however, in Austria's KAMPTAL, KREMSTAL, and the WACHAU, where the soil and cool climate bring out all the lentilly, white-peppery aromas in the fruit.

GUELBENZU *Spain* Family-owned bodega making good Guelbenzu Crianza★, from Tempranillo, Cabernet and Merlot, and rich concentrated Evo★, made mostly from Cabernet Sauvignon. The new Lautus★ is made from old vines and incorporates Garnacha in the blend. In 2001, the owners decided to leave the NAVARRA DO and move to a generic *vino de mesa* appellation to protest against existing DO regulations in Spain. Best years: (Evo) 1999 **98 97 96 95** 94.

GUIGAL *Côte-Rôtie AC, Rhône Valley, France* Marcel Guigal is among the most famous names in the RHONE, producing wines from his company's own vineyards in COTE-ROTIE under the Château d'Ampuis label as well as the Guigal range from purchased grapes. Northern Rhône holdings have been tripled with the recent acquisition of  the J-L Grippat and de Vallouit operations. La Mouline, la Turque and la Landonne all rate ★★★ in most critics' opinions, but I have to add the proviso that with all these oaky wines I find the unique beauty and fragrance of Côte-Rôtie difficult to discern. However, many of the top Côte-Rôtie producers have, predictably, decided to follow Guigal's new oil route. I'm more of a fan of the fragrant CONDRIEU★★ (la Doriane★★★). HERMITAGE★★ is also good, as is the cheaper COTES DU RHONE★. GIGONDAS★ is reasonably chunky. Best years: (top reds) (2000) 99 98 97 95 **94 91 90 89 88 85 83 82**.

CH. GUIRAUD★★ *Sauternes AC, 1er Cru Classé, Bordeaux, France* A property that was hauled up from near extinction by the Canadian Narby family, convinced that Guiraud could be one of SAUTERNES' greatest wines. Selecting only the best grapes and using 50% new oak each year, they have returned Guiraud to the top-quality fold. Keep best vintages for 10 years or more. Second wine (dry): G de Guiraud. Best years: (2001) 99 98 97 96 **95 90 89 88 86 85 83**.

GUNDERLOCH *Nackenheim, Rheinhessen, Germany* Fritz and Agnes Hasselbach's estate has become one of Germany's best. Sensationally concentrated and luscious Beerenauslese★★★ and Trockenbeerenauslese★★★ dessert Rieslings are among the world's most expensive wines. Dry and off-dry Rieslings, at least ★, however, are good value. Late-harvest Spätlese and Auslese are ★★ year in, year out. Best years: (Spätlese, Auslese) (2001) (00) **99 98 97** 96 **95 94 93 92 90 89**.

GUNDLACH-BUNDSCHU *Sonoma Valley AVA, California, USA* Family-owned winery, founded in 1858. From the Rhinefarm Vineyards comes outstanding juicy, fruity Cabernet Sauvignon★★, a rich and tightly structured Merlot★★, a Zinfandel★ and Pinot Noir★. Also produced are 2 Chardonnay★ bottlings and attractive Riesling and Gewürztraminer★. The Bundschu family has created a small boutique winery, Bartholomew Park.

FRITZ HAAG *Brauneberg, Mosel, Germany* MOSEL grower with vineyards in the BRAUNEBERGER Juffer and Brauneberger Juffer Sonnenuhr. Pure, elegant Rieslings at least ★ quality, Auslese reaching ★★ or ★★★. Best years: (Auslese) (2001) 00 99 98 **97 96 95 94 93 92 91 90 88 85 83**.

REINHOLD HAART *Piesport, Mosel, Germany* Theo Haart produces sensational Rieslings – with blackcurrant, peach and citrus aromas – from the great Piesporter Goldtröpfchen★★ vineyard. Ausleses are usually ★★★, but 1999 suffered a bit from heat stress and young vines. Best years: (Spätlese, Auslese) (2001) 00 98 **97 96 95 94 93 91 90 89**.

HAMILTON RUSSELL VINEYARDS *Walker Bay, Overberg WO, South Africa* Owner Anthony Hamilton Russell and winemaker Kevin Grant pursue their goal of classic Pinot Noir and Chardonnay with fierce dedication. From 1999, new Burgundian clones provide a fruitier profile and higher quality plateau to the Pinot Noir★. The Chardonnay★ maintains the restrained house style – expect both to rise to ★★ in future vintages. The Southern Right label focuses on Pinotage and Sauvignon Blanc from bought-in grapes. Best years: (Pinot Noir) **2000 99 98 97 96 95**; (Chardonnay) 2001 **00 99 98 97 96 95**.

HANDLEY *Mendocino County, California, USA* Outstanding producer of sparkling wines, including one of California's best Brut Rosés★ and a delicious Blanc de Blancs★★. An aromatic Gewürztraminer★★ is one of the state's finest. Two bottlings of Chardonnay, from the DRY CREEK VALLEY★★ and ANDERSON VALLEY★, are worth seeking out. The Anderson Valley estate Pinot Noirs (regular★, Reserve★★) are in a lighter, more subtle style. Best years: (Pinot Noir Reserve) 2000 99 **98 96**.

HANGING ROCK *Macedon Ranges, Victoria, Australia* Highly individual, gutsy sparkling wine, Macedon Cuvée★★ stands out at John and Anne (née Tyrrell) Ellis's ultra-cool-climate vineyard high in the Macedon

Ranges. Tangy estate-grown 'The Jim Jim' Sauvignon Blanc★ is mouthwatering stuff, while Heathcote Shiraz★★, from a warmer neighbouring region, is the best red.

HARDYS *McLaren Vale, South Australia* Despite the worrying tie-up with American giant Canandaigua, wines under the Hardys flagship label still taste reassuringly Australian. Varietals under the Siegersdorf and Nottage Hill labels are among Australia's most reliably good gluggers. Top of the tree are the commemorative Eileen Hardy Shiraz★★★ and Thomas Hardy Cabernet★★★, both dense reds for hedonists. Eileen Hardy Chardonnay★★ is rich, heady, oak-perfumed and complex. Newer releases include the attractively packaged Tintara Shiraz★★ and Grenache★★, plus 'ecologically aware' Banrock Station★, the inexpensive Insignia wines and great-value sparkling wine under the Omni label. Other BRL Hardy brands include HOUGHTON, LEASINGHAM, REYNELL, Stonehaven, Yarra Burn, and the company also has stakes in BAROSSA VALLEY ESTATE and Brookland Valley. Best years: (Eileen Hardy Shiraz) 1998 97 96 95 **93 88 87 81 79 70**.

HARLAN ESTATE *Oakville AVA, California, USA* Estate in the western hills of OAKVILLE, whose BORDEAUX blend has become one of California's most sought-after reds. Full-bodied and rather tannic, Harlan Estate★★★ offers layers of ripe black fruits and heaps of new French oak. Rough upon release, the wine is built to develop for 10–20 years.

HARTENBERG ESTATE *Stellenbosch WO, South Africa* After a promising start in 1994 under a young and enthusiastic team, this old winery has been marking time of late. New vineyards should see them on the catch-up trail again shortly. Shiraz★, Merlot★★ and Cabernet perform well in the warm Bottelary Hills. More unusual are Zinfandel and the Cape's sole Pontac. Whites are well served by a firm, flavoursome Chardonnay and, unusually for these north-facing slopes, a vigorous, limy Riesling★. Best years: (premium reds) **1998 97 96 95 94**.

HARTFORD COURT *Russian River AVA, California, USA* Boutique winery focusing on very limited-production wines from RUSSIAN RIVER and SONOMA COAST fruit. Pinot Noirs include the stylish Marin County★★ bottling and the massive Arrendell Vineyard★★★. Seascape Vineyard Chardonnay★★ has textbook cool-climate intensity and acidity. Hartford Zinfandels include Highwire★ and Fanucchi Wood★★.

HATTENHEIM *Rheingau, Germany* Fine RHEINGAU village with 13 vineyard sites, including a share of the famous Marcobrunn vineyard. Best producers: SCHLOSS REINHARTSHAUSEN★★, Schloss Schönborn★. Best years: (Spätlese, Auslese) (2001) **99** 98 96 **95 94 93 92 90**.

CH. HAUT-BAGES-LIBÉRAL★ *Pauillac AC, 5ème Cru Classé, Haut-Médoc, Bordeaux, France* Little-known PAUILLAC property that has quietly been gathering plaudits for some years now: loads of unbridled delicious fruit, a positively hedonistic style – and its lack of renown keeps the price just about reasonable. The wines will age well, especially the latest vintages. Best years: 2000 99 98 96 **95 94 90 89 86 85**.

CH. HAUT-BAILLY★★ *Pessac-Léognan AC, Cru Classé de Graves, Bordeaux, France* The softest and most charming among the GRAVES Classed Growths, which has been on good form right through the 1990s. Drinkable very early, but ages well. Second wine: la Parde-de-Haut-Bailly. Best years: 2000 99 98 96 **95 93 90 89 88 86 85 83 82**.

CH. HAUT-BATAILLEY★ *Pauillac AC, 5ème Cru Classé, Haut-Médoc, Bordeaux, France* Despite being owned by the Borie family of DUCRU-BEAUCAILLOU, this estate has produced too many wines that are light, pleasant, attractively spicy, but lacking real class and concentration. Recent vintages have shown improvement and the wine is becoming a bit more substantial. Best years: 2000 99 96 **95 90 89 85 83 82**.

CH. HAUT-BRION *Pessac-Léognan AC, 1er Cru Classé, Graves, Bordeaux, France* The only Bordeaux property outside the MEDOC and SAUTERNES to be included in the great 1855 Classification, when it was accorded First Growth status. The excellent gravel-based vineyard is now part of Bordeaux's suburbs. The red wine★★★ almost always deserves its exalted status, and there is also a small amount of white★★★ which, at its best, is magically rich yet marvellously dry, blossoming out over 5–10 years. Second wine: (red) Bahans-Haut-Brion. Best years: (red) 2000 99 98 96 95 94 **93 90 89 88 86 85 83 78**; (white) 2000 99 98 **96 95 94 90 89 88**.

CH. HAUT-MARBUZET★ *St-Estèphe AC, Cru Bourgeois, Haut-Médoc, Bordeaux, France* Impressive ST-ESTEPHE wine with great, rich, mouthfilling blasts of flavour and lots of new oak. Best years: 2000 99 98 **97** 96 **95 94 93 90 89 88 86 85 83 82**.

HAUT-MÉDOC AC *Bordeaux, France* The finest gravelly soil is here in the southern half of the MÉDOC peninsula, and Haut-Médoc AC covers all the decent vineyard land not included in the 6 village ACs (MARGAUX, MOULIS, LISTRAC, ST-JULIEN, PAUILLAC and ST-ESTEPHE). The wines vary in quality and style. Best producers: Beaumont, Belgrave★, Bernadotte★, Cambon la Pelouse★, Camensac, CANTEMERLE★, Charmail★, Cissac★, Citran★, Coufran★, la LAGUNE★★, Lanessan★, Malescasse, Maucamps★, Sénéjac, SOCIANDO-MALLET★★, la Tour-Carnet, la Tour-du-Haut-Moulin★, Verdignan, Villegeorge. Best years: 2000 **96 95 94 90 89 88 86 85**.

HAUT-MONTRAVEL AC See Montravel AC.
HAUTES-CÔTES DE BEAUNE AC See Bourgogne-Hautes-Côtes de Beaune AC.
HAUTES-CÔTES DE NUITS AC See Bourgogne-Hautes-Côtes de Nuits AC.

HAWKES BAY *North Island, New Zealand* One of New Zealand's most prestigious wine regions. The high number of sunshine hours, moderately predictable weather during ripening and a complex array of soil patterns make it ideal for a wide range of winemaking styles. Chardonnay, Cabernet Sauvignon and Merlot are the area's greatest strengths, although Syrah has good potential. Free-draining Gimblett Gravels area is especially promising. Best producers: Alpha Domus★, CHURCH ROAD★, Clearview★, CRAGGY RANGE★, Esk Valley★★, Matariki★, MATUA VALLEY★★, MORTON ESTATE★, Newton-Forrest★, NGATARAWA★, C J Pask, Sacred Hill★, SILENI★, TE MATA★★, Trinity Hill, Unison★★, Vidal★, VILLA MARIA★★. Best years: (premium reds) (2000) 99 **98 96 95 94**.

DR HEGER *Ihringen, Baden, Germany* Joachim Heger specializes in powerful, dry Grauburgunder (Pinot Gris), Weissburgunder (Pinot Blanc and red Spätburgunder (Pinot Noir)★ with Riesling a sideline. Grauburgunder from the Winklerberg★★ is serious stuff.

CHARLES HEIDSIECK *Champagne AC, Champagne, France* Charles Heidsieck, under Rémy Cointreau ownership, is the most consistently fine of all the major houses, with ★★★ vintage Champagne. The non-vintage★★ is regularly of vintage quality, especially those cuvées★★ marked by a bottling date (for example, Mis en Cave en 1996); these age well for 5 years. Best years: (1996) **95 90 89 88 85 82**.

HEITZ CELLARS *Napa Valley AVA, California, USA* Star attraction here is the Martha's Vineyard Cabernet Sauvignon★★. Heitz also produces a Bella Oaks Vineyard Cabernet Sauvignon★, a Trailside Vineyard

Cabernet★ and a straight Cabernet★ that takes time to understand but can be good. After 1992, phylloxera forced the replanting of Martha's Vineyard and bottling only resumed in 1996. Many believe that early bottlings of Martha's Vineyard are among the best wines ever produced in CALIFORNIA. Grignolino Rosé is an attractive picnic wine. Best years: (Martha's Vineyard) (1997) 96 92 91 **86 85 75**.

HENRIQUES & HENRIQUES *Madeira DOC, Madeira, Portugal* The wines to look for are the 10-year-old★★ and 15-year-old★★ versions of the classic varieties. Vibrant Sercial and Verdelho, and rich Malmsey and Bual are all fine examples of their styles. Henriques & Henriques also has vintage Madeiras of extraordinary quality.

HENRY OF PELHAM *Niagara Peninsula VQA, Ontario, Canada* Winery making concentrated wines from low-yielding vines. Best are Reserve Chardonnay★, Proprietor's Reserve Riesling★, Riesling Icewine★ and a Cabernet-Merlot blend. Best years: (Riesling Icewine) 1999 98 **97 95**.

HENSCHKE *Eden Valley, South Australia* Fifth-generation winemaker Stephen Henschke and his viticulturist wife Prue make some of Australia's grandest reds from old vines in Eden Valley. Top wine, HILL OF GRACE★★★, is stunning, and Mount Edelstone Shiraz★★★ and Cyril Henschke Cabernet★★ and Keyneton Estate★ are also brilliant wines. The whites are full and intensely flavoured too, led by the seductive, perfumed Julius Riesling★★, the toasty yet fruity Louis Semillon★★ and Croft Chardonnay★. Best years: (Mount Edelstone) 1998 97 **96 94** **92 91 90 88 86 84 82 80 78**.

HÉRAULT, VIN DE PAYS DE L' *Languedoc, France* A huge region, covering the entire Hérault *département*. Red wines predominate, based on Carignan, Grenache and Cinsaut, and most of the wine is sold in bulk. But things are changing. There are lots of hilly vineyards with great potential, and MAS DE DAUMAS GASSAC is merely the first of many exciting reds from the region. The whites are improving too. Best producers: Bosc, Capion★, la Fadèze, GRANGE DES PERES★★, Jany, Limbardié★, MAS DE DAUMAS GASSAC★★, Moulines.

HERMITAGE AC *Rhône Valley, France* Great Hermitage, from steep vineyards above the town of Tain l'Hermitage in the northern RHONE, is revered throughout the world as a rare, rich red wine – expensive, memorable and classic. Not all Hermitage achieves such an exciting blend of flavours, but the best growers, with mature red Syrah vines, can create superbly original wine, needing 5–10 years' aging even in a light year and a minimum of 15 years in a ripe vintage. White Hermitage, from Marsanne and Roussanne, is less famous but the best wines, made by traditionalists, can outlive the reds, sometimes lasting as long as 40 years. Best producers: A Belle★★, CHAPOUTIER★★, B Chave★★, J-L CHAVE★★★, Colombier★★, COLOMBO★★, DELAS★★ (les Bessards★★★), B Faurie★★, Fayolle★★, M Ferraton★, GRAILLOT★★, J-L Grippat★★, GUIGAL★★, JABOULET (la Chapelle★★★), Remizières, J-M Sorrel★★, M Sorrel★★★, TAIN L'HERMITAGE co-op★★, Tardieu-Laurent★★, les Vins de Vienne★★. Best years: (reds) (2001) 00 99 98 97 **96 95 94 92** **91 90 89 88 85 83 82 78 71 70**.

JAMES HERRICK *Vin de Pays d'Oc, Languedoc, France* When Herrick and his Aussie partners planted 175ha (435 acres) of Chardonnay between Narbonne and Béziers, many locals thought he was mad. The wines turned out to be a big success, and the brand and vineyards are now part of the Southcorp/Rosemount group, Australia's leading wine company. Chardonnay is an attractive blend of tropical fruit and

French elegance. A Reserve bottling★ is more concentrated. Syrah-based red blend Cuvée Simone has disappointed.

THE HESS COLLECTION *Mount Veeder AVA, California, USA* NAPA VALLEY producer earning rave reviews for its Cabernet Sauvignon★★, which shows all the intense lime and black cherry originality of its MOUNT VEEDER fruit, without coating it with impenetrable tannins. The Chardonnay★ is ripe with tropical fruit and balanced oak. Hess Select is the budget label. Best years: (Cabernet) (2000) (99) 98 97 **96 95 94 93 91 90**.

HESSISCHE BERGSTRASSE *Germany* Small, warm wine region near Darmstadt. Much of the winemaking is by the co-op, Bergsträsser Winzer, although the Staatsweingut also makes some good wines. There has been less flirtation with new grape varieties here than elsewhere in Germany, and Riesling is still the most prized grape. Eisweins are a speciality.

HEURIGER *Austria* Fresh, young wine drunk in the many taverns in the Viennese hills. Once the wine is a year old it is called der Alte, or 'old chap'. No really good wine is sold as Heuriger, yet a few swift jugs of it can make for a great evening – but keep the aspirin handy.

HEYL ZU HERRNSHEIM *Nierstein, Rheinhessen, Germany* Historical estate whose main strength is substantial dry whites from the Riesling, Weissburgunder (Pinot Blanc) and Silvaner grapes. However, Auslese and higher Prädikat wines of recent vintages have been of ★★ and – sometimes – ★★★ quality. In future only wines from the top sites (Brudersberg, Pettenthal, Hipping, Oelberg) will carry the vineyard designation. Other high-quality dry wines will be sold under the 'Rotschiefer' name. Best years: (Riesling Auslese) (2001) 99 98 97 96 **93 90 89**.

HIDALGO *Jerez y Manzanilla DO, Andalucía, Spain* Hidalgo's Manzanilla La Gitana★★ is deservedly one of the best-selling manzanillas in Spain. Hidalgo is still family-owned, and only uses grapes from its own vineyards. Brands include Mariscal★, Fino Especial and Miraflores, Amontillado Napoleon★★, Oloroso Viejo★★ and Jerez Cortado★★.

HILL OF GRACE★★★ *Eden Valley, South Australia* A stunning wine with dark, exotic flavours made by HENSCHKE from a single plot of Shiraz. The Hill of Grace vineyard was first planted in the 1860s, and the old vines produce a powerful, structured wine with superb ripe fruit, chocolate, coffee, earth, leather and the rest. Can be cellared for 20 years or longer. Best years: (1997) 96 95 94 **93 92 91 90 88 86 85 82 78 72**.

HILLTOP *Neszmély, Hungary* This dynamic company, with its showpiece winery, has been Hungary's leader in providing fresh, bright wines, especially white, at friendly prices. Based in the Aszár-Neszmély wine region, aromatic varieties such as Irsai Oliver and Gewürztraminer thrive alongside Sauvignon Blanc, Chardonnay and Merlot on the protected slopes between the Danube and the Transdanubian Mountains. Grapes are also bought in from other regions. Chief winemaker Akos Kamocsay is one of Hungary's most respected. Hilltop also produces a good but controversial TOKAJI.

HILLTOPS *New South Wales, Australia* Promising high-altitude cherry-growing region with a small but fast-growing area of vineyards around the town of Young. Good potential for reds from Cabernet Sauvignon and Shiraz. Best producers: Demondrille, Grove Estates, MCWILLIAM'S (Barwang vineyard), Woodonga Hill.

FRANZ HIRTZBERGER *Wachau, Niederösterreich, Austria*   One of the WACHAU's top growers. Hirtzberger's finest wines are the concentrated, elegant Smaragd Rieslings from Singerriedel★★★ and Hochrain★★. The best Grüner Veltliner comes from the Honivogl site★★★. Best years: (Riesling Smaragd) (2001) 00 99 98 **97 96 95 94 93 92 91 90 88**.

HOCHHEIM *Rheingau, Germany*   Village best known for having given the English the word 'Hock' for Rhine wine, but with good individual vineyard sites, especially Domdechaney, Hölle (or Hell!) and Kirchenstück. Best producers: Franz KUNSTLER★★★, W H Schafer, Domdechant Werner. Best years: (2001) 99 98 97 96 **94 93 92 90 88**.

HOGUE CELLARS *Yakima Valley AVA, Washington State, USA*   A large winery producing nearly 400,000 cases a year, Hogue Cellars makes a crisp Fumé Blanc, brambly Reserve Cabernet Sauvignon★ and decent Merlot. A peppery Syrah★ and spicy Viognier★ have been added to the mix. Best years: (top reds) 2000 99 97 **96 95**.

HOLLICK *Coonawarra, South Australia*   Run by viticulturist Ian Hollick, this winery makes a broader range of good wines than is usually found in COONAWARRA: an irresistible sparkling Merlot★ (yes, *Merlot*), subtle Chardonnay★, tobaccoey Cabernet-Merlot★ and a richer Ravenswood Cabernet Sauvignon★★. Also attractive Sauvignon-Semillon and good limy Riesling★. Best years: (Ravenswood) 1998 **96 94 93 91 90 88**.

DOM. DE L'HORTUS *Pic St-Loup, Coteaux du Languedoc AC, Languedoc, France*   From a first vintage in 1990, Jean and Marie-Thérèse Orliac have created one of the leading estates in this booming region. Cuvée Classique★, a ready-to-drink unoaked Mourvèdre-Syrah-Grenache blend, has delightful flavours of herbs, plums and cherries. Big brother Grande Cuvée★★ needs some time for the fruit and oak to come into harmony. Promising new white l'Hortus Grande Cuvée★ is a blend of Chardonnay and Viognier. Best years: (Grande Cuvée red) 2000 99 98 **97 96 95 94 93**.

HOSPICES DE BEAUNE *Côte de Beaune, Burgundy, France*   Scene of a theatrical auction on the third Sunday in November each year, the Hospices is an historical foundation which sells wine from its holdings in the COTE D'OR to finance its charitable works. The quality of the wine-making has increased immeasurably since 1994, partly thanks to the building of a new state-of-the-art winery on the outskirts of Beaune. The wines are matured and bottled by the purchaser, which can cause variations in quality, and pricing reflects charitable status rather than common sense.

HOUGHTON *Swan District, Western Australia*   WESTERN AUSTRALIA's biggest winery, wholly owned by BRL Hardy, with a huge output of tasty 'White Burgundy'★ (called Houghton's HWB in the EU). Good Sauvignon-Semillon★ and Chenin Blanc; also recently improved Chardonnay and attractive Riesling★. Reds are much improved, especially Houghton and Moondah Brook Cabernets★ and Shiraz★. The super-duper Jack Mann commemorative Cabernet blend★★ was released in 1997 to a well-deserved fanfare. Best years: (Jack Mann) **1996 95 94**.

VON HÖVEL *Konz-Oberemmel, Saar, Germany*   Eberhard von Kunow owns some top sites, including Oberemmeler Hütte. He has always made unusually rich, succulent wines for a region renowned for steely Rieslings, but since 1993 quality has taken another leap; wines are now almost all ★★. Most wines age impressively for 10 years or more. Best years: (Auslese) (2000) 99 97 96 95 **94 93 90 89 88 85**.

HOWARD PARK *Great Southern, Western Australia* Howard Park has been an important player in high-quality Australian Cabernet over the last 15 years, and new owners have expanded the winery. The classic Cabernet Sauvignon-Merlot★★★, built for long cellaring, is matched by intense, floral Riesling★★★, and a classy Chardonnay★★ is not far behind. Scotsdale Cabernet Sauvignon★ and Leston Shiraz★ are part of a new regional push. Second label Madfish is good for Shiraz★ and dry whites (Chardonnay★). Best years: (Cabernet-Merlot) 1998 97 96 94 93 92 **90 89 88 86**; (Riesling) 2001 **00 98 97 96 95 94 93 91 90 88 86**.

HOWELL MOUNTAIN AVA *Napa Valley, California, USA* NAPA's north-eastern corner is noted for powerhouse Cabernet Sauvignon and Zinfandel as well as exotic, full-flavoured Merlot. Best producers: BERINGER (Merlot★★), DUCKHORN★, DUNN★★, La Jota★★, Liparita★, PINE RIDGE (Cabernet Sauvignon★), Viader★★★. Best years: (reds) (2000) 99 98 97 96 **95 94 93 92 91 90**.

HUADONG WINERY *Shandong Province, China* The first producer of varietal and vintage wines in China, Huadong has received massive investment from its multinational joint owners (Allied Domecq) as well as state support. Money, however, can't change climates, and excessive moisture from the summer rainy season causes problems. Even so, Riesling and Chardonnay (under the Tsingtao label) are not at all bad and have achieved some export sales.

HUET L'ECHANSONNE *Vouvray AC, Loire Valley, France* Gaston Huet has passed this estate to his son-in-law, Noël Pinguet, but still takes a keen interest in the complex, traditional Vouvrays which can age for decades. Wines are produced from 3 excellent sites – le Haut-Lieu, Clos du Bourg and le Mont – which can be dry★★, medium-dry★★ or sweet★★★, depending on the vintage. Also very good Vouvray Mousseux★★. Best years: 2000 **99 98 97** 96 **95 93 90 89 88 85 76 64 61 59 47**.

HUGEL ET FILS *Alsace AC, Alsace, France* Arguably the most famous name in Alsace. As well as wines from its own vineyards, Hugel buys in grapes for basic wines. Best wines are sweet ALSACE VENDANGE TARDIVE★★ and Sélection de Grains Nobles★★★. The Tradition wines are generally rather dull, but the Jubilée wines are often of ★★ quality. Best years: (Vendange Tardive Riesling) (2000) 99 98 97 96 **95 90 89 88**.

HUNTER VALLEY *New South Wales, Australia* NEW SOUTH WALES' oldest wine region overcomes a tricky climate to make fascinating, ageworthy Semillon and rich, buttery Chardonnay. The reds meet less universal approval. Shiraz is the mainstay, aging well but often developing a leathery overtone; Cabernet can deliver occasional success. Premium region is the Lower Hunter Valley; the Upper Hunter has few wineries but extensive vineyards. Best producers: Allandale★★, BROKENWOOD★★, De Iuliis, Kulkunbulla, LAKE'S FOLLY★, LINDEMANS★★, Lowe Family, MCWILLIAM'S★, Meerea Park★, ROSEMOUNT★★, ROTHBURY★, TYRRELL'S★★. Best years: (Shiraz) 2000 99 98 97 **96 95 94 93 91**.

HUNTER'S *Marlborough, South Island, New Zealand* One of MARLBOROUGH's stars, with fine, if austere, Sauvignon★★, savoury, Burgundian Chardonnay★★, vibrant Riesling★ and sophisticated Pinot Noir★. Also attractive fizz★.

INNISKILLIN *Niagara Peninsula, Ontario, Canada* One of Canada's leading wineries, producing good Pinot Noir★, beautifully rounded Klose Vineyard Chardonnay★ and thick, rich, Vidal Icewine★★. Winemaker Karl Kaiser is also achieving good results with Cabernet Franc. Another Inniskillin winery is in the OKANAGAN VALLEY in British Columbia, a partnership between the winery and the Inkameep Indian Band. Best years: (Vidal Icewine) 1999 **98 97 95 94 92 89**.

IPHOFEN *Franken, Germany* One of the 2 most important wine towns in FRANKEN for dry Riesling and Silvaner. Both are powerful, with a pronounced earthiness. Best producers: JULIUSSPITAL★, Johann Ruck★, Hans Wirsching★. Best years: (2001) **00** 99 **98 97 94 93 92 90**.

IRANCY AC *Burgundy, France* Formerly known as Bourgogne-Irancy and labelled simply Irancy from 1996, this northern outpost of vineyards, just south-west of CHABLIS, is an unlikely champion of the clear, pure flavours of the Pinot Noir grape. But red Irancy can be delicate and lightly touched by the ripeness of plums and strawberries, and can age well. There is also a little rosé. Best producers: Bienvenu, J-M BROCARD, Cantin, A & J-P Colinot★, Delaloge, Patrice Fort★, Simonnet-Febvre. Best years: (2001) 00 99 **98 96**.

IRON HORSE VINEYARDS *Sonoma County, California, USA* Outstanding sparkling wines with Brut★★ and the Blanc de Blancs★★ delicious on release but highly suitable for aging. The LD★★★ (Late Disgorged) is a heavenly mouthful of sparkling wine – yeasty and complex. A blanc de noirs★ called 'Wedding Cuvée' and a Brut Rosé★ complete the line-up. Table wines include a lovely Pinot Noir★★, a barrel-fermented Chardonnay★, a zesty Sauvignon and a seductive Viognier★★.

IROULÉGUY AC *South-West France* A small AC in the Basque Pyrenees. Cabernet Sauvignon, Cabernet Franc and Tannat give robust reds that are softer than MADIRAN. Production of white from Petit Courbu and Manseng has recently restarted. Best producers: Arretxea★, Brana★, Etxegaraya, Ilarria★, Irouléguy co-op (Mignaberry★). Best years: (reds) 2000 **98 97 96 95**.

ISABEL ESTATE *Marlborough, New Zealand* Grapegrowers (for CLOUDY BAY) turned award-winning winemakers Michael and Robyn Tiller are blazing a trail with Sauvignon Blanc★★ that equals the country's best. Aromatic, plum-and-cherry Pinot Noir★★, stylish, concentrated Chardonnay★★, and promising Riesling★ and Pinot Gris★ complete the impressive line-up. An estate to follow. Best years: (Pinot Noir) (2001) 00 **99 98 96 94**.

ISOLE E OLENA *Chianti Classico DOCG, Tuscany, Italy* Paolo De Marchi has long been one of the pacesetters in Chianti Classico. His CHIANTI CLASSICO★★, characterized by clean, elegant and spicily perfumed fruit, excels in every vintage. The powerful SUPER-TUSCAN Cepparello★★★, made from 100% Sangiovese, is the top wine. Excellent Syrah★★, Cabernet Sauvignon★★★, Chardonnay★★, and VIN SANTO★★★. Best years: (Cepparello) (2000) 99 98 97 **96 95 94 93 91 90 88 86**.

CH. D'ISSAN★ *Margaux AC, 3ème Cru Classé, Haut-Médoc, Bordeaux France* This lovely moated property has disappointed me far too often in the past but is beginning to pull its socks up. When successful, the wine can be one of the most delicate and scented in the MARGAUX AC. Best years: 2000 99 98 96 **95 90 89 85 83 82 78**.

PAUL JABOULET AÎNÉ *Rhône Valley, France* During the 1970s, Jaboulet led the way in raising the world's awareness of the great quality of RHONE wines, yet during the 80s the quality of wine faltered, and though many of the wines are still good, they are no longer the star in any appellation. Best wines are top red HERMITAGE la Chapelle★★ and white Chevalier de Stérimberg★★. CROZES-HERMITAGE Thalabert★ is famous, but occasional release Vieilles Vignes★★ is much better nowadays, as are whites Mule Blanche★ and Raymond Roure★. Attractive CORNAS Dom. St-Pierre★ and sweet, perfumed MUSCAT DE BEAUMES-DE-VENISE★★. Best years: (la Chapelle) (2000) 99 98 97 96 95 **94 91 90 89 88 78.**

JACKSON ESTATE *Marlborough, South Island, New Zealand* An established grapegrower with vineyards in MARLBOROUGH's most prestigious district, Jackson Estate turned its hand to winemaking in 1991, making appley Sauvignon Blanc★ that improves with a little age, restrained Chardonnay and Pinot Noir★ and complex traditional-method fizz★.

JACQUESSON *Champagne AC, Champagne, France* Venerable Champagne house owned by the Chiquet family since 1974. The ultra-reliable non-vintage Brut★ and Rosé★ are rather presumptuously called Perfection. The vintage Blanc de Blancs★★ is a classic example of this style, and vintage Signature Brut★★★ is a full-bodied biscuity Champagne of class and longevity. Best years: 1995 **93 90 89 88 85.**

LOUIS JADOT *Beaune, Burgundy, France*   A leading merchant based in Beaune with a broad range matched only by DROUHIN, with with rights to some estate wines of the Duc de Magenta★★. Jadot has extensive vineyard holdings for red wines, but it is the firm's whites which have earned its reputation. Excellent in Grands Crus like BATARD-MONTRACHET★★★ and CORTON-CHARLEMAGNE★★ but Jadot also shows a more egalitarian side by producing good wines in lesser ACs like ST-AUBIN★ and RULLY★. After leading white Burgundy in quality during the 1970s, the 80s were less thrilling, but in the 90s Jadot returned to form. Best years: (top reds) (2001) 00 99 98 97 96 **95 93 90 89.**

JAFFELIN *Beaune, Burgundy, France* Owned by BOISSET, Jaffelin produces a large range of wines from the CÔTE D'OR, the CÔTE CHALONNAISE and BEAUJOLAIS, including a sound range of Village wines.

JAMET *Côte-Rôtie AC, Rhône Valley, France* Jean-Paul and Jean-Luc Jamet are 2 of the most talented growers of CÔTE-ROTIE. If anything, the wines★★★ from this excellent estate have improved since they took over from their father, Joseph. The wines age well for a decade or more. Best years: (2000) 99 98 97 96 95 **94 91 90 89 88 87 85 83 82.**

JARDIN DE LA FRANCE, VIN DE PAYS DU *Loire Valley, France* This vin de pays covers most of the LOIRE VALLEY, and production often exceeds 80 million bottles – mostly of white wine, from Chenin Blanc and Sauvignon Blanc, and usually fairly cheap to buy. There is an increasing amount of good Chardonnay made here, too. The few reds and rosés are generally light and sharp. Best producers: Ackerman-Laurance, Bablut, Couillaud, Forges, Hauts de Sanziers, Touche Noire.

JASNIÈRES AC *Loire Valley, France* Tiny AC north of Tours making long-lived, bone-dry whites from Chenin Blanc. Sweet wine may be made in good years. Best producers: Bellivière★★, J Gigou★★. Best years: (2000) **99 98 97** 96 **95 93 92 90 89.**

ROBERT JAYER-GILLES *Côte de Nuits, Burgundy, France* Robert Jayer-Gilles produces expensive but sought-after wines, heavily dominated by new oak. Good ALIGOTE★, wonderful Hautes-Côtes de Nuits Blanc★★, as well as sensuous reds, including ECHEZEAUX★★★ and NUITS-ST-GEORGES les Damodes★★. Best years: (top reds) (2001) 00 99 98 **97** 96 **95 93.**

JEREZ Y MANZANILLA DO/SHERRY See pages 158–9.

JEREZ Y MANZANILLA DO/SHERRY

Andalucía, Spain

 The Spanish now own the name outright. From 1996 'British sherry' and 'Irish sherry' ceased to exist. At least in the EU, the only wines that can be sold as sherry come from the triangle of vineyard land between the Andalucian towns of inland Jerez de la Frontera, and Sanlúcar de Barrameda and Puerto de Santa María by the sea.

The best sherries can be spectacular. Three main factors contribute to the high quality potential of wines from this region: the chalky-spongy albariza soil where the best vines grow, the Palomino Fino grape – unexciting for table wines but potentially great once transformed by the sherry-making processes – and a natural yeast called flor. All sherry must be a minimum of 3 years old, but fine sherries age in barrel for much longer. Sherries must be blended through a solera system. About a third of the wine from the oldest barrels is bottled, and the barrels topped up with slightly younger wine from another set of barrels and so on, for a minimum of 3 sets of barrels. The idea is that the younger wine takes on the character of older wine, as well as keeping the blend refreshed.

MAIN SHERRY STYLES

Fino and manzanilla Fino sherries derive their extraordinary, tangy, pungent flavours from flor. Young, newly fermented wines destined for these styles of sherry are deliberately fortified very sparingly to just 15–15.5% alcohol before being put in barrels for their minimum of 3 years' maturation. The thin, soft, oatmeal-coloured mush of flor grows on the surface of the wines, protecting them from the air (and therefore keeping them pale) and giving them a characteristic sharp, pungent tang. The addition of younger wine each year feeds the flor, maintaining an even layer. Manzanillas are fino-style wines that have matured in the cooler seaside conditions of Sanlúcar de Barrameda, where the flor grows thickest and the fine, salty tang is most accentuated.

Amontillado True amontillados are simply fino sherries that have continued to age after the flor has died (after about 5 years) and so finish their aging period in contact with air. These should all be bone dry. Medium-sweet amontillados are merely concoctions for the export market; the dry sherry is sweetened with mistela, a blend of grape juice and alcohol.

Oloroso This type of sherry is strongly fortified after fermentation to deter the growth of flor. Olorosos therefore mature in barrel in contact with the air, which gradually darkens them while they develop rich, intense, nutty and raisiny flavours.

Other styles Manzanilla pasada is aged manzanilla, with greater depth and nuttiness. Palo cortado is an unusual, deliciously nutty, dry style somewhere in between amontillado and oloroso. Sweet oloroso creams and pale creams are almost without exception enriched solely for the export market. Sweet varietal wines are made from sun-dried Pedro Ximénez or Moscatel.

See also individual producers.

BEST PRODUCERS AND WINES

Argüeso (Manzanilla San León, Manzanilla Fina Las Medallas).

BARBADILLO (Manzanilla Eva, Solear Manzanilla Fina Vieja, Amontillado Príncipe, Amontillado de Sanlúcar, Cuco Oloroso Seco, Palo Cortado Obispo Gascon).

Delgado Zuleta (Manzanilla Pasada La Goya).

Díez Mérito (Don Zoilo Imperial Amontillado, Imperial Fino, Victoria Regina Oloroso).

DOMECQ (Amontillado 51-1A, Sibarita Palo Cortado, Fino La Ina, Venerable Pedro Ximénez).

Garvey (Palo Cortado, Amontillado Tio Guillermo, Pedro Ximénez Gran Orden).

GONZALEZ BYASS (Tio Pepe Fino, Matusalem Oloroso Muy Viejo, Apóstoles Oloroso Viejo, Amontillado del Duque Seco y Muy Viejo, Noé Pedro Ximénez, Oloroso Viejo de Añado).

HIDALGO (Amontillado Napoleon, Oloroso Viejo, Manzanilla La Gitana, Manzanilla Pasada, Jerez Cortado).

LUSTAU (Almacenista single-producer wines, Old East India Cream, Puerto Fino).

OSBORNE (Amontillado Coquinero, Fino Quinta, Bailén Oloroso, Solera India, Pedro Ximénez).

Sánchez Romate (Pedro Ximénez Cardenal Cisneros).

VALDESPINO (Amontillado Coliseo, Amontillado Tio Diego, Amontillado Don Tomás, Cardenal Palo Cortado, Inocente Fino, Oloroso Don Gonzalo, Pedro Ximénez Solera Superior).

Williams & Humbert (Pando Fino, Manzanilla Alegria).

159

JERMANN *Friuli-Venezia Giulia, Italy* Silvio Jermann, in the COLLIO zone of north-east Italy, produces non-DOC Chardonnay★, Sauvignon Blanc★, Pinot Bianco★ and Pinot Grigio★. Deep, long-lived Vintage Tunina★★ is based on Sauvignon-Chardonnay but includes Ribolla, Malvasia and Picolit. Barrel-fermented Chardonnay★★ was called 'Where the dreams have no end' but has, incredibly, been renamed 'Were dreams, now it is just wine'. Vinnae★ is based on Ribolla; Capo Martino★ is also a blend of local varieties. The wines are plump but pricy.

JOHANNISBERG *Rheingau, Germany* Probably the best known of all the Rhine wine villages, with 10 vineyard sites, including the famous Schloss Johannisberg. Best producers: Prinz von Hessen★, Johannishof★★, Schloss Johannisberg★. Best years: (2001) 99 98 **97 96 94 93 90**.

KARL H JOHNER *Bischoffingen, Baden, Germany* Johner specializes in new oak-aged wines from his native BADEN. The vividly fruity Pinot Noir★ and Pinot Blanc★ are excellent, the Chardonnay SJ★ is one of Germany's best examples of this varietal, and the rich, silky Pinot Noir SJ★★ can be one of Germany's finest reds. Best years: (Pinot Noir SJ) (2001) 00 99 98 **97 96 93 90**.

JORDAN *Alexander Valley AVA, Sonoma, California, USA* Ripe, fruity Cabernet Sauvignon★ with a cedar character rare in California. The Chardonnay★ is balanced and attractive. J★ fizz is an attractive mouthful, now made independently by Judy Jordan's J Wine Co. Best years: (Cabernet) (2000) 99 **97 96 95 94 91 87 86**.

JORDAN *Stellenbosch WO, South Africa* Ted and Shelagh Jordan bought this farm in the early 1980s. The premium varieties they planted are now bearing fruit for their son and daughter-in-law, Gary and Kathy. The strong white range is headed by a nutty Chardonnay★. Cabernet Sauvignon★, Merlot★ and Cobblers Hill★, a BORDEAUX blend, show elegant understatement but deepen with a little age. Best years: (Chardonnay) **2000 99 98 97 96**; (Cobblers Hill) 1999 98 **97**.

TONI JOST *Bacharach, Mittelrhein, Germany* Husband and wife team Peter and Linde Jost have put the MITTELRHEIN on the map. From the Bacharacher Hahn site come some delicious, racy Rieslings★ including well-structured Halbtrockens★; Auslese★★ adds creaminess without losing that pine-needle scent. Best years: (2001) 99 98 **97 96 94 93 92 90 89**.

J P VINHOS *Terras do Sado, Portugal* Forward-looking operation, using Portuguese and foreign grapes with equal ease. Quinta da Bacalhôa★ is an oaky, meaty Cabernet-Merlot blend; Tinto da Ânfora★ a rich and figgy ALENTEJO red (Grande Escolha★★ version is powerful and cedary); and Cova da Ursa★ a toasty, rich Chardonnay, if now more subdued than previously. Portugal's finest sparkling wine, vintage-dated Loridos Extra Bruto★, is a pretty decent Champagne lookalike, made from Chardonnay. New is SÓ (which means 'only' in Portuguese, as in 'only Syrah'), characterful if atypical. Also decent Moscatel de SETUBAL★.

JULIÉNAS AC *Beaujolais, Burgundy, France* One of the more northerly BEAUJOLAIS Crus, Juliénas makes delicious, 'serious' Beaujolais which can be big and tannic enough to develop in bottle. Best producers: G Descombes★, DUBOEUF★, P Granger★, Ch. de Juliénas★, J P Margerand★, R Monnet★, Pelletier★, B Santé★, M Tête★. Best years (2001) **00 99 98**.

JULIUSSPITAL *Würzburg, Franken, Germany* A 16th-century charitable foundation known for its dry wines – especially Silvaners from IPHOFEN and WURZBURG. Look out for the Würzburger Stein vineyard wines, sappy

Müller-Thurgau, grapefruity Silvaners★★ and petrolly Rieslings★★. Back on form in 1999, after curiously disappointing 1998 and 97 vintages. Best years: (2001) 00 99 **94 93 92 90.**

JUMILLA DO *Murcia and Castilla-La Mancha, Spain* Jumilla's reputation in Spain is for big alcoholic reds. Reds and fruity rosés are made from Monastrell (Mourvèdre), so the potential is there. Whites are mostly boring. Best producers: Casa de la Ermita★, Induvasa (Finca Luzón★), Agapito Rico, Julia Roch (Casa Castillo★★). Best years: 2000 **99 98 96.**

JURA See Arbois, Château-Chalon, Côtes du Jura, l'Étoile.

JURANÇON AC *South-West France* The sweet white wine made from late-harvested and occasionally botrytized grapes can be heavenly, with floral, spicy, apricot-quince flavours. The rapidly improving dry wine, Jurançon Sec, can be ageworthy. Best producers: Bellegarde★, Bru-Baché★★, Castera★, CAUHAPE★★, Clos Lapeyre★, Clos Thou★, CLOS UROULAT★★, Larrédya★, Souch★. Best years: (sweet) 2000 **99 98 96 95.**

JUVÉ Y CAMPS *Cava DO and Penedès DO, Cataluña, Spain* Juvé y Camps is ultra-traditional – and expensive. Unusually among the Catalan companies, most of the grapes come from its own vineyards. Fruitiest CAVA is Reserva de la Familia Extra Brut★, but the rosé and the top brand white Cava Gran Juvé are also good. Ermita d'Espiells is a neutral, dry white wine.

KAISERSTUHL *Baden, Germany* A 4000ha (10,000-acre) volcanic stump rising to 600m (2000ft) and overlooking the Rhine plain and south BADEN. Best producers: BERCHER★★, Bickensohl co-op, Dr HEGER★★, Karl H JOHNER★, Franz Keller★, Königsschaffhausen co-op, Salwey★. Best years: (dry whites) (2001) **99 98 97 96 93.**

KALLSTADT *Pfalz, Germany* A warm climate combined with the excellent Saumagen site results in the richest dry Rieslings in Germany. These, and the dry Weissburgunder (Pinot Blanc) and Muskateller (Muscat), can stand beside the very best from ALSACE. Pinot Noir is also showing it likes the chalk soil. Best producer: KOEHLER-RUPRECHT★★★. Best years: (2001) 00 **99 98 97 96 95 93 92 90 89 88 85 83.**

KAMPTAL *Niederösterreich, Austria* Wine region centred on the town of Langenlois, making some impressive dry whites, particularly Riesling and Grüner Veltliner. Best producers: BRUNDLMAYER★★, Ehn★★, Hirsch★, Fred Loimer★, Schloss Gobelsburg★. Best years: 2000 99 98 **97 95 94 93.**

KANONKOP *Stellenbosch WO, South Africa* Longevity is apparent on many fronts at this premium Stellenbosch estate. Beyers Truter has been its winemaker for 21 years; his favourite Pinotage★★ (standard and Auction Reserve) comes from 50-year-old vines, and the muscular, savoury red BORDEAUX blend Paul Sauer★★ and Auction Reserve★★ version really do mature for 10 years or more. Cabernet Sauvignon★ adds to an enviable red wine reputation. The Krige brothers, owners of the estate, and Truter are partners in nearby BEYERSKLOOF and a third red wine property, Bouwland, also specializing in Pinotage and a Cabernet-Merlot blend. Best years: (Paul Sauer) **1998 97 96 95 94 92 91.**

KARTHÄUSERHOF *Trier, Ruwer, Germany* Top Ruwer estate which has gone from strength to strength since Christoph Tyrell and winemaker Ludwig Breiling took charge in 1986. Rieslings combine aromatic extravagance with racy brilliance. Since 1993 most wines are ★★, some Auslese and Eiswein ★★★. Best years: (2001) 99 **97** 96 95 **94 93 90 89 88 86.**

KATNOOK ESTATE *Coonawarra, South Australia* Chardonnay★★ has consistently been the best of the fairly expensive whites here, though the Riesling★ and Sauvignon★ are pretty good, too. Reds are led by well-structured Cabernet Sauvignon★ and treacly Shiraz★, with flagship reds, Odyssey Cabernet Sauvignon★★ and Prodigy Shiraz★★, reaching a higher level. Best years: (Odyssey) 1997 96 **94 92 91**.

KÉKFRANKOS See Blaufränkisch.

KENDALL-JACKSON *Sonoma County, California, USA* Jess Jackson founded KJ in bucolic Lake County in 1982 after buying a vineyard there. The operation has since grown from under 10,000 cases to over 2 million. Early success with the Vintner's Reserve Chardonnay was fuelled by a style of winemaking favouring sweetness, but lately the wines have become more challenging. Today's Chardonnays are barrel fermented and oak aged. The Grand Reserve wines are blends from several AVAs. Kendall-Jackson owns several other wineries in California, including La Crema (Chardonnay★, Pinot Noir★) and Robert Pepi, as well as Chile (Calina) and Argentina (Tapiz).

KENWOOD *Sonoma Valley AVA, California, USA* Owned by Gary Heck of Korbel sparkling wine fame, this winery has always represented very good quality at reasonable prices. The Sauvignon Blanc★ highlights floral and melon flavours with a slightly earthy finish, while the new Massara Merlot★ offers nice complexity in a subtle style. The range of Zinfandels is impressive (Jack London★★, Mazzoni★, Nuns Canyon★), while the flagship red remains the long-lived Artist Series Cabernet Sauvignon★★. Best years: (Zinfandel) (2001) 00 99 **98 97 96 95 94**.

VON KESSELSTATT *Trier, Mosel, Germany* Good Riesling★ and rich, fragrant Spätlese and Auslese★★ wines from some top sites at GRAACH (Josephshöfer) in the MOSEL, Scharzhofberg in the Saar and at Kasel in the Ruwer. Best years: (Riesling Spätlese) (2001) 99 98 **97 96 95 94 93**.

KHAN KRUM *Black Sea Region, Bulgaria* An all-Bulgarian winemaking team produces some of Bulgaria's best modern whites, such as the oaky Reserve Chardonnay and perfumed, apricotty Riesling-Dimiat Country Wine.

KIEDRICH *Rheingau, Germany* Small village whose top vineyard is the Gräfenberg, giving extremely long-lived, mineral Rieslings. Wines from Sandgrub and Wasseros are also often good. Best producers: Knyphausen, WEIL★★. Best years: (Riesling Spätlese, Auslese) (2001) 99 98 **97** 96 **95 94 93 92 90**.

KING ESTATE *Oregon, USA* OREGON's biggest producer of Pinot Gris★ and Pinot Noir. Both wines are made in a user-friendly style but the Pinot Noir is inconsistent. The Reserve Pinot Noir and Reserve Pinot Gris★ offer greater depth. The Domaine Pinot Noir★ is a selection of the best barrels and can be quite good. Best years: (Reserve Pinot Noir) 2000 99 98 **96 94**.

KIONA *Yakima Valley AVA, Washington State, USA* A small operation in sagebrush country, Kiona has a reputation for its barrel-fermented Chardonnay★, big, full Cabernet Sauvignon★, brambly Lemberger★ and delightful dry Rieslings★. Its forte is in the production of good-value late-harvest wines, notably Chenin Blanc★, Riesling★★ and Gewürztraminer★★. Best years: (Late Harvest wines) 2000 99 97.

KISTLER *Sonoma Valley AVA, California, USA* One of California's hottest Chardonnay producers. Wines are made from many different vineyards (Kistler Vineyard, Durell Vineyard and Dutton Ranch can be ★★★; McCrea Vineyard and the ultra-cool-climate Camp Meeting

Ridge Vineyard ★★). All possess great complexity with good aging potential. Kistler also makes a number of single-vineyard Pinot Noirs★★ that go from good to very good. Best years: (Kistler Vineyard Chardonnay) (2001) 00 99 **98** 97 96 **95 94 91 90**.

KLEIN CONSTANTIA *Constantia WO, South Africa* Since 1980, the Jooste family have turned this winery into a South African showpiece. Sauvignon Blanc★, usually crisp and tangy, though sometimes a little ripe, benefits from winemaker Ross Gower's experience in New Zealand. A decent Chardonnay, attractive, off-dry Riesling★ and Vin de Constance★, a Muscat dessert wine based on the 18th-century CONSTANTIA examples, highlight the area's aptitude for white wine. Of the reds, recently released Shiraz★ looks promising. Best years: (Vin de Constance) **1997 96 95 94 93 92 91 90**.

KNAPPSTEIN *Clare Valley, South Australia* In 1995 Tim Knappstein quit the company, now part of PETALUMA, to focus on his own LENSWOOD VINEYARDS, high in the ADELAIDE HILLS. However, the Knappstein brand is still a market leader, with fine Riesling★★ and Gewürztraminer★, subtly-oaked Semillon-Sauvignon★, Cabernet-Merlot and Chardonnay, plus the premium Enterprise pair, Shiraz★ and Cabernet Sauvignon★. Former Petaluma winemaker Andrew Hardy took charge in 1996, and he has pumped new enthusiasm into the wines. Best years: (Enterprise Cabernet Sauvignon) 1999 98 **97**.

EMMERICH KNOLL *Unterloiben, Wachau, Niederösterreich, Austria* Since the late 1970s publicity-shy Emmerich Knoll has made some of the greatest Austrian dry white wines. His Riesling and Grüner Veltliner are packed with fruit and are rich and complex. They rarely fail to reach ★★ quality, with Grüner Veltliner and Riesling from both the Loibenberg and Schütt sites ★★★. They repay keeping for 5 years or more. Best years: (Riesling Smaragd) (2001) 00 99 98 97 **96 95 94 93 92 90 89 88 86 85**.

KOEHLER-RUPRECHT *Kallstadt, Pfalz, Germany* Bernd Philippi makes powerful, very concentrated dry Rieslings★★★ from the Kallstadter Saumagen site, the oak-aged botrytized Elysium★★ and, since 1991, Burgundian-style Pinot Noirs★. Philippi is also co-winemaker (with Bernhard Breuer) at Mont du Toit in South Africa, where they have been producing ground-breaking wines since 1998. Best years: (Riesling Auslese trocken) (2001) **99** 98 **97** 96 **95 93 90 89 88**.

ALOIS KRACHER *Illmitz, Burgenland, Austria* Austria's greatest sweet winemaker. Nouvelle Vague wines are aged in barriques while Zwischen den Seen wines are spared oak. The Scheurebe Beerenauslesen and TBAs, and the Welschrieslings, Chardonnay-Welschrieslings and Grande Cuvée are all ★★★. The Bouviers★ (often labelled Kracher Beerenauslese) are also good. With the 97 vintage Kracher catapulted himself into the first rank of Austrian red wine producers. Best years: (whites) (2000) (99) 98 **96 95 94 93 91 89 86 81**.

KREMSTAL *Niederösterreich, Austria* Wine region on both sides of the Danube around the town of Krems, producing some of Austria's best whites, particularly dry Riesling and Grüner Veltliner. Best producers: Mantlerhof★, Sepp Moser★, Nigl★, NIKOLAIHOF★★, Franz Proidl★, Fritz Salomon★★. Best years: (2001) 00 99 98 **97 95 94 93**.

KRUG *Champagne AC, Champagne, France*   Serious CHAMPAGNE house, making seriously expensive wines. The non-vintage, Grande Cuvée★★, used to knock spots off most other de luxe brands but has begun to get a bit too cumbersome for its own good. Also an impressive vintage★★, a rosé★★★ and ethereal single-vineyard Clos du Mesnil★★★ Blanc de Blancs. Now owned by LVMH, so the style may change and – heretical as it is to say so – maybe for the better. Best years: (1990) **89 88 85 82 81 79**.

KUENTZ-BAS *Alsace AC, Alsace, France*   A small négociant, with high-quality wines from its own vineyards (labelled Réserve Personnelle) and from purchased grapes (Cuvée Tradition). Look out for the Eichberg Grand Cru★★ and the excellent ALSACE VENDANGE TARDIVE★★ wines. Best years: (Grand Cru Gewurztraminer) (2000) 98 **97 96 95 94 93 90 89**.

PETER JAKOB KÜHN *Oestrich, Rheingau, Germany*   During the late 1990s Kühn was the rising star of the RHEINGAU, frequently making headlines with his substantial dry Rieslings and full, juicy Spätlese. These wines are usually ★, sometimes ★★. Best years: (2001) 99 98 **97 96 94 93 92**.

KUMEU/HUAPAI *Auckland, North Island, New Zealand*   A small but significant viticultural area north-west of Auckland. The 11 wineries profit from their proximity to New Zealand's largest city. Most producers make little or no wine from their home region. Best producers: COOPERS CREEK★, Harrier Rise, KUMEU RIVER★, MATUA VALLEY★★, NOBILO. Best years: (reds) 2000 **99 98 96 94 93**.

KUMEU RIVER *Kumeu, Auckland, North Island, New Zealand*   This family winery has been transformed by New Zealand's first Master of Wine, Michael Brajkovich, who has created a range of adventurous, high-quality wines: a big, complex, award-winning Chardonnay★★★ (Maté's Vineyard★★★), softly stylish Merlot★, complex oak-aged Pinot Gris★ and a newly released premium Merlot-Malbec-Cabernet Franc blend called Melba★★. Only Pinot Noir disappoints so far. Best years: (Chardonnay) **2000 99 98 96**.

KUNDE ESTATE *Sonoma Valley, California, USA*   The Kunde family have grown wine-grapes in SONOMA COUNTY for at least 100 years; in 1990 they started producing wines, with spectacular results. The Chardonnays are all impressive – Kinneybrook★★, Wildwood★★ and the powerful, buttery Reserve★★. The Century Vines Zinfandel★★ gets rave reviews, as does the peppery Syrah★★ and the explosively fruity Viognier★★. Best years: (Zinfandel) (2001) 00 99 97 **96 95 94**.

FRANZ KÜNSTLER *Hochheim, Rheingau, Germany*   Gunter Künstler makes some of the best dry Rieslings in the RHEINGAU. They are powerful, mineral wines★★, with everything from the Hölle site worthy of ★★★. In 1996 he bought the run-down Aschrott estate, which more than doubled his vineyard area. The sweet wine quality has been erratic lately, but the best are fantastic. Best years: (Riesling Spätlese trocken, Auslese trocken) (2001) 99 98 97 96 **94 93 92 90 89 88**.

KWV *Paarl, South Africa*   The KWV severely rationalized its standard range after converting from co-op to company. The grander Cathedral Cellar line-up has been enlarged and overall quality improved. Best are the bright-fruited, well-oaked Triptych★ (Cabernet-Merlot-Shiraz), rich, bold Cabernet★ and modern-style Pinotage. Among whites, barrel-fermented Chardonnay shows pleasing fruit/oak balance. Topping everything, in price if in no other way, is the single-vineyard Perold; so far only one vintage, a Shiraz, has been released. Port-style fortifieds remain superb value, particularly Vintage★★.

LA AGRÍCOLA *Mendoza, Argentina* One of Argentina's great success stories. Dynamic owner José Zuccardi saw the potential for export before his compatriots and set about creating a range of utterly enjoyable easy-drinking wines. La Agrícola now exports about 70% of its wine under a number of labels, including Santa Julia and Picajuan Peak. Its greatest success is its basic reds★, often from Italian or Spanish grape varieties. Reserves and top of the line 'Q' are good but should improve dramatically with a new barrel-aging facility from the 2001 vintage. Whites are good but less exciting.

CH. LABÉGORCE-ZÉDÉ★ *Margaux AC, Bordeaux, France* Although not situated on the best MARGAUX soil, this property has been carefully cherished and improved by Luc Thienpont from POMEROL. The wine isn't that perfumed but the balance between concentration and finesse is always good. Age for 5 years or more. Second wine: Domaine Zédé. A third wine, Z de Zédé, is a simple BORDEAUX AC. Best years: 2000 99 98 97 96 **95 94 90 89 88**.

LABOURÉ-ROI *Nuits-St-Georges, Burgundy, France* Price-conscious and generally reliable merchant, yet no longer so consistent as before as supply struggles to keep up with demand. The CHABLIS★ and MEURSAULT★ are very correct wines, and NUITS-ST-GEORGES★, CHAMBOLLE-MUSIGNY★, GEVREY-CHAMBERTIN★, BEAUNE★ and VOLNAY★ are usually good.

LADOIX AC *Côte de Beaune, Burgundy, France* Most northerly village in the COTE DE BEAUNE and one of the least known. The village includes some of the Grand Cru CORTON, and the lesser vineyards may be sold as Ladoix-Côte de Beaune or COTE DE BEAUNE-VILLAGES. There are several good growers, and Ladoix wine, mainly red, quite light in colour and a little lean in style, is reasonably priced. Best producers: (reds) P André★, Cachat-Ocquidant★, E Cornu★, Prince Florent de Merode★, A & J-R Nudant★; (whites) P André★, E Cornu, R & R Jacob★, VERGET★. Best years: (reds) (2001) 99 **98 97 96 95.**

MICHEL LAFARGE *Côte de Beaune, Burgundy, France* The doyen of VOLNAY, Michel Lafarge has now virtually handed over to his son, Frédéric. The MEURSAULT produced under this label is not thrilling, but the red wines can be outstanding, notably Volnay Clos des Chênes★★★, Volnay Clos du Château des Ducs★★★ (a monopole) and less fashionable BEAUNE Grèves★★. BOURGOGNE Rouge★ is good value. Top wines are accessible when young but can age up to 10 years or more. Best years: (top reds) 1999 98 97 96 95 **93 91 90 89 88**.

CH. LAFAURIE-PEYRAGUEY★★★ *Sauternes AC, 1er Cru Classé, Bordeaux, France* One of the most improved SAUTERNES properties of the 1980s and now frequently one of the best Sauternes of all, sumptuous and rich when young, and marvellously deep and satisfying with age. Best years: (2001) 99 98 97 96 **95 90 89 88 86 85 83**.

CH. LAFITE-ROTHSCHILD★★★ *Pauillac AC, 1er Cru Classé, Haut-Médoc, Bordeaux, France* This PAUILLAC First Growth is frequently cited as the epitome of elegance, indulgence and expense. If vintages of the late 1980s were excellent, those of the late 90s have been superb, with added depth and body to match the wine's traditional finesse. Second wine: les Carruades de Lafite-Rothschild. Best years: 2000 99 98 97 96 95 94 **90 89 88 86 85 82**.

CH. LAFLEUR★★★ *Pomerol AC, Bordeaux, France* Using some of POMEROL's most traditional winemaking, this tiny estate can seriously rival the great PETRUS for sheer power and flavour, and indeed in certain years has nudged ahead of Pétrus for hedonistic richness and concentration. Best years: 2000 99 98 97 96 95 **94 93 90 89 88 86 85**.

LAFON *Meursault, Côte de Beaune, Burgundy, France* A leading producer in MEURSAULT and one of Burgundy's current superstars, with a reputation and prices to match. From biodynamic viticulture Dominique Lafon produces rich, powerful Meursaults that spend as long as 2 years in barrel and age superbly in bottle. As well as excellent Meursault, especially Clos de la Barre★★, les Charmes★★★ and les Perrières★★★, Lafon makes a tiny amount of le MONTRACHET★★★ and some really individual and exciting red wines from VOLNAY★★ (Santenots du Milieu★★★) and MONTHELIE★★. Since 1999 the Lafons also own a MACON★ domaine. Best years: (whites) (2001) 00 99 97 96 95 **93 92**; (reds) 99 98 97 96 95 93 **92 91**.

CH. LAFON-ROCHET ★ *St-Estèphe AC, 4ème Cru Classé, Haut-Médoc, Bordeaux, France* Good-value, affordable Classed Growth claret. Recent vintages have seen an increase of Merlot in the blend, making the wine less austere. Delicious and blackcurranty after 10 years. Best years: 2000 98 97 96 **05 94 90 89 88 86 85 83 82**.

LAGEDER *Alto Adige DOC, Trentino-Alto Adige, Italy* Leading producer in ALTO ADIGE. Produces medium-priced varietals under the Lageder label, and pricy estate and single-vineyard wines including Cabernet★ and Chardonnay★★ under the Löwengang label, Sauvignon Lehenhof★★, Cabernet Cor Römigberg★★, Pinot Bianco Haberlehof★★ and Pinot Grigio Benefizium Porer★★. Also owns the historic Casòn Hirschprunn estate, source of excellent Alto Adige blends. Premium white Contest★★ is based on Pinot Grigio and Chardonnay but also includes small amounts of Marsanne and Roussanne. The red equivalent, Casòn★★, is Merlot-Cabernet based; a second red, Corolle★, and white Etelle★★ show similar style.

LAGO DI CALDARO DOC *Trentino-Alto Adige, Italy* At its best a lovely, barely red, youthful glugger from the Schiava grape, tasting of straw-berries and cream and bacon smoke. However, far too much Caldaro is overproduced. Known in German as Kalterersee. Kalterersee Auslese (Lago di Caldaro Scelto) is not sweet, but has 0.5% more alcohol. Best producers: Caldaro co-op★, LAGEDER★, Prima & Nuova/Erste & Neue★, San Michele Appiano co-op, Schloss Sallegg★.

CH. LAGRANGE★★ *St-Julien AC, 3ème Cru Classé, Haut-Médoc, Bordeaux, France* Since the Japanese company Suntory purchased this large estate in 1983, the leap in quality has been astonishing. No longer an amiable, shambling ST-JULIEN, this is now a single-minded wine of good fruit, meticulous winemaking and fine quality. Second wine: les Fiefs de Lagrange. Best years: 2000 99 98 96 95 **94 93 90 89 88 86 85**.

LAGREIN Highly individual black grape variety, planted only in Italy's Trentino-Alto Adige region, producing deep-coloured, brambly, chocolaty reds called Lagrein Dunkel, and full-bodied yet attractively scented rosé (known as Kretzer). Best producers: Colterenzio co-op (Cornell★), Graziano Fontana★, Franz Gojer★, Gries co-op★, Hofstätter★, LAGEDER★, Laimburg★, Muri-Gries★, J Niedermayr★, I Niedriest★, Plattner-Waldgries★, Hans Rottensteiner★, Santa Maddalena co-op★, Simoncelli★, Terlano co-op★★, Thurnhof★★, Tiefenbrunner★, Zemmer★

CH. LAGREZETTE *Cahors AC, South-West France* Splendid CAHORS estate owned by Alain-Dominique Perrin, boss of luxury jewellers Cartier. Since 1991, wines have been made in a modern cellar under the eye of Michel Rolland. There's supple, fruity Moulin Lagrezette, oak-aged Chevaliers and Ch. Lagrezette★. Sometimes, Cuvée Dame Honneur★★ and le Pigeonnier★★ are also produced, mainly from Auxerrois.

CH. LA LAGUNE★★ *Haut-Médoc AC, 3ème Cru Classé, Haut-Médoc, Bordeaux, France* Wine from this Classed Growth, the closest in the MEDOC to Bordeaux city, has been consistently good. The best vintages are full of the charry, chestnut warmth of good oak and a deep, cherry-blackcurrant-plum sweetness which, after 10 years or so, becomes outstanding claret. Second wine: Moulin de la Lagune. Best years: 2000 98 96 **95 94 90 89 88 86 85 83 82**.

LAKE'S FOLLY *Hunter Valley, New South Wales, Australia* Charismatic founder Dr Max Lake sold out to Perth businessman Peter Fogarty in 2000. In best years, austere Chardonnay★★ ages slowly to a masterly antipodean yet Burgundy-like peak. The red is generally ★, but not consistent. Best years: (red) 1999 98 97 **96 93 91 89 85 83 81**; (white) 1999 98 **97 96 94 92 91**.

LALANDE-DE-POMEROL AC *Bordeaux, France* To the north of its more famous neighbour POMEROL, this AC produces full, ripe wines with an unmistakable mineral edge that are very attractive to drink at 3–4 years old, but age reasonably well too. Even though they lack the concentration of top Pomerols, the wines are not particularly cheap. Best producers: Annereaux★, Belles-Graves, Bertineau-St-Vincent★, Clos de l'Église, la Croix-Chenevelle, la Croix-St-André★, la Fleur de Boüard★, Fougeailles, Garraud★, Grand Ormeau★, Haut-Chaigneau★, Haut-Surget, les Hauts Conseillants, Sergant, Siaurac, Tournefeuille, Viaud★. Best years: 2000 98 **96 95 94 90 89 88 85 83 82**.

LAMBRUSCO *Emilia-Romagna, Italy* Lambrusco is actually the name of a black grape variety, grown in 4 DOC zones on the plains of Emilia, and 1 around Mantova in LOMBARDY, but it is the screwcap bottles of red and white non-DOC Lambrusco that have made the name famous, even though some of them may contain no wine from the Lambrusco grape at all. Originally a dry or semi-sweet fizzy red wine, whose high acidity partnered the rich local food, good dry Lambrusco (especially Lambrusco di Sorbaia and Grasparossa di Castelvetro) is worth trying. Best producers: Barbieri, Barbolini, F Bellei★, Casali, Cavicchioli★, Chiarli, Vittorio Graziano★, Oreste Lini, Stefano Spezia, Venturini Baldini.

LAMOREAUX LANDING *Finger Lakes AVA, New York State, USA* One of the most important wineries in FINGER LAKES. Its Chardonnay Reserve★ is a consistent medal winner, and the Pinot Noir★ is arguably the region's best. Merlot★ and Cabernet Franc★ are also attractive, as are Riesling★ and good, quaffable fizz. Best years: (2001) **00 99 98**.

LANDMARK *Sonoma County, California, USA* Mid-size producer in Sonoma concentrating on Chardonnay and Pinot Noir. Chardonnays include Overlook★★, known for its restraint, and the oakier Damaris Reserve★★ and San Lorenzo★★. Both Pinot Noirs – the Kastania Vineyard in the SONOMA COAST AVA and Grand Detour★★ from Sonoma Mountain AVA – are beautifully focused.

LANGHE DOC *Piedmont, Italy* Important DOC covering wines from the Langhe hills around Alba. The range of varietals such as Chardonnay, Barbera and Nebbiolo embrace many former vino da tavola blends of the highest order. Best producers: (reds) ALTARE★★, Boglietti (Buio★★), Bongiovanni (Falletto★★), CERETTO★★, CHIARLO★, Cigliuti★★, CLERICO★★, Aldo CONTERNO★★, Conterno-Fantino (Monprà★★), Luigi Einaudi★, GAJA★★★, A Ghisolfi★★, Marchesi di Gresy (Virtus★★), F Nada (Seifile★★), Parusso (Bricco Rovella★★), Rocche dei Manzoni (Quatr Nas★), Vajra★, Gianni Voerzio (Serrapiu★★), Roberto VOERZIO★★. Best years: (reds) (2001) 00 99 **98 97 96 95 93 90**.

CH. LANGOA-BARTON ★★ *St-Julien AC, 3ème Cru Classé, Haut-Médoc, Bordeaux, France* Owned by the Barton family since 1821, Langoa-Barton is usually lighter in style than its ST-JULIEN stablemate LEOVILLE-BARTON, but it is still extremely impressive and reasonably priced. Drink after 7 or 8 years, although it may keep for 15. Second wine: Réserve de Léoville-Barton (a blend from the young vines of both Barton properties). Best years: 2000 99 98 96 **95 90 89 88 86 85 83 82**.

LANGUEDOC-ROUSSILLON *Midi, France* This vast area of southern France, running from Nîmes to the Spanish border and covering the *départements* of the GARD, HÉRAULT, Aude and Pyrénées-Orientales, is still a source of undistinguished cheap wine, but is also one of France's most exciting wine regions. The transformation is the result of better grape varieties, temperature-controlled vinification and ambitious producers, from the heights of MAS DE DAUMAS GASSAC to very good local co-ops. The best wines are the reds, particularly those from CORBIÈRES, FAUGÈRES, MINERVOIS and PIC ST-LOUP, and some new-wave Cabernets, Merlots and Syrahs, as well as the more traditional *vins doux naturels*, such as BANYULS, MAURY and MUSCAT DE RIVESALTES; but we are now seeing exciting whites as well, particularly as new plantings of Chardonnay, Marsanne, Roussanne, Viognier and Sauvignon Blanc mature. See also Bouches-du-Rhône, Collioure, Costières de Nîmes, Coteaux du Languedoc, Côtes du Roussillon, Côtes du Roussillon-Villages, Côtes de Thongue, Fitou, Muscat de Frontignan, Muscat de Mireval, Oc, Rivesaltes, Roussillon, St-Chinian.

LANSON *Champagne AC, Champagne, France* Owners Marne & Champagne are the dominant force in own-label cheap Champagne, producing 20 million bottles each year under numerous labels. Fortunately they seem determined to maintain Lanson as their quality flagship. Non-vintage Black Label ★ is reliable stuff and, like the rosé ★ and vintage ★★ wines, especially de luxe Noble Cuvée ★★, improves greatly with aging. Best years: (1996) (95) **93 90 89 88 85 83 82**.

LA ROSA *Cachapoal, Rapel, Chile* Old family operation rejuvenated by a new winery, La Palmeria. Unoaked Chardonnay★ is pure apricots and figs, and the Merlot★ is one of the better wines from RAPEL. Reserva and Gran Reserva wines (often ★★) are a step up in quality.

CH. LASCOMBES *Margaux AC, 2ème Cru Classé, Haut-Médoc, Bordeaux, France* One of the great underachievers in MARGAUX, with little worth drinking in the 1980s and 90s. New American ownership and investment might make the difference – at least the 2000 is the best in many years. Best years: 2000 96 95 **90 89 88 86 85**.

CH. DE LASTOURS *Corbières AC, Languedoc, France* Large CORBIÈRES estate, with some exciting wines. The top white is Blanc de Blancs, but the best wines are the reds – particularly concentrated old Grenache-

Carignan Ch. de Lastours★, fruity Cuvée Simone Descamps ★ and oaky la Grande Rompue. Best years: (reds) 2000 99 **98 96 95 94 93 90**.

CH. LATOUR ★★★ *Pauillac AC, 1er Cru Classé, Haut-Médoc, Bordeaux, France* Latour's great reputation is based on powerful, long-lasting classic wines. Throughout the 1950s, 60s and 70s the property stood for consistency and a refusal to compromise in the face of financial pressure. Strangely, in the early 80s there was an attempt to make lighter, more fashionable wines, with mixed results. The late 80s saw a return to classic Latour, much to my relief. Its reputation for making fine wine in less successful vintages is well deserved. After 30 years in British hands, it is now French-owned. Second wine: les Forts de Latour. Best years: 2000 99 98 97 96 95 94 **93** 90 **89 88 86 82 78 75 70**.

LOUIS LATOUR *Beaune, Burgundy, France* Unfashionable merchant almost as well known for his COTEAUX DE L'ARDECHE Chardonnays as for his Burgundies. Latour's white Burgundies are much better than the reds, although the red CORTON-Grancey★★ can be very good. Latour's oaky CORTON-CHARLEMAGNE ★★, from his own vineyard, is his top wine, but there is also good CHEVALIER-MONTRACHET ★★, BATARD-MONTRACHET ★★ and le MONTRACHET ★★. Even so, as these are the greatest white vineyards in Burgundy, there really should be more top performances. Best years: (top whites) (2001) 00 99 **97** 96 **95 92**.

CH. LATOUR-MARTILLAC *Pessac-Léognan AC, Cru Classé de Graves, Bordeaux, France* A GRAVES Classed Growth that for many years positively cultivated an old-fashioned image but which is now a property to watch. The vineyard is strictly organic, and has many ancient vines. In the past, the reds★ were deep, dark and well structured but they lacked charm. Things improved considerably in the 1980s and again in the late 90s. The whites★★ are thoroughly modern and of fine quality. Best years: (reds) 2000 99 98 96 **95 90 88 86 85 83**; (whites) 2000 99 **98 96 95 94 93 90 89 88**.

CH. LATOUR-À-POMEROL ★★ *Pomerol AC, Bordeaux, France* Directed by Christian MOUEIX of PETRUS fame, this property makes luscious wines with loads of gorgeous fruit and enough tannin to age well. Best years: 2000 99 98 96 **95 94 90 89 88 85 83 82**.

LATRICIÈRES-CHAMBERTIN AC See Chambertin AC.

LAUREL GLEN *Sonoma Mountain AVA, California, USA* Owner/wine-maker Patrick Campbell makes only Cabernet★★ at his mountaintop winery. This is rich wine with deep fruit flavours, aging after 6–10 years to a perfumed, complex BORDEAUX style. Counterpoint is a label for wine that does not make it into the top-level Cabernet. Terra Rosa is made from bought-in wine and bargain-label Reds has been made from wines from Chile and Argentina. Best years: (1999) 98 97 96 **95 94 93 92 91 90**.

LAURENT-PERRIER *Champagne AC, Champagne, France* Large, family-owned CHAMPAGNE house, offering flavour and quality at reasonable prices. Non-vintage★ is a bit lean and dry, but the vintage★★ is delicious, and the top wine, Cuvée Grand Siècle★★★, is among the finest Champagnes of all. Good rosé, as non-vintage★★ and vintage Grand Siècle Alexandra★★★. Best years: (1996) 95 **93 90 88 85 82**.

L'AVENIR *Stellenbosch WO, South Africa* Owner and former sugar broker Marc Wiehe, and winemaker and former pharmacist François Naudé, successfully adapted to their new roles and quickly gained plaudits. Pinotage★ and Chenin Blanc★ are Naudé's passion, but Cabernet★ and Chardonnay★ are also stylish and well made. Best years: (Pinotage) **2000 99 98 97 96 95 94**.

CH. LAVILLE-HAUT-BRION★★★ *Pessac-Léognan AC, Cru Classé de Graves, Bordeaux, France* The white wine of la MISSION-HAUT-BRION, one of the finest white PESSAC-LEOGNANS, with a price tag to match. Fermented in barrel, it needs 10 years or more to reach its savoury but luscious peak. Best years: 2000 99 98 97 96 95 **94 93 90 89 85**.

LAZIO *Italy* Region best known for FRASCATI, Rome's white glugger. There are also various bland whites from Trebbiano and Malvasia, such as EST! EST!! EST!!! DI MONTEFIASCONE. The region's best are red table wines based on Cabernet and Merlot or Sangiovese from the likes of Castel de Paolis (Quattro Morio★★), Paolo di Mauro (Vigna del Vassallo★★), Cerveteri co-op (Tertium★), Falesco (Montiano★★) as well as wines from Casale del Giglio★, Pietra Pinta★ and Trappolini★.

LEASINGHAM *Clare Valley, South Australia* A wing of BRL HARDY, Leasingham is CLARE VALLEY's biggest winery, and is well respected. Bin 56 Cabernet-Malbec★ and Bin 61 Shiraz★, once great bargains, are rising in price, while recently minted Classic Clare Shiraz★★ and Cabernet★ are high-alcohol, heavily oaked, overpriced blockbusters; Bastion Shiraz-Cabernet★ is better value. Riesling★★ can be among the area's best; respectable Chardonnay★ and Semillon-Sauvignon as well. Sparkling Shiraz is excellent.

L'ECOLE NO 41 *Columbia Valley AVA, Washington State, USA* The velvety and deeply flavoured Seven Hills Merlot★ from this winery can be good, as can the Cabernet Sauvignon★. A BORDEAUX-style blend called Apogee★★ from the Pepper Bridge vineyard in WALLA WALLA is more interesting. The best wines are the Semillons: the barrel-fermented★ is rich and woody but preference goes to the exciting single-vineyard Fries Vineyard Semillon★★ and Seven Hills Vineyard Semillon★★. The Chardonnay★ is pleasant, if simple. Best years: (top reds) 2000 99 97 **96 95**.

LECONFIELD *Coonawarra, South Australia* Leconfield's popular appeal continues under winemaker Phillippa Treadwell. Cabernet★ is finely crafted, Merlot★ is delightful, and peppery Shiraz★★ is set to hit the heights in years to come. Best years: (Shiraz) 1999 98 **96 95 94 91**.

LEDA *Castilla y León, Spain* A small winery launched by a bunch of young, enthusiastic wine professionals, including the sons of Mariano Garcia (of VEGA SICILIA and MAURO fame). It has taken the country by storm with its profound red Viñas Viejas★★ from very old Tempranillo vines in small plots throughout the Duero region. Best years: 1999 **98**.

LEEUWIN ESTATE *Margaret River, Western Australia* MARGARET RIVER's high flier, with pricy Chardonnay (Art Series★★★) that gets Burgundy lovers drooling into their bibs. The Cabernets have been patchy, but at best are ★★, blackcurranty yet with a cool, lean edge. Art Series Riesling★★ is complex and fine. Best years: (Art Series Chardonnay) **1998 96 95 94 92 90 89 87 85 83 82 81 80**.

DOM. LEFLAIVE *Puligny-Montrachet, Côte de Beaune, Burgundy, France* Famous white Burgundy producer, with extensive holdings in some of the world's greatest vineyards (including, since 1990, le MONTRACHET). The price of the wines is correspondingly high, although 1986–92 produced many disappointing wines. A new winemaking team, led by

Anne-Claude Leflaive and including the talented Pierre Morey, and the adoption of biodynamic growing soon turned things around. The top wines here – les Pucelles★★★, CHEVALIER-MONTRACHET★★★, BATARD-MONTRACHET★★★ and Bienvenues-Bâtard-Montrachet★★★ – are consistently delicious and can age for up to 20 years. Best years: (2001) 00 99 98 97 96 95 **94**.

OLIVIER LEFLAIVE FRÈRES *Puligny-Montrachet, Côte de Beaune, Burgundy, France* Former co-manager of Dom. LEFLAIVE, négociant Olivier Leflaive specializes in crisp, modern white wines from the COTE D'OR and the COTE CHALONNAISE, but standards are far from consistent. Lesser ACs – ST-ROMAIN, MONTAGNY★, ST-AUBIN★ and RULLY★ – offer good value, but the rich, oaky BATARD-MONTRACHET★★★ is the star turn of winemaker Franck Grux. Best years: (top whites) (2001) 00 99 **97** 96 **95**.

PETER LEHMANN *Barossa Valley, South Australia* BAROSSA doyen Lehmann buys grapes from many local growers and owns the superb Stonewell plot, main source of his best Shiraz★★. Splendidly juicy, old-fashioned, fruit-packed reds include Grenache★, Mentor★★ and Eight Songs Shiraz★★. Also lemony Semillon★★ and dry, long-lived Riesling★★ from Eden Valley. Best years: (Stonewell Shiraz) (1998) 96 94 **93 92 91** 90 89.

JOSEF LEITZ *Rüdesheim, Rheingau, Germany* The Leitz family makes the best dry and off-dry Rieslings in RÜDESHEIM, especially from the Berg Rottland★★ and Berg Schlossberg★★ sites. Many wines offer excellent value for money. Best years: (Riesling Spätlese) (2001) 00 99 98 **97** 96 **94 93** 92 90 89.

LEIWEN *Mosel, Germany* This unspectacular village, which was once a mass producer of cheap wines, has become a hotbed of the MOSEL Riesling revolution. Nowhere else in the region is there such a concentration of dynamic estates and new ideas. Best producers: GRANS-FASSIAN★★, Carl Loewen, Josef Rosch, St Urbans-Hof, Heinz Schmitt.

LEMBERGER See Blaufränkisch.

LENSWOOD VINEYARDS *Adelaide Hills, South Australia* Tim and Annie KNAPPSTEIN quickly established a fine reputation for Chardonnay★★ and Pinot Noir★★, and The Palatine★★ red blend, Sauvignon Blanc★★, Semillon★ and Cabernets★ are well on the way. Recent vintages of the Pinot Noir should be causing YARRA VALLEY producers sleepless nights. Best years: (Pinot Noir) 1999 98 **97 96 95 94 93**.

LENZ WINERY *Long Island AVA, New York State, USA* A leading LONG ISLAND winery going from strength to strength. The Merlot★ is elegant and powerful with soft, balanced tannins; dry Gewürztraminer★ is spicy and tasty. In good vintages the Pinot Noir★ has deep, ripe fruit. Chardonnay★ is mostly good and Cabernet Franc is appealing. Brut-style sparkling wine★ is hard to find, but worth the search. Best years: (Merlot) 1999 98 97 **96 95**.

LEONETTI CELLAR *Washington State, USA* The Cabernet Sauvignon★★★ and Merlot★★ produced here are immense, with concentrated fruit and enough tannin to chew on but not be blasted by. The tiny production is usually sold out within hours. Sangiovese★ is also pretty interesting. Best years: (Cabernet) 2000 99 98 97 **96 95 94 93** 92.

CH. LÉOVILLE-BARTON★★★ *St-Julien AC, 2ème Cru Classé, Haut-Médoc, Bordeaux, France* Made by Anthony Barton, whose family has run this ST-JULIEN property since 1826, this fine claret is a traditionalist's delight. Dark, dry and tannic, the wines are difficult to taste young, therefore often underestimated, but over 10–15 years they achieve a lean yet sensitively proportioned beauty rarely equalled in Bordeaux. Moreover, they are extremely fairly priced. Second wine: Réserve de Léoville-Barton. Best years: 2000 99 98 96 95 **94 93 90 89 88 86**.

CH. LÉOVILLE-LAS-CASES★★★ *St-Julien AC, 2ème Cru Classé, Haut-Médoc, Bordeaux, France*   The largest of the 3 Léoville properties, with the highest profile of all the ST-JULIENS, making wines of startlingly deep, dark concentration. I now find them so dense and thick in texture that it is difficult to identify them as St-Julien. Second wine: Clos du Marquis. The death of Michel Delon, the genius behind the property, in 2000, may have an effect on the wine style. We shall see. Best years: 2000 99 98 96 95 **94 93 90 89 88 86 85 83 82**.

CH. LÉOVILLE-POYFERRÉ★★ *St-Julien AC, 2ème Cru Classé, Haut-Médoc, Bordeaux, France*   Since the 1986 vintage Didier Cuvelier has gradually increased the richness of the wine without wavering from its austere style. A string of excellent wines in the 90s frequently show more classic ST-JULIEN style than those of illustrious neighbour LEOVILLE-LAS-CASES. Second wine: Moulin-Riche. Best years: 2000 99 98 96 95 **94 90 89 86 85 83 82**.

DOM. LEROY *Vosne-Romanée, Côte de Nuits, Burgundy, France*   In 1988 Lalou Bize-Leroy bought the former Dom. Noëllat in VOSNE-ROMANÉE, renaming it Domaine Leroy, which should not be confused with her négociant house, Maison LEROY, or the Dom. d'Auvenay, her personal estate. Here she produces fiendishly expensive, though fabulously concentrated, wines with biodynamic methods and almost ludicrously low yields from top vineyards such as CHAMBERTIN★★★, CLOS DE VOUGEOT★★★, MUSIGNY★★★, RICHEBOURG★★★ and ROMANEE-ST-VIVANT★★★. Best years: (top reds) (2001) 00 99 98 97 96 95 93 90 **89**.

MAISON LEROY *Auxey-Duresses, Côte de Beaune, Burgundy, France*   Négociant tucked away in the back streets of AUXEY-DURESSES, Leroy co-owns Dom. de la ROMANEE-CONTI, though is no longer involved in its management. However, its own cellar contains an extraordinary range of gems, often terrifyingly expensive, dating back to the beginning of the century. Best years: (reds) **1990 85 71 59 49 47 45**.

LIEBFRAUMILCH *Pfalz, Rheinhessen, Nahe and Rheingau, Germany*   Sweetish and low in acidity, Liebfraumilch now has a down-market image and sales are plummeting. It can come from the PFALZ, RHEINHESSEN, NAHE or the RHEINGAU and must be made of 70% Riesling, Silvaner, Müller-Thurgau or Kerner grapes.

LIGURIA *Italy*   Thin coastal strip of north-west Italy, running from the French border at Ventimiglia to the Tuscan border. Best-known wines are the Cinqueterre, Colli di Luna, Riviera Ligure di Ponente and Rossese di Dolceacqua DOCs.

LIMESTONE COAST *South Australia*   Newly defined zone for the south-east of South Australia, taking in PADTHAWAY, COONAWARRA, Wrattonbully and exciting new regions along the coast at Mt Benson, Robe, Kingston and Mt Gambier. Many of the new vineyards in this far-flung area have Coonawarra-like terra rossa soil with great potential for quality. Southcorp, Beringer Blass, YALUMBA, BRL HARDY and Cranswick are all involved.

LIMOUX AC *Languedoc, France*   The first AC in the LANGUEDOC to allow producers to use Chardonnay and Chenin Blanc, which must be vinified in oak. Production is dominated by the SIEUR D'ARQUES CO-OP.

whose best wines, Toques et Clochers★, fetch high prices at the annual charity auction. Other good producers include Dom. Bégude★ and Dom. de l'Aigle★ (recently bought by RODET) with promising Pinot Noir, Syrah and Chardonnay.

LINDEMANS *Murray River, Victoria, Australia*   Large, historic company that is a key part of Southcorp. Wines come from various regions. Best include HUNTER VALLEY Shiraz (Steven Vineyard★); Classic Hunter Semillon★★; mineral COONAWARRA St George Cabernet★; spicy Limestone Ridge Shiraz-Cabernet★★; and flagship Pyrus★ – a BORDEAUX blend. Also an impressive, if oaky, PADTHAWAY Chardonnay★ and the mass-market Bin 65 Chardonnay – several million cases a year and growing, and it still tastes pretty good! Best years: (Hunter Shiraz) (1998) 97 96 **95 94 91** 87 86 83 82 80 79 73 70 65; (Hunter Semillon) (1999) 98 96 95 91 **90 89 87 86** 80 79 78 75 72 68; (Coonawarra reds) 1998 96 **94 93 91 90 88 86 85 82**.

JEAN LIONNET *Cornas, Rhône Valley, France*   Jean Lionnet produces dense, tannic CORNAS★★ in a fairly modern style. The emphasis here is on new oak aging. Because the wines can seem closed when young, it's worth waiting for 6–7 years, especially for his Dom. de Rochepertuis★★. Lionnet also produces impressive COTES DU RHONE★ from his younger Cornas vines, and a little white ST-PERAY★. Best years: (Rochepertuis) (2000) 99 98 97 **96 95 94 92 91 90 89 88 85 83**.

LIRAC AC *Rhône Valley, France*   An excellent but underrated AC between TAVEL and CHATEAUNEUF-DU-PAPE. The reds have the dusty, spicy fruit of Châteauneuf without quite achieving the intensity of the best examples. They age well but are delicious young. The rosé is refreshing, with a lovely strawberry fruit, and the white can be good – drink them young before the perfume goes. Best producers: Amido★, Aquéria★, Bouchassy★, la Genestière, Lafond-Roc-Epine★, Maby, Mont-Redon★, la Mordorée★★, Pélaquié★, Roger Sabon★★, St-Roch★, Ségriès★, Tavel co-op★. Best years: (2001) 00 **98 97 96 95 94 93 91 90**.

LISTRAC-MÉDOC AC *Haut-Médoc, Bordeaux, France*   Set back from the Gironde and away from the best gravel ridges, Listrac is 1 of the 6 specific ACs within the HAUT-MEDOC. The wines can be good without ever being thrilling, and are marked by solid fruit, a slightly coarse tannin and an earthy flavour. More Merlot is now being used to soften the style. Best producers: CLARKE, Ducluzeau, Fonréaud, Fourcas-Dupré★, Fourcas-Hosten, Fourcas-Loubaney, Grand Listrac co-op, Mayne-Lalande★, Saransot-Dupré. Best years: 2000 96 **95 90 89 88 86 85**.

LOIRE VALLEY *France*   The Loire river cuts right through the heart of France. The middle reaches are the home of world-famous SANCERRE and POUILLY-FUME. The region of TOURAINE makes good Sauvignon Blanc and Gamay, while at VOUVRAY and MONTLOUIS the Chenin Blanc makes some pretty good fizz and still whites, ranging from sweet to very dry. The Loire's best reds are made in SAUMUR-CHAMPIGNY, CHINON and BOURGUEIL, mainly from Cabernet Franc, with ANJOU-VILLAGES improving fast. Anjou is famous for rosé, but the best wines are white, either sweet from the Layon Valley or very dry from SAVENNIERES. Near the mouth of the river around Nantes is MUSCADET. See also Anjou Blanc, Anjou Rouge, Bonnezeaux, Cabernet d'Anjou, Cheverny, Côte Roannaise, Coteaux de l'Aubance, Coteaux du Layon, Crémant de Loire, Gros Plant du Pays Nantais, Jardin de la France, Jasnières, Menetou-Salon, Muscadet, Pouilly-sur-Loire, Quarts de Chaume, Quincy, Reuilly, Rosé de Loire, St-Nicolas-de-Bourgueil, Saumur, Saumur Mousseux, Touraine.

LOMBARDY *Italy* Lombardy, richest and most populous of Italian regions, is a larger consumer than producer. Many of the best grapes go to provide base wine for Italy's thriving *spumante* industry. However, there are some interesting wines in OLTREPO PAVESE, VALTELLINA, LUGANA and high-quality sparkling and still wines in FRANCIACORTA.

LONG ISLAND *New York State, USA* Long Island has 2 AVAs: the Hamptons, and North Fork, which has more maritime exposure. This cool region has a long growing season and concentration of fruit in the wines can be wonderful in a good year. However, hurricanes have ruined some vintages. Best grapes are Chardonnay, Merlot and Cabernet Franc. Best producers: BEDELL★★, CASTELLO DI BORGHESE/HARGRAVE, GALLUCCIO/GRISTINA★, LENZ★, Palmer★, Pellegrini★, Pindar, Schneider★. Best years: (reds) 2000 **98 97 95 94 93**.

DR LOOSEN *Bernkastel, Mosel, Germany* Loosen's estate has portions of some of the MOSEL's most famous vineyards: Treppchen and Prälat in ERDEN, Würzgarten in URZIG, Sonnenuhr in WEHLEN, Himmelreich in GRAACH and Lay in BERNKASTEL. Most of Ernst Loosen's wines achieve ★★, and Spätlese and Auslese from Wehlen, Ürzig and Erden frequently ★★★. One of Germany's foremost protagonists of organic methods, his simple Riesling is great, year in year out. A joint venture with CHATEAU STE MICHELLE in WASHINGTON is proving exciting. Best years: (2000) 99 98 97 96 95 **94 93 92 90 89 88 85 76**. See also J L Wolf.

LÓPEZ DE HEREDIA *Rioja DOC, Rioja, Spain* Family-owned RIOJA company, still aging wines in old oak casks. Younger red wines are called Viña Cubillo★, and mature wines Viña Tondonia★ and Viña Bosconia★. Good, oaky whites, especially Viña Gravonia★★. Best years: (Viña Tondonia) 1994 **93 91 87 86 85**.

LOUPIAC AC *Bordeaux, France* A sweet wine area across the Garonne river from BARSAC. The wines are attractively sweet without being gooey. Drink young in general, though they can age. Best producers: Clos Jean★, Cros★, Loupiac-Gaudiet, Mémoires★, Noble★, Ricaud, les Roques. Best years: (2001) 99 98 **97 96 95 90 89 88 86**.

CH. LA LOUVIÈRE *Pessac-Léognan AC, Bordeaux, France* The star of PESSAC-LEOGNAN's non-classified estates, its reputation almost entirely due to André Lurton. Well-structured reds★★ and fresh, Sauvignon-based whites★★ are excellent value. Best years: (reds) 2000 99 98 **96 95 94 93 90 89 88 86 85**; (whites) 2000 99 98 **96 95 94 93 90 89 88**.

LUGANA DOC *Lombardy, Italy* Dry white (occasionally sparkling) from the Trebbiano di Lugana grape. Well-structured wines from the better producers can develop excitingly over a few years. Best producers: Ca' dei Frati★★, Ottella★, Provenza★, Visconti★, Zenato★.

LUNA *Napa Valley, California, USA* Led by winemaker John Kongsgaard (ex-NEWTON), Luna has attracted attention with its ambitious SUPER-TUSCAN-style Sangiovese★, stylish Pinot Grigio and attractive Merlot. Best years: (reds) 1999 98 **97 96**.

PIERRE LUNEAU-PAPIN *Muscadet Sèvre-et-Maine AC and Muscadet Coteaux de la Loire AC, Loire Valley, France* Meticulous producer who specializes in unoaked Muscadets for the long haul: his top wine, le 'L d'Or★, ages very well. Oak-fermented wines, although interesting, are variable. Best years: ('L' d'Or) 2000 **99 98 97 96 95 90**.

LUNGAROTTI *Torgiano DOC, Umbria, Italy* Leading producer of TORGIANO. The Torgiano Riserva (Vigna Monticchio★★) is now DOCG. Also makes red San Giorgio★ (Cabernet-Sangiovese) and Chardonnay Palazzi★.

LUSSAC-ST-ÉMILION AC *Bordeaux, France*   Much of the wine from this
AC, which tastes like a lighter ST-EMILION, is made by the first-rate local
co-op and should be drunk within 4 years of the vintage; certain
properties are worth seeking out. Best producers: Barbe-Blanche★,
Bel-Air, Bellevue, Courlat, Croix-de-Rambeau, la Grenière, Haut-Milon,
Lyonnat★, Vieux-Ch.-Chambeau. Best years: 2000 **98 96 95 90 89 88**.

EMILIO LUSTAU *Jerez y Manzanilla DO, Andalucía, Spain*   Specializes in
supplying 'own-label' wines to supermarkets. Quality is generally good,
and there are some real stars at the top, especially the Almacenista
range★★: very individual sherries from small, private producers.

CH. LYNCH-BAGES *Pauillac AC, 5ème Cru Classé, Haut-Médoc, Bordeaux,
France*   I am a great fan of Lynch-Bages red★★★ – with its almost
succulent richness, its gentle texture and its starburst of flavours, all
butter, blackcurrants and mint, and it is now one of PAUILLAC's most
popular wines. Because of its Fifth Growth status, it was inclined to be
underpriced; I couldn't say that now, but it's still worth the money. It
is impressive at 5 years, beautiful at 10 and irresistible at 20. Second
wine: Haut-Bages-Avérous. White wine: Blanc de Lynch-Bages★. Best
years: (reds) 2000 99 98 96 95 **94 90 89 88 86 85 83 82**.

MÂCON AC *Mâconnais, Burgundy, France*   The basic Mâconnais AC, but
most whites in the region are labelled under the superior MACON-VILLAGES
AC. The wines are rarely exciting. Chardonnay-based Mâcon Blanc,
especially, is a rather expensive basic quaffer. Drink young. Mâcon
Supérieur has a slightly higher minimum alcohol level. Best producers:
Bertillonnes, Bruyère, DUBOEUF, LAFON★. Best years: (2001) 00 **99**.

MÂCON-VILLAGES AC *Mâconnais, Burgundy, France*   Mâcon-Villages
should be an enjoyable, fruity, fresh wine for everyday drinking, but
because it is made from Chardonnay, the wines are often overpriced.
The name can be used by 43 villages, which may also append their
own name, as in Mâcon-Lugny. Co-ops dominate production. Best
villages: Chaintré, Chardonnay, Charnay, Clessé, Davayé, Igé, Lugny,
Prissé, la Roche Vineuse, St-Gengoux-de-Scissé, Uchizy, Viré. Best
producers: D & M Barraud★★, A Bonhomme★★, Deux Roches★, E
Gillet★, la Greffière★★, LAFON★, J-J Litaud★, Jean Manciat★, O
Merlin★★, Robert-Denogent★★, Rijckaert★, Roally★, Saumaize-
Michelin★, la Soufrandière★, J Thévenet★★, Valette★★, VERGET★★,
J-J Vincent★. Best years: (2000) 99 **98 97 96 95**. See also Viré-Clessé.

MACULAN *Breganze DOC, Veneto, Italy*   Fausto Maculan makes an
impressive range of BREGANZE DOC led by Cabernet-Merlot blend
Fratta★★ and Cabernet Palazzotto★, along with excellent reds★★ and
whites★★ from the Ferrata vineyards, but his most impressive wines
are sweet Torcolato★★ and outstanding Acininobili★★★ made
mainly from botrytized Vespaiolo grapes.

MADEIRA DOC *Madeira, Portugal*   The subtropical holiday island of
Madeira seems an unlikely place to find a serious wine. However,
Madeiras are very serious indeed and the best can survive to a great
age. Internationally famous by the 17th century, modern Madeira was
shaped by the phylloxera epidemic 100 years ago, which wiped out the
vineyards. Replantation was with hybrid vines inferior to the 'noble'
and traditional Malvasia (or Malmsey), Boal (or Bual), Verdelho and
Sercial varieties. There are incentives to replant with noble grapes, but
progress is slow (having now crept up to 15% of total plantings). The
typically burnt, tangy taste of inexpensive Madeira comes from the
process of heating in huge vats. The better wines are aged naturally in

the subtropical warmth. All the wines are fortified early on and may be sweetened with fortified grape juice before bottling. Basic 3-year-old Madeira is made mainly from Tinta Negra Mole, whereas higher-quality 5-year-old (Reserva), 10-year-old (Reserva Velha), 15-year-old (Extra Reserva) and vintage wines (from a single year, aged in cask for at least 20 years) tend to be made from 1 of the 4 'noble' grapes. Best producers: Barbeito, Barros e Souza, H M Borges, HENRIQUES & HENRIQUES, Vinhos Justino Henriques, MADEIRA WINE COMPANY, Pereira d'Oliveira.

MADEIRA WINE COMPANY *Madeira DOC, Madeira, Portugal* This company ships more than half of all Madeira exported in bottle. Among the brand names are Blandy's, Cossart Gordon, Leacock and Miles. Now controlled by the Symington family from the mainland. Big improvements are taking place in 5-, 10- and 15-year-old wines.

MADIRAN AC *South-West France* In the gentle hills of Vic-Bilh, north of Pau, there has been a steady revival of the Madiran AC. Several of the best producers are now using new oak and micro-oxygenation, and this certainly helps to soften the rather aggressive wine, based on the tannic Tannat grape. Best producers: Aydie★★, Barréjat★, Berthoumieu★, Bouscassé★★, Capmartin★, CHAPELLE LENCLOS★★, du Crampilh★, Caves de Crouseilles, Laffitte-Teston★, MONTUS★★, Mouréou★, Producteurs PLAIMONT. Best years: 2000 98 **97 96 95 94 90 89 88 85**.

CH. MAGDELAINE★★ *St-Émilion Grand Cru AC, 1er Grand Cru Classé, Bordeaux, France* Owned by the quality-conscious company of MOUEIX, these are dark, rich, aggressive wines, yet with a load of luscious fruit and oaky spice. In lighter years the wine has a gushing, easy, tender fruit and can be enjoyed at 5–10 years. Best years: 2000 99 98 96 95 **90 89 88 85 82 75**.

MAIPO, VALLE DEL *Valle Central, Chile* Birthplace of the Chilean wine industry and increasingly encroached upon by Chile's capital, Santiago. Cabernet is king and many of Chile's premium-priced reds come from here. Good Chardonnay is produced from vineyards close to the Andes. Best producers: ALMAVIVA★★, CARMEN★, Clos Quebrada de Macul★, CONCHA Y TORO★, SANTA CAROLINA, SANTA INES/DE MARTINO★, SANTA RITA★, TARAPACA.

MÁLAGA DO *Andalucía, Spain* Málaga is a curious blend of sweet wine, alcohol and juices (some boiled up and concentrated, some fortified, some made from dried grapes) and production is dwindling. The label generally states colour and sweetness. The best are intensely nutty, raisiny and caramelly. Best producers: Gomara★, López Hermanos★★, Telmo RODRIGUEZ★★.

CH. MALARTIC-LAGRAVIÈRE★ *Pessac-Léognan AC, Cru Classé de Graves, Bordeaux, France* A change of ownership in 1997 and massive investment in the vineyard and cellars has seen a steady improvement here since the 1998 vintage. The tiny amount of white★ is made from 100% Sauvignon Blanc and usually softens after 3–4 years into a lovely nutty wine. Best years: (reds) 2000 99 98 97 **96 90 89**; (whites) 2000 99 98 **96 95 94**.

MALBEC A red grape, rich in tannin and flavour, from South-West France. A major ingredient in CAHORS wines, it is also known as Côt or Auxerrois. At its best in Argentina and Chile, where it produces lush textured, ripe, perfumed, damsony reds. In CALIFORNIA, Australia and New Zealand it sometimes appears in BORDEAUX-style blends. In South Africa it is used both in blends and for varietal wines.

CH. MALESCOT ST-EXUPÉRY★★ *Margaux AC, 3ème Cru Classé, Haut-Médoc, Bordeaux, France* Once one of the most scented, exotic reds in Bordeaux, a model of perfumed MARGAUX. In the 1980s Malescot lost its reputation as the wine became pale, dilute and uninspired, but since 1995 it has begun to rediscover that cassis and violet perfume and return to its former glory. Best years: 2000 99 98 96 95 **90**.

MALVASIA This grape is widely planted in Italy and is found there in many guises, both white and red. In Fruili, it is known as the Malvasia Istriana and produces light, fragrant wines of great charm, while in TUSCANY, UMBRIA and the rest of central Italy it is used to improve the blend for wines like ORVIETO and FRASCATI. On the islands, Malvasia is used in the production of rich, dry or sweet wines in Bosa and Cagliari (in SARDINIA) and in Lipari off the coast of SICILY to make really tasty, apricotty sweet wines. As a black grape, Malvasia Nera is blended with Negroamaro in southern PUGLIA, while in PIEDMONT a paler-skinned relation produces frothing light reds in Castelnuovo Don Bosco, just outside Turin. Variants of Malvasia also grow in Spain and mainland Portugal. On the island of MADEIRA it produces sweet, varietal fortified wine, usually known by its English name: Malmsey.

LA MANCHA DO *Castilla-La Mancha, Spain* Spain's vast central plateau is Europe's biggest delimited wine area. Whites are never exciting but nowadays are often fresh and attractive. Reds can be light and fruity, or richer. Since 1995, DO regulations have allowed for irrigation and the planting of new grape varieties, including Viura, Chardonnay, Cabernet Sauvignon, Merlot, Petit Verdot and Syrah. There is still some rough, old-style wine, but progress is fast. Best producers: Ayuso Roig (Viña Q, Estola), Vinícola de Castilla (Castillo de Alhambra, Señorío de Guadianeja★), la Magdalena co-op, Nuestra Señora de la Cabeza co-op (Casa Gualda), Parra Jiménez★, Rodriguez & Berger (Santa Elena), Torres Filoso (Arboles de Castillejo★), Casa de la Viña.

DOM. ALBERT MANN *Alsace AC, Alsace, France* Powerful, flavoursome and ageworthy wines from a range of Grand Cru vineyards, including intense, mineral Rieslings from Furstentum★★ and Rosenberg★★ and rich Furstentum Gewurztraminer★★. An impressive range of Pinot Gris culminates in astonishingly concentrated Sélection de Grains Nobles from Furstentum★★★. Best years: (Sélection de Grains Nobles Gewurztraminer) 1998 97 94 **89**.

MANZANO, FATTORIA DI *Tuscany, Italy* Massive investment and the freedom to plant and replant with a New World abandon has resulted in the world clamouring for Tuscan Syrah (Podere Il Bosco★★), Viognier★★ and even Gamay (Podere Il Vescovo★), as well as Chardonnay (Podere Fontarca★) and Sauvignon blend Podere Le Terrazze★. Best years: (Podere Il Bosco) **1999 98 97 96 95 92**.

MARANGES AC *Côte de Beaune, Burgundy, France* AC in the southern CÔTE DE BEAUNE. Slightly tough red wines of medium depth, sometimes sold as CÔTE DE BEAUNE-VILLAGES. Less than 5% of production is white. Best producers: B Bachelet★, M Charleux★, Contat-Grangé★, DROUHIN, GIRARDIN★★. Best years: (reds) (2001) 99 **97 96 95**.

MARCASSIN *Sonoma County, California, USA* Helen Turley focuses on cool-climate Chardonnay and Pinot Noir. Incredible depth and restrained power are the hallmarks here. Tiny quantities of single-vineyard Chardonnays from Gauer Ranch Upper Barn, Hudson Vineyard, Lorenzo Vineyard and Marcassin Vineyard (the last two both SONOMA COAST) often rank ★★★. Best years: (2001) 00 99 98 **97 96 95**.

MARCHE *Italy* Adriatic region producing increasingly good white VERDICCHIO and reds from Montepulciano and Sangiovese led by ROSSO CONERO and ROSSO PICENO. Good wines from international varieties such as Cabernet, Chardonnay and Sauvignon Blanc and sold under the Marche IGT are becoming more common. Still others may add Merlot, Sangiovese or even Syrah to Montepulciano. The best include Boccadigabbia's Akronte★★ (Cabernet), Oasi degli Angeli's Kurni★★ (Montepulciano), Umani Ronchi's Pelago★★ (Montepulciano-Cabernet-Merlot), La Monacesca's Camerte★★ (Sangiovese-Merlot) and Le Terrazze's Chaos★★ (Montepulciano-Merlot-Syrah).

MARCILLAC AC *South-West France* Strong, dry red wines (and a little rosé), largely made from a local grape, Fer. The reds are rustic but full of fruit and should be drunk at 2–5 years old. Best producers: Michel Laurens, Marcillac-Vallon co-op, Jean-Luc Matha, Philippe Teulier.

MARGARET RIVER *Western Australia* Planted on the advice of agronomists in the late 1960s, this coastal community quickly established its name as a leading area for Cabernet, with marvellously deep, BORDEAUX-like structured reds. Now Chardonnay, concentrated and opulent, vies with Cabernet for top spot, but there is also fine grassy Semillon, often blended with citrus zest Sauvignon and lean but fruity Verdelho. Best producers: Amberley Estate★, Brookland Valley★, CAPE MENTELLE★★, CULLEN★★, Devil's Lair★, EVANS & TATE★, Hay Shed Hill, LEEUWIN ESTATE★★, MOSS WOOD★★, PIERRO★★, VASSE FELIX★★, Voyager Estate, Xanadu★. Best years: (Cabernet-based reds) (2000) 99 98 96 **95 94 93 91 90**.

MARGAUX AC *Haut-Médoc, Bordeaux, France* AC centred on the village of Margaux but including Soussans and Cantenac, Labarde and Arsac. Gravel banks dotted through the vineyards mean that the wines are rarely heavy and should have a divine perfume when mature at 7–12 years. Best producers: (Classed Growths) BRANE-CANTENAC★★, Dauzac★, FERRIERE★★, Giscours★, ISSAN★, Kirwan★, LASCOMBES★, MALESCOT ST-EXUPERY★★, MARGAUX★★★, PALMER★★, PRIEURE-LICHINE★, RAUZAN-SEGLA★★, Tertre★; (others) ANGLUDET★, Bel-Air Marquis d'Aligre★, la Gurgue★, LABEGORCE-ZEDE★, Monbrison★, SIRAN★. Best years: 2000 99 96 95 **90 89**.

CH. MARGAUX★★★ *Margaux AC, 1er Cru Classé, Haut-Médoc, Bordeaux, France* The greatest wine in the MEDOC. Has produced almost flawless wines since 1978, and inspired winemaker Paul Pontallier continues to produce the best from this great *terroir*. There is also some delicious white, Pavillon Blanc★★, made from Sauvignon Blanc, but it must be the most expensive BORDEAUX AC wine by a mile. Second wine: (red) Pavillon Rouge★★. Best years: (reds) 2000 99 98 96 95 94 **93** 90 **89 88 86 85 83 82 81 79 78**; (whites) 2000 99 98 **96 95 94 90 89 88**.

MARLBOROUGH *South Island, New Zealand* Marlborough has enjoyed such spectacular success as a quality wine region that it is difficult to imagine that the first vines were planted as recently as 1973. Its long, cool and relatively dry ripening season and free-draining stony soils are the major assets. Its snappy, aromatic Sauvignon Blanc first brought the region fame worldwide. Fine-flavoured Chardonnay, steely Riesling, elegant Champagne-method fizz and luscious botrytized wines are the other successes. Pinot Noir is improving every year. Best producers: CELLIER LE BRUN, Clifford Bay★★, CLOUDY BAY★★, DELEGAT'S★, Forrest Estate★★, Fromm★★, GROVE MILL★, HUNTER'S★★, ISABEL★★, JACKSON ESTATE★, Lawson's Dry Hills★, MONTANA, Nautilus★, SERESIN★★, Stoneleigh★, VAVASOUR★★, WITHER HILLS★★. Best years: (Chardonnay) 2001 00 **99 98 97 96 94**; (Pinot Noir) (2001) 00 **99 98 97 96 94**.

MARQUÉS DE CÁCERES *Rioja DOC, Rioja, Spain*   Go-ahead RIOJA winery making crisp, aromatic, modern whites★ and rosés★, and fleshy, fruity reds (Reservas★) with the emphasis on aging in bottle, not barrel. There is a new luxury red, Gaudium★. Best years: (reds) 1998 **96 95 94 92 91 90 89 87 85 82 78**.

MARQUÉS DE GRIÑÓN *Rioja DOC, Rioja and Rueda DO, Castilla y León, Spain*   From his home, non-DO estate at Malpica, near Toledo, Carlos Falcó (the eponymous Marqués de Griñón) has expanded into the Duero and now into RIOJA, after selling a stake in his company to BERBERANA. Minty Cabernet de Valdepusa★★ and Durius red (blended from TORO and RIBERA DEL DUERO) have been joined by barrel-fermented Chardonnay, Petit Verdot★★, Syrah★★ and the top blend, Eméritus★★, from his own estate, 2 Marqués de Griñón red Riojas (a lightly oaked young wine★ and a Reserva★), and white non-DO Durius★. Best years: (Valdepusa Eméritus) 1998 **97**.

MARQUÉS DE MURRIETA *Rioja DOC, Rioja, Spain*   The RIOJA bodega that most faithfully preserves the traditional style of long aging. Ultra-conservative, yet sporting glistening new fermentation vats and a Californian bottling line. The splendidly ornate Castillo de Ygay★★ label now includes wines other than the Gran Reserva. A more modern-styled, up-market cuvée, Dalmau★★, was introduced in 1999. Whites are dauntingly oaky, reds packed with savoury mulberry fruit. Best years: (reds) 1996 **95 94 92 91 89 87 85 68 64**.

MARQUÉS DE RISCAL *Rioja DOC, País Vasco and Rueda DO, Castilla y León, Spain*   A producer which has restored its reputation for classic pungent RIOJA reds (Reserva★). The expensive, Cabernet-based Barón de Chirel★★ cuvée is made only in selected years. Increasingly aromatic RUEDA whites★. Cellar problems during the 1990s are now presumed to have been corrected. Best years: (Barón de Chirel) **1996 95 94 91**.

MARSALA DOC *Sicily, Italy*   Fortified wines, once as esteemed as sherry or Madeira. A taste of an old Vergine (unsweetened) Marsala, fine and complex, will show why. Today most is sweetened. Purists say this mars its delicate nuances, but DOC regulations allow for sweetening Fine and Superiore versions. Best producers: DE BARTOLI★, Florio (Baglio Florio★, Terre Arse★), Pellegrino (Soleras★, Vintage★).

MARSANNAY AC *Côte de Nuits, Burgundy, France*   Village almost in Dijon, best known for its rosé, pleasant but quite austere and dry. But the reds are much better, frequently proving to be one of Burgundy's most fragrant wines. There is a little white. Best producers: R Bouvier★, P Charlopin★★, CLAIR★★, Collotte★, Fougeray de Beauclair★, Geantet-Pansiot★★, JADOT, D Mortet★★, J & J-L Trapet★. Best years: (reds) (2001) 00 **99 97 96**.

MARSANNE Undervalued grape yielding rich, nutty wines in the northern Rhône (HERMITAGE, CROZES-HERMITAGE, ST-JOSEPH and ST-PERAY), often with the more lively Roussanne. Also used in PIC ST-LOUP and other Languedoc wines, and performs well in Australia at MITCHELTON★★ and TAHBILK★★. As Ermitage, it produces some good wines in Swiss VALAIS.

MARTINBOROUGH *North Island, New Zealand* A cool, dry climate, free-draining soil and a passion for quality are this region's greatest assets. Mild autumn weather promotes intense flavours balanced by good acidity in all varieties: top Pinot Noir and complex Chardonnay, intense Cabernet, full Sauvignon Blanc and honeyed Riesling. Best producers: ATA RANGI★★, DRY RIVER★★★, MARTINBOROUGH VINEYARD★★, Nga Waka★, PALLISER ESTATE★★, Te Kairanga★. Best years: (Pinot Noir) (2001) 00 **99 98 97 96 94**.

MARTINBOROUGH VINEYARD *Martinborough, North Island, New Zealand* Famous for Pinot Noir★★ but also makes impressive Chardonnay★★, spicy Riesling★, and luscious botrytized styles★★ when vintage conditions allow. Winemaker Claire Mulholland has brought added elegance to the often-blockbuster wines of this high-flying producer. Best years: (Pinot Noir) (2001) 99 **98 96 94**.

MARTÍNEZ BUJANDA *Rioja DOC, Pais Vasco, Spain* Family-owned firm that makes some of the best modern RIOJA. Whites and rosés are young and crisp, reds★ are full of fruit *and* age well. The single-vineyard Finca Valpiedra★★ is a major newcomer. The family has now purchased a large estate in La MANCHA. Best years: (reds) **1998 96 95 94 92 91 90 87 86 85**.

MARZEMINO This red grape of northern Italy's TRENTINO province makes deep-coloured, plummy and zesty reds that are best drunk within 3–5 years. Best producers: Battistotti★, La Cadalora★, Cavit★, Concilio Vini★, Isera co-op★, Letrari★, Mezzacorona, Eugenio Rosi★, Simoncelli★, Spagnolli★, De Tarczal★, Vallarom★, Vallis Agri★.

MAS BRUGUIÈRE *Pic St-Loup, Coteaux du Languedoc AC, Languedoc, France* One of the top domaines in this quality-oriented region. The basic red★ has rich, spicy Syrah character, while top-of-the-range La Grenadière★★ develops buckets of black fruit and spice after 3 years. Calcadiz is an easy-drinking red from young vines. The Roussanne white Les Mûriers★ is aromatic, fruity and refreshingly crisp.

MAS DE DAUMAS GASSAC *Vin de Pays de l'Hérault, Languedoc, France* Aimé Guibert is the longest established quality producer in the Languedoc, proving that the HERAULT, normally associated with cheap table wine, is capable of producing great red wines that can age in bottle. The tannic yet rich Cabernet Sauvignon-based red★★ and the fabulously scented white★★ (Viognier, Muscat, Chardonnay and Petit Manseng) are usually impressive, if expensive. Sweet Vin de Laurance★★ is a new triumph. Best years: (reds) 2000 99 98 97 96 95 **94 93 90**.

MAS JULLIEN *Coteaux du Languedoc AC, Languedoc, France* Olivier Jullien makes fine wines from traditional MIDI varieties, with such success that bottles have to be rationed. The red Mas Jullien at best rates ★★★, while the États d'Ame★ is more forward and fruit driven White★ is also good stuff. Also late-harvest Clairette Beudelle. Best years: (reds) 2000 99 98 97 **96 95 94 93 91**.

BARTOLO MASCARELLO *Barolo DOCG, Piedmont, Italy* One of the great old-fashioned producers of BAROLO★★★, yet the wines have an exquisite perfume and balance. The Dolcetto★ and Barbera★ can need a little time to soften. Best years: (Barolo) (2000) (99) 98 97 96 95 **93 90 89 88 86 85 82 78**.

GIUSEPPE MASCARELLO *Barolo DOCG, Piedmont, Italy* The old house of Giuseppe Mascarello (now run by grandson Mauro) is renowned for dense, vibrant Dolcetto d'Alba (Bricco★★) and intense Barbera (Codana★★), but the pride of the house is BAROLO from the Monprivato★★★ vineyard. A little is now produced as a Riserva, Cà d'Morissio★★★ in top years. Small amounts of Barolo are also made from the Bricco, Santo Stefano di Perno and Villero vineyards. Best years: (Monprivato) (2000) (99) 98 97 96 **95 93 91 90 89 88 85 82 78**.

MASI *Veneto, Italy* Family firm, one of the driving forces in VALPOLICELLA. Brolo di Campofiorin★ (effectively if not legally a *ripasso* Valpolicella) is worth looking out for, as is AMARONE (Mazzano★★ and Campolongo di Torbe★★). Valpolicella's Corvina grape is also used in red blends Toar★ and Osar★. The wines of Serègo Alighieri★★ are also produced by Masi. Best years (Amarone): 1997 **95 93 90 88 86 85**.

MASTROBERARDINO *Campania, Italy* This family firm has long flown the flag for CAMPANIA in southern Italy, though it has now been joined by others. Best known for red TAURASI★★ and white Greco di Tufo★ and Fiano di Avellino★. Best years: (Taurasi Radici) 1997 96 95 **94 93 90 89 88 86 85 83 82 81 79**.

MATANZAS CREEK *Sonoma Valley AVA, California, USA* Sauvignon Blanc★ is taken seriously here, and the results show in a complex, zesty wine; Chardonnay★★ is rich and toasty but not overblown. Merlot★★ has a high reputation, with its silky, mouthfilling richness. Limited-edition Journey Chardonnay★★ and Merlot★★ are opulent but pricy. In 2000 Jess Jackson (of KENDALL-JACKSON) gained control of the winery. Best years: (Chardonnay) 2000 99 **98 97 96 95 94 93 91 90**; (Merlot) (2000) 99 97 96 **95 94 93 92 91 90**.

MATUA VALLEY *Auckland, North Island, New Zealand* In 2001 Matua became part of the Beringer Blass empire; the change in ownership (but not in management) is unlikely to affect the adventurous range of wines, at least in the short term. Best are the sensuous, scented Ararimu Chardonnay★★, lush and strongly varietal Gewürztraminer★, a creamy oak-aged Sauvignon Blanc★, tangy MARLBOROUGH Sauvignon Blanc★ (Shingle Peak), fine Merlot★ and Ararimu Merlot-Cabernet Sauvignon★★. Best years: (Ararimu Merlot-Cabernet) 1998 **96 94 91**.

CH. MAUCAILLOU★ *Moulis AC, Cru Bourgeois, Haut-Médoc, Bordeaux, France* Maucaillou shows that you don't have to be a Classed Growth to make high-quality claret. Expertly made by the Dourthe family, it is soft but classically flavoured. It is accessible early on but ages well for 10–12 years. Best years: 2000 99 98 96 **95 90 89**.

MAULE, VALLE DEL *Valle Central, Chile* The most southerly sub-region of Valle CENTRAL, with wet winters and a large day/night temperature difference. White varieties (mostly Chardonnay and Sauvignon Blanc) outnumber red by nearly 2 to 1, but Merlot's success on clay soils looks set to shift the balance. Best producers: (whites) J Bouchon, Calina★ (KENDALL-JACKSON), CARMEN★, SANTA RITA★, Terra Noble.

MAURO *Castilla y León, Spain* After making a name for himself as VEGA SICILIA's winemaker for 30 years, Mariano García has propelled his family's estate to the forefront in Spain and abroad. Wines include Crianza★★, Vendimia Seleccionada★★ and Terreus★★★. Best years: 1999 **98 97 96 95 94**.

MAURY AC *Roussillon, France* A *vin doux naturel* made mainly from Grenache Noir. This strong, sweetish wine can be made in either a young, fresh style or the locally revered old *rancio* style. Best producers: Mas Amiel★★, la Coume du Roy★, Maury co-op★, Maurydoré★, la Pleiade★.

MAXIMIN GRÜNHAUS *Grünhaus, Ruwer, Germany* The best estate in the Ruwer valley and one of Germany's greatest. Dr Carl von Schubert vinifies separately the wines of his 3 vineyards (Abtsberg, Bruderberg and Herrenberg), making chiefly dry and medium-dry wines of great subtlety. In good vintages the wines are easily ★★★ and the Auslese will age for decades; even QbA and Kabinett wines can age for many years. Best years: (2001) 00 97 96 95 **94 93 92** 90 **89 88 85 83 79 76 75 71**.

MAZIS-CHAMBERTIN AC See Chambertin AC.

MAZOYÈRES-CHAMBERTIN AC See Chambertin AC.

McLAREN VALE *South Australia* Sunny maritime region south of Adelaide, producing full-bodied wines from Chardonnay, Sauvignon Blanc, Shiraz, Grenache and Cabernet. About 50 small wineries, plus big boys HARDYS, Southcorp/ROSEMOUNT and BLASS. Best producers: Cascabel, CHAPEL HILL★★, CLARENDON HILLS★★, Coriole★, D'ARENBERG★★, FOX CREEK★★, Andrew Garrett, HARDYS★★, Kangarilla Road★, Maxwell★, Geoff MERRILL★, REYNELL★★, ROSEMOUNT★★, Tatachilla★, WIRRA WIRRA★★.

McWILLIAM'S *Riverina, New South Wales, Australia* Large family winery, now tied up with California's E & J GALLO. Best wines are the Mount Pleasant range from the Lower HUNTER VALLEY: classic bottle-aged Semillons (Elizabeth★★, Lovedale★★), buttery Chardonnays★ and special-vineyard Shirazes★ – Old Paddock & Old Hill, Maurice O'Shea (★★ in the best years) and Rosehill. Classy liqueur Muscat★★ from RIVERINA, and good table wines from their HILLTOPS Barwang★ vineyard. Best years: (Elizabeth Semillon) 1997 95 94 93 **91 89 86 83 82 81 79**.

MÉDOC AC *Bordeaux, France* The Médoc peninsula north of Bordeaux on the left bank of the Gironde river produces a good fistful of the world's most famous reds. These are all situated in the HAUT-MÉDOC, the southern, more gravelly half of the area. The Médoc AC, for reds only, covers the northern part. Here, in these flat clay vineyards, the Merlot grape dominates. The wines can be attractive in warm years: dry but juicy. Best at 3–5 years old. Best producers: la Cardonne, Escurac, les Grands Chênes★, Greysac, Lacombe-Noaillac, Lafon★, Loudenne, les Ormes-Sorbet★, Patache d'Aux, POTENSAC★★, Ramafort, Rollan-de-By★, la Tour-de-By★, la Tour-Haut-Caussan★, la Tour-St-Bonnet, Vieux-Robin. Best years: 2000 **96 95 90 89 88 86 85 82**.

MEERLUST *Stellenbosch WO, South Africa* Owner Hannes Myburgh maintains his late father's faith in the BORDEAUX varieties: his complex Rubicon★★ was one of the Cape's first Bordeaux blends. Italian cellarmaster Giorgio Dalla Cia's passion is refined Merlot★; there's also impressive Chardonnay★★ and ripe Pinot Noir★. Best years: (Rubicon) **1998 97 96 95 94 92 91**; (Chardonnay) **1999 98 97 96**.

ALPHONSE MELLOT *Sancerre AC, Loire Valley, France* Long-established grower and négociant. The négociant business includes decent wines from POUILLY-FUMÉ and MENETOU-SALON, but the most interesting come

182

from the family's own vineyards in SANCERRE. Dom. la Moussière★ is unoaked, with fresh, intense citrus flavours; the oaked Cuvée Edmond★★ can seem overly wooded at first and needs a few years to mature to a fascinating, fully integrated flavour. Red Génération XIX is much improved. Best years: (Cuvée Edmond) 2000 **99 98 97 96 95 90 89**.

CHARLES MELTON *Barossa Valley, South Australia*   One of the leading lights in the renaissance of hand-crafted Shiraz, Grenache and Mourvèdre in the BAROSSA. Fruity Grenache rosé Rose of Virginia★, RHONE blend Nine Popes★★, varietal Grenache★★ and smoky Shiraz★★ have all attained cult status. Cabernet Sauvignon is variable, but ★★ at best. Best years: (Nine Popes) 1999 98 **96 95 94 93 92 91 90**.

MENDOCINO COUNTY *California, USA*   The northernmost county of the North Coast AVA. It includes the cool-climate ANDERSON VALLEY AVA, excellent for sparkling wines and the occasional Pinot Noir; and the warmer Redwood Valley AVA, with good Zinfandel and Cabernet. Best producers: FETZER, Fife★, Goldeneye, HANDLEY★★, Husch, Lazy Creek★, McDowell Valley★, Navarro★★, PACIFIC ECHO★, Parducci, ROEDERER★★. Best years: (reds) (2000) 99 **97 96 95 94 93 92 91 90**.

MENDOZA *Argentina*   The most important wine region in Argentina, accounting for about 75% of fine wine production. Situated in the eastern foothills of the Andes on a similar latitude to Chile's Santiago, the region's bone-dry climate produces powerful, high-alcohol red wines. Just south of Mendoza city, Maipú and Luján de Cuyo are ideal for Malbec, Syrah and Cabernet Sauvignon. High-altitude sub-regions nearer the Andes, such as Tupungato, now produce better whites, particularly Chardonnay. Best producers: Luigi Bosca, CATENA★★, DOMAINE VISTALBA★, Finca El Retiro★, LA AGRICOLA★, Nieto Senetiner (Cadus★★), NORTON★, Terrazas de los Andes★.

MENETOU-SALON AC *Loire Valley, France*   Extremely attractive, chalky-clean Sauvignon whites and cherry-fresh Pinot Noir reds and rosés from west of SANCERRE. Best producers: Chatenoy★, Chavet★, J-P Gilbert★, H Pellé★, J-M Roger★, J Teiller★, Tour St-Martin★.

MÉO-CAMUZET *Vosne-Romanée, Côte de Nuits, Burgundy, France*   Super-quality estate, run by Jean-Nicolas Méo since 1989. New oak barrels and luscious, rich fruit combine in superb wines, which also age well. CLOS DE VOUGEOT★★★, RICHEBOURG★★★ and CORTON★★ are the grandest wines, along with the VOSNE-ROMANEE Premiers Crus, aux Brulées★★, Cros Parantoux★★★ and les Chaumes★★. Also fine NUITS-ST-GEORGES aux Boudots★★ and aux Murgers★★, and now also offering some less expensive négociant wines. Best years: (2001) 00 99 98 97 96 95 93 **90**.

MERCUREY AC *Côte Chalonnaise, Burgundy, France*   Most important of the 4 main COTE CHALONNAISE villages. The red is usually pleasant and strawberry-flavoured, sometimes rustic, and can take some aging. There is not much white but I like its buttery, even spicy, taste. Best at 3–4 years old. Best producers: (reds) FAIVELEY★★, E Juillot★, M Juillot★★, Lorenzon★★, F Raquillet★, RODET, de Suremain★★, de Villaine★★; (whites) FAIVELEY (Clos Rochette★), Genot-Boulanger★, M Juillot★, O LEFLAIVE★, RODET (Chamirey★). Best years: (reds) 2000 99 98 **97 96 95**.

MERLOT   See pages 184–5.

GEOFF MERRILL *McLaren Vale, South Australia*   High-profile winemaker with an instinctive feel for wine. Under the Geoff Merrill brand he fields nicely bottle-aged Reserve Cabernet★ in a light, early-picked, slightly eccentric style, Reserve Shiraz★ and Chardonnay★ (Reserve★★). The cheaper Mount Hurtle brand has a moreish Grenache rosé.

MERLOT

 Red wine without tears. That's the reason Merlot has vaulted from being merely Bordeaux's red wine support act, well behind Cabernet Sauvignon in terms of class, to being the red wine drinker's darling, planted like fury all over the world. It is able to claim some seriousness and pedigree, but – crucially – can make wine of a fat, juicy character mercifully low in tannic bitterness, which can be glugged with gay abandon almost as soon as the juice has squirted from the press. Yet this doesn't mean that Merlot is the jelly baby of red wine grapes. Far from it.

WINE STYLES

Bordeaux Merlot The great wines of Pomerol and St-Émilion, on the Right Bank of the Dordogne, are largely based on Merlot and the best of these – for example, Château Pétrus, which is almost 100% Merlot – can mature for 20–30 years. In fact there is more Merlot than Cabernet Sauvignon planted throughout Bordeaux, and I doubt if there is a single red wine property that does not have some growing, because the variety ripens early, can cope with cool conditions and is able to bear a heavy crop of fruit. In a cool, damp area like Bordeaux, Cabernet Sauvignon cannot always ripen, so the soft, mellow character of Merlot is a fundamental component of the blend even in the best, Cabernet-dominated, Médoc estates, imparting a supple richness and approachability to the wines, even when young.

Other European Merlots The south of France has briskly adopted the variety, producing easy-drinking, fruit-driven wines, but in the hot Languedoc the grape often ripens too fast to express its full personality and can seem a little simple and even raw-edged. Italy has long used very high-crop Merlot to produce a simple, light quaffer in the north, particularly in the Veneto, though Friuli and Alto Adige make fuller styles and there are some very impressive Tuscan examples. The Italian-speaking Swiss canton of Ticino is often unjustly overlooked for its intensely fruity, oak-aged versions. Eastern Europe has the potential to provide fertile pastures for Merlot and so far the most convincing, albeit simple, styles have come from Hungary and Bulgaria, although the younger examples are almost invariably better than the old. Spain has developed good Merlot credentials since the mid-1990s.

New World Merlots Youth is also important in the New World, nowhere more so than in Chile. Chilean Merlot, mostly blended with Carmenère, has leapt to the front of the pack of New World examples with gorgeous garnet-red wines of unbelievable crunchy fruit richness that cry out to be drunk virtually in their infancy. California Merlots often have more serious pretensions, but the nature of the grape is such that its soft, juicy quality still shines through. The cooler conditions in Washington State have produced some impressive wines, and the east coast of the US has produced good examples from places such as Long Island. With some French input, South Africa is starting to get Merlot right, and in New Zealand, despite the cool, damp conditions, some gorgeous rich examples have been made. Only Australia seems to find Merlot problematic, but there are some fine exceptions from cooler areas, including some surprisingly good fizzes.

BEST PRODUCERS

France

Bordeaux (St-Émilion) ANGELUS, AUSONE, BEAU-SEJOUR BECOT, MAGDELAINE, TERTRE-ROTEBOEUF, TROPLONG-MONDOT; (Pomerol) le BON PASTEUR, l'EGLISE-CLINET, l'EVANGILE, la FLEUR-PETRUS, GAZIN, LAFLEUR, LATOUR-A-POMEROL, PETIT-VILLAGE, PETRUS, le PIN, TROTANOY, VIEUX-CHATEAU-CERTAN.

Other European Merlots

Italy (Friuli) Livio FELLUGA; (Tuscany) AMA, AVIGNONESI, CASTELGIOCONDO, Ghizzano, Le Macchiole, ORNELLAIA, Petrolo, San Giusto a Rentennano, Tua Rita; (Lazio) Falesco.

Spain (Penedès) Can Ràfols dels Caus; (Somontano) ENATE.

Switzerland Daniel Huber, Werner Stucky, Christian Zundel.

New World Merlots

USA (California) ARROWOOD, BERINGER, CHATEAU ST JEAN, DUCKHORN, FERRARI-CARANO, MATANZAS CREEK, MERRYVALE, NEWTON, Pahlmeyer, SHAFER, STERLING; (Washington) ANDREW WILL, CANOE RIDGE, LEONETTI; (New York) BEDELL, LENZ.

Australia Brookland Valley, CLARENDON HILLS, James Irvine, KATNOOK ESTATE, PARKER COONAWARRA ESTATE, PETALUMA, Tatachilla, YARRA YERING.

New Zealand Esk Valley (VILLA MARIA), GOLDWATER, C J Pask, VILLA MARIA.

South Africa MORGENHOF, SAXENBURG (Private Collection), STEENBERG, THELEMA, VEENWOUDEN, VERGELEGEN.

Chile CARMEN, CASA LAPOSTOLLE (Cuvée Alexandre, Clos Apalta), Casa Silva, CONO SUR (Reserva), ERRAZURIZ, LA ROSA (La Palmeria), VALDIVIESO, VINA CASABLANCA.

MERRYVALE *Napa Valley AVA, California, USA* A Chardonnay powerhouse (Reserve★★, Silhouette★★★, Starmont★★), but reds are not far behind, with BORDEAUX-blend Profile★★ and juicy Reserve Merlot★★. Best years: (Chardonnay) (2001) 00 99 **98 97 96 95**.

LOUIS MÉTAIREAU *Muscadet Sèvre-et-Maine AC, Loire Valley, France* Classic Muscadets with considerable intensity, thanks to low yields and careful winemaking. Styles range from lighter Petit Mouton to concentrated Cuvée LM★ and Cuvée One★.

MEURSAULT AC *Côte de Beaune, Burgundy, France* The biggest and most popular white wine village in the CÔTE D'OR. There are no Grands Crus, but a whole cluster of Premiers Crus. The general standard is better than in neighbouring Puligny. The golden wine is lovely to drink young but better aged for 5–8 years. Virtually no Meursault red is now made. Best producers: R Ampeau★★, Michel Bouzereau★★, Boyer-Martenot★★, Coche-Debord★★, COCHE-DURY★★★, DROUHIN★, A Ente★★, J-P Fichet★★, V GIRARDIN★★, JADOT★★, P Javillier★★, François Jobard★★, Rémi Jobard★★★, LAFON★★★, Matrot★★, Pierre Morey★★, G Roulot★★★. Best years: (2001) 00 99 **97** 96 **95 92** 89.

CH. MEYNEY★ *St-Estèphe AC, Cru Bourgeois, Haut-Médoc, Bordeaux, France* One of the most reliable ST-ESTEPHES, producing broad-flavoured wine with dark, plummy fruit. Second wine: Prieur de Meyney. Best years: 2000 99 96 **95 94 90** 89 88.

PETER MICHAEL WINERY *Sonoma County, California, USA* British-born Sir Peter Michael caught the wine bug and turned a country retreat into an impressive winery known for its small-batch wines. Les Pavots★★ is the estate red BORDEAUX blend, and Mon Plaisir★★ and Cuvée Indigne★ are his top Chardonnays, both noted for their deep, layered flavours. Best years: (Les Pavots) 1997 **96 95 94 93 92 91 90**.

LOUIS MICHEL *Chablis AC, Burgundy, France* The prime exponent of unoaked CHABLIS. The top Crus – Montmains★★★, Montée de Tonnerre★★★ and les Clos★★★ – are wonderfully fresh, mineral and they age triumphantly. Best years: (top crus) 2000 99 98 **97** 96 **95 90** .

MIDI *France* A loose geographical term, virtually synonymous with LANGUEDOC-ROUSSILLON, covering the vast, sunbaked area of southern France between the Pyrenees and the RHONE VALLEY.

MILLTON *Gisborne, North Island, New Zealand* Organic vineyard using biodynamic methods, whose top wines include the sophisticated Clos St Anne Chardonnay★★, botrytized Opou Vineyard Riesling★★ and complex barrel-fermented Chenin Blanc★. Recent vertical tastings of Chardonnays and Rieslings spanning over a decade indicated just how well both wines age. Best years: (whites) **1999 98 96 94**.

MINER FAMILY VINEYARDS *Oakville AVA, California, USA* Dave Miner has 32ha (80 acres) planted on a ranch 305m (1000 feet) above the OAKVILLE Valley floor. Highlights include a yeasty, full-bodied Chardonnay★★ as well as intense Merlot★★ and Cabernet Sauvignon★★ that demand a decade of aging. A stylish Viognier★★ from purchased fruit is also made.

MINERVOIS AC *Languedoc, France* Attractive, mostly red wines from north-east of Carcassonne. Big companies like Nicolas have worked with local co-ops to produce good, juicy, quaffing wine at reasonable prices. The best wines are made by the estates: full of ripe, red fruit and pine-dust perfume, for drinking young. It can age, especially if a little new oak has been used. Since 1997, a village denomination, La Livinière, covering 4 communes, can be appended to the Minervoi label. Best producers: (reds) Aires Hautes★, CLOS CENTEILLES★★, Coupe-Roses★, Pierre Cros★, Fabas★, Gourgazaud★, la Grave, Maris★, Oupia★, Piccinini★, Pujol, Ste-Eulalie★, la TOUR BOISÉE★, Vassière, Villerambert-Julien★, Violet★. Best years: 2000 **99 98 96 95**.

CH. LA MISSION-HAUT-BRION★★★ *Pessac-Léognan AC, Cru Classé de Graves, Bordeaux, France* Traditionally I have found la Mission's wines long on power but short on grace, but in the difficult years of the 1990s they showed consistency allied to intensity and fragrance. Best years: 2000 99 98 96 95 94 **93 90 89 88 85**.

MISSION HILL *British Columbia, Canada* Spring 2001 saw the expansion of Mission Hill's winery, allowing it to process grapes from its extensive vineyard holdings in the OKANAGAN VALLEY. Kiwi winemaker John Simes has strengthened the winery's red wines of late: excellent Chardonnay★★, Pinot Blanc★ and Pinot Gris★ are joined by Merlot★, Cabernet Sauvignon, Shiraz★, including separate bottlings from 100% estate-grown grapes, and a red meritage blend, Oculus★★.

MITCHELL *Clare Valley, South Australia* Jane and Andrew Mitchell turn out some of CLARE VALLEY's most ageworthy Watervale Riesling★ and a classy barrel-fermented Growers Semillon★. Growers Grenache★ is a huge unwooded and spirity lump of fruit, but if you're in the mood... Peppertree Shiraz★★ and Sevenhill Cabernet Sauvignon★ are plump, chocolaty and typical of the region.

MITCHELTON *Goulburn Valley, Victoria, Australia* VICTORIA's most consistently fine Riesling (Blackwood Park★★), but mature Marsanne★★, Roussanne★★ and Viognier★ are the specialities here, alone or in blends. Print Label Shiraz★★ and Reserve Cabernet★ are increasingly deep and structured, as are Shiraz, Mourvèdre and Grenache blends. Best years: (Print Label) 1998 96 **95 92 91 90**.

MITTELRHEIN *Germany* Small, northerly wine region. Almost 75% of the wine here is Riesling but, unlike other German regions, the Mittelrhein has been in decline over the last few decades. The vineyard sites are steep and difficult to work – although breathtaking. The best growers (like Toni JOST★★) cluster around Bacharach in the south and Boppard in the north, and produce wines of a striking mineral tang and dry, fruity intensity. Best years: (Riesling Spätlese) (2001) 98 **97 93 90**.

MOËT & CHANDON *Champagne AC, Champagne, France* Moët & Chandon dominates the CHAMPAGNE market (more than 25 million bottles a year), and has become a major producer of sparkling wine in CALIFORNIA and Australia too. Good non-vintage★ can be delightful – soft, creamy and a little spicy, and consistency is pretty good. The vintage★★ usually has considerable style, while the rosé★★ can show a Pinot Noir floral fragrance depressingly rare in modern Champagne. Dom Pérignon★★★ is the de luxe cuvée. It can be one of the greatest Champagnes of all, but you've got to age it for a number of years or you're wasting your money. Best years: (1996) **95 93 92 90 88 86 85 82**.

MONBAZILLAC AC *South-West France* BERGERAC's leading sweet wine. Most is light, pleasant, but forgettable, from the efficient co-op. This style won't age, but a truly rich, late-harvested Monbazillac can last 10 years. Best producers: l'Ancienne Cure★, Bélingard (Blanche de Bosredon★), la Borderie★, Grande Maison★, Haut-Bernasse, Hébras, Theulet★, Tirecul-la-Gravière★★, Treuil-de-Nailhac★. Best years: 1999 98 **97 96 95 90**.

187

CH. MONBOUSQUET★★ *St-Émilion Grand Cru AC, Bordeaux, France*
Gérard Perse, who also owns Ch. PAVIE, has transformed this struggling estate on the Dordogne plain into one of ST-ÉMILION's 'super-crus'. Rich, voluptuous and very expensive, the wine is drinkable from 3–4 years but will age longer. There is also a tiny volume of white. Best years: 2000 99 98 **97 96 95 94**.

ROBERT MONDAVI *Napa Valley, California, USA*   Robert Mondavi is a Californian institution, based in NAPA. Best known for the regular Cabernet Sauvignon★, open and fruity with the emphasis on early drinkability, and the Reserve Cabernet★★★, possessing enormous depth and power. A regular★ and a Reserve★ Pinot Noir are velvety smooth and supple wines with style, perfume and balance. For many years the Mondavi trademark wine was Fumé (Sauvignon Blanc) (Reserve Fumé★), but in recent years Chardonnay★ (Reserve★★) has become the winery leader, although, as with most of the wines, I'd like a little more personality to shine through. Mondavi also owns ARROWOOD in SONOMA, BYRON in SANTA BARBARA COUNTY, OPUS ONE in Napa in partnership with the Rothschilds, as well as the Mondavi Woodbridge winery, where inexpensive varietal wines are produced. The La Famiglia range, made in Napa, is based chiefly on Italian varietals. Mondavi is involved in SENA in Chile, and in Italy has associations with FRESCOBALDI (CASTELGIOCONDO), producing a SUPER-TUSCAN named Luce, and with ORNELLAIA. Best years: (Cabernet Sauvignon Reserve) (2001) (00) 99 98 97 96 95 94 **92 91 88 87 86 85 84**.

MONTAGNE-ST-ÉMILION AC *Bordeaux, France*   A ST-ÉMILION satellite which can produce rather good red wines. The wines are normally ready to drink in 4 years but age quite well in their slightly earthy way. Best producers: Calon, Corbin, Faizeau★, Laurets, Moines, Montaiguillon, Négrit, Roc-de-Calon, Rocher Corbin, Roudier, Vieux-Ch.-St-André. Best years: 2000 **98 96 95 94 90 89 88**.

MONTAGNY AC *Côte Chalonnaise, Burgundy, France*   Wines from this Côte Chalonnaise village can be rather lean, but are greatly improved now that some producers are aging their wines for a few months in new oak. Generally best with 2–5 years' bottle age. Best producers: S Aladame★★, BOUCHARD PERE ET FILS★, BUXY CO-OP★, Davenay★, FAIVELEY, LATOUR★, O LEFLAIVE★, A Roy★, J Vachet★. Best years: (2001) 00 **99 96**.

MONTALCINO See Brunello di Montalcino DOCG.

MONTANA *Auckland, Gisborne, Hawkes Bay and Marlborough, New Zealand*
Montana crushes an estimated 50% of New Zealand's total grape production. In 2001 ownership of this efficient and at times innovative winery passed to the large international distributor Allied Domecq. Montana's MARLBOROUGH Sauvignon Blanc★ and GISBORNE Chardonnay★ are in a considerable way to thank for putting New Zealand on the international map. To show that big can try to be best, the company established CHURCH ROAD★, a small (by Montana standards) winery in HAWKES BAY. Estate bottlings, particularly Ormond Estate Chardonnay★★, also bode well. Makes consistent Lindauer fizz and, with the help of the CHAMPAGNE house DEUTZ, austere yet full-bodied Deutz Marlborough Cuvée NV Brut★.

MONTECARLO DOC *Tuscany, Italy*   Both reds (Sangiovese with Syrah and whites (Trebbiano with Sémillon and Pinot Grigio) are distinctive Non-DOC wines can include Cabernet, Merlot, Pinot Bianco, Roussanne and Vermentino. Best producers: Buonamico★, Carmignani★ Montechiari★, Wandanna★. Best years: (reds) (2001) 00 **99 98 97 96 95 93**.

MONTECILLO *Rioja DOC, Rioja, Spain* Owned by sherry firm OSBORNE, making high-quality RIOJAS in young and mature styles. Red and white Crianza★ is young and fruity. Rich, fruity red Gran Reservas★ are aged in French oak barrels and combine delicacy with flavour. The Viña Cumbrero and Viña Monty brands were abandoned in 2000. Best years: (reds) 1999 **98 96 95 94 91 88 87 86 82 81**.

MONTEFALCO DOC *Umbria, Italy* Sangiovese-based Montefalco Rosso, often good, is outclassed by dry Sagrantino di Montefalco (now DOCG) and Sagrantino Passito, a glorious sweet red made from dried grapes. Best producers: (Sagrantino) Adanti★, Antonelli★, Caprai★★ (25 Anni★★★), Colpetrone★★. Best years: (Sagrantino) (2000) 99 98 97 96 95 **94 93 91 90 88**.

MONTEPULCIANO Grape, grown mostly in eastern Italy (unconnected with TUSCANY's Sangiovese-based wine VINO NOBILE DI MONTEPULCIANO). Can produce deep-coloured, fleshy, spicy wines with moderate tannin and acidity. Besides MONTEPULCIANO D'ABRUZZO, it is used in ROSSO CONERO and ROSSO PICENO in the MARCHE and also in UMBRIA, Molise and PUGLIA.

MONTEPULCIANO D'ABRUZZO DOC *Abruzzo, Italy* The Montepulciano grape's most important manifestation. Quality varies from the insipid or rustic to the concentrated and characterful. Best producers: Cataldi Madonna★, Cornacchia★, Filomusi Guelfi★, Illuminati★, Marramiero★, Masciarelli★★, A & E Monti★, Montori★, Nicodemi★, Cantina Tollo★, Umani Ronchi★, Roxan★, La Valentina★, Valentini★★★, L Valori★, Ciccio Zaccagnini★. Best years: (2001) 00 99 **98 97 95 94 93 90 88 85**.

MONTEREY COUNTY *California, USA* Large CENTRAL COAST county south of San Francisco Bay in the Salinas Valley. The most important AVAs are Arroyo Seco, Chalone, Carmel Valley and Santa Lucia Highlands. Best grapes are Chardonnay, Riesling and Pinot Blanc, with some good Cabernet Sauvignon, Merlot in Carmel Valley and Pinot Noir in the Santa Lucia Highlands in the cool middle of the county. Best producers: Barnett Vineyard★, Bernardus★★, CHALONE★★, Estancia★, Heller★, Jekel★, Mer Soleil★★, Morgan★, TALBOTT★★, Testarossa★★. Best years: (reds) (2000) 99 **97 96 95 94 92 91 90**.

MONTES *Curicó, Chile* One of Chile's pioneering wineries in the modern era, focused right from the start on the export market. Most important for innovative development of top-quality vineyard land on the steep Apalta slopes of COLCHAGUA and the virgin country of Marchihue out towards the Pacific. Sauvignon Blanc★  and Chardonnay★ are good and fruit-led; all the reds are more austere and need bottle age. Top-of-the-line Montes Alpha M★ is now beginning to shine after a slow start, but the best wines are Montes Alpha Syrah★★ and a new Syrah called Montes Folly★★.

MONTEVERTINE *Tuscany, Italy* Based in the heart of CHIANTI CLASSICO, Montevertine is famous for its non-DOC wines, particularly Le Pergole Torte★★★. This was the first of the SUPER-TUSCANS made solely with the Sangiovese grape, and it remains one of the best. A little Canaiolo is included in the excellent Il Sodaccio★★ and Montevertine Riserva★★. Best years: (Le Pergole Torte) (1999) 98 97 96 **95 93 92 90 88 86 85**.

MONTGRAS *Rapel, Chile* Reds are, so far, well ahead of the whites at this superbly equipped new winery in COLCHAGUA. Reserva Merlot★ and Cabernet★ are oaky but with good plum and berry fruit. New plantings on Ninquén hill, including Syrah, with much lower yields, will provide the real excitement in upcoming vintages.

MONTHELIE AC *Côte de Beaune, Burgundy, France* Attractive, mainly red wine village lying halfway along the COTE DE BEAUNE behind MEURSAULT and VOLNAY. The wines generally have a lovely cherry fruit and make pleasant drinking at a good price. Best producers: COCHE-DURY★, Darviot-Perrin★, P Garaudet★, R Jobard★, LAFON★, Olivier LEFLAIVE★, Monthelie-Douhairet★, Potinet-Ampeau★, G Roulot★★, de Suremain★. Best years: (reds) 1999 98 **97 96 95**; (whites) (2001) 00 99 **97**.

MONTILLA-MORILES DO *Andalucía, Spain* Sherry-style wines that are sold almost entirely as lower-priced sherry substitutes. However, the wines *can* be superb, particularly the top dry amontillado, oloroso and rich Pedro Ximénez styles. Best producers: Alvear (top labels★★), Aragón, Gracia Hermanos, Pérez Barquero★, Toro Albalá★★.

MONTLOUIS AC *Loire Valley, France* Situated on the opposite bank of the Loire to the VOUVRAY AC, Montlouis wines are made from the same Chenin grape and in similar styles (dry, medium and sweet and Champagne-method fizz) but tend to be a touch more rustic. Two-thirds of the production is Mousseux, a green, appley fizz which is best drunk young. The still wines need aging for 5–10 years, particularly the sweet (Moelleux) version. Best producers: Chidaine★, Delétang★★, Levasseur★, des Liards/Berger★ (Vendange Tardive★★), Moyer★, Taille aux Loups★★. Best years: 2000 99 **98 97 96 95 90 89 88 86 85**.

MONTRACHET AC *Côte de Beaune, Burgundy, France* This world-famous Grand Cru straddles the boundary between the villages of CHASSAGNE-MONTRACHET and PULIGNY-MONTRACHET. Produces wines with a unique combination of concentration, finesse and perfume; white Burgundy at its most sublime. Another Grand Cru, Chevalier-Montrachet, immediately above it on the slope yields a slightly leaner wine that is less explosive in its youth, but good examples will become ever more fascinating over 20 years or more. Best producers: G Amiot★★★, Colin★★★, DROUHIN (Laguiche)★★★, LAFON★★★, LATOUR★★, Dom. LEFLAIVE★★★, RAMONET★★★, Dom. de la ROMANÉE-CONTI★★★, Thénard★★★. Best years: (2001) 00 99 98 97 96 95 **92 90 89 86 85**.

MONTRAVEL AC *South-West France* Dry, medium-dry and sweet white wines from the western end of the BERGERAC region. Sweet ones from Côtes de Montravel AC and Haut-Montravel AC. Production is declining. Best producers: le Bondieu, Gourgueil, Moulin Caresse, Perreau, Pique-Sègue, Puy-Servain★, le Raz. Best years: 2000 **98 96 95**.

CH. MONTROSE★★ *St-Estèphe AC, 2ème Cru Classé, Haut-Médoc, Bordeaux, France* A leading ST-ESTEPHE property, once famous for its dark, brooding wine that would take around 30 years to reach its prime. In the late 1970s and early 80s the wines became lighter, but Montrose has now returned to a powerful style, though softer than before. Recent vintages have been extremely good. Second wine: la Dame de Montrose. Best years: 2000 99 98 96 95 94 90 **89 86**.

MONT TAUCH, LES PRODUCTEURS DU *Fitou, Languedoc-Roussillon, France* A big, quality-conscious co-op producing a large range of MIDI wines, from good gutsy FITOU★ and CORBIERES to rich MUSCAT DE RIVESALTES★ and light but gluggable Vin de Pays du Torgan. Top wine: Terroir de Tuchan★. Best years: (Terroir de Tuchan) 2000 99 98 **97 96 95**.

CH. MONTUS *Madiran AC, South-West France*　Alain Brumont has led MADIRAN's revival, using 100% Tannat and deft public relations. The top wine is aged in new oak. He has 3 properties: Montus (Cuvée Prestige★★), Bouscassé (Vieilles Vignes★★) and Meinjarre. Montus and Bouscassé also make enjoyable dry PACHERENC DU VIC-BILH★, while Bouscassé has fine Moelleux★★. Best years: (Cuvée Prestige) 2000 99 98 97 96 **95 94 93 91 90 89 88 85**.

MORELLINO DI SCANSANO DOC *Tuscany, Italy*　Morellino is the local name for the Sangiovese grape in the south-west of TUSCANY. The wines can be broad and robust, but more and more delightfully perfumed examples are appearing. Best producers: E Banti★, Carletti/Poliziano (Lohsa★), Cecchi★, Il Macereto★, Mantellassi★, Mazzei/FONTERUTOLI★, Morellino di Scansano co-op★, Moris Farms★★, Poggio Argentaria★★, Le Pupille★★. Best years: (2000) 99 **98 97 96 95 93 90**.

MOREY-ST-DENIS AC *Côte de Nuits, Burgundy, France*　Morey has 5 Grands Crus (Clos des Lambrays, CLOS DE LA ROCHE, CLOS ST-DENIS, Clos de Tart and a share of BONNES-MARES) as well as some very good Premiers Crus. Basic village wine is sometimes unexciting, but from a quality grower the wine has good fruit and acquires an attractive depth as it ages. A tiny amount of startling nutty white wine is also made. Best producers: Pierre Amiot★, Arlaud★★, CLAIR★★, DUJAC★★★, Dom. des Lambrays★★, G Lignier★★, H Lignier★★★, H Perrot-Minot★★, Ponsot★★, Rossignol-Trapet★, ROUMIER★★, ROUSSEAU★★, Sérafin★★. Best years: (2001) 00 99 98 **97** 96 **95 93 90**.

MORGENHOF *Stellenbosch WO, South Africa*　A 300-year-old Cape farm grandly restored and run with French flair by owner Anne Cointreau-Huchon. Winemaker Rianie Strydom's equally stylish range spans Cap Classique sparkling to port styles. Best are a well-oaked, muscular Chenin Blanc, structured Merlot★ and the dark-berried, supple Première Sélection★, a BORDEAUX-style blend.

MORGON AC *Beaujolais, Burgundy, France*　Most wine from this BEAUJOLAIS Cru has a soft, cherry fruit for very easy drinking, but from a good grower and from the slopes of the Mont du Py the wine can be thick and dark, acquiring a perfume of cherries as it ages. Best producers: G Brun★, Calot★, la Chanaise (Piron★), G Charvet★, Collonge★, L-C Desvignes★, DUBOEUF (Jean Descombes★), J Foillard★, M Lapierre★, Plateau de Bel-Air★, N Potel★, P Savoye★. Best years: (2001) 00 99 98 **97 96 95**.

MORNINGTON PENINSULA *Victoria, Australia*　Exciting cool-climate maritime region dotted with small vineyards, often owned by monied Melbourne hobbyists. Chardonnay here runs the gamut from honeyed to harsh; Pinot Noir can be very stylish indeed in warmer years. Best producers: DROMANA★, Main Ridge★, Moorooduc★, Paringa Estate, Port Phillip Estate★, STONIER★★, T'Gallant★, Tuck's Ridge. Best years: (Pinot Noir) 2000 99 **98 97 95 94**.

MORRIS *Rutherglen, Victoria, Australia*　Historic winery, ORLANDO-owned, making traditional favourites like liqueur Muscat★★ and Tokay★★ (Old Premium is ★★★), 'ports', 'sherries' and robust table wines from Shiraz★, Cabernet★, Durif★ and Blue Imperial (Cinsaut).

MORTON ESTATE *Katikati, North Island, New Zealand*　The winery is in the tiny town of Katikati; the vineyards are in HAWKES BAY. Morton Estate now produces New Zealand's most expensive Chardonnay, Coniglio★★★, a Burgundy lookalike that is made in minute quantities. Other good wines are the robust, complex Black Label Chardonnay★★, a rich and gamy Black Label Merlot★, the best

Hawkes Bay Pinot Noir★ yet, berries and cedar Black Label Merlot-Cabernet Sauvignon★★ and a successful fizz★★. Best years: (Black Label Merlot-Cabernet) 2000 99 98 **96 95 94**.

GEORG MOSBACHER *Deidesheim, Pfalz, Germany*   This small estate makes dry white and dessert wines in the wine village of FORST. Best of all are the dry Rieslings★★ from the Forster Ungeheuer site, which are among the lushest in Germany. Delicious young, but worth cellaring for more than 3 years. Best years: (2001) 99 98 **97 96 94 93 90**.

MOSCATO D'ASTI DOCG *Piedmont, Italy*   Utterly beguiling, delicately scented, gently bubbling wine, made from Moscato Bianco grapes grown in the hills between Asti and Alba in north-west Italy. The DOCG is the same as for ASTI Spumante, but only select grapes go into this wine, which is frizzante (semi-sparkling) rather than fully sparkling. Drink while they're bubbling with youthful fragrance. Best producers: Araldica/Alasia★, ASCHERI★, Bava★, Bera★, Braida★, Cascina Castlèt★, Caudrina★★, Giuseppe Contratto★, Coppo★, Cascina Fonda★, Forteto della Luja★, Icardi★, Marenco★, Beppe Marino★, La Morandina★, Marco Negri★, Perrone★, Cascina Pian d'Or★, Saracco★★, Scagliola★, La Spinetta★★, I Vignaioli di Santo Stefano★.

MOSCATO PASSITO DI PANTELLERIA DOC *Sicily, Italy*   The Muscat of Alexandria grape is used to make this powerful dessert wine. Pantelleria is a small island south-west of SICILY, closer to Africa than it is to Italy. The grapes are picked in mid-August and laid out in the hot sun to dry and shrivel for a couple of weeks. They are then crushed and fermented to give an amber-coloured, intensely flavoured sweet Muscat. The wines are best drunk within 5–7 years of the vintage. Best producers: Benanti★, D'Ancona★, DE BARTOLI★★, Donnafugata (Ben Ryé★), MID (Tanit), Murana, Nuova Agricoltura co-op★, Pellegrino.

MOSEL-SAAR-RUWER *Germany*   Not a coherent wine region, but a collection of vineyard areas on the Mosel and its tributaries, the Saar and the Ruwer. The Mosel river rises in the French Vosges before forming the border between Germany and Luxembourg. In its first German incarnation in the Upper Mosel the light, tart Elbling grape holds sway, but with the Middle Mosel begins a series of villages responsible for some of the world's very best Riesling wines: PIESPORT, BRAUNEBERG, BERNKASTEL, GRAACH, WEHLEN, URZIG and ERDEN. The wines are not big or powerful, but in good years they have tremendous slatiness and an ability to blend the greenness of citrus leaves and fruits with the golden warmth of honey. Great wines are rarer in the lower part of the valley as the Mosel swings round into Koblenz, although Winningen is an island of excellence. The Saar can produce wonderful, piercing wines in villages such as Serrig, AYL, OCKFEN and Wiltingen. The Ruwer produces slightly softer wines; the estates of MAXIMIN GRUNHAUS and KARTHAUSERHOF are on every list of the best in Germany.

MOSS WOOD *Margaret River, Western Australia*   Pioneer winery with silky smooth, rich but structured Cabernet★★★. Chardonnay★★ can be rich and peachy; Pinot Noir★ can be erratic but is magical at best. Semillon★★, both oaked and unoaked, is consistently fascinating. Best years: (Cabernet) 1998 96 95 **94 93 91 90 85**.

J P MOUEIX *Bordeaux, France*   As well as owning PETRUS, la FLEUR-PETRUS, MAGDELAINE, TROTANOY and other properties, the Moueix family runs a thriving merchant business specializing in the wines of the right bank, particularly POMEROL and FRONSAC. Quality is generally high.

MOULIN-À-VENT AC *Beaujolais, Burgundy, France* BEAUJOLAIS Cru that
can resemble a full, chocolaty Burgundy, tasting more of Pinot Noir
than Gamay, after 6–10 years' bottle age. Best producers: Bertola★,
Cellier des Samsons★, L Champagnon★, G Charvet★, Chauvet★,
Desperrier★, Diochon★, DUBOEUF (single domaines★), Gay-Coperet★,
P Granger★, Ch. des Jacques★, Janin★, Janodet★, Margerand★, Ch. du
Moulin-à-Vent★, B Santé★, la Tour du Bief★, R Trichard★, Vissoux/
P-M Chermette★. Best years: (2001) 00 **99 98 97 96 95**.

MOULIS AC *Haut-Médoc, Bordeaux, France* Small AC within the HAUT-MEDOC.
Much of the wine is excellent – delicious at 5–6 years old, though good
examples can age 10–20 years – and not overpriced. Best producers:
Anthonic, Biston-Brillette, Brillette, CHASSE-SPLEEN★, Duplessis, Dutruch-
Grand-Poujeau, Gressier-Grand-Poujeaux, MAUCAILLOU★, Ch. Moulin-à-
Vent, POUJEAUX★★. Best years: 2000 96 **95 94 90 89 88 86 85 83 82**.

MOUNTADAM *Eden Valley, South Australia* The late David Wynn and
his Bordeaux-educated son Adam planted this property high in the
Eden Valley from scratch. It is now a subsidiary of CAPE MENTELLE. Rich,
buttery Chardonnay★★ has a worldwide reputation. There is also
sumptuous Pinot Noir★, bold Cabernet-Merlot blend The Red★, and
the fruity David Wynn wines. Patriarch★★ is a rich, fruit-laden
premium Shiraz. Best years: (Patriarch) 1998 97 96 **94 93 91 90 87 84**;
(Chardonnay) **1998 97 94 93 92 91 90**.

MOUNT LANGI GHIRAN *Grampians, Victoria,*
Australia This winery made its reputation
with remarkable dark plum, chocolate and
pepper Shiraz★★; later releases are still good,
though can be erratic. Delightful Riesling★,
honeyed Pinot Gris★ and melony unwooded
Chardonnay★. Joanna★★ Cabernet is dark
and intriguing. Best years: (Shiraz) 1999 98 97 96 95 **94 93 90 89 86**.

MOUNT MARY *Yarra Valley, Victoria, Australia* Classic property using
only estate-grown grapes along BORDEAUX lines, with dry white
Triolet★★ blended from Sauvignon Blanc, Semillon and Muscadelle,
and Quintet (★★★ for committed Francophiles) from all 5 Bordeaux
red grapes that ages beautifully. The Pinot Noir★★ is almost as good.
Best years: (Quintet) 1998 97 95 **94 91 90 88 84 80**.

MOUNT VEEDER AVA *Napa Valley, California, USA* Small AVA in south-
west NAPA, with Cabernet Sauvignon and Zinfandel wines in a typical
rough-hewn style. Best producers: Chateau Potelle★, Robert Craig★★,
HESS COLLECTION★★, Lokoya★★, Mayacamas★, Mount Veeder Vineyards★.

MOURVÈDRE The variety originated in Spain, where it is called
Monastrell. It dominates the JUMILLA DO and also Alicante, Bullas and
Yecla. It needs lots of sunshine to ripen, which is why it performs well
on the Mediterranean coast at BANDOL. It is increasingly important as a
source of body and tarry, pine-needle flavour in the wines of
CHATEAUNEUF-DU-PAPE and parts of the MIDI. It is beginning to make a
reputation in Australia and CALIFORNIA, where it is sometimes known as
Mataro, and is just starting to make its presence felt in South Africa.

MOUTON-CADET *Bordeaux AC, Bordeaux, France* The most widely sold
red BORDEAUX in the world was created by Baron Philippe de Rothschild
in the 1930s. Blended from the entire Bordeaux region, the wine is
correct but uninspiring – and never cheap. Also a white and rosé.

CH. MOUTON-ROTHSCHILD★★★ *Pauillac AC, 1er Cru Classé, Haut-Médoc, Bordeaux, France* Baron Philippe de Rothschild died in 1988, having raised Mouton from a run-down Second Growth to its promotion to First Growth in 1973, and a reputation as one of the greatest wines in the world. It can still be the most magnificently opulent of the great MEDOC reds, although there were signs of inconsistency in the early 90s. Recent vintages have been back on top form. When young, this wine is rich and indulgent on the palate, aging after 15–20 years to a complex bouquet of blackcurrant and cigar box. There is also a white wine, Aile d'Argent. Second wine: Petit-Mouton. Best years: (red) 2000 99 98 96 95 94 **90 89 88 86 85 83 82 70**.

MUDGEE *New South Wales, Australia* Small, long-overlooked region neighbouring HUNTER VALLEY, with a higher altitude and marginally cooler temperatures. Major new plantings are giving it a fresh lease of life; ROSEMOUNT is leading the charge with impressive Mountain Blue Shiraz-Cabernet★★ and the Hill of Gold★★ range of varietals. Other producers are beginning to make the best use of very good fruit. Best producers: Andrew Harris★, Huntington Estate★, Miramar★, ORLANDO★, Elliot Rocke, ROSEMOUNT★★, Thistle Hill.

MUGA *Rioja DOC, Rioja, Spain* A traditional family winery making high-quality, rich red RIOJA★, especially the Gran Reserva, Prado Enea★. It is the only bodega in Rioja where every step of red winemaking is still carried out in oak containers. Whites and rosés are good too. The modern Torre Muga Reserva★ marks a major stylistic change. Best years: (Torre Muga Reserva) 1996 **95 94 91**.

MULDERBOSCH *Stellenbosch WO, South Africa* Winemaker Mike Dobrovic has chalked up a decade at this small winery. Consistency is the hallmark of the almost entirely white range. The sleek, gooseberry-infused Sauvignon Blanc★★ is deservedly a cult wine; drink young and fresh. Purity and intensity are the distinguishing features of Chardonnay★★ and Steen-op-Hout★ (Chenin Blanc brushed with oak). Faithful Hound, a Cabernet-Merlot blend and the sole red, is BORDEAUX-like, though easy-drinking. Best years: (Chardonnay) **1999 98 97 96 95**.

EGON MÜLLER-SCHARZHOF *Scharzhofberg, Saar, Germany* Some of the greatest German wines, but also the most expensive. The ultimate sweet versions are the estate's Auslese, Beerenauslese, Trockenbeerenauslese and Eiswein, all ★★★. Regular Kabinett and Spätlese wines are pricy but classic. Best years: (Auslese) (2001) 99 97 95 **93** 90 **89 88 83 76 75 71**.

MÜLLER-CATOIR *Neustadt-Haardt, Pfalz, Germany* An eye-opener for those who are sceptical about Germany's ability to make wines in an international idiom. Produces wine of a piercing fruit flavour and powerful structure unsurpassed in Germany, including ★★★ Riesling, Scheurebe and Rieslaner; ★★ Gewürztraminer, Muskateller and Pinot Noir; Weissburgunder★. Best years: (Riesling Spätlese) (2001) **99 98 97 96 94 93 92 90 89**.

MÜLLER-THURGAU The workhorse grape of Germany, largely responsible for LIEBFRAUMILCH. When yields are low it produces pleasant floral wines; but this is rare since modern clones are all super-productive. It is occasionally better in England – though the odd good examples, with a slightly green edge to the grapy flavour, come from Austria, Switzerland, Luxembourg and Italy's ALTO ADIGE. New Zealand used to pride itself on making the world's best Müller-Thurgau, but acreage is in terminal decline.

G H MUMM *Champagne AC, Champagne, France*   Mumm's top-selling non-vintage brand, Cordon Rouge, is usually disappointing. It has been under new ownership since 1999 and a new winemaker has set about improving quality, but he's got a long way to go. Best years: 1996 **95 90 89 88 85 82**.

MUMM NAPA *Napa Valley AVA, California, USA*   The French CHAMPAGNE house MUMM and Seagram Classic Wines of California started Mumm Napa in 1983. Some reports have it that the French owners are sorry they did because the bubbly coming out of California has been simply too good. The style has now become leaner and drier, which is a pity, but both Cuvée Napa Brut Prestige and Vintage Reserve★ are good. Blanc de Noirs★ is better than most pink Champagnes. Tête de Cuvée DVX★ is the flagship.

RENÉ MURÉ *Alsace AC, Alsace, France*   In recent years this domaine in Rouffach has been making spectacular wines. Its pride and joy is the Clos St-Landelin, a parcel within the Grand Cru Vorbourg. The Clos is the source of lush, concentrated wines from all the major varieties, including a very oaky Pinot Noir★. The Muscat Vendange Tardive★★ is rare and remarkable, as is the opulent old-vine Sylvaner Cuvée Oscar★. The Vendange Tardive★★ and Sélection de Grains Nobles★★★ wines are among the best in Alsace. Best years: (Clos St-Landelin Riesling) (2001) 00 99 **97** 96 95 **94 92 90 89 88**.

MURFATLAR *Romania*   Region to the west of the Black Sea, producing excellent late-harvest wines (including botrytized versions) from Pinot Gris★, Chardonnay and Muscat Ottonel. Sparkling wines are being made, too. Murfatlar can also be a source of ripe, soft, low-acid reds.

ANDREW MURRAY VINEYARDS *Santa Barbara County, California, USA* Working with RHONE varieties, winemaker Andrew Murray has created an impressive array of wines since the initial 1994 vintage. Rich, aromatic Viognier★ and Roussanne★★ as well as several Syrahs, including Roasted Slope★★ and Hillside Reserve★★. Esperance★ is a spicy blend patterned after a serious COTES DU RHONE. Best years: (Syrah) (2000) 99 98 97 96 **94**.

MUSCADET AC *Loire Valley, France*   Muscadet is the general AC for the region around Nantes in north-west France, with 3 high-quality zones: Muscadet Coteaux de la Loire, Muscadet Côtes de Grand Lieu and Muscadet Sèvre-et-Maine. Producers who make basic Muscadet AC are allowed higher yields but cannot use the term *sur lie* on the labels. Generally inexpensive and best drunk young and fresh, a perfect match for the local seafood – but the best can age several years. Best producers: Serge Bâtard★, Chéreau-Carré★, Dorices★, l'ECU/Guy Bossard★, Gadais, Jacques Guindon, Hautes-Noëlles, Herbauges★, l'Hyvernière★, LUNEAU-PAPIN★, METAIREAU★, la Preuille, Quatre Routes★, la Ragotière★, Sauvion★, la Touché★. Best years: (*sur lie*) (2001) **00 99 98 97 96**.

MUSCAT See pages 196–7.

MUSCAT OF ALEXANDRIA   Muscat of Alexandria rarely shines in its own right but performs a useful job worldwide, adding perfume and fruit to what would otherwise be dull, neutral white wines. It is common for sweet and fortified wines throughout the Mediterranean basin and in South Africa (where it is also known as Hanepoot), as well as being a fruity, perfumed bulk producer there and in Australia, where it is known as Gordo Blanco or Lexia.

195

MUSCAT

It's strange, but there's hardly a wine grape in the world which makes wine that actually tastes of the grape itself. Yet there's one variety which is so joyously, exultantly grapy that it more than makes up for all the others – the Muscat, generally thought to be the original wine vine. In fact there seem to be about 200 different branches of the Muscat family worldwide, but the noblest of these and the one that always makes the most exciting wine is called Muscat Blanc à Petits Grains (the Muscat with the small berries). These berries can be crunchily green, golden yellow, pink or even brown – as a result Muscat has a large number of synonyms. The wines they make may be pale and dry, rich and golden, subtly aromatic or as dark and sweet as treacle.

WINE STYLES

France Muscat is grown from the far north-east right down to the Spanish border, yet is rarely accorded great respect in France. This is a pity because the dry, light, hauntingly grapy Muscats of Alsace are some of France's most delicately beautiful wines. It pops up sporadically in the Rhône Valley, especially in the sparkling wine enclave of Die. Mixed with Clairette, the Clairette de Die Tradition is a fragrant grapy fizz that should be better known. Muscat de Beaumes-de-Venise is another well-known version, this time fortified, fragrant and sweet. Its success has encouraged the traditional fortified winemakers of Languedoc-Roussillon, especially in Frontignan and Rivesaltes, to make fresher, more perfumed wines rather than the usual flat and syrupy ones they've produced for generations.

Italy Muscat is grown in Italy for fragrantly sweet or (rarely) dry table wines in the north and for *passito*-style wines (though the less fine Muscat of Alexandria makes most of the rich southern Moscato). Yet the greatest Muscats in Italy are those of Asti, where it is called Moscato Bianco. As either Asti Spumante or Moscato d'Asti, this brilliantly fresh fizz can be a blissful drink. Italy also has red varieties: the Moscato Nero for rare sweet wines in Lazio, Lombardy and Piedmont; and Moscato Rosa/Rosenmuskateller and Moscato Giallo/Goldmuskateller for delicately sweet wines in Trentino-Alto Adige and Friuli-Venezia Giulia.

Other regions Elsewhere in Europe, Muscat is a component of some Tokajis in Hungary, Crimea has shown how good it can be in the Massandra fortified wines, and the rich golden Muscats of Samos and Patras are among Greece's finest wines. As Muskateller in Austria and Germany it makes primarily dry, subtly aromatic wines. In Spain, Moscatel de Valencia is sweet, light and sensational value, Moscatel de Grano Menudo is on the resurgence in Navarra and it has also been introduced in Mallorca. Portugal's Moscatel de Setúbal is also wonderfully rich and complex. California grows Muscat, often calling it Muscat Canelli, but South Africa and Australia make better use of it. With darker berries, and called Brown Muscat in Australia and Muscadel in South Africa, it makes some of the world's most sweet and luscious fortified wines especially in the north-east Victoria regions of Rutherglen and Glenrowan in Australia.

MUSCAT DE BEAUMES-DE-VENISE AC *Rhône Valley, France* Delicious Muscat *vin doux naturel* from BEAUMES-DE-VENISE in the southern Rhône. It has a fruity acidity and a bright fresh feel, and is best drunk young to get all that lovely grapy perfume at its peak. Best producers: Baumalric★, Beaumes-de-Venise co-op, Bernardins★, CHAPOUTIER★, Coyeux★, DELAS★, Durban★★, Fenouillet★, JABOULET★★, Vidal-Fleury★.

MUSCAT BLANC À PETITS GRAINS See Muscat.

MUSCAT DE FRONTIGNAN AC *Languedoc, France* Well-known Muscat *vin doux naturel* on the Mediterranean coast. With colours ranging from bright gold to deep orange, it is quite impressive but can seem rather cloying. Muscat de Mireval AC, a little further inland, can have a touch more acid freshness, and quite an alcoholic kick. Best producers: (Frontignan) Cave du Muscat de Frontignan, la Peyrade★, Robiscau; (Mireval) la Capelle, Mas des Pigeonniers, Moulinas.

MUSCAT DE MIREVAL AC See Muscat de Frontignan AC.

MUSCAT DE RIVESALTES AC *Roussillon, France* Made from Muscat Blanc à Petits Grains and Muscat of Alexandria, the wine can be very good indeed, especially since several go-ahead producers are now allowing the aromatic skins to stay in the juice for longer periods, thereby gaining perfume and fruit. Most delicious when young. Best producers: Cave de Baixas (Dom Brial★, Ch. les Pins★), CASENOVE★, CAZES★★, Chênes★, Destavel, Fontanel★, Forca Réal★, Jau★, Laporte★, Mas Rous, MONT TAUCH co-op★, Piquemal★, Sarda-Malet★.

MUSCAT DE ST-JEAN-DE-MINERVOIS AC *Languedoc, France* Up in the remote Minervois hills, a small AC for fortified Muscat made from Muscat Blanc à Petits Grains. Less cloying than some Muscats from the plains of LANGUEDOC-ROUSSILLON, more tangerine and floral. Best producers: Barroubio, CLOS BAGATELLE, Vignerons de Septimanie.

MUSIGNY AC *Grand Cru, Côte de Nuits, Burgundy, France* One of a handful of truly great Grands Crus, combining power with an exceptional depth of fruit and lacy elegance – an iron fist in a velvet glove. Understandably expensive. A tiny amount of white Musigny is produced by de VOGUE. Best producers: DROUHIN★★★, JADOT★★★, D Laurent★★★, Dom. LEROY★★★, J-F Mugnier★★★, J Prieur★★, ROUMIER★★★, VOGUE★★★, Vougeraie★★. Best years: (2001) 00 99 98 97 96 95 93 **90 89 88**.

NAHE *Germany* Wine region named after the River Nahe which rises below Birkenfeld and joins the Rhine by BINGEN, just opposite RÜDESHEIM in the RHEINGAU. Riesling, Müller-Thurgau and Silvaner are the main grapes, but the Rieslings from this geologically complex region are considered some of Germany's best. The finest vineyards are those of Niederhausen and SCHLOSSBÖCKELHEIM, situated in the dramatic, rocky Upper Nahe Valley, and at Dorheim and Münster in the lower Nahe.

CH. NAIRAC★★ *Barsac AC, 2ème Cru Classé, Bordeaux, France* An established star in BARSAC which, by dint of enormous effort and considerable investment, produces a wine sometimes on a par with the First Growths. The influence of aging in new oak casks, adding spice and even a little tannin, makes this sweet wine a good candidate for aging 10–15 years. Best years: (2001) 99 98 97 96 **95 90 89 88 86 83**.

NAPA VALLEY See pages 200–1.

NAPA VALLEY AVA *California, USA* An AVA designed to be so inclusive that it is almost completely irrelevant. It includes vineyards that are outside the Napa River drainage system – such as Pope Valley and

Chiles Valley. Because of this a number of sub-AVAs have been and are in the process of being created; a few such as CARNEROS and STAGS LEAP DISTRICT are discernibly different from their neighbours, but many are similar in nature, and many fear that these sub-AVAs will simply dilute the magic of Napa's name. See also Howell Mountain, Mount Veeder, Napa Valley, Oakville, Rutherford.

NAVARRA DO *Navarra, Spain* This buzzing region has increasing numbers of vineyards planted to Cabernet Sauvignon, Merlot and Chardonnay in addition to Tempranillo, Garnacha and Moscatel (Muscat). This translates into a wealth of juicy reds, barrel-fermented whites and modern sweet Muscats, but quality is still more haphazard than it should be. Best producers: Camilo Castilla (Capricho de Goya Muscat★★), CHIVITE★, Magaña★, Vicente Malumbres, Alvaro Marino★, Castillo de Monjardin★, Vinícola Navarra, Nekeas co-op, Ochoa, Palacio de la Vega★, Piedemonte Olite co-op, Príncipe de Viana★, Señorío de Otazu★. Best years: (reds) 1999 **98 96 95 94 93**.

NEBBIOLO The grape variety responsible for the majestic wines of BAROLO and BARBARESCO, found almost nowhere outside north-west Italy. Its name derives from the Italian for fog, *nebbia*, because it ripens late when the hills are shrouded in autumn mists. It needs a thick skin to withstand this fog, so often gives very tannic wines that need years to soften. When grown in the limestone soils of the Langhe hills around Alba, Nebbiolo produces wines that are only moderately deep in colour but have a wonderful array of perfumes and an ability to develop great complexity with age – rivalled only by Pinot Noir and Syrah. Barolo is usually considered the best and longest-lived of the Nebbiolo wines; the myth that it needs a decade or more to be drinkable has been dispelled by new-style Barolo, yet the best of the traditional styles are more than worth the wait. Barbaresco, Barolo's neighbour, also varies widely in style between the traditional and the new. NEBBIOLO D'ALBA and ROERO produce lighter styles. The variety is also used for special barrique-aged blends, often with Barbera and/or Cabernet and sold under the LANGHE DOC. Nebbiolo is also the principal grape for reds of northern PIEDMONT – CAREMA, GATTINARA and GHEMME. In LOMBARDY it is known as Chiavennasca and is the main variety of the Valtellina DOC and VALTELLINA SUPERIORE DOCG wines. Outside Italy, rare good examples have been made in Australia and CALIFORNIA.

NEBBIOLO D'ALBA DOC *Piedmont, Italy* Red wine from Nebbiolo grown around Alba, but excluding the BAROLO and BARBARESCO zones. Vineyards in the LANGHE and ROERO hills, by the Tanaro river, are noted for sandy soils that produce a fragrant, fruity style for early drinking, though some growers make wines that improve for 5 years or more. Best producers: Alario★, ASCHERI, Bricco Maiolica★★, Cascina Chicco★, CERETTO, Correggia★★, GIACOSA★, Giuseppe MASCARELLO★, PRUNOTTO★, RATTI, SANDRONE★, Vietti★. Best years: (2000) (99) **98 97 96 95**.

NELSON *South Island, New Zealand* A range of mountains separates Nelson from MARLBOROUGH at the northern end of South Island. Nelson is made up of a series of small hills and valleys with a wide range of mesoclimates. Pinot Noir, Chardonnay, Riesling and Sauvignon Blanc do well. Best producers: Greenhough, NEUDORF★★, SEIFRIED★/Redwood Valley. Best years: (whites) 2001 00 **99 98 97**.

NAPA VALLEY

California, USA

 From the earliest days of California wine, and through all its up and downs, the Napa Valley has been the standard-bearer for the whole industry and the driving force behind quality and progress. The magical Napa name – derived from an Indian word for plenty – applies to the fertile valley itself, the county in which it is found and the AVA for the overall area, but the region is so viticulturally diverse that the appellation is virtually meaningless.

The valley was first settled by immigrants in the 1830s, and by the late 19th century Napa, and in particular the area around the communities of Rutherford and Oakville, had gained a reputation for exciting Cabernet Sauvignon. Despite the long, dark years of Prohibition, this reputation survived and when the US interest in wine revived during the 1970s, Napa was ready to lead the charge.

GRAPE VARIETIES

Most of the classic French grapes are grown and recent replantings have done much to match varieties to the most suitable locations. Cabernet Sauvignon is planted in profusion and Napa's strongest reputation is for varietal Cabernet and Bordeaux-style (or Meritage) blends, mostly Cabernet-Merlot. Pinot Noir and Chardonnay, for both still and sparkling wines, do best in the south, from Yountville down to Carneros. Zinfandel is grown mostly at the north end of the valley. Syrah and Sangiovese are relatively new here.

SUB-REGIONS

The most significant vine-growing area is the valley floor running from Calistoga in the north down to Carneros, below which the Napa River flows out into San Pablo Bay. It has been said that there are more soil types in Napa than in the whole of France, but much of the soil in the valley is heavy, clayish, over-fertile and difficult to drain and really not fit to make great wine. Some of the best vineyards are tucked into the mountain slopes at the valley sides or in selected spots at higher altitudes.

There is as much as a 10° temperature difference between torrid Calistoga and Carneros at the mouth of the valley, cooled by Pacific fog and a benchmark for US Pinot Noir and cool-climate Chardonnay. About 20 major sub-areas have been identified along the valley floor and in the mountains, although there is much debate over how many have a real claim to individuality. Rutherford, Oakville and Yountville in the mid-valley produce Cabernet redolent of dust, dried sage and ultra-ripe blackcurrants. Softer flavours come from Stags Leap to the east. The higher-altitude vineyards of Diamond Mountain, Spring Mountain and Mount Veeder along the Mayacamas mountain range to the west produce deep Cabernets, while Howell Mountain in the north-east has stunning Zinfandel and Merlot.

See also CARNEROS AVA, HOWELL MOUNTAIN AVA, MOUNT VEEDER AVA, NAPA VALLEY AVA, OAKVILLE AVA, RUTHERFORD AVA, STAGS LEAP DISTRICT AVA; and individual producers.

ESTATE 1998 BOTTLED

EISELE VINEYARD
NAPA VALLEY

Cabernet Sauvignon

ARAUJO
ESTATE WINES

BEST YEARS

(2001) (00) 99 97 **95 94 92 91 90 87 86**

BEST PRODUCERS

Cabernet Sauvignon and Meritage blends
Abreu, Altamura, Anderson's Conn Valley, S Anderson, ARAUJO, Barnett (Rattlesnake Hill), BEAULIEU, BERINGER, Bryant Family, Buehler (Reserve), Burgess Cellars, Cafaro, CAIN CELLARS, Cakebread, CAYMUS, CHATEAU MONTELENA, Chateau Potelle (VGS), CHIMNEY ROCK, CLOS DU VAL, Clos Pegase, Colgin, Conn Creek (Anthology), Corison, Cosentino, Robert Craig, DALLA VALLE, Del Dotto, DIAMOND CREEK, DOMINUS, DUCKHORN, DUNN, Elyse, Etude, Far Niente, Fisher, FLORA SPRINGS, Forman, Freemark Abbey, Frog's Leap, Grace Family, Groth, HARLAN ESTATE, Hartwell, HEITZ, HESS, Jarvis, La Jota, Lewis Cellars, Livingston, Lokoya, Long Meadow Ranch, Long Vineyards, Markham, Mayacamas, MERRYVALE, Peter MICHAEL, MINER, MONDAVI, Monticello, Mount Veeder Winery (FRANCISCAN), NEWTON, NIEBAUM-COPPOLA, Oakford, Oakville Ranch (MINER), OPUS ONE, Pahlmeyer, Paradigm, Robert Pecota, Peju Province (HB Vineyard), PHELPS, PINE RIDGE, Plumpjack, Pride Mountain, Quintessa, Raymond, Rombauer (Meilleur du Chai), Rudd Estate, Saddleback, St Clement, SCREAMING EAGLE, Seavey, SHAFER, SILVER OAK, SILVERADO, SPOTTSWOODE, Staglin Family, STAG'S LEAP WINE CELLARS, STERLING, Swanson, The Terraces, Philip Togni, Turnbull, Viader, Villa Mt Eden (Signature Series), Vine Cliff, Vineyard 29, Von Strasser, Whitehall Lane, ZD.

NERO D'AVOLA The name of SICILY's great red grape derives from the town of Avola near Siracusa, although it is now planted all over the island. Its deep colour, high sugars and acidity make it useful for blending, especially with the lower-acid Nerello Mascalese, but also with Cabernet, Merlot and Syrah. On its own, and from the right soils, it can be brilliant, with a soft, ripe, spicy black-fruit character. Examples range from simple quaffers to many of Sicily's top reds.

NEUCHÂTEL *Switzerland* Swiss canton with high-altitude vineyards, mainly Chasselas whites and Pinot Noir reds. Best producers: Ch. d'Auvernier, Thierry Grosjean, Montmillon, Porret.

NEUDORF *Nelson, South Island, New Zealand* Owners Tim and Judy Finn make stylish and often innovative wines and have resisted the temptation to expand production, preferring instead to fine-tune the quality of their wines by careful vineyard and winery management. Best are gorgeous, honeyed Chardonnay★★, Sauvignon Blanc★★, rich but scented Pinot Noir★★ and Riesling★. Best years: (Chardonnay) 2001 00 **99 98 96 94**; (Pinot Noir) (2001) 00 **99 98 97**.

NEW SOUTH WALES *Australia* Australia's most populous state. The RIVERINA, a hot, irrigated area of 9000ha (22,000 acres) grows 14% of Australia's grapes and is definitely showing signs of improvement. The HUNTER VALLEY, MUDGEE, COWRA and HILLTOPS are smaller, premium-quality regions hugging the coastal highlands. Orange is a high-altitude inland district. Fashionable CANBERRA is an area of tiny vineyards at chilly altitudes, as is Tumbarumba at the base of the Snowy Mountains.

NEWTON *Napa Valley AVA, California, USA* Spectacular winery and vineyards above St Helena. Estate Cabernet Sauvignon★★, Merlot★★ and Claret★ are some of California's most balanced and ageworthy examples. Even better is new single-vineyard BORDEAUX-blend Le Puzzle★★★. Newton pioneered the unfiltered Chardonnay★★★ style and this lush mouthful remains one of California's best. Newtonian★ is the excellent second label, sold chiefly in export markets. French luxury giant LVMH took a controlling interest in 2000. Age the Chardonnays for up to 5 years, reds for 10–15. Best years: (Cabernet Sauvignon) (2000) (99) 97 96 **95 94 92 91 90**.

NEW YORK STATE *USA* Wine grapes were first planted on Manhattan Island in the mid-17th century but it wasn't until the early 1950s that a serious wine industry began to develop in the state as vinifera grapes were planted to replace natives such as *Vitis labrusca*. The most important region is the FINGER LAKES in the north of the state, with the Hudson River also showing some form, but LONG ISLAND is the most exciting area. Quality has increased markedly in recent years, as improved vineyard practices help growers cope with the sometimes erratic weather. Best producer: (Hudson Valley) Millbrook★. See also Finger Lakes, Long Island.

NGATARAWA *Hawke's Bay, North Island, New Zealand* One of HAWKE'S BAY's better producers. Viticulture is organic, with Chardonnay, botrytized Riesling and a Cabernet-Merlot blend produced under the premium Alwyn Reserve label. The Glazebrook range includes attractive Chardonnay★ and Cabernet-Merlot★, both of which are best drunk within 5 years. Best years: (reds) (2000) **99 98 96**.

NIAGARA PENINSULA *Ontario, Canada* Sandwiched between lakes Erie and Ontario, the Niagara Peninsula benefits from regular through-breezes created by the Niagara escarpment, the cool climate bringing out distinctive characteristics in the wine. Chardonnay leads the way in dry whites, with Riesling and Vidal making good icewine. Pinot Noir is proving the most successful red grape, but Merlot and Cabernet Sauvignon are improving. Best producers: Cave Spring★, Chateau des Charmes★, HENRY OF PELHAM★, INNISKILLIN★, Konzelmann★, Marynissen, Reif Estate★, Southbrook★, Stoney Ridge, THIRTY BENCH WINERY★. Best years: (reds) 2000 99 98 **97**.

NIEBAUM-COPPOLA ESTATE *Rutherford AVA, California, USA* Movie director Coppola has turned the historical Inglenook Niebaum winery into an elaborate tourist destination. Rubicon★★, a BORDEAUX blend, lacked grace in the early vintages but with Coppola's greater involvement in the 1990s the wine has taken on a more exciting personality. It still needs 5–6 years of aging. Coppola offers Zinfandel★ under the Edizione Pennino label and Cabernet Franc★ under Coppola Family Wines. Diamond series (especially Syrah and Claret) are good buys. Best years: (Rubicon) (2000) (99) 97 96 95 **94 92 91 86**.

NIEPOORT *Port DOC, Douro, Portugal* Remarkable small PORT shipper of Dutch origin, run by the widely respected Dirk van der Niepoort. Outstanding Vintage ports★★★, old tawnies★★★ and Colheitas★★★ and a single-quinta wine: Quinta do Passadouro★★. Unfiltered LBVs★★ are among the best in their class – intense and complex. He also produces fine red★★ and white★★ DOURO Redoma and red Passadouro★★. Best years: (Vintage) (2000) 97 94 92 91 87 85 83 **82 80 77 70 66 63 58 55 45 42 27**; (Passadouro) 1997 **95 94 92**.

NIERSTEIN *Rheinhessen, Germany* Both a small town and a large Bereich which includes the infamous Grosslage Gutes Domtal. The town boasts 23 vineyard sites and the top ones (Oelberg, Orbel, Brudersberg, Hipping and Pettenthal) are some of the best in the whole Rhine Valley. Best producers: Heinrich Braun★, GUNDERLOCH★★, HEYL ZU HERRNSHEIM★★, ST ANTONY★★. Best years: 1999 98 **97** 96 **94 93**.

NIKOLAIHOF *Wachau, Niederösterreich, Austria* The Saahs family of Mautern makes some of the best wines in the WACHAU as well as in nearby Krems-Stein in KREMSTAL, including steely, intense Rieslings from their small plot in the famous Steiner Hund vineyard, always ★★. Best years: (Steiner Hund Riesling Spätlese) (2001) 99 98 **97 95 94 92 91 90 86 79 77**.

NOBILO *Kumeu/Huapai, Auckland, North Island, New Zealand* New Zealand's third-largest winery produces a wide range of wines, from popular medium-dry White Cloud to single-vineyard varietals. Lush, intensely flavoured Dixon Vineyard Chardonnay★★ is Nobilo's 'prestige' label. Sleek Sauvignon Blanc★ and Chardonnay★ from Nobilo's newly developed MARLBOROUGH vineyard are rapidly moving toward centre-stage. In 1998 Nobilo bought SELAKS, a mid-sized company with wineries in AUCKLAND and MARLBOROUGH. Nobilo itself is now owned by Australian giant BRL HARDY.

NORTON *Luján de Cuyo, Mendoza, Argentina* Austrian-owned winery which is investing heavily in new equipment and vineyards. So far the quality of the viticulture outstrips the winemaking, but Norton's chief winemaker, Jorge Riccitelli, works hard at their ever-improving line-up. Reds impress more than whites, but new Torrontés★, snappy Sauvignon Blanc★ and 100% barrique-fermented and oak-aged Reserva

Chardonnay★ show potential. In reds, the Porteño label Sangiovese-Malbec is excellent value. Under the Norton label there is good, chocolaty Sangiovese, soft, rich Merlot★ and good Barbera. Reserva Merlot★ and Malbec★ are ripe and full; top-of-the-line Privada★★ is approachable young but worthy of aging.

NOVAL, QUINTA DO *Port DOC, Douro, Portugal* Owned by French insurance giant AXA's subsidiary AXA-Millésimes, this immaculate property is the source of extraordinary Quinta do Noval Nacional★★★, made from ungrafted vines – some say the best vintage PORT made, but virtually unobtainable except at auction. Other Noval ports (including Noval Vintage★★★ and single-quinta Silval★★) are now excellent too. Also fine Colheitas★★ and some stunning 40-year-old tawnies★★★. Best years: (Nacional) (2000) 97 94 87 85 **70 66 63 62 60 31**; (Vintage) (2000) 97 95 94 91 **87 85 70 66 63 60**.

NUITS-ST-GEORGES AC *Côte de Nuits, Burgundy, France* This large AC is one of the few relatively reliable 'village' names in Burgundy. Although it has no Grands Crus, many of its Premiers Crus (it has 38!) are extremely good. The red can be rather slow to open out, often needing at least 5 years. Minuscule amounts of white are made by Gouges★, l'Arlot, Chevillon and RION. Best producers: l'Arlot★★, R Arnoux★★, J Chauvenet★★, R Chevillon★★★, J-J Confuron★★, FAIVELEY★★, Gouges★★, GRIVOT★★, JAYER-GILLES★★, D Laurent★★, MEO-CAMUZET★★, A Michelot★, Mugneret★★, RION★★, THOMAS-MOILLARD★★. Best years: (reds) (2001) 00 99 98 **97** 96 **95 93 90**.

NYETIMBER *West Sussex, England* Often referred to as the best winery in England, Nyetimber lives on although Stuart and Sandy Moss have sold their estate and manor house. They will be concentrating on making and marketing their award-winning wines: Classic Cuvée★★, a Chardonnay-Pinot blend that spends at least 6 years on its lees, and Aurora Cuvée Blanc de Blancs★. Latest release is a summery pink fizz.

OAKVILLE AVA *Napa Valley, California, USA* This region is cooler than RUTHERFORD, which lies immediately to the north. Planted primarily to Cabernet Sauvignon, the area contains some of the best vineyards, both on the valley floor (MONDAVI, OPUS ONE, SCREAMING EAGLE) and hillsides (HARLAN ESTATE, DALLA VALLE), producing wines that display lush, ripe black fruits and firm tannins. Best years: (Cabernet Sauvignon) (2001) (00) 99 97 96 95 94 91 **90**.

OC, VIN DE PAYS D' *Languedoc-Roussillon, France* Vin de Pays which intended to concentrate on good quality from international varieties, but problems of overproduction and consequently underripeness have dogged attempts to smarten up its reputation. Occasional fine red or white shows what can be done. Best producers: l'Aigle★, Dom. de la BAUME (whites★), Clovallon★, HERRICK★, J Lurton, Mas Cremat★, Ormesson★, Pech-Céleyran (Viognier★), Quatre Sous★, St-Saturnin★, SKALLI-FORTANT, VAL D'ORBIEU (top reds★), Virginie.

OCKFEN *Saar, Germany* Village with one famous individual vineyard site, the Bockstein. The wines can be superb in a sunny year, never losing their cold steely streak but packing in delightful full-flavoured fruit as well. Best producers: Dr Fischer, Dr Heinz Wagner★★, St Urbans-Hof★, ZILLIKEN★★. Best years: 1999 **97 95 93 90**.

OKANAGAN VALLEY *British Columbia, Canada* The oldest and most important wine-producing region of British Columbia and first home of Canada's rich, honeyed icewine. The Okanagan Lake helps temper the bitterly cold nights but October frosts can be a problem.

Chardonnay, Pinot Blanc, Pinot Gris and Pinot Noir are the top-performing grapes. South of the lake, Cabernet and Merlot are now being grown successfully. **Best producers:** Blue Mountain★, Burrowing Owl★, Gehringer★, INNISKILLIN, MISSION HILL★, Quail's Gate, SUMAC RIDGE★, Tinhorn Creek. **Best years:** (reds) 2000 **98**.

OLTREPÒ PAVESE DOC *Lombardy, Italy* Oltrepò Pavese is Italy's main source of Pinot Nero, used mainly for sparkling wines that may be called Classese when made by the Champagne method here, though base wines supply *spumante* industries elsewhere. The region supplies Milan's everyday wines, often fizzy, though still reds from Barbera, Bonarda and Pinot Nero and whites from the Pinots, Riesling and Chardonnay can be impressive. **Best producers:** Cà di Frara★, Le Fracce★, Frecciarossa★, Fugazza, Mazzolino★, Monsupello★, Montelio★, Vercesi del Castellazzo★, Bruno Verdi★. **Best years:** (reds) (2001) 00 99 **98 97 96 95**.

OMAR KHAYYAM *Maharashtra, India* Traditional-method sparkling wine produced from a blend of Chardonnay, Ugni Blanc, Pinot Noir, Pinot Meunier – and Thompson Seedless grapes grown at high altitudes. The Thompson is being used less and less as plantings of the other varieties come on stream. Technology, introduced by CHAMPAGNE consultants PIPER-HEIDSIECK, has resulted in a fresh, chunky sparkler – though quality is somewhat erratic. A remarkably good pink and a demi-sec fizz are also produced, plus red and white table wines.

WILLI OPITZ *Neusiedlersee, Austria* The eccentric and publicity-conscious Willi Opitz produces a remarkable, unusual range of dessert wines from his tiny 2ha (5-acre) vineyard, including red Eiswein. The best are ★★, but dry wines are simpler and less consistent.

OPUS ONE★★ *Oakville AVA, California, USA* Joint venture between Robert MONDAVI and the late Baron Philippe de Rothschild of MOUTON-ROTHSCHILD. The first vintage (1979) was released in 1983. At that time, the $50 price was the most expensive for any California wine, though others have reached way beyond it now. The various Opus bottlings since 1979 have been in the ★★ range but have rarely reached the standard of the Mondavi Reserve Cabernet. **Best years:** (2000) (99) 98 97 96 95 94 93 **92** 91 **90 88 87 86 85 84**.

DOM. DE L'ORATOIRE ST-MARTIN *Côtes du Rhône AC, Rhône Valley, France* Careful fruit selection in the vineyard is the secret of Frédéric and François Alary's concentrated COTES DU RHONE-VILLAGES reds and whites. The Haut-Coustias white★ is ripe with aromas of peach and exotic fruits, while the red★★ is a luscious mouthful of raspberries, herbs and spice. Top red Cuvée Prestige★★ is deep and intense with darkly spicy fruit. **Best years:** (Cuvée Prestige) (2000) 99 98 **97 96 95 94 93 90 89 88**.

OREGON *USA* Oregon shot to international stardom in the early 1980s following some perhaps overly generous praise of its Pinot Noir, but it is only with the release of 3 fine vintages in a row – 1998, 99 and 2000 – and some soul-searching by the winemakers about what style they should be pursuing that we can now begin to accept that some of the hype was deserved. Chardonnay can be quite good in an austere, understated style. The rising star is Pinot Gris which, in Oregon's cool climate, can be delicious, with surprising complexity. Pinot Blanc is also gaining momentum. The WILLAMETTE VALLEY is considered the best growing region, although the more Bordeaux-like climate of the Umpqua and Rogue Valleys can produce good Cabernet Sauvignon and Merlot. Best producers: (Rogue, Umpqua) Abacela★, Bridgeview Vineyards★, Calahan Ridge, Foris★, Henry Estate, Valley View Winery. Best years: (reds) 2000 99 98 **96 94**.

ORLANDO *Barossa Valley, South Australia*   Australia's second-biggest wine company and the force behind export colossus Jacob's Creek is owned by Pernod-Ricard. It encompasses MORRIS, Russet Ridge, Wickham Hill, Gramp's, Richmond Grove and Wyndham Estate, and MUDGEE wines Craigmoor, Poet's Corner, Henry Lawson and Montrose. Top wines under the Orlando name include COONAWARRA reds St Hugo★ and Jacaranda Ridge★, and individualistic Eden Valley Rieslings St Helga★ and Steingarten★★, but Orlando has lacked strength at the premium end. Rich Centenary Hill Barossa Shiraz★★ might change that, as might renewed efforts in Mudgee. Jacob's Creek Reserve and Limited Release★ wines are excellent, though basic Jacob's Creek seems a bit stretched as Australia's most successful export brand. Best years: (St Hugo Cabernet) **1998 96 94 92 91 90 88 86**.

ORNELLAIA, TENUTA DELL' *Bolgheri, Tuscany, Italy*   This beautiful property was developed by Lodovico Antinori, brother of Piero, after he left the family firm, ANTINORI, to strike out on his own. The red Ornellaia★★★, a Cabernet-Merlot blend, bears comparison with neighbouring SASSICAIA. The white Poggio alle Gazze★★ is made solely with Sauvignon. An outstanding Merlot, Masseto★★★, is produced in small quantities. Bought by MONDAVI in 2002 – let's hope quality stays up. Best years: (Ornellaia) (2000) 99 98 97 96 95 **94 93 90 88**.

ORTENAU *Baden, Germany*   A chain of steep granitic hills between Baden-Baden and Offenburg, which produce the most elegant (generally dry) Rieslings in BADEN, along with fragrant, fruity, medium-bodied Spätburgunder (Pinot Noir) reds. Best producers: Laible★★, Nägelsförst, Schloss Neuweier.

ORVIETO DOC *Umbria, Italy*   Traditionally a lightly sweet *abboccato* white wine, Orvieto is now usually dry and characterless. In the superior Classico zone, however, the potential for richer, more biscuity wines exists. Not generally a wine for aging. There are also some very good botrytis-affected examples. Best producers: (dry) Barberani-Vallesanta★, La Carraia★, Decugnano dei Barbi★, Palazzone★, Castello della SALA★, Salviano★, Conte Vaselli★, Le Velette★; (sweet) Barberani-Vallesanta★, Decugnano dei Barbi★, Palazzone★★, Castello della SALA★★.

OSBORNE *Jerez y Manzanilla DO, Andalucía, Spain*   The biggest drinks company in Spain, Osborne does most of its business in brandy and other spirits. Its sherry arm in Puerto de Santa María specializes in the light Fino Quinta★. Amontillado Coquinero★, rich, intense Bailén Oloroso★★ and Solera India★★ are very good indeed.

OVERBERG WO *South Africa*   South Africa's most southerly wine district, prized for cool-climate viticulture, embracing the upland area of Elgin as well as the coastal ward of Walker Bay. In Elgin, more apple orchards are being turned over to vines; Sauvignon, Chardonnay, Riesling and Pinot Noir vindicate this decision. In Walker Bay, Pinot Noir is the holy grail of the majority, although Chardonnay and Pinotage are also doing well. Best producers: (Elgin) Paul Cluver★, Neil ELLIS; (Walker Bay) BOUCHARD FINLAYSON★, HAMILTON RUSSELL★, Newton Johnson★. Best years: (Pinot Noir) 2000 99 98 **97**.

PAARL WO *South Africa*   Paarl is now South Africa's most densely planted region, accounting for 16.5% of all vineyards. There is great diversity of soil and climate here, favouring everything from Cap Classique sparkling wines to sherry styles, but reds are starting to set the quality pace, especially Shiraz. Its white RHONE counterpart, Viognier, is also performing well. Wellington and FRANSCHHOEK are smaller designated areas (wards) within the Paarl district. Best producers: (Paarl) Backsberg, BOSCHENDAL, FAIRVIEW★★, GLEN CARLOU★★, DISTELL (Plaisir de Merle, Nederburg), VEENWOUDEN★★, VILLIERA★, Welgemeend★; (Wellington) Claridge, Diemersfontein★. Best years: (premium reds) 2000 99 98 **97**.

PACHERENC DU VIC-BILH AC *South-West France*   Individual whites from an area overlapping the MADIRAN AC in north-east Béarn. The wines are mainly dry but there are some medium-sweet/sweet late-harvest wines. Most Pacherenc is best drunk young. Best producers: Aydie★, Berthoumieu★, Brumont (Bouscassé★★, Montus★), du Crampilh★, Damiens, Laffitte-Teston★, Producteurs PLAIMONT★, Sergent★. Best years: 2000 **97 96 95**.

PACIFIC ECHO *Anderson Valley AVA, California, USA*   Known until 1998 as Scharffenberger Cellars, this winery produced a string of attractive, toasty sparklers. POMMERY's investment has consolidated this performance. The Brut★★, with lovely toasty depth, the exuberant Rosé★★, and the blanc de blancs Prestige Cuvée★★ are all excellent.

PADTHAWAY *South Australia*   This wine region has always been the alter-ego of nearby COONAWARRA, growing whites to complement Coonawarra's reds. Padthaway Sauvignon Blanc is some of Australia's tastiest. But today some excellent reds are made; even GRANGE has included some Padthaway grapes. ORLANDO's premium Henry Lawson Shiraz★ is 100% Padthaway, HARDYS' Eileen Hardy Shiraz★★★ is half Padthaway and LINDEMANS' Padthaway Chardonnay★ is a serious white. Best producers: Browns of Padthaway, HARDYS★★, Henry's Drive★★, LINDEMANS★, ORLANDO★, Padthaway Estate, SEPPELT.

BRUNO PAILLARD *Champagne AC, Champagne, France*   Bruno Paillard is one of the very few individuals who has created a new CHAMPAGNE house over the past century. Paillard still does the blending himself. The non-vintage Première Cuvée★ is lemony and crisp, the Réserve Privée★ is a blanc de blancs; the vintage Brut★★ is a serious wine, and in 2000 he launched a de luxe cuvée, Ne Plus Ultra★★, a barrel-fermented blend of Grands Crus from the 1990 vintage. Best years: 1995 **90 89 88**.

ALVARO PALACIOS *Priorat DOC, Cataluña, Spain*   The young Alvaro Palacios was already a veteran with Bordeaux and Napa experience when he launched his boutique winery in the rough hills of southern CATALUNA in the late 1980s. He is now one of the driving forces of the area's sensational rebirth. His expensive, highly concentrated reds (L'Ermita★★★, Finca Dofi★★, Les Terrasses★) from old Garnacha vines and a dollop of Cabernet Sauvignon, Merlot and Syrah have won a cult following. Best years: 1999 98 **97 96 95 94 93**.

PALETTE AC *Provence, France*   Tiny AC just east of Aix-en-Provence. Even though the local market pays high prices, I find the reds and rosés rather tough and charmless. However, Ch. Simone, the only producer of white Palette, manages to achieve a wine of some flavour from basic southern grapes. Best producers: Crémade, Ch. Simone★.

207

PALLISER ESTATE *Martinborough, North Island, New Zealand* State-of-the-art winery producing some of New Zealand's best Sauvignon Blanc★★ (certainly the best outside MARLBOROUGH) and Riesling★, with some impressive, rich-textured Pinot Noir★★. Exciting botrytized dessert wines appear in favourable vintages. Méthode★ fizz is also impressive. Best years: (Pinot Noir) (2001) 00 **99 98 96 94**.

PALLISER ESTATE

MARTINBOROUGH
SAUVIGNON BLANC
2000

e750ml   13.5% Vol

CH. PALMER★★ *Margaux AC, 3ème Cru Classé, Haut-Médoc, Bordeaux, France* This estate was named after a British major-general who fought in the Napoleonic Wars. Palmer was the leading property in MARGAUX AC during the 1960s and 70s until the Mentzelopolous family took over at Ch. MARGAUX in 1977. The wine is wonderfully perfumed, with irresistible plump fruit. The very best vintages can age for 30 years or more. Second wine: Alter Ego (previously Réserve-du-Général). Best years: 2000 99 98 96 95 91 **90 89 88 86 85 83 82 79 78**.

PANTHER CREEK *Willamette Valley AVA, Oregon, USA* Sourcing wine from well-placed vineyards in OREGON and WASHINGTON, Panther Creek specializes in cherryish Pinot Noir★★. Single-vineyard wines Shea★★★, Bednarik★★, Freedom Hill★ and Nysa★ have extra complexity and length. Small amounts of Chardonnay from Celilo Vineyard (in Washington), Melón, Pinot Gris and a frothy traditional-method bubbly round out the range. Best years (Pinot Noir) 2000 99 98 **97 96 94**.

CH. PAPE-CLÉMENT *Pessac-Léognan AC, Cru Classé de Graves, Bordeaux, France* The expensive red wine★★ from this GRAVES property has not always been as consistent as it should be – but things settled down into a high-quality groove during the 1990s. In style it is mid-way between the refinement of HAUT-BRION and the firmness of la MISSION-HAUT-BRION. Also a small production of a much-improved white wine★★. Second wine: (red) Clémentin. Best years: (reds) 2000 99 98 97 96 95 **90 89 88 86**; (white) 2000 99 98 **96**.

PARELLADA This Catalan exclusivity is the lightest of the trio of simple white grapes that go to make CAVA wines in north-eastern Spain. It also makes still wines, light, fresh and gently floral, with good acidity. Drink it as young as possible, while it still has the benefit of freshness.

PARKER COONAWARRA ESTATE *Coonawarra, South Australia* Red wine specialist whose top label, cheekily named First Growth★★ in imitation of illustrious BORDEAUX reds, has enjoyed much critical acclaim and auction success. It is released only in better years and is built to age well. Second label Terra Rossa Cabernet Sauvignon★ is lighter and leafier, and Merlot★ is good too. Best years: (First Growth) (1998) **96 93 91 90 88**.

PASO ROBLES AVA *California, USA* A large AVA at the northern end of SAN LUIS OBISPO COUNTY. Cabernet Sauvignon and Zinfandel perform well in this warm region, and Syrah is now gaining a foothold as well. The Perrin family from Ch. de BEAUCASTEL selected this AVA to plant Rhône varieties for their California project, Tablas Creek, whose whites so far outshine the reds. Best producers: Adelaida★, Eberle★, Justin★, J Lohr★, Peachy Canyon★, Tablas Creek★, Wild Horse★.

LUIS PATO *Bairrada, Beira Litoral, Portugal*　Leading 'modernist' in BAIRRADA, passionately convinced of the Baga grape's ability to make great reds on clay soil. Wines such as the Vinhas Velhas★, Vinha Barrosa★★, Vinha Pan★★ and the flagship Quinta do Ribeirinho Pé Franco★★ (from ungrafted vines) now rank among Portugal's finest new reds. Homenagem★★ combines Baga with an equal amount of Touriga Nacional from Quinta de Cabriz (DÃO). Exciting white, Vinha Formal★★, is 100% Bical. Best years: (reds) 2000 97 **96 95 92**.

PAUILLAC AC *Haut-Médoc, Bordeaux, France*　The deep gravel banks around the town of Pauillac in the HAUT-MEDOC are the heartland of Cabernet Sauvignon. For many wine lovers, the king of red wine grapes finds its ultimate expression in the 3 Pauillac First Growths (LATOUR, LAFITE-ROTHSCHILD and MOUTON-ROTHSCHILD). The large AC also contains 15 other Classed Growths, including PICHON-LONGUEVILLE-LALANDE, PICHON-LONGUEVILLE and LYNCH-BAGES. The uniting characteristic of Pauillac wines is their intense blackcurrant flavour and heady cedar and pencil-shavings perfume. These are the longest-lived of Bordeaux's great red wines. Best producers: Armailhac★, BATAILLEY★, Clerc-Milon★, Duhart-Milon★, Fonbadet, GRAND-PUY-DUCASSE★, GRAND-PUY-LACOSTE★★, HAUT-BAGES-LIBERAL★, HAUT-BATAILLEY★, LAFITE-ROTHSCHILD★★★, LATOUR★★★, LYNCH-BAGES★★★, MOUTON-ROTHSCHILD★★★, Pibran★, PICHON-LONGUEVILLE★★★, PICHON-LONGUEVILLE-LALANDE★★★, PONTET-CANET★★. Best years: 2000 96 95 **90 89 88 86 85 83 82**.

CH. PAVIE★★ *St-Émilion Grand Cru AC, 1er Grand Cru Classé, Bordeaux, France*　Pavie has had its ups and downs in recent years, but a change of ownership in 1998 (it is now part of the same team as Pavie-Decesse★ and MONBOUSQUET★) has put it in the top flight again. The wines are rich and concentrated, but for some a little *too* extracted. Best years: 2000 99 98 96 95 **90 89 88 86 85 83 82**.

CH. PAVIE-MACQUIN★★ *St-Émilion Grand Cru AC, Grand Cru Classé, Bordeaux, France*　This has become one of the stars of the ST-ÉMILION GRAND CRU since the 1990s. Management and winemaking are in the hands of Nicolas Thienpont (of BORDEAUX-COTES DE FRANCS) and Stéphane Derenoncourt, who consults to CANON-LA-GAFFELIERE and PRIEURÉ-LICHINE, among others. Rich, firm and reserved, the wines need 7–8 years to open up and will age longer. Best years: 2000 99 98 97 96 95 **94 90**.

PÉCHARMANT AC *South-West France*　Lovely red wines from this small AC north-east of BERGERAC. The wines are quite light in body but have a delicious, full, piercing flavour of blackcurrants and attractive grassy acidity. Good vintages will easily last 10 years and end up indistinguishable from a good HAUT-MEDOC. Best producers: Beauportail, Bertranoux, Costes, Grand Jaure, Haut-Pécharmant, la Tilleraie, Tiregand★. Best years: 2000 98 **96 95 90**.

PEDROSA *Ribera del Duero DO, Castilla y León, Spain*　Delicious, elegant reds★ (Pérez Pascuas Gran Reserva★★), both young and oak-aged, from a family winery in the little hill village of Pedrosa del Duero. The wines are not cheap, but far less pricy than some stars of this fashionable region. Best years: (Pérez Pascuas) 1996 **95 94 91 90**.

PEGASUS BAY *Waipara, Canterbury, New Zealand*　Matthew Donaldson and Lynette Hudson fashion lush, mouthfilling Chardonnay★★, an almost chewy Pinot Noir★ and its even richer big brother Prima Donna Pinot Noir★★, a powerful Sauvignon Blanc-Semillon★★ and a very stylish Riesling★★ – an impressive portfolio from this upcoming region. All will age well. Best years: (Pinot Noir) (2001) 00 **99 98 97 96**.

209

PEMBERTON *Western Australia* Exciting emergent region, deep in the karri forests of the south-west, full of promise for cool-climate Pinot Noir, Chardonnay, Merlot and Sauvignon Blanc. Leading wineries include SALITAGE, run by Denis (LEEUWIN ESTATE) Horgan's brother John; Picardy, founded by Bill Pannell of MOSS WOOD fame; Chestnut Grove, part-owned by the Langes from Alkoomi; Smithbrook, part-owned by PETALUMA; and Bronzewing Estate, owned by John Kosovich of SWAN winery Westfield. Some large outfits such as HOUGHTON have moved in.

PEÑAFLOR *Mendoza, Argentina* The biggest wine producer in Argentina; BRIGHT BROTHERS make a good range of wines for export markets. Investment in its fine wine arm, Trapiche, along with the expertise of Bordeaux enologist Michel Rolland, is beginning to deliver results. Iscay★, a Merlot-Malbec blend, is Trapiche's new flagship red. Also a punchy Sauvignon Blanc and melony Chardonnay.

PENEDÈS DO *Cataluña, Spain* The wealthy CAVA industry is based in Penedès, and the majority of the still wines are white, made from the Cava trio of Parellada, Macabeo and Xarel-lo, clean and fresh when young, but never exciting. Better whites are made from Chardonnay. The reds are variable, the best made from Cabernet Sauvignon and/or Tempranillo and Merlot. Best producers: Albet i Noya★, Can Feixes★, Can Ràfols dels Caus★ (Caus Lubis Merlot★★), Cavas Hill, JUVE Y CAMPS, Jean León★, Marques de Monistrol, Masía Bach★, Albert Milá i Mallofré, Puig y Roca★, TORRES★★, Vallformosa, Jané Ventura★.

PENFOLDS *Barossa Valley, South Australia* Part of Australia's giant Southcorp group, Penfolds has always proved that quality *can* go in hand with quantity; since merging with ROSEMOUNT, the world waits and prays to see this continue. Makes the country's greatest red wine, GRANGE★★★, and a welter of superbly rich, structured reds from Magill Estate★★ through St Henri★, Bin 707 Cabernet★★★, Bin 389 Cabernet-Shiraz★★, Bin 28 Kalimna★ and Bin 128 Coonawarra Shiraz★ to Koonunga Hill and Rawson's Retreat cheapies (Riesling★). Still very much a red wine name, although a spirited bid for white wine fame was made with Chardonnay and Semillon from ADELAIDE HILLS, led by overpriced Yattarna★★, dubbed, with tongue in cheek, the 'white Grange'. Also makes tasty wooded Semillon★★ and lemony Semillon-Chardonnay★. Best years: (reds) 1998 96 **94 93 92 91 90 88 86 84 83 82 80 78 76 71**.

PENLEY ESTATE *Coonawarra, South Australia* Kym Tolley, a member of the PENFOLD family, combined the names when he left Southcorp and launched Penley Estate in 1991. From 1997 Cabernet Sauvignon★★ has been outstanding and matches its lavish packaging. Chardonnay and Hyland Shiraz can reach ★★; fizz★ is also worth a try, as is the recently released Merlot★. Best years: (Cabernet) 1998 **96 94 93 92 91**.

PERNAND-VERGELESSES AC *Côte de Beaune, Burgundy, France* The little-known village of Pernand-Vergelesses contains a decent chunk of the great Corton hill, including much of the best white CORTON-CHARLEMAGNE Grand Cru vineyard. The red wines sold under the village name are very attractive when young with a nice raspberry pastille fruit and a slight earthiness, and will age for 6–10 years. As no one ever links poor old Pernand with the heady heights of Corton-Charlemagne, the whites sold under the village name can be a bargain. The wines can be a bit lean and dry to start with but fatten up beautifully after 2–4 years in bottle. Best producers: (reds) Champy, CHANDON DE BRIAILLES★★, C Cornu★, Denis Père et Fils★, Dubreuil-Fontaine★, Laleure-Piot★

Rapet★, Rollin★; (whites) CHANDON DE BRIAILLES★★, Dubreuil-Fontaine★, GERMAIN, A Guyon, JADOT, Laleure-Piot★, J-M Pavelot★, Rapet★, Rollin★★. Best years: (reds) (2001) 99 98 **97 96 95**; (whites) (2001) 00 **99 97 96 95**.

JOSEPH PERRIER *Champagne AC, Champagne, France*   This is the sole CHAMPAGNE house left in Châlons-en-Champagne (previously called Châlons-sur-Marne). In 1998 Alain Thiénot took a controlling interest in the house. The NV Cuvée★ is biscuity and creamy, Prestige Cuvée Josephine★★ has length and complexity, but the much cheaper Cuvée Royale Vintage★★ is the best deal. Best years: 1995 **90 89 88 85 82**.

PERRIER-JOUËT *Champagne AC, Champagne, France*   Until 1999, Perrier-Jouët was owned by the Seagram group, and performance was generally lacklustre, although the vintage could be quite good, the Blason de France rosé★ charming and the de luxe cuvée Belle Époque★★, white and rosé, was still classy. There's a new winemaker as well as new owners, so there's hope that quality will begin to improve throughout the range. Best years: (1996) **95 92 90 89 85 82**.

PERVINI *Primitivo di Manduria DOC, Puglia, Italy*   Premium venture from the Perrucci family, long-established bulk shippers of basic Puglian wines. There's real quality and a modern outlook across the range of Primitivo-based reds (PRIMITIVO DI MANDURIA★★). Whites and rosés are decent, simple wines to drink young. Best years: (reds) 2001 00 **99 98 97 96**.

PESQUERA *Ribera del Duero DO, Castilla y León, Spain*   Tinto Pesquera reds, richly coloured, firm, fragrant and plummy-tobaccoey, are among Spain's best. Made by the small firm of Alejandro Fernández, they are 100% Tempranillo and sold as Crianzas★★, with expensive Reservas★★ and Pesquera Janus★★ in the best years. Condado de Haza (Alenza★★) is a separate estate and new ventures have also been launched in Zamora (Dehesa La Granja) and La MANCHA (Vínculo). Best years: (Pesquera Crianza) (1999) 96 **95 94 93 92 91 90 89 86 85**.

PESSAC-LÉOGNAN AC *Bordeaux, France*   AC created in 1987 for the northern (and best) part of the GRAVES region and including all the Graves Classed Growths. The supremely gravelly soil tends to favour red wines over the rest of the Graves. Now, thanks to cool fermentation and the use of new oak barrels, this is also one of the most exciting areas of Francerobinson for top-class white wines. Best producers: (reds) Brown, les Carmes Haut-Brion★, Dom. de CHEVALIER★★, FIEUZAL★, HAUT-BAILLY★★, HAUT-BRION★★★, Larrivet Haut-Brion★, LATOUR-MARTILLAC★, la LOUVIERE★★, MALARTIC-LAGRAVIERE★, la MISSION-HAUT-BRION★★★, PAPE-CLEMENT★★, SMITH-HAUT-LAFITTE★★, la Tour-Haut-Brion★★; (whites) CARBONNIEUX★, Dom. de CHEVALIER★★★, Couhins-Lurton★★, FIEUZAL★★, HAUT-BRION★★★, LATOUR-MARTILLAC★★, LAVILLE-HAUT-BRION★★★, la LOUVIERE★★, MALARTIC-LAGRAVIERE★, PAPE-CLEMENT★★, Rochemorin★, SMITH-HAUT-LAFITTE★★. Best years: (reds) 2000 99 98 96 95 **90 89 88**; (whites) 2000 99 98 **96 95 94 93 90**.

PETALUMA *Adelaide Hills, South Australia*   This public company, which includes KNAPPSTEIN and MITCHELTON and has major interests in WESTERN AUSTRALIA and MORNINGTON PENINSULA wineries, was founded by Brian Croser, probably Australia's most influential winemaker. It was taken over by brewer Lion Nathan in late 2001. Champagne-method Croser★ is stylish but lean. The Chardonnay★★ and COONAWARRA (Cabernet-Merlot)★★ are consistently outstanding and CLARE Riesling★★ is at the fuller end of the spectrum and matures superbly. Vineyard Selection Tiers Chardonnay★★★ is ridiculously expensive. Best years: (Coonawarra) 1999 97 **95 94 92 91 90 88**.

PETITE ARVINE Swiss variety from the VALAIS, found mainly between the communes of Sion and Martigny. Petite Arvine has a bouquet of peach and apricot, and develops a spicy, honeyed character with age. Dry, medium or sweet, the wines have good aging potential. Best producers: Chappaz★, Caves Imesch★, Dom. du Mont d'Or★.

PETITE SIRAH Long used as a blending grape in California but used also for varietal wines, Petite Sirah is often confused with the Durif of southern France. At its best in California and Mexico, the wine has great depth and strength; at worst it can be monstrously huge and unfriendly. Best producers: L A CETTO (Mexico), DeLoach★, Fife, FETZER, Foppiano, RAVENSWOOD★★, RIDGE★★, Stags' Leap Winery★★, TURLEY★★.

PETIT VERDOT A rich, tannic red variety, grown mainly in Bordeaux's HAUT-MEDOC to add depth, colour and violet fragrance to top wines. Late ripening and erratic yield limit its popularity, but warmer-climate plantings in Australia, California, Chile, Argentina, Spain and Italy are giving exciting results.

CH. PETIT-VILLAGE★★ *Pomerol AC, Bordeaux, France* This top POMEROL wine is sterner in style than its neighbours. In general it is worth aging the wine for 8–10 years at least. Best years: 2000 99 98 96 95 **94 90 89 88 85 82**.

CH. PÉTRUS★★★ *Pomerol AC, Bordeaux, France* Now one of the most expensive red wines in the world (alongside other superstars from POMEROL, such as le PIN), but only 40 years ago Pétrus was virtually unknown. The powerful, concentrated wine produced here is the result of the caring genius of Pétrus' owners, the MOUEIX family, who have maximized the potential of the vineyard of almost solid clay, although the impressive average age of the vines has been much reduced by recent replantings. Drinkable for its astonishingly rich, dizzying blend of fruit and spice flavours after a decade, but top years will age for much longer, developing exotic scents of tobacco and chocolate and truffles as they mature. Best years: 2000 99 98 97 96 95 94 **93** 90 **89 88 86 85 82 79 75 71**.

DOM. PEYRE ROSE *Coteaux du Languedoc AC, Languedoc, France* Organic viticulture, ultra-low yields and total absence of oak are all marks of the individuality of Marlène Soria's wines. Syrah is the dominant grape in both the raisin- and plum-scented Clos des Cistes★★ and the dense, velvety Clos Syrah Léone★★. An attractive white★ is a recent addition to the range. Best years: (reds) 1999 98 **97 96 95 94 93**.

CH. DE PEZ★ *St-Estèphe AC, Cru Bourgeois, Haut-Médoc, Bordeaux, France* One of ST-ESTEPHE's leading non-Classed Growths, de Pez makes mouthfilling, satisfying claret with sturdy fruit. Slow to evolve, good vintages often need 10 years or more to mature. Now owned by CHAMPAGNE house ROEDERER. Best years: 2000 98 97 96 95 **94 90 89 88**.

PFALZ *Germany* Germany's most productive wine region makes a lot of mediocre wine, but the quality estates are capable of matching the best that Germany has to offer. The Mittelhaardt has a reputation for Riesling especially round the villages of WACHENHEIM, FORST and Deidesheim, though Freinsheim, KALLSTADT, Ungstein, Gimmeldingen and Haardt also produce fine Riesling as well as Scheurebe, Rieslaner and Pinot Gris. In the Südliche

Weinstrasse the warm climate makes the area an ideal testing ground for Spät-, Weiss- and Grauburgunder (Pinot Noir, Pinot Blanc and Pinot Gris), as well as Gewürztraminer, Scheurebe, Muscat and red Dornfelder, the last often dark and tannic, if not elegant, sometimes with oak barrique influence. See also Bad Dürkheim, Burrweiler.

JOSEPH PHELPS *Napa Valley AVA, California, USA* Joseph Phelps' Insignia★★ (Cabernet, Merlot and Cabernet Franc) is consistently one of California's top reds, strongly fruit-driven with a lively spicy background. Phelps' pure Cabernets include Napa Valley★ and Backus Vineyard★★, beautifully balanced with solid ripe fruit. The Vin du Mistral line of RHONE varietals includes an intensely fruity Viognier★ and a lightly spiced Syrah★ that improves with short-term cellaring. Best years: (Insignia) (2000) 99 97 96 95 94 93 92 **91 85**.

CH. DE PIBARNON *Bandol AC, Provence, France* Blessed with excellently located vineyards, Pibarnon is one of BANDOL's leading properties. The reds★★, extremely attractive when young, develop a truffly, wild herb character with age. Average white and a ripe, strawberryish rosé. Best years: (red) (2000) 99 98 97 **96 95 94 93 91 90 89 88 85 82**.

FRANZ X PICHLER *Wachau, Niederösterreich, Austria* Austria's most famous producer of dry wines has a reputation as the country's 'bad boy'. Demand for his Rieslings and Grüner Veltliners far outstrips supply. Top wines Grüner Veltliner 'M'★★★ (for monumental) and Riesling Unendlich★★★ (endless), an alcoholically potent but perfectly balanced dry Riesling, are amazing. Since 1997 he has teamed up with Szemes and TEMENT in BURGENLAND to make red Arachon★★. Best years: (Riesling/Grüner Veltliner Smaragd) (2001) 00 99 98 **97 95 94 93 92 90 86**.

CH. PICHON-LONGUEVILLE★★★ *Pauillac AC, 2ème Cru Classé, Haut-Médoc, Bordeaux, France* Despite its superb vineyards with the potential for making great PAUILLAC, Pichon-Longueville (called Pichon-Baron until 1988) wines were 'also-rans' for a long time. In 1987 the management was taken over by Jean-Michel Cazes of LYNCH-BAGES and, since then, there has been a remarkable change in fortune. Recent vintages have been of First Growth standard, with firm tannic structure and rich dark fruit. Cellar for at least 10 years, although it is likely to keep for 30. Second wine: les Tourelles de Pichon. Best years: 2000 99 98 97 96 95 **90 89 88 86 82**.

CH. PICHON-LONGUEVILLE-LALANDE★★★ *Pauillac AC, 2ème Cru Classé, Haut-Médoc, Bordeaux, France* Pichon-Longueville-Lalande has been run since 1978 by the inspirational figure of Madame de Lencquesaing, who has led the property ever upwards through her superlative vineyard management and winemaking sensitivity. Divinely scented and lush at 6–7 years, the wines usually last for 20 at least. Things dipped at the end of the 1980s, but recent efforts have been excellent. Second wine: Réserve de la Comtesse. Best years: 2000 99 98 97 96 95 **90 89 88 86 85 83 82 81**.

PIC ST-LOUP *Coteaux du Languedoc AC, Languedoc, France* The vineyards of this Cru, arranged around a steep outcrop of limestone north of Montpellier, produce some of the best reds in the Languedoc. This is one of the coolest growing zones in the MIDI. Syrah is the dominant variety,

213

along with Grenache and Mourvèdre. Whites from Marsanne, Roussanne, Rolle and Viognier are showing promise. Best producers: Cazeneuve★, l'Euzière, l'HORTUS★, Lascaux★, Lavabre★, MAS BRUGUIERE★, Mas de Mortiès★. Best years: (reds) 2001 00 99 **98 96 95 93 90**.

PIEDMONT *Italy* This is the most important Italian region for the tradition of quality wines. In the north, there is CAREMA, GHEMME and GATTINARA. To the south, in the LANGHE hills, there's BAROLO and BARBARESCO, both masterful examples of the Nebbiolo grape, and other wines from Dolcetto and Barbera grapes. In the Monferrato hills, in the provinces of Asti and Alessandria, the Barbera, Moscato and Cortese grapes hold sway. Recent changes in the system have created the broad new DOCs of Colline Novaresi in the north, Langhe and Monferrato in the south and the regionwide Piemonte appellation designed to classify all wines of quality from a great range of grape varieties. See also Asti, Erbaluce di Caluso, Gavi, Moscato d'Asti, Nebbiolo d'Alba, Roero.

PIEROPAN *Veneto, Italy* Leonildo and Teresita Pieropan produce excellent SOAVE Classico★ and, from 2 single vineyards, Calvarino★★ and La Rocca★★. There is an excellent RECIOTO DI SOAVE Le Colombare★★, and an opulent Passito della Rocca★★, a barrique-aged blend of Sauvignon, Riesling Italico and Trebbiano di Soave. Single-vineyard Soaves can improve for 5 years or more, as can the Recioto and other sweet styles.

PIERRO *Margaret River, Western Australia* Mike Peterkin makes Pierro Chardonnay★★★ by the hatful, yet still it is a masterpiece of power and complexity. The LTC Semillon-Sauvignon-Chardonnay blend★ is full with just a hint of leafiness, while Pinot Noir★ continues to improve as the vines age. Dark, dense Cabernets★★ is the serious, BORDEAUX-like member of the family. Fire Gully is the second label, using bought-in grapes. Best years: (Chardonnay) **1999 97 96 94 93**.

PIESPORT *Mosel, Germany* The generic Piesporter Michelsberg wines, soft, sweet and easy-drinking, have nothing to do with the excellent Rieslings from the top Goldtröpfchen site. With their intense peach and blackcurrant aromas they are unique among MOSEL wines. Best producers: GRANS-FASSIAN★, Reinhold HAART★★, Kurt Hain★, von KESSELSTATT★, St Urbans-Hof★, Weller-Lehnert. Best years: (Riesling Spätlese) (2001) 00 **99 98 97 96 95 93 92 90 89**.

CH. LE PIN★★★ *Pomerol AC, Bordeaux, France* Now one of the most expensive wines in the world, with prices at auction overtaking those for PETRUS. The 1979 was the first vintage and the wines, which are concentrated but elegant, are produced from 100% Merlot. The tiny 2ha (5-acre) vineyard lies close to those of TROTANOY and VIEUX-CH.-CERTAN. Best years: 2000 99 98 97 96 95 **94 90 89 88 86 85 83 82 81**.

PINE RIDGE WINERY *Stags Leap District AVA, California, USA* Within an ever-changing roster, Pine Ridge offers wines from several NAPA AVAs, but its flagship Cabernet remains the supple, plummy Stags Leap District★★. Andrus Reserve Cabernet★★ has more richness and power. CARNEROS Merlot★★ is spicy and cherry fruited, and Carneros Chardonnay★ looks good. Oregon's ARCHERY SUMMIT is a sister label. Best years: (Stags Leap Cabernet) (2000) (99) 97 96 **95 94 91**.

PINGUS, DOMINIO DE *Ribera del Duero DO, Castilla y León, Spain* Peter Sisseck's tiny vineyards and winery have attracted worldwide attention since 1995 due to the extraordinary depth and character of the cult wine they produce, Pingus★★. Second wine Flor de Pingus★★ is also super. Best years: (Pingus) (2000) 99 **98 97 96 95**.

PINOT BIANCO See Pinot Blanc.

PINOT BLANC Wine made from the Pinot Blanc grape has a clear, yeasty, appley taste, and good examples can age to a delicious honeyed fullness. In France its chief power-base is in ALSACE, where it is taking over the 'workhorse' role from Sylvaner and Chasselas. Most CRÉMANT D'ALSACE now uses it as the principal variety. Important in northern Italy as Pinot Bianco, but it is probably taken most seriously in southern Germany and Austria (as Weissburgunder), producing imposing wines with ripe pear and peach fruit and a distinct nutty character. Also successful in Hungary, Slovakia, Slovenia and the Czech Republic. Promising new plantings in CALIFORNIA, OREGON and Canada.

PINOT GRIGIO See Pinot Gris.

PINOT GRIS At its finest in France's ALSACE; with reasonable acidity and a deep colour the grape produces fat, rich wines that mature wonderfully. It is very occasionally used in BURGUNDY (called Pinot Beurot) to add fatness to a wine. As Pinot Grigio it is grown in northern Italy, where it produces some of the country's most popular yet boring dry whites, but also some of the most exciting. Also successful in Austria and Germany as Ruländer or Grauer Burgunder, and as Malvoisie in the Swiss VALAIS. There are some good Romanian and Czech examples, as well as spirited ones in Hungary (as Szürkebarát). In a crisp style, it is very successful in OREGON and showing some promise in CALIFORNIA and Canada's OKANAGAN VALLEY. Becoming fashionable in New Zealand and in the cooler regions of Australia.

PINOT MEUNIER The most widely planted grape in the CHAMPAGNE region. A vital ingredient in Champagne, along with Pinot Noir and Chardonnay – though it is the least well known of the 3.

PINOT NERO See Pinot Noir.
PINOT NOIR See pages 216–17.

PINOTAGE A Pinot Noir x Cinsaut cross, conceived in South Africa in 1925 but not widely planted until the 1950s. Currently enjoying international popularity, the variety's champion is Beyers Truter of KANONKOP. New-style Pinotage, wooded or unwooded, has plum, banana and marshmallow flavours. There are several examples from New Zealand, a few from CALIFORNIA and Canada, and a little is grown in Brazil and Zimbabwe. Best South African producers: Graham BECK★ (sparkling, Old Road★), Bellingham (Premium★), BEYERSKLOOF★, Clos Malverne★, Diemersfontein★, FAIRVIEW★, GRANGEHURST★, Kaapzicht★, KANONKOP★★, L'AVENIR★, Newton Johnson★, Simonsig★, SPICE ROUTE★, Stony Brook★, Tukulu, Uiterwyk★ (Top of the Hill★★), WARWICK.

PIPER-HEIDSIECK *Champagne AC, Champagne, France* Traditionally one of CHAMPAGNE's least distinguished brands, though the owners, Rémy, have made great improvements. The non-vintage★ is gentler and more biscuity than it used to be, and can develop complexity. De luxe cuvée Champagne Rare★★ is pretty good. Best years: (1995) **90 89 85 82**.

PINOT NOIR

There's this myth about Pinot Noir that I think I'd better lay to rest. It goes something like this. Pinot Noir is an incredibly tricky grape to grow and even more difficult grape to vinify; in fact Pinot Noir is such a difficult customer that the only place that regularly achieves magical results is the thin stretch of land known as the Côte d'Or, between Dijon and Chagny in France, where mesoclimate, soil conditions and 2000 years of experience weave an inimitable web of pleasure.

This just isn't so. The thin-skinned, early-ripening Pinot Noir is undoubtedly more difficult to grow than other great varieties like Cabernet or Chardonnay, but that doesn't mean that it's impossible to grow elsewhere – you just have to work at it with more sensitivity and seek out the right growing conditions. And although great red Burgundy is a hauntingly beautiful wine, many Burgundians completely fail to deliver the magic, and the glorious thing about places like New Zealand, California, Oregon, Australia and Germany is that we are seeing an ever increasing number of wines that are thrillingly different from anything produced in Burgundy, yet with flavours that are unique to Pinot Noir.

WINE STYLES
France All France's great Pinot Noir wines do come from Burgundy's Côte d'Or. Rarely deep in colour, they should nonetheless possess a wonderful fruit quality when young – raspberry, strawberry, cherry or plum – that becomes more scented and exotic with age, the plums turning to figs and pine, and the richness of chocolate mingling perilously with truffles and well-hung game. Strange, challenging, hedonistic. France's other Pinots – in north and south Burgundy, the Loire, Jura, Savoie, Alsace and now occasionally in the south of France – are lighter and milder, and in Champagne its pale, thin wine is used to make sparkling wine.
Other European regions During the 1990s, helped by good vintages, German winemakers made considerable efforts to produce serious Pinot Noir (generally called Spätburgunder). Italy, where it is called Pinot Nero, and Switzerland (as Blauburgunder) both have fair success with the variety. Austria and Spain have produced a couple of good examples, and Romania, the Czech Republic and Hungary produce significant amounts of Pinot Noir, though of generally low quality.
New World Light, fragrant wines have bestowed upon Oregon the reputation for being 'another Burgundy'; but I get more excited about the sensual wines of California. The cool, fog-affected areas stand out: the ripe, stylish Russian River Valley examples; the marvellously fruity, exotically scented wines of Carneros; and the startlingly original offerings from Santa Barbara County.

New Zealand is the most important southern hemisphere producer, with wines of thrilling fruit and individuality, most notably from Martinborough, Canterbury's Waipara district and Central Otago. In the cooler regions of Australia – including Yarra Valley, Adelaide Hills, Nourt-East Victoria and Tasmania – producers are beginning to find their way with the variety. New Burgundian clones now reaching maturity bode well for South African Pinot Noir. Chile also has a few fine producers.

BEST PRODUCERS

France *Burgundy* (growers) B Ambroise, d'ANGERVILLE, Comte Armand, D Bachelet, G Barthod, J-M Boillot, CHANDON DE BRIAILLES, R Chevillon, CLAIR, J-J Confuron, C Dugat, B Dugat-Py, DUJAC, Engel, Anne Gros, GRIVOT, Hudelot-Noëllat, Michel LAFARGE, LAFON, Dom. LEROY, H Lignier, MEO-CAMUZET, Montille, Denis Mortet, J-F Mugnier, Ponsot, RION, Dom. de la ROMANEE-CONTI, E Rouget, ROUMIER, ROUSSEAU, TOLLOT-BEAUT, de VOGUE; (merchants) DROUHIN, FAIVELEY, V GIRARDIN, JADOT, LABOURE-ROI, D Laurent, RODET.

Germany FURST, JOHNER, Meyer-Näkel, MULLER-CATOIR, REBHOLZ.

Italy CA' DEL BOSCO, Hofstätter, Marchesi Pancrazi, Castello della SALA.

New World Pinot Noirs
USA (California) ACACIA, AU BON CLIMAT, Babcock, BYRON, CALERA, CHALONE, Davis Bynum, DEHLINGER, Merry Edwards, Etude, Gary Farrell, FLOWERS, HARTFORD COURT, KISTLER, LANDMARK, Lane Tanner, Littorai, MARCASSIN, Patz & Hall, Kent RASMUSSEN, ROCHIOLI, SAINTSBURY, SANFORD, Joseph SWAN, Talley, WILLIAMS SELYEM; (Oregon) BEAUX FRERES, BETHEL HEIGHTS, CRISTOM, DOMAINE DROUHIN, PANTHER CREEK, Rex Hill, Torii Mor, Ken WRIGHT.

Australia Ashton Hills, BANNOCKBURN, Bass Phillip, COLDSTREAM HILLS, Diamond Valley, Freycinet, Giaconda, LENSWOOD, Paringa Estate, TARRAWARRA, YARRA YERING.

New Zealand ATA RANGI, DRY RIVER, FELTON ROAD, Fromm, ISABEL, Kaituna Valley, MARTINBOROUGH VINEYARD, NEUDORF, PALLISER ESTATE, PEGASUS BAY, WITHER HILLS.

South Africa BOUCHARD FINLAYSON, HAMILTON RUSSELL.

Chile CONO SUR, VALDIVIESO, VILLARD ESTATE.

PIPERS BROOK VINEYARD *Northern Tasmania, Australia*   Keenly sought wines combining highish prices, clever marketing and skilled winemaking by Andrew Pirie. Steely Riesling★★, classically reserved Chardonnay★★, fragrant Gewürztraminer★ and refreshing Pinot Gris★ are highlights, as well as increasingly good Pinot Noir (Reserve, Blackwood★ and the Lyre★★). Its traditional-method sparkling wine, Pirie★★, may achieve ★★★ with a little extra age. Ninth Island is good second label. Best years: (Riesling) **2000 99 97 95 94 93 92 91 90**.

PLAIMONT, PRODUCTEURS *Madiran AC, Côtes de St-Mont VDQS and Vin de Pays des Côtes de Gascogne, South-West France*   This grouping of 3 Gascon co-ops is the largest, most reliable and most go-ahead producer of COTES DE GASCOGNE and COTES DE ST-MONT. The whites, full of crisp fruit, are reasonably priced and are best drunk young. The reds, especially Ch. St-Go★ and de Sabazan★, are very good too. Also good MADIRAN★★, and PACHERENC DU VIC-BILH.

PLANETA *Sicily, Italy*   Rapidly expanding, young and dynamic estate. Chardonnay★★ is already one of the best in southern Italy; Cabernet Sauvignon★ and Merlot★ are improving every year. Rich, peppery Santa Cecilia★★ (Nero d'Avola-Syrah) is aiming for international stardom. Basic La Segreta red★ and white★ are marvellously fruity. Latest addition is a fascinating Sicilian version of FIANO, Cometa★★.

PLANTAGENET *Great Southern, Western Australia*   Influential winery in the GREAT SOUTHERN region, contract-making wine for smaller outfits and producing its own flavourful range, notably spicy Shiraz★★, limy Riesling★★, melony/nutty Chardonnay★★, plump Pinot Noir★★ and classy Cabernet Sauvignon★★. Omrah is the second label, made from bought-in grapes. Best years: (Cabernet Sauvignon) 1998 97 **96 95 94 93 91 90 86 85**.

POLIZIANO *Vino Nobile di Montepulciano, Tuscany, Italy*   A leading light in Montepulciano. VINO NOBILE★★ is far better than average, especially the Riserva Vigna Asinone★★. SUPER-TUSCAN Le Stanze★★★ (Cabernet Sauvignon-Merlot) has been outstanding in recent vintages – the fruit in part coming from owner Carletti's other estate, Lohsa, in MORELLINO DI SCANSANO. Best years: (Vino Nobile) (1999) (98) 97 **96 95 93 90**.

POL ROGER *Champagne AC, Champagne, France*   Makers of Winston Churchill's favourite CHAMPAGNE and for many years a great favourite of the British market. The non-vintage White Foil★ is biscuity and dependable rather than thrilling. Pol Roger also produces a vintage★★, a vintage rosé★★, a vintage Grand Cru Chardonnay★★ and a vintage Réserve Spécial★★ (50% Chardonnay). Its top Champagne, the Pinot-dominated Cuvée Sir Winston Churchill★★, is a deliciously refined drink. All vintage wines will improve with another 5 years' keeping or more. Best years: (1996) 95 **93 90 89 88 86 85 82**.

POLZ *Steiermark, Austria*   Brothers Erich and Walter Polz are probably the most consistent producers of aromatic dry white wines in Styria. Few wines here fail to reach ★, and with Weissburgunder (Pinot Blanc), Morillon (Chardonnay) and Sauvignon Blanc the combination of intensity and elegance frequently deserves ★★. Steirische Klassik indicates wines vinified without any new oak. Best years: (Morillon, Sauvignon Blanc) (2001) 00 **99 97**.

POMEROL AC *Bordeaux, France*   One of the most famous and expensive of the BORDEAUX ACs, Pomerol includes some of the world's most sought-after red wines. Pomerol's unique quality lies in its deep clay in which the Merlot grape flourishes. The result is seductively rich, almost creamy wine with wonderful mouthfilling fruit flavours. Best producers: Beauregard★, Bonalgue, le BON PASTEUR★★, Certan-de-May★★, Clinet★★, Clos l'Église★, Clos René★, la CONSEILLANTE★★, l'EGLISE-CLINET★★★, l'EVANGILE★★, la FLEUR-PETRUS★★, GAZIN★★, Hosanna★ (previously Certan-Guiraud), LAFLEUR★★★, LATOUR-A-POMEROL★★, Montviel, Nénin★ (since 1990), PETIT-VILLAGE★★, PETRUS★★★, Le PIN★★★, Sales★, TROTANOY★★, VIEUX-CHATEAU-CERTAN★★. Best years: 2000 98 96 95 **94 90 89 88 86 85 83 82**.

POMINO DOC See Chianti Rufina.

POMMARD AC *Côte de Beaune, Burgundy, France* The first village south of Beaune. At their best, the wines should have full, round, beefy flavours. Can age well, often for 10 years or more. There are no Grands Crus but les Rugiens Bas and les Épenots (both Premiers Crus) occupy the best sites. Best producers: Comte Armand★★★, J-M Boillot★★, Courcel★★, Dancer★, P Garaudet★, M Gaunoux★, V GIRARDIN★★★, LAFARGE★★, D Laurent★★, Lejeune★, Montille★★, A Mussy★, J & A Parent★, Ch. de Pommard★, Pothier-Rieusset★. Best years: 1999 98 97 96 95 **93 90 89 88**.

POMMERY *Champagne AC, Champagne, France* Warmly regarded CHAMPAGNE house, performing well under the innovative leadership of winemaker Prince Alain de Polignac, a descendant of the celebrated Madame Pommery. Restrained non-vintage Brut Royal★ is often surpassed by another non-vintage, Apanage★, but 'Summertime' Blanc de Blancs and 'Wintertime' Blanc de Noirs seem superfluous additions to the range. Austere vintage Brut★★ is delicious, and the prestige cuvée Louise, both white★★ and rosé★★, is the epitome of discreet, perfumed elegance. Best years: (1996) 95 **92 90 89 88 85 82 76 75**.

CH. PONTET-CANET★★ *Pauillac AC, 5ème Cru Classé, Haut-Médoc, Bordeaux, France* The vineyards of this property are located close to those of MOUTON-ROTHSCHILD. The wines used to be rather lean and uninteresting but since 1979, when the Tesserons of LAFON-ROCHET bought the property, there has been a gradual return to form – big, chewy, intense claret which develops a beautiful blackcurrant fruit. Now one of the best value of the Classed Growths. Best years: 2000 99 98 97 96 95 **94 90 89 86 85 83 82**.

PORT See pages 220–1.

CH. POTENSAC★★ *Médoc AC, Cru Bourgeois, Bordeaux, France* Potensac's fabulous success is based on quality, consistency and value for money. Owned and run by the Delon family, of LEOVILLE-LAS-CASES, the wine can be drunk at 4–5 years, but fine vintages will improve for at least 10 years. Best years: 2000 99 98 97 96 95 **90 89 88 86**.

POUILLY-FUISSÉ AC *Mâconnais, Burgundy, France* Chardonnay from 5 villages, including Pouilly and Fuissé. For several years high prices and low quality meant this was a wine to avoid, but now it is beginning to find a sensible price level and there are some committed growers producing buttery, creamy wines that can be delicious at 2 years but will often develop beautifully for up to 10. Best producers: D & M Barraud★★, Corsin★★, C & T Drouin★, J-A Ferret★★★, M Forest★★, Ch. FUISSE★★, Guffens-Heynen (VERGET)★★★, R Lassarat★★, Léger-Plumet★, R Luquet★, Merlin★★, Robert-Denogent★★, Saumaize-Michelin★★, la Soufrandière★★, Valette★★★. Best years: (2000) **99 98 97 96 95 94 93 90**.

PORT DOC

Douro, Portugal

 The Douro region in northern Portugal, where the grapes for port are grown, is wild and beautiful. Steep hills covered in vineyard terraces plunge dramatically down to the Douro river. Grapes are one of the only crops that will grow in the inhospitable climate, which gets progressively drier the further inland you travel. But not all the Douro's grapes qualify to be made into increasingly good port. A quota is established every year, and the rest are made into table wines.

Red port grapes include Touriga Francesa, Tinta Roriz, Touriga Nacional, Tinta Barroca, Tinta Cão and Tinta Amarela. Grapes for white port include Malvasia Dorada, Malvasia Fina, Goureio and Rabigato. The grapes are partially fermented, and then *aguardente* (grape spirit) is added – fortifying the wine, stopping the fermentation and leaving sweet, unfermented grape sugar in the finished port.

PORT STYLES

Vintage Finest of the ports matured in bottle, made from grapes from the best vineyards. Vintage port is not 'declared' every year (usually there are 3 or 4 declarations per decade), but only during the second year in cask, if the shipper thinks the standard is high enough. It is bottled after 2 years, and may be consumed soon afterwards, not uncommon in the USA; at this stage it packs quite a punch. The British custom of aging for 20 years or more can yield exceptional mellowness.

Single quinta A true single-quinta wine comes from an individual estate; however, many shippers sell their vintage port under a quinta name in years which are not declared as a vintage, even though it may be sourced from 2 or 3 different vineyards. It is quite possible for these 'off vintage' ports to equal or even surpass the vintage wines from the same house.

Aged Tawny Matured in cask for 10, 20 or 30 years before bottling and sale, older tawnies have delicious nut and fig flavours.

Colheita Tawny from a single vintage, matured in cask for at least 7 years – potentially the finest of the aged tawnies.

Late Bottled Vintage (LBV)/Late Bottled Port matured for 4–6 years in cask then usually filtered to avoid sediment forming in the bottle. Traditional unfiltered LBV has much more flavour and like vintage port requires decanting. If released young, LBV can often be aged for another 5 years or more.

Crusted Rarely seen today, this is a blend of good ports from 2–3 vintages, bottled without filtration after 3–4 years in cask. A deposit (crust) forms in the bottle and the wine should be decanted.

Vintage Character (also known as Premium Ruby) has an average of 3–5 years' age. A handful represent good value.

Ruby The youngest red port with only 1–3 years' age. Ruby port should be bursting with young, almost peppery fruit but rarely achieves this level of quality.

Tawny Cheap tawny is a blend of ruby and white port and is both dilute and raw.

White Only the best taste dry and nutty from wood-aging; most are coarse and alcoholic, best drunk chilled or with tonic water.

BEST PRODUCERS

Vintage BURMESTER, CHURCHILL, COCKBURN, CRASTO, CROFT, Delaforce, DOW, FERREIRA, FONSECA, Gould Campbell, GRAHAM, Quarles Harris, Infantado, Martinez, NIEPOORT, NOVAL (including Nacional), Osborne, RAMOS PINTO, Roriz, ROSA, SMITH WOODHOUSE, TAYLOR, Vale Dona Maria, VESUVIO, WARRE.

Single quinta BURMESTER (Quinta Nova de Nossa Senhora do Carmo), CHURCHILL (Agua Alta), COCKBURN (Quinta dos Canais), CROFT (Quinta da Roêda), Delaforce (Quinta da Corte), DOW (Quinta do Bomfim), FONSECA (Guimaraens), GRAHAM (Malvedos), Martinez (Quinta da Eira Velha), NIEPOORT (Quinta do Passadouro), NOVAL (Silval), SMITH WOODHOUSE (Santa Madalena), TAYLOR (Quinta da Terra Feita, Quinta de Vargellas), WARRE (Quinta da Cavadinha).

Aged tawny Barros, BURMESTER, COCKBURN, DOW, FERREIRA, FONSECA, GRAHAM, Krohn, NIEPOORT, NOVAL, RAMOS PINTO, ROSA, SANDEMAN, TAYLOR, WARRE.

Colheita Barros, BURMESTER, Feist, Krohn, NIEPOORT, NOVAL.

Traditional Late Bottled Vintage CHURCHILL, CRASTO, Infantado, NIEPOORT, NOVAL, RAMOS PINTO, ROSA, SMITH WOODHOUSE, Vale da Mina, WARRE.

Crusted CHURCHILL, WARRE.

Ruby FONSECA, GRAHAM, TAYLOR, WARRE.

White CHURCHILL, NIEPOORT.

POUILLY-FUMÉ AC *Loire Valley, France* Fumé means 'smoked' in
French and a good Pouilly-Fumé has a pungent smell often likened to
gunflint. The only grape allowed is the Sauvignon Blanc, and the
extra smokiness comes from a flinty soil called silex. Despite the efforts
of a few producers, this is a seriously underperforming and overpriced
AC. Best producers: Berthiers★, G Blanchet★, Henri Bourgeois★,
A Cailbourdin★, J-C Chatelain★, Didier DAGUENEAU★★★, Serge
Dagueneau★, M Deschamps★, Ladoucette★, Landrat-Guyollot★,
Masson-Blondelet★, M Redde★, Tinel-Blondelet★, Ch. de Tracy★. Best
years: 2000 99 **98 97 96 95 90**.

POUILLY-SUR-LOIRE AC *Loire Valley, France* Light appley wines from
the Chasselas grape from vineyards around Pouilly-sur-Loire, the town
which gave its name to POUILLY-FUME. Drink as young as possible.

POUILLY-VINZELLES AC *Mâconnais, Burgundy, France* A small
appellation which, with its neighbour Pouilly-Loché (whose wines
may also be sold as Pouilly-Vinzelles), lies somewhat in the shadow of
big brother POUILLY-FUISSE. Most of the wines come through the local
co-operative, but there are now some good domaines offering rich
white wines from the steep east-facing slopes. Best producers: Cave
des Grands Crus, la Soufrandière★★, Tripoz★, Valette★. Best years:
(2000) **99 98 97**.

CH. POUJEAUX★★ *Moulis AC, Cru Bourgeois, Haut-Médoc, Bordeaux,
France* Poujeaux is one reason why MOULIS AC is attracting attention:
the wines have a delicious chunky fruit and new-oak sweetness.
Attractive at 6–7 years old, good vintages can easily last for 20–30
years. Best years: 2000 98 97 96 **95 94 93 90 89 88 86 85 83 82**.

PRAGER *Wachau, Niederösterreich, Austria* Toni Bodenstein is one of
the pioneers of the region, producing the first Riesling
Trockenbeerenauslese★★★ in the WACHAU in 1993. Also top dry
Rieslings from the Achleiten and Klaus vineyards★★★ and excellent
Grüner Veltliners from the Achleiten vineyard★★. Best years:
(Smaragd whites) (2001) 00 99 98 **97 96 95 93 92 90 86**.

PREMIÈRES CÔTES DE BLAYE AC *Bordeaux, France* An improving AC
on the right bank of the Gironde. The fresh, Merlot-based reds are
ready at 2–3 years but will age for more. The whites can be sold under
the COTES DE BLAYE AC. Best producers: Bel-Air la Royère★, Haut-
Bertinerie★, Haut-Grelot, Haut-Sociando, Jonqueyres★, Loumède,
Mondésir-Gazin★, Rolande-la-Garde, Segonzac★, Sociondo, Tourtes.
Best years: 2000 **98 96 95 94 90 89 88**.

PREMIÈRES CÔTES DE BORDEAUX AC *Bordeaux, France* Hilly region
overlooking GRAVES and SAUTERNES across the Garonne. For a long time
the AC was best known for its Sauternes-style sweet wines, particularly
from the communes of CADILLAC, LOUPIAC and STE-CROIX-DU-MONT, but the
juicy reds and rosés have now forged ahead. These are usually
delicious at 2–3 years old but should last for 5–6 years. Dry whites are
designated BORDEAUX AC. Best producers: (reds) Brethous★, CARSIN★,
Chelivette, Clos Ste-Anne, Grand-Mouëys★, Haux★, Jonchet, Juge
(Dupleich), Lamothe-de-Haux★, Langoiran, Melin, Puy-Bardens★,
REYNON★, le Sens, Suau, Tanesse. Best years: (reds) 2000 **98 96 95 94 90**.

CH. PRIEURÉ-LICHINE★ *Margaux AC, 4ème Cru Classé, Haut-Médoc,
Bordeaux, France* Seriously underachieving property that saw
several false dawns before being sold in 1999. Right Bank specialist
Stéphane Derenoncourt of PAVIE-MACQUIN and CANON-LA-GAFFELIERE fame
is now the consultant winemaker, and hopefully the wine will return

at very least to its traditional gentle, perfumed style. Best years: 2000 99 98 96 95 **94 90 89 88 86 85 83 82**.

PRIEURÉ DE ST-JEAN DE BÉBIAN *Coteaux du Languedoc AC, Languedoc, France* One of the pioneering estates in the MIDI, now owned by former wine writer Chantal Lecouty and her husband. It took a dip in the early 1990s but is now clearly back on form, producing an intense, spicy, generous red★★. The second wine is La Chapelle de Bébian, and there is also a barrel-fermented white★. Best years: (red) 2000 99 98 **97 96 95**.

PRIMITIVO DI MANDURIA DOC *Puglia, Italy* The most important appellation for PUGLIA's Primitivo grape, which has been enjoying a renaissance of interest since it was found to be identical to California's Zinfandel. The best wines combine outstanding ripeness and concentration with a knockout alcohol level. Good Primitivo is also sold as IGT Primitivo del Tarantino. Best producers: Felline★★, PERVINI★★, Giovanni Soloperto. Best years: (2001) 00 **99 98 97 96**.

PRIMO ESTATE *Adelaide Plains, South Australia* Innovative Joe Grilli stuck his winery in one of Australia's hottest climates but works miracles with his own grapes and those from outlying areas. The premium label is Joseph: Grilli adapts the Italian *amarone* method for Moda Amarone Cabernet-Merlot★★ (★★★ with 10 years age!) and makes a dense, eye-popping Joseph Red fizz★. He also does a sensuous Botrytis Riesling La Magia★★, fabulous honeyed fortified Fronti★★★, surprising dry white Colombard★, and a cherry-ripe blend of Shiraz and Sangiovese★ – and superb olive oils★★★. Best years: (Cabernet-Merlot Joseph) 1999 98 97 **96 95 94 93 91 90**.

PRIORAT DOC *Cataluña, Spain* A hilly, isolated district with very low-yielding vineyards planted on precipitous slopes of deep slate soil. Old-style fortified *rancio* wines used to attract little attention. Then in the 1980s a group of young winemakers revolutionized the area, bringing in state-of-the-art winemaking methods and grape varieties such as Cabernet Sauvignon to back up the native Garnacha and Cariñena. Their rare, expensive wines have taken the world by storm. Ready at 5 years old, the best will last much longer. The region was elevated to DOC status in 2001. Best producers: Bodegas B G (Gueta-Lupía★), Capafons-Ossó★, Cims de Porrera★★, CLOS MOGADOR★★★, La Conreria d'Scala Dei★, Clos i Terrasses (Clos Erasmus★★★), Costers del Siurana (Clos de l'Obac★★), J M Fuentes (Gran Clos★★), Mas Doix★★, Mas d'en Gil (Clos Fontà★★), Mas Martinet (Clos Martinet★★), Alvaro PALACIOS★★★, Pasanau Germans (Finca la Planeta★★), Rotllan Torra★★, Scala Dei★, VALL-LLACH★★. Best years: (reds) (2000) 99 98 **96 95 94 93 90**.

PROSECCO DI CONEGLIANO-VALDOBBIADENE DOC *Veneto, Italy* The Prosecco grape gives soft, scented wine made sparkling by a second fermentation in tank, though Prosecco can also be still, or *tranquillo*. Generally, however, it is a *spumante* or *frizzante* for drinking young. Cartizze, from a vineyard area of that name, is the most refined. Best producers: Adami★, Bernardi★, Bisol★, Carpenè Malvolti★, Le Colture, Col Vetoraz★, Nino Franco★, Ruggeri & C★, Tanorè★, Zardetto★.

PROVENCE *France* Provence is home to France's oldest vineyards but the region is better known for its nudist beaches and arts festivals than for its wines. However, it seems even Provence is caught up in the revolution sweeping through the vineyards of southern France. The area has 5 small ACs (BANDOL, les BAUX-DE-PROVENCE, BELLET, CASSIS and PALETTE), but most of the wine comes from the much larger areas of the COTES DE PROVENCE, COTEAUX VAROIS, Coteaux de Pierrevert and COTEAUX D'AIX-EN-PROVENCE. VdP des BOUCHES-DU-RHONE is also becoming increasingly important. Provençal reds are generally better than whites and rosés.

J J PRÜM *Bernkastel, Mosel, Germany* Estate making some of Germany's best Riesling in sites like the Sonnenuhr★★★ in WEHLEN, Himmelreich★★ in GRAACH and Lay★★ and Badstube★★ in BERNKASTEL. All have great aging potential. Best years: (2001) 00 99 98 97 96 95 **94 93 90 88 85 83 79 76 71**.

S A PRÜM *Wehlen, Mosel, Germany* There are a confusing number of Prüms in the MOSEL – the best known is J J PRUM, but Raimund Prüm of S A Prüm comes a decent second. The estate's most interesting wines are Riesling from WEHLENer Sonnenuhr, especially Auslese★★, but it also makes good wine from sites in BERNKASTEL★, GRAACH★ and Zeltingen★. Best years: (2001) 99 **97 95 93 90 88 86 85**.

PRUNOTTO *Barolo DOCG, Piedmont, Italy* One of the great BAROLO producers, now ably run by Albiera, the eldest of Piero ANTINORI's 3 daughters. Highlights include BARBERA D'ALBA Pian Romualdo★★, BARBERA D'ASTI Costamiòle★★, NEBBIOLO D'ALBA Occhetti★, Barolo Bussia★★★ and Cannubi★★ and new BARBARESCO Bric Turot★★. Also produces good MOSCATO D'ASTI★, BARBERA D'ASTI Fiulot★ and ROERO Arneis★. Best years: (Barolo) (2000) 99 98 97 96 **95 94 93 90 89 88 85**.

PUGLIA *Italy* This southern region is a prolific source of blending wines, but exciting progress has been made with native varieties: Uva di Troia in CASTEL DEL MONTE; Negroamaro in SALICE SALENTINO and other reds and rosés of the Salento peninsula; white Greco for characterful Gravina, revived by Botromagno; and Verdeca and Bianco d'Alessano for Locorotondo and Martina Franca. But it is the red Primitivo (CALIFORNIA's Zinfandel), led by examples from the likes of PERVINI and Felline, that is set to make the biggest impact, whether under the PRIMITIVO DI MANDURIA DOC or more general IGTs.

PUISSEGUIN-ST-ÉMILION AC *Bordeaux, France* Small ST-EMILION satellite AC. The wines are generally fairly solid but with an attractive chunky fruit and usually make good drinking at 3–5 years. Best producers: Bel-Air, Branda, Durand-Laplagne★, Fongaban, Guibeau-la-Fourvieille, Laurets, la Mauriane★, Producteurs Réunis, Soleil. Best years: 2000 **98 96 95**.

PULIGNY-MONTRACHET AC *Côte de Beaune, Burgundy, France* Puligny is one of the finest white wine villages in the world and adds the name of its greatest Grand Cru, le MONTRACHET, to its own. There are 3 other Grands Crus (BATARD-MONTRACHET, Bienvenues-BATARD-MONTRACHET and Chevalier-MONTRACHET) and 11 Premiers Crus. The flatter vineyards use the Puligny-Montrachet AC. Good vintages really need 5 years' aging, while Premiers Crus and Grands Crus may need 10 years and can last for 20 or more. Only about 3% of the AC is red wine. Best producers: J-M Boillot★★, CARILLON★★★, J Chartron★, G Chavy★, DROUHIN★★, A Ente★★, B Ente★, JADOT★★, Larue★★, LATOUR★, Dom. LEFLAIVE★★★ (since 1994), O LEFLAIVE★, P Pernot★★, Ch. de Puligny-Montrachet★★, RAMONET★★, SAUZET★★. Best years: (2001) 00 99 **97** 96 **95** 92.

QUARTS DE CHAUME AC *Loire Valley, France* The Chenin Blanc grape finds one of its most rewarding mesoclimates here. Quarts de Chaume is a 40ha (100-acre) AC within the larger COTEAUX DU LAYON AC and, as autumn mists begin to curl off the river Layon, noble rot attacks the grapes. The result is intense, sweet wines which can last for longer than almost any in the world – although many can be drunk after 5 years. Best producers: BAUMARD★★★, Bellerive★★, Laffourcade★, Pierre-Bise★★,

J Pithon★★★, Plaisance★, F Poirel★★, Joseph Renou★★. Best years: (2001) 00 99 **97 96 95 94 93 90 89 88 85 83 81 78 76 70 69 64 59 47**.

QUEENSLAND *Australia* Queensland still has the smallest production of all Australia's wine-producing states, but is catching up fast. About 30 wineries perch on rocky hills in the main region, the Granite Belt, near the NEW SOUTH WALES border. New regions South Burnett, north-west of Brisbane, Mount Cotton, Mount Tamborine and Toowoomba are showing some promise. Best producers: Bald Mountain, Clovely Estate, Kominos, Mount Cotton, Preston Peak, Robinsons Family, Stone Ridge, Windermere, Winewood.

QUERCIABELLA *Chianti Classico DOCG, Tuscany, Italy* This model of a modern CHIANTI producer serves up a gorgeously scented, rich-fruited Chianti Classico★★ and Riserva★★. But it has made an even greater splash with its two SUPER-TUSCANS: BURGUNDY-like white Batàr★★ from Pinot Bianco and Chardonnay, and tobaccoey, spicy Sangiovese-Cabernet blend Camartina★★★. Best years: (Camartina) 1997 96 95 **94 93 91 90 88**.

QUILCEDA CREEK *Washington State, USA* This tiny winery has built a cult following in Washington because of a big, rich Cabernet Sauvignon★★★. The wine can be a bit overpowering, but it does open up to stunning effect after a while in the glass and it has good aging potential. Since 1997 a less expensive Columbia Valley Red★★ has been produced from a blend of Cabernets Sauvignon and Franc and Merlot. Best years: (Cabernet) (2000) 99 98 97 96 95 **94 92**.

QUINCY AC *Loire Valley, France* Intensely flavoured, dry white wine from Sauvignon Blanc vineyards west of Bourges. Can age for a year or two but always keeps a rather aggressive gooseberry flavour. Best producers: H Bourgeois★, Mardon★, J Rouzé, Troterau★. Best years: (2001) **00 99 97 96**.

QUINTARELLI *Valpolicella DOC, Veneto, Italy* Giuseppe Quintarelli is the great traditional winemaker of VALPOLICELLA. His philosophy is one of vinifying only the very best grapes and leaving nature to do the rest. His Classico Superiore★★ is left in cask for about 4 years and his famed AMARONE★★★ and RECIOTO★★ for 7 years or more before release. There is also Alzero★★, a spectacular Amarone-style wine made from Cabernets Franc and Sauvignon. Best years: (Amarone) **1995 93 91 90 88 86 85 83**.

QUIVIRA *Dry Creek Valley AVA, California, USA* Among the best of the new-wave Zinfandel★ producers; established the trend for bright, fruity early-drinking wine under former winemaker Doug Nalle. The wines are immediately delicious and have the balance to age well. The Dry Creek Cuvée★ (Grenache, Mourvèdre, Syrah and Zinfandel) is dangerously delightful. Lively Sauvignon Blanc★ is another crowd-pleaser. Best years: (Zinfandel) **1999 98 97 96 95 94 91 90**.

QUPÉ *Santa Maria Valley AVA, California, USA* Owner/winemaker Bob Lindquist makes a gorgeously tasty Bien Nacido Reserve Syrah★★★. His Reserve Chardonnay★★ and Bien Nacido Cuvée★★ (two-thirds Chardonnay, one-third Viognier) have sublime appley fruit and perfume. A leading exponent of RHONE-style wines, he also makes Viognier★, Mourvèdre★ and Marsanne★. Best years: (Reserve Syrah) (2000) 99 98 97 **96 95 94 92 91 90**.

RAÏMAT *Costers del Segre DO, Cataluña, Spain* Owned by CODORNIU, this large, irrigated estate makes pleasant but surprisingly lean wines from Tempranillo, Cabernet Sauvignon (Mas Castell vineyard★) and Chardonnay. Also lean but okay fizz. 4 Varietales is a new upscale red blend. Best years: (reds) 1999 **98 97 96 95 94 92 91 90**.

RAMONET *Chassagne-Montrachet, Côte de Beaune, Burgundy, France* The Ramonets (father and sons) produce some of the most complex of all white Burgundies from 3 Grands Crus (BATARD-MONTRACHET★★★, Bienvenues-BATARD-MONTRACHET★★★ and le MONTRACHET★★★) and Premiers Crus including Ruchottes★★★, Caillerets★★★, Boudriotte★★, Vergers★★, Morgeot★★ and Chaumées★★★. If you want to spare your wallet try the ST-AUBIN★★ or the CHASSAGNE-MONTRACHET white★★ or red★★. Best years: (whites) (2001) 00 99 98 97 96 95 **93 92 90 89**.

JOÃO PORTUGAL RAMOS *Alentejo, Portugal* João Portugal Ramos has the potential to become Portugal's foremost winemaker. At least a dozen producers draw on his expertise as a consultant, but he is now making his mark with his own winery and vineyards. Smoky, peppery Trincadeira★★, spicy Aragonês (Tempranillo)★, powerful Syrah★, and intensely dark-fruited Vila Santa★★ (a blend of the previous two wines topped up with Cabernet Sauvignon and Alicante Bouschet) are all superb. Marquês de Borba★ is the label for everyday red and white wines, though a small amount of a brilliant red Reserva★★ is also made. João Ramos has also taken charge of the potentially outstanding Pegos Claros★★ from the neighbouring TERRAS DO SADO region. Best years: (2001) 00 99 **97**.

RAMOS PINTO *Douro DOC and Port DOC, Douro, Portugal* Innovative PORT company now controlled by ROEDERER, making complex, full-bodied Late Bottled Vintage★ and aged tawny (Quinta do Bom Retiro★★). The 1994 Vintage★★ and Quinta da Ervamoira★★ are of a different order to older vintage efforts. Table wines Duas Quintas (Reserva★) and Bons Ares★ (Reserva★) are variable and no longer cheap. Best years: (Vintage) (2000) 97 95 94 **83**.

RAMPOLLA, CASTELLO DEI *Chianti Classico DOCG, Tuscany, Italy* One of the outstanding CHIANTI CLASSICO★★ estates. SUPER-TUSCAN Sammarco, sometimes ★★★, is mostly Cabernet with some Sangiovese, while the extraordinary Vigna d'Alceo★★★ adds Petit Verdot to Cabernet Sauvignon. Best years: (Sammarco) 1998 97 96 95 **94 90 88 86 85**; (Vigna d'Alceo) 1999 98 97 **96**.

RANDERSACKER *Franken, Germany* Important wine village in FRANKEN, producing excellent medium-bodied dry Rieslings, dry Silvaners, spicy Traminer and piercingly intense Rieslaner. Best producers: JULIUSSPITAL★, Robert Schmitt★, Schmitt's Kinder★. Best years: (Riesling Spätlese trocken) (2001) 00 99 **98 97 94 93 92 90**.

RAPEL, VALLE DEL *Valle Central, Chile* Proving to be one of Chile's most exciting red wine regions, Rapel is split between Valle del Cachapoal to the north and Valle de COLCHAGUA to the south. Both are excellent for Cabernet Sauvignon, Merlot and Carmenère. Best producers:

CASA LAPOSTOLLE★, CONCHA Y TORO★★, Gracia, LA ROSA★, MONTES★, Porta, Viu Manent★.

KENT RASMUSSEN *Carneros AVA, California, USA*　Tightly structured Burgundian-style Chardonnay★★ capable of considerable aging and a fascinating juicy Pinot Noir★★ are made by ultra-traditional methods. Also occasional delightful oddities like Pinotage, Alicante and Dolcetto under the Ramsay label. Best years: (Pinot Noir) (2001) 00 99 98 97 **95 94 92 91 90**.

RASTEAU AC *Rhône Valley, France*　Rasteau is one of the original 16 villages entitled to the COTES DU RHONE-VILLAGES AC. The single-village AC is for a fortified red or white and a *rancio* version which is left in barrel for 2 or more years. Best producers: Beaurenard★, Cave des Vignerons, Rabasse-Charavin, la Soumade★, du Trapadis★.

RENATO RATTI *Barolo DOCG, Piedmont, Italy*　The late Renato Ratti led the revolution in winemaking in the Alba area with BAROLO and BARBARESCO of better balance, colour and richness and softer in tannins than the traditional models. Today his son Pietro and nephew Massimo Martinelli produce sound modern Barolo★★ from the Marcenasco vineyards at La Morra, as well as good BARBERA D'ALBA (Torriglione★), Dolcetto d'Alba (Colombé★) and NEBBIOLO D'ALBA (Ochetti★). Villa Pattono★ is a blend of Barbera and Freisa from Monferrato.

RAUENTHAL *Rheingau, Germany*　Sadly, only a few producers live up to the reputation earned by this RHEINGAU wine village's great Baiken and Gehrn sites, for intense, spicy Rieslings. Best producers: J B BECKER★, Georg BREUER★★, August Eser. Best years: (2001) 00 99 98 **97 96 94 93 90**.

CH. RAUZAN-SÉGLA★★ *Margaux AC, 2ème Cru Classé, Haut-Médoc, Bordeaux, France*　A dynamic change of winemaking regime in 1982 and the purchase of the property by Chanel in 1994 have propelled Rauzan-Ségla up the quality ladder. Now the wines have a rich blackcurrant fruit, almost tarry, thick tannins and weight, excellent woody spice and superb concentration. Second wine: Ségla. Best years: 2000 99 98 96 95 **94 90 89 88 86 85 83**.

JEAN-MARIE RAVENEAU *Chablis AC, Burgundy, France*　One of the outstanding growers in CHABLIS, producing beautifully nuanced wines from 3 Grands Crus (Blanchot★★★, les Clos★★★ and Valmur★★★) and 4 Premiers Crus (Montée de Tonnerre★★★, Vaillons★★, Butteaux★★★ and Chapelot★★), using a combination of old oak and stainless-steel fermentation. The wines can easily age for a decade or more. Best years: (top crus) (2001) 00 99 98 97 96 **95 92 90 89**.

RAVENSWOOD *Sonoma Valley AVA, California, USA*　Joel Peterson, one of California's best-known Zin experts, established Ravenswood in 1976. During the lean years, when most Zinfandel was pink and sweet, he added an intense Chardonnay, a sometimes very good Cabernet Sauvignon★ and several tasty Merlots (Sangiacomo★★). But Zinfandel remains the trump card. Peterson makes several, varying the menu from year to year, but recent offerings seem to have lost some of their depth and pungency – pleasant, but not memorable. Interestingly, Amador County★ and Lodi★ offerings showed more intensity than most of the Sonoma products. In 2001, Franciscan Estates purchased the winery. Best years: (Zins) (2000) 99 **97 96 95 94 92 91 90**.

CH. RAYAS *Châteauneuf-du-Pape, Rhône Valley, France*　The most famous estate in CHATEAUNEUF-DU-PAPE. Emmanuel Reynaud, nephew of the eccentric Jacques Reynaud, is running this estate in his uncle's inimitable rule-breaking style, producing big, alcoholic, exotically rich reds★★★ and whites★★ which also age well. However, prices are not cheap and the wines are not consistent, but at its best Rayas is worth the money. The red is made entirely from low-yielding Grenache vines – the only such wine in the AC – while the white is a blend of Clairette, Grenache Blanc and (so rumour has it) Chardonnay. Second label Pignan can also be impressive. COTES DU RHONE Ch. de Fonsalette★★ is usually wonderful. Best years: (Châteauneuf-du-Pape) (2000) 99 98 96 95 **94 93 91** 90 **89 88 86**; (whites) 2000 99 98 97 96 95 **94 93 91** 90 **89 86**.

REBHOLZ *Siebeldingen, Pfalz, Germany*   This estate in the southern PFALZ produces fine dry Riesling★★, Weissburgunder★★ and Grauburgunder★, all crystalline in their clarity, with vibrant fruit aromas. Top of the range are intensely mineral dry Riesling★★★ from the Kastanienbusch vineyard, powerful dry Gewürztraminer★★ and extravagantly aromatic, crisp, dry Muskateller★★. Also produces Germany's finest barrel-fermented Chardonnay★★ and most serious Spätburgunder★★ (Pinot Noir) reds. Best years: (whites) (2001) 00 **99** 98 **97 96 95** 94 **93** 92 90 **89**; (reds) (2001) 00 99 98 97 **96 94 93**.

RECIOTO DELLA VALPOLICELLA DOC *Veneto, Italy*   The great sweet wine of VALPOLICELLA, made from grapes picked earlier than usual and left to dry on straw mats until the end of January. The wines are deep in colour, with a rich, bitter-sweet cherryish fruit. They age well for 5–8 years, but most are best drunk young. As with Valpolicella, the Classico tag is all important. Best producers: Accordini★, ALLEGRINI★★, Bolla (Spumante★★), Brigaldara★, Tommaso Bussola★★, Michele Castellani★★, DAL FORNO★★★, MASI★, QUINTARELLI★, Le Ragose★, Le Salette★, Serègo Alighieri★★, Speri★, Tedeschi★, Tommasi★, Villa Monteleone★★, Viviani★. Best years: 2000 **97 95 93** 90 **88 85**.

RECIOTO DI SOAVE DOCG *Veneto, Italy*   Sweet white wine made in the SOAVE zone from dried grapes, like RECIOTO DELLA VALPOLICELLA. Garganega grapes give wonderfully delicate yet intense wines that age well for up to a decade. The best, ANSELMI's I Capitelli, is now sold as IGT Veneto. Best producers: ANSELMI★★, La Cappuccina★★, Cà Rugate★, Coffele★, Gini★★, PIEROPAN★, Bruno Sartori★, Tamellini★★. Best years: 2000 **98 97 95 93** 90 **88**.

DOM. DE LA RECTORIE *Banyuls AC and Collioure AC, Roussillon, France*   Marc and Thierry Parcé are distant relations of Dr A Parcé of Mas Blanc, a famous name in BANYULS. Their COLLIOURE cuvées (la Coume Pascole★★ and le Seris★★) are made for keeping, while the Banyuls Cuvée Léon Parcé★★ can be enjoyed for its youthful fruit or kept for future pleasure. The vin de pays Grenache Gris, Cuvée l'Argile★, is one of the best whites in ROUSSILLON. Best years: (la Coume Pascole) 2000 99 98 **97 96 95 93**.

RÉGNIÉ AC *Beaujolais, Burgundy, France*   The wines of this BEAUJOLAIS Cru are generally light and attractive but in poor years not up to scratch. Best producers: DUBOEUF★ (des Buyats★), H & J-P Dubost★, Rochette★. Best years: (2001) **00 99**.

DOM. LA RÉMÉJEANNE *Côtes du Rhône AC, Rhône Valley, France*   First-class property making a range of strikingly individual wines. COTES DU RHONE-VILLAGES les Genèvriers★★ has the weight and texture of good CHATEAUNEUF-DU-PAPE, while COTES DU RHONE Syrah les Eglantiers★★ is superb. Both need at least 3–5 years' aging. Also good Côtes du Rhône les Chèvrefeuilles★ and les Arbousiers (red and white). Best years: (les Eglantiers) (2000) 99 98 **96**.

REMELLURI *Rioja DOC, País Vasco, Spain* Organic ʀɪᴏᴊᴀ estate producing red wines with far more fruit than usual and good concentration for aging – the best are ★★. There is also a delicate, barrel-fermented white blend★. Best years: (Reserva) 1996 **95 94 91 89**.

RETSINA *Greece* Resinated white (and some rosé) wine common all over Greece – although both production and sales are falling steadily. Poor Retsina is diabolical but the best are deliciously oily and piny. Drink young.

REUILLY AC *Loire Valley, France* Extremely dry but with the odd attractive Sauvignon from west of sᴀɴᴄᴇʀʀᴇ. Also some pale Pinot Noir red and Pinot Gris rosé. Best producers: H Beurdin★, C Lafond★. Best years: (2001) 00 **99 98 97 96 95**.

REYNELL *McLaren Vale, South Australia* Pioneer John Reynell established Chateau Reynella in 1838. Now HQ of the BRL ʜᴀʀᴅʏ empire, wines are labelled Reynell in Australia, although the Chateau Reynella name is still used for export. Prices have shot up lately, but they're not unreasonable given the quality. Basket Pressed Cabernet★★, Merlot★★ and Shiraz★★ are concentrated, tannic, ageworthy reds from low-yielding vines, some of which were planted in the 1930s. Best years: (reds) (1998) **96 95 94**.

CH. REYNON *Premières Côtes de Bordeaux AC, Bordeaux, France* Property of enology professor Denis Dubourdieu, white wine specialist and consultant to a number of ɢʀᴀᴠᴇs Classed Growths. The dry whites, particularly the barrel-fermented Vieilles Vignes★, are superb and the red has come on tremendously since 1997. In the same stable is the quality Graves Clos Floridène★, which is vinified at Reynon. Best years: (reds) 2000 99 98 **97 96 95**; (whites) 2000 **99 98 96 95**.

RHEINGAU *Germany* Wine region on a south-facing stretch of the Rhine flanking the city of Wiesbaden, planted with 79% Riesling and 11% Spätburgunder (Pinot Noir). Traditionally considered Germany's most aristocratic wine region, both in terms of the racy, slow-maturing wines and because of the number of noble estate owners. But famous names here are no longer a guarantee of top quality, as a new generation now produces the best wines. See also Eltville, Erbach, Geisenheim, Hochheim, Johannisberg, Kiedrich, Rauenthal, Rüdesheim, Winkel. Best years: (Riesling Spätlese) (2001) **99** 98 **97** 96 **93 90**.

RHEINHESSEN *Germany* Large wine region to the south and west of Mainz. On the Rheinterrasse between Mainz and Worms are a number of very famous top-quality estates, especially at Bodenheim, Nackenheim, ɴɪᴇʀsᴛᴇɪɴ and Oppenheim. ʙɪɴɢᴇɴ, to the north-west, also has a fine vineyard area along the left bank of the Rhine. However, Riesling accounts for only 10% of the vineyard area; Weissburgunder (Pinot Blanc) is the rising star. Best years: (Riesling Spätlese) (2001) 00 **99** 98 **97 96 94 93 90**.

RHÔNE VALLEY *France* The Rhône starts out as a river in Switzerland, ambling through Lake Geneva before hurtling southwards into France. In the area south of Lyon, between Vienne and Avignon, the valley becomes one of France's great wine regions. In the northern part, where vertigo-inducing slopes overhang the river, there is not much wine produced but the little that is made is of remarkable individuality. The Syrah grape reigns here in COTE-ROTIE and on the great hill of HERMITAGE. ST-JOSEPH, CROZES-HERMITAGE and CORNAS also make excellent reds, while the white Viognier grape yields perfumed, delicate wine at CONDRIEU and at the tiny AC CHATEAU-GRILLET. In the southern part the steep slopes give way to wide plains, where the vines swelter in the hot sun, with hills both in the west and east. Most of these vineyards are either COTES DU RHONE or COTES DU RHONE-VILLAGES, reds, whites and rosés, but there are also specific ACs. The most well known of these are CHATEAUNEUF-DU-PAPE and the luscious, golden dessert wine, MUSCAT DE BEAUMES-DE-VENISE. See also Clairette de Die, Coteaux de l'Ardèche, Coteaux du Tricastin, Côtes du Lubéron, Gigondas, Lirac, Rasteau, St-Péray, Tavel, Vacqueyras.

RÍAS BAIXAS DO *Galicia, Spain*   The best of GALICIA's 5 DOs, Rías Baixas is making increasing quantities of Spain's best whites (apart from a few Chardonnays in the north-east). The magic ingredient is the characterful Albariño grape, making dry, fruity whites with a glorious fragrance and citrus tang. Drink young or with short aging. Best producers: Adegas Galegas★, Agro de Bazán★★, Quinta de Couselo★★, Granxa Fillaboa★, Lagar de Fornelos★ (La RIOJA ALTA), Lusco do Miño★★, Martin Códax★★, Gerardo Méndez Lázaro (Do Ferreiro Cepas Vellas★★), Pazo de Barrantes★ (MARQUES DE MURRIETA), Pazo de Señorans★, Bodegas Salnesur (Condes de Albarei★), Santiago Ruiz★★ (Lan), Terras Gauda★★.

RIBATEJO *Portugal*   Portugal's second-largest wine region, now with its own DOC, straddles the river Tagus (Tejo). Hotter and drier than ESTREMADURA to the west, prolific vineyards on the fertile soils alongside the river are producing volumes of improving everyday reds and whites. There are several sub-regional DOCs. Best producers: (reds) Almeirim co-op, BRIGHT BROTHERS, Casa Cadaval★, Quinta do Casal Branco (Falcoaria★), D F J VINHOS, Falua (Reserva★), Quinta Grande, Horta da Nazaré, Quinta da Lagoalva★.

RIBERA DEL DUERO DO *Castilla y León, Spain*   The dark, mouthfilling reds in this DO, from Tinto Fino (Tempranillo), sometimes with Cabernet Sauvignon and Merlot, are nowadays generally more exciting than those of RIOJA. But excessive expansion of vineyards and increase in yields may threaten its supremacy. Best producers: Alión★★, ARROYO★★, Arzuaga★, Balbás★, Hijos de Antonio Barceló★, Briego★★, Felix Callejo★, Convento San Francisco★, Hermanos Cuadrado García★★, Dehesa de los Canónigos★, Del Campo★, Fuentespina★, Hacienda Monasterio★, Emilio Moro★, Pago de Carraovejas★, PEDROSA★★, PESQUERA★★★, PINGUS★★★, Protos★, Teófilo Reyes★★, Rodero★, Telmo RODRIGUEZ★★, Hermanos Sastre★★, Tarsus★★, Valderiz★★, Valduero★, Valtravieso★, VEGA SICILIA★★★, Viñedos y Bodegas★. Best years: (2001) 00 99 **96 95 94 91 90 89 86 85**.

BARONE RICASOLI *Chianti Classico DOCG, Tuscany, Italy*   The estate where modern CHIANTI was perfected by Baron Bettino Ricasoli in the mid-19th century has recovered its lost form. 1993 saw the start of the renaissance under the guidance of Francesco Ricasoli. The flagship wine is now Castello di Brolio Chianti Classico★; that labelled simply Brolio is effectively a second selection. Chianti Classico Riserva Guicciarda★ is good value. Casalferro★★, a Sangiovese-Merlot red, looks certain to join the SUPER-TUSCAN élite. Best years: (Casalferro) (2000) 99 98 97 **96 95 94 93**.

DOM. RICHEAUME *Côtes de Provence AC, Provence, France* German-owned property, run on organic principles and producing impressively deep-coloured wines★ (Colomelle★★) full of smoky spice and power. Best years: (Colomelle) (2000) 99 98 **97 95**.

RICHEBOURG AC *Grand Cru, Côte de Nuits, Burgundy, France* Rich, fleshy wine from the northern end of VOSNE-ROMANEE. Most domaine-bottlings are exceptional. Best producers: GRIVOT★★★, Anne Gros★★★, A-F Gros★★★, Hudelot-Noëllat★★, Dom. LEROY★★★, MEO-CAMUZET★★★, Mongeard-Mugneret★, Dom. de la ROMANEE-CONTI★★★. Best years: (2001) 00 99 98 97 96 95 93 **91** 90 **89 88 85**.

DOM. RICHOU *Loire Valley, France* One of the leading domaines in the LOIRE, producing consistently good wines. Best are the ANJOU-VILLAGES Vieilles Vignes★★ and sweet COTEAUX DE L'AUBANCE les Trois Demoiselles★★. Best years: (les Trois Demoiselles) 1999 **97** 96 **95 94 93 90** 89 88.

MAX FERD RICHTER *Mülheim, Mosel-Saar-Ruwer, Germany* Racy Rieslings from some of the best sites in the MOSEL, including WEHLENer Sonnenuhr★★, BRAUNEBERGer Juffer★★ and GRAACHer Domprobst★★. Richter's Mülheimer Helenenkloster vineyard produces a magical Eiswein★★★ virtually every year – although not in 1999. Best years: (Riesling Spätlese) (2001) 99 98 **97** 96 **95 94 93 90 89 88**.

RIDGE VINEYARDS *Santa Cruz Mountains AVA, California, USA* Once a Zinfandel-only winery, winemaker Paul Draper moved into Cabernet Sauvignon★★ and Petite Sirah★★ in the late 60s. The Zinfandels★★★, made with grapes from various sources, have great intensity and long life, and the other reds, led by Monte Bello Cabernet★★★, show impressive originality. Fine Chardonnay★★, too. Best years: (Monte Bello) (2000) (99) 98 97 **95 94 93 92 91 90 89 87 85 84**.

RIDGEVIEW ESTATE *West Sussex, England* Christine and Michael Roberts are emulating CHAMPAGNE every step of the way at their South Downs vineyard. Bloomsbury★ and Belgravia blends of Chardonnay, Pinot Noir and Pinot Meunier are produced under the Cuvée Merret label. Also delicious Fitzrovia rosé and Cavendish, a Pinot Noir-based sparkler.

RIECINE *Chianti DOCG, Tuscany, Italy* Small estate in Gaiole making exquisite CHIANTI. Yields are low, so there is a great intensity of fruit and a superb definition of spiced cherry flavours. New American owners have retained Irish winemaker Sean O'Callaghan, who continues to fashion still better CHIANTI CLASSICO★★, Riserva★★★ and barrique-aged La Gioia★★★. Best years: (La Gioia) (1999) 98 97 96 **95 94 90 88 85**.

RIESLING See pages 232–3.

RIESLING ITALICO Known as Welschriesling in the rest of Europe, and not in any way related to the great Riesling of the Rhine, this grape is widely planted in northern Italy, where it produces decent dry whites. In Austria it makes some of the very best sweet wines, but tends to be rather dull and thin as a dry wine. In Hungary, where is it called Olasz Rizling, it is highly esteemed.

CH. RIEUSSEC★★★ *Sauternes AC, 1er Cru Classé, Bordeaux, France* Apart from the peerless Ch. d'YQUEM, Rieussec is often the richest, most succulent wine of SAUTERNES. Other estates can now rival it in quality but rarely make such extravagantly rich wines. Cellar for at least 10 years. Dry white 'R' is inexplicably dull. Second wine: Clos Labère. Owned since 1984 by LAFITE-ROTHSCHILD. Best years: (2001) 99 98 97 96 95 **90 89 88 86 85 83**.

RIESLING

I'm sad to have to make this bald statement at the start, but I feel I must. If you have tasted wines with names like Laski Riesling, Olasz Riesling, Welschriesling, Gray Riesling, Riesling Italico and the like and found them bland or unappetizing – do not blame the Riesling grape. These wines have filched Riesling's name, but have nothing whatsoever to do with the great grape itself.

Riesling is Germany's finest contribution to the world of wine – and herein lies the second problem. German wines have fallen to such a low level of general esteem through the proliferation of wines like Liebfraumilch that Riesling, even true German Riesling, has been dragged down with it.

So what *is* true Riesling? It is a very ancient German grape, probably the descendant of wild vines growing in the Rhine Valley. It certainly performs best in the cool vineyard regions of Germany's Rhine and Mosel Valleys, and in Alsace and Austria. It also does well in Canada, New Zealand and cool parts of Australia; yet it is widely planted in California, South Africa and Italy, and the warmer parts of Australia also grow it to good effect.

Young Rieslings often show a delightful floral perfume, sometimes blended with the crispness of green apples, often lime, peach, nectarine or apricot, sometimes even raisin, honey or spice depending upon the ripeness of the grapes. As the wines age, the lime often intensifies, and a flavour perhaps of slate, perhaps of petrol/kerosene intrudes. In general Rieslings may be drunk young, but top dry wines can improve for many years, and the truly sweet German styles can age for generations.

WINE STYLES

Germany These wines are based on a marvellous perfume and an ability to hold on to a piercing acidity, even at high ripeness levels, so long as the ripening period has been warm and gradual rather than broiling and rushed. German Rieslings can be bone dry, through to medium and even lusciously sweet, but if they are dry, they must be made from fully ripe grapes, otherwise the acidity is excessive and the wine's body insufficient. Styles range from crisp elegant Mosels to riper, fuller wines from the Pfalz and Baden regions in the south. The very sweet Trockenbeerenauslese (TBA) Rieslings are made from grapes affected by noble rot; for Eiswein (icewine), also intensely sweet, the grapes are picked and pressed while frozen.

Other regions In the valleys of the Danube in Austria, Riesling gives stunning dry wines that combine richness with elegance, but the most fragrant wines, apart from German examples, come from France's Alsace. The mountain vineyards of northern Italy, and the cool vineyards of the Czech Republic, Slovakia and Switzerland can show a floral sharp style, as can New Zealand. America's Pacific Northwest and New York State are having some success, and California generally produces a grapy style which is usually best when sweet. Canada's icewines can be stunning. Australia's cooler spots are looking increasingly good for lean, limy Rieslings. Riesling is in decline in South Africa, but cooler sites produce delicate dry styles and some good late-harvest and botrytized Rieslings.

BEST PRODUCERS

Germany

Dry BASSERMANN-JORDAN, Georg BREUER, Heymann-Löwenstein, KOEHLER-RUPRECHT, KUNSTLER, J LEITZ, MULLER-CATOIR, REBHOLZ, ST ANTONY, SAUER, J L WOLF.

Non-dry DIEL, DONNHOFF, GUNDERLOCH, HAAG, HAART, Heymann-Löwenstein, JOST, KARTHAUSERHOF, C Loewen, VON KESSELSTATT, KUNSTLER, Dr LOOSEN, MAXIMIN GRUNHAUS, MULLER-CATOIR, Egon MULLER-SCHARZHOF, J J PRUM, RICHTER, Willi SCHAEFER, WEIL.

Austria

Dry BRUNDLMAYER, HIRTZBERGER, J Högl, KNOLL, Nigl, NIKOLAIHOF, F-X PICHLER, Rudi Pichler, PRAGER, Freie Weingärtner WACHAU.

France

(Alsace) *Dry* P BLANCK, A Boxler, DEISS, Dirler, HUGEL, Kientzler, Kreydenweiss, KUENTZ-BAS, A Mann, MURÉ, Ostertag, SCHOFFIT, TRIMBACH, WEINBACH, ZIND-HUMBRECHT.

Non-dry Léon Beyer, DEISS, HUGEL, Ostertag, TRIMBACH, WEINBACH, ZIND-HUMBRECHT.

Australia

Tim ADAMS, Wolf BLASS, Leo Buring, DELATITE, GROSSET, HENSCHKE, HOWARD PARK, LEEUWIN, MITCHELTON, Mount Horrocks, MOUNT LANGHI GHIRAN, ORLANDO, PETALUMA, PIPERS BROOK, PLANTAGENET, Geoff WEAVER, Wilson Vineyard, YALUMBA.

New Zealand

CLOUDY BAY, CORBANS (Stoneleigh), DRY RIVER, FELTON ROAD, Fromm, GIESEN, MILLTON, PEGASUS BAY, VILLA MARIA, Waipara West.

South Africa

Avontuur (Above Royalty), Neethlingshof.

USA

(Washington) CHATEAU STE MICHELLE (Eroica), KIONA.

RIOJA DOC *Rioja, Navarra, País Vasco and Castilla y León, Spain* Rioja, in northern Spain, is not all oaky, creamy white wines and elegant, barrel-aged reds, combining oak flavours with wild strawberry and prune fruit. Over half Rioja's red wine is sold young, never having seen the inside of a barrel, and most of the white is fairly anonymous. Wine quality, as could be expected from such a large region with more than 300 producers, is inconsistent. There is far too much mediocre Rioja on the market as large producers and co-ops try to milk Rioja's reputation. However, a bevy of new producers with great ambitions is changing the regional hierarchy and they, at least, are taking quality seriously. Best producers: (reds) ALLENDE★★, Altos de Lanzaga★★ (Telmo RODRIGUEZ), Amézola de la Mora, ARTADI★★, Baron de Ley★, BERBERANA★, Beronia, Bodegas Bilbaínas, CAMPILLO★, CAMPO VIEJO★, Luis Cañas, CONTINO★★, El Coto★, CVNE, DOMECQ★, FAUSTINO★, Lan (Culmen★), LOPEZ DE HEREDIA★, MARQUES DE CACERES★, MARQUES DE GRINON★, MARQUES DE MURRIETA★, MARQUES DE RISCAL★★, Marqués de Vargas★★, MARTINEZ BUJANDA★★, MONTECILLO★, MUGA★, Navajas, Palacio, REMELLURI★★, Fernando Remírez de Ganuza★★, La RIOJA ALTA★★, RIOJANAS★, Roda★★, Señorío de San Vicente★★, Viña Ijalba; (whites) Beronia, CAMPO VIEJO★, CVNE★, LOPEZ DE HEREDIA★, MARQUES DE CACERES★, MARQUES DE MURRIETA★, MARTINEZ BUJANDA★★, MONTECILLO★, La RIOJA ALTA★, RIOJANAS★. Best years: (reds) (2001) **96 95 94 91 89 87 86 85 83 82 81 78**.

LA RIOJA ALTA *Rioja DOC, Rioja, Spain* One of the best of the older RIOJA producers, making mainly Reservas and Gran Reservas. Its only Crianza, Viña Alberdi, fulfils the minimum age requirements for a Reserva anyway. There is a little good, lemony-oaky Viña Ardanza Reserva★ white. Red Reservas, Viña Arana★ and Viña Ardanza★★, age splendidly, and Gran Reservas, Reserva 904★★ and Reserva 890★★★ (made only in exceptional years), are among the very best of Rioja wines. Best years: (Gran Reserva 890) **1987 85 82 81 78**.

RIOJANAS *Rioja DOC, Rioja, Spain* Quality winery producing Reservas and Gran Reservas in 2 styles – elegant Viña Albina★ and richer Monte Real★ – plus the new, refined Gran Albina★★. White Monte Real Blanco Crianza★ is one of RIOJA's best. The whites and Reservas can be kept for 5 years after release, Gran Reservas for 10 or more. Best years: (Monte Real Gran Reserva) **1994 91 89 87 85 83 82 81**.

RION *Nuits-St-Georges, Côte de Nuits, Burgundy, France* Patrice Rion was the winemaker at Dom. Daniel Rion from 1979 to 2000, making consistently fine but often austere reds such as VOSNE-ROMANEE les Beaumonts★★ and les Chaumes★★, NUITS-ST-GEORGES Clos des Argillières★★ and latterly ECHEZEAUX★★ and CLOS DE VOUGEOT★★★. Under his own Patrice Rion label he makes richly concentrated BOURGOGNE Rouge and CHAMBOLLE-MUSIGNY les Cras★★ from his own vines as well as, since 2000, a small range of négociant wines. Best years: (top reds) (2000) 99 98 97 96 **95 93 90 88**.

RIVERA *Puglia, Italy* One of southern Italy's most dynamic producers. The CASTEL DEL MONTE Riserva Il Falcone★★ is an excellent, full-blooded southern red. Also a series of varietals under the Terre al Monte label, best of which are Aglianico★, Pinot Bianco and Sauvignon Blanc.

RIVERINA *New South Wales, Australia* Along with RIVERLAND, this extensive irrigated region, fed by the Murrumbidgee River and also known as Big Rivers, provides the bulk of Australia's basic table wines. Many of Australia's best-known brands, from companies like HARDYS, MCWILLIAM'S, ORLANDO and PENFOLDS, though not mentioning eithe

Riverina or Riverland on the label, are based on wines from these areas. There are also some remarkable sweet wines such as Noble One Botrytis Semillon★★★ from DE BORTOLI. Other leading producers are Cranswick Estate, Gramp's, Lillypilly and Miranda.

RIVERLAND *Australia* A vast irrigated region along the Murray River, straddling 3 states (SOUTH AUSTRALIA, VICTORIA and NEW SOUTH WALES), and producing a third of the national grape crush. Mainly given over to casks and cheaper bottles of table and fortified wine, though an increasing number of producers are bringing out high-quality special selections. Best producers: Angove's, Bonneyview, Deakin Estate, HARDYS (Banrock Station), Kingston Estate, YALUMBA (Oxford Landing).

RIVESALTES AC *Languedoc-Roussillon, France* *Vin doux naturel* from a large area around the town of Rivesaltes. These fortified wines are some of southern France's best and can be made from an assortment of grapes, mainly white Muscat (when it is called MUSCAT DE RIVESALTES) and Grenache Noir, Gris and Blanc. A *rancio* style ages well. Best producers: CASENOVE★, CAZES★★, Chênes★, Fontanel★, Forca Réal★, GAUBY★, Ch. de Jau★, Joliette★, Laporte, Rivesaltes co-op, Sarda-Malet★, Terrats co-op, Trouillas co-op.

ROBERTSON WO *South Africa* Hot, dry inland area with lime-rich soils, uncommon in the Cape, that are ideal for vines. Chenin Blanc and Colombard are the major white wine varieties, and Chardonnay performs well (for both still and sparkling styles), as can Sauvignon in leafy, aggressive form. The traditional Muscadel (Muscat Blanc à Petits Grains) yields a benchmark fortified wine. A red revolution is currently under way; Shiraz, Merlot and Cabernet have made an excellent start. Best producers: Bon Courage, Graham BECK★, De Wetshof, Robertson Winery, SPRINGFIELD ESTATE★, Van Loveren, Zandvliet.

CH. ROC DE CAMBES★★ *Côtes de Bourg AC, Bordeaux, France* François Mitjavile of TERTRE-ROTEBOEUF has applied enthusiasm and diligence to this property since he acquired it in 1988. Full and concentrated, with ripe dark fruit, this wine takes the COTES DE BOURG appellation to new heights. Best years: 2000 99 98 **97 96 95 94 93 91 90 89**.

J ROCHIOLI VINEYARDS *Russian River Valley AVA, California, USA* Meticulous growers still selling grapes, the Rochioli family are equally good at winemaking, offering silky, black cherry Pinot Noir★★ and a richer, dramatic West Block Reserve Pinot★★★. All wines stand out, including a fine Sauvignon Blanc★★ and a range of cult Chardonnays★★. Best years: (Pinot Noir) (2001) 00 99 98 **97 95 94 92**.

ROCKFORD *Barossa Valley, South Australia* Wonderfully nostalgic wines from the stone winery of Robert O'Callaghan, a great respecter of the old vines so plentiful in the BAROSSA, who delights in using antique machinery. Masterful Basket Press Shiraz★★, Riesling★, Moppa Springs★ (a Grenache-Shiraz-Mourvèdre blend) and cult sparkling Black Shiraz★★★. Best years: (Basket Press Shiraz) (1998) 96 **95 92 91 90 86**.

ANTONIN RODET *Mercurey, Côte Chalonnaise, Burgundy, France* Merchant based in the village of MERCUREY, specializing in COTE CHALONNAISE, but with an excellent range from throughout Burgundy. Rodet owns or co-owns 5 domaines – Ch. de Rully★, Ch. de Chamirey★, Ch. de Mercey★, Dom. de Perdrix★ and Jacques Prieur★★ – which are the source of the best wines. BOURGOGNE Vieilles Vignes★ is one of the best inexpensive Chardonnays available. Recently purchased Dom. de l'Aigle in LIMOUX. Best years: (reds) 1999 98 **97** 96 **95 93 90**; (whites) (2001) 00 99 **97** 96 **95**.

TELMO RODRÍGUEZ *Spain*   The former winemaker for REMELLURI has now formed a 'wine company' that is active throughout Spain and Portugal. With a team of enologists and viticulturists, it forms joint ventures with local growers and manages the whole winemaking process. The results are often spectacular. Top wines: Molino Real★★ (MALAGA), Alto Matallana★★ (RIBERA DEL DUERO), Altos de Lanzaga★★ (RIOJA), Dehesa Gago Pago La Jara★★ (TORO), Viña 105★ (Cigales), Basa (RUEDA).

LOUIS ROEDERER *Champagne AC, Champagne, France*   Renowned firm making some of the best, full-flavoured CHAMPAGNES around. As well as the excellent non-vintage★★ and pale vintage rosé★, it also makes a big, exciting vintage★★, delicious vintage Blanc de Blancs★★ and the famous Roederer Cristal★★★, a de luxe cuvée which is nearly always magnificent. Both the vintage wines and Cristal can usually be aged for 10 years or more; the non-vintage benefits from a bit of aging, too. Best years: (1996) 95 **93 90 89 88 86 85**.

ROEDERER ESTATE *Anderson Valley AVA, California, USA*   Californian offshoot of Louis ROEDERER. The Brut★★ (sold in the UK as Quartet) is impressive though austere, a step back from the upfront fruit of many California sparklers, but it will age beautifully if you can wait. The top bottling, or tête de cuvée , L'Ermitage★★★, is a stunning addition to the range of California fizz. Best years: (L'Ermitage) (1996) **94 92 91**.

ROERO DOC *Piedmont, Italy*   The Roero hills lie across the Tanaro river from the LANGHE hills, home of BAROLO and BARBARESCO. Long noted as a source of Nebbiolo in supple, fruity red wines to drink in 2–5 years, Roero has recently made its mark with the white Arneis grape. Best producers: (reds) G Almondo★, Ca' Rossa★, Cascina Chicco★, Correggia★, Deltetto★, Funtanin★, F Gallino★, Malvirà★, Monchiero Carbone★, Angelo Negro★, Porello★. Best years: (reds) (2001) **00 99 98 97 96**. See also Arneis.

ROMAGNA *Emilia-Romagna, Italy*   Romagna's wine production is centred on 4 DOCs and 1 DOCG. The whites are from Trebbiano (ineffably dull), Pagadebit (showing promise as both a dry and sweet wine) and Albana (ALBANA DI ROMAGNA can be dry or sweet). The reds are dominated by the Sangiovese grape, and range from young and fresh through to wines that can rival good CHIANTI CLASSICO. Best producers: (Sangiovese) La Berta★, Castelluccio★★, L Conti★, Drei Donà-La Palazza★, G Madonia★, San Patrignano co-op–Terre del Cedro★ (Avi★★), Tre Monti★, Zerbina★★.

LA ROMANÉE-CONTI AC *Grand Cru, Côte de Nuits, Burgundy, France*   For many extremely wealthy wine lovers this is the pinnacle of red Burgundy★★★. It is an incredibly complex wine with great structure and pure, clearly defined fruit flavour, but you've got to age it 15 years to see what all the fuss is about. The vineyard covers only 1.8ha (4½ acres), which is one reason for the high prices. Wholly owned by Dom. de la ROMANÉE-CONTI. Best years: (2001) 00 99 98 97 96 95 93 **91** 90 **89** 88 **85 78 72**.

DOM. DE LA ROMANÉE-CONTI *Vosne-Romanée, Côte de Nuits, Burgundy, France*   This famous red wine domaine owns a string of Grands Crus in VOSNE-ROMANEE (la TACHE★★★, RICHEBOURG★★★, ROMANEE-CONTI★★★, ROMANEE-ST-VIVANT★★★, ECHEZEAUX★★★ and Grands-Échézeaux★★★) as well as a small parcel of le MONTRACHET★★★. The wines are ludicrously expensive but can be quite sublime – full of fruit when young, but capable of aging for 15 years or more to an astonishing marriage made in the heaven and hell of richness and decay. Best years: (reds) (2001) 00 99 98 97 96 95 93 90 **89** 88 **85 78**.

ROMANÉE-ST-VIVANT AC *Grand Cru, Côte de Nuits, Burgundy, France* By far the largest of VOSNE-ROMANÉE's 6 Grands Crus. At 10–15 years old the wines should reveal the keenly balanced brilliance of which the vineyard is capable, but a surly, rough edge sometimes gets in the way. Best producers: l'Arlot★★, R Arnoux★★★, S Cathiard★★★, J-J Confuron★★★, DROUHIN★★★, Hudelot-Noëllat★★★, JADOT★★★, Dom. LEROY★★★, Dom. de la ROMANÉE-CONTI★★★, THOMAS-MOILLARD★★. Best years: (2001) 00 99 98 97 96 95 93 **91** 90 **89 88**.

ROQUES, QUINTA DOS *Dão DOC, Beira Alta, Portugal* Now the DAO's finest producer, the wines of 2 estates with quite different characters are made here. Quinta dos Roques red★ is ripe and supple, while Quinta das Maias★ is a smoky, peppery red. The top wines are the dos Roques Reserva★★, made from old vines and aged in 100% new oak, and Touriga Nacional★★. Both estates also have a decent dry white, especially Roques Encruzado★. Best years: (2001) 00 97 **96**.

ROSA, QUINTA DE LA *Douro DOC and Port DOC, Douro, Portugal* The Bergqvist family have transformed this property into a small but serious producer of both PORT and DOURO★ (Reserva★★) table wines. The Vintage Port★★ is excellent, as is unfiltered LBV★★, while Finest Reserve and 10-year-old tawny★ are also good. A special selection vintage port, Vale do Inferno★★, was made in 1999 and shows a lovely old vine intensity. Best years: (Vintage) (2000) 97 96 95 94 92 **91**.

ROSÉ DE LOIRE AC *Loire Valley, France* Dry rosé from ANJOU, SAUMUR and TOURAINE. It can be a lovely drink, full of red berry fruits, but drink as young as possible and chill well. It's far superior to Rosé d'Anjou AC, which is usually sweetish, without much flavour. Best producers: l'Echalier, Haute-Perche, Ogereau, Passavant, RICHOU, Sauveroy.

ROSÉ DES RICEYS AC *Champagne, France* This is a curiosity and an expensive one at that. It's a still, dark pink wine made from Pinot Noir grapes in the southern part of the CHAMPAGNE region. Best producers: Alexandre Bonnet★, Devaux★, Guy de Forez, Morel.

ROSEMOUNT ESTATE *Hunter Valley, New South Wales, Australia* Winery buying and growing grapes in several regions to produce some of Australia's most popular wines, but appears to have taken a new and unfortunate direction recently with many wines seeming sweeter and flatter than before. Top are complex, weighty Roxburgh★★ and Show Reserve★ Chardonnays; blackcurranty COONAWARRA Cabernet★ and gutsy Balmoral Syrah★★. Rose label Chardonnay★★ from the Orange region can be very good, as is MCLAREN VALE Show Reserve Shiraz★★. Mountain Blue Shiraz-Cabernet★★ and Hill of Gold varietals★★ are the most exciting new wines to come out of MUDGEE for a long time and GSM★★ (Grenache, Syrah, Mourvèdre) is a knockout. The recent merger with Southcorp creates a high-quality giant. Let's hope the quality stays high, not too many old favourites get culled and prices don't get silly. Best years: (Balmoral Syrah) 1998 97 **96 94 92 91 90**.

ROSSO CÒNERO DOC *Marche, Italy* The best wines in this zone, on the Adriatic coast just south of Ancona, are made solely from Montepulciano, and have a wonderfully spicy richness. Best producers: Fazi Battaglia★, Garofoli★ (Grosso Agontano★★), Lanari★ (Fibbio★★),

Leopardi Dittajuti★, Malacari★, Mecella (Rubelliano★), Moroder★ (Dorico★★), Le Terrazze★ (Sassi Neri★★, Visions of J★★), Umani Ronchi★ (Cúmaro★★). Best years: (2001) 00 **99 98 97 95 90**.

ROSSO DI MONTALCINO DOC *Tuscany, Italy* The little brother of BRUNELLO DI MONTALCINO spends much less time aging in wood, so enabling the wines to retain a wonderful exuberance of flavour that Brunello may lose through its longer cask-aging. Best producers: Altesino★, ARGIANO★, Caparzo★, Casanova di Neri★★, Ciacci Piccolomini d'Aragona★★, Col d'Orcia★, Collemattoni★, COSTANTI★, Fuligni★, Gorelli-Due Portine★, M Lambardi★★, Lisini★, Siro Pacenti★★, Agostina Pieri★, Poggio Antico★, Il Poggione★, Poggio Salvi★, Salicutti★★, San Filippo-Fanti★, Talenti★, Valdicava★. Best years: (2001) 00 **99 98 97 96 95**.

ROSSO DI MONTEPULCIANO DOC *Tuscany, Italy* Some VINO NOBILE producers use this DOC in order to improve selection for the main wine; the best Rossos deliver delightfully plummy, chocolaty flavours. Best producers: La Braccesca★, Dei★, Del Cerro★, Fassati★, Nottola★, Palazzo Vecchio★, POLIZIANO★, Salcheto★, Valdipiatta★, Villa Sant'Anna★. Best years: (2001) **00 99 98 97**.

ROSSO PICENO DOC *Marche, Italy* This red is often considered a poor relative of ROSSO CONERO, since Sangiovese tends to be lean and harsh in the Marche. But when the full complement (40%) of Montepulciano is used, Rosso Piceno can be rich and seductive. Best producers: Boccadigabbia★ (Villamagna★★), Le Caniette★, Laurentina★, Saladini Pilastri★, Velenosi★. Best years: (2001) 00 **99 98 97 95 94 93 90**.

RENÉ ROSTAING *Côte-Rôtie AC, Rhône Valley, France* René Rostaing produces modern, rich, ripe wines marked by their deep colour and soft fruit flavours. With vines in some of the best sites in CÔTE-ROTIE, he produces 4 wines: classic Côte-Rôtie★★, la Viallère★★, Côte Blonde★★★ and la Landonne★★★. There's a very good CONDRIEU★★ too. Best years: (top crus) (2000) 99 98 97 96 **95 94 91 90 88 85**.

ROTHBURY ESTATE *Hunter Valley, New South Wales, Australia* Len Evans' brainchild (now owned by Fosters) has struggled to find its way in recent years. The premium Brokenback HUNTER VALLEY range (Shiraz★, Semillon★, Chardonnay) has led a new quality charge. Hunter Valley Semillon★ is legendary; the Verdelho has life and zest; also inexpensive varietals from MUDGEE and COWRA (Chardonnay★).

GEORGES ROUMIER *Chambolle-Musigny AC, Côte de Nuits, Burgundy, France* Christophe Roumier has long been recognized as one of Burgundy's top winemakers, devoting as much attention to his vineyards as to cellar technique, believing in severe pruning, low yields and stringent grape selection. Roumier never uses more than one-third new oak. His best wine is often BONNES-MARES★★★, but his other Grands Crus include MUSIGNY★★★, Ruchottes-Chambertin★★ and CORTON-CHARLEMAGNE★★. The best value are usually the village Chambolle★★ and an exclusively owned Premier Cru in MOREY-ST-DENIS, Clos de la Bussière★★. Best years: (reds) (2001) 00 99 98 97 96 95 **93 90 89 88**.

ROUSSANNE The RHONE VALLEY's best white grape variety, frequently blended with Marsanne. Roussanne is the more aromatic and elegant of the two, less prone to oxidation and with better acidity, but growers usually prefer Marsanne due to its higher yields. Now being planted in the MIDI. There are some examples in Australia and, while much of the Roussanne planted in California has been identified as Viognier, there are a few true plantings that produce fascinating wines.

ARMAND ROUSSEAU *Gevrey-Chambertin AC, Côte de Nuits, Burgundy, France* One of the most highly respected and important CHAMBERTIN estates, with vineyards in Clos-de-Bèze★★★, Mazis-Chambertin★★ and Charmes-Chambertin★★ as well as CLOS DE LA ROCHE★★★ in MOREY-ST-DENIS and GEVREY-CHAMBERTIN Clos St-Jacques★★★. The outstandingly harmonious, elegant, yet rich wines are made in a traditional style and enjoy an enviable reputation for longevity. The Chambertin★★★ is exceptionally fine. Charles Rousseau has been at the helm since 1957, though recent vintages have been slightly inconsistent. Best years: (2001) 00 99 98 96 93 **91 90 89 88 85**.

ROUSSILLON *France* The snow-covered peaks of the Pyrenees form a spectacular backdrop to the ancient region of Roussillon, now the Pyrénées-Orientales *département*. The vineyards produce a wide range of fairly priced wines, mainly red, ranging from the ripe, raisin-rich *vins doux naturels* to light, fruity-fresh vins de pays, and there are now some really exciting table wines, both white and red, being made in Roussillon, especially by individual estates. See also Banyuls, Collioure, Côtes du Roussillon, Côtes du Roussillon-Villages, Maury, Muscat de Rivesaltes, Rivesaltes.

RUCHOTTES-CHAMBERTIN AC See Chambertin AC.

RÜDESHEIM *Rheingau, Germany* Village producing silky, aromatic wines from some famous sites (Berg Schlossberg, Berg Rottland, Berg Roseneck and Bischofsberg). Not to be confused with the NAHE village of the same name. During the 1990s a group of young winemakers dramatically improved standards here. Best producers: Georg BREUER★★, Johannishof★, Josef LEITZ★★. Best years: (Riesling Spätlese) (2001) 00 99 98 **97** 96 **94 93 90**.

RUEDA DO *Castilla y León, Spain* The RIOJA firm of MARQUES DE RISCAL launched the reputation of this white-wine-only region in the 1970s, first by rescuing the almost extinct local grape, Verdejo, then by introducing Sauvignon Blanc. Fresh young whites have been joined by barrel-fermented wines aiming for a longer life, particularly those made at Castilla La Vieja and Belondrade y Lurton. Best producers: Alvarez y Diez★, Antaño (Viña Mocén★), Belondrade y Lurton, Cerrosol (Doña Beatriz), Hermanos Lurton★, MARQUES DE RISCAL★, Bodegas de Crianza Castilla La Vieja (Palacio de Bornos Vendimia Seleccionada★★), Javier Sanz Cantalapiedra★, Viñedos de Nieva★, Viños Sanz, Angel Rodríguez Vidal (Martinsancho★).

RUFFINO *Tuscany, Italy* Huge, long-established winemaking concern recently divided between two sides of the Folonari family. Brothers Marco and Paolo continue to produce CHIANTI CLASSICO from Santedame★ and the classic Riserva Ducale Oro★★. SUPER-TUSCANS include promising new Chardonnay, La Solatia★; new Sangiovese-Cabernet-Merlot blend Modus★; Pinot Noir Nero del Tondo★; and the unique blend of Colorino and Sangiovese, Romitorio di Santedame★★★. The Ruffino operation also includes VINO NOBILE estate Lodola Nuova, BRUNELLO Il Greppone Mazzi and now Borgo Conventi in COLLIO. The newly created Tenute Ambrogio & Giovanni Folonari includes the Cabreo (Sangiovese-Cabernet Il Borgo★, Chardonnay La Pietra★) and Nozzole (powerful, long-lived Cabernet Il Pareto★★) properties in Chianti Classico, but also extends to Vino Nobile estate Gracciano-Svetoni, newly established BOLGHERI estate Campo del Mare and, since 2001, Brunello producer La Fuga.

RUINART *Champagne AC, Champagne, France* This is one of the oldest CHAMPAGNE houses. Ruinart has a surprisingly low profile, given the quality of its wines. The non-vintage★★ is very good, as is the new Blanc de Blancs non-vintage★★, but the top wines here are the classy Dom Ruinart Blanc de Blancs★★★ and the Dom Ruinart Rosé★★★. Best years: (1996) **95 93 92 90 88 86 85 83 82**.

RULLY AC *Côte Chalonnaise, Burgundy, France* One of Burgundy's most improved ACs with good-quality, reasonably priced wine. Once famous for sparkling wines, it is now best known for its still whites, often oak-aged. Reds are light, with a fleeting strawberry and cherry perfume. Best producers: (whites) Allaines★, J-C Brelière★, DROUHIN★, Dureuil-Janthial★, Duvernay, FAIVELEY★, V GIRARDIN★, JADOT★, JAFFELIN★, Olivier LEFLAIVE★, RODET★★, Villaine★; (reds) A Delorme, Dureuil-Janthial★, Duvernay, la Folie, H & P Jacqueson★. Best years: (whites) (2001) 00 **99**; (reds) (2001) 00 **99**.

RUSSIAN RIVER VALLEY AVA *Sonoma County, California, USA* Beginning south of Healdsburg along the Russian River as it flows south-west, this valley cools as it meanders toward the Pacific. It is now challenging CARNEROS as the top spot for Pinot Noir and Chardonnay. Best producers: Davis Bynum★, DEHLINGER★★★, De Loach★, Dutton-Goldfield★, Gary Farrell★★, IRON HORSE★★, ROCHIOLI★★, SONOMA-CUTRER★, Rodney Strong★, Joseph SWAN★, Marimar TORRES★, WILLIAMS SELYEM★★. Best years: (Pinot Noir) (2001) (00) 99 **97 95 94 93 92 91 90**.

RUSTENBERG *Stellenbosch WO, South Africa* Local youngster Adi Badenhorst, with experience in California and Bordeaux, heads up the new cellar, a beautiful renovation in the old dairy. The vineyards too are being overhauled: a massive 53ha (130 acres) were planted with Rustenberg's imported vines in 2001. Majestic Peter Barlow Cabernet★★, BORDEAUX-style blend John X Merriman★★, and the new-look, classically styled single-vineyard Five Soldiers★ (Chardonnay), put this producer in the premier league. The Brampton range represents good value. Best years: (Peter Barlow) **1999 98 97 96**; (Five Soldiers) **2000 99 98 97**.

RUST EN VREDE *Stellenbosch WO, South Africa* The youthful team, headed by Jean Engelbrecht, is giving this red-only property a new lease of life. Young, virus-free vines are doing likewise in the vineyards and contributing to fresher fruit and suppler tannins. Shiraz★ and Rust en Vrede★, a Cabernet-based blend designed to show off the *terroir*, are stars, but Merlot and Cabernet are catching up fast. Best years: (Rust en Vrede estate wine) **1998 97 96 95 94 92**.

RUTHERFORD AVA *Napa Valley, California, USA* This viticultural area in mid-NAPA VALLEY has inspired hours of argument over whether it has a distinct identity. The heart of the area, the Rutherford Bench, does seem to be a prime Cabernet Sauvignon zone, and many traditional old Napa Cabernets have come from here and exhibit the 'Rutherford Dust' flavour. Best producers: BEAULIEU★★, Cakebread, FLORA SPRINGS★★, Freemark Abbey, NIEBAUM-COPPOLA★★, Staglin★★. Best years: (Cabernet) (2000) 99 97 96 **95 94 93 92 91 90 87 86**.

RUTHERGLEN *Victoria, Australia* This region in north-east VICTORIA is the home of heroic reds from Shiraz, Cabernet and Durif, and luscious world-beating fortifieds from Muscat and Tokay (Muscadelle). Good sherry-style and vintage port-style wines. Also home of Giaconda, maker of already legendary Chardonnay★★. Best producers: (fortified) ALL SAINTS★★, Buller's★, Campbells★★, CHAMBERS★★, MORRIS★★, Stanton & Killeen★★.

SAALE-UNSTRUT *Germany*   Located in the former East Germany, Saale-Unstrut's vineyards have been extensively replanted since reunification in 1989, but these vineyards must mature before first-class wines can be produced. Weissburgunder (Pinot Blanc) is the most important quality grape, with 11% of total vineyard area. Best producer: Lützkendorf★.

SACHSEN *Germany*   Until recently one of Europe's forgotten wine regions on the river Elbe in former East Germany. Now beginning to produce some good wines, the best being dry Riesling, Gewürztraminer, Weissburgunder (Pinot Blanc) and Grauburgunder (Pinot Gris) with surprisingly generous alcoholic content. Best producers: Schloss Proschwitz★, Schloss Wackerbarth★, Klaus Zimmerling★.

ST-AMOUR AC *Beaujolais, Burgundy, France*   The northernmost BEAUJOLAIS Cru, producing juicy, soft-fruited wine which lasts well for 2–3 years. Best producers: Billards/Loron★, DUBOEUF★ (des Sablons★), H Fessy (Mongenie★), J Patissier★, J-G Revillon★, M Tête★. Best years: (2001) **00 99**.

ST ANTONY *Nierstein, Rheinhessen, Germany*   Dr Alex Michalsky runs one of RHEINHESSEN's finest estates, making dry and off-dry Rieslings (frequently ★★) with unusual power and richness from the top sites of NIERSTEIN. Occasional sweet Auslese and higher Prädikat wines are always expansive and luscious. All wines except the regular dry Riesling★ have at least 5 years' aging potential. Best years: (Riesling Spätlese trocken) (2001) 00 99 98 **97 96 94 93 92 90 89**.

ST-AUBIN AC *Côte de Beaune, Burgundy, France*   Some of Burgundy's best-value wines. Good reds, especially from Premiers Crus like les Frionnes and les Murgers des Dents de Chien. Also reasonably priced, oak-aged white wines. Best producers: Bernard Bachelet, D & F Clair★★, M Colin★★, DROUHIN★, JADOT★, Lamy-Pillot★, Larue★★, Olivier LEFLAIVE★, B Morey★, H Prudhon★, RAMONET★★, Roux★, G Thomas★. Best years: (reds) (2001) 99 **98 97 96**; (whites) (2001) 00 **99 97**.

ST-CHINIAN AC *Languedoc, France*   Large AC for strong, spicy red wines with more personality and fruit than run-of-the-mill HERAULT. Best producers: Berloup co-op, Borie la Vitarèle★, CANET-VALETTE★★, Cazal-Viel★, CLOS BAGATELLE, Combebelle, Jougla★, la Madura, Mas Champart★, Maurel Fonsalade★, Moulin de Ciffre, Navarre, Rimbert★, Roquebrun co-op, St-Chinian co-op. Best years: 2001 00 99 **98 96 95 94 93**.

ST-DÉSIRAT, CAVE DE *St-Joseph, Rhône Valley, France*   St-Désirat is one of the best co-ops in the RHONE VALLEY. The intense, smoky red St-Joseph★ is a fantastic bargain, as are local vins de pays.

ST-ÉMILION AC *Bordeaux, France*   The scenic Roman hill town of St-Émilion is the centre of Bordeaux's most historic wine region. The finest vineyards are on the plateau and *côtes*, or steep slopes, around the town, although an area to the west, called the *graves*, contains 2 famous properties, CHEVAL BLANC and FIGEAC. It is a region of smallholdings, with over 1000 properties, and consequently the co-operative plays an important part. The dominant early-ripening Merlot grape gives wines with a 'come hither' softness and sweetness

241

rare in red Bordeaux. St-Émilion AC is the basic generic AC, with 4 'satellites' (LUSSAC, MONTAGNE, PUISSEGUIN, ST-GEORGES) allowed to annex their name to it. The best producers, including the Classed Growths, are found in the more tightly controlled ST-EMILION GRAND CRU AC category. Best years: 2000 **98 96 95 94 90 89 88 86 85**.

ST-ÉMILION GRAND CRU AC *Bordeaux, France* St-Émilion's top-quality AC, which includes the estates classified as Grand Cru Classé and Premier Grand Cru Classé. The 1996 Classification lists 55 Grands Crus Classés. It also includes most of the new wave of limited edition *vins de garage*. Best producers: (Grands Crus Classés) l'ARROSEE★★, Balestard-la-Tonnelle★, CANON-LA-GAFFELIERE★★, Clos de l'Oratoire★, la Clotte★, la Dominique★★, Grand Mayne★★, Grand Pontet★, Larmande★, Pavie-Decesse★, PAVIE-MACQUIN★★, Soutard★, la Tour Figeac★, TROPLONG-MONDOT★★; (others) Faugères★, Fleur Cardinale★, Fombrauge★, la Gomerie★, Gracia★, MONBOUSQUET★★, La Mondotte★★, Moulin St-Georges★★, Quinault l'Enclos★, Rol Valentin★★, TERTRE-ROTEBOEUF★★, Teyssier, VALANDRAUD★★. Best years: 2000 99 98 96 **95 94 90 89 88 86 85**. See also St-Émilion Premier Grand Cru Classé.

ST-ÉMILION PREMIER GRAND CRU CLASSÉ *Bordeaux, France* The St-Émilion élite level, divided into 2 categories – 'A' and 'B' – with only the much more expensive CHEVAL BLANC and AUSONE in category 'A'. There are 11 'B' châteaux, with ANGELUS and BEAU-SEJOUR BECOT added in the 1996 Classification. Best producers: ANGELUS★★★, AUSONE★★★, BEAU-SEJOUR BECOT★★, Beauséjour★★, BELAIR★, CANON★, CHEVAL BLANC★★★, Clos Fourtet★, FIGEAC★★, la Gaffelière★, MAGDELAINE★★, PAVIE★★. Best years: 2000 99 98 96 95 **94 90 89 88 86 85 83 82**.

ST-ESTÈPHE AC *Haut-Médoc, Bordeaux, France* Large AC north of PAUILLAC with 5 Classed Growths. St-Estèphe wines have high tannin levels, but less weight. They are drinkable at 2–3 years, but given time (10–20 years) those sought-after flavours of blackcurrant and cedarwood do peek out. More Merlot has been planted to soften the wines. Best producers: CALON-SEGUR★★, COS D'ESTOURNEL★★, Cos Labory★, HAUT-MARBUZET★, LAFON-ROCHET★, Lilian-Ladouys★, Marbuzet★, MEYNEY★, MONTROSE★★, les Ormes-de-Pez★, PEZ★, Phélan Ségur★. Best years: 2000 96 **95 94 90 89 88 86 85 83 82**.

DOM. ST-GAYAN *Gigondas AC, Rhône Valley, France* The Meffre family have substantial holdings of vines in GIGONDAS and the COTES DU RHONE. Old-vine fruit lends power to the Gigondas★ (★★ in top years), but the extensive period of barrel-aging really only suits the ripest vintages. Côtes du Rhône (red and white) and Côtes du Rhône-Villages RASTEAU are usually good value. Best years: (Gigondas): 1998 97 96 95 **93 91 90**.

ST-GEORGES-ST-ÉMILION AC *Bordeaux, France* The best satellite of ST-EMILION, with lovely, soft wines that can nevertheless age for 6–10 years. Best producers: Calon, Griffe de Cap d'Or, Macquin St-Georges★, St-André Corbin, Ch. St-Georges★, Tour-du-Pas-St-Georges★, Vieux-Montaiguillon. Best years: 2000 98 **96 95 94 90 89 88 85**.

ST HALLETT *Barossa Valley, South Australia* Change is afoot at the home of the venerable Old Block Shiraz★★ and its Shiraz siblings Blackwell★ and Faith★. Following a merger with MCLAREN VALE's Tatachilla, then a joint takeover of ADELAIDE HILLS' Hillstowe, all 3 wineries have been snapped up by brewer Lion Nathan (as has PETALUMA). Let's hope the wines, including the bargain Gamekeeper's Reserve★ red, Poacher's Blend★ white, EDEN VALLEY Riesling★ and The Reward Cabernet★★, don't suffer. Best years: (Old Block) (1999) 98 **96 94 93 91 90**.

ST-JOSEPH AC *Rhône Valley, France* Large, mainly red AC, on the opposite bank of the Rhône to HERMITAGE. Made from Syrah, the reds have mouthfilling fruit with irresistible blackcurrant richness. Brilliant at 1–2 years, they can last for up to 8. Only a little white is made and, with up-to-date winemaking, these are usually pleasant, flowery wines to drink young, although an increasing number can age. Best producers: (reds) CHAPOUTIER★, J-L CHAVE★★, Chêne★★, L Chèze★, COLOMBO★, Courbis★, COURSODON★★, CUILLERON★★, DELAS★★, E & J Durand★, Florentin★, P Gaillard★★, GRAILLOT★★, B Gripa★★, J-L Grippat★★, JABOULET★, Monteillet★★, Paret★★, A Perret★, P Pichon★, ST-DÉSIRAT co-op★, TAIN L'HERMITAGE co-op★, Tardieu-Laurent★★, Tunnel★, F Villard★★; (whites) Chêne★★, L Chèze★, Courbis★, CUILLERON★★, DELAS★, E & J Durand★, Ferraton★, Florentin★, P Gaillard★★, B Gripa★, J-L Grippat★, JABOULET★, Monteillet★, A Perret★, Trollat★, Villard★★. Best years: (reds) (2001) 00 99 98 **97 96 95** 94; (whites) (2001) 00 **99 98 97 96 95**.

ST-JULIEN AC *Haut-Médoc, Bordeaux, France* For many, St-Julien produces perfect claret, with an ideal balance between opulence and austerity and between the brashness of youth and the genius of maturity. It is the smallest of the HAUT-MÉDOC ACs but almost all is first-rate vineyard land and quality is high. Best producers: BEYCHEVELLE★, BRANAIRE★★, DUCRU-BEAUCAILLOU★★, GLORIA★★, GRUAUD-LAROSE★★, LAGRANGE★★, LANGOA-BARTON★★, LEOVILLE-BARTON★★★, LEOVILLE-LAS-CASES★★★, LEOVILLE-POYFERRE★★, ST-PIERRE★★, TALBOT★. Best years: 2000 99 98 97 96 95 **94 90 89 88 86 85 83 82**.

ST-NICOLAS-DE-BOURGUEIL AC *Loire Valley, France* An enclave of just under 500ha (1250 acres) within the larger BOURGUEIL AC. Almost all the wine is red and with the same piercing red fruit flavours of Bourgueil, and much better after 7–10 years, especially in warm vintages. Best producers: M Cognard★, P Jamet★, F Mabileau★, J-C Mabileau★, Taluau & Foltzenlogel★, Vallée★. Best years: (2001) 00 99 **97 96 95 90 89 85**.

ST-PÉRAY AC *Rhône Valley, France* Rather hefty, Champagne-method fizz from Marsanne and Roussanne grapes. Still white is usually dry and stolid. Best producers: Biguet★, CLAPE★, COLOMBO (La Belle de Mai★), DELAS, Fauterie★, B Gripa, J Lemenicier★, LIONNET★, J-L Thiers★, A Voge★. Best years: (2001) 00 99 **98 97 96 95**.

CH. ST-PIERRE★★ *St-Julien AC, 4ème Cru Classé, Haut-Médoc, Bordeaux, France* Small ST-JULIEN property making wines that have become a byword for ripe, lush fruit wrapped round with the spice of new oak. Drinkable early, but top vintages can improve for 20 years. Best years: 2000 99 98 97 96 95 **94 90 89 88 86 83 82**.

ST-ROMAIN AC *Côte de Beaune, Burgundy, France* Out-of-the-way village producing red wines with a firm, bittersweet cherrystone fruit and flinty-dry whites varying between austerely acid and quirkily old-style. Usually good value by Burgundian standards, but take a few years to open out. Best producers: (whites) Allaines★, Bazenet★, H & G Buisson, Chassouney★★, A Gras★★, JAFFELIN★, O LEFLAIVE★, P Taupenot, VERGET★★; (reds) A Gras★. Best years: (whites) (2000) 99 **97 96 95**; (reds) 1999 98 **97 96 95**.

ST-VÉRAN AC *Mâconnais, Burgundy, France* Often thought of as a POUILLY-FUISSÉ understudy. This is gentle, fairly fruity, normally unoaked Mâconnais Chardonnay at its best, and the overall quality is good. The price is fair, too. Best to drink young. Best producers: D & M Barraud★, G Chagny, Corsin★★, Deux Roches★, B & J-M Drouin★,

DUBOEUF★, G Guérin★, Lassarat★, Saumaize-Michelin★, J C Thévenet★★, J-L Tissier★, VERGET★, J-J Vincent★. Best years: (2001) 00 **99**.

STE-CROIX-DU-MONT AC *Bordeaux, France* Best of the 3 sweet wine ♀ ACs that gaze jealously at SAUTERNES and BARSAC across the Garonne river (the others are CADILLAC and LOUPIAC). The wine is mildly sweet rather than splendidly rich. Top wines can age for at least a decade. Best producers: Crabitan-Bellevue, Loubens★, Lousteau-Vieil, Mailles, Mont, Pavillon★, la Rame★. Best years: (2001) 99 98 **97 96 95 90 89 88**.

SAINTSBURY *Carneros AVA, California, USA* New-wave, deeply 🍷 committed winery using only CARNEROS fruit. Its Pinot Noirs★★ are brilliant examples of the perfume and fruit quality of Carneros; the Reserve★★★ and the exquisite Brown Ranch★★★ are deeper and oakier, while Garnet★ is a delicious, lighter style. Chardonnay★★ and Reserve Chardonnay★★ are also impressive, best after 2–3 years. Best years: (Pinot Noir Reserve) (2000) 99 98 **97 96 95 94 92 91**.

SALA, CASTELLO DELLA *Orvieto DOC, Umbria, Italy* Belongs to the ♀ ANTINORI family, making good ORVIETO★ and outstanding oak-aged Cervaro della Sala★★★ (Chardonnay and a little Grechetto). Also impressive Pinot Nero★ and sweet Muffato della Sala★★.

SALAPARUTA, DUCA DI *Sicily, Italy* Corvo is the brand name for Sicilian 🍷 wines made by this firm. Red and white Corvo are pretty basic, but there are superior whites, Colomba Platino★ and Bianca di Valguarnera★, and 2 fine reds, Terre d'Agala★ and Duca Enrico★★.

SALICE SALENTINO DOC *Puglia, Italy* One of the better DOCs in the 🍷 Salento peninsula, turning out wines (made with Negroamaro and tempered with a dash of perfumed Malvasia Nera) that are ripe and chocolaty, acquiring hints of roast chestnuts and prunes with age. Drink after 3–4 years, although they may last as long again. The DOCs of Alezio, Brindisi, Copertino, Leverano and Squinzano have similar Rosso and Rosato. Best producers: Candido★, Casale Bevagna★, Leone De Castris★, Due Palme★, Taurino★, Vallone★, Conti Zecca. Best years: (reds) (2001) 00 99 **98 97 96 95**.

SALITAGE *Pemberton, Western Australia* An original partner with his ♀ brother Denis in MARGARET RIVER'S LEEUWIN ESTATE, John Horgan established PEMBERTON's first and largest winery in 1989. The wines are good, sometimes excellent. There's a no-holds-barred barrel-fermented Chardonnay★★, an Unwooded Chardonnay★, Pinot Noir★ and Cabernet Blend★★ (Cabernet Sauvignon, Cabernet Franc, Merlot and Petit Verdot). A second label, Treehouse, produces good Chardonnay-Verdelho. Top reds will age for 3–7 years.

SAMOS *Greece* The island of Samos was granted an appellation in 1982, ♀ but its reputation for producing rich, sweet dessert wines from the Muscat grape stretches back centuries. The 2 wineries of the Samos co-op make similar Muscat-based wines. Pale green Samena dry white is made from early-picked Muscat; deep gold, honeyed Samos Nectar★★ is made from sun-dried grapes; the rarer version, Palaio, is aged for up to 20 years and very apricotty in nature; and seductively complex Samos Anthemis★ is fortified and cask-aged for up to 5 years.

SANCERRE AC *Loire Valley, France* Sancerre mania broke out in the 🍷 1970s, first with the white wine which can provide the perfect expression of the bright green tang of the Sauvignon grape, then with the reds and rosés, which are made from Pinot Noir. The whites, from a good grower in one of the best villages like Bué, Chavignol, Verdigny or Ménétréol in the chalky land around the hill town of

Sancerre, can be deliciously refreshing; so too can the rare Pinot Noir rosé. Reds are now being taken more seriously, but still really need fine, dry years to show best. The wines are now more consistent than those of neighbouring POUILLY. **Best producers:** F & J Bailly★, Balland-Chapuis★, H

Bourgeois★★, R Champault★, F Cotat★★, L CROCHET★★, Delaporte★, Gitton★, P Jolivet★, A MELLOT★, J Mellot★, P Millérioux★, H Natter★, A & F Neveu★, R Neveu★, V Pinard★, H Reverdy★, P & N Reverdy★, Reverdy-Cadet★, J-M Roger★, Vacheron★★, André Vatan★, Edmond Vatan★. **Best years:** 2000 **99 98 97 96 95 90**.

SANDEMAN *Port DOC, Douro, Portugal and Jerez y Manzanilla DO, Spain* No longer one of the leading PORT houses, but there are definite signs of improvement. Best are the aged tawnies, Imperial Aged Reserve Tawny★ and 20-year-old★★, and the single-quinta Vau★★, while Signature★ is a good premium ruby style. Terraços do Douro is a new label for red and white DOURO. Recently purchased by SOGRAPE.

LUCIANO SANDRONE *Barolo DOCG, Piedmont, Italy* Luciano Sandrone has become one of PIEDMONT's leading wine stylists, renowned for his BAROLO Cannubi Boschis★★★ and Le Vigne★★★, as well as BARBERA D'ALBA★★ and Dolcetto d'Alba★★, which rank with the best.

SANFORD *Santa Rita Hills AVA, California, USA* Richard Sanford planted the great Benedict vineyard in the Santa Ynez Valley in 1971, thus establishing Santa Ynez and SANTA BARBARA as potentially top-quality vineyard regions. Sanford now makes sharply focused, dark-fruited Pinot Noir★★, Chardonnay★★ and Sauvignon Blanc★. A new series of 'Signature' Barrel Select Pinot Noir★★ is especially impressive. **Best years:** (Pinot Noir) (1999) 98 **97 96 95 94 92 91**.

SANGIOVESE Sangiovese rivals Trebbiano as the most widely planted grape variety in Italy, but it reaches its greatest heights in central TUSCANY. This grape has produced a wide variety of clones that make generalization difficult. Much care is being taken in the current wave of replanting, whether in CHIANTI CLASSICO, BRUNELLO DI MONTALCINO or VINO NOBILE DI MONTEPULCIANO. Styles range from pale, lively and cherryish, through the vivacious, mid-range Chiantis, to excellent top Riservas and SUPER-TUSCANS. A number of fine examples are also produced in ROMAGNA. CALIFORNIA producers like ATLAS PEAK, SHAFER, Robert Pepi and SEGHESIO are now working some of their magic on this grape. Australia is taking a keen interest, with good examples from King Valley in VICTORIA (Gary Crittenden, Pizzini) and MCLAREN VALE (Coriole). Some interesting examples are also grown in Argentina and the grape is starting to appear in South African vineyards.

SAN LUIS OBISPO COUNTY *California, USA* CENTRAL COAST county best known for Chardonnay, Pinot Noir, a bit of old-vine Zinfandel and Cabernet Sauvignon. There are 5 AVAs – Edna Valley, PASO ROBLES, SANTA MARIA VALLEY (shared with SANTA BARBARA COUNTY), Arroyo Grande Valley and York Mountain – each of which has already grown some outstanding grapes and will surely grow a lot more. **Best producers:** Clairborne & Churchill★, Creston Vineyards★, Eberle★, Edna Valley★★, Justin★★, J Lohr (Hilltop Cabernet Sauvignon★★), Meridian★★,

Norman★, Sausalito Canyon★, Savannah-Chanel★, Serin Peaks★★, Talley★★, Wild Horse★. Best years: (reds) (2000) 99 **98 97 95 94 92**.

SAN PEDRO *Curicó, Chile* A takeover by Chile's biggest brewer, along with Jacques Lurton as consultant since 1994, turned the fortunes of San Pedro around, leading to another 1000ha (2470 acres) of planting and new facilities. A recent joint venture with Ch. d'Assault of Bordeaux will produce a couple of red wines in a new vineyard in the foothills of the Andes in the RAPEL valley. Crisp, clean 35 Sur Sauvignon Blanc, Reserva Chardonnay★, and Cabernet and Merlot★ in the Castillo de Molina range are best, though basic Gato and 35 Sur reds aren't bad, either.

SANTA BARBARA COUNTY *California, USA* CENTRAL COAST county, north-west of Los Angeles, known for Chardonnay, Riesling, Pinot Noir and Syrah. The main AVAs are Santa Ynez Valley and most of SANTA MARIA VALLEY (the remainder is in SAN LUIS OBISPO COUNTY), both leading areas for Pinot Noir. Best producers: AU BON CLIMAT★★, Babcock★, BYRON★★, CAMBRIA★, Foxen★★, Gainey★, Hitching Post★★, Longona★, Andrew MURRAY★★, Fess Parker★, QUPE★★, SANFORD★★, Whitcraft★★, Zaca Mesa★. Best years: (Pinot Noir) (2000) 99 98 **97 95 94 92**.

SANTA CAROLINA *Maipo, Chile* Long-established winery that is at last catching up with the modern world. You'll find fresh Reserva whites★ with good fruit definition, including an excellent sweet Semillon-Sauvignon★★ from Lontué, and substantial, ripe, if oaky, Barrica Selection reds★.

SANTA CRUZ MOUNTAINS AVA *California, USA* A sub-region of the CENTRAL COAST AVA. Long-lived Chardonnays and Cabernet Sauvignons are the most notable wines; the most famous is the stunning Montebello Cabernet from RIDGE. Small amounts of robust Pinot Noir are also produced here. Best producers: BONNY DOON★★, David Bruce★★, Kathryn Kennedy★★, Mount Eden Vineyards★★, RIDGE★★★, Santa Cruz Mountain Vineyard★.

SANTA INÉS/DE MARTINO *Maipo, Chile* Owned by the de Martino family, who came to Chile from Italy more than 60 years ago. The Reserva de Familia de Martino Cabernet Sauvignon★ leads the reds together with a sweet, soft Reserva de Familia Carmenère★ and good-value Cabernet Sauvignon Legado de Armida★. Also a crisp Santa Inés Sauvignon Blanc and warm, floral de Martino Viognier★ from Marchihue.

SANTA MADDALENA *Alto Adige DOC, Italy* Light, delicate wine from the Schiava grape grown in the hills above Bolzano. It has a perfume of black cherries, cream and bacon smoke, and can be improved with the addition of up to 10% of Lagrein. Drink young, but some vintages will age. Best producers: Egger-Ramer★, Franz Gojer★, LAGEDER★, Josephus Mayr★, Josef Niedermayr★, Plattner Waldgries★, Hans Rottensteiner★, Heinrich Rottensteiner★, Santa Maddalena co-op★.

SANTA MARIA VALLEY AVA *Santa Barbara County and San Luis Obispo County, California, USA* Cool Santa Maria Valley is coming on strong as a producer of Chardonnay, Pinot Noir and Syrah. Look for wines made from grapes grown in Bien Nacido vineyards by several small wineries. Best producers: AU BON CLIMAT★★, BYRON★★, CAMBRIA★, Camelot (KENDALL-JACKSON)★, Foxen★★, Lane Tanner (Pinot Noir★★), Longona★, QUPE★★.

SANTA RITA *Maipo, Chile* Long-established MAIPO giant, now revitalized under winemaker Andrés Ilabaca. Plummy new red blends such as Triple C★★ (Cabernet Franc, Cabernet Sauvignon, Carmenère) and

Syrah-Cabernet Sauvignon-Carmenère★ show real flair, and a trio of red blends in the Floresta★★ range are exciting and packed with flavour. Top-of-the-range Cabernet Sauvignon Casa Real★ is not quite back on form yet.

SANTENAY AC *Côte de Beaune, Burgundy, France* Red Santenay wines often promise good ripe flavour, though they don't always deliver it, but are worth aging for 4–6 years in the hope that the wine will open out. Many of the best wines, both red and white, come from les Gravières Premier Cru on the border with CHASSAGNE-MONTRACHET. Best producers: (reds) R Belland★★, D & F Clair★, M Colin★, J Girardin★, V GIRARDIN★★, Monnot★, B Morey★★, L Muzard★★, Prieur-Brunet, Roux Père et Fils★; (whites) V GIRARDIN★, JAFFELIN, René Lequin-Colin★. Best years: (reds) (2001) 99 98 **97 96 95**; (whites) (2001) 00 **99 97 96**.

CASA SANTOS LIMA *Alenquer DOC, Estremadura, Portugal* A beautiful estate with an expanding range. Espiga reds and whites are light, fruity and tasty, but for more character look to the spicy red★★ and creamy, perfumed white Palha-Canas, or to red and white Quinta das Setencostas★. New reds sold under the Casa Santos Lima label include Touriz★ (from DOURO varieties) and varietal Touriga Nacional★, Touriga Francesa★, Trincadeira★ and Tinta Roriz★. Also a promising peachy, herby Chardonnay★. Best years: (2001) **00 98 97**.

SÃO JOÃO, CAVES *Beira Litoral, Portugal* A traditional-seeming but discreetly modernist company. It was a pioneer of cool-fermented, white BAIRRADA, and has made some very good Cabernet Sauvignons from its own vines. Rich, complex reds include outstanding Reserva★★ and Frei João★ from Bairrada and Porta dos Cavalheiros★★ from DAO – they demand at least 10 years' age to show their quality.

SARDINIA *Italy* Grapes of Spanish origin, like the white Vermentino and Torbato and the red Monica, Cannonau and Carignano, dominate production on this huge, hilly Mediterranean island, but they vie with a Malvasia of Greek origin and natives like Nuragus and Vernaccia. The cooler northern part favours whites, especially Vermentino, while the southern and eastern parts are best suited to reds from Cannonau and Monica. The wines used to be powerful, alcoholic monsters, but the current trend is for a lighter, modern, more international style. Foremost among those in pursuit of quality are ARGIOLAS, SELLA & MOSCA and the Santadi co-op. See also Carignano del Sulcis, Vernaccia di Oristano.

SASSICAIA DOC★★★ *Tuscany, Italy* This Cabernet Sauvignon-Cabernet Franc blend from the coast has done more than any other wine to gain credibility abroad for Italy. Vines were planted in 1944 to satisfy the Marchese Incisa della Rocchetta's thirst for fine red Bordeaux, which was in short supply during the war. The wine remained purely for family consumption until nephew Piero Antinori (of ANTINORI) and winemaker Giacomo Tachis persuaded the Marchese to refine production practices and to release several thousand bottles from the 1968 vintage. Since then, Sassicaia's fame has increased as it proved itself, with a few weak vintage exceptions, to be one of the world's great Cabernets, combining a blackcurrant power of blistering intensity with a heavenly scent of cigars. It is the first Italian single-owner estate wine to have its own DOC, within the BOLGHERI appellation, from the 1995 vintage. Best years: (1999) 98 97 95 **90 88 85** 84 83 82 81 78 75 71 68.

HORST SAUER *Escherndorf, Franken, Germany* His wines from the late 1990s shot the ebullient and energetic Horst Sauer to stardom. Top of the range are his dry Rieslings★★ and Silvaners★, which are unusually juicy and fresh for a region renowned for blunt, earthy wines. His late-harvest wines are unchallenged in the region and sometimes ★★★; they will easily live a decade, sometimes much more. Best years: (Riesling, Silvaner) (2001) 00 **99 98 97**.

SAUMUR AC *Loire Valley, France* Improving dry white wines, made mainly from Chenin Blanc, but up to 20% Chardonnay can be added. The reds are lighter than those of SAUMUR-CHAMPIGNY. Also dry to off-dry Cabernet rosé, and sweet Coteaux de Saumur in good years. Best producers: Clos Rougeard★★, FILLIATREAU★, Hureau★★, Langlois-Château★, R-N Legrand★, Nerleux★, la Paleine★ la Perruche★, la Renière★, Retiveau-Rétif★, Roches Neuves★, St-Just★, P Vatan★★, VILLENEUVE★★. Best years: (whites) (2001) **00 99 97 96 95 90**.

SAUMUR-CHAMPIGNY AC *Loire Valley, France* Saumur's best red wine. Cabernet Franc is the main grape, and in hot years the wine can be superb, with a piercing scent of blackcurrants and raspberries easily overpowering the earthy finish. Delicious young, it can age for 6–10 years. Best producers: Clos Rougeard★★, Clos des Cordeliers★, Drouineau★, FILLIATREAU★, des Galmoises★, Hureau★, R-N Legrand★, Retiveau-Rétif★, Roches Neuves★★, St-Just★, de Targé★, P Vadé★, VILLENEUVE★★. Best years: (2001) **00 99 97 96 95 90**.

SAUMUR MOUSSEUX AC *Loire Valley, France* Reasonable Champagne-method sparkling wines made mainly from Chenin Blanc. Adding Chardonnay and Cabernet Franc makes Saumur Mousseux softer and more interesting. Usually non-vintage. Small quantities of rosé are also made. Best producers: BOUVET-LADUBAY★, GRATIEN & MEYER★, Grenelle★, la Paleine★, la Perruche★, St-Cyr-en-Bourg co-op★.

SAUTERNES AC *Bordeaux, France* The name Sauternes is synonymous with the best sweet wines in the world. Sauternes and BARSAC both lie on the banks of the little river Ciron and are 2 of the very few areas in France where noble rot occurs naturally. Production of these intense, sweet, luscious wines from botrytized grapes is a risk-laden and extremely expensive affair, and the wines are never going to be cheap. From good producers (most of which are Crus Classés) the wines are worth their high price – as well as 14% alcohol they have a richness full of flavours of pineapples, peaches, syrup and spice. Good vintages should be aged for 5–10 years, and they can often last twice as long. Best producers: BASTOR-LAMONTAGNE★, Clos Haut-Peyraguey★★, Cru Barréjats★, DOISY-DAENE★★, DOISY-VEDRINES★★, FARGUES★★, GILETTE★★, GUIRAUD★★, Haut-Bergeron★, les Justices★, LAFAURIE-PEYRAGUEY★★★, Lamothe-Guignard★, Malle★, Rabaud-Promis★, Raymond-Lafon★★, Rayne-Vigneau★, RIEUSSEC★★★, Sigalas Rabaud★★, SUDUIRAUT★★, la TOUR BLANCHE★★, YQUEM★★★. Best years: (2001) 99 98 97 **96 95 90** 89 88 86 83.

SAUVIGNON BLANC See pages 250–1.

SAUZET *Côte de Beaune, Burgundy, France* A producer with a reputation for classic, rich, full-flavoured white Burgundies, made in an opulent, fat style, that don't always age as well as they should. Sauzet owns prime sites in PULIGNY-MONTRACHET★ and CHASSAGNE-MONTRACHET★, as well as small parcels of BATARD-MONTRACHET★★★ and Bienvenues-BATARD-MONTRACHET★★★, and supplements grapes from its own vineyards with bought-in supplies.

SAVENNIÈRES AC *Loire Valley, France* Wines from Chenin Blanc, produced on steep vineyards south of Anjou. Usually steely and dry, although they also used to appear in semi-sweet and sweet styles, and since the great 1989 and 90 vintages we've seen a revival of these. The top wines usually need at least 8 years to mature, and can age for longer. There are 2 extremely good vineyards with their own ACs: la Coulée-de-Serrant and la Roche-aux-Moines. Best producers: BAUMARD★★, Clos de Coulaine★, CLOS DE LA COULEE-DE-SERRANT★★, Closel★★, Épiré★★, Forges★★, Laffourcade★, Dom. aux Moines★, F Moron/des Maurières★, Pierre-Bise★★, P Soulez★, P-Y Tijou★★, Varennes★. Best years: (2000) 99 **97 96 95** 93 90 89 88 85 83 82 78 76 71 70 69 66.

SAVIGNY-LÈS-BEAUNE AC *Côte de Beaune, Burgundy, France* This large village concentrates on red wines; they are usually middle weight and best drunk 4–10 years after the vintage. The top Premiers Crus are more substantial. The white wines show a bit of dry, nutty class after 3–4 years. The wines are generally reasonably priced. Best producers: S Bize★, Camus-Bruchon★★, Champy★, CHANDON DE BRIAILLES★, B CLAIR★★, M Écard★★, J J Girard★, P Girard★, V GIRARDIN★, L Jacob★★, D Laurent★★, C Maréchal★, J-M Pavelot★★, TOLLOT-BEAUT★★. Best years: (reds) (2001) 99 98 **97 96 95** 93.

SAVOIE *France* Savoie's high Alpine vineyards, which are scattered between Lake Geneva and Grenoble and on the banks of the Rhône and Isère rivers, produce fresh, snappy white wines with loads of flavour, when made from the Altesse (or Roussette) grape. Drink them young. There are some attractive light reds and rosés, too, mainly from a group of villages south of Chambéry and, in hot years, some positively Rhône-like reds from the Mondeuse grape. Most of the better wines use the Vin de Savoie AC and should be drunk young or with 3–4 years' age. The 15 best villages, including Abymes, Apremont, Arbin, Chignin, Cruet and Montmélian, can add their own name to the AC name. Between Lyon and Savoie are the vineyards of the Vin du Bugey VDQS, which produce light, easy-drinking reds and whites. Best producers: Boniface★, Bouvet★, Dupasquier★, Magnin★, C Marandon★, Monin, Neyroud, Perret★, A & M Quénard★, R Quénard★, Ripaille★, Rocailles★, C Trosset★. See also Seyssel.

SAXENBURG *Stellenbosch WO, South Africa* Winemaker Nico van der Merwe manages 2 harvests a year in different hemispheres. Locally, he creates some of the Cape's most sought-after reds, led by Shiraz; the headily scented, burly Private Collection Shiraz★★ and an even richer, bigger Shiraz Select★★. Also excellent Cabernet★★, Merlot★, Sauvignon Blanc★★ and Chardonnay★ under the Private Collection label. Nico is producing equally good results at Swiss businessman Adrian Bührer's other estate, Ch. Capion in the LANGUEDOC. Drink whites young; reds will improve for 5–8 years. Best years: (premium reds) 1999 98 **97 96 95** 94 93 92 91.

WILLI SCHAEFER *Graach, Mosel, Germany* Schaefer's naturally sweet Riesling Spätlese and Auslese from the great Domprobst vineyard in GRAACH are classic MOSEL wines. The balance of piercing acidity and lavish fruit is every bit as dramatic as Domprobst's precipitous slope. Made in tiny quantities and extremely long-lived, they're frequently ★★★, as is the sensational Beerenauslese Schaefer produces in good vintages. Even the QbA wines here are ★. Best years: (Riesling Spätlese, Auslese) (2001) 00 99 98 97 96 95 **94 93 92** 90 **89 88** 83 76 71.

SAUVIGNON BLANC

 Of all the world's grapes, the Sauvignon Blanc is leader of the 'love it or loathe it' pack. It veers from being wildly fashionable to totally out of favour depending upon where it is grown and which country's consumers are being consulted. But Sauvignon is always at its best when full rein is allowed to its very particular talents because this grape does give intense, sometimes shocking flavours, and doesn't take kindly to being put into a straitjacket. One difficulty with the grape is that it must be picked perfectly ripe. Sometimes Loire Sauvignon Blanc is associated with a pungent 'catty' smell. This is a sure sign that the fruit was not fully ripe when picked. On the other hand, if the grapes are too ripe, they begin to lose the acidity that makes the wines so irresistibly snappy and refreshing.

WINE STYLES

Sancerre-style Sauvignon Although it had long been used as a blending grape in Bordeaux, where its characteristic green tang injected a bit of life into the blander, waxier Sémillon, Sauvignon first became trendy as the grape used for Sancerre, a bone-dry Loire white whose green gooseberry fruit and slightly smoky perfume inspired the winemakers of other countries to try to emulate, then often surpass the original model.

But Sauvignon is only successful where it is respected. The grape is not as easy to grow as Chardonnay, and the flavours are not so adaptable. Yet the range of styles Sauvignon produces is as wide, if less subtly nuanced, as those of Chardonnay. It is highly successful when picked not too ripe, fermented cool in stainless steel, and bottled early. This is the Sancerre model followed by growers elsewhere. New Zealand is now regarded as the top Sauvignon country, and most new producers in countries like Australia, South Africa, southern France, Hungary and Chile try to emulate this powerful mix of passionfruit, gooseberry and lime.

Using oak Sauvignon also lends itself to fermentation in barrel and aging in new oak, though less happily than does Chardonnay. This is the model of the Graves region of Bordeaux, although generally here Sémillon would be blended in with Sauvignon to good effect.

New Zealand again excels at this style, though there are good examples from California, Australia, northern Italy and South Africa. In Austria, a handful of producers in southern Styria (Steiermark) make powerful, aromatic versions with a touch of oak. In all these regions, the acidity that is Sauvignon's great strength should remain, with a dried apricots fruit and a spicy, biscuity softness from the oak. These oaky styles are best drunk either within about a year, or after aging for 5 years or so, and can produce remarkable, strongly individual flavours that you'll either love or loathe.

Sweet wines Sauvignon is also a crucial ingredient in the great sweet wines of Sauternes and Barsac from Bordeaux, though it is less susceptible than its partner Sémillon to the sweetness-enhancing 'noble rot' fungus, botrytis.

Sweet wines from the USA, South Africa, Australia and, inevitably, New Zealand range from the interesting to the out-standing – but the characteristic green tang of the Sauvignon should stay in the wine even at ultra-sweet levels.

250

BEST PRODUCERS

France
Pouilly-Fumé J-C Chatelain, Didier DAGUENEAU, Ladoucette, Masson-Blondelet, de Tracy; *Sancerre* H Bourgeois, F Cotat, CROCHET, A MELLOT, Pinard, Jean-Max Roger, Vacheron; *Pessac-Léognan* Dom. de CHEVALIER, Couhins-Lurton, FIEUZAL, HAUT-BRION, LAVILLE-HAUT-BRION, SMITH-HAUT-LAFITTE.

Other European Sauvignons
Austria Gross, Lackner-Tinnacher, POLZ, E & M TEMENT.

Italy Colterenzio co-op, Peter Dipoli, GRAVNER, Edi Kante, LAGEDER, ORNELLAIA, SCHIOPETTO, Vie di Romans, Villa Russiz.

Spain (Rueda) MARQUES DE RISCAL, Hermanos Lurton; (Penedès) TORRES (Fransola).

New Zealand
Cairnbrae, CLOUDY BAY, Forrest Estate, GROVE MILL, HUNTER'S, ISABEL, Lawson's Dry Hills, MONTANA, Nautilus, NEUDORF, NOBILO, PALLISER ESTATE, Saint Clair, Allan Scott, SEIFRIED, SELAKS, SERESIN, VAVASOUR, VILLA MARIA, WITHER HILLS.

Australia
Bridgewater Mill, CHAIN OF PONDS, Dalrymple, HANGING ROCK, Hill Smith Estate, KATNOOK ESTATE, LENSWOOD VINEYARDS, Ravenswood Lane, SHAW & SMITH, Geoff WEAVER.

USA
California Abreu, ARAUJO, Babcock, FLORA SPRINGS (Soliloquy), KENWOOD, MATANZAS CREEK, Robert MONDAVI (Reserve Fumé), Murphy-Goode, Navarro, QUIVIRA, ROCHIOLI, SPOTTSWOODE.

Chile
CONCHA Y TORO (Terrunyo), VIÑA CASABLANCA.

South Africa
Neil ELLIS, Flagstone, MULDERBOSCH, SAXENBURG, SPRINGFIELD ESTATE, STEENBERG, THELEMA, VERGELEGEN, VILLIERA.

SCHEUREBE Very popular Silvaner x Riesling crossing most widespread in Germany's RHEINHESSEN and PFALZ. Also planted in Austria, where it is sometimes sold under the name Sämling 88. At its best in Trockenbeerenauslese and Eiswein. When ripe, it has a marvellous flavour of honey, exotic fruits and the pinkest of pink grapefruit.

SCHIOPETTO *Friuli-Venezia Giulia, Italy* One of the legends of Italian wine, who pioneered the development of scented varietals and, above all, high-quality, intensely concentrated white wines from COLLIO. Most outstanding are Tocai★★, Pinot Bianco★★ and Sauvignon★★ which open out with age to display fascinating flavours. New COLLI ORIENTALI vineyards Poderi dei Blumeri can only add further prestige.

SCHLOSSBÖCKELHEIM *Nahe, Germany* This NAHE village's top sites are the Felsenberg and Kupfergrube, but good wines also come from Mühlberg and Königsfels. Best producers: Dr CRUSIUS★, DONNHOFF★★★, Gutsverwaltung Niederhausen-Schlossböckelheim★. Best years: (2001) 00 **99** 98 **96 95 94**.

SCHLOSS LIESER *Lieser, Mosel, Germany* Since Thomas Haag (son of Wilhelm, of the Fritz HAAG estate) took over the winemaking in 1992, this small estate has shot to the top. MOSEL Rieslings★★ marry richness with great elegance. Best years: (2001) 99 **98 97 96 95 94 93**.

SCHLOSS REINHARTSHAUSEN *Erbach, Rheingau, Germany* Estate formerly owned by the Hohenzollern family, which ruled Prussia, then Germany until 1918. There are several fine vineyard sites, including the great ERBACHer Marcobrunn. Interesting organic Weissburgunder-Chardonnay blend from its vines in Erbacher Rheinhell, an island in the middle of the Rhine. Good Rieslings (Auslese, Beerenauslese, TBA ★★★) and Sekt★. Best years: (2001) **99** 98 **97** 96 **95 94 93 92 90 89**.

SCHLOSS SAARSTEIN *Serrig, Mosel-Saar-Ruwer, Germany* Fine Saar estate whose Riesling trocken can taste a little austere; better balanced are wines like the Serriger Riesling Kabinett★ or Spätlese★ and Auslese★★, which keep the startling acidity but coat it with fruit, often with the aromas of slightly unripe white peaches. Saarstein makes the occasional spectacular Eiswein★★★. Best years: 1999 **97 95 93 92 90 89 88 86 85**.

SCHLOSS VOLLRADS *Oestrich-Winkel, Rheingau, Germany* Following the sudden death of owner Erwein Graf Matuschka-Greiffenclau before the 1997 harvest, the running of this historic estate was taken up by its banker, Rowald Hepp, who continues to direct it. Quality seems to have got back on track from the 1999 vintage.

DOM. SCHOFFIT *Alsace AC, Alsace, France* One of the two main owners of the outstanding Rangen Grand Cru vineyard, also making a range of deliciously fruity non-cru wines. Top-of-the-tree Clos St-Théobald wines from Rangen are often ★★★ and will improve for at least 5–6 years after release, Rieslings for even longer. The Cuvée Alexandre range is essentially declassified ALSACE VENDANGE TARDIVE. Best years: (Clos St-Théobald Riesling) (2000) 99 **99** 98 **97 96 95 94**.

SCHRAMSBERG *Napa Valley AVA, California, USA* The first CALIFORNIA winery to make really excellent CHAMPAGNE-method sparklers from the classic grapes. Though all releases do not achieve the same heights, the best of these wines are among the best in California, and as good as most in Champagne. The Crémant★ is an attractive sweetish sparkler, the Blanc de Noirs★★ and the Blanc de Blancs★ are more classic. Top of the line is the Reserve Brut★★, which can be world class. In a bold, powerful style is J Schram★★ – rich and flavoursome and increasingly good. Vintage-dated wines can be drunk with up to 10 years' age.

SCREAMING EAGLE *Oakville AVA, California, USA* Real estate agent Jean Phillips first produced a Cabernet Sauvignon from her OAKVILLE valley floor vineyard in 1992. Made in very limited quantities, the wine is California's most sought-after Cabernet each vintage. Made by Heidi Peterson Barrett, winemaker for Grace Family Vineyards and Paradigm, the Cabernet Sauvignon★★★ is a huge, brooding wine that displays all the lush fruit of Oakville.

SEAVIEW *McLaren Vale, South Australia* Best known for good, mass-market Brut fizz★, excellent Pinot-Chardonnay★★ and Vintage Reserve Blanc de Blancs★★. There has been some confusion over rebranding following the Southcorp-ROSEMOUNT merger, but the Edwards & Chaffey label is now used for premium sparklers★★, rich Shiraz★★, Cabernet★★ and unfiltered Chardonnay★★.

SEGHESIO *Sonoma County, California, USA* Having grown grapes in SONOMA COUNTY for a century, the Seghesio family is today known for its own Zinfandel. All bottlings, from Sonoma County★★ to the single-vineyard San Lorenzo★★ and Cortina★★, display textbook black fruit and peppery spice. Sangiovese from 1905 vines, known as Chianti Station★, is one of the best in the state. Also look for crisp Italian whites such as Pinot Grigio★ and Arneis★.

SEIFRIED *Nelson, South Island, New Zealand* Estate founded in 1974 by Austrian Hermann Seifried and his New Zealand wife Agnes. The best wines include Sauvignon Blanc★, Gewürztraminer★ and botrytized Riesling★★. The Redwood Valley label is used in export markets.

SELAKS *Kumeu/Huapai, Auckland, North Island, New Zealand* A long-established winery making fine Sauvignon Blanc-Semillon★★ and snappy Sauvignon Blanc★★; also Chardonnay★ and Riesling★. Bought by NOBILO in 1998, but wine styles and quality have been maintained. Best years: (Sauvignon Blanc-Semillon) (2001) **99 97 96 94**.

SELBACH-OSTER *Zeltingen, Mosel, Germany* Johannes Selbach is one of the MOSEL's new generation of star winemakers, producing very pure, elegant Riesling★ from the Zeltinger Sonnenuhr site. Also good wine from WEHLEN, GRAACH and BERNKASTEL. Best years: (Riesling Spätlese) (2001) 00 99 98 **97 96 95 94 93 92 91 90 89 88 85**.

SELLA & MOSCA *Sardinia, Italy* Apart from the rich, port-like Anghelu Ruju★ made from semi-dried Cannonau grapes, this much-modernized old firm produces excellent dry whites, Terre Bianche★ (Torbato), La Cala★ (Vermentino) and oak-aged reds, Marchese di Villamarina★★ (Cabernet) and Tanca Farrà★★ (Cannonau-Cabernet). Best years: (Marchese di Villamarina) 1997 96 **95 93 92 90**.

SELVAPIANA *Chianti DOCG, Tuscany, Italy* This estate in CHIANTI RUFINA has always produced excellent wines that are typical of the zone. But since 1990 it has vaulted into the top rank of Tuscan estates, particularly with the Riserva★★ and 2 single-vineyard Riservas, Vigneto Bucerchiale★★★ and Fornace★★. VIN SANTO★★ is very good. Best years: (Bucerchiale) (1999) 98 96 95 **94 93 91 90 88 85**.

SÉMILLON Found mainly in South-West France, especially in the sweet wines of SAUTERNES and BARSAC, because it is prone to noble rot (*Botrytis cinerea*). Also blended for its waxy texture with Sauvignon Blanc to make dry wine – almost all the great GRAVES Classed Growths are based on this blend. Performs well in Australia (aged Semillon from the

HUNTER, BAROSSA and CLARE VALLEY can be wonderful) on its own or as a blender with Chardonnay (the accent over the é is dropped on New World labels). Sémillon is also blended with Sauvignon in Australia, New Zealand, CALIFORNIA and WASHINGTON STATE. In South Africa it is primarily a bulk blender, but varietal wines, often barrel-fermented, and blends with Sauvignon are producing some outstanding results.

SEÑA★ *Valle del Aconcagua, Aconcagua, Chile* A MONDAVI and Chadwick family (ERRÁZURIZ) partnership, currently sourced from Errázuriz's Don Maximiano vineyards, Seña is a Cabernet-Carmenère blend. By 2005, it should be composed of 5 different varieties from a single estate. It has fruit intensity and quality is high, although not enough to justify the price. Cellar for 5–10 years. Best years: 1999 **96 95**.

SEPPELT *Barossa Valley, South Australia and Grampians, Victoria* Historic Australian company, now part of Southcorp, best known for making classy fizz and fortifieds. Sparklers include tank-fermented crowd pleaser Great Western, through tasty Fleur de Lys★ up to the pristine, subtly yeasty Salinger★★, made by the Champagne method from Pinot Noir and Chardonnay. Also makes great sparkling red, including the wonderful Show Reserve Shiraz★★★. Top-notch fortifieds, from dry 'sherry' to aged 'port' styles, include the DP Show series★★★ and the legendary 100-year-old Para Liqueur Tawny★★★. Table wines are good, too, especially Great Western Shiraz★★ and Corella Ridge Chardonnay★, Dorrien Cabernet★, Partalunga Chardonnay★ and wines from super-cool Drumborg.

SERESIN *Marlborough, South Island, New Zealand* Film producer Michael Seresin's winery is making a big impact on the MARLBOROUGH scene. Intense Sauvignon Blanc★★ is best within a year or two of the vintage, but creamy Chardonnay★★, succulent Pinot Gris★ and rich, oaky Pinot Noir★★ will age for up to 3 years.

SETÚBAL DOC *Terras do Sado, Portugal* Fortified wine from the Setúbal Peninsula south of Lisbon, which is called 'Moscatel de Setúbal' when made from at least 85% Moscatel, and 'Setúbal' when it's not. Best producers: José Maria da FONSECA★★, J P VINHOS★.

SEYSSEL AC *Savoie, France* Known for its feather-light, sparkling wine, Seyssel Mousseux. With the lovely sharp, peppery bite of the Molette and Altesse grapes smoothed out with a creamy yeast, it is an ideal summer gulper. The still white is light and floral, and made only from Altesse. Best producers: Mollex★, Varichon & Clerc★.

SEYVAL BLANC Hybrid grape (Seibel 5656 x Rayon d'Or) whose disease resistance and ability to continue ripening in a damp autumn make it a useful variety in England, Canada and NEW YORK STATE and other areas in the eastern US. Gives clean, sappy, grapefruit-edged wines that are sometimes a very passable imitation of bone-dry CHABLIS.

SHAFER *Stags Leap District AVA, California, USA* One of the best NAPA wineries, making unusually fruity STAGS LEAP DISTRICT Cabernet★★ and a Reserve-style Hillside Select★★★. Merlot★★ and Firebreak★★ (Sangiovese-Cabernet) are also important. Chardonnay★★★, from Red Shoulder Ranch, is classic CARNEROS style. Beginning with the 1999 vintage, estate-grown Syrah has been added to the line-up. Best years: (Cabernet Hillside Select) (2000) (99) 98 97 96 95 94 **93 92 91 90 85 84**.

SHAW & SMITH *Adelaide Hills, South Australia* Cousins Michael Hill Smith – Australia's first MW – and Martin Shaw had a runaway success with their tangy Sauvignon Blanc★ from the first vintage in 1989. They gradually added an unwooded Chardonnay★, a Reserve★ and now a single-vineyard M3★ to the list, and now have an impressive new winery and a lot more wines, including a promising second label, Incognito, with a Merlot★ and a Chardonnay. Best years: (Reserve Chardonnay) **1999 98 97 96 95 94 92**.

SHERRY See Jerez y Manzanilla DO, pages 158–9.

SHIRAZ See Syrah, pages 266–7.

SICILY *Italy* Sicily is emerging with a renewed spirit and attitude to wine production. Those who lead the way, such as PLANETA, Duca di SALAPARUTA and TASCA D'ALMERITA, have been joined by others, including Donnafugata, the revitalized Spadafora and transformed Settesoli (headed by Diego Planeta) as well as other exciting estates. These include Abbazia Santa Anastasia, especially noted for its Cabernet Sauvignon-Nero d'Avola blend, Litra★★; Cottanera, for excellent varietal Merlot (Grammonte★★), Mondeuse (L'Ardenza★★) and Syrah (Sole di Sesta★★); Cusumano, for 100% Nero d'Avola (Sàgana★) and a Nero d'Avola-Cabernet-Merlot blend (Noà★); Morgante, for another pure Nero d'Avola (Don Antonio★★); and Ceuso, for a Nero d'Avola-Merlot-Cabernet blend (Ceuso Custera★). Firriato, aided by Kym Milne, also makes excellent reds★ and whites★. See also Marsala, Moscato Passito di Pantelleria.

SIEUR D'ARQUES, LES VIGNERONS DU *Limoux AC and Blanquette de Limoux AC, Languedoc, France* This modern co-op makes around 90% of the still and sparkling wines of LIMOUX. The BLANQUETTE DE LIMOUX★ and CREMANT DE LIMOUX★ are both reliable, but the real excitement comes with the Toques et Clochers Chardonnays★ (occasionally ★★). The co-op also makes a range of white and red varietal vins de pays.

SILENI *Hawkes Bay, North Island, New Zealand* Established by millionaire Graeme Avery, with a view to making nothing but the best, this modern winery brings a touch of the NAPA VALLEY to HAWKES BAY. A sleek and stylish Chardonnay★ and ripe, mouthfilling Semillon★ both impress. Best of all is the EV Merlot-Cabernet Franc★★, a dense yet elegant red with a classy oak influence.

SILVER OAK CELLARS *Napa Valley, California, USA* One of California's best Cabernet Sauvignon producers, with bottlings from ALEXANDER VALLEY★★ and NAPA VALLEY★★ grapes. Forward, generous, fruity wines, impossible not to enjoy young, yet with great staying power. Best years: (Napa Valley) (2000) (99) 97 96 95 **94 93 92 91 90 87 86 85 84 82**.

SILVERADO VINEYARDS *Stags Leap District AVA, California, USA* This estate winery makes good Cabernet Sauvignon and Chardonnay. The regular Cabernet★ has intense fruit and is drinkable fairly young; Limited Reserve★★ has more depth and is capable of some aging. The Chardonnay★ has soft, inviting fruit and a silky finish. Also a fruity Merlot★ and a refreshing Sauvignon Blanc★. A new STAGS LEAP DISTRICT Cabernet Sauvignon★★ displays the cherry fruit and supple tannins of this area. Best years: (Reserve Cabernet) (1999) (98) 97 96 95 94 **93 91 90**.

SIMI *Alexander Valley AVA, California, USA*   Historic winery recently sold to Canandaigua, although winemaker Nick Goldschmidt has stayed. The Cabernet Sauvignon★, Chardonnay★★ and Sauvignon Blanc★ (Sendal★★) attain high standards; Chardonnay Reserve occasionally reaches ★★★. Best years: (reds) (1999) 97 95 94 **92 91 90**.

SIMONSIG *Stellenbosch WO, South Africa*   Family-run estate, producing a large, well-made range of wines. Winemaker Johan Malan's forte is reds: among the best are regular Shiraz and lavishly American-oaked Merindol Syrah, a delicious unwooded Pinotage and plusher Redhill Pinotage★, and 2 blends featuring BORDEAUX varieties – the svelte Tiara★ and bright-fruited Frans Malan Reserve★, containing a good injection of Pinotage. Whites are sound if less exciting. Cap Classique sparklers, Kaapse Vonkel and Cuvée Royale, are biscuity and creamy.

CH. SIRAN★ *Margaux AC, Cru Bourgeois, Haut-Médoc, Bordeaux, France*   Consistently good claret, approachable young, but with enough structure to last for as long as 20 years. Second wine: Ch. Bellegarde. Best years: 2000 98 96 95 **90 89 86 85 83 82**.

SKALLI-FORTANT DE FRANCE *Languedoc-Roussillon, France*   Now one of the most important producers in the south of France, Robert Skalli was an early pioneer of varietal wines in the MIDI. Modern winemaking and the planting of international grape varieties were the keys to success. The Fortant de France brand includes a range of single-variety Vins de Pays d'OC. Grenache and Chardonnay are among the best, but I am yet to be fully convinced by the top reds.

CH. SMITH-HAUT-LAFITTE *Pessac-Léognan AC, Cru Classé de Graves, Bordeaux, France*   Large property best known for its reds★★, now one of the most improved and innovative estates in PESSAC-LEOGNAN since a change of ownership in 1990. There is only a little white★★ (from 100% Sauvignon) but it is a shining example of tip-top modern white Bordeaux. Best years: (reds) 2000 99 98 97 96 **95 94 90 89**; (whites) 2000 99 **98 96 95 94 93 92**.

SMITH WOODHOUSE *Port DOC, Portugal*   Underrated but consistently satisfying PORT from this shipper in the Symington group. The Vintage★★ is always worth looking out for, as is single-quinta Santa Madalena (made since 1995), and its Late Bottled Vintage Port★★ is the rich and characterful, figgy, unfiltered type. Best years: (Vintage) (2000) 97 94 92 91 **85 83 80 77 70 63**; (Santa Madalena) (1999) 98 95.

SOAVE DOC *Veneto, Italy*   In the hilly Soave Classico zone near Verona, the Garganega and Trebbiano di Soave grapes can produce ripe, nutty, scented wines. However, 70% of all Soave comes from the flat fertile plains, and much of this is blended into a limp, tasteless white. Since 1992, the blend may include 30% Chardonnay, and good examples are definitely on the increase. Best producers: Bertani★, Ca' Rugate★, La Cappuccina★, Gini★★, Inama★, MASI★, Pasqua/Cecilia Beretta★, PIEROPAN★★, Portinari★, Prà★, Suavia★, Tamellini★. See also Recioto di Soave DOCG, ANSELMI.

CH. SOCIANDO-MALLET★★ *Haut-Médoc AC, Cru Bourgeois, Haut-Médoc, Bordeaux, France*   Owner Jean Gautreau has made this one of BORDEAUX's star Crus Bourgeois. The wine shows every sign of great red Bordeaux flavours to come if you can hang on for 10–15 years. Best years: 2000 99 98 97 96 95 **94 93 90 89 88 86 85 83 82**.

SOGRAPE *Portugal*   Portuguese giant Sogrape can be credited with revolutionizing quality in some of Portugal's most reactionary wine regions. Mateus Rosé is still the company's golden egg, but Sogrape makes good to very good wines in BAIRRADA (Reserva Branco★), DOURO (Reserva Tinto★) and VINHO VERDE as well. Subsidiaries FERREIRA and Offley provide top-flight PORTS and Casa Ferreirinha table wines. From the high-tech Quinta dos Carvalhais winery in DAO come improved Duque de Viseu★ and Grão Vasco reds and whites, but also the company's premium wines under the Quinta dos Carvalhais label: varietal Encruzado★ (white) and reds Tinta Roriz★ and Touriga Nacional are promising but inconsistent. A (red) Reserva is a further step up, but in price as well as quality. Sogrape also makes Vinha do Monte from the ALENTEJO. Also owns Finca Flichman in Argentina.

SOLAIA★★★ *Tuscany, Italy* One of ANTINORI's much-admired SUPER-TUSCANS, sourced, like TIGNANELLO, from the Santa Cristina vineyard. Solaia is a blend of Cabernet Sauvignon, Sangiovese and Cabernet Franc. Intense, with rich fruit and a classic structure, it is not produced in every vintage. Best years: (1999) 98 97 96 95 **94 93 91 90 88 86 85**.

SOMONTANO DO *Aragón, Spain* In the foothills of the Pyrenees, this region is an up-and-coming star. Reds and rosés from the local grapes (Moristel and Tempranillo) can be light, fresh and flavourful, and international varieties such as Chardonnay and Gewürztraminer are already yielding promising wines. An interesting development is the rediscovery of the soft native red grape, Moristel, and the powerful Parraleta (RIOJA's Graciano). Best producers: ENATE★, Bodega Pirineos★, VIÑAS DEL VERO★. Best years: (reds) 1999 **98 97 96 95 94**.

SONOMA COAST AVA *California, USA* A huge appellation defined on its western boundary by the Pacific Ocean, that attempts to bring together the coolest regions of SONOMA COUNTY. It encompasses the Sonoma part of CARNEROS and overlaps parts of SONOMA VALLEY and RUSSIAN RIVER. The heart of the appellation are vineyards on the high coastal ridge only a few miles from the Pacific. Intense Chardonnays and Pinot Noirs are the focus. Best producers: FLOWERS★★, HARTFORD COURT★★, KISTLER (Hirsch Vineyard Pinot Noir★★★), Littorai (Hirsch Pinot Noir★★★), MARCASSIN★★, W H Smith★★, Wild Hog★.

SONOMA COUNTY *California, USA* Sonoma's vine-growing area is big and sprawling, with dozens of soil types and mesoclimates, from the fairly warm SONOMA VALLEY and ALEXANDER VALLEY regions to the cool Green Valley and lower RUSSIAN RIVER VALLEY. The best wines are from Chardonnay, Sauvignon Blanc, Cabernet Sauvignon, Pinot Noir and Zinfandel. Often the equal of rival NAPA in quality and originality of flavours. See also Carneros, Dry Creek Valley.

SONOMA-CUTRER *Russian River Valley AVA, Sonoma County, California, USA* Crisp, pleasant but often overrated Chardonnay from 3 vineyards. Les Pierres is the most complex and richest of the 3, often worth ★★; Cutrer★★ can also have a complexity worth waiting for. Russian River Ranches★ can be rather flat and ordinary, though much improved in recent releases. Best years: (2001) 00 99 **98 97 95 94**.

SONOMA VALLEY AVA *California, USA* The oldest wine region north of San Francisco, Sonoma Valley is situated on the western side of the Mayacamas Mountains, which separate it from NAPA VALLEY. Best varieties are Chardonnay and Zinfandel, with Cabernet and Merlot from hillside sites also good. Best producers: ARROWOOD★★, CARMENET★★, CHATEAU ST JEAN★, B R Cohn, Fisher★, GUNDLACH-BUNDSCHU★, KENWOOD★, KUNDE★, LANDMARK★, LAUREL GLEN★★, MATANZAS CREEK★★, RAVENSWOOD★★, St Francis★, Sebastiani★. Best years: (Zinfandel) (2001) 00 99 **98 97 96 95 94**.

SPARKLING WINES OF THE WORLD ___

Made by the Traditional (Champagne) Method

Although Champagne is still the benchmark for top-class sparkling wines all over the world, the Champagne houses themselves have taken the message to California, Australia and New Zealand via wineries they've established in these regions. However, Champagne-method fizz doesn't necessarily have to feature the traditional Champagne grape varieties (Chardonnay, Pinot Noir and Pinot Meunier), and this allows a host of other places to join the party. Describing a wine as Champagne method is now strictly speaking no longer allowed (only original Champagne from France is officially sanctioned to do this), but the use of a phrase like Traditional Method should not distract from the fact that these wines are still painstakingly produced using the complex system of secondary fermentation in the bottle itself.

STYLES OF SPARKLING WINE
France French fizz ranges from the sublime to the near-ridiculous. The best examples have great finesse and include grapy Crémant d'Alsace, produced from Pinot Blanc and Riesling; often inexpensive yet eminently drinkable Crémant de Bourgogne, based mainly on Chardonnay; and some stylish examples from the Loire, notably in Saumur and Vouvray. Clairette de Die and Blanquette de Limoux in the south confuse the issue by following their own idiosyncratic method of production, but the result is delicious.
Rest of Europe Franciacorta DOCG is a success story for Italy. Most metodo classico sparkling wine is confined to the north, where ripening conditions are closer to those of Champagne, but a few good examples do pop up in unexpected places – Sicily, for instance. Asti and Lambrusco are not Champagne-method wines. In Spain, the Cava wines of Cataluña offer an affordable style for everyday drinking. German Sekt comes in two basic styles: one made from Riesling grapes, the other using Champagne varieties. England is proving naturally suited to growing grapes for sparkling wine.
Australia and New Zealand Australia has a wide range of styles though there is still little overt varietal definition. Blends are still being produced using fruit from many areas, but regional characters are starting to emerge. Cool Tasmania is the star performer, making some top fizz from local grapes. Red sparklers, notably those made from Shiraz, are an irresistible Australian curiosity with an alcoholic kick. Cool-climate New Zealand is coming up fast for fizz with some premium and pricy examples; as in Australia, some have Champagne connections.
USA In California, some magnificent examples are produced – the best ones using grapes from Carneros or the Anderson Valley. Quality has been transformed by the efforts of French Champagne houses. Oregon is also a contender in the sparkling stakes.
South Africa Cap Classique is the local name for the Champagne method. Many producers are jumping on the fizz bandwagon and the best are very good, but there are problems with consistency.

See also individual producers.

VINTAGE 1996

PIRIE

TASMANIA

IMPORTED BY [...]

BEST PRODUCERS

Australia Blue Pyrenees, BROWN BROTHERS, Cope-Williams, GREEN POINT, HANGING ROCK, Charles MELTON, PETALUMA (Croser), PIPERS BROOK (Pirie), ROCKFORD (Sparkling Shiraz), SEAVIEW, SEPPELT, TALTARNI (Clover Hill), YALUMBA (Jansz), Yarrabank, YELLOWGLEN.

Austria BRUNDLMAYER.

France (Alsace) Ostertag; (Burgundy) Caves de Bailly, Caves de Lugny; (Saumur) BOUVET-LADUBAY, GRATIEN & MEYER; (Die) Clairette de Die co-op; (Limoux) SIEUR D'ARQUES co-op; (Vouvray) Clos Naudin, HUET.

Germany (Franken) Rudolf FURST; (Pfalz) Bergdolt, KOEHLER-RUPRECHT; (Saar) Dr Heinz Wagner.

Italy (Franciacorta) BELLAVISTA, CA' DEL BOSCO; (Trento) FERRARI; (Sicily) TASCA D'ALMERITA.

New Zealand CELLIER LE BRUN, CLOUDY BAY (Pelorus), CORBANS (Amadeus), MONTANA (Deutz), MORTON ESTATE, Nautilus, PALLISER.

Portugal Caves ALIANCA, J P VINHOS.

South Africa Graham BECK, J C le ROUX (Pongrácz), Twee Jonge Gezellen, VILLIERA.

Spain (Cava) CODORNIU, FREIXENET, JUVE Y CAMPS, Raventós i Blanc.

UK CHAPEL DOWN, NYETIMBER, RIDGEVIEW, VALLEY VINEYARDS.

USA (California) S Anderson, DOMAINE CARNEROS, DOMAINE CHANDON, HANDLEY, IRON HORSE, J Wine, Laetitia, MUMM NAPA, PACIFIC ECHO, ROEDERER ESTATE, SCHRAMSBERG; (Oregon) Argyle.

SOUTH AUSTRALIA Australia's biggest grape-growing state, with some 60,000ha (150,000 acres) of vineyards. Covers many climates and most wine styles, from bulk wines to the very best. Established areas are ADELAIDE HILLS, Adelaide Plains, CLARE, BAROSSA and Eden Valleys, MCLAREN VALE, Langhorne Creek, COONAWARRA, PADTHAWAY and RIVERLAND. Newer districts creating excitement include Mount Benson, Robe and Kangaroo Island; the recently planted Wrattonbully is producing promising red wines and is, like Coonawarra, made up of terra rossa soil over limestone. See also Limestone Coast.

SOUTH-WEST FRANCE As well as the world-famous wines of BORDEAUX, South-West France has many lesser-known, inexpensive ACs, VDQS and VdPs, over 10 *départements* from the Atlantic coast to LANGUEDOC-ROUSSILLON. Bordeaux grapes (Cabernet Sauvignon, Merlot and Cabernet Franc for reds; Sauvignon Blanc, Sémillon and Muscadelle for whites) are common, but there are lots of interesting local varieties as well, such as Tannat (in MADIRAN), Petit Manseng (in JURANÇON) and Mauzac (in GAILLAC). See also Bergerac, Cahors, Côtes de Duras, Côtes du Frontonnais, Irouléguy, Monbazillac, Montravel, Pacherenc du Vic-Bilh.

SPÄTBURGUNDER See Pinot Noir.

SPICE ROUTE WINE COMPANY *Swartland WO, South Africa* High-profile operation owned by Charles Back, of FAIRVIEW. White wines are strongly represented by sumptuous Chenin Blanc★ and tangy Sauvignon★, but the real quality lies in top reds, the big yet classically styled Flagship duo of Pinotage★★ and Syrah★★; the Merlot is not quite so successful. Best years: (Flagship reds) **1999 98**.

SPOTTSWOODE *Napa Valley AVA, California, USA* Replanted in the mid-1990s, this beautifully situated 16ha (40-acre) vineyard west of St Helena has not missed a beat since the winery opened in 1982. Deep, blackberry and cherry-fruited Cabernet Sauvignon★★★ is wonderful to drink early, but is best at 5–10 years. Sauvignon Blanc★★ (blended with a little Semillon and barrel fermented) is a sophisticated treat. Best years: (Cabernet) (2000) (99) 98 97 96 **95 94 93 92 91**.

SPRINGFIELD ESTATE *Robertson WO, South Africa* Abrie Bruwer lives dangerously, using hands-off methods to capture his vineyards' *terroir* in this distinctive range. His approach is tested to the utmost in the Méthode Ancienne Chardonnay★★, barrel fermented with vineyard yeasts and bottled without any fining or filtration. Not every vintage makes it! The unwooded Wild Yeast Chardonnay★ has expressive pineapple and paw paw flavours. The farm's rocky soils are reflected in the flinty, lively Life from Stone Sauvignon Blanc★. Ever-improving Cabernet Sauvignon – also made as Méthode Ancienne★.

STAGS LEAP DISTRICT AVA *Napa County, California, USA* Created in 1989, this is one of California's best-defined appellations. Located in south-eastern NAPA VALLEY, it is cooler than OAKVILLE or RUTHERFORD to the north, so the red wines here are more elegant in nature. A little Sauvignon Blanc and Chardonnay are grown here, but the true stars are Cabernet Sauvignon and Merlot. Best producers: CHIMNEY ROCK★★, CLOS DU VAL★, Hartwell★★, PINE RIDGE★★, SHAFER★★★, SILVERADO★, Robert Sinskey★★, STAG'S LEAP WINE CELLARS★★, Stags' Leap Winery★.

STAG'S LEAP WINE CELLARS *Stags Leap District AVA, California, USA* The winery rose to fame when its Cabernet Sauvignon came first at the Paris tasting of 1976. Cabernet Sauvignon★★ can be stunning, particularly the SLV★★★ from estate vineyards and the Fay★★; the Cask 23 Cabernet Sauvignon★ can be very good, but is overhyped. After a dip in quality, late 1990s vintages seem back on form. A lot of work has gone into the Chardonnay★★ and the style is one of NAPA's most successful. Best years: (Cabernet) (2000) 99 98 97 96 **95 94 91 90 87 86**.

STEELE WINES *Lake County, California, USA* Owner and winemaker Jed Steele is a master blender. He sources grapes from all over California and shapes them into exciting wines, usually featuring vivid fruit with supple mouthfeel. But he also offers single-vineyard wines and has, in current release, 4–6 Chardonnays, most ★★. His Zinfandels★★ are often very good, as are his Pinot Noirs★★ (CARNEROS, SANTA MARIA VALLEY). The Shooting Star label provides remarkable value in a ready-to-drink style.

STEENBERG *Constantia WO, South Africa* The oldest farm in the CONSTANTIA valley is seeing great results from total vineyard replanting in the early 1990s. Sauvignon Blanc Reserve★★, firmly established as one of South Africa's best, is smoky and flinty with underlying fruit richness; straight Sauvignon★ is upfront fruit. Semillon★★ and Chardonnay★ are impressive. An irresistible, minty Merlot★★ has been joined by BORDEAUX-blend Catharina★ and exciting, smoky Shiraz★★. Best years: (whites) **2001 00 99 98 97 96**.

STEIERMARK *Austria* Known as Styria in English, this wine region in south-east Austria formerly covered much of Slovenia's vineyards, too. It includes the regions of Süd-Oststeiermark, Süd-Steiermark and West-Steiermark. It is the warmest of the 4 Austrian wine zones, but the best vineyards are in cool, high-altitude sites. The best wines are Morillon (unoaked Chardonnay, though oak is catching on here as well), Sauvignon Blanc and Gelber Muskateller (Muscat Blanc à Petits Grains). Best producers: Gross★, Lackner-Tinnacher★★, POLZ★, TEMENT★★, Winkler-Hermaden★.

STELLENBOSCH WO *South Africa* Considered the hub of the South African wine industry, this fine red wine district boasts the greatest concentration of wineries in the Cape, though only third in vineyard area; the vineyards straddle valley floors and stretch up the many mountain slopes. Climates and soils are as diverse as wine styles; smaller units of origin – wards – are now being demarcated to more accurately reflect this diversity. The renowned reds are matched by some excellent Sauvignon Blanc and Chardonnay, as well as modern Chenin Blanc and Semillon. Best producers: BEYERSKLOOF★, De Trafford★, Dornier★, EIKENDAL★, Neil ELLIS★★, Ken Forrester★, GRANGEHURST★★, HARTENBERG★, JORDAN★, KANONKOP★★, L'AVENIR★, Le Bonheur★, Le Riche★, Lievland★, Longridge★, MEERLUST★★, Meinert★, MORGENHOF★, MULDERBOSCH★★, Neethlingshof★, Overgaauw★, RUSTEN-BERG★★, RUST-EN-VREDE★, SAXENBURG★★, SIMONSIG★, STELLENZICHT★★, THELEMA★★, Uiterwyk★, VERGELEGEN★★, WARWICK★, Waterford★.

STELLENZICHT *Stellenbosch WO, South Africa* Winemaker Guy Webber aims for fruit and perfume rather than power in his wines. This is evident in his silky, lemony Sémillon★ and smoky, spicy Syrah★★. Sauvignon Blanc★ with gooseberry intensity and bold perfumed Golden Triangle Pinotage★ are also very enjoyable. Best years: (Syrah) 1999 **98 97 95 94**.

SUPER-TUSCANS

Tuscany, Italy

The term 'Super-Tuscans', first used by English and American writers, has now been adopted by Italians themselves to describe the new-style red wines of Tuscany. The 1970s and 80s were a time when enormous strides were being made in Bordeaux, Australia and California, yet these changes threatened to bypass Italy completely because of its restrictive wine laws. A group of winemakers, led by Piero Antinori – who created the inspirational Tignanello and Solaia from vineyards within the Chianti Classico DOCG – abandoned tradition to put their best efforts and best grapes into creative wines styled for modern tastes.

Old large oak casks were replaced with French barriques, while Cabernet Sauvignon and other trendy varieties, such as Merlot, Pinot Noir and Syrah, were planted alongside Sangiovese in vineyards that emerged with sudden grandeur as crus. Since the DOC specifically forbade such innovations, producers were forced to label their wines as plain Vino da Tavola. The 'Super-Tuscan' Vino da Tavolas, as they were quickly dubbed, were a phenomenal success: brilliant in flavour with an approachable, upfront style. Some found it hard to believe that table wines with no official credentials could outrank DOCG Chianti. A single mouthful was usually enough to convince them.

WINE STYLES
Sangiovese and Cabernet Sauvignon are the basis for most Super-Tuscans, one usually making up the balance with the other. Both also appear varietally, with Sangiovese forming the largest group of top-quality Super-Tuscans. To some Sangiovese-based wines, a small percentage of other native varieties such as Colorino, Canaiolo or Malvasia Nera is added. Merlot has long been used as the complement to Cabernet in the Bordeaux mould but more recently has been combined with Sangiovese in exactly the same way. Syrah is of growing importance, mostly varietally, but also in innovative new blends such as Argiano's Solengo. Super-Tuscan wines also show considerable differences in vinification and aging. Top wines are invariably based on ripe, concentrated grapes from a site with special attributes.

CLASSIFICATIONS
A law passed in 1992 has finally brought the Super-Tuscans into line with official classifications. Sassicaia now has its own DOC under Bolgheri. Chianti Classico's newly independent DOCG could cover many a Sangiovese-based Super-Tuscan, but the majority are currently sold under the region-wide IGT Toscana alongside wines made from international varieties. There are also 3 sub-regional IGTs, but only a few producers use these.

The situation for consumers remains confused in the short term because some examples labelled vino da tavola are still being sold.

See also BOLGHERI, CHIANTI CLASSICO, SASSICAIA, SOLAIA, SYRAH, TIGNANELLO; and individual producers.

2000 99 98 97 96 **95 93 90 88 85**

BEST PRODUCERS

Sangiovese and other Tuscan varieties Badia a Coltibuono (Sangioveto), BOSCARELLI, CASTELLARE (I Sodi di San Niccolò), FELSINA (Fontalloro), FONTODI (Flaccianello della Pieve), ISOLE E OLENA (Cepparello), Lilliano (Anagallis), MONTEVERTINE (Le Pergole Torte, Il Sodaccio), Paneretta (Quattrocentenario, Terrine), Poggio Scalette (Il Carbonaione), Querceto (La Corte), RIECINE (La Gioia), RUFFINO (Romitorio di Santedame), San Giusto a Rentennano (Percarlo), VOLPAIA (Coltassala).

Sangiovese-Cabernet and Sangiovese-Merlot blends ARGIANO (Solengo), BANFI (Summus), Colombaio di Cencio (Il Futuro), FONTERUTOLI (Siepi), Gagliole, Montepeloso (Nardo), QUERCIABELLA (Camartina); Sette Ponti (Oreno), TIGNANELLO.

Cabernet Col d'Orcia (Olmaia), Fossi (Sassoforte), ISOLE E OLENA (Collezione), Nozzole (Il Pareto), RAMPOLLA (Sammarco, Vigna d'Alceo), SOLAIA.

Merlot AMA (L'Apparita), Le Macchiole (Messorio), ORNELLAIA (Masseto), Petrolo (Galatrona), Tua Rita (Redigaffi).

Cabernet-Merlot blends ANTINORI (Guado al Tasso), BANFI (Excelsus), Capezzana (Ghiaie della Furba), ORNELLAIA (Ornellaia), Poggio al Sole (Seraselva), POLIZIANO (Le Stanze), Le Pupille (Saffredi), Trinoro, Tua Rita (Giusto di Notri).

STERLING VINEYARDS *Napa Valley AVA, California, USA*   Merlot is the focus here, with Three Palms★★ and Reserve★★, both impressively packed with ripe, dense fruit, leading the way. Reserve Cabernet★ is generally good, and the regular bottling is improving, as is Winery Lake Pinot Noir★. The NAPA VALLEY Chardonnay★ can be rich and intense. Best years: (Three Palms) (2000) 99 97 96 **95 94**.

STONIER *Mornington Peninsula, Victoria, Australia*   The peninsula's biggest winery and one of its best, and though Lion Nathan, via PETALUMA, now has a controlling interest, Tod Dexter is still at the winemaking helm. Reserve Chardonnay★★ and Reserve Pinot★★ are usually outstanding, and there are fine standard bottlings in warm vintages. Cabernet, in the rather herbaceous style typical of the region, continues to improve.

STONYRIDGE *Waiheke Island, Auckland, North Island, New Zealand*   The leading winery on WAIHEKE ISLAND, Stonyridge specializes in reds made from Cabernet Sauvignon, Merlot, Petit Verdot, Malbec and Cabernet Franc. The top label, Larose★★★, is a remarkably BORDEAUX-like red of real intensity; it is one of New Zealand's most expensive wines. Best years: (Larose) (2000) 99 **98 96 94 93 91**.

CH. SUDUIRAUT★★ *Sauternes AC, 1er Cru Classé, Bordeaux, France*   Together with RIEUSSEC, Suduiraut is regarded as a close runner-up to d'YQUEM. Although the wines are delicious at only a few years old, the richness and excitement increase enormously after a decade or so. Seemed to be under-performing in the 1980s and mid-90s but now owned by AXA (see PICHON-LONGUEVILLE) and back on song. Best years: (2001) 99 98 97 **96 95 90 89 88 86 82 81**.

SUHINDOL *Danube Plain Region, Bulgaria*   Established in 1909, this former co-operative was privatized in 1991. With its 3 wineries, it is one of Bulgaria's largest producers. It also owns more than 40% of its own vineyards, which is rare in Bulgaria, with 1500ha (3700 acres) already producing. New technology and judicious use of oak have improved quality enormously, as the Craftsman's Creek, Copper Crossing and regional wines show. The Gamza and Gamza-Merlot blends are worth trying, and it is now developing some premium Cabernet and Merlot reds.

SUMAC RIDGE *Okanagan Valley VQA, British Columbia, Canada*   Winemaker Mark Wendenberg produces excellent Sauvignon Blanc★ and Gewürztraminer Reserve★, fine Pinot Blanc and one of Canada's best Champagne-method fizzes, Steller's Jay Brut★. Top reds include Cabernet Sauvignon, Cabernet Franc, Merlot, Pinot Noir and Meritage★.

SUNTORY *Japan*   Red Tomi and sweet white Noble d'Or (made from botrytized grapes) are top brand names here for wine made exclusively from grapes grown in Japan; this is a rarity in a country where imported wine can legally be blended with Japanese and sold as Japanese. The grapes are classic varieties: Cabernet Sauvignon, Cabernet Franc, Semillon and Sauvignon.

SUPER-TUSCANS See pages 262–3.

SUTTER HOME *Napa County, California, USA*   There is a range of light, sound everyday wines but the winery is best known for its White Zinfandel, producing over 5 million cases a year.

SWAN DISTRICT *Western Australia*   The original WESTERN AUSTRALIA wine region and the hottest stretch of vineyards in Australia, spread along the torrid, fertile silty flats of Perth's Swan River. It used to specialize in fortified wines, but SOUTH AUSTRALIA and north-east VICTORIA both do them better. New-wave whites and reds, especially from Moondah Brook and HOUGHTON, are fresh and generous. Best producers: Paul Conti, HOUGHTON★, Lamont, Moondah Brook★, Sandalford, Westfield.

JOSEPH SWAN VINEYARDS *Russian River Valley AVA, California, USA* Joseph Swan made legendary Zinfandel in the 1970s and was one of the first to age Zinfandel★★ in French oak. In the 1980s he turned to Pinot Noir★★ which is now probably the winery's best offering. Since Swan's death in 1989, his son-in-law, Rod Berglund, has proved a worthy successor. Best years: (Zinfandel) (1999) 98 97 **96 95 94 93 92 91**.

SYRAH See pages 266–7.

LA TÂCHE AC★★★ *Grand Cru, Côte de Nuits, Burgundy, France* Along with la ROMANÉE-CONTI, the greatest of the great VOSNE-ROMANÉE Grands Crus, owned by Dom. de la ROMANÉE-CONTI. The wine has the rare ability to provide layer on layer of flavours; keep it for 10 years or you'll only experience a fraction of the pleasure you paid big money for. Best years: (2001) 00 99 98 97 96 95 93 90 **89** 88 **85 78**.

TAHBILK *Goulburn Valley, Victoria, Australia* Wonderfully old-fashioned family company making traditionally big, gumleafy/minty reds, matured in old wood. Shiraz★ (1860 Vines★★) and Cabernet★ are full of character, even if they need years of cellaring. White Marsanne★★ is perfumed and attractive, as is a floral-scented Viognier★. Other whites tend to lack finesse. Best years: (1860 Vines) 1995 **92 91** 86 84 82.

TAIN L'HERMITAGE, CAVE DE *Hermitage, Rhône Valley, France* Progressive co-op producing an extensive range of wines from throughout the northern Rhône. Quality is surprisingly high, despite production of 500,000 cases annually. Top cuvées are marketed under the Nobles Rives label. Impressive CROZES-HERMITAGE les Haut du Fief★, fine CORNAS★★ and both red and white HERMITAGE★★. Topping the range are an old-vine red Hermitage Gambert de Loche★★ and a fine Vin de Paille★★. Best years: (top reds) (2000) 99 98 97 **95**.

TAITTINGER *Champagne AC, Champagne, France* The top wine, Comtes de Champagne Blanc de Blancs★★★, can be memorable for its creamy, foaming pleasures and the Comtes de Champagne rosé★★ is elegant and oozing class. Ordinary non-vintage★ is soft and honeyed but has been unusually inconsistent for a while now. Another de luxe cuvée, called Vintage Collection★, is simply the vintage Brut in a fancy bottle. Best years: 1996 **95 92 90 89 88 86 85 82 79**.

CH. TALBOT★ *St-Julien AC, 4ème Cru Classé, Haut-Médoc, Bordeaux, France* Chunky, soft-centred but sturdy, capable of aging well for 10–20 years. There is also an interesting and good-value white wine, Caillou Blanc de Talbot★. Second wine: Connétable Talbot. Best years: 2000 99 98 96 95 **90 89 88 86 85 83 82**.

TALBOTT *Monterey County, California, USA* Founded in 1980, this estate is known for its Chardonnays from vineyards near Gonzales and the Santa Lucia Highlands in MONTEREY COUNTY. Sleepy Hollow Vineyard★★, Cuvée Cynthia★★ and Diamond T Estate★★★ are all packed with ripe tropical fruit and ample oak. Chardonnay and Pinot Noir are also produced under the Logan label.

TALTARNI *Pyrenees, Victoria, Australia* Specializing in classic, deep-flavoured, European-style Cabernet★, Shiraz★ and Merlot; also a Malbec rosé and respected fizz, especially Clover Hill★ and pink Brut Tâché★ from TASMANIA. Sauvignon Blanc★ is tangy and gooseberry-like. Best years: (Shiraz) 1999 98 96 **92 91 90** 88 84.

SYRAH/SHIRAZ

Syrah now produces world-class wines in 3 countries and its popularity is rising fast. In France, where Hermitage and Côte-Rôtie are 2 of the world's great reds; in Australia, where as Shiraz it produces some of the New World's most remarkable reds; and now in California, too. And wherever Syrah appears it trumpets a proud and wilful personality based on loads of flavour and unmistakable originality.

When the late-ripening Syrah grape is grown in the coolest, most marginal areas for full ripening, such as Côte-Rôtie, it is capable of producing wines of immense class and elegance. However, producers must ensure low yields if they are to produce high-quality wines.

Syrah's spread round the warmer wine regions of the world has so far been limited. Syrah's heartland – Hermitage and Côte-Rôtie in the Rhône Valley – comprises a mere 270ha (670 acres) of steeply terraced vineyards, producing hardly enough wine to make more than a very rarefied reputation for themselves. This may be one reason for its relatively slow uptake by growers in other countries who simply had no idea as to what kind of flavour the Syrah grape produced, so didn't copy it. But the situation is rapidly changing.

WINE STYLES

French Syrah The flavours of Syrah are most individual, but with modern vineyard practices and modern winemaking techniques they are far less daunting than they used to be. Traditional Syrah had a savage, almost coarse, throaty roar of a flavour. And from the very low-yielding Hermitage vineyards, the small grapes often showed a bitter tannic quality. But better selections of clones in the vineyard and improved winemaking have revealed that Syrah in fact gives a wine with a majestic depth of fruit – all blackberry and damson, loganberry and plum – some quite strong tannin, and some tangy smoke, but also a warm creamy aftertaste, and a promise of chocolate and occasionally a scent of violets. It is these characteristics that have made Syrah popular throughout the south of France as an 'improving' variety for its rather rustic red wines.

Australian Shiraz Australia's most widely planted red variety has become, in many respects, its premium varietal. Shiraz gives spectacularly good results when taken seriously – especially in the Barossa, Clare, Eden Valley and McLaren Vale regions of South Australia. An increasingly diverse range of high-quality examples are also coming from Victoria's warmer vineyards, more traditional examples from New South Wales' Hunter Valley and Mudgee, and exciting, more restrained styles from Western Australia's Margaret River and Great Southern regions, as well as cooler high-country spots. Flavours are rich, intense, thick sweet fruit coated with chocolate, and seasoned with leather, herbs and spice. And here in Australia it is often blended with Cabernet Sauvignon.

Other regions In California producers are turning out superb Rhône blends as well as varietal Syrahs modelled closely on Côte-Rôtie or Hermitage. In South Africa, more exciting wines appear every vintage. Italy, Spain, Argentina, Chile and New Zealand are also beginning to shine.

QUPÉ

19   97

SYRAH

Santa Barbara County
Bien Nacido Reserve

PRODUCED AND BOTTLED BY ROBERT N. LINDQUIST
SANTA MARIA, CALIFORNIA BW 6009 ALC. 14.5% BY VOL.

BEST PRODUCERS

France

Rhône ALLEMAND, R Balthazar, G Barge, A Belle, L Burgaud, CHAPOUTIER, B Chave, J-L CHAVE, Chêne, CLAPE, Clusel-Roch, du Colombier, COLOMBO, Combier, Courbis, COURSODON, CUILLERON, DELAS, E & J Durand, B Faurie, Gaillard, J-M Gerin, GRAILLOT, J-L Grippat, GUIGAL, JABOULET, JAMET, Jasmin, Monteillet, ROSTAING, M Sorrel, Tardieu-Laurent, VERSET, F Villard, les Vins de Vienne.

Languedoc Ch. des ESTANILLES, GAUBY, l'HORTUS.

Other European Syrah

Italy Bertelli, FONTODI, Fossi, ISOLE E OLENA, Le Macchiole, MANZANO, Poggio al Sole.

Spain Albet i Noya, MARQUES DE GRINON, Enrique Mendoza.

New World Syrah/Shiraz

Australia Tim ADAMS, BAROSSA VALLEY ESTATE, Jim BARRY, BEST'S, BOWEN, BROKENWOOD, Grant BURGE, CHAPEL HILL, Charles Cimicky, CLARENDON HILLS, Coriole, Craiglee, Dalwhinnie, D'ARENBERG, FOX CREEK, HARDYS, HENSCHKE, Hewitson, Jasper Hill, LECONFIELD, Peter LEHMANN, MCWILLIAM'S, Charles MELTON, MITCHELTON, MOUNT LANGI GHIRAN, PENFOLDS, PLANTAGENET, ROCKFORD, ROSEMOUNT, ST HALLETT, SEPPELT, TALTARNI, TYRRELL'S, VERITAS, WENDOUREE, The Willows, WIRRA WIRRA, WYNNS, YARRA YERING, Zema.

New Zealand DRY RIVER, Fromm, Stonecroft, TE MATA, Trinity Hill.

South Africa BOEKENHOUTSKLOOF, Diemersfontein, Eben Sadie, SAXENBURG, SPICE ROUTE, STEENBERG, STELLENZICHT.

USA (California) ALBAN, ARAUJO, DEHLINGER, Edmunds St John, Havens, Jade Mountain, Lewis Cellars, Andrew MURRAY, Ojai, Fess Parker, QUPE, Swanson, Thackrey, Truchard, Zaca Mesa.

Chile MONTES, Viu Manent.

267

TARAPACÁ *Maipo, Chile* No expense has been spared in recent vineyard and winery improvements at this long-established company, and the wine, too, is improving under the guidance of Sergio Correa. New premium reds include Reserva Privada Syrah★ and Last Edition★ – an unusual blend of Cabernet, Merlot, Syrah and Mourvèdre.

TARRAWARRA *Yarra Valley, Victoria, Australia* Clothing magnate and arts patron Marc Besen wanted to make a MONTRACHET, and hang the expense. The winemakers are on the right track: Tarrawarra Chardonnay★★ is deep and multi-faceted, but Pinot Noir★ is just as good, with almost COTE DE NUITS flavour and concentration. Tin Cows is a less pricy brand for both these grapes, plus Shiraz and Merlot. Best years: (Pinot Noir) **1998 97 96 94 92**.

TASCA D'ALMERITA *Sicily, Italy* The estate of the Conte Tasca d'Almerita in the highlands of central SICILY makes some of southern Italy's best wines. From native grape varieties come excellent Rosso del Conte★★ (based on Nero d'Avola) and white Nozze d'Oro★ (based on Inzolia), but the range extends to Chardonnay★★ and Cabernet Sauvignon★★ of extraordinary intensity and elegance. Almerita Brut★ (Chardonnay) is a fine Italian Champagne-method sparkler. Relatively simple Regaleali Bianco and Rosato are good value.

TASMANIA *Australia* Tasmania may be a minor state viticulturally, with only 800ha (2000 acres) of vines, but the island has a diverse range of mesoclimates and sub-regions. The generally cool climate has always attracted seekers of greatness in Pinot Noir and Chardonnay, and good results are becoming more consistent. Riesling, Gewürztraminer and Pinot Gris perform well, but the real star here is fabulous premium fizz. Best producers: Elsewhere Vineyard★, Freycinet★★, Iron Pot Bay, Stefano Lubiana★, Moorilla★, Notley Gorge★, PIPERS BROOK★★, Spring ·Vale★, Wellington★. Best years: (Pinot Noir) 2000 99 **98 97 95 94 93 92 91**.

TAURASI DOCG *Campania, Italy* Remarkably, it was a single producer, MASTROBERARDINO, and a single vintage, 1968, that created the reputation for this red. Now the great potential of the Aglianico grape is being exploited by others, both within this DOCG and elsewhere in CAMPANIA. Drink at 5–10 years. Best producers: A Caggiano★★, Feudi di San Gregorio★★, MASTROBERARDINO★, S Molettieri★, Struzziero, Terre Dora di Paolo★. Best years: (1999) 98 97 96 **95 94 93 92 90 89 88 86**.

TAVEL AC *Rhône Valley, France* Big, alcoholic rosé from north-west of Avignon. Grenache and Cinsaut are the main grapes. Drink Tavel at one year old if you want it cheerful, heady, yet refreshing. Best producers: Aquéria★, la Forcadière★, Genestière★, GUIGAL, la Mordorée★, Vignerons de Tavel, Trinquevedel, Vieux Moulin.

TAYLOR FLADGATE & YEATMAN *Port DOC, Douro, Portugal* The aristocrat of the PORT industry, 300 years old and still going strong. Its Vintage★★★ is superb; Quinta de Vargellas★★ is an elegant, cedary, single-quinta vintage port made in the best of the 'off-vintages'. Quinta da Terra Feita★★, the other main component of Taylor's Vintage, is also often released as a single-quinta in non-declared years. Taylor's 20-year-old★★ is a very fine aged tawny. First Estate is a successful premium ruby. The best vintage ports can be kept for at least 25 years. Best years: (Vintage) (2000) 97 94 92 **85 83 80 77 75 70 66 63 60 55 48 45 27**; (Vargellas) 1998 96 95 91 **88 87 86 82 78 67 64 61**.

TE MATA *Hawkes Bay, North Island, New Zealand* HAWKES BAY's glamour
winery, its best-known wines are the reds, Coleraine★★★ and
Awatea★★, both based on Cabernet Sauvignon with varying
proportions of Merlot and Cabernet Franc. Also outstanding is Elston
Chardonnay★★, a superbly crafted, toasty, ageable wine. Exceptional
vintages of all 3 wines might be aged for 5–10 years. Bullnose Syrah★
is an elegant, peppery red, and an initial release of Viognier shows
potential. Best years: (Coleraine) 1998 **96 95 94 91 90 89**.

E & M TEMENT *Ehrenhausen, Steiermark, Austria* Fanatical Manfred
Tement makes Austria's best Sauvignon Blanc★★ (single-site
Zieregg★★★) and Morillon (Chardonnay)★★ in a spectacular new
hilltop winery. Both varieties are fermented and aged in oak, giving
power, depth and subtle oak character. Also makes red Arachon★★ in
a joint venture with F X PICHLER and Szemes in BURGENLAND. Best years:
(Morillon Ried Zieregg) (2001) 00 99 **97 95 94**.

DOM. TEMPIER *Bandol AC, Provence, France* Leading BANDOL estate,
run by the Péyraud family and making rich, ageworthy reds from a
high percentage of Mourvèdre. The top wines are Migoua★★,
Cabassou★★ and la Tourtine★★, and they do need aging – otherwise
the Mourvèdre can be a bit overpowering. The rosé★ is one of Provence's
best. Best years: (2000) 99 98 97 96 **95 93 92 90 89 88 85 83 82**.

TEMPRANILLO Spain's best native red grape can make wonderful wine,
with wild strawberry and spicy, tobaccoey flavours. It is important in
RIOJA, PENEDES (as Ull de Llebre), RIBERA DEL DUERO (as Tinto Fino or Tinta
del País), La MANCHA and VALDEPENAS (as Cencibel), NAVARRA, SOMONTANO,
UTIEL-REQUENA and TORO (as Tinta de Toro). In Portugal it is found in the
DOURO, DAO and ESTREMADURA (as Tinta Roriz) and in ALENTEJO (as
Aragonês). Wines can be deliciously fruity for drinking young, but
Tempranillo also matures well, and its flavours blend happily with oak.
It is now being taken more seriously in Argentina, and new plantings
have been made in CALIFORNIA, OREGON, Australia and South Africa.

TEROLDEGO ROTALIANO DOC *Trentino-Alto Adige, Italy* Teroldego is a
native TRENTINO grape variety, producing deep-coloured, grassy,
blackberry-flavoured wine on the gravel soils of the Rotaliano plain.
Best producers: Barone di Cles★, M Donati★, Dorigati★, Endrizzi★,
FORADORI★★, Conti Martini★, Mezzacorona (Riserva★), Cantina
Rotaliana★, A & R Zeni★. Best years: 2000 99 **97 96 95 94 93 91 90**.

TERRAS DO SADO *Setúbal Peninsula, Portugal* Warm, maritime-
influenced area south of Lisbon. SETUBAL produces fine sweet fortified wine.
Many of the better reds, mostly based on Castelão, come from the Palmela
DOC. A few good whites are also made. Best producers: (reds) Caves
ALIANCA (Palmela Particular★), BRIGHT BROTHERS (Reserva★), D F J VINHOS, José
Maria da FONSECA★, Hero do Castanheiro, J P VINHOS★, Pegões co-op, João
Portugal RAMOS (Pegos Claros★★). Best years: (2001) 00 99 **97 96 95 94 92**.

TERRICCIO, CASTELLO DEL *Tuscany, Italy* High in the hills south of
Livorno, this producer has transformed itself from bulk red and white
wines to the status of Tuscan superstar. However, changes in
philosophy seem to have stripped both the top red Lupicaia★
(Cabernet-Merlot) and the less pricy Tassinaia★ (Sangiovese-Cabernet-
Merlot) of much of their exciting scented personality. Hopefully things

will revert to their potential ★★★ again. The barrique-fermented Chardonnay Saluccio★★ and varietal Sauvignon Blanc Con Vento★ are the most interesting whites. Best years: (Lupicaia) 1997 **96 95 94 93**.

CH. LE TERTRE-RÔTEBOEUF★★ *St-Émilion Grand Cru AC, Bordeaux, France* ST-EMILION's most exceptional unclassified estate. The richly seductive, Merlot-based wines sell at the same price as the Premiers Grands Crus Classés. Under the same ownership as the outstanding ROC DE CAMBES. Best years: 2000 99 98 97 96 95 **94 90 89 88 86 85**.

TEXAS *USA* Since the planting of an experimental vineyard in 1975, Texas has risen to fifth in the ranks of US wine-producing states. The state has 5 AVAs, of which Texas High Plains is most significant, 36 wineries and some fine Chardonnay and Riesling. Thunderstorms are a menace, capable of destroying entire crops in minutes. Best producers: Cap Rock, Fall Creek, Llano Estacado, Messina Hof, Pheasant Ridge, Ste-Genevieve.

THELEMA *Stellenbosch WO, South Africa* Family-run winery, high in the Simonsberg mountains. Meticulous attention is paid to the vineyards, where CALIFORNIA's Phil Freese helps with innovative ideas. Winemaker Gyles Webb's rich blackcurrant Cabernet Sauvignon★★, ripe fleshy Merlot★, barrel-fermented Chardonnay★★, vibrant Sauvignon Blanc★★ and less-hyped Riesling★ are now part of modern Cape wine industry's history. These are set to be joined by a Shiraz in 2002. Best years: (Cabernet Sauvignon) **1999 98 97 96 95 94 93 92 91**; (Chardonnay) **2000 99 98 97 96 95**.

THERMENREGION *Niederösterreich, Austria* This region, south of Vienna, takes its name from the thermal spa towns of Baden and Bad Vöslau. Near Vienna is the village of Gumpoldskirchen with its rich and often sweet white wines. The red wine area around Baden produces large amounts of Blauer Portugieser together with a couple of good examples of Pinot Noir and Cabernet. Best producers: Biegler, Fischer, Hofer, Johanneshof★, Schellmann, Stadlmann★. Best years: (sweet whites) (2000) 99 **98 96 95**.

THIRTY BENCH WINERY *Niagara Peninsula VQA, Ontario, Canada* A collaboration of 3 winemakers, Thirty Bench is known for its low yields and intense wines. Excellent Riesling, including Late Harvest and Icewine★, has been joined by BORDEAUX-style red Reserve Blend★ and a fine barrel-fermented Chardonnay.

DOMAINE THOMAS-MOILLARD *Nuits-St-Georges AC, Côte de Nuits, Burgundy, France* This is the label for wines from the family-owned vineyards of négociant house Moillard-Grivot. The wines are not consistent across the range, but the best, including ROMANEE-ST-VIVANT★★★ and BONNES-MARES★★★, are very fine, in an old-fashioned, long-lived, robust style. Other good reds include NUITS-ST-GEORGES Clos de Thorey★★, BEAUNE Grèves★ and VOSNE-ROMANEE Malconsorts★★. Red and white HAUTES-COTES DE NUITS★ stand out at the simpler end of the range. Best years: (top reds) (2001) 00 99 98 **97** 96 95 **93 90**.

THREE CHOIRS *Gloucestershire, England* Martin Fowke makes an impressive range of wines at this state-of-the-art winery set in a 28ha (70-acre) vineyard. These include lovely dry single varietals (Bacchus, Madeleine Angevine, Schönburger and Phoenix), lightly oaked Estate Reserve wines and experimental

THREE CHOIRS

reds. There is even a zingy white Anglais Nouveau, released in November at the same time as BEAUJOLAIS NOUVEAU. Sparkling wines, both non-vintage Classic Cuvée and Vintage Reserve, are based on Seyval Blanc but include Pinot Noir.

TICINO *Switzerland* Italian-speaking, southerly canton of Switzerland. The most important wine of the region is Merlot del Ticino, usually soft and gluggable, but sometimes more serious with some oak barrel-aging. Best producers: Daniel Huber★, Werner Stucky★, Christian Zündel★. Best years: (2000) **97 96**.

TIGNANELLO★★ *Tuscany, Italy* The wine that broke the mould in Tuscany. Piero ANTINORI employed the previously unheard of practice of aging in small French oak barrels and used Cabernet Sauvignon (20%) in the blend with Sangiovese. Initially labelled as simple vino da tavola, the quality was superb and Tignanello's success sparked off the SUPER-TUSCAN movement that has produced many of Italy's most exciting wines. Top vintages are truly great: lesser years are of decent CHIANTI CLASSICO quality. Best years: (2000) 99 98 97 **96 95 94 93 90 88 86 85**.

TINTA RORIZ See Tempranillo.

TOCAI FRIULANO Unrelated to Hungary's TOKAJI, Tocai Friulano is a north-east Italian grape producing dry, nutty, oily whites of great character in COLLIO and COLLI ORIENTALI and good wines in the Veneto's COLLI EUGANEI, as well as lots of neutral stuff in Piave. Best producers: Borgo San Daniele★, Borgo del Tiglio★, Dorigo★, Drius★, Livio FELLUGA★, JERMANN★, Edi Keber★★, Miani★★, Princic★, Ronchi di Manzano★, Paolo Rodaro★, Ronco del Gelso★★, Russiz Superiore★★, SCHIOPETTO★★, Specogna★, Villa Russiz★, Le Vigne di Zamò★★.

TOKAJI *Hungary* Hungary's classic, liquorous wine of historical reputation, with its unique, sweet-and-sour, sherry-like tang, comes from 28 villages on the Hungarian-Slovak border. Mists from the Bodrog river ensure that noble rot on the Furmint, Hárslevelü and Muscotaly (Muscat Ottonel) grapes is a fairly common occurrence. Degrees of sweetness are measured in *puttunyos*. Discussions continue about traditional oxidized styles versus fresher modern versions. Best producers: Disznókö★★, Château Megyer★★, Oremus★, Château Pajzos★★, Royal Tokaji Wine Company★★, Istvan Szepsy (6 Puttonyos 95★★★, Essencia★★★), Tokaji Kereskedöház★★. Best years: 1999 **97 93**.

TOLLOT-BEAUT & FILS *Chorey-lès-Beaune, Burgundy, France* High-quality COTE DE BEAUNE reds with lots of fruit and a pronounced new oak character. The village-level CHOREY-LES-BEAUNE★★, ALOXE-CORTON★★ and SAVIGNY-LES-BEAUNE★★ wines are all excellent, as is the top BEAUNE Premier Cru Clos du Roi★★. Best years: (reds) (2001) 99 98 **97 96 95 93 90**.

TORGIANO DOC & DOCG *Umbria, Italy* A zone near Perugia dominated by one producer, LUNGAROTTI. Lungarotti's basic Rubesco Torgiano★ is ripely fruity, the Riserva Vigna Monticchio★★ is a fine black cherry-flavoured wine. Torgiano Riserva Rosso has been accorded DOCG.

TORO DO *Castilla y León, Spain* Mainly red wines, which are robust, full of colour and tannin, and pretty high in alcohol. The main grape, Tinta de Toro, is a local variant of Tempranillo, and there is some Garnacha. Whites from the Malvasia grape are generally heavy. Best producers: Viña Bajoz★, Fariña★, Frutos Villar (Muruve★), Maurodos★★, Telmo RODRIGUEZ★, Toresanas/Bodegas de Crianza Castilla la Vieja★, Vega Saúco★, Vega de Toro/Señorío de San Vicente (Numanthia★★).

TORRES *Penedès DO, Cataluña, Spain* Large family winery led by visionary Miguel Torres, making good wines with local grapes, Parellada and Tempranillo, but also renowned for French varieties. Viña Sol★ is a good, citrony quaffer, Viña Esmeralda★ (Muscat Blanc à Petits Grains and Gewürztraminer) is grapy and spicy, Fransola★★ (Sauvignon Blanc with some Parellada) is rich yet leafy, and Milmanda★★ is a delicate, expensive Chardonnay. Successful reds are Gran Coronas★, soft, oaky and blackcurranty (Tempranillo and Cabernet); fine, relatively rich Mas la Plana★★ (Cabernet Sauvignon); floral, perfumed Mas Borrás (Pinot Noir); and raisiny Atrium★ (Merlot). The new top-line reds, Grans Muralles★, from a blend of Catalan grapes, and Reserva Real★★, a BORDEAUX-style red blend, are interesting but expensive. Best years: (Mas la Plana) 1996 95 **94 91 90** 88 87 83 81 79 76.

MARIMAR TORRES ESTATE *Sonoma County, California, USA* The sister of Spanish winemaker Miguel TORRES has established her own winery in the cool Green Valley region of SONOMA COUNTY, only a few miles from the Pacific Ocean. She specializes in Chardonnay and Pinot Noir, the best of which are from the Don Miguel Vineyard. The Chardonnay★★ is big and intense, perhaps a shade heavy on the oak, best with 2–4 years' age. The full-bodied Pinot Noir also achieves ★★ quality. Best years: (2001) 00 99 98 97 96 **95 94**.

MIGUEL TORRES *Curicó, Chile* After a long period of under-achievement from the man who re-awoke the Chilean wine industry, we are at last seeing good snappy Sauvignon Blanc★ once more, grassy, fruity Santa Digna rosé★ and a lean but blackcurranty Manso de Velasco Cabernet★, as well as exciting, sonorous old Carignan-based Cordillera. Best years: (Manso) (1999) 97 **96 95 94**.

TOURAINE AC *Loire Valley, France* General AC for Touraine wines in the central LOIRE. There are 6140ha (15,170 acres) of AC vineyards, divided half and half between red or rosé and white. Most of the reds are from the Gamay and in hot years these can be juicy, rustic-fruited wines. There is a fair amount of red from Cabernets Sauvignon and Franc, too, and some good Côt (Malbec). The reds are best drunk young. Fairly decent whites come from the Chenin Blanc but the best wines are from Sauvignon Blanc. These can be a good SANCERRE substitute at half the price. Drink at one year old, though Chenin wines can last longer. White and rosé sparkling wines are made by the traditional method, but are rarely as good as the best VOUVRAY and CREMANT DE LOIRE. Best producers: (reds and rosés) Ch. de Chenonceau★, Corbillières, J Delaunay★, Robert Denis★, Marcadet★, Marionnet/la Charmoise★, Pavy★, Roche Blanche★; (whites) des Acacias★, Baron Briare, Ch. de Chenonceau★, X Frissant, Marcadet★, Marionnet/la Charmoise★, Octavie★, Oisly-et-Thésée co-op★, Pibaleau★, Pré Baron★, J Preys★, Roche Blanche★. Best years: (reds) (2001) **00 99 98 97 96 95**.

CH. LA TOUR BLANCHE★★ *Sauternes AC, 1er Cru Classé, Bordeaux, France* This estate regained top form in the 1980s with the introduction of new oak barrels for fermentation, lower yields and greater selection. Full-bodied, rich and aromatic, it now ranks with the best of the Classed Growths. Second wine: Les Charmilles. Best years: (2001) 99 98 97 96 **95 90 89 88 86**.

DOM. LA TOUR-BOISÉE *Minervois AC, Languedoc, France* Jean-Louis Poudou is one of the pioneering producers in MINERVOIS. Of most interest here is the red Cuvée Marie-Claude★, aged for 12 months in barrel, the white Cuvée Marie-Claude★, which has a hint of Muscat Blanc à Petits Grains for added aroma, and the fruity Cuvée Marielle et Frédérique★, produced from Grenache and Syrah.

CH. TOUR DES GENDRES *Bergerac AC, South-West France* Luc de Conti's BERGERACS are made with as much sophistication as is found in the better Crus Classés of BORDEAUX. Generously fruity Moulin des Dames★ and the more earnest la Gloire de Mon Père★ reds are mostly Cabernet Sauvignon. Full, fruity and elegant Moulin des Dames★ white is a classic Bordeaux blend of Sémillon, Sauvignon Blanc and Muscadelle. Best years: (la Gloire de Mon Père) 2000 99 98 **97 96 95 94 90 89 88**.

TOURIGA NACIONAL High-quality red Portuguese grape which is rich in aroma and fruit. It is prized for PORT production as it contributes deep colour and tannin to the blend, and is rapidly increasing in importance for table wines both in the DOURO and elsewhere in Portugal.

TOWER ESTATE *Hunter Valley, New South Wales, Australia* Len Evans' latest venture, in partnership with a syndicate that includes British super-chef Rick Stein, features de luxe accommodation and focuses on sourcing top-notch grapes from their ideal regions. So, there is powerful, stylish COONAWARRA Cabernet★★, top-flight BAROSSA Shiraz★★ (sourced via Peter LEHMANN), fine floral CLARE Riesling★★, fruity ADELAIDE HILLS Sauvignon Blanc★ and classic Semillon★★, Shiraz★ and Chardonnay★ from the HUNTER.

TRÁS-OS-MONTES *Portugal* Impoverished north-eastern province, traditionally a supplier of grapes for Mateus Rosé, with 3 IPR regions, Valpaços, Chaves and Planalto-Mirandês, but producing pretty rustic stuff. However, the Vinho Regional Trás-os-Montes/Terras Durienses covers a handful of very good DOURO-sourced reds. Best producers: RAMOS PINTO (Bons Ares★ and Reserva★), Quinta de Cidrô (Chardonnay★), Valle Pradinhos.

TREBBIANO The most widely planted white Italian grape variety – far too widely, in fact, for Italy's good. As the Trebbiano Toscano, it is used as the base for EST! EST!! EST!!! and any number of other neutral, dry whites, as well as in VIN SANTO. But there are also a number of grapes masquerading under the Trebbiano name that aren't anything like as neutral. The most notable are the Trebbianos from LUGANA and ABRUZZO – both grapes capable of full-bodied, fragrant wines. Called Ugni Blanc in France, and primarily used for distilling, as it should be.

TRENTINO *Italy* This northern region is officially linked with ALTO ADIGE, but they are completely different. The wines rarely have the verve or perfume of Alto Adige examples, but can make up for this with riper, softer flavours, where vineyard yields have been kept in check. The Trentino DOC covers 20 different styles of wine, including whites Pinot Bianco and Grigio, Chardonnay, Moscato Giallo, Müller-Thurgau and Nosiola, and reds Schiava, Lagrein, Marzemino, Teroldego and Cabernet. Trento Classico is a special DOC for Champagne-method fizz. Best producers: N Balter★, N Bolognani★, La Cadalora★, Castel Noarna★, Cavit co-op, De Tarczal★, Dorigati, FERRARI★★, Graziano Fontana★, FORADORI★★, Isera co-op★, Letrari★, Longariva★, Conti Martini★, Maso Cantanghel★★, Maso Furli★, Maso Roveri★, Mezzacorona, Pojer & Sandri★, Pravis★, San Leonardo★★, Simoncelli★, E Spagnolli★, Vallarom★, La Vis co-op. See also Teroldego Rotaliano.

DOM. DE TRÉVALLON *Provence, France* Iconoclastic Parisian Eloi
Dürrbach makes brilliant reds★★ (at best ★★★) – mixing herbal
wildness with a sweetness of blackberry, blackcurrant and black, black
plums – and a tiny quantity of white★★★. Dürrbach's tradition-
busting blend of Cabernet Sauvignon and Syrah, no longer accepted
by the appellation les BAUX-DE-PROVENCE, is now VdP des BOUCHES-DU-
RHONE. The wines age extremely well, but are intriguingly drinkable in
their youth. Best years: (reds) (2000) 99 98 **97 96 95 94 93 90 89 88**.

TRIMBACH *Alsace AC, Alsace, France* An excellent grower/merchant
whose trademark is beautifully structured, subtly perfumed elegance.
Riesling and Gewurztraminer are the specialities, but the Pinot Gris
and Pinot Blanc are first-rate too. Top wines are Gewurztraminer
Cuvée des Seigneurs de Ribeaupierre★★, Riesling Cuvée Frédéric
Émile★★ and Riesling Clos St-Hune★★★. Also very good ALSACE
VENDANGE TARDIVE★★ and Sélection de Grains Nobles★★. Best years:
(Clos St-Hune) 1998 97 96 95 **93 92 90 89 88 85 83 81 76**.

TRITTENHEIM *Mosel, Germany* Important MOSEL wine village with some
excellent vineyard sites, most notably the Apotheke (pharmacy) and
Leiterchen (little ladder). The wines are sleek, with crisp acidity and
plenty of fruit. Best producers: Ernst Clüsserath★, Clüsserath-Weiler★,
GRANS-FASSIAN★, Milz-Laurentiushof★. Best years: (2001) 00 99 98 **97 95
93 90**.

CH. TROPLONG-MONDOT★★ *St-Émilion Grand Cru AC, Bordeaux, France*
Consistently one of the best of ST-EMILION's Grands Crus Classés and
contentiously denied promotion to Premier Grand Cru Classé status
in 1996. The wines are beautifully structured and mouthfillingly
textured for long aging. Best years: 2000 99 98 97 96 95 **94 90 89 88
86 85**.

CH. TROTANOY★★ *Pomerol AC, Bordeaux, France* Another POMEROL
estate (along with PETRUS, la FLEUR-PETRUS, LATOUR-A-POMEROL and
others) which has benefited from the brilliant touch of the MOUEIX
family. After a dip in the mid-1980s, recent vintages are getting back
on form. Best years: 2000 99 98 97 96 95 **94 93 90 89 88 82**.

CAVE VINICOLE DE TURCKHEIM *Alsace AC, Alsace, France* Very
important co-op with a reputation for good Pinot Blanc★, Pinot Gris★
and Gewurztraminer★. Brand★★ and Hengst★★ bottlings of the last
two are rich and concentrated. Riesling is less reliable, but reds, rosés
and CREMANT D'ALSACE★ are consistent. Best years: (Grand Cru
Gewurztraminer) (2000) 99 98 **97 95 94 93 90 89**.

TURLEY CELLARS *Napa Valley AVA, California, USA* Larry Turley
specializes in powerful Zinfandel and Petite Sirah. After early
assistance from his talented winemaking sister Helen (now based at
MARCASSIN), Turley has gone on to produce ultra-ripe Zins★★ from a
number of old vineyards. They pack a wallop and are either praised
for their profound power and depth or damned for their tannic, high-
alcohol, PORT-like nature. Petite Sirah★★ is similarly built, and all the
wines can last a decade or more. Best years: (Zins) (2000) (99) 98 97 96
95 **94 93**.

TURSAN VDQS *South-West France* Restaurateur Michel Guérard (3-star
Michelin), with his Baron de Bachen label, has helped preserve and
promote these wines, made on the edge of les Landes, the sandy
coastal area south of Bordeaux. The white is the most interesting:
made from the Baroque grape, it is clean, crisp and refreshing. Best
producers: Baron de Bachen★, Dulucq, Tursan co-op.

TUSCANY *Italy*   Tuscany's rolling hills, clad with vines, olive trees and cypresses, have produced wine since at least Etruscan times, and today Tuscany leads the way in promoting the new image of Italian wines. Its many DOC/DOCGs are based on the red Sangiovese grape and are led by CHIANTI CLASSICO, BRUNELLO DI MONTALCINO and VINO NOBILE DI MONTEPULCIANO, as well as famous SUPER-TUSCANS like ORNELLAIA and TIGNANELLO. White wines, despite sweet VIN SANTO, and the occasional excellent Chardonnay and Sauvignon, do not figure highly. See also Bolgheri, Carmignano, Montecarlo, Morellino di Scansano, Rosso di Montalcino, Rosso di Montepulciano, Sassicaia, Solaia, Vernaccia di San Gimignano.

TYRRELL'S *Hunter Valley, New South Wales, Australia*   Stalwart family-owned company with prime Lower HUNTER vineyards. Comprehensive range from basic Long Flat quaffers through the Individual Vineyard range (★), up to the superb Vat 1 Semillon★★★, generally excellent

Vat 47 Chardonnay★★, and Vat 5★ and Vat 9★★ Shiraz. Vat 6 Pinot Noir★ is variable. Best years: (Vat 1 Semillon) 1996 95 94 93 **92 91 90 89 87 86 77 76 75**; (Vat 47 Chardonnay) (1999) 98 97 **96 95 94 91 89**.

UCO VALLEY *Mendoza, Argentina*   This valley, in the foothills of the Andes, is an old secret of Argentine viticulture, newly rediscovered. With vineyards at 1000–1500m (3200–4900 ft) above sea level, clearly whites are going to be important, and the Chardonnays are Argentina's best. Reds are also showing fascinating flavours, with Merlot, Malbec, Syrah and Pinot Noir promising to be exceptional. Best producers: CATENA★★, La Celia★, Salentein★, Terrazas de los Andes★.

UGNI BLANC   See Trebbiano.

UMBRIA *Italy*   Wine production in this Italian region is dominated by ORVIETO, accounting for almost 70% of DOC wines. However, some of the most characterful wines are reds from TORGIANO and MONTEFALCO. Latest interest centres on remarkable new reds made by the outstanding Riccardo Cotarella at estates such as Pieve del Vescovo (Lucciaio★★), La Carraia (Fobiano★★), Lamborghini (Campoleone★★) and La Palazzola (Rubino★★).

ÜRZIG *Mosel, Germany*   Middle MOSEL village with the famous Würzgarten (spice garden) vineyard tumbling spectacularly down to the river and producing marvellously spicy Riesling. Drink young or with at least 5 years' age. Best producers: Bischöfliche Weinguter★, J J Christoffel★★, Dr LOOSEN★★★, Mönchhof★★, Peter Nicolay★. Best years: (2001) 00 99 98 **97** 96 95 **94 93**.

UTIEL-REQUENA DO *Valencia, Spain*   Inland from Valencia, Utiel-Requena is renowned for its rosés, mostly made from the Bobal grape. Recent plantings of Tempranillo are improving the reds. Best producers: Vicente Gandía Pla, Mustiguillo★, Bodegas Palmera (L'Angelet★), Schenk, Torre Oria, Vinival.

VACQUEYRAS AC *Rhône Valley, France*   The most important of the COTES DU RHONE-VILLAGES communes was promoted to its own AC in 1990. Red wines account for 95% of production; dark in colour, they have a warm, spicy bouquet and a rich deep flavour that seems infused with the herbs and pine dust of the south. Lovely to drink at 2–3 years, though good wines will age for 5 years or more. Best producers: Armouriers★, la Charbonnière★, Clos des Cazaux★, Couroulu★, DELAS★, la Fourmone (Roger Combe)★, la Garrigue★, JABOULET★, Montmirail★, Montvac★, Sang des Cailloux★, Tardieu-Laurent★★, Ch. des Tours★, Vacqueyras co-op★, Verquière★. Best years: (2001) 00 99 98 **97 96 95 94**.

VALAIS *Switzerland* Swiss canton flanking the Rhône above Lake Geneva. Between Martigny and Sierre the valley turns north-east, creating an Alpine suntrap, and this short stretch of terraced vineyard land provides many of Switzerland's most individual wines from Fendant, Johannisberger (the local name for Silvaner), Pinot Noir and Gamay, and several stunning examples from Syrah, Chardonnay, Ermitage (Marsanne) and Petite Arvine. Best producers: Michel Clavien★, J Germanier★, R Gilliard, Caves Imesch, Didier Joris★★, Mathier, Dom. du Mont d'Or★, Raymond, Zufferey.

CH. DE VALANDRAUD★★ *St-Émilion Grand Cru AC, Bordeaux, France*
The precursor of the 'garage wine' sensation in ST-ÉMILION, a big, rich, extracted wine from low yields, from grapes mainly grown on the less favoured Dordogne plain. The first vintage was in 1991 and since then prices have rocketed. Best years: 2000 99 98 97 96 95 **94 93 92**.

VALDEPEÑAS DO *Castilla-La Mancha, Spain* Valdepeñas offers some of Spain's best inexpensive oak-aged reds, but these are a small drop in a sea of less exciting stuff. In fact there are more whites than reds, at least some of them modern, fresh and fruity. Best producers: Miguel Calatayud, Los Llanos★, Luís Megía, Real, Félix Solís, Casa de la Viña.

VALDESPINO *Jerez y Manzanilla DO, Andalucía, Spain* Old-fashioned, high-quality sherry firm. Delicious wines include Inocente Fino★★, Tio Diego Amontillado★★, the expensive but concentrated Palo Cortado Cardenal★★, dry amontillados Coliseo★★★ and Don Tomás★★, Don Gonzalo Old Dry Oloroso★★ and Pedro Ximénez Solera Superior★★.

VALDIVIESO *Curicó, Chile* Part of the Mitjan group and recipient of huge investment both in their Lontué winery and Curicó Valley vineyards. Best known for smooth Pinot Noir★ and Chardonnay, but exciting Merlot★, Cabernet Franc★ and Malbec★★ in the single-vineyard Reserves. Multi-varietal blend Caballo Loco★ is good but a long way from its goal of being Chile's answer to GRANGE. V Series Malbec★★ and Pinot Noir★★ show smoothly honed complexity, but at a price. Although sparkling wines have been made here for 100 years, Champagne-method fizz is a recent introduction.

VAL D'ORBIEU, LES VIGNERONS DU *Languedoc-Roussillon, France*
This growers' association is France's largest wine exporting company, selling in excess of 20 million cases of (mostly uninspiring) wine a year. Membership includes several of the MIDI's best co-ops (Cucugnan, Cuxac, Ribauté and Montredon) and individual producers (Dom. de Fontsainte, Ch. la VOULTE-GASPARETS). It also owns Cordier (BORDEAUX) and Listel. Also marketed by Val d'Orbieu are Château de Jau and the excellent BANYULS and COLLIOURE estate, Clos de Paulilles. Its range of blended wines (Cuvée Chouette★, Chorus★, Pas de Deux, Elysices★, Réserve St-Martin★ and la Cuvée Mythique★) are a judicious mix of traditional Mediterranean varieties with Cabernet or Merlot and show welcome signs of ambition to raise quality.

VALENCIA *Spain* The best wines from Valencia DO in the south-east of Spain are the inexpensive, sweet, grapy Moscatels. Simple, fruity whites, reds and rosés are also good. Alicante DO to the south produces a little-known treasure, the Fondillón dry or semi-dry fortified wine, as well as a cluster of wines from native and foreign varieties made by a few quality-conscious modern wineries. Monastrell (Mourvèdre) is the main red grape variety. UTIEL-REQUENA DO specializes in rosés and light reds. Best producers: (Valencia) Vicente Gandía Pla, Los Pinos★, Schenk, Cherubino Valsangiacomo (Marqués de Caro); (Alicante) Bocopa★, Gutiérrez de la Vega (Casta Diva Muscat★★), Enrique Mendoza★★, Salvador Poveda★, Primitivo Quiles★.

VALLE D'AOSTA *Italy* Tiny Alpine valley sandwiched between PIEDMONT and the French Alps in northern Italy. The regional DOC covers 17 wine styles, referring either to a specific grape variety (like Gamay or Pinot Nero) or to a delimited region like Donnaz, a northern extension of Piedmont's CAREMA, producing a light red from the Nebbiolo grape. Perhaps the finest wine from these steep slopes is the sweet Chambave Moscato. Best producers: R Anselmet★, C Charrère★, Les Crêtes★, La Crotta di Vegneron★, Grosjean, Institut Agricole Regional★, Onze Communes co-op, Ezio Voyat★.

VALLEY VINEYARDS *Berkshire, England* Eighteen grape varieties planted over 13ha (32 acres) from which 2 Aussies – viticulturist and owner Jon Leighton and consultant winemaker John Worontschak – produce full-flavoured wines, many with antipodean-style use of oak. Fumé is an excellent oaked white; Bacchus-based Regatta really refreshing; and the bottle-fermented sparkling wines Ascot, Heritage Brut and Heritage Rosé are all good and reasonably priced.

VALL-LLACH *Priorat DOC, Spain* The tiny winery, owned by Catalan folk singer Lluís Llach, with young Sara Pérez as winemaker, has joined the ranks of the best PRIORAT producers with its powerful reds★★ dominated by old-vine Cariñena. Best years: 1999 **98**.

VALPOLICELLA DOC *Veneto, Italy* This wine can range in style from a light, cherryish red to the rich, port-like RECIOTO and AMARONE Valpolicellas. Most of the better examples are Valpolicella Classico from the hills and are made predominantly from Corvina (the best grape). The most concentrated, ageworthy examples are made either from a particular vineyard, or by refermenting the wine on the skins and lees of the Amarone, a style called *ripasso*, or simply by using a portion of dried grapes. Best producers: Accordini★, ALLEGRINI★★, Bertani★, Brigaldara★, Brunelli★, Tommaso Bussola★, M Castellani★, DAL FORNO★★, Guerrieri-Rizzardi★, MASI★, Mazzi★, Pasqua/Cecilia Beretta★, QUINTARELLI★★, Le Ragose★, Le Salette★, Serègo Alighieri★, Speri★, Tedeschi★, Villa Monteleone★, Zenato★, Fratelli Zeni★. Best years: 2000 97 95 93 90 88.

VALTELLINA SUPERIORE DOCG *Lombardy, Italy* Red wine produced on the precipitous slopes of northern LOMBARDY. There is a basic, light Valtellina DOC red, made from at least 70% Nebbiolo (here called Chiavennasca), but the best wines are made under the Valtellina Superiore DOCG as Grumello, Inferno, Sassella and Valgella. From top vintages the wines are attractively perfumed and approachable. Sfursat or Sforzato is a dense, high-alcohol red (up to 14.5%) made from semi-dried grapes. Best producers: La Castellina★, Enologica Valtellinese★, Fay★, Nino Negri★, Nera★, Rainoldi★, Conti Sertoli Salis★, Triacca★. Best years: (1998) 97 96 95 93 90 89 88 85.

VASSE FELIX *Margaret River, Western Australia* One of the originals responsible for MARGARET RIVER rocketing to fame, with decadently rich, profound Cabernet Sauvignon★★ and oak-led Shiraz★. Flagship red is the delicious Heytesbury★★, with a Chardonnay★★ to match. I'm still waiting for Vasse Felix consistently to reach the next level up. Best years: (Heytesbury) 1999 98 97 96 **95**.

VAUD *Switzerland* With the exception of the canton of Geneva, the Vaud accounts for the vineyards bordering Lake Geneva. There are 5 regions: la Côte, Lavaux, CHABLAIS, Côtes de l'Orbe-Bonvillars and Vully. Delightful light white wines are made from Chasselas; at DEZALEY it gains some real depth and character. Reds are from Gamay and Pinot Noir. Best producers: Henri Badoux, Louis Bovard★, Conne, Delarze, Dubois Fils, Grognuz, Massy, Obrist, Pinget, J & P Testuz.

VAVASOUR *Marlborough, South Island, New Zealand* First winery in the Awatere Valley, near MARLBOROUGH's main wine area, now enjoying spectacular success. One of New Zealand's best Chardonnays★★, a fine Pinot Noir★★ and palate-tingling oak-aged Sauvignon Blanc★★. Second label Dashwood also impresses, particularly with the tangy Dashwood Sauvignon Blanc★★.

VEENWOUDEN *Paarl WO, South Africa* This tiny cellar, which can double as a concert 'hall', is owned by inernational opera singer Deon van der Walt. His brother Marcel, an ex-golf pro, crafts 3 reds based on BORDEAUX varieties: sumptuous, well-oaked Merlot★★, firm and silky-fruited Veenwouden Classic★★ and Vivat Bacchus★, with a distinctive Malbec component. All are made to mature, the first 2 for up to 10 years. A tiny quantity of fine Chardonnay★ is also made. Best years: (Merlot, Classic) **1999** 98 97 96 95 94 93.

VEGA SICILIA *Ribera del Duero DO, Castilla y León, Spain* Among Spain's most expensive red wines, rich, fragrant, complex and very slow to mature, and by no means always easy to appreciate. This estate was the first in Spain to introduce French varieties, and over a quarter of the vines are now Cabernet Sauvignon, two-thirds are Tempranillo and the rest Malbec and Merlot. Vega Sicilia Unico★★★ – the top wine – has traditionally been given about 10 years' wood aging, but this has now been reduced to 5 and volatility evident in some vintages should now no longer occur. Second wine: Valbuena★★. A subsidiary winery produces the more modern-style Alión★★. Best years: (Unico) **1990** 86 85 83 82 81 80 79 76 75 74 70 68.

VELICH *Neuseidlersee, Burgenland, Austria* Former casino croupiers Roland and Heinz Velich make not only Austria's most mineral and sophisticated Chardonnay★★ from old vines in the Tiglat vineyard, but since 1995 also spectacular dessert wines of ★★ and ★★★ quality. Best years: (Tiglat Chardonnay) (2001) 00 99 **97** 95 93 92; (sweet whites) (2000) 99 98 **96** 95 94 91.

VENETO *Italy* This region takes in the wine zones of SOAVE, VALPOLICELLA, BARDOLINO and Piave in north-east Italy. It is the source of a great deal of inexpensive wine, but the Soave and Valpolicella hills are also capable of producing small quantities of high-quality wine. Other hilly areas like Colli Berici and COLLI EUGANEI produce mainly large quantities of dull staple varietal wines, but can offer the odd flash of brilliance. The great dry red of this zone is AMARONE. See also Bianco di Custoza, Breganze, Prosecco di Conegliano-Valdobbiadene, Recioto della Valpolicella, Recioto di Soave.

VERDICCHIO DEI CASTELLI DI JESI DOC *Marche, Italy* Verdicchio, grown in the hills near the Adriatic around Jesi and in the Apennine enclave of Matelica, has blossomed into central Italy's most promising white variety. When fresh and fruity it is the ideal wine with fish, but some Verdicchio can age into a white of surprising depth of flavours. A few producers, notably Garofoli with Serra Fiorese★★, age it in oak, but even without wood it can develop an almost Burgundy-like complexity. Jesi is the classical zone, but the rarer Verdicchio di Matelica can be as impressive. A little is made sparkling. Best producers: (Jesi) Brunori★, Bucci★, Colonnara★, Coroncino★, Fazi Battaglia★, Garofoli★★, Mancinelli★, Terre Cortesi Moncaro★, Monte Schiavo★, Santa Barbara★, Sartarelli★★, Tavignano★, Umani Ronchi★, Fratelli Zaccagnini★; (Matelica) Belisario★, Bisci★, Mecella★, La Monacesca★★.

VERGELEGEN *Stellenbosch WO, South Africa* Winemaker Andre van Rensburg is busy making this historic Anglo American-owned farm one of the greats of the new century. His 2 Sauvignon Blancs are already considered benchmarks: the regular bottling★★ is aggressive and racy, streaked with sleek tropical fruit; the single-vineyard★★ flinty, dry and powerful. There is also a ripe-textured, stylish Chardonnay Reserve★★. The reds are even more attention-grabbing. Vergelegen★★, the BORDEAUX-blend flagship, shows classic mineral restraint. Merlot★★ and Cabernet★★ are some of the best in South Africa. Van Rensburg has only been here since 1998; several of these wines will reach ★★★ status in future vintages. Best years: (premium reds) **2000 99 98 97 95 94**; (Chardonnay Reserve) **2000 99 98 97 96**.

VERGET *Mâconnais, Burgundy, France* A négociant house specializing in white Burgundies, run by Jean-Marie Guffens-Heynen, an exuberant character with his own domaine. The Guffens-Heynen wines include excellent MACON-VILLAGES★ and POUILLY-FUISSE★★ but the Verget range extends to outstanding Premiers Crus and Grands Crus from the COTE D'OR, notably CHASSAGNE-MONTRACHET★★ and BATARD-MONTRACHET★★★. But beware, the wines are made in a *very* individualistic style.

VERITAS *Barossa, South Australia* In vino veritas (In wine there is truth), say the Binder family. There's certainly truth in the bottom of a bottle of Hanisch Vineyard Shiraz★★★ or Heysen Vineyard Shiraz★★★, both blindingly good wines. The Shiraz-Mourvèdre★★ (known locally as Bulls' Blood) and Shiraz-Grenache★★ blends are lovely big reds; Cabernet-Merlot★★ is also good. Under the Christa-Rolf label, Shiraz-Grenache★ is good and spicy with attractive, forward black fruit.

VERMENTINO The best dry white wines of SARDINIA generally come from the Vermentino grape. Light, dry, perfumed and nutty, the best examples tend to be from the north of the island, where the Vermentino di Gallura zone is located. Occasionally it is made sweet or sparkling. Vermentino is also grown in LIGURIA and TUSCANY, though its character is quite different. It is believed to be the same as Rolle, found in many blends in LANGUEDOC-ROUSSILLON. Best producers: (Sardinia) ARGIOLAS★, Capichera★, Cherchi★, Gallura co-op, Piero Mancini★, Pedra Majore★, Santadi co-op★, SELLA & MOSCA★, Vermentino co-op.

VERNACCIA DI ORISTANO DOC *Sardinia, Italy* Outstanding, oxidized, almost sherry-like wines from the west of the island, which acquire complexity and colour through long aging in wood. Amber-coloured and dry, nutty and long on the finish. Best producer: Contini★.

279

VERNACCIA DI SAN GIMIGNANO DOCG *Tuscany, Italy* Dry white wines – generally light quaffers – made from the Vernaccia grape grown in the hills around San Gimignano. It is debatable whether the allowance of up to 10% Chardonnay in the blend is a forward step. There is a San Gimignano DOC for the zone's up-and-coming reds, though the best SUPER-TUSCANS are sold as IGT wines. Best producers: Cà del Vispo★, Le Calcinaie★, Casale-Falchini★, V Cesani★, La Lastra (Riserva★), Melini (Le Grillaie★), Montenidoli★, G Panizzi★, Il Paradiso★, Pietrafitta★, La Rampa di Fugnano★, Guicciardini Strozzi★, Teruzzi & Puthod (Terre di Tufi★★), Casa alle Vacche★, Vagnoni★.

NOËL VERSET *Cornas AC, Rhône Valley, France* Powerful, concentrated reds★★ from some of the oldest and best-sited vines in CORNAS. Yields are tiny and it shows in the depth that Verset achieves. Worth aging for 10 years or more. Best years: 1999 98 97 96 95 94 91 90 **89 88 85**.

VESUVIO DOC *Campania, Italy* Red wines based on Piedirosso and whites from Coda di Volpe and Verdeca. The evocative name Lacryma Christi del Vesuvio is now only for superior versions. Best producers: Cantine Caputo, Cantina Grotta del Sole, MASTROBERARDINO.

VESÚVIO, QUINTA DO★★★ *Port DOC, Douro, Portugal* A consistently top performer, it differs from Symington stablemates DOW, GRAHAM and WARRE in that it appears whenever the high quality can be maintained (and not just in officially declared years). A brilliant port, best with at least 10 years' age. Best years: (2000) 99 98 97 96 95 94 92 **91 90**.

VEUVE CLICQUOT *Champagne AC, Champagne, France* Produced by the LVMH luxury goods group, these Champagnes can still live up to the high standards set by the original Widow Clicquot at the beginning of the 19th century, although many are released too young. The non-vintage★ is full, toasty and satisfyingly weighty, or lean and raw, depending on your luck: the vintage★★ is fuller and the de luxe Grande Dame★★★ is both powerful and elegant. Grande Dame Rosé★★★ is exquisite. Best years: (1996) 95 **93 91 90 89 88 85 82**.

VICTORIA *Australia* Despite its relatively small area, Victoria has arguably more land suited to quality grape-growing than any other state in Australia, with climates ranging from hot Sunraysia and RUTHERGLEN on the Murray River to cool MORNINGTON PENINSULA and GIPPSLAND in the south. The range of flavours is similarly wide and exciting. With more than 200 wineries, Victoria leads the boutique winery boom, particularly in Mornington Peninsula. See also Bendigo, Central Victoria, Geelong, Grampians and Pyrenees, Yarra Valley.

VIEUX-CHÂTEAU-CERTAN★★ *Pomerol AC, Bordeaux, France* Slow-developing, tannic red with up to 30% Cabernet Franc and 10% Cabernet Sauvignon in the blend, which after 15–20 years finally resembles more a fragrant refined MEDOC than a hedonistic POMEROL. Best years: 2000 99 98 96 95 **90 89 88 86 85 83 82**.

VIEUX TÉLÉGRAPHE *Châteauneuf-du-Pape AC, Rhône Valley, France* One of the top names in the AC, less tannic than BEAUCASTEL perhaps, but with just as much aging potential. The vines are some of the oldest in CHATEAUNEUF and the Grenache-based red★★★ is among the best modern-style wines produced in the RHONE VALLEY. There is also a small amount of white★★, which is heavenly when very young. Also owns la Roquette (Châteauneuf-du-Pape★★) and les Pallières★ in GIGONDAS. Best years: (reds) (2000) 99 98 97 **96 95 93 90 89 88**.

VILLA MARIA *Auckland, North Island, New Zealand* Founder George
Fistonich also owns Esk Valley and Vidal. Villa Maria Reserve
Cabernet★★★, Esk Valley The Terraces★★★ (a BORDEAUX-style blend)
and Vidal Merlot-Cabernet★★ are superb. Reserve Chardonnay from
Vidal★★ and Villa Maria★ are power-packed wines. Also produces 2
outstanding examples of MARLBOROUGH Sauvignon Blanc: Wairau
Valley★★ and even more concentrated Clifford Bay Reserve★★. Also
from Marlborough, impressive Riesling★★ and stunning Late Harvest
Riesling★★★. Best years: (Hawkes Bay reds) (2000) **99 98 96**.

VILLARD ESTATE *Casablanca, Chile* Owner Thierry Villard (formerly of
ORLANDO in South Australia) has created one of Chile's most successful
boutique wineries. Big, buttery Chardonnay Reserve★ and clean, crisp
Sauvignon Blanc★, both from CASABLANCA. Also good Casablanca Pinot
Noir★, MAIPO Merlot★ and superb El Noble★★ sweetie.

CH. DE VILLENEUVE *Saumur-Champigny AC, Loire Valley, France*
During the 1990s this property emerged as one of the very best in the
region. The secret lies in low yields, picked when properly ripe. First-
class SAUMUR-CHAMPIGNY★, with concentrated, mineral Vieilles
Vignes★★ and le Grand Clos★★. Also good white, stainless steel-
fermented SAUMUR★ and barrel-fermented Saumur Les Cormiers★★.

VILLIERA *Stellenbosch WO, South Africa* Quality and value for money are
non-negotiables in this varied range. The speciality is Cap Classique
sparklers under the Tradition label; the flagship vintage Monro Brut★
is a Pinot Noir-Chardonnay blend with rich, biscuity flavours.
Winemaker Jeff Grier is known for Sauvignon Blanc (Bush Vine★);
there's also a consistent Riesling★ and 2 delicious Chenin Blancs with
different degrees of oaking. Reds are equally good, especially the
intense yet succulent BORDEAUX-style Cru Monro★ and newcomer
Merlot-Pinotage★. Best years: (Cru Monro) **1999 98 97 96 95 94**.

VIN SANTO *Tuscany, Italy* The 'holy wine' of TUSCANY can be one of the
world's great sweet wines – just occasionally, that is, for it is also one
of the most wantonly abused wine terms in Italy (in particular avoid
anything called *liquoroso*). Made from grapes either hung from rafters
or laid on mats after harvest to dry, the resulting wines, fermented and
aged in small barrels (*caratelli*) for up to 7–8 years, should be nutty,
oxidized, full of the flavours of dried apricots and crystallized orange
peel, concentrated and long. Also produced in UMBRIA and in TRENTINO as
Vino Santo. Best producers: Castello di AMA★, AVIGNONESI★★★, Fattoria
Basciano★★, Cacchiano★, Capezzana★★, Fattoria del Cerro★★,
Corzano & Paterno★★, FONTODI★★, ISOLE E OLENA★★★, Rocca di
Montegrossi★, San Felice★★, San Giusto a Rentennano★★★,
SELVAPIANA★★, Villa Pillo★, Villa Sant'Anna★★, VOLPAIA★.

VIÑA CASABLANCA *Casablanca, Chile* This much-acclaimed estate owes
its reputation to Ignacio Recabarren, now departed to CONCHA Y TORO.
Only top wines use CASABLANCA-sourced fruit. White Label wines use
vineyards in Lontué, MAIPO and San Fernando. There is rose- and lychee-
filled Gewürztraminer★, excellent tangy, intense Sauvignon Blanc★,
quince-edged Santa Isabel Estate Chardonnay★★ and barrel-fermented
Chardonnay★ from the same estate. Reds include inky-black Cabernet
Sauvignon★ and low-yield White Label Merlot★, together with the
minty, exotic Merlot★★ and Cabernet★★ from the Santa Isabel Estate.

VIÑAS DEL VERO *Somontano DO, Aragón, Spain* SOMONTANO's largest
company, specializing in New World-inspired wines. A buttery but
mineral unoaked Chardonnay and its toasty barrel-fermented

counterpart★ are joined by more original whites such as Clarión★, a blend of Chardonnay, Gewürztraminer and Macabeo. Flavours have unfortunately been lightening up recently, but top reds – Gran Vos★ (Merlot-Cabernet-Pinot Noir) and the new red blend★★ made by its subsidiary Blecua – still deliver the goods.

VINHO VERDE DOC *Minho and Douro Litoral, Portugal* 'Vinho Verde' can be red *or* white. 'Green' only in the sense of being young, demarcated Vinhos Verde come from north-west Portugal. The whites are the most widely seen outside Portugal and range from sulphured and acidic to aromatic, flowery and fruity. One or two that fall outside the DOC regulations are sold as Vinho Regional Minho. Best producers: Quinta de Alderiz, Quinta da Aveleda, Quinta da Baguinha★, Encostas dos Castelos, Quinta da Franqueira★, Moncão co-op (Deu la Deu Alvarinho★), Muros de Melgaço (Alvarinho★), Quintas de Melgaço, Palácio de Brejoeira, Dom Salvador, Casa de Sezim★, Soalheiro, SOGRAPE (Gazela, Quinta de Azevedo★), Quinta do Tamariz (Loureiro★).

VINO NOBILE DI MONTEPULCIANO DOCG *Tuscany, Italy* The 'noble wine' from the hills around the town of Montepulciano is made from the Sangiovese grape, known locally as the Prugnolo, with the help of a little Canaiolo and Mammolo. At its best, it combines the power and structure of BRUNELLO DI MONTALCINO with the finesse and complexity found in top CHIANTI. Unfortunately, the best was a rare beast until relatively recently, though the rate of improvement has been impressive. The introduction of what is essentially a second wine, ROSSO DI MONTEPULCIANO, has certainly helped. Best producers: AVIGNONESI★★, Bindella★, BOSCARELLI★★, La Braccesca/ANTINORI★, Le Casalte★, La Ciarlina★, Contucci★★, Dei★★, Del Cerro★, Fassati★, Il Macchione★, Nottola★★, Palazzo Vecchio★, POLIZIANO★★, Redi★, Romeo★, Salcheto★, Trerose★, Valdipiatta★, Villa Sant'Anna★. Best years: (2001) 00 99 98 **97 95 93 90 88**.

VIOGNIER A poor yielder, prone to disease and difficult to vinify. The wine can be delicious: peachy, apricotty with a soft, almost waxy texture, usually a fragrance of spring flowers and sometimes a taste like crème fraîche. Traditionally grown only in the northern RHONE, it is now found in LANGUEDOC-ROUSSILLON, Ardèche and the southern Rhône as well as in CALIFORNIA, Argentina, Chile, Australia and South Africa.

VIRÉ-CLESSÉ *Mâconnais, Burgundy, France* Appellation created in 1998 out of 2 of the best MACON VILLAGES. Controversially, the rules have outlawed wines with residual sugar, thus excluding Jean Thévenet's extraordinary cuvées. Best producers: Bonhomme★★, Chazelles★, Cave de Viré★, Ch. de Viré★, Merlin★, Michel★★, Rijckaert★.

ROBERTO VOERZIO *Barolo DOCG, Piedmont, Italy* One of the best of the new wave of BAROLO producers that came to prominence in the late 1980s. Dolcetto (Priavino★) is successful, as is Vignaserra★★ – barrique-aged Nebbiolo with a little Cabernet – and the outstanding new BARBERA D'ALBA Riserva Vigneto Pozzo dell'Annunziata★★★. Barriques are also used for fashioning his Barolo, but such is the quality and concentration of fruit coming from densely planted vineyards that the oak does not overwhelm. Single-vineyard examples made in the best years are Brunate★★, Cerequio★★★, La Serra★★ and new Riserva Capalot★★★. Best years: (Barolo) (2000) 99 98 97 96 **95 93 91 90 89 88 85**.

COMTE GEORGES DE VOGÜÉ *Chambolle-Musigny AC, Côte de Nuits, Burgundy, France* De Vogüé owns substantial holdings in 2 Grands Crus, BONNES-MARES★★★ and MUSIGNY★★★, as well as in Chambolle's top Premier Cru, les Amoureuses★★★. Since 1990 the domaine has been on magnificent form. It is the sole producer of minute quantities of Musigny Blanc★★★, but because of recent replanting the wine is now being sold as (very expensive) BOURGOGNE Blanc. Best years: (Musigny) (2001) 00 99 98 97 96 95 93 **92 91 90**.

VOLNAY AC *Côte de Beaune, Burgundy, France* Volnay is home to the finest red wines of the COTE DE BEAUNE in terms of elegance and class. Attractive when young, the best examples can age well. The top Premiers Crus are Caillerets, Champans, Clos des Chênes, Santenots (which actually lies in MEURSAULT) and Taillepieds. Best producers: R Ampeau★★, d'ANGERVILLE★★, J-M Boillot★★, J-M Bouley★★, Carré-Courhin★, COCHE-DURY★★, V GIRARDIN★★, LAFARGE★★★, LAFON★★★, Dom. Matrot★★, Montille★★, N Potel★★, J Prieur★★, Roblet-Monnot★, J Voillot★★. Best years: 1999 98 97 96 **95 93 91 90 89 88**.

VOLPAIA, CASTELLO DI *Chianti Classico DOCG, Tuscany, Italy* Light, perfumed but refined CHIANTI CLASSICO★ (Riserva★★). Two stylish SUPER-TUSCANS, Balifico★★ and Coltassala★★, are both predominantly Sangiovese. Sometimes good but not great VIN SANTO★.

VOSNE-ROMANÉE AC *Côte de Nuits, Burgundy, France* The greatest village in the COTE DE NUITS, with 6 Grands Crus and 13 Premiers Crus (notably les Malconsorts, aux Brûlées and les Suchots) which are often as good as other villages' Grands Crus. The quality of the village wine is also high. In good years the wines need at least 6 years' aging and 10–15 would be better. Best producers: R Arnoux★★★, Cacheux-Sirugue★★, Sylvain Cathiard★★, Champy★★, B Clavelier★★, R Engel★★, GRIVOT★★★, Anne Gros★★★, A-F Gros★★, Haegelen-Jayer★★, F Lamarche★★, Dom. LEROY★★★, MEO-CAMUZET★★★, Mugneret-Gibourg★★, RION★★, Dom. de la ROMANEE-CONTI★★★, E Rouget★★★, THOMAS-MOILLARD★. Best years: (2001) 00 99 98 97 96 95 **93 91 90**.

VOUGEOT AC *Côte de Nuits, Burgundy, France* Outside the walls of CLOS DE VOUGEOT there are 11ha (27 acres) of Premier Cru and 5ha (12 acres) of other vines. Look out for Premier Cru Les Cras (red) and the Clos Blanc de Vougeot, first planted with white grapes in 1110. Best producers: Bertagna★★, Chopin-Groffier★★, C Clerget★, Vougeraie★★. Best years: (reds) (2000) 99 98 97 96 95 **93 91 90 89 88**.

CH. LA VOULTE-GASPARETS *Corbières AC, Languedoc, France* One of the MIDI's most consistent properties, producing CORBIERES with flavours of thyme and baked earth from old hillside vines. The Cuvée Réservée★ and Romain Pauc★★ are the most expensive wines, but the basic Voulte-Gasparets★ is also good. Can be drunk young, but ages well. Best years: (Romain Pauc) 2000 98 **96 95 93 91**.

VOUVRAY AC *Loire Valley, France* Dry, medium-dry, sweet and sparkling wines from Chenin grapes east of Tours. The dry wines acquire beautifully rounded flavours after 6–8 years. Medium-dry wines, when properly made from a single domaine, are worth aging for 20 years or more. Spectacular noble-rot-affected sweet wines can be produced in years such as 1995, 96 and 97. The fizz is some of the

LOIRE's best. Best producers: Aubuisières★★, Bourillon-Dorléans★★, Champalou★★, Clos Naudin★★, P Delaleu★, la Fontainerie★★, Ch. Gaudrelle★★, Gautier★★, HUET★★, Nerisson★, Pichot★★, F Pinon★★. Best years: 2001 99 **98 97 96 95** 93 90 89 88 85 83 78 76 75 70.

WACHAU *Niederösterreich, Austria* This stunning stretch of the Danube between Krems-Stein and the monastery of Melk is Austria's top region for dry whites. Riesling is the grape here, followed by Grüner Veltliner. Best producers: F HIRTZBERGER★★★, Högl★★, Emmerich KNOLL★★★, NIKOLAIHOF★★, F X PICHLER★★★, PRAGER★★★, Freie Weingärtner WACHAU★★. Best years: (2001) 00 99 **98 97 95 94** 93 92 90 88 86 83 79 77.

WACHAU, FREIE WEINGÄRTNER *Wachau, Niederösterreich, Austria* Co-op long producing fine WACHAU white wines, especially vineyard-designated Grüner Veltliners and Rieslings★★. Best years: (2000) 99 **98 97 96 95** 93 92 91 90 88 86 79.

WACHENHEIM *Pfalz, Germany* Wine village made famous by the BÜRKLIN-WOLF estate, its best vineyards are capable of producing rich yet beautifully balanced Rieslings. Best producers: Josef BIFFAR★, BÜRKLIN-WOLF★★, Karl Schaefer★, J L WOLF★★. Best years: (1999) 98 **97** 96 **94** 93 90.

WAIHEKE ISLAND *North Island, New Zealand* GOLDWATER pioneered wine-making on this island in Auckland harbour in the early 1980s. Hot, dry ripening conditions have made high-quality Cabernet-based reds that sell for high prices. An increasing quantity of Chardonnay is appearing, together with experimental plots of Shiraz and Viognier. A tiny, highly fashionable region that will soon be home to over 30 winemakers. Best producers: Fenton★★, GOLDWATER★★, Obsidian, STONYRIDGE★★★, Te Whau★. Best years: (reds) 2000 99 98 **96 94** 93.

WALLA WALLA VALLEY AVA *Washington State, USA* Walla Walla has more than 35 of WASHINGTON's wineries, but 22 of these have only been producing since 1999. Vineyard acreage has trebled since 1999 – and is still growing. If you think there's a gold-rush feel about this clearly exciting area you wouldn't be far wrong. Best producers: CANOE RIDGE★, Dunham Cellars★, L'ECOLE NO 41★★, LEONETTI CELLAR★★★, Pepper Bridge Winery★, WOODWARD CANYON★★.

WARRE *Port DOC, Douro, Portugal* Top-quality Vintage PORT★★★, and a good 'off-vintage' port from Quinta da Cavadinha★★. Crusted★★ and LBV★★ are very welcome traditional, full-bodied ports. Warrior★ is a reliable ruby. Otima, an adequate 10-year-old tawny, is most remarkable for its unconventional clear bottle presentation. Age Vintage port for 15–30 years. Best years: (Vintage) (2000) 97 94 91 85 83 80 **77 70 66 63**; (Cavadinha) (1999) 98 95 92 **90 88 87 86 82 78**.

WARWICK *Stellenbosch WO, South Africa* This farm focuses on reds from the heart of the Cape's best red wine country. Traditional BORDEAUX varieties are responsible for the complex Trilogy★ blend, and a refined, fragrant, varietal Cabernet Franc★. Old Bush Vine Pinotage is less consistent but, at best, is plummy and perfumed; Pinotage also plays a role in the new red blend, Three Cape Ladies★, with Cabernet Sauvignon and Merlot. Whites are represented by a full-bodied yet lightly oaked Chardonnay★. Best years: (Trilogy) 1999 98 **97 96 95 94**.

WASHINGTON STATE *USA* Second-largest premium wine-producing state in the US. The chief growing areas are in irrigated high desert, east of the Cascade Mountains, where the COLUMBIA VALLEY AVA encompasses the smaller AVAs of YAKIMA VALLEY, WALLA WALLA VALLEY and Red Mountain. Although the heat is not as intense as in CALIFORNIA, long summer days with extra hours of sunshine due to the northern latitude seem to increase the intensity of fruit flavours and result in both red and white wines of great depth. Cabernet, Merlot, Chardonnay, Sauvignon Blanc and Semillon produce very good wines here.

GEOFF WEAVER *Adelaide Hills, South Australia* Geoff Weaver crafts fine wines from grapes grown at his Lenswood vineyard. Quality fruit from low-yielding vines produces limy Riesling★★, crisply gooseberryish Sauvignon★★ and stylish cool-climate Chardonnay★★. Cabernet-Merlot★ is restrained but tasty, Pinot Noir promising.

WEGELER *Bernkastel, Mosel; Oestrich-Winkel, Rheingau; Deidesheim, Pfalz, Germany* In 1997 the Wegeler family sold their share of the huge Deinhard wine empire to concentrate on wines from their own vineyards. All 3 estates are dedicated primarily to Riesling, and today dry wines make up the bulk of production. Whether dry or naturally sweet Auslese, the best merit ★★ and will develop well with 5 or more years of aging. The MOSEL estate achieves the best standard of the 3 estates; nearly all the wines are ★. Best years: (Mosel-Saar-Ruwer) (2001) 99 98 **97 96 95 93 90 89 88 83 76**.

WEHLEN *Mosel, Germany* Village whose steep Sonnenuhr vineyard produces some of the most powerful Rieslings in Germany. Best producers: Kerpen, Dr LOOSEN★★★, J J PRUM★★★, S A PRUM★, Max Ferd RICHTER★★, SELBACH-OSTER★★, WEGELER★, Dr Weins-Prüm★. Best years: (2000) 99 98 **97** 96 95 **94 93 92 90 89 88 85 83 76**.

ROBERT WEIL *Kiedrich, Rheingau, Germany* This estate has enjoyed huge investment from Japanese drinks giant Suntory which, coupled with Wilhelm Weil's devotion to quality, has made it the brightest jewel in the RHEINGAU's crown. Majestic sweet Auslese, Beerenauslese and Trockenbeerenauslese Rieslings★★★, and dry Rieslings★ are crisp and elegant, although the regular wines have been a little disappointing in recent vintages. Best years: (2001) **99** 98 **97** 96 **95 94 93 90 89**.

WEINBACH *Alsace AC, Alsace, France* This Kaysersberg estate, which produces some of the most classic wines of ALSACE, is run by Mme Colette Faller and her two daughters. The range is quite complicated. Some wines are named in honour of Mme Faller's late husband Théo★★; others are labelled Ste-Cathérine★★, and are late picked, though not technically Vendange Tardive. Also very fine are the Gewurztraminer Altenbourg Laurence★★ and the Pinot Gris Cuvée Laurence★★. The Riesling Grand Cru Schlossberg★★★ is the finest dry wine. In certain vintages the estate produces Quintessence – a super-concentrated Sélection de Grains Nobles – from Pinot Gris★★★ and Gewurztraminer★★★. All the wines are exceptionally balanced and can be aged for many years. Best years: (Grand Cru Riesling) 1999 98 97 96 **95 94 93 92 90 89 88 85 83**. See also Alsace Vendange Tardive.

WEISSBURGUNDER See Pinot Blanc.

WELSCHRIESLING See Riesling Italico.

WENDOUREE *Clare Valley, South Australia* Small winery using old-fashioned methods to make enormous, ageworthy reds★★★ from paltry yields off their own very old Shiraz, Cabernet, Malbec and Mataro (Mourvèdre) vines, plus tiny amounts of sweet Muscat★. Reds can, and do, age beautifully for 30 years or more. Best years: (reds) 1998 96 95 94 **92 91 90 86 83 82 81 80 78 76 75**.

WESTERN AUSTRALIA Only the south-west corner of this vast state is suited to vines, the SWAN DISTRICT and Perth environs being the oldest and hottest area, with present attention (and more than 100 wineries) focused on GREAT SOUTHERN, MARGARET RIVER, Geographe and PEMBERTON.

WIEN *Austria* Region within the city limits of Wien (Vienna). The best wines come from south-facing sites in Grinzing, Nussdorf and Weiden; and the Bisamberg hill east of the Danube. Best producers: Bernreiter, Kierlinger, Mayer, Schilling, Wieninger★. Best years: (2001) 00 **99 97 95 94 93**. See also Heuriger.

WILLAMETTE VALLEY AVA *Oregon, USA* This viticultural area is typical of OREGON's maritime climate. Wet winters, generally dry summers, and a good chance of long, cool autumn days provide sound growing conditions for cool-climate varieties such as Pinot Noir, Pinot Gris and Chardonnay. Dundee Hills, with its volcanic hillsides, is considered the best sub-region. Best producers: ADELSHEIM★, AMITY★, Argyle★, BEAUX FRERES★★, BETHEL HEIGHTS★, Cameron★, CRISTOM★, DOMAINE DROUHIN★★, ELK COVE★★, EYRIE★, KING ESTATE, PANTHER CREEK★, Ponzi, Rex Hill★, Sokol Blosser, Torii Mor★, WillaKenzie★, Ken WRIGHT★, Yamhill Valley★. Best years: (reds) 2000 99 98 **96 94**.

WILLIAMS SELYEM *Russian River Valley AVA, California, USA* Purchased in 1998 by John Dyson of New York, it looks as if the cult following for the Pinot Noirs★★, especially the J Rochioli Vineyard★★★, has diminished somewhat. Traditionally the wine is big, sometimes very fruity and sometimes just a bit off the wall. Impressive Zinfandel★★, too. Best years: (Pinot Noir) (1999) 98 97 **96 95 94 92 91**.

WINKEL *Rheingau, Germany* RHEINGAU village whose best vineyard is the large Hasensprung but the most famous one is Schloss Vollrads – an ancient estate that does not use the village name on its label. Best producers: August Eser, Johannishof★★, SCHLOSS VOLLRADS★ (since 1999), WEGELER★. Best years: (2001) **99** 98 96 **93 90**.

WIRRA WIRRA *McLaren Vale, South Australia* Consistent maker of whites with more finesse than is customary in the region; now reds are as good, too. Recent years have seen rapid expansion. Well-balanced Sauvignon Blanc★, ageworthy Semillon blend★, buttery Chardonnay★★ and soft reds led by delicious The Angelus Cabernet★★, chocolaty RSW Shiraz★★, decadent Original Blend Grenache-Shiraz★, and seductive Allawah BAROSSA Grenache★★. Best years: (The Angelus) 1999 98 97 **96 95 92 91 90**.

WITHER HILLS *Marlborough, South Island, New Zealand* Brent Marris launched his Wither Hills label while working for DELEGAT'S. A trio of stylish MARLBOROUGH wines – concentrated, pungent Sauvignon Blanc★★, fine, fruit-focused Chardonnay★★ and vibrant Pinot Noir★★ – rapidly established his reputation as one of the region's top producers. With a new winery and grapes from extensive vineyards owned by his father, Marris is taking the world by storm.

J L WOLF *Wachenheim, Pfalz, Germany* Ernst Loosen, of Dr LOOSEN in the MOSEL, took over this underperforming estate in 1996. A string of concentrated dry and naturally sweet Rieslings★★ have won it a place among the region's top producers. Best years: (2001) 00 99 98 **97 96**.

WOODWARD CANYON *Walla Walla Valley AVA, Washington State, USA* Big, barrel-fermented Chardonnays, one from Estate★ fruit and the other from Celilo Vineyard★, were the trademark wines for many years, but today the focus is on reds, with a fine Artist Series★ Cabernet Sauvignon and Dedication★★ Cabernet Sauvignon leading the line-up. Merlot can be velvety and deeply perfumed. White and red★ BORDEAUX-style blends are labelled Charbonneau, the name of the vineyard where the fruit is grown. Best years: (Cabernet Sauvignon) 2000 99 98 97 **96 95**.

KEN WRIGHT CELLARS *Willamette Valley AVA, Oregon, USA* Ken Wright produces more than a dozen succulent, single-vineyard Pinot Noirs. Bold and rich with new oak flavour, they range from good to ethereal, led by the Carter★★★, Shea★★★, Arcus★★ and McCrone★★. Fine WASHINGTON Chardonnay from the Celilo Vineyard★★, expressive French clone OREGON Chardonnays from Carabella★ and McCrone★ and a zesty Pinot Blanc from Freedom Hill Vineyard★ make up the portfolio of whites. Best years: (Pinot Noir) (2001) 99 98 **97 94 93 90**.

WÜRTTEMBERG *Germany* Underperforming wine region centred on the river Neckar. More than half the wine made is red, and the best comes from Lemberger (Blaufränkisch), Dornfelder or Spätburgunder (Pinot Noir) grapes. Massive yields are often responsible for pallid wines. However, a few of the many marvellously steep sites produce perfumed reds and racy Riesling. Best years: (reds) (2001) 99 98 **97 94 93 90**.

WÜRZBURG *Franken, Germany* The centre of FRANKEN wines. Some Rieslings can be great, but the real star is Silvaner. Best producers: Bürgerspital, JULIUSSPITAL★, Staatlicher Hofkeller, Weingut am Stein★. Best years: (2001) 00 99 97 **94 93 92 90**.

WYNNS *Coonawarra, South Australia* This name is synonymous with COONAWARRA. After a low period in the 1970s, standard Cabernet★★ and Shiraz★ have returned to form, so that they are among the best value in the land. They also age well: better vintages from the 1950s and 60s are still alive and kicking. In peak years the cream of the Cabernet is released as John Riddoch★★★ and Shiraz as Michael★★, both powerful reds, the latter incredibly oaky. There is also Chardonnay★ in an attractive, fruit-driven style, plus cheap, delightful Riesling★. Best years: (John Riddoch) 1998 96 94 **91 90 88 86 82**.

YAKIMA VALLEY AVA *Washington State, USA* This valley lies within the much larger COLUMBIA VALLEY AVA. Yakima is planted mostly to Chardonnay, Merlot and Cabernet Sauvignon and has around 30 wineries. Best producers: Bonair, Chinook★, Hedges Cellars★, HOGUE CELLARS★, Kestrel★, KIONA★, Porteous★, Wineglass Cellars★.

YALUMBA *Barossa Valley, South Australia* Distinguished old firm, owned by the Hill-Smith family, making a wide range of wines under its own name, as well as the Heggies (restrained Riesling★, nice plump Merlot★, opulent Viognier★ and botrytis Riesling★★), Hill-Smith Estate (Sauvignon Blanc★) and Pewsey Vale (fine Riesling★ and Cabernet Sauvignon★) ranges. Flagship reds are The Signature Cabernet-Shiraz★★, Octavius Shiraz★★ and The Menzies Cabernet★★ and all cellar well. New premiums include Old Vine Grenache★★, Contour Riesling★★ and a Shiraz Viognier★. From here down to reliable quaffers like Galway Shiraz, Oxford Landing Chardonnay, Sauvignon★, Viognier★★, Merlot and Cabernet-Shiraz, Yalumba is consistently impressive. Angas Brut remains big-volume enjoyable fizz for the masses (me included); Yalumba D seems to be recovering from a crisis of confidence, while the acquisition of TASMANIA's Jansz★ has added a class act to the flight. Fortified wines are excellent, notably Muscat★★. Best years: (The Signature red) 1997 96 **95 93 92 91 90 88**.

YARRA VALLEY *Victoria, Australia*   With its cool climate, the fashionable Yarra is asking to be judged as Australia's best Pinot Noir region. Exciting also for Chardonnay and Cabernet-Merlot blends and as a supplier of base wine for sparklers. Best producers: Arthur's Creek★★, COLDSTREAM HILLS★, DE BORTOLI★★, Diamond Valley, GREEN POINT VINEYARDS★, Métier, MOUNT MARY★★, Oakridge★, St Huberts★, Seville Estate★, TARRAWARRA★★, Yarra Burn★, Yarra Ridge★, YARRA YERING★★, Yeringberg★, Yering Station★.

YARRA YERING *Yarra Valley, Victoria, Australia*   Bailey Carrodus creates extraordinary wines from his exceptional vineyard. Dry Red No. 1★★★ (Cabernet-based) and Dry Red No. 2★★★ (Shiraz-based) are profound, concentrated, ageworthy, packed with unnervingly self-confident fruit and memorable perfume. Pinot Noir★★ is expensive but gets finer and wilder by the vintage. Chardonnay★ is erratic, occasionally delicious. Best years: (No. 1) 1999 98 97 96 **94 93 91 90 89 86.**

YELLOWGLEN *Ballarat, Victoria, Australia*   Big Champagne-method fizz producer owned by Beringer Blass. Pinot Chardonnay NV, Yellow NV, Y Sparkling Burgundy and Red NV are basic but well made. Cuvée Victoria★ is the finest. Best years: (Cuvée Victoria) **1996 95 92 91 90 88.**

CH. D'YQUEM★★★ *Sauternes AC, 1er Cru Supérieur, Bordeaux, France*   Often rated the most sublime sweet wine in the world, no one can question Yquem's total commitment to quality. Despite a large vineyard (100ha/250 acres), production is tiny. Only fully noble-rotted grapes are picked, often berry by berry, and low yield means each vine produces only a glass of wine! This precious liquid is then fermented in new oak barrels and left to mature for 3½ years before bottling. It is one of the world's most expensive wines, in constant demand because of its richness and exotic flavours. A dry white, Ygrec, is made in some years. In 1999 LVMH won a 3-year takeover battle with the Lur-Saluces family, owners for 406 years. Best years: 1996 95 94 93 **91 90 89 88 86 83 82 81 80 79 76 75 71 70 67 62.**

ZILLIKEN *Saarburg, Mosel-Saar-Ruwer, Germany*   Estate specializing in Rieslings★★ (Auslese, Eiswein often ★★★) from the Saarburger Rausch vineyard. Best years: (2001) 99 97 95 **94 93 91 90 89 88 85 83 79 76.**

ZIND-HUMBRECHT *Alsace AC, Alsace, France*   Olivier Humbrecht is one of France's outstanding winemakers. The family owns vines in 4 Grand Cru sites – Rangen, Goldert, Hengst and Brand – and these wines (Riesling★★, Gewurztraminer★★★, Pinot Gris★★★ and Muscat★★) are excellent, as is a range of wines from specific vineyards and *lieux dits*, such as Gewurztraminer or Riesling Clos Windsbuhl★★★ and Pinot Gris Clos Windsbuhl or Clos Jebsal★★. ALSACE VENDANGE TARDIVE wines are almost invariably of ★★★ quality. Even basic Sylvaners★ and Pinot Blancs★★ are fine. Best years (Clos Windsbuhl Gewurztraminer): 1999 98 **97 96 95 94 93 92 90 89.**

ZINFANDEL CALIFORNIA's versatile red grape can make big, juicy, fruit-packed wine – or insipid, sweetish 'blush' or even late-harvest dessert wine. Some Zinfandel is now made in other countries, with notable examples in Australia and South Africa. Best producers: (California) Brown★★, Cline Cellars★★, Dashe★★, DRY CREEK VINEYARD★, FETZER★, Martinelli★★, Nalle★★, Preston★, QUIVIRA★, Rafanelli★★, RAVENSWOOD★★, RIDGE★★★, Rosenblum★★, Saddleback★★, St Francis★★, SEGHESIO★★, TURLEY★★, WILLIAMS SELYEM★★; (Australia) CAPE MENTELLE★, Kangarilla Road, Nepenthe. See also Primitivo di Manduria.

GLOSSARY OF WINE TERMS

AC/AOC (APPELLA-TION D'ORIGINE CONTRÔLÉE) The top category of French wines, defined by regulations covering vineyard yields, grape varieties, geographical boundaries, alcohol content and production method. Guarantees origin and style of a wine, but not its quality.

ACID/ACIDITY Naturally present in grapes and essential to wine, providing balance and stability and giving the refreshing tang in white wines and the appetizing grip in reds.

ADEGA Portuguese for winery.

AGING An alternative term for maturation.

ALCOHOLIC CONTENT The alcoholic strength of wine, expressed as a percentage of the total volume of the wine. Typically in the range of 7–15%.

ALCOHOLIC FERMENTATION The process whereby yeasts, natural or added, convert the grape sugars into alcohol (Ethyl alcohol, or Ethanol) and carbon dioxide.

AMONTILLADO Traditionally dry style of sherry. *See* Jerez y Manzanilla in main A–Z.

ANBAUGEBIET German for growing region; these names will appear on labels of all QbA and QmP wines. There are 13 *Anbaugebiete*: Ahr, Baden, Franken, Hessische Bergstrasse, Mittelrhein, Mosel-Saar-Ruwer, Nahe, Pfalz, Rheinhessen, Saale-Unstrut, Sachsen and Württemberg.

AUSBRUCH Austrian Prädikat category used for sweet wines.

AUSLESE German and Austrian Prädikat cat-egory meaning that the grapes were 'selected' for their higher ripeness.

AVA (AMERICAN VITICULTURAL AREA) System of appellations of origin for US wines.

AZIENDA AGRICOLA Italian for estate or farm. It also indicates wine made from grapes grown by the proprietor.

BARREL AGING Time spent maturing in wood, usually oak, during which the wines take on flavours from the wood.

BARREL FERMENTA-TION Oak barrels may be used for fermentation instead of stainless steel to give a rich, oaky flavour to the wine.

BARRIQUE The *barrique bordelaise* is the traditional Bordeaux oak barrel of 225 litres (50 gallons) capacity.

BAUMÉ A scale measuring must weight (the amount of sugar in grape juice) to estimate potential alcohol content.

BEERENAUSLESE German and Austrian Prädikat category applied to wines made from 'individually selected' berries (i.e. grapes) affected by noble rot (*Edelfäule* in German). The wines are rich and sweet.

Beerenauslese wines are only produced in the best years in Germany, but in Austria they are a regular occurrence.

BEREICH German for region or district within a wine region or *Anbaugebiet*. Bereichs tend to be large, and the use of a Bereich name, such as Bereich Bingen, without qualification is seldom an indication of quality – in most cases, quite the reverse.

BIODYNAMIC VITI-CULTURE This approach works with the movement of the planets and cosmic forces to achieve health and balance in the soil and in the vine. Vines are treated with infusions of mineral, animal and plant materials, applied in homeopathic quantities.

BLANC DE BLANCS White wine made from one or more white grape varieties. Used especially for sparkling wines; in Champagne, denotes wine made entirely from the Chardonnay grape.

BLANC DE NOIRS White wine made from black grapes only – the juice is separated from

BOTTLE SIZES

CHAMPAGNE

Magnum	1.5 litres	2 bottles
Jeroboam	3 litres	4 bottles
Rehoboam	4.5 litres	6 bottles
Methuselah	6 litres	8 bottles
Salmanazar	9 litres	12 bottles
Balthazar	12 litres	16 bottles
Nebuchadnezzar	15 litres	20 bottles

BORDEAUX

Magnum	1.5 litres	2 bottles
Marie-Jeanne	2.25 litres	3 bottles
Double-magnum	3 litres	4 bottles
Jeroboam	4.5 litres	6 bottles
Imperial	6 litres	8 bottles

the skins to avoid extracting any colour. Most often seen in Champagne, where it describes wine made from Pinot Noir and/or Pinot Meunier.

BLENDING (assemblage) The art of mixing together wines of different origin, styles or age, often to balance out acidity, weight etc.

BODEGA Spanish for winery.

BOTRYTIS *See* noble rot.

BRUT French term for dry sparkling wines, especially Champagne.

CARBONIC MACERATION Winemaking method used to produce fresh fruity reds for drinking young. Whole (uncrushed) bunches of grapes are fermented in closed containers – a process that extracts lots of fruit and colour, but little tannin.

CAVE CO-OPÉRATIVE French for co-operative cellar, where members bring their grapes for vinification and bottling under a collective label. In terms of quantity, the French wine industry is dominated by co-ops. Often use less workaday titles, such as Caves des Vignerons, Producteurs Réunis, Union des Producteurs or Cellier des Vignerons.

CHAMPAGNE METHOD Traditional method used for all of the world's finest sparkling wines. A second fermentation takes place in the bottle, producing carbon dioxide which, kept in solution under pressure, gives the wine its fizz.

CHAPTALIZATION Legal addition of sugar during fermentation to raise a wine's alcoholic strength. More necessary in cool climates

where lack of sun produces insufficient natural sugar in the grape.

CHARTA A German organization founded to protect the image of the best Rheingau Rieslings in 1984, recognizable by a double-window motif on the bottle or label. The accent is on dry wines that go with food. Now merged with VDP to form VDP-Rheingau, but the Charta symbol remains in use.

CHÂTEAU French for castle, used to describe a variety of wine estates.

CHIARETTO Italian for a rosé wine of medium pink colour.

CLARET English for red Bordeaux wines, from the French *clairet*, which was traditionally used to describe a lighter style of red Bordeaux.

CLARIFICATION Term covering any wine-making process (such as filtering or fining) that involves the removal of solid matter either from the must or the wine.

CLONE Strain of grape species. The term is usually taken to mean laboratory-produced, virus-free clones, selected to produce higher or lower quantity, or selected for resistance to frost or disease.

CLOS French for a walled vineyard – as in Burgundy's Clos de Vougeot – also commonly incorporated into the names of estates (e.g. Clos des Papes), regardless of whether they are walled or not.

COLD FERMENTATION Long, slow fermentation at low temperature to extract maximum freshness from the grapes.

COLHEITA Aged tawny port from a single vintage. *See* Port in main A–Z.

COMMUNE A French village and its surrounding area or parish.

CORKED/CORKY Wine fault derived from a cork which has become contaminated, usually with Trichloroanisole or TCA, and nothing to do with pieces of cork in the wine. The mouldy, stale smell is unmistakable.

COSECHA Spanish for vintage.

CÔTE French word for a slope or hillside, which is where many, but not all, of the country's best vineyards are to be found.

CRÉMANT French term for traditional-method sparkling wine from Alsace, Bordeaux, Burgundy, Die, Jura, Limoux, Loire and Luxembourg.

CRIANZA Spanish term for the youngest official category of oak-matured wine. A red Crianza wine must have had at least 2 years' aging (1 in oak, 1 in bottle) before sale; a white or rosé, 1 year.

CRU French for growth, meaning a specific plot of land or particular estate. In Burgundy, growths are divided into Grands (great) and Premiers (first) Crus, and apply solely to the actual land. In Champagne the same terms are used for whole villages. In Bordeaux there are various hierarchical levels of Cru referring to estates rather than their vineyards.

CRU BOURGEOIS French term for wines from the Médoc and Sauternes that are ranked immediately below the Crus Classés. Many are excellent value for money.

CRU CLASSÉ The Classed Growths are the aristocracy of Bordeaux, ennobled by the Classifications of 1855 (for the Médoc, Barsac and Sauternes), 1955, 1969, 1986 and 1996 (for St-Émilion) and 1947, 1953 and 1959 (for Graves). Curiously, Pomerol has never been classified. The modern classifications are more reliable than the 1855 version, which was based solely on the price of the wines at the time of the Great Exhibition in Paris, but in terms of prestige the 1855 Classification remains the most important. With the exception of a single alteration in 1973, when Ch. Mouton-Rothschild was elevated to First Growth status, the list has not changed since 1855. It certainly needs revising.

CUVE CLOSE A bulk process used to produce inexpensive sparkling wines. The second fermentation, which produces the bubbles, takes place in tank rather than in the bottle.

CUVÉE French for the contents of a single vat or tank, but usually indicates a wine blended from either different grape varieties or the best barrels of wine.

DÉGORGEMENT Stage in the production of Champagne-method wines when the sediment, collected in the neck of the bottle during *remuage*, is removed.

DEMI-SEC French for medium-dry.

DO (DENOMINACIÓN DE ORIGEN) Spain's equivalent of the French AC quality category, regulating origin and production methods.

DOC (DENOMINAÇÃO DE ORIGEM CONTROLADA) The top regional classification for Portuguese wines.

DOC (DENOMINACIÓN DE ORIGEN CALIFICADA) Spanish quality wine category, intended to be one step up from DO. So far only Rioja and Priorat qualify.

DOC (DENOMINAZIONE DI ORIGINE CONTROLLATA) Italian quality wine category, regulating origin, grape varieties, yield and production methods.

DOCG (DENOMINAZIONE DI ORIGINE CONTROLLATA E GARANTITA) The top tier of the Italian classification system.

DOSAGE A sugar and wine mixture added to sparkling wine after *dégorgement* which affects how sweet or dry it will be.

EDELZWICKER Blended wine from Alsace in France, usually bland.

EINZELLAGE German for an individual vineyard site which is generally farmed by several growers. The name is preceded on the label by that of the village; for example, the Wehlener Sonnenuhr is the Sonnenuhr vineyard in Wehlen. The mention of a particular site should signify a superior wine. Sadly, this is not necessarily so.

EISWEIN Rare, chiefly German and Austrian, late-harvested wine made by picking the grapes and pressing them while frozen. This concentrates the sweetness of the grape as most of the liquid is removed as ice. *See also* Icewine.

ESCOLHA Portuguese for selection.

FILTERING Removal of yeasts, solids and any impurities from a wine before bottling.

FINING Method of clarifying wine by adding a coagulant (e.g. egg whites, isinglass or bentonite) to remove soluble particles such as proteins and excessive tannins.

FINO The lightest, freshest style of sherry. *See* Jerez y Manzanilla in main A–Z.

FLOR A film of yeast which forms on the top of fino sherries (and some other wines), preventing oxidation and imparting a unique tangy, dry flavour.

FLYING WINEMAKER Term coined in the late 1980s to describe enologists, many Australian-trained, brought in to improve the quality of wines in many underperforming wine regions.

FORTIFIED WINE Wine which has high-alcohol grape spirit added, usually before the initial fermentation is completed, thereby preserving sweetness.

FRIZZANTE Italian for semi-sparkling wine, usually made dry, but sometimes sweet.

GARAGE WINE *See* vin de garage.

GARRAFEIRA Portuguese term for wine from an outstanding vintage, with 0.5% more alcohol than the minimum required, and 2 years' aging in vat or barrel followed by 1 year in bottle for reds, and 6 months of each for whites. Also used by merchants for their best blended and aged wines. Use of the term is in decline as producers opt for the more readily recognized Reserva as an alternative on the label.

GRAN RESERVA Top category of Spanish wines from a top vintage, with at least 5 years' aging (2 of them in cask) for reds and 4 for whites.

GRAND CRU French for great growth.

Supposedly the best vineyard sites in Alsace, Burgundy, Champagne and parts of Bordeaux and should produce the most exciting wines.

GRANDES MARQUES Great brands – the Syndicat des Grandes Marques was once Champagne's self-appointed élite. It disbanded in 1997.

GROSSLAGE German term for a grouping of vineyards. Some are not too big, and have the advantage of allowing small amounts of higher QmP wines to be made from the grapes from several vineyards. But sometimes the use of vast Grosslage names (e.g. Niersteiner Gutes Domtal) deceives consumers into believing they are buying something special.

HALBTROCKEN German for medium dry. In Germany and Austria medium-dry wine has 9–18g per litre of residual sugar, though sparkling wine is allowed up to 50g per litre. But the high acid levels in German wines can make them seem rather dry and lean.

ICEWINE A speciality of Canada, produced from juice squeezed from ripe grapes that have frozen on the vine. See also Eiswein.

IGT (INDICAZIONE GEOGRAFICA TIPICA) The Italian equivalent of the French vin de pays. As in the Midi, both premium and everyday wines may share the same appellation. Many of the Super-Tuscan vini da tavola are now sold under a regional IGT.

IPR (INDICAÇÃO DE PROVENIÊNCIA REGULAMENTADA) The second tier in the Portuguese wine classification regulations, covering grape varieties,

yields and aging requirements.

KABINETT Term used for the lowest level of QmP wines in Germany.

LANDWEIN German or Austrian country wine; the equivalent of French vin de pays. The wine must have a territorial definition and may be chaptalized to give it more alcohol.

LATE HARVEST See Vendange Tardive.

LAYING DOWN The storing of wine which will improve with age.

LEES Sediment – dead yeast cells, grape pips (seeds), pulp and tartrates – thrown by wine during fermentation and left behind after racking. Some wines are left on the fine lees for as long as possible to take on extra flavour.

MALOLACTIC FERMENTATION Secondary fermentation whereby harsh malic acid is converted into mild lactic acid and carbon dioxide. Normal in red wines but often prevented in whites to preserve a fresh, fruity taste.

MANZANILLA The tangiest style of sherry, similar to fino. See Jerez y Manzanilla in main A–Z.

MATURATION Positive term for the beneficial aging of wine.

MERITAGE American term for red or white wines made from a blend of Bordeaux grape varieties.

MESOCLIMATE The climate of a specific geographical area, be it a vineyard or simply a hillside or valley.

MOELLEUX French for soft or mellow, used to describe sweet or medium-sweet wines.

MOUSSEUX French for sparkling wine.

MUST The mixture of grape juice, skins, pips and pulp produced after crushing (but prior to completion of fermentation), which will eventually become wine.

MUST WEIGHT An indicator of the sugar content of juice – and therefore the ripeness of grapes.

NÉGOCIANT French term for a merchant who buys and sells wine. A négociant-éléveur is a merchant who buys, makes, ages and sells wine.

NEW WORLD When used as a geographical term, New World includes the Americas, South Africa, Australia and New Zealand. By extension, it is also a term used to describe the clean, fruity, upfront style now in evidence all over the world, but pioneered in the USA and Australia.

NOBLE ROT (Botrytis cinerea) Fungus which, when it attacks ripe white grapes, shrivels the fruit and intensifies their sugar while adding a distinctive flavour. A vital factor in creating many of the world's finest sweet wines, such as Sauternes and Trockenbeerenauslese.

OAK The wood used almost exclusively to make barrels for fermenting and aging fine wines.

OECHSLE German scale measuring must weight.

OLOROSO The darkest, most heavily fortified style of sherry. See Jerez y Manzanilla in main A–Z.

OXIDATION Over-exposure of wine to air, causing loss of fruit and flavour. Slight oxidation, such as occurs through the wood of a barrel or during racking, is part of the aging process and, in wines of sufficient structure, enhances flavour and complexity.

PASSITO Italian term for wine made from dried grapes. The result is usually a sweet wine with a raisiny intensity of fruit. *See also* Moscato Passito di Pantelleria, Recioto di Soave, Recioto della Valpolicella and Vin Santo in main A–Z.

PERLWEIN German for a lightly sparkling wine.

PÉTILLANT French for a slightly sparkling wine.

PHYLLOXERA The vine aphid *Phylloxera vastatrix* attacks vine roots. It devastated European and consequently other vineyards around the world in the late 1800s soon after it arrived from America. Since then, the vulnerable *Vitis vinifera* has generally been grafted on to vinously inferior, but phylloxera-resistant, American rootstocks.

PRÄDIKAT Grades defining quality wines in Germany and Austria. These are (in ascending order) Kabinett (not considered as Prädikat in Austria), Spätlese, Auslese, Beerenauslese, the Austrian-only category Ausbruch, and Trockenbeerenauslese. Strohwein and Eiswein are also Prädikat wines. Some Spätleses and even a few Ausleses are now made as dry wines.

PREMIER CRU First Growth; the top quality classification in parts of Bordeaux, but second to Grand Cru in Burgundy. Used in Champagne to designate vineyards just below Grand Cru.

PRIMEUR French term for a young wine, often released for sale within a few weeks of the harvest. Beaujolais Nouveau is the best-known example.

QbA (QUALITÄTSWEIN BESTIMMTER ANBAUGEBIETE) German for quality wine from designated regions. Sugar can be added to increase the alcohol content. Usually pretty ordinary, but from top estates this category offers excellent value for money. In Austria *Qualitätswein* is equivalent to the German QbA.

QmP (QUALITÄTSWEIN MIT PRÄDIKAT) German for quality wine with distinction. A higher category than QbA, with controlled yields and no sugar addition. QmP covers 6 levels based on the ripeness of the grapes: *see* Prädikat.

QUINTA Portuguese for farm or estate.

RACKING Gradual clarification of a quality wine; the wine is transferred from one barrel or container to another, leaving the lees behind.

RANCIO A fortified wine deliberately exposed to the effects of oxidation, found mainly in Languedoc-Roussillon, Cataluña and southern Spain.

REMUAGE Process in Champagne-making whereby the bottles, stored on their sides and at a progressively steeper angle in *pupitres*, are twisted, or riddled, each day so that the sediment moves down the sides and collects in the neck of the bottle on the cap, ready for *dégorgement*.

RESERVA Spanish wines that have fulfilled certain aging requirements: reds must have at least 3 years' aging before sale, of which one must be in oak barrels; whites and rosés must have at least

2 years' age, of which 6 months must be in oak.

RÉSERVE French for what is, in theory at least, a winemaker's finest wine. The word has no legal definition in France.

RIPASSO A method used in Valpolicella to make wines with extra depth. Wine is passed over the lees of Amarone della Valpolicella, adding extra alcohol and flavour, though also extra tannin and a risk of higher acidity and oxidation.

RISERVA An Italian term, recognized in many DOCs and DOCGs, for a special selection of superior-quality wine that has been aged longer before release. It is only a promise of a more pleasurable drink if the wine had enough fruit and structure in the first place.

SEC French for dry. When applied to Champagne, it actually means medium-dry.

'SECOND' WINES A second selection from a designated vineyard, usually lighter and quicker-maturing than the main wine.

SEDIMENT Usually refers to residue thrown by a wine, particularly red, as it ages in bottle.

SEKT German for sparkling wine. The wine will be entirely German only if it is called Deutscher Sekt or Sekt bA. The best wines are traditional-method made from 100% Riesling or from 100% Weissburgunder (Pinot Blanc).

SÉLECTION DE GRAINS NOBLES A super-ripe category for sweet Alsace wines, now also being used by some producers of Coteaux du Layon in the Loire for the most concentrated wines. *See also* Alsace Vendange Tardive in main A–Z.

SMARAGD The top of the three categories of wine from the Wachau in Austria, the lower two being Federspiel and Steinfeder. Made from very ripe and usually late-harvested grapes.

SOLERA Traditional Spanish system of blending fortified wines, especially sherry and Montilla-Moriles.

SPÄTLESE German for late-picked (therefore riper) grapes. Often moderately sweet, though there are now dry versions.

SPUMANTE Italian for sparkling. Bottle-fermented wines are often referred to as *metodo classico* or *metodo tradizionale*.

SUPÉRIEUR French for a wine with a slightly higher alcohol content than the basic AC.

SUPERIORE Italian DOC wines with higher alcohol or more age potential.

SUR LIE French for on the lees, meaning wine bottled direct from the cask/fermentation vat to gain extra flavour from the lees. Common with quality Muscadet, white Burgundy, similar barrel-aged whites and, increasingly, commercial bulk whites.

TAFELWEIN German for table wine.

TANNIN Harsh, bitter, mouth-puckering element in red wine, derived from grape skins and stems, and from oak barrels. Tannins soften with age and are essential for long-term development in red wines.

TERROIR A French term used to denote the combination of soil, climate and exposure to the sun – that is, the natural physical environment of the vine.

TROCKEN German for dry. In most parts of Germany and Austria Trocken matches the standard EU definition of dryness – less than 9g per litre residual sugar.

TROCKENBEEREN-AUSLESE (TBA) German for 'dry berry selected', denoting grapes affected by noble rot (*Edelfäule* in German) – the wines will be lusciously sweet although low in alcohol.

VARIETAL Wine made from, and named after, a single or dominant grape variety.

VDP German organization recognizable on the label by a Prussian eagle bearing grapes. The quality of estates included is usually – but not always – high. Now merged with the Charta organization.

VDQS (VIN DÉLIMITÉ DE QUALITÉ SUPÉRIEURE) The second-highest classification for French wines, behind AC.

VELHO Portuguese for old. Legally applied only to wines with at least 3 years' aging for reds and 2 years for whites.

VENDANGE TARDIVE French for late harvest. Grapes are left on the vines beyond the normal harvest time to concentrate flavours and sugars. The term is traditional in Alsace. *See also* Alsace Vendange Tardive in main A–Z.

VIEILLES VIGNES French term for a wine made from vines at least 20 years old. Should have greater concentration than wine from younger vines.

VIÑA Spanish for vineyard.

VIN DE GARAGE Wines made on so small a scale they could be made in one's garage. Such wines may be made from vineyards of a couple of hectares or less, and are often of extreme concentration.

VIN DE PAILLE Sweet wine found mainly in the Jura region of France. Traditionally, the grapes are left for 2–3 months on straw (*paille*) mats before fermentation to dehydrate, thus concentrating the sugars. The wines are sweet but slightly nutty.

VIN DE PAYS The term gives a regional identity to wine from the country districts of France. It is a particularly useful category for adventurous winemakers who want to use good-quality grapes not allowed under the frequently restrictive AC regulations. Many are labelled with the grape variety.

VIN DE TABLE French for table wine, the lowest quality level.

VIN DOUX NATUREL (VDN) French for a fortified wine, where fermentation has been stopped by the addition of alcohol, leaving the wine 'naturally' sweet, although you could argue that stopping fermentation with a slug of powerful spirit is distinctly unnatural.

VIN JAUNE A speciality of the Jura region in France, made from the Savagnin grape. In Château-Chalon it is the only permitted style. Made in a similar way to fino sherry but not fortified. Unlike fino, *vin jaune* usually ages well.

VINIFICATION The process of turning grapes into wine.

VINO DA TAVOLA The Italian term for table wine, officially Italy's lowest level of production, is a catch-all that until recently applied to more than 80% of the nation's wine, with virtually no regulations controlling quality. Yet this category also provided the arena in the 1970s for the biggest revolution in quality that Italy has ever seen, with the creation of innovative, DOC-busting Super-Tuscans. *See* Super-Tuscans in main A–Z.

VINTAGE The year's grape harvest, also used to describe wines of a single year. 'Off-vintage' is a year not generally declared as vintage. *See* Port in main A–Z.

VITICULTURE Vine-growing and vineyard management.

VITIS VINIFERA Vine species, native to Europe and Central Asia, from which almost all the world's quality wine is made.

VQA (VINTNERS QUALITY ALLIANCE) Canadian equivalent of France's AC system, defining quality standards and designated viticultural areas.

WEISSHERBST German rosé wine, a speciality of Baden.

WO (WINE OF ORIGIN) South African system of appellations which certifies area of origin, grape variety and vintage.

YIELD The amount of fruit, and ultimately wine, produced from a vineyard. Measured in hectolitres per hectare (hl/ha) in most of Europe and in the New World as tons/acre or tonnes/hectare. Yield may vary from year to year, and depends on grape variety, age and density of the vines, and viticultural practices.

WHO OWNS WHAT

The world's major drinks companies are getting bigger and, frankly, I'm worried. As these vast wine conglomerates stride across continents, it seems highly likely that local traditions will – for purely business reasons – be pared away, along with individuality of flavour. It's not all bad news: in some cases wineries have benefited from the huge resources that come with corporate ownership, but I can't help feeling nervous knowing that the fate of a winery rests in the hands of distant institutional investors. Below I have listed some of the names that crop up again and again – and will no doubt continue to do so, as they aggressively pursue their grasp of market share.

Other wine companies – which bottle wines under their own names and therefore feature in the main A–Z – are gradually spreading their nets. KENDALL-JACKSON of California, for example, owns wineries in Chile, Argentina, Italy and Australia. GALLO, the biggest wine producer in the world, now has an agreement with MCWILLIAM'S of Australia, and several areas report Gallo's interest in wineries. Robert MONDAVI is most famous for his wineries in California, but he also has interests in Italy and Chile, and, with the Rothschild family, co-owns OPUS ONE. The Rothschilds, in partnership with CONCHA Y TORO, produce ALMAVIVA in Chile, and have other interests in France besides the renowned Ch. MOUTON-ROTHSCHILD.

Cross-ownership is making it enormously difficult to know which companies remain independent, and the never-ending whirl of joint ventures, mergers and takeovers shows no signs of slowing down, which means that the following can only be a snapshot at the time of going to press. In 12 months time this list will probably look substantially different, as new players enter the arena and one giant gets gobbled up by another.

ALLIED DOMECQ UK-based group with a global wines and spirits portfolio. In 2001 it purchased New Zealand's MONTANA and Spain's Bodegas y Bebidas group (AGE, CAMPO VIEJO), and the prestigious Tarsus winery in Ribera del Duero). Allied Domecq brands include: ATLAS PEAK, Buena Vista, CLOS DU BOIS, William Hill and MUMM NAPA (California), Balbi and Graffigna (Argentina), COCKBURN (port), DOMECQ and Harveys (sherry), MUMM and PERRIER-JOUET (Champagne). Allied Domecq has stakes in a number of Australian wineries, including Peter LEHMANN.

AXA-MILLESIMES The French insurance group owns Bordeaux châteaux PICHON-LONGUEVILLE, Pibran, Cantenac-Brown and SUDUIRAUT, as well as TOKAJI producer Disznókö in Hungary and port producer Quinta do NOVAL.

BERINGER BLASS The wine division of Foster's, the brewers, takes its name from California's BERINGER and Australia's Wolf BLASS. In California it owns CHATEAU ST JEAN, Chateau Souverain, Meridian, St Clement, Stags' Leap Winery. Australian brands include Annie's Lane, BAILEYS of Glenrowan, Jamiesons Run, Mamre Brook, Metala, ROTHBURY ESTATE, Saltram, Yellowglen. It also owns wineries in Italy and New Zealand (MATUA VALLEY).

BRL HARDY Australian company with many famous brands, including HARDYS, Banrock Station, BAROSSA VALLEY ESTATE, HOUGHTON, LEASINGHAM, Moondah Brook, REYNELL, Stonehaven, Yarra Burn, New Zealand's NOBILO and SELAKS, Dom. de la BAUME in Languedoc. Linked with Constellation in the USA.

CONSTELLATION US-based wine, beer and spirits group. Its Canandaigua division includes US brands Paul Masson, Almaden, Inglenook and Covey Run. The FRANCISCAN division makes wines under its own name from its Oakville estate in Napa Valley, and also owns the Estancia, RAVENSWOOD and Simi wineries in California and Veramonte in Chile. One of the UK's largest drinks wholesalers/distributors, Matthew Clark – which has a distribution agreement with Southcorp – also comes under the Constellation umbrella. Also linked in a joint venture with BRL Hardy of Australia.

FREIXENET Spanish wine producer making a bid for global market share, with some of Spain's biggest names (including Castellblanch, Conde de Caralt, Segura Viudas, René Barbier) and wine companies in California and Mexico. It also owns the Champagne house of Henri Abelé, Bordeaux négociant/producer Yvon Mau and Australia's Wingara Wine Group (Deakin Estate, KATNOOK ESTATE, Riddoch Estate).

LVMH French luxury goods group Louis Vuitton-Moët Hennessy owns Champagne houses MOET & CHANDON (including Dom Pérignon), KRUG, Canard-Duchêne, Mercier, RUINART and VEUVE CLICQUOT, and has established DOMAINE CHANDON sparkling wine companies in California, Australia, Argentina and Spain. The purchase of Ch. d'YQUEM in 1999 was a major coup. It also owns CAPE MENTELLE and MOUNTADAM in Australia, CLOUDY BAY in New Zealand, NEWTON in California, and promising Argentinian winery Terrazas de los Andes.

PERNOD RICARD The French spirits giant owns the ORLANDO Wyndham Group (Australia), with its Jacob's Creek brand; Etchart (Argentina); Long Mountain (South Africa); and has interests in wineries in China and Georgia.

SOUTHCORP Australia's biggest wine conglomerate, which merged with Rosemount in 2001. Brands include: Leo Buring, COLDSTREAM HILLS, Devil's Lair, James HERRICK (Languedoc-Roussillon), Killawarra, LINDEMANS, PENFOLDS, Queen Adelaide, ROSEMOUNT ESTATE, Rouge Homme, SEAVIEW, SEPPELT, Seven Peaks (CENTRAL COAST, California), Tollana, WYNNS.

INDEX OF PRODUCERS

298

301

307

M

Mabileau, F *243*
Mabileau, J-C *243*
Maby, Dom. *173*
Macay, Ch. *117*
Le Macchiole *66, 185, 263, 267*
Il Macchione *282*
Il Macereto *191*
Maclé, Jean *98, 117*
Macquin St-Georges, Ch. *242*
Maculan *75, 85, **175***
Madeira Wine Co. ***176***
Madone, Dom. de la *61*
Madonia, Giovanna *45, 236*
La Madura *241*
Maestracci *113*
Maffini, L *134*
Magaña *199*
Magdalena co-op *177*
Magdelaine, Ch. *69, **176**, 185, 192, 242*
Magence, Ch. *146*
Magenta, Duc de *53, 98*
Magneau, Ch. *71, 146*
Magnin *249*
Maias, Quinta das *122*
Maillard Père & Fils *104*
Mailles, Ch. des *244*
Mailly co-op *97*
Main Ridge *191*
Maire, H *51, 98*
Majella *112*
Malacari *238*
Malandes *94*
Malartic-Lagravière, Ch. *71, **176**, 211*
Malescasse, Ch. *151*
Malescot St-Exupéry, Ch. *69, **177**, 178*
Malle, Ch. de *248*
Malumbres, Vicente *199*
Malvirà *51, 236*
Manciat, Jean *175*
Mancinelli *279*
Mancini, Piero *279*
Mann, Dom. Albert *47, **177**, 233*
Manos, Ch. *71, 82*
Mansenoble *113*
Mantellassi *191*
Mantlerhof *163*
Manzaneque, Manuel *90, 101*
Manzano, Fattoria di ***177**, 267*
Marandon, C *249*
Maravenne *118*
Marbuzet, Ch. *242*
Marcadet *272*
Marcarini, B *125*
Marcassin *101, **178**, 217, 257, 274*
Marchand-Grillot *95*
Marcillac, Cave de *116*
Marcillac-Vallon co-op *178*
Marcoux, Dom. de *99*

Mardon, Dom. *225*
Maréchal, Claude *249*
Marenco, G *74, 192*
Marengo, M *57*
Margaine, A *97*
Margaux, Ch. *69, 71, 72, 85, **178***
Margerand, J P *160, 193*
Marino, Alvaro *199*
Marino, Beppe *192*
Marionnet, Henry *272*
Maris *187*
Markham *201*
Markowitsch *89*
Marqués de Cáceres ***179**, 234*
Marqués de Griñon *63, 85, 90, **179**, 234, 267*
Marqués de Monistrol *91, 210, 259*
Marqués de Murrieta ***179**, 234*
Marqués de Riscal ***179**, 234, 239, 251*
Marqués de Vargas *234*
Marramiero *189*
Marsau, Ch. *72*
Martin Códax *230*
Martinborough Vineyard ***180**, 217*
Martinelli *288*
Martinetti, Franco *56*
Martinez *221*
Martínez Bujanda ***180**, 234*
Martini, Conti *269, 273*
Martini & Rossi *52*
Martinolles, Dom. de *65, 120*
Marynissen *203*
Mas Amiel *182*
Mas Blanc *55, 110*
Mas de Boudard *90*
Mas des Bressades *114, 141*
Mas Bruguière *116, **180**, 214*
Mas Carlot *114*
Mas Champart *241*
Mas des Chimères *116*
Mas Crémat *118, 119, 204*
Mas de la Dame *60*
Mas de Daumas Gassac *152, **180***
Mas Doix *223*
Mas Fontcreuse *90*
Mas d'en Gil *223*
Mas de Gourgonnier *60*
Mas Jullien *116, **180***
Mas de Lavabre *214*
Mas de Libian *118*
Mas Martinet *223*
Mas de Mortiès *116, 214*
Mas des Pigeonniers *198*
Mas Pignou *139*
Mas Redorne *55*
Mas de Rey *73*
Mas Rous *198*
Mas Ste-Berthe *60*
Mascarello, Bartolo *57, 125, **181***

Mascarello, Giuseppe *56, 57, 125, 137, **181**, 199*
Masciarelli *189*
Masi *49, 56, **181**, 228, 256, 277*
Masía Bach *210*
Maso Cantanghel *273*
Maso Furli *273*
Maso Roveri *273*
La Massa *103*
Masson-Blondelet *222, 251*
Massy *278*
Mastroberardino *134, **181**, 268, 280*
Mastrojanni *80*
Masùt da Rive *138*
Matanzas Creek *101, **181**, 185, 251, 257*
Matariki *151*
Matha, Jean-Luc *178*
Mathier *125, 276*
Mathieu *97*
Matijaz Tercic *110*
Matrot, Dom. *65, 79, 186, 283*
Matthews Cellars *110*
Matua Valley *85, 151, 164, **181***
Maucaillou, Ch. **181**, 193*
Maucamps, Ch. *151*
Maurel Fonsalade, Ch. *241*
Mauriane, La *224*
Maurières, des *249*
Mauro *90, 170, **182***
Maurodós *211*
Maury co-op *182*
Maurydoré *182*
Maximin Grünhaus ***182**, 233*
Maxwell *182*
Mayacamas *193*
Maye & Fils *133*
Mayer *286*
Mayne-Lalande, Ch. *173*
Mayne-Vieil, Ch. *138*
Mayr, Josephus *246*
Mazzei/Fonterutoli *191*
Mazzi *277*
Mazziotti *131*
Mazzolino *205*
McAlister *143*
McDonald Winery *see* Church Road
McDowell Valley *183*
McWilliam's *75, 153, 155, **182**, 197, 234, 267*
Mecella *238, 279*
Meerea Park *155*
Meerlust *85, 101, **182**, 261*
Megía, Luís *276*
Megyer, Château *271*
Meinert *261*
Meinjarre *191*
Melgaço, Quintas de *282*
Melin, Ch. *222*
Melini *103, 280*
Mellot, A ***182**, 245, 251*

311

313

317

ACKNOWLEDGEMENTS

Editor Maggie Ramsay; *Desktop Publishing* Keith Bambury; *Additional Editorial Work* Lorna Bateson; *Cartographer* Andrew Thompson; *Proofreader* Hugh Morgan; *Indexer* Angie Hipkin; *Production* Sara Granger; *Art Director* Nigel O'Gorman; *Photography* Nigel James; *Managing Editor* Anne Lawrance.

OLDER VINTAGE CHARTS *(top wines only)*

FRANCE

Alsace	90	89	88	85	83	81	76	71	69	61
	10♦	9♦	8♦	8♦	9♦	7◇	10♦	9♦	8◇	9◇
Champagne (vintage)	90	89	88	86	85	83	82	81	76	75
	9♦	8♦	8♦	7♦	8♦	7◇	10♦	7♦	9◇	9◇

Bordeaux	90	89	88	86	85	83	82	81	79	78
Margaux	10◇	8◇	7♦	8◇	8♦	9♦	8♦	7◇	6◇	7♦
St.-Jul., Pauillac, St-Est.	10◇	9◇	8♦	9◇	8♦	8♦	10♦	7♦	7♦	7♦
Graves/Pessac-L. (red)	8◇	8◇	8♦	6♦	8♦	8♦	9♦	7◇	7◇	8♦
St-Émilion, Pomerol	10◇	9◇	8♦	7♦	9♦	7♦	9♦	7◇	7◇	7♦

Bordeaux (cont.)	75	70	66	62	61	59	55	53	49	47
Margaux (cont.)	6◇	8♦	7◇	8◇	10♦	8◇	6◇	8◇	9◇	8◇
St.-Jul. etc. (cont.)	8♦	8♦	8♦	9◇	10♦	9◇	8◇	9◇	10◇	9◇
Graves etc. (R) (cont.)	6◇	8♦	8◇	8◇	10♦	9◇	8◇	8◇	10◇	9◇
St-Émilion etc. (cont.)	8♦	8♦	6◇	8◇	10◇	7◇	7◇	8◇	9◇	10◇

Sauternes	90	89	88	86	83	82	81	80	76	75
	10♦	9◇	9◇	9◇	9◇	5♦	6◇	7♦	8♦	8♦
Sauternes (cont.)	71	67	62	59	55	53	49	47	45	37
	8♦	9◇	8◇	9◇	8◇	8◇	10◇	10◇	9◇	10◇

Burgundy

Chablis	90	89	88	87	86	85	83	81	78	71
	10♦	8♦	8◇	5◇	7◇	9♦	7◇	8◇	9◇	9◇
Côte de Beaune (wh.)	90	89	88	86	85	82	79	78	73	71
	8♦	9♦	6◇	8◇	9◇	6◇	8◇	8◇	8◇	9◇
Côte de Nuits (red)	90	89	88	85	83	80	78	76	71	69
	10◇	8♦	8◇	8♦	6◇	6◇	9♦	6◇	9◇	8◇